OUR PARISH
PRAYS and SINGS

OUR PARISH PRAYS and SINGS

A SERVICE BOOK FOR LITURGICAL WORSHIP

with official texts, hymns, psalms and paraliturgies

THE LITURGICAL PRESS

Collegeville   Minnesota

To the many contributors whose generous assistance and cooperation made this edition of *Our Parish Prays and Sings* possible, the editors and publisher are sincerely grateful. With special appreciation acknowledgement is made of the following material held under copyright:

GREGORIAN INSTITUTE OF AMERICA, 2132 Jefferson Avenue, Toledo, Ohio, Nos. 59, 60, 130, 131, 132, 133, 134, 135, 136, 137, 138, 139, 140, 141, 142, 143, 144, 145, 146, 147, 148, 149, 150, text and melody.

REV. CYRIL A. REILLY, Loras College, Dubuque, Iowa, No. 65 text and melody.

CROSIER FATHERS, Onamia, Minnesota, Nos. 258, 267 text and melody.

RIGHT REV. MONSIGNOR MARTIN B. HELLRIEGEL, 8115 Church Road, St. Louis, Missouri, No. 83.

BURNS & OATES, LTD., London, England, Nos. 37, 71, 198, 251

LE CENTRE CATHOLIQUE DE L'UNIVERSITE D'OTTAWA, 1 rue Stewart, Ottawa, Canada, No. 31.

OXFORD UNIVERSITY PRESS, London, England, Nos. 270, 280

EAST ASIAN PASTORAL INSTITUTE, P. O. Box 1815, Manila, Philippines, No. 4 text; Bible vigils, Nos. 1, 2, 3, 8

REV. GREGORY MURRAY, O.S.B., Ealing Abbey, London, England, No. 57, 283

CHARLES SCRIBNER'S SONS, New York, New York, No. 290

J. CURWEN & SONS, LTD., London, England, Nos. 266, 278

THE ORTHODOX PRESBYTERIAN CHURCH, 7401 Old York Road, Philadelphia Pennsylvania, Nos. 182, 190

NOVELLO & CO., LTD., London, England, No. 177

WORLD LIBRARY OF SACRED MUSIC, INC., 1846 Westwood Avenue, Cincinnati, Ohio, Nos. 284, 285, 286

TARDY ET ACTION CATHOLIQUE RURAL, Bourges, France, readings, collects, prefaces, explanatory notes translated from *Missel Biblique de tous les jours.*

LAWRENCE DALEIDEN CO., 218 West Madison Street, Chicago, Illinois, No. 241

Liturgical texts released by the National Conference of Bishops of the United States of America and published by authority of the Bishops' Commission on the Liturgical Apostolate, 1312 Massachusetts Avenue, Washington, D.C., are reproduced in this volume; all such official texts consisting of excerpts from Sacred Scripture are © Copyright 1964 by the Confraternity of Christian Doctrine, Washington, D.C. Passages from or adapted from the Book of Psalms © Copyright 1950, 1955 by the Confraternity of Christian Doctrine, Washington, D.C.

© Copyright 1965 by The Order of St. Benedict, Inc., Collegeville, Minnesota. Printed in the U.S.A.

To the following authors of texts and composers of melodies we extend particular recognition and gratitude:

Texts:

DAVID RICHO, 311 Howard Avenue, New Haven, Connecticut, Nos. 14, 15, 16, 17

REV. ROGER SCHOENBECHLER, O.S.B., Mount St. Benedict, Crookston, Minnesota, Nos. 19, 63, 170

REV. BERNARD MISCHKE, O.S.C., Crosier Fathers, Onamia, Minnesota, Nos. 258, 267

REV. GERARD FARRELL, O.S.B., and J. ROBERTS, No. 264

REV. BENEDICT AVERY, O.S.B., St. John's University, Collegeville, Minnesota, Nos. 227, 229, 231

REV. CLAUDE EARLS, O.S.B., Colegio del Tepeyac, Callao 842, Mexico, D.F., Nos. 7, 8, 9, 10, 11, 12, 13, 53

SISTER M. TERESINE, O.S.F., Alverno College, 1501 South Layton Boulevard, Milwaukee, Wisconsin, Nos. 55, 196, 239

REV. IRVIN UDULUTSCH, O.F.M.CAP., St. Anthony's Monastery, Marathon, Wisconsin, Nos. 70, 172, 175, 191, 195, 201, 202, 217, 221, 273

REV. JAMES DONOHUE, Loras College, Dubuque, Iowa.

Melodies:

REV. CLAUDE EARLS, O.S.B., Colegio del Tepeyac, Callao 842, Mexico, D.F., Nos. 46, 69, 171, 173, 174, 178, 193, 199, 200, 203, 215, 223, 234, 236, 248, 261, 272, 275

SISTER M. JOY, O.S.B., St. Benedict's Convent, St. Joseph, Minnesota, Nos. 2, 22, 23, 26

FRANK GORTON, 1404 Atwater Street, Bloomington, Indiana, Nos. 3, All Saints' Litany

GERHARD TRACK, St. John's University, Collegeville, Minnesota, Nos. 4, 25, 38, 87, 227

REV. EUGENE LINDUSKY, O.S.C., Crosier Fathers, Onamia, Minnesota, Nos. 258, 267

SISTER M. OCTAVIA, F.S.P.A., Viterbo College, LaCrosse, Wisconsin, Nos. 18, 24

JOHN LEE, 22 Chester Place, Los Angeles, California, Nos. 20, 21, 29, 98, 99, 100, 101, 102, 226, 231

SISTER MARIENNE, O.S.F., St. Joseph's Convent, 1501 South Layton Boulevard, Milwaukee, Wisconsin, No. 33

REV. JULES MARTEL, O.M.I., 1 rue Stewart, Ottawa, Canada, No. 31

REV. GERARD FARRELL, O.S.B., St. John's University, Collegeville, Minnesota, Nos. 27, 260, 264

SISTER M. CLARISSIMA, O.S.F., Alverno College, 1501 South Layton Boulevard, Milwaukee, Wisconsin, Nos. 28

REV. QUENTIN DITTBERNER, O.S.B., Sacred Heart Convent, Fargo, North Dakota, No. 34, The Divine Praises

SISTER MARY CECILIA, S.S.N.D., 5522 West Bluemound Road, Milwaukee, Wisconsin, No. 30

BROTHER GERARD WOJCHOWSKI, O.S.B., St. John's Abbey, Collegeville, Minnesota, No. 66

REV. HIPPOLYTUS DORITY, O.S.B., Scholasticat S. Vincent de Paul, 2555 Chemin Ste. Foy, Quebec, Canada, No. 263

REV. IRVIN UDULUTSCH, O.F.M.CAP., St. Anthony's Monastery, Marathon, Wisconsin, No. 245

SISTER MARY VICTORIA, C.S.J., 1515 West Ogden Avenue, LaGrange Park, Illinois, No. 32

Text and melodies:

REVS. E. ARRONDO and A. DANOZ, Covarrubias 19, Madrid 10, Spain, Nos. 7, 8, 9, 10, 11, 12, 13

SISTER MARY VICTORIA, C.S.J., 1515 West Ogden Avenue, LaGrange Park Illinois, Nos. 39, 56, 58, 92

REV. GERARD FARRELL, O.S.B., St. John's University, Collegeville, Minnesota, Nos. 73, 74, 75, 76, 77, 78, 79, 80, 81, 82, 152, 153, 154, 155, 156, 157, 158, 159, 160, 161, 162, 163, 164, 165, 166, 255, 264, 289, 290, 291, 292, 293, 294, 295, 296, 297, 298, 299, 300, 301, 302

JOHN LEE, 22 Chester Place, Los Angeles, California, Nos. 98, 99, 100, 101, 102

SISTER M. THEOPHANE, O.S.F., Alverno College, 1501 South Layton Boulevard Milwaukee, Wisconsin, Nos. 237, 238

REV. CHRISTOPHER COELHO, O.F.M., St. Louis Friary, Palmaner, Chittoor District, India, Nos. 276, 287, 288

Because the process of arriving at certainty with regard to the current ownership of copyrighted text and/or music for hymns is difficult, the editors of *Our Parish Prays and Sings* ask indulgence for any possible omission or oversight in making due acknowledgement and request that such omission be brought to their attention for correction in subsequent printings.

The majority of texts and/or melodies in public domain have been edited and modified by the contributors to *Our Parish Prays and Sings;* all such modifications in text or melody together with texts and melodies produced for this edition but not specifically accredited above are under the copyright proper to this publication.

Nihil obstat: John Eidenschink, O.S.B., J.C.D., *Censor deputatus. Imprimi potest:* † Baldwin Dworschak, O.S.B., Abbot of St. John's Abbey. *Imprimatur:* † Peter W. Bartholome, D.D., Bishop of St. Cloud. August 27, 1965.

Typography and layout by the North Central Publishing Company, St. Paul, Minn. Printed by the Webb Publishing Company, St. Paul, Minn. Bound by A. J. Dahl, Minneapolis, Minn.

THE USE OF
VERNACULAR AT MASS[1]

I. *Understanding Liturgical Texts in the Vernacular*

The Constitution on the Liturgy, issued by the Second Vatican Council, states that it is of the highest importance that the faithful understand the rites because the sacraments "not only presuppose faith but by words and objects they also nourish, strengthen, and express it"; moreover, "they do indeed impart grace, but in addition, the very act of celebrating them most effectively disposes the faithful to receive this grace in a fruitful manner, to worship God duly, and to practice charity" (59). Another basic principle taught by the Constitution is that "Christ is always present in his Church, especially in her liturgical celebrations." Among the ways he is present is "in his word, since it is he himself who speaks when the Holy Scriptures are read in the Church." He is present also "when the Church prays and sings, for he promised: 'Where two or three are gathered together in my name, there am I in the midst of them'" (7).

The widespread interest in the Council and particularly in the discussions on vernacular in the liturgy have prepared the people for changes. Many are filled with hope for a great advance in meaningful participation by all the people in the sacred rites. At the same time it is evident or will soon be evident that beyond use of the language which the people understand there must be developed an understanding of the "language" of the liturgy in a deeper sense. No one can find the meaning in the allusions to Abraham's bosom or to Jerusalem in the funeral rites unless he knows Abraham as our father and Jerusalem as the place of God's presence with his people, the prefiguring of the Church on earth and in heaven. We all know how necessary is a grasp of scriptural idiom to understand the Epistles. This is also necessary to appreciate the use of water, oil, bread, and wine, and to know the significance of such phrases as "new and eternal covenant" and "Lamb of God." The simple phrase, "through Christ our Lord," or "through him and with him and in him," expresses a direction in devotion, a union with Christ's worship of the Father that is not yet the spontaneous manner of praying among our people. The same is true of praying the psalms as Christian prayers.

Understanding the liturgy is not merely a matter of vocabulary or of remembering biblical events. Christ's earthly life followed in large part its Old Testament prefigurings and he established the basic rites of his Church on the basis of meanings already indicated in the Scriptures. He made the inspired psalms and canticles his own prayers. His great act of worship and sacrifice for mankind, "the paschal mystery" (5, 6, 47, 61, 102, 106), was intended as a new Exodus, a passing from this world to the Father, and it took place at the time of the Passover celebration.

Because of the scriptural basis of liturgical language and actions, the Constitution on the Liturgy provides for more extensive reading of Scrip-

[1] A statement by the *Bishops' Commission on the Liturgical Apostolate.*

ture in the liturgy and also for the integration of preaching with Scripture. It states that the sermon is part of the liturgical service and that it "should draw its content mainly from scriptural and liturgical sources, and its character should be that of a proclamation of God's wonderful works in the history of salvation, the mystery of Christ, ever made present and active within us, especially in the celebration of the liturgy" (35).

The Constitution also states that Bible services should be encouraged (35) which include of their nature a sermon on the texts read to the people and said or sung by them. And it states that it is essential to "promote that warm and living love for Scripture to which the venerable tradition of both Eastern and Western rites gives testimony" (24) — a love which may be possessed by the simplest as well as the most learned members of the Church, as history shows us.

Since, as the Constitution states, it is now a primary pastoral duty to enable the people to take their full internal and external part in the liturgy (14, 19), it is clearly our duty to equip ourselves at once to carry out this task and to begin to carry it out among our people. Providentially, the scriptural, catechetical, and liturgical renewals of recent decades have already produced an abundance of reading matter, at many levels, which can serve to enrich our basic structure of rites and prayers and, at the same time, help us to inform our people.

But what is most necessary of all is that we begin, if we have not begun already, to meet with Christ as he speaks to us through the liturgical rites and the inspired word of Scripture. This should best start with the use of the primal form of Christian "mental prayer" or "meditation," traditionally known as *lectio divina* (or, as we might call it in English, "praying the Bible"). This means, very simply, prayerfully "hearing," by slow meditative reading, a biblical or liturgical passage as Christ's word here and now: asking ourselves, for example, what is he telling us here about himself, about the Father, about the divine plan for our own salvation and that of our people? How does he ask us to respond to this word of God's love with him, now in our prayer and also in our life?

Such a form of meditation, especially when the passages chosen are those which the priest is to explain and open out to his people in Sunday Mass, or at a baptism or wedding or funeral, or at a Bible service, will, experience shows, serve to integrate the priest's prayer-life in itself and with his work for his people as "minister of the word." Any *study* of the liturgical texts and of sacred Scripture then serves to enrich and deepen both the priest's own prayer and worship and the sermons in which he opens out God's word to his people.

The question, obviously, is not one of making biblical scholars either of all priests or of the faithful. It is one simply of restoring that living familiarity with Scripture and, through it, with Christ, which is our rightful inheritance.

II. *Reading and Praying in the Vernacular*

The introduction of the common language into liturgical rites is an event of numerous and important implications. Clearly it was the intention of the Fathers of the Second Vatican Council to provide the people with rites of sacred worship which would be meaningful and intelligible to them (36, 54, 63, 101, 113). Both those parts of the liturgy which instruct the faithful and those parts which express their prayer and devotion are to be spoken or sung in the vernacular language. This reform in our custom is intended to bring the people into more effective contact with the sacred Scripture and the holy texts of the liturgy, thereby fostering deeper faith, greater knowledge, and more sincere prayer.

But these worthy objectives will not automatically be achieved by the use of the vernacular. Such prayer and readings will have to be done in a more meaningful and appropriate manner than has unfortunately been employed by some priests when reciting Latin texts. To celebrate the liturgy in a manner that is apparently hasty, matter-of-fact, and without attention to the meaning of the words would, of course, be irreverent and improper no matter what the language; however, when the vernacular is used, there is the greatest possibility of scandal. These observations, which must be honestly admitted, are commonly expressed whenever the vernacular is discussed and both clergy and laity are surely anxious not only to avoid the danger but, first of all, to seek the fullest advantages the vernacular can bring. For this reason, the following comments are offered on the manner of speaking the English tongue in liturgical services, in the hope that they might serve as a guide to all. For the purposes of these remarks, there is a basic difference between reading the word of God and reading other texts.

A. *Reading the Word of God*

All Scripture readings are to be proclamations, not mere recitations. Lectors and priests should approach the public reading of the Bible with full awareness that it is their honored task to render the official proclamation of the revealed word of God to his assembled holy people. The character of this reading is such that it must convey that special reverence which is due the sacred Scriptures above all other words.

1. It is of fundamental importance that the reader communicate the fullest meaning of the passage. Without exaggerated emphasis or affectation, he must convey the particular significance of those words, phrases, clauses or sentences which constitute the point being made. Careful phrasing and inflection are necessary to enable the listener to follow every thought and the relationships among them. Patterns of speech, especially monotonous patterns of speech, must be avoided, and the pattern of thought in the text must be adhered to. The message in all its meaning must be earnestly communicated.

2. The manner of speaking and tone of voice should be clear and firm, never indifferent or uncertain. The reader should not draw attention to himself either by being nervous and awkward or by being obviously conscious of a talent for dramatic reading. It is the message that should be remembered, not the one who reads it. The voice should be reverent without being unctuous, loud without shouting, authoritative without being offensive or overbearing. The pace must be geared to understanding — never hurried, never dragged.

3. By his voice, attitude, and physical bearing, the reader should convey the dignity and sacredness of the occasion. His role is that of a herald of the word of God, his function to provide a meaningful encounter with that living word. Perfection in this mission may not always be achieved, but it must always and seriously be sought.

B. *Praying and Speaking Aloud*

When the celebrant leads the people in prayer, or speaks to them, or addresses God in their behalf, his manner of speaking will differ somewhat in each case. In every instance, however, he should convey that he sincerely means what he says. This sincerity is crucially important; it makes the difference between a matter-of-fact, ritualized, indifferent celebration and one that is truly an expression of faith and devotion.

1. *Dialogue.* In the greetings and verbal exchange between celebrant and congregation, all participants should speak their parts with meaning. When the priest says, "The Lord be with you," for example, he must convey that he is really addressing the people, that he sincerely means the greeting, and that he invites response. The tone and inflection of voice must be natural and convincing. At the same time, dialogue should never become extremely informal; all must be aware that the words they speak are part of a sacred rite. The liturgy must always be characterized by dignity and reverence as well as meaningful and sincere speech.

2. *Prayer.* When reading the orations, Preface, and the like, the priest should speak in a manner befitting his sacerdotal role. His tone of voice should be more formal, more reverent; yet he must remember he is speaking to a Person, not merely reciting formulas. Note that this applies no matter which language is used in the prayer; it applies equally to the Canon as to the Collect or the Lord's Prayer. The latter prayer is gravely abused by a sing-song recitation which pays little attention to the praises and petitions actually contained in the words. The conclusions of prayers, although in set formulas, must never be hurried, or routinely said. Since the affirmative response of the people is expected, the rhythm and tone of the priest should be sufficiently strong to encourage and facilitate the response.

III. *Extent of Liturgical Use of English*

The extent to which it is lawful to use English in the liturgy throughout the dioceses of the United States is determined in the decrees of the Na-tional Conference of Bishops, enacted April 2, 1964, and confirmed by the *Consilium* for the implementation of the Constitution on the Sacred Liturgy in a rescript of May 1, 1964. The following paragraphs summarize and specify what is found in the decrees, which should be consulted for additional details. (The use of officially approved vernaculars other than English, although conceded by the body of Bishops, is dependent upon the judgment and permission of the individual local Ordinary in accord with n. 6 of the Decree).

A. *Divine Office*

The entire text of the Divine Office may be sung or said in English, according to the terms of the Constitution and the decrees. In the case of the clergy, however, the faculty to use English must be obtained from the Ordinary, local or religious. This permission is not needed if the cleric takes part in the Office with a group of the faithful or of religious who lawfully use the English Office.

The editions of the breviary in English issued by two publishers, Benziger Brothers and The Liturgical Press, have been approved by the Conference of Bishops.

B. *Sacraments and Sacramentals*

The entire rite of the sacraments and sacramentals, other than the Eucharist (below), may be celebrated in English, including the essential forms of the sacraments. It is always required, however, that the approved text be used.

The text approved for the sacraments and sacramentals is the official *Collectio Rituum* newly edited and published. The Bishops' Commission on the Liturgical Apostolate has authorized four editions of the *Collectio Rituum,* issued by the following publishers: Benziger Brothers, Bruce Publishing Company, Catholic Book

Publishing Co., and The Liturgical Press.

For the rites of the sacraments and sacramentals which are not contained in the official *Collectio Rituum*, the English translations found in *The Roman Ritual* by the Reverend Philip Weller (Bruce Publishing Co.) have been approved for liturgical use.

C. *The Holy Eucharist*

In the celebration of Mass it is lawful to use English in the lessons, in the prayer of the faithful, and in the ordinary and proper parts which pertain to the people. In sequence, the use of English and the retention of Latin for these parts may be enumerated as follows:

Entrance Rite—Preparatory prayers at the foot of the altar—Latin
    Introit antiphon, Kyrie and Gloria—English
    Prayer or Collect (including the introductory *Dominus vobiscum* and *Et cum spiritu tuo*)—Latin

The Word of God
    Epistle and other lessons—English
    Gradual, Alleluia, and other chants—English
    Munda cor meum, etc.—Latin
    Gospel (including the introductory versicles and responses)—English
    (Homily) Creed—English

The Preparation of the Gifts
    The Lord be with you and response, and *Let us pray*—English
    Offertory antiphon—English
    Silent prayers of the priest—Latin
    Prayer over the gifts or Secret prayer—Latin

The Eucharistic Prayer
    Preface of the Canon (including the introductory dialogue and response beginning *Dominus vobiscum*)—Latin
    Sanctus—English
    Silent prayers of the Canon and the conclusion—Latin

The Eucharistic Banquet
    Lord's Prayer (with the invitation *Let us pray*, etc.)—English
    Libera nos, quaesumus (with the versicle *Pax Domini* and response)—Latin
    Haec commixtio—Latin
    Agnus Dei—English
    Silent prayers of the priest before Communion (and during the ablutions afterward)—Latin
    Communion of the faithful (including *Behold the Lamb of God* etc. and the formula for Communion)—English
    Communion antiphon—English
    Postcommunion (including the introductory *Dominus vobiscum* and *Et cum spiritu tuo*)—Latin
    Dismissal (*The Lord be with you, Go, the Mass is ended,* etc. with the responses)—English
    Placeat—Latin
    Blessing—English

Where it is used, the "common prayer" or prayer of the faithful mentioned in art. 53 of the Constitution on the Liturgy may likewise be in English.

The English translation of the parts permitted in the vernacular is given in the *Roman Missal* newly edited and published for use in the dioceses of the United States. Two editions of the official altar missal have been authorized by the Bishops' Commission: Benziger Brothers, and Catholic Book Publishing Co.

IV. *Directives Concerning the Use of the Vernacular at Mass*

1. In the dioceses of the United States of America it is lawful to use English, to the extent described in the decree of April 2, 1964, at all Masses at which the people are present, beginning on the First Sunday of Advent, November 29, 1964. (The clause "at which the people are present" —in the Constitution "adstante populo"— may be interpreted as applying to all scheduled parish or institutional Masses.)

2. The Lessons, Epistle, and Gospel in English should be proclaimed facing the people at both low and sung Masses.

3. At low Masses and at sung Masses without a subdeacon, it is possible and even desirable that the (Lesson or Lessons before the Epistle, if any, and the) Epistle should be proclaimed by a reader, whether clerical or lay, other than the celebrant. The reading of the Gospel should be reserved to the deacon or, in his absence, to the celebrant.

4. Although the use of English is permitted to the same extent in low Masses and in sung Masses, the vernacular texts of the Ordinary and Proper must be sung to melodies or settings approved by the competent ecclesiastical authority, i.e., the National Conference of Bishops.

5. It remains lawful to sing the Proper chants *recto tono* or to psalm tones in the absence of appropriate settings.

6. At both high Masses and solemn Masses, the Lessons, Epistle, and Gospel may be recited in a loud, clear, and solemn tone of voice without chant.

7. The English greetings, versicles, etc., may be sung *recto tono* in the absence of appropriate settings.

8. Especially on Sundays and feast days it is desirable, at least at the principal low Masses, that psalms or hymns appropriate to the respective parts of Mass should be sung by the people. This is particularly applicable at the entrance of the priest (and during the preparatory prayers which remain in Latin), between the Lessons, at the Offertory, during Communion, and as a recessional (that is, immediately after the blessing and during the recession of the celebrant).

9. At low Masses, where possible it is desirable that the congregation or the choir or other group, or a cantor recite the Proper chants, adding psalm verses as needed.

10. Psalms or psalm verses added to the Proper antiphons of the Roman Missal, whether sung or recited, should follow the text of the Book of Psalms published by the Confraternity of Christian Doctrine, from which the respective antiphons have been adopted.

11. For the present, the form of the common prayer or prayer of the faithful may be determined by the individual Bishops. For example, the invocations of the third part of the Litany of the Saints may be used, or the variants of the Byzantine Litany already employed in some places.

12. Since the Collects, etc., and the Preface of the Canon remain in Latin, it is desirable that the commentator, in addition to his other duties, should very briefly summarize these prayers for the benefit of the faithful.

POSITIONS OF THE FAITHFUL AT HOLY MASS

At sung or *High Masses* it is customary and desirable for the people to follow the same postures as the clergy, as these are listed in the Roman Missal in the new code of rubrics (1960). This we recommend for accepted usage around the country, when Mass is offered as a sung Mass.

With regard to recited or *Low Masses*, which will be the usual manner for the offering of the participated Mass, a very practical problem presents itself. For the Low Mass, the Missal formerly gave only one rule: that those present should kneel throughout, except at the Gospel. This direction, which was made obsolete by various local customs, was suppressed in 1960, so that now it is appropriate to adapt the postures of the sung Mass to congregational use at the Low Mass in participated fashion.

The problem has been somewhat complicated in the practical order by some liturgists, who with every good intention and quite properly stress standing as the posture most expressive of the spirit of public prayer. As the priest stands, it seems proper that the people should stand when they pray, sing or speak with him. However, this does not take into consideration the very practical problem which standing poses for the older members of the congregation, and indeed many of its younger members.

Accordingly, then, the following usage is recommended with a view to making it as simple as possible.

POSITIONS OF THE FAITHFUL AT LOW MASS
THE LITURGY OF THE WORD

Entrance Rite (up to the Epistle) — STAND
(If no hymn is sung, kneel during the celebrant's prayers at the foot of the altar)

The Word of God (up to the Offertory Antiphon)
Epistle — SIT
Gospel — STAND
Homily — SIT
Creed — STAND
(Common Prayer, or Prayer of the Faithful) — STAND

THE LITURGY OF THE EUCHARIST

Preparation of the Gifts (up to the Preface)
Offertory Prayers — SIT
Prayer over the Gifts (Secret) — STAND

Eucharistic Prayer (CANON)
Preface and Sanctus — STAND
After Sanctus through the great "Amen" — KNEEL

Eucharistic Banquet (COMMUNION)
The Lord's Prayer — STAND
After Agnus Dei — KNEEL
Postcommunion and dismissal — STAND
Blessing — KNEEL
Recessional — STAND

Reception of Holy Communion

Whether the individual communicant kneels or stands while receiving Holy Communion depends on local custom and circumstances. Obviously, the Ordinary can decide for his diocese.

Additional Kneeling

For Requiem Masses, and on certain penitential weekdays, the rubrics of the Missal prescribe kneeling during the Collect and the Postcommunion. The rubrics are naturally extended to cover the Prayer over the gifts also, now that this prayer is said aloud.

This rule applies on the weekdays of Advent, Lent, Passiontide, September Ember days, Vigils of the second and third class outside of Paschaltide, and in Masses for the dead.

PROPER OF THE SEASON

The officially approved text for the Entrance antiphon, Gradual, Alleluia verse, Tract, Sequence, Offertory and Communion antiphon, Prayer over the Assembly, Prayer over the Offerings, Prayer after the Communion for all Sundays and feasts that may displace a Sunday are given below. Explanatory notes and readings are taken from the original Missel Biblique *published by Tardy.*

The full text for the common ending **Per Dóminum (This we ask of you through our Lord)** *is as follows:*

Per Dóminum nostrum Iesum Christum Fílium tuum, qui tecum vivit et regnat in unitáte Spíritus Sancti, Deus, per ómnia sǽcula sæculórum. Amen.

This we ask of you through our Lord Jesus Christ, your Son, who lives and reigns with you in the unity of the Holy Spirit, God, forever. Amen.

FIRST SUNDAY OF ADVENT

ENTRANCE ANTIPHON *Ps. 24:1-3, 4*

To you I lift up my soul; in you, O my God, I trust; let me not be put to shame; let not my enemies exult over me. No one who waits for you shall be put to shame.

Ps. Your ways, O Lord, make known to me; teach me your paths.

Glory be to the Father and to the Son and to the Holy Spirit. As it was in the beginning, is now and ever shall be, world without end. Amen. To you . . .

Prayer over the Assembly

Excita, quǽsumus, Dómine, poténtiam tuam, et veni: ut ab imminéntibus peccatórum nostrórum perículis, te mereámur protegénte éripi, te liberánte salvári: Qui vivis et regnas cum Deo Patre in unitáte Spíritus Sancti, Deus, per ómnia sǽcula sæculórum.

Rouse up your power, Lord, and come. Protect us, and we shall be rescued from the perils to which our sins are exposing us; deliver us, and we shall be saved. This we ask of you, Lord Jesus, living and reigning with the Father in the unity of the Holy Spirit, God, forever.

EPISTLE   Romans 13:11-14

Christians must prepare for the return of Christ. The Church invites her members to look forward to this day, "dispelling the darkness by the light of their life."

A reading from the letter of the apostle Paul to the Christians of Rome
Brethren,
You should know that it is time now for us to wake up from our sleep.
Salvation is closer to us today than it was when we began to believe.
The night is fading: the day approaches. Let us therefore reject the
things that are done in the dark, and put on the armor of light.[1] Let us
behave honorably, as people do in broad daylight. Let there be no excess
in eating or in drinking, no debauchery or impurity, no quarrels or jealousy.
Renounce all this, to put on the Lord Jesus Christ.

Gradual Ps. 24:3, 4
No one who waits for you shall be put to shame. Your ways, O Lord,
make known to me; teach me your paths.

Alleluia Ps. 84:8
Alleluia, alleluia. Show us, O Lord, your kindness, and grant us your
salvation. Alleluia.

GOSPEL   Luke 21:25-33
*From the very beginning of the liturgical year, the Church focuses our
attention upon the "parousia," Christ's return at the end of time. For it is
that final stage of things that truly illumines the whole history of the world.*

*The birth of Jesus Christ introduced us into messianic times, that period
of history during which he is establishing God's kingdom, first of all
through his own life on earth, then through his Church, which is his Body.
These times will come to an end only with the return of Christ, when he will
turn the kingdom over to his Father. Because the Lord has come, we know
that he will come again.*

A reading from the holy Gospel according to Luke
At that time Jesus said to his disciples:
"Prodigies will appear in the sun, the moon and the stars; and on the
earth the nations will be in anguish at the strange roaring of the sea and
the waves. Everyone's tongue will be parched with fear, in expectation of
that which is threatening the universe; for the powers of the heavens will
be set in motion.
"Then it is that they will see the 'Son of Man coming on the clouds,' in
all the brilliance of his power and his glory.
"As for you, when all this begins to happen, open your eyes and lift up
your head, for your liberation is approaching!"
And Jesus used a comparison:
"When the fig tree and the other trees bud, you know that summer is
near. In the same way, when you see all these things happening, know how
to recognize that God's reign is near.
"It is a solemn truth that I tell you: this generation shall not pass till all
these things have happened. Sky and earth will pass away; my words shall
not."

[1] The arms necessary for the spiritual fight, in the first place: faith, hope, charity.

OFFERTORY ANTIPHON *Ps. 24:1-3*

To you I lift up my soul; in you, O my God, I trust; let me not be put to shame; let not my enemies exult over me. No one who waits for you shall be put to shame.

Prayer over the Offerings

Hæc sacra nos, Dómine, poténti virtúte mundátos, ad suum fáciant puríores veníre princípium. Per Dóminum.

May the sanctifying power of these consecrated offerings make us clean, O Lord, and bring us with purer souls to the God who created them. This we ask of you through our Lord.

COMMUNION ANTIPHON *Ps. 84:13*

The Lord will give his benefits: and our land shall yield its increase.

Prayer after the Communion

Suscipiámus, Dómine, misericórdiam tuam in médio templi tui: ut reparatiónis nostræ ventúra solémnia cóngruis honóribus præcedámus. Per Dóminum.

May we sense the impact of your mercy, Lord, in the midst of your temple, that with fitting praises we may prepare for the coming celebration of our reinstatement into divine favor. This we ask of you through our Lord.

SECOND SUNDAY OF ADVENT

ENTRANCE ANTIPHON *Is. 30:30; Ps. 79:2*

People of Sion, behold the Lord shall come to save the nations; and the Lord shall make the glory of his voice to be heard, in the joy of your heart.

Ps. O shepherd of Israel, hearken, O guide of the flock of Joseph!

Glory be to the Father and to the Son and to the Holy Spirit. As it was in the beginning, is now and ever shall be, world without end. Amen. People of Sion . . .

Prayer over the Assembly

Excita, Dómine, corda nostra ad præparándas Unigéniti tui vias: ut per eius advéntum purificátis tibi méntibus servíre mereámur: Qui tecum vivit et regnat in unitáte Spíritus Sancti, Deus, per ómnia sǽcula sæculórum.

Lord, make our hearts more diligent in preparing the way for your only-begotten Son, since his coming will enable us to serve you with purified souls. This we ask of you through him, who lives and reigns with you in the unity of the Holy Spirit, God, forever.

EPISTLE

Romans 15:4-13

St. Paul announces that the great event has happened: Christ has come. He has come to save the Jews who were waiting for him; and, out of pure mercy, he has also saved the pagans who were not waiting for him.

In the name of all men, the Church, the new Jerusalem, now awaits the final coming of Christ. It is by increasing the amount of charity in the world that she is able to prepare for final and definitive redemption.

A reading from the letter of the apostle Paul to the Christians of Rome

Brethren,

Everything that has been written [in the Bible] has been written for our instruction, that, through the stability and the consolation provided for us in the Scriptures, we may attain to hope.

May God, the source of that stability and consolation, grant that you understand one another after the example of Christ Jesus, in order that, with one heart and one voice, you may give glory to God, the Father of our Lord Jesus Christ!

Be concerned about one another, therefore; Christ was deeply concerned about you in order to promote God's glory. For Christ placed himself at the service of the Jews, in order to keep the promises made by his Father to their ancestors. As for the pagans, it is because of God's mercy that they glorify him, in accordance with these words of Scripture: "Among all the nations, Lord, I shall praise you and sing the glory of your name." [1] And again: "Pagan nations, come and share the joy of the chosen people!" [2] And elsewhere: "Nations of the whole world, praise the Lord! Glorify him, peoples of the universe!" [3] Isaiah in turn wrote: "He will come, the Son of Jesse; he will rise up to rule the world. In him all the nations will put their hope." [4]

May the God of hope, then, cause you to find in your faith the fullness of joy and of peace! May he fill you with hope by the power of the Holy Spirit!

Gradual Ps. 49:2-3, 5

From Sion, perfect in beauty, God shines forth. Gather his faithful ones before him, those who have made a covenant with him by sacrifice.

Alleluia Ps. 121:1

Alleluia, alleluia. I rejoiced because they said to me: "We will go up to the house of the Lord." Alleluia.

GOSPEL

Matthew 11:2-10

Jesus is indeed the one announced by the prophets; of these the last and greatest was John the Baptist. Mankind, then, has entered the messianic age. The complete and perfect fulfillment of this age is now being awaited. But human hope can sustain itself on the pledges already fulfilled: God has, in fact, answered our expectations by his advent in Christ.

---

[1] 2 Sam. 22:50 and Ps. 17:50.   [3] Ps. 116:1.
[2] Deut. 32:43.   [4] Is. 11:10.

A reading from the holy Gospel according to Matthew

At that time when John the Baptist in his prison cell heard of the miracles performed by Christ, he sent two of his disciples to ask him, "Are you the one who is to come, or must we wait for another?"

Jesus answered them, "Go and tell John what you hear and see: the blind see, the lame walk, the lepers are cured, the deaf hear, the dead rise, the poor receive the good news. Blessed is the one for whom I am not a stumbling-block!"

Upon their departure, Jesus began to speak to the crowd about John: "What did you go out to see in the desert? A reed bending to every whim of the wind? Now what did you go out to see? A man in costly clothing? No, you know that people who wear fine clothes live in the palaces of kings. Then what were you going out to see? A prophet? Yes, I tell you, and more than a prophet! This is the one of whom it is written: 'See, I am sending my messenger before you; he is to prepare the way for you!' "

OFFERTORY ANTIPHON *Ps. 84:7-8*

Will you not, O God, give us life; and shall not your people rejoice in you? Show us, O Lord, your kindness, and grant us your salvation.

Prayer over the Offerings

Placáre, quǽsumus, Dómine, humilitátis nostræ précibus et hóstiis: et ubi nulla súppetunt suffrágia meritórum, tuis nobis succúrre præsídiis. Per Dóminum.

Let your heart be touched, Lord, by our poor prayers and our simple offerings. We cannot lay claim to any merit; but do aid us with your assistance. This we ask of you through our Lord.

COMMUNION ANTIPHON *Bar. 5:5; 4:36*

Up, Jerusalem! Stand upon the heights; and behold the joy that comes to you from your God.

Prayer after the Communion

Repléti cibo spirituális alimóniæ, súpplices te, Dómine, deprecámur: ut, huius participatióne mystérii, dóceas nos terréna despícere et amáre cæléstia. Per Dóminum.

Strengthened by this spiritual food, we entreat you, Lord, that our participation in this sacrifice may teach us detachment from the things of earth and affection for heavenly values. This we ask of you through our Lord.

THIRD SUNDAY OF ADVENT

ENTRANCE ANTIPHON *Phil. 4:4-6; Ps. 84:2*

Rejoice in the Lord always: again I say, rejoice. Let your moderation be known to all men: for the Lord is near. Have no anxiety, but in everything, by prayer let your petitions be made known to God.

Ps. You have favored, O Lord, your land; you have restored the well-being of Jacob.

Glory be to the Father and to the Son and to the Holy Spirit. As it was in the beginning, is now and ever shall be, world without end. Amen. Rejoice . . .

Prayer over the Assembly

Aurem tuam, quǽsumus, Dómine, précibus nostris accómmoda: et mentis nostræ ténebras grátia tuæ visitatiónis illústra: Qui vivis et regnas cum Deo Patre in unitáte Spíritus Sancti, Deus, per ómnia sǽcula sæculórum.

Lord, give ear to our prayers and by the grace of your coming enlighten the darkness of our souls. This we ask of you, Lord Jesus, living and reigning with the Father in the unity of the Holy Spirit, God, forever.

EPISTLE   Philippians 4:4-7

Though unseen, the Lord is close to those who trust in him. By their joy, their love and their spirit of peace, may Christians bear witness before all men to the presence of God in the world!

A reading from the letter of the apostle Paul to the Christians of Philippi
Brethren,

Rejoice always in the Lord! I tell you again, rejoice!

Let everyone recognize you by your unaffected and thoughtful manners: the Lord is near!

Whatever happens, do not be upset! But if you need anything, ask God for it in a prayer of entreaty, already filled with thankfulness.

And may God's inexpressible peace guard your hearts and your minds in Christ Jesus our Lord!

Gradual *Ps. 79:2-3, 2*

From your throne, O Lord, upon the Cherubim, rouse your power, and come. O shepherd of Israel, hearken, O guide of the flock of Joseph!

Alleluia *Ps. 79:2*

Alleluia, alleluia. Rouse, O Lord, your power, and come to save us. Alleluia.

GOSPEL   John 1:19-28

The message of John the Baptist links our Christian hope to the great expectation of Jewish messianism. Our faith too is given assurance that Christ is already here, even if we experience difficulty in sensing his presence.

A reading from the holy Gospel according to John

At that time the Jews sent priests and levites from Jerusalem to ask John the Baptist, "Who are you?"

John declared categorically, "I am not the Messiah."

"What then?" they asked. "Are you Elijah?"

"Of course not," he replied.

"Are you the Prophet?" [1]

"No."

They insisted: "Who are you, then? We must take back some answer to those who sent us. Who do you claim to be?"

John replied, "I am, as the prophet Isaiah said, the voice that cries in the desert, 'Smooth out the road for the Lord!' " [2]

Those who had been sent were pharisees; they wanted to know more: "If you are neither the Messiah, nor Elijah, nor the Prophet, by what right do you baptize?"

"My baptism," replied John, "is only a baptism of water; but in your midst there stands someone whom you do not know. It is he who is to come after me, although he was in existence before me; and as for me, I am not worthy to untie the strap of his sandal."

This took place at Bethany, beyond the Jordan, where John was baptizing.

OFFERTORY ANTIPHON *Ps. 84:2*

You have favored, O Lord, your land; you have restored the well-being of Jacob. You have forgiven the guilt of your people.

Prayer over the Offerings

Devotiónis nostræ tibi, quǽsumus, Dómine, hóstia iúgiter immolétur: quæ et sacri péragat institúta mystérii, et salutáre tuum in nobis mirabíliter operétur. Per Dóminum.

With whole-hearted love, O Lord, we bring you this offering. May it always be presented to you in sacrifice, fulfilling what your heart desired when you instituted this mystery; and may the wonderful work of your salvation find realization in us. This we ask of you through our Lord.

COMMUNION ANTIPHON *Is. 35:4*

Say to those who are frightened: Be strong, fear not! Here is our God, he comes to save us.

Prayer after the Communion

Implorámus, Dómine, cleméntiam tuam: ut hæc divína subsídia, a vítiis expiátos, ad festa ventúra nos prǽparent. Per Dóminum.

We implore your clemency, Lord; may your Eucharist purify us of our sins and prepare us for the coming feasts. This we ask of you through our Lord.

[1] It is believed that Elijah (Malachi 4:5-6) or the great Prophet (Deuteronomy 18:15) would return to prepare for the coming of the Messiah.

[2] Isaiah 40:3. See this text later on, p. 23.

FOURTH SUNDAY OF ADVENT

ENTRANCE ANTIPHON *Is. 45:8; Ps. 18:2*

Drop down dew, you heavens, from above, and let the clouds rain the Just: let the earth be opened and bud forth a savior.

Ps. The heavens declare the glory of God, and the firmament proclaims his handiwork.

Glory be to the Father and to the Son and to the Holy Spirit. As it was in the beginning, is now and ever shall be, world without end. Amen. Drop down dew . . .

Prayer over the Assembly

Excita, quǽsumus, Dómine, poténtiam tuam, et veni: et magna nobis virtúte succúrre; ut per auxílium grátiæ tuæ, quod nostra peccáta præpédiunt, indulgéntia tuæ propitiatiónis accéleret: Qui vivis et regnas cum Deo Patre in unitáte Spíritus Sancti, Deus, per ómnia sǽcula sæculórum.

Rouse up your power, Lord, and come; help us with all the force of your grace. Then, by your indulgent mercy, we shall quickly be granted the blessings now obstructed by our sins. This we ask of you, Lord Jesus, living and reigning with the Father in the unity of the Holy Spirit, God, forever.

EPISTLE   1 Corinthians 4:1-5

Cliques were forming in the community at Corinth. Individuals boasted of belonging to a certain apostle or preacher rather than to the Church as such. St. Paul reminded the Corinthians that such pettiness had no place if one gave any thought to Christ's return; for Christ alone can judge the merits of each person. His reminder is just as timely for Christians of our day as it was for the Corinthians.

A reading from the first letter of the apostle Paul to the Christians of Corinth
Brethren,

We should be regarded merely as servants of Christ, charged with transmitting to others the mysteries of God. Now what is expected of a servant is that he be trustworthy.

As for me, I am not much disturbed at being judged by you or by any human tribunal. Nor am I capable of judging myself. Though I have no pangs of conscience, it is not by a clear conscience that I am justified — the one who judges me is the Lord.

Do not be too eager to judge, therefore. Wait for the Lord's return. He it is who will bring to light what is hidden in the dark, and reveal the true dispositions of men's hearts. Then everyone will receive from God himself the praise that he deserves.

Gradual Ps. 144:18, 21

The Lord is near to all who call upon him, to all who call upon him in truth. May my mouth speak the praise of the Lord, and may all flesh bless his holy name.

Alleluia

Alleluia, alleluia. Come, O Lord, and delay not; forgive the sins of your people Israel. Alleluia.

GOSPEL Luke 3:1-6

The Gospel provides data for determining the exact date of Christ's historical coming on earth. It asks us also to "prepare the road for the Lord," that his advent in mystery may continue to take place today.

A reading from the holy Gospel according to Luke

In the fifteenth year of the reign of Emperor Tiberius — when Pontius Pilate was governor of Judea; Herod, tetrarch of Galilee; his brother Philip, tetrarch of Iturea and Trachonitis; and Lysanias, tetrarch of Abilene — Annas and Caiphas being high priests of the Jews, the word of God came to John, son of Zachary, in the desert.

He went about the whole Jordan region, preaching a baptism of repentance for the forgiveness of sins, according to what is written in the book of the oracles of the prophet Isaiah:

"A voice cries in the desert:
Prepare the road for the Lord, straighten out his paths!
Fill up all the hollows, level off the mountains and the hills!
Make the crooked ways straight, make the rough roads smooth!
And every man will see the salvation that God is sending!" [1]

OFFERTORY ANTIPHON *Luke 1:28*

Hail, Mary, full of grace, the Lord is with you, blessed are you among women, and blessed is the fruit of your womb.

Prayer over the Offerings

Sacrifíciis præséntibus, quæsumus, Dómine, placátus inténde: ut et devotióni nostræ profíciant, et salúti. Per Dóminum.

Here are the offerings for the sacrifice, Lord. Look favorably on them, we implore you: may they increase our fervor and be useful for our salvation. This we ask of you through our Lord.

COMMUNION ANTIPHON *Is. 7:14*

Behold, a virgin shall be with child and bear a son, and shall name him Emmanuel.

Prayer after the Communion

Sumptis munéribus, quæsumus, Dómine: ut cum frequentatióne mystérii, crescat nostræ salútis efféctus. Per Dóminum.

We have received your gifts, Lord: may our frequent communions bring about an increase of your saving grace. This we ask of you through our Lord.

[1] Isaiah 40:3-5.

DECEMBER 24

THE VIGIL OF CHRISTMAS

ENTRANCE ANTIPHON *Exod. 16:6, 7; Ps. 23:1*

This day you shall know that the Lord will come, and save us: and in the morning you shall see his glory.

Ps. The Lord's are the earth and its fullness; the world and those who dwell in it.

Glory be to the Father and to the Son and to the Holy Spirit. As it was in the beginning, is now and ever shall be, world without end. Amen. This day . . .

Prayer over the Assembly

Deus, qui nos redemptiónis nostræ ánnua expectatióne lætíficas: præsta; ut Unigénitum tuum, quem Redemptórem læti suscípimus, veniéntem quoque Iúdicem secúri videámus, Dóminum nostrum Iesum Christum, Fílium tuum: Qui tecum vivit et regnat in unitáte Spíritus Sancti, Deus, per ómnia sǽcula sæculórum.

O Lord, you make us happy every year in the expectation of our redemption. We welcome joyfully as our Redeemer your only-begotten Son, our Lord Jesus Christ. Give us the grace to be without fear when we see him coming again to judge us. This we ask of you through him, who lives and reigns with you in the unity of the Holy Spirit, God, forever.

EPISTLE   Romans 1:1-6

The Savior who is coming is Jesus. He is man like us; and, at the same time, he is God's Son. His coming emphasizes the fact that God wants to establish a relationship of love with men.

A reading from the letter of the apostle Paul to the Christians of Rome

I am Paul, a servant of Jesus Christ. My vocation is to be an apostle, to be set apart for the service of the gospel, that good news which God had promised beforehand through his prophets in the Scripture.

That good news is his Son, a descendant of David by his human birth, whom the Spirit of holiness established in full power as the Son of God after his resurrection from the dead: it is Jesus Christ our Lord.

He it is who has given me the grace and the mission of an apostle, to subject all nations to him in the faith for the glory of his name. And you are among those nations, for Jesus Christ our Lord is calling you also!

Gradual Exod. 16:6, 7; Ps. 79:2-3

This day you shall know that the Lord will come and save us: and in the morning you shall see his glory. O shepherd of Israel, hearken, O guide of the flock of Joseph! From your throne upon the Cherubim, shine forth before Ephraim, Benjamin and Manasseh.

Alleluia

Alleluia, alleluia. Tomorrow shall the wickedness of the earth be abolished: and the savior of the world shall reign over us. Alleluia.

GOSPEL Matthew 1:18-21

The Gospel takes us back to the days that preceded the birth of Jesus. It places the event in its historical setting and emphasizes the role of Savior that Jesus is going to take.

A reading from the holy Gospel according to Matthew

When Mary, the Mother of Jesus, was only engaged to Joseph and they had not yet lived together, it was found that she had become pregnant by the action of the Holy Spirit. Joseph, her husband, who was a just man, did not want to disgrace her, and he decided on a quiet separation. This was his intention, when the angel of the Lord appeared to him in a dream and said, "Joseph, son of David, do not be afraid to take Mary, your wife, into your home; for the life that she carries within her is the fruit of the Holy Spirit. She will give birth to a Son, and you shall call him Jesus; for it is he who will save his people from their sins."

OFFERTORY ANTIPHON *Ps. 23:7*

Lift up, O gates, your lintels; reach up, you ancient portals, that the king of glory may come in.

Prayer over the Offerings

Da nobis, quǽsumus, omnípotens Deus: ut, sicut adoránda Fílii tui natalítia prævenímus, sic eius múnera capiámus sempitérna gaudéntes: Qui tecum vivit et regnat in unitáte Spíritus Sancti, Deus, per ómnia sǽcula sæculórum.

Lord, this is the vigil of the honored birthday of your Son. It prepares for the joy of Christmas; may it lead us also to the joys of heaven. This we ask of you through him, who lives and reigns with you in the unity of the Holy Spirit, God, forever.

COMMUNION ANTIPHON *Is. 40:5*

The glory of the Lord shall be revealed, and all mankind shall see the salvation of our God.

Prayer after the Communion

Da nobis, quǽsumus, Dómine: unigéniti Fílii tui recensíta nativitáte respiráre; cuius cælésti mystério páscimur et potámur. Per eúndem Dóminum nostrum Iesum Christum Fílium tuum, qui tecum vivit et regnat in unitáte Spíritus Sancti, Deus, per ómnia sǽcula sæculórum.

O Lord, make our hearts light with new joy as we celebrate the birth of your Son, who has made himself our food and drink in this heavenly, eucharistic mystery. This we ask of you through the same Jesus Christ, our Lord and your Son, who lives and reigns with you in the unity of the Holy Spirit, God, forever.

DECEMBER 25

THE BIRTH OF THE LORD
FIRST MASS: AT MIDNIGHT

ENTRANCE ANTIPHON *Ps. 2:7, 1*

The Lord said to me, "You are my son; this day I have begotten you."

Ps. Why do nations rage and the people utter folly?

Glory be to the Father and to the Son and to the Holy Spirit. As it was in the beginning, is now and ever shall be, world without end. Amen. The Lord . . .

Prayer over the Assembly

Deus, qui hanc sacratíssimam noctem veri lúminis fecísti illustratióne claréscere: da, quæsumus; ut, cuius lucis mystéria in terra cognóvimus, eius quoque gáudiis in cælo perfruámur: Qui tecum vivit et regnat in unitáte Spíritus Sancti, Deus, per ómnia sæcula sæculórum.

O God, you have caused this most holy night to glow with the brightness of the true light. After allowing us a glimpse of your divine light on earth, give us the full enjoyment of it in the happiness of heaven. This we ask of you through him who is your light, who lives and reigns with you in the unity of the Holy Spirit, God, forever.

EPISTLE   Titus 2:11-15

The Epistle points up how Christ's nativity manifests salvation. That historical event, the import of which is perceived only by faith, changed the divine-human equation; moreover, it heralded the perfect triumph of salvation which will take place on the last day.

A reading from the letter of the apostle Paul to his disciple Titus

Beloved friend,

See, God's grace has appeared, ready to save all men!

It teaches us to reject wickedness and worldly ambitions, to live here on earth in sobriety, justice and love toward God.

It makes us look to the happiness that we hope for: of seeing Christ Jesus, our great God, our Savior, revealed in his glory; of seeing him who gave himself for us, in order to free us from all sin and to make of us a purified people who will really be his people, a people dedicated to doing good.

It is in this way that you should speak and exhort, in Christ Jesus our Lord!

Gradual Ps. 109:3, 1

Yours is princely power in the day of your birth, in holy splendor; before the daystar, I have begotten you. The Lord said to my Lord, "Sit at my right hand, till I make your enemies your footstool."

Alleluia Ps. 2:7

Alleluia, alleluia. The Lord said to me, "You are my son; this day I have begotten you." Alleluia.

GOSPEL   Luke 2:1-14

The majesty of the eternal birth of the Word was brought to mind by the psalm texts of the Gradual, while the Gospel recounts the birth of Jesus at Bethlehem — at once humble and glorious. Mary and Joseph are the first to know that the day of salvation has come.

A reading from the holy Gospel according to Luke

At that time an edict was issued by Caesar Augustus, ordering a census of the whole world. This first census took place while Cyrinus was governor of Syria. Everyone had to be registered in the country of his origin.

Joseph, therefore, being of the family and the line of David, left the village of Nazareth in Galilee and went up to Judea, to Bethlehem, the city of David, to be registered with Mary, his wife, who was about to become a mother.

It was during their stay at Bethlehem that the time came for her to give birth.

Mary brought her firstborn Son into the world, wrapped him in swaddling clothes and laid him in the stable manger, for there was no room for them in the inn.

In the countryside nearby, there were shepherds staying awake all night to watch their flocks. Suddenly an angel of the Lord stood by them, and the glory of the Lord surrounded them with light. They trembled with fear, but the angel said to them, "Do not be afraid, for I bring you good news, which will be a great joy for all the people: today, in the city of David, there is born to you a Savior: the Messiah, the Lord! Here is how you will recognize him: you will find a newborn infant, wrapped in swaddling clothes and laid in a manger."

Suddenly a band of heavenly spirits joined the angel; they were praising God, saying:

"Glory to God in the heights of heaven, and peace on earth to men of good will!"

OFFERTORY ANTIPHON Ps. 95:11, 13

Let the heavens be glad and the earth rejoice before the Lord, for he comes.

Prayer over the Offerings

Accépta tibi sit, Dómine, quǽsumus, hodiérnæ festivitátis oblátio: ut, tua grátia largiénte, per hæc sacrosáncta commércia, in illíus inveniámur forma, in quo tecum est nostra substántia: Qui

Be pleased to receive, O Lord, the offering which we present to you on this great feast. In this holy service heaven and earth engage in a sacred exchange: may your grace, here generously bestowed, cause us to resem-

tecum vivit re regnat in unitáte Spíritus Sancti, Deus, per ómnia sǽcula sæculórum.

ble your Son, through whom our human nature is united to you. This we ask of you through him, who lives and reigns with you in the unity of the Holy Spirit, God, forever.

COMMUNION ANTIPHON *Ps. 109:3*

In holy splendor, before the day-star I have begotten you.

Prayer after the Communion

Da nobis, quǽsumus, Dómine Deus noster: ut, qui Nativitátem Dómini nostri Iesu Christi mystériis nos frequentáre gaudémus; dignis conversatiónibus ad eius mereámur perveníre consórtium: Qui tecum vivit et regnat in unitáte Spíritus Sancti, Deus, per ómnia sǽcula sæculórum.

Lord, our God, we are happy to celebrate in this Mass the birth of your Son, our Lord Jesus Christ. Make us fit, by the holiness of our life, to share with him the happiness of heaven. This we ask of you through him, who lives and reigns with you in the unity of the Holy Spirit, God, forever.

SECOND MASS: AT DAWN

ENTRANCE ANTIPHON *Is. 9:2, 6; Ps. 92:1*

A light shall shine upon us this day: for the Lord is born to us. And he shall be called wonderful, God, prince of peace, Father of the world to come: of whose reign there shall be no end.

Ps. The Lord is king, in splendor robed; robed is the Lord and girt about with strength.

Glory be to the Father and to the Son and to the Holy Spirit. As it was in the beginning, is now and ever shall be, world without end. Amen. A light . . .

Prayer over the Assembly

Da nobis, quǽsumus, omnípotens Deus: ut, qui nova incarnáti Verbi tui luce perfúndimur; hoc in nostro respléndeat ópere, quod per fidem fulget in mente. Per eúndem Dóminum nostrum Iesum Christum Fílium tuum, qui tecum vivit et regnat in unitáte Spíritus Sancti, Deus, per ómnia sǽcula sæculórum.

Lord, the new light of your Word-made-flesh penetrates to the depth of our souls. Please make this light of our faith shine through every action of our life. This we ask of you through the same Jesus Christ, our Lord and your Son, who lives and reigns with you in the unity of the Holy Spirit, God, forever.

Commemoration of St. Anastasia, martyr

Da quǽsumus, omnípotens Deus: ut, qui beátæ Anastásiæ Márty-

God all-powerful, we celebrate the memory of your martyr St. Anastasia;

ris tuæ solémnia cólimus; eius apud te patrocínia sentiámus. Per Dóminum. make us experience her protection. This we ask of you through our Lord.

EPISTLE Titus 3:4-7

"God became man," says St. Irenaeus, "that man might become God." It was through baptism that we were born into the life of God and became his children.

A reading from the letter of the apostle Paul to his disciple Titus

Beloved friend,

See, the goodness of God, our Savior, has become manifest, his love for men revealed! What saves us is not the good actions we ourselves have performed; it is his pure goodness; it is that baptism of rebirth in which the Holy Spirit makes us new men.

This Spirit he has poured out generously on us through Jesus Christ, our Savior, to make us saints by his grace — saints whose heritage, in hope, is life eternal; in Christ Jesus our Lord.

Gradual Ps. 117:26, 27, 23

Blessed is he who comes in the name of the Lord; the Lord is God, and he has given us light. By the Lord has this been done; it is wonderful in our eyes.

Alleluia Ps. 92:1

Alleluia, alleluia. The Lord is king, in splendor robed; robed is the Lord and girt about with strength. Alleluia.

GOSPEL Luke 2:15-20

Following a chronological order of events, the Gospel of this second Mass recounts the arrival of the shepherds at the crib. This episode highlights the fact that salvation had come to the "poor" of Israel, to those who put all their trust in God's help.

A reading from the holy Gospel according to Luke

At that time [after the angels had left], the shepherds said to one another, "Let's go right to Bethlehem and see what has happened — this thing that the Lord has just announced to us." They hurried over, and found Mary and Joseph, and the newborn infant laid in the manger. Having seen for themselves, they proceeded to tell what had been said to them about this child; and all those who heard them were amazed at these things.

As for Mary, she was keeping all these memories carefully and meditating on them in her heart.

The shepherds then returned, glorifying and praising God for everything that had been proclaimed to them, which they had now seen and heard.

OFFERTORY ANTIPHON *Ps. 92:1-2*

God has made the world firm, not to be moved. Your throne, O God, stands firm from of old; from everlasting you are.

Prayer over the Offerings

Múnera nostra, quǽsumus, Dómine, Nativitátis hodiérnæ mystériis apta provéniant, et pacem nobis semper infúndant: ut, sicut homo génitus idem refúlsit et Deus, sic nobis hæc terréna substántia cónferat, quod divínum est. Per eúndem Dóminum nostrum Iesum Christum Fílium tuum, qui tecum vivit et regnat in unitáte Spíritus Sancti, Deus, per ómnia sǽcula sæculórum.

Lord, may our offerings be suitable for the mysteries of Christmas; may they always pour out your peace on us. He who was born of our humanity is the same who made his divinity shine forth; may the earthly substance of these offerings also become a heavenly food for us. This we ask of you through the same Jesus Christ, our Lord and your Son, who lives and reigns with you in the unity of the Holy Spirit, God, forever.

Commemoration of St. Anastasia

Accipe, quǽsumus, Dómine, múnera dignánter obláta: et beátæ Anastásiæ Mártyris tuæ suffragántibus méritis, ad nostræ salútis auxílium proveníre concéde. Per Dóminum.

Please accept our offering, Lord; may it help toward our salvation. This we ask of you through the merits of your martyr St. Anastasia. We address our prayer to you through our Lord.

COMMUNION ANTIPHON *Zach. 9:9*

Rejoice heartily, O daughter Sion, shout for joy, O daughter Jerusalem! See, your king shall come, a just savior of the world is he.

Prayer after the Communion

Huius nos, Dómine, sacraménti semper nóvitas natális instáuret: cuius Natívitas singuláris humánam répulit vetustátem. Per eúndem Dóminum nostrum Iesum Christum Fílium tuum, qui tecum vivit et regnat in unitáte Spíritus Sancti, Deus, per ómnia sǽcula sæculórum.

Lord, the wondrous birth of your Son has delivered mankind from their old enslavement. May his sacrament always bring us a new life. This we ask of you through the same Jesus Christ, our Lord and your Son, who lives and reigns with you in the unity of the Holy Spirit, God, forever.

Commemoration of St. Anastasia

Satiásti, Dómine, famíliam tuam munéribus sacris: eius, quǽsumus, semper interventióne nos réfove, cuius solémnia celebrámus. Per Dóminum.

You have nourished your family, Lord, with the holy Eucharist. Make our souls more ardent through the intercession of the saint whose feast we are celebrating. This we ask of you through our Lord.

THIRD MASS: THE MASS OF THE DAY

ENTRANCE ANTIPHON *Is. 9:6; Ps. 97:1*

A child is born to us, a son is given to us; upon his shoulder dominion rests; and his name shall be called the angel of great counsel.

Ps. Sing to the Lord a new song, for he has done wondrous deeds.

Glory be to the Father and to the Son and to the Holy Spirit. As it was in the beginning, is now and ever shall be, world without end. Amen. A child . . .

Prayer over the Assembly

Concéde, quǽsumus, omnípotens Deus: ut nos Unigéniti tui nova per carnem Natívitas líberet; quos sub peccáti iugo vetústa sérvitus tenet. Per eúndem Dóminum nostrum Iesum Christum Fílium tuum, qui tecum vivit et regnat in unitáte Spíritus Sancti, Deus, per ómnia sǽcula sæculórum.

We entreat you, God all-powerful: may the new and wonderful birth of your incarnate Son deliver us from the old slavery which holds us down under the yoke of sin! This we ask of you through the same Jesus Christ, our Lord and your Son, who lives and reigns with you in the unity of the Holy Spirit, God, forever.

EPISTLE   Hebrews 1:1-12

In solemn phrases we are invited to contemplate Christ, (a) as the Son who is the perfect image of the Father; (b) as the Word that creates; (c) as the Mediator of the new covenant.

A reading from the letter of the apostle Paul to the Hebrews

When God spoke to our fathers, he did so through the prophets, giving his message at frequent intervals and clothing it in a variety of forms. Now in our times, which are the last times, he has spoken to us through his own Son, the Son by whom he created the world and in whom all creation is to find its goal.

That Son, who is the shining reflection of God's glory, the perfect image of his nature, that Son, whose all-powerful word sustains every creature, purified us of our sins and then claimed his seat in the heavens, at the right hand of the divine majesty, being placed above all the angels in the eminence of his title as Son.

For to which of his angels has God ever said, "You are my Son; today I have begotten You" [1]? And again, "I shall be his Father, and he will be my Son" [2]? Moreover, when he introduces his only-begotten Son into the world, he says, "Let all the angels of God adore him!" [3]

As far as angels are concerned, the psalm says, "He makes his angels a mighty wind; he makes his servants a leaping flame." [4] But where the Son is concerned, "Your throne, O God, is an eternal throne, and your royal scepter a scepter of justice. You love justice and detest evil, Lord; therefore

[1] Psalm 2:7.
[2] 2 Samuel 7:14.
[3] Psalm 96:7.
[4] Psalm 103:4.

your God has chosen you above all the rest and consecrated you King in gladness." [1] And again, "It was you, Lord, who made the earth in the beginning; and the heavens are the work of your hands. They will perish; but you remain. They will wear out, like a garment; you will cast them off like a cloak that one changes. But you, for your part, remain the same; there will be no end to your years." [2]

Gradual *Ps. 97:3-4, 2*

All the ends of the earth have seen the salvation by our God. Sing joyfully to God, all you lands. The Lord has made his salvation known: in the sight of the nations he has revealed his justice.

Alleluia

Alleluia, alleluia. A sanctified day has shone upon us. Come, you nations, and adore the Lord: for this day a great light has descended upon the earth. Alleluia.

GOSPEL   John 1:1-14

The Gospel begins by having us meditate on the mysterious, intimate ties that unite the Word to the Father. Then it tells us how the Word of God was progressively manifested in the world: first through the work of creation, then by the revelation made to the people of Israel, finally "by becoming flesh and dwelling among us."

A reading from the holy Gospel according to John

Before all things, there was the Word; the Word was united to God, and the Word was God. From all eternity he was with God. It was through him that [the Creator] made all things; and nothing that exists was made without him. In him was life, and that life is the light of men. That light shines in the darkness, and the darkness has not been able to stop it.

There came a man sent from God: he was called John the Baptist. He came to serve as a witness, to bear witness on behalf of the light, that through him all men might have faith. He was not the light, but he was here to bear witness on behalf of the light.

[The Word], the true light that enlightens every man, was making his entrance into this world. He was in the world — this world which God had created through him — and the world did not recognize him. He came home, and his own people did not welcome him.

But to all those who did welcome him he gave the power to become sons of God. For those who believe in him are not sons of blood or of carnal desire or of a human will; they are the sons of God. [3]

Yes, the Word was made flesh and he established his dwelling-place

[1] Psalm 44:7-8.
[2] Psalm 101:26-28.
[3] Most modern exegetes read, "But to all those who did welcome him he gave the power to become sons of God; to those, that is, who believe in *him* who is born not of blood nor of carnal desire nor of a human will, but of God."

among us. We have seen his glory, the glory which the Father has given his only-begotten Son by filling him with grace and truth.

OFFERTORY ANTIPHON *Ps. 88:12, 15*

Yours are the heavens, and yours is the earth; the world and its fullness you have founded. Justice and judgment are the foundation of your throne.

Prayer over the Offerings

Obláta, Dómine, múnera, nova Unigéniti tui Nativitáte sanctífica: nosque a peccatórum nostrórum máculis emúnda. Per eúndem Dóminum nostrum Iesum Christum Fílium tuum, qui tecum vivit et regnat in unitáte Spíritus Sancti, Deus, per ómnia sǽcula sæculórum.

Sanctify these offerings, Lord, through the birth of your only-begotten Son, and purify us from the stains of our sins. This we ask of you through the same Jesus Christ, our Lord and your Son, who lives and reigns with you in the unity of the Holy Spirit, God, forever.

COMMUNION ANTIPHON *Ps. 97:3*

All the ends of the earth have seen the salvation by our God.

Prayer after the Communion

Præsta, quǽsumus, omnípotens Deus: ut natus hódie Salvátor mundi, sicut divínæ nobis generatiónis est auctor; ita et immortalitátis sit ipse largítor: Qui tecum vivit et regnat in unitáte Spíritus Sancti, Deus, per ómnia sǽcula sæculórum.

Listen to our prayer, all-powerful Lord: the Savior of the world by his birth today has brought us into the family of God; may he grant us a share in immortality also. This we ask of you through him, who lives and reigns with you in the unity of the Holy Spirit, God, forever.

SUNDAY WITHIN THE OCTAVE OF THE BIRTH OF THE LORD

ENTRANCE ANTIPHON *Wis. 18:14-15; Ps. 92:1*

When a profound stillness compassed everything and the night in its swift course was half spent, your all-powerful word, O Lord, bounded from heaven's royal throne.

Ps. The Lord is king, in splendor robed; robed is the Lord and girt about with strength.

Glory be to the Father and to the Son and to the Holy Spirit. As it was in the beginning, is now and ever shall be, world without end. Amen. When a profound stillness . . .

Prayer over the Assembly

Omnípotens sempitérne Deus, dírige actus nostros in beneplácito tuo: ut in nómine diléti Fílii tui mereámur bonis opéribus abundáre: Qui tecum vivit et regnat in unitáte Spíritus Sancti, Deus, per ómnia sæcula sæculórum.

All-powerful, eternal God, direct our actions according to your will, and we shall be able to multiply our good works by the grace of your beloved Son, our Lord Jesus Christ, who lives and reigns with you in the unity of the Holy Spirit, God, forever.

For possible commemorations, see pages 166–168.

EPISTLE   Galatians 4:1-7

The Epistle highlights the fact that the incarnation of the Word has brought mankind into the last phase of salvation. The old alliance, a preparatory stage, held the people of God under the law. Like a governess, the law was teaching men to live as God's children. But now that God has become man, the Holy Spirit himself, being communicated to Christians, is teaching them to be sons of the Father and is sustaining their love.

A reading from the letter of the apostle Paul to the Christians of Galatia

Brethren,

[If you belong to Christ, it is you who are the "offspring" of Abraham, the "heirs" of the promise made to him (3:29).] [1]

But as long as the heir is not yet of age, he is treated as a servant, even though he is master of the whole estate. Until the time set by his father, he will remain under the charge of his tutors and of those to whom his education is entrusted.

It has been the same for the people of God: as long as we were in our childhood, we remained subject to the material prescriptions [of the Jewish law].

But at the time which he had set, God sent his Son. He caused him to be born of a woman and subjected him to the law, in order to deliver us from the servitude of the old law and to make us true sons by adoption.

And the proof that you are really sons is this, that God has sent into your hearts the Spirit of his Son, that Spirit which [from your inmost beings] cries out to God and calls him: "Father!"

You are no longer a slave, therefore, but a son; and, if you are a son, you are an heir, by God's choice.

Gradual Ps. 44:3, 2

Fairer in beauty are you than the sons of men: grace is poured out upon your lips. My heart overflows with a goodly theme; as I sing my ode to the king, my tongue is nimble as the pen of a skillful scribe.

---

[1] As an aid to the understanding of this Epistle, the verse which precedes it has been added.

Alleluia Ps. 92:1

Alleluia, alleluia. The Lord is king, in splendor robed; robed is the Lord and girt about with strength. Alleluia.

GOSPEL   Luke 2:33-40

The liturgy wants us to understand, even now at Christmas time, an essential lesson: the Incarnation cannot be separated from the Redemption. Christ achieved the salvation of the world only by accepting the Cross; and, however disconcerting such a Savior as this may be, all men must take a stand for or against him and his method.

A reading from the holy Gospel according to Luke

At that time [when they presented Jesus in the temple], Joseph and Mary, the Mother of Jesus, were astonished at what was being said about him.

The aged Simeon blessed them and said to Mary, his Mother, "This child will be the cause either of the fall or of the rise of every man in Israel. Everyone will take sides for or against him. — A sword of sorrow will pierce your soul. — Thus the inmost dispositions of each one will one day be brought to light."

There was also a prophetess, Anna, daughter of Phanuel, of the tribe of Aser. Having remained a widow after only seven years of marriage, she had reached the advanced age of eighty-four years; never did she leave the temple, but served God day and night by fasting and prayer. She also came upon the scene just at this time, and blessed God; and she spoke about the child to all those who were awaiting the liberation of the people of Israel.

Having done all that the law commanded, Mary and Joseph returned home to Nazareth in Galilee.

The boy kept growing and becoming stronger; he was filled with wisdom, and God's grace was in him.

OFFERTORY ANTIPHON *Ps. 92:1-2*

God has made the world firm, not to be moved. Your throne, O God, stands firm from of old; from everlasting you are.

Prayer over the Offerings

Concéde, quǽsumus, omnípotens Deus: ut óculis tuæ maiestátis munus oblátum, et grátiam nobis piæ devotiónis obtíneat, et efféctum beátæ perennitátis acquírat. Per Dóminum.

God all-powerful, before your majesty we bring our offerings; may they obtain for us the grace of a more fervent piety and ensure us an eternity of happiness. This we ask of you through our Lord.

COMMUNION ANTIPHON *Matthew 2:20*

Take the child and his mother, and go into the land of Israel, for those who sought the child's life are dead.

Prayer after the Communion

Per huius Dómine, operatiónem mystérii, et vítia nostra purgéntur, et iusta desidéria compleántur. Per Dóminum.	Lord, by the impact of this mystery purify us from our vices and fulfill our just desires. This we ask of you through our Lord.

JANUARY 1

THE OCTAVE OF THE BIRTH OF THE LORD

ENTRANCE ANTIPHON *Is. 9:6; Ps. 97:1*

A child is born to us, a son is given to us; upon his shoulder dominion rests; and his name shall be called the angel of great counsel.

Ps. Sing to the Lord a new song, for he has done wondrous deeds.

Glory be to the Father and to the Son and to the Holy Spirit. As it was in the beginning, is now and ever shall be, world without end. Amen. A child . . .

Prayer over the Assembly

Deus, qui salútis ætérnæ, beátæ Maríæ virginitáte fecúnda, humáno géneri prǽmia præstitísti: tríbue, quǽsumus; ut ipsam pro nobis intercédere sentiámus, per quam merúimus auctórem vitæ suscípere, Dóminum nostrum Iesum Christum, Fílium tuum: Qui tecum vivit et regnat in unitáte Spíritus Sancti, Deus, per ómnia sǽcula sæculórum.	O God, who through the fruitful virginity of Blessed Mary gave all men the riches of eternal salvation, we entreat you to let us feel the intercession of her who gave us the author of life, our Lord Jesus Christ, your Son, who lives and reigns with you in the unity of the Holy Spirit, God, forever.

EPISTLE   Titus 2:11-15

By the name which he received officially on the day of the circumcision, Jesus became known to all as the Savior.

A reading from the letter of the apostle Paul to his disciple Titus
Beloved friend,

See, God's grace has appeared, ready to save all men!

It teaches us to reject wickedness and worldly ambitions, to live here on earth in sobriety, justice and love toward God.

It makes us look to the happiness that we hope for: of seeing Christ Jesus, our great God, our Savior, revealed anew in his glory; of seeing him who gave himself for us, in order to free us from all sin and to make of us a purified people who will really be his people, a people dedicated to doing good.

It is in this way that you should speak and exhort, in Christ Jesus our Lord!

Gradual *Ps. 97:3-4, 2*

All the ends of the earth have seen the salvation by our God. Sing joyfully to God, all you lands. The Lord has made his salvation known: in the sight of the nations he has revealed his justice.

Alleluia *Heb. 1:1-2*

Alleluia, alleluia. God, who in diverse ways spoke in times past to the fathers by the prophets, last of all, in these days, has spoken to us by his son. Alleluia.

GOSPEL   Luke 2:21

It was the Father's own choice that his Son be known among men by the name: Savior.

A reading from the holy Gospel according to Luke

At that time, the eighth day after his birth, the day on which the infant was to be circumcised, he received the name of Jesus [God saves us]. It was the name the angel had indicated before the child was conceived in his Mother's womb.

OFFERTORY ANTIPHON *Ps. 88:12, 15*

Yours are the heavens, and yours is the earth; the world and its fullness you have founded. Justice and judgment are the foundation of your throne.

Prayer over the Offerings

Munéribus nostris, quǽsumus, Dómine, precibúsque suscéptis: et cæléstibus nos munda mystériis, et cleménter exáudi. Per Dóminum.

Be pleased to accept our offerings and our prayers and in your kindness purify us, Lord, through this holy sacrifice. This we ask of you through our Lord.

COMMUNION ANTIPHON *Ps. 97:3*

All the ends of the earth have seen the salvation by our God.

Prayer after the Communion

Hæc nos commúnio, Dómine, purget a crímine: et, intercedénte beáta Vírgine Dei Genetríce María, cæléstis remédii fáciat esse consórtes. Per eúndem Dóminum nostrum Iesum Christum Fílium tuum, qui tecum vivit et regnat in unitáte Spíritus Sancti, Deus, per ómnia sǽcula sæculórum.

May this communion, Lord, cleanse us of our sins; through the intercession of the blessed Virgin Mary, Mother of God, may it heal our souls and make them share in the happiness of heaven. This we ask of You through the same Jesus Christ, our Lord and your Son, who lives and reigns with you in the unity of the Holy Spirit, God, forever.

SUNDAY BETWEEN JANUARY 2 AND 5

THE HOLY NAME OF JESUS

This feast is celebrated on the Sunday between January 2 and 5; when no Sunday occurs it falls on January 2.

ENTRANCE ANTIPHON   *Phil. 2:10-11; Ps. 8:2*

At the name of Jesus every knee should bend of those in heaven, on earth, and under the earth, and every tongue should confess that the Lord Jesus Christ is in the glory of God the Father.

Ps. O Lord, our Lord, how glorious is your name over all the earth!

Glory be to the Father and to the Son and to the Holy Spirit. As it was in the beginning, is now and ever shall be, world without end. Amen. At the name . . .

Prayer over the Assembly

Deus, qui unigénitum Fílium tuum constituísti humáni géneris Salvatórem, et Iesum vocári iussísti: concéde propítius; ut, cuius sanctum nomen venerámur in terris, eius quoque aspéctu perfruámur in cælis. Per eúndem Dóminum nostrum Iesum Christum Fílium tuum, qui tecum vivit et regnat in unitáte Spíritus Sancti, Deus, per ómnia sǽcula sæculórum.

O God, you made your only-begotten Son the Savior of the human race and decreed for him the name of Jesus. Grant us the grace of seeing in the happiness of heaven the one whose holy name we venerate on earth. This we ask of you through the same Jesus Christ, our Lord and your Son, who lives and reigns with you in the unity of the Holy Spirit, God, forever.

EPISTLE   Acts 4:8-12

"In the name of Jesus of Nazareth, stand up and walk," St. Peter had said to the cripple who was begging at the temple gate. And the man had got up, healed. The healing of bodies is the sign of the salvation Jesus brings to the world, that salvation which is the liberation from all evil.

A reading from the Acts of the Apostles

Then Peter, filled with the Holy Spirit, answered [the judges]:

"Rulers of the people and elders. Since an inquiry is being made today into the case of this cripple and it is asked by what means he was healed, be informed, all of you, and the whole people of Israel: it is in the name of Jesus Christ of Nazareth, whom you crucified and whom God has raised from the dead, it is by the power of this name that the man is standing before you, healed!

"This Jesus is 'the stone that was rejected by you, the builders, which has become the cornerstone.' [1]

[1] See Psalm 117:22 and Matthew 21:42.

"Aside from him, there is no salvation, for there is no other name given to men under heaven by which we can be saved!"

Gradual *Ps. 105:47; Is. 63:16*

Save us, O Lord, our God, and gather us from among the nations, that we may give thanks to your holy name and glory in praising you. You, O Lord, are our Father and our redeemer, from everlasting is your name.

Alleluia *Ps. 144:21*

Alleluia, alleluia. May my mouth speak the praise of the Lord, and may all flesh bless his holy name. Alleluia.

GOSPEL Luke 2:21

The Father himself willed that his Son be known among men by the name: Savior.

A reading from the holy Gospel according to Luke

At that time, the eighth day after his birth, the day on which the infant was to be circumcised, he received the name of Jesus [God saves us]. It was the name the angel had indicated before the child was conceived in his Mother's womb.

OFFERTORY ANTIPHON *Ps. 85:12, 15*

I will give thanks to you, O Lord my God, with all my heart, and I will glorify your name forever. For you, O Lord, are good and forgiving, abounding in kindness to all who call upon you. Alleluia.

Prayer over the Offerings

Benedíctio tua, clementíssime Deus, qua omnis viget creatúra, sanctíficet, quǽsumus, hoc sacrifícium nostrum, quod ad glóriam nóminis Fílii tui, Dómini nostri Iesu Christi, offérimus tibi: ut maiestáti tuæ placére possit ad laudem, et nobis profícere ad salútem. Per eúndem Dóminum nostrum Iesum Christum Fílium tuum, qui tecum vivit et regnat in unitáte Spíritus Sancti, Deus, per ómnia sǽcula sæculórum.

You are supremely good, O Lord, and your blessing has given life to all creatures. May it sanctify this sacrifice which we offer for the glory of the name of our Lord Jesus Christ, your Son; may it make this sacrifice pleasing to your majesty and profitable for our salvation! This we ask of you through the same Jesus Christ, our Lord and your Son, who lives and reigns with you in the unity of the Holy Spirit, God, forever.

COMMUNION ANTIPHON *Ps. 85:9-10*

All the nations you have made shall come and worship you, O Lord, and glorify your name. For you are great and do wondrous deeds; you alone are God. Alleluia.

Prayer after the Communion

Omnípotens ætérne Deus, qui creásti et redemísti nos, réspice propítius vota nostra: et sacrifícium salutáris hóstiæ, quod in honórem nóminis Fílii tui, Dómini nostri Iesu Christi, maiestáti tuæ obtúlimus, plácido et benígno vultu suscípere dignéris; ut grátia tua nobis infúsa, sub glorióso nómine Iesu, ætérnæ prædestinatiónis título gaudeámus nómina nostra scripta esse in cælis. Per eúndem Dóminum nostrum Iesum Christum Fílium tuum, qui tecum vivit et regnat in unitáte Spíritus Sancti, Deus, per ómnia sǽcula sæculórum.

All-powerful, eternal God, our Creator and Redeemer, please accept our prayers and the sacrifice which we have offered to your divine majesty in honor of the name of your Son, our Lord Jesus Christ. You have poured out your grace on us; by your grace may we have the joy of seeing our name written in heaven in the book of the elect under the glorious name of Jesus. This we ask of you through the same Jesus Christ, our Lord and your Son, who lives and reigns with you in the unity of the Holy Spirit, God, forever.

JANUARY 6

THE EPIPHANY OF THE LORD

ENTRANCE ANTIPHON *Mal. 3:1; 1 Par. 29:12; Ps. 71:1*

Behold, the Lord the ruler is come; and the kingdom is in his hand, and power, and dominion.

Ps. O God, with your judgment endow the king, and with your justice, the king's son.

Glory be to the Father and to the Son and to the Holy Spirit. As it was in the beginning, is now and ever shall be, world without end. Amen. Behold . . .

Prayer over the Assembly

Deus, qui hodiérna die Unigénitum tuum géntibus stella duce revelásti: concéde propítius; ut, qui iam te ex fide cognóvimus, usque ad contemplándam spéciem tuæ celsitúdinis perducámur. Per eúndem Dóminum nostrum Iesum Christum Fílium tuum, qui tecum vivit et regnat in unitáte Spíritus Sancti, Deus, per ómnia sǽcula sæculórum.

O God, who by the guidance of a star revealed to the pagan peoples the birth of your Son, grant that those who already know you by faith may ultimately be brought to the contemplation of your glory. This we ask of you through the same Jesus Christ, our Lord and your Son, who lives and reigns with you in the unity of the Holy Spirit, God, forever.

EPISTLE   Isaiah 60:1-6

After their return from captivity, the Jews put their whole heart into rebuilding Jerusalem and its temple. To encourage them, prophets de-

scribed the wonderful future of this new Jerusalem: it would become the center of the world, where their God would be adored by all the peoples of earth as the one true God. In this way Israel's last prophets indicated how the gentiles would be assimilated into the people of God and how the era of universal salvation would begin. We are part of that age in which this prophecy is being fulfilled.

A reading from the prophet Isaiah

Arise, Jerusalem, and be radiant,
see, your light has come:
God is shining on you like a rising sun!

Darkness covers the earth,
and the nations know only the night.
But over you the Lord is rising;
and his brightness shines on you.

The nations will turn toward your light,
and the kings will march
in the splendor of your dawn.

Lift up your eyes, look about you!
All are gathering and coming toward you:
your sons and your daughters are hastening from all sides.

Look at them and rejoice!
Be astounded and let your heart swell!
Here are treasures coming from across the seas,
and the wealth of the nations.

Caravans of camels will overwhelm you,
the dromedaries of Madian and of Epha.
Throngs will come from Saba,
bearing gold and frankincense
and singing the praises of the Lord.

Gradual Is. 60:6, 1

All from Saba shall come, bringing gold and frankincense, and proclaiming the praises of the Lord. Rise up in splendor, O Jerusalem, for the glory of the Lord shines upon you.

Alleluia Matthew 2:2

Alleluia, alleluia. We have seen his star in the East: and have come with gifts to worship the Lord. Alleluia.

GOSPEL   Matthew 2:1-12

The Gospel which tells of the coming of the Magi to Bethlehem is the center of this Mass. The texts of the choir chants bring out the full import of this event, by showing that the prophecies about the universality of salvation are here fulfilled and by affirming that Christ is the King of all nations.

A reading from the holy Gospel according to Matthew

After the birth of Jesus at Bethlehem of Juda, under the reign of Herod, Magi from the East arrived in Jerusalem, asking, "Where can we find the King of the Jews who has just been born? For we have seen his star in the East, and we have come to pay homage to him."

At this news King Herod was disturbed, and all Jerusalem with him. He called together the chief priests and the scribes and asked them where the Christ was to be born.

"In Bethlehem of Juda," they answered. "For the prophet has written, 'And you, Bethlehem, land of Juda, you are not the least of the towns of Juda; for from you shall come forth a leader, the shepherd of Israel, my people.' " [1]

Then Herod had the Magi come to him secretly, and he found out from them the exact date on which they had seen this star. And he told them to go to Bethlehem. "Go and make careful inquiries about this child," he said; "and, when you have found him, report to me, that I too may go and pay him homage."

After listening to the king, the Magi set out on their way again. And there was the star they had seen in the East, moving along before them, until it came to where the child was; then it stopped. The sight of the star filled them with joy.

Entering the house, they found the child with his Mother Mary; and they fell to their knees and paid him homage. Then, opening their treasures, they offered him gold, frankincense and myrrh.

They were advised in a dream not to return to Herod; and so they went back to their country by another route.

OFFERTORY ANTIPHON *Ps. 71:10-11*

The kings of Tharsis and the isles shall offer gifts; the kings of Arabia and Saba shall bring tribute. All kings shall pay him homage, all nations shall serve him.

Prayer over the Offerings

Ecclésiæ tuæ, quǽsumus, Dómine, dona propítius intuére: quibus non iam aurum, thus, et myrrha profértur: sed quod eísdem munéribus declarátur, immolátur et súmitur, Iesus Christus Fílius tuus Dóminus noster: Qui tecum vivit et regnat in unitáte Spíritus Sancti, Deus, per ómnia sǽcula sæculórum.

Look favorably, Lord, on the offering of your Church. It is no longer gold, frankincense and myrrh: this offering today is he himself of whom these gifts are a figure, he who is offered, immolated and given as food, Jesus Christ, your Son, our Lord, who lives and reigns with you in the unity of the Holy Spirit, God, forever.

COMMUNION ANTIPHON *Matthew 2:2*

We have seen his star in the East and have come with gifts to worship the Lord.

[1] Micah 5:1.

Prayer after the Communion

Præsta, quǽsumus, omnípotens Deus: ut quæ solémni celebrámus offício, purificátæ mentis intellegéntia consequámur. Per Dóminum.

Enable us, all-powerful God, in the clarity of our purified souls to understand the lessons of this great feast which we celebrate each year. This we ask of you through our Lord.

FIRST SUNDAY AFTER EPIPHANY

THE HOLY FAMILY OF JESUS, MARY AND JOSEPH

ENTRANCE ANTIPHON *Prov. 23:24, 25; Ps. 83:2-3*
The father of the just will exult with glee; let your father and mother have joy; let her who bore you exult.

Ps. How lovely is your dwelling place, O Lord of hosts! My soul yearns and pines for the courts of the Lord.

Glory be to the Father and to the Son and to the Holy Spirit. As it was in the beginning, is now and ever shall be, world without end. Amen. The father . . .

Prayer over the Assembly

Dómine Iesu Christe, qui, Maríæ et Ioseph súbditus, domésticam vitam ineffabílibus virtútibus consecrásti: fac nos, utriúsque auxílio, Famíliæ sanctæ tuæ exémplis ínstrui: et consórtium cónsequi sempitérnum: Qui vivis et regnas cum Deo Patre in unitáte Spíritus Sancti, Deus, per ómnia sǽcula sæculórum.

Lord Jesus Christ, in obeying Mary and Joseph you consecrated family life with admirable virtues. Grant that with the help of both of them we may learn from the example of your holy Family and so become a part of it for eternity. This we ask of you, Lord Jesus, living and reigning with the Father in the unity of the Holy Spirit, God, forever.

EPISTLE Colossians 3:12-17
The family of God's children is the Church. Here we must live out the unity and the love characteristic of genuine family life.

A reading from the letter of the apostle Paul to the Christians of Colossae
Brethren,

Since God has chosen you, since he has made you his saints and his beloved, have nothing in your hearts but mercy, tenderness, humility, kindness and patience. Support one another and forgive one another for any wrongs that may be committed. The Lord has forgiven you. Do as he has done.

Above all, have charity; it is the bond of all the virtues. And let the peace of Christ reign in your hearts, that peace to which God calls you to make you all one body! Live in a state of thanksgiving.

May Christ's word dwell in your soul with all its riches! Study it, and encourage one another in your efforts toward perfection. With all your hearts, sing: let your thanks rise up to God in psalms, hymns and canticles! And whatever you do or say, let it be in the name of the Lord Jesus; let it be in thanksgiving, through him, to God the Father.

Gradual *Ps. 26:4; Ps. 83:5*

One thing I ask of the Lord; this I seek: to dwell in the house of the Lord all the days of my life. Happy they who dwell in your house, O Lord! continually they praise you.

Alleluia *Is. 45:15*

Alleluia, alleluia. Truly you are a hidden God, the God of Israel, the savior. Alleluia.

GOSPEL   Luke 2:42-52

For different reasons, the temple and the house at Nazareth are entitled to be called the house of God. In both of them, Jesus seeks the will of his Father. His submission to his parents is the expression of his filial love.

A reading from the holy Gospel according to Luke

When he was twelve years old, Jesus went up to Jerusalem with his parents, who were going there, as they did every year, for the feast of the Passover.

When they set out on their way back after the feast, the child Jesus remained in Jerusalem. His parents did not notice this fact, but went along all day thinking that he was in the caravan. Then they looked for him among their relatives and acquaintances. Not finding him, they went back in search of him, all the way to Jerusalem.

It was the third day when they found him in the temple. Seated in the midst of the doctors, he was listening to them and asking them questions. All those who heard him were amazed at his intelligence and his answers.

When they saw him, his parents were deeply moved. "My Son," exclaimed his Mother, "why have you done such a thing to us? Oh, how anxious your father and I were, looking for you!"

"Why were you looking for me?," he answered. "Did you not know that I must be in my Father's house?" They did not understand this reply.

Then he went down with them to Nazareth; and he was subject to them.

His Mother kept all these memories faithfully in her heart. As he grew older, Jesus progressed also in wisdom and in grace, both in God's eyes and in the eyes of men.

OFFERTORY ANTIPHON *Luke 2:22*

The parents of Jesus took him up to Jerusalem, to present him to the Lord.

Prayer over the Offerings

Placatiónis hóstiam offérimus tibi, Dómine, supplíciter depre-

Lord, we offer you this sacrifice and our humble prayers. Through the

cántes: ut, per intercessiónem Deíparæ Vírginis cum beáto Ioseph, famílias nostras in pace grátia tua fírmiter constítuas. Per eúndem Dóminum nostrum Iesum Christum Fílium tuum, qui tecum vivit et regnat in unitáte Spíritus Sancti, Deus, per ómnia sǽcula sæculórum.

intercession of the Mother of God, the Virgin Mary, and of St. Joseph, be pleased to establish our families securely in your grace and your peace. This we ask of you through the same Jesus Christ, our Lord and your Son, who lives and reigns with you in the unity of the Holy Spirit, God, forever.

COMMUNION ANTIPHON *Luke 2:51*

Jesus went down with them, and came to Nazareth and was subject to them.

Prayer after the Communion

Quos cæléstibus réficis sacraméntis, fac, Dómine Iesu, sanctæ Famíliæ tuæ exémpla iúgiter imitári: ut, in hora mortis nostræ, occurrénte gloriósa Vírgine Matre tua cum beáto Ioseph; per te in ætérna tabernácula récipi mereámur: Qui vivis et regnas cum Deo Patre in unitáte Spíritus Sancti, Deus, per ómnia sǽcula sæculórum.

Lord Jesus, you nourish our souls on your Eucharist. Grant us the grace to imitate faithfully the example of your holy Family, that we may be welcomed at the hour of our death by the glorious Virgin Mary, your Mother, and by St. Joseph, and may be received by you into our everlasting home. This we ask of you, Lord Jesus, living and reigning with the Father in the unity of the Holy Spirit, God, forever.

SECOND SUNDAY AFTER EPIPHANY

ENTRANCE ANTIPHON *Ps. 65:4, 1-2*

Let all on earth worship you, O God, and sing praise to you, sing praise to your name, Most High.

Ps. Shout joyfully to God, all you on earth, sing praise to the glory of his name; proclaim his glorious praise.

Glory be to the Father and to the Son and to the Holy Spirit. As it was in the beginning, is now and ever shall be, world without end. Amen. Let all . . .

Prayer over the Assembly

Omnípotens sempitérne Deus, qui cæléstia simul et terréna moderáris: supplicatiónes pópuli tui cleménter exáudi; et pacem tuam nostris concéde tempóribus. Per Dóminum.

All-powerful, eternal God, you govern all things both in heaven and on earth. Listen with fatherly kindness to the prayers of your people and grant peace to men in our time. This we ask of you through our Lord.

EPISTLE   Romans 12:6-16

St. Paul here reminds us that each one must put to the service of the community the divine gifts he has received. Thus the Church bears witness in the world to the charity of God.

A reading from the letter of the apostle Paul to the Christians of Rome
Brethren,
According to the special grace which God grants him, each one of us possesses different gifts.

One has the gift of prophecy;[1] let him submit himself to the rules of the faith! Another has the gift of rendering service; let him be devoted to that work! Let him who is learned teach! Let him who has the gift of exhorting, strengthen others! Let the rich one give with simplicity! Let the leader think of others! Let him who aids the unfortunate add a smile to his aid!

In a word, we must love truly, and not just pretend to love. Have a horror of evil and a passion for the good. Love one another with a brotherly love, each one ready to give way to the rest, with a warm heart, not concerned about his own discomfort. Actually it is the Lord whom you are serving.

Your hope gives you joy. Know how to stand fast in trials, therefore, and to persevere in prayer. Sustain your brethren in their need and be hospitable. Bless those who do evil to you; bless, never curse. Laugh with those who laugh, weep with those who weep: have your joys and your sorrows in common. Do not get a taste for grandeur, but be content to live with lowly people.

Gradual *Ps. 106:20-21*

The Lord sent forth his word to heal them and to snatch them from destruction. Let them give thanks to the Lord for his kindness and his wondrous deeds to the children of men.

Alleluia *Ps. 148:2*

Alleluia, alleluia. Praise the Lord, all you his angels, praise him, all you his hosts. Alleluia.

GOSPEL   John 2:1-11

After telling about the marriage feast at Cana, St. John points out that by this first miracle Jesus manifested his "glory," that is to say, his messianic mission of being the divinely sent Savior of men.

A reading from the holy Gospel according to John
At that time a wedding took place at Cana in Galilee. The Mother of Jesus was there, and Jesus himself was invited, with his disciples. It happened that when the wine gave out, the Mother of Jesus mentioned to him, "They have no more wine."

[1] A spiritual favor, the aim of which is teaching, exhortation and sometimes prediction.

"Woman," replied Jesus, "is that your affair, or mine either? My hour has not yet come!"

Mary, however, said to the servants, "Do whatever he tells you."

Now there were six stone water-jars placed there, for the ablutions required by Jewish ritual, each with a capacity of two or three measures.[1]

Jesus said to the servants, "Fill those jars with water." They filled them to the brim. "Now," he added, "draw some out and take it to the chief steward." This they did.

When the steward had tasted the water made wine (he did not know where this wine had come from, but the servants who had drawn the water knew), he summoned the bridegroom. "Everyone serves the good wine first," he said. "Then, when the company have become rather gay, the inferior stuff is passed off on them. But you have kept the best wine for the end of the feast!"

Such was the first miracle of Jesus, that of Cana in Galilee. He revealed his divine glory, and his disciples believed in him.

OFFERTORY ANTIPHON *Ps. 65:1-2, 16*

Shout joyfully to God, all you on earth, sing praise to the glory of his name. Hear now, all you who fear God, while I declare what the Lord has done for me.

Prayer over the Offerings

Obláta, Dómine, múnera sanctífica: nosque a peccatórum nostrórum máculis emúnda. Per Dóminum.

Sanctify our offerings, Lord, and purify us from the stains of our sins. This we ask of you through our Lord.

COMMUNION ANTIPHON *John 2:7, 8, 9, 10-11*

The Lord said, "Fill the jars with water and take to the chief steward."

When the chief steward had tasted the water after it had become wine, he said to the bridegroom, "You have kept the good wine until now."

This first miracle Jesus worked in the presence of his disciples.

Prayer after the Communion

Augeátur in nobis, quǽsumus, Dómine, tuæ virtútis operátio: ut, divínis vegetáti sacraméntis, ad eórum promíssa capiénda, tuo múnere præparémur. Per Dóminum.

May your power, Lord, be more and more active in our souls; nourished on this divine sacrament, may they be prepared by your grace for the promises of eternal life. This we ask of you through our Lord.

[1] About 20 to 30 gallons apiece.

THIRD SUNDAY AFTER EPIPHANY

ENTRANCE ANTIPHON *Ps. 96:7-8, 1*

Adore God, all you his angels: Sion hears and is glad, and the cities of Juda rejoice.

Ps. The Lord is king; let the earth rejoice; let the many isles be glad.

Glory be to the Father and to the Son and to the Holy Spirit. As it was in the beginning, is now and ever shall be, world without end. Amen. Adore God . . .

Prayer over the Assembly

Omnípotens sempitérne Deus, infirmitátem nostram propítius réspice: atque ad protegéndum nos déxteram tuæ maiestátis exténde. Per Dóminum.

All-powerful, eternal God, look down with mercy on our weakness and stretch forth the right hand of your majesty to help us. This we ask of you through our Lord.

EPISTLE   Romans 12:16-21

This text follows last Sunday's. It tells us that it is by loving our brethren, the hostile ones included, that we shall aid the development of God's kingdom on earth.

A reading from the letter of the apostle Paul to the Christians of Rome
Brethren,

Do not let yourselves be guided by your own wisdom, and do not repay anyone evil for evil. Put your effort into doing good, not only before God, but before the whole world. Do the impossible to live at peace with all. Do not avenge yourselves, beloved brethren, but let the justice of God be done. For it is written, " 'Mine is vengeance, mine the task of doing justice,' says the Lord." [1] And elsewhere, "Is your enemy hungry? Give him something to eat. Is he thirsty? Give him something to drink. By doing so, you are heaping coals of fire on his head [you are stirring up in him the fire of remorse]." [2] Do not let yourself be conquered by evil, but conquer evil by doing good.

Gradual Ps. 101:16-17

The nations shall revere your name, O Lord, and all the kings of the earth your glory. For the Lord has rebuilt Sion, and he shall appear in his glory.

Alleluia Ps. 96:1

Alleluia, alleluia. The Lord is king; let the earth rejoice; let the many isles be glad. Alleluia.

[1] Deuteronomy 32:35.
[2] Proverbs 25:21-22.

GOSPEL   Matthew 8:1-13

The leper is the image of sinful man whom Christ has come to save.
Our Lord's words remind us that salvation is offered not only to the Jews,
but also to the pagans, represented here by the centurion.

A reading from the holy Gospel according to Matthew

At that time Jesus came down from the mountain and a great crowd
followed him.

Just then a leper came forward and, lying prostrate at his feet, said,
"Lord, if you want to, you can heal me."

Jesus stretched out his hand, touched him and said, "Such is my will.
Be healed." At once his leprosy disappeared. "Be sure not to tell anyone
about this," Jesus added. "But go and show yourself to the priest and
make the offering prescribed by Moses to bear witness to your healing."

When Jesus had just entered Capharnaum, a [Roman] centurion approached him and begged him, "Lord, my servant is lying in bed at my
house; he is paralyzed, and suffering a great deal."

"I will go and heal him," replied Jesus.

But the centurion objected, "Lord, I am not worthy that you should enter
my house. Only say a word, and my servant will be healed. It is the same
with me: I am merely a subaltern, but I have soldiers under my command,
and I need only say to one of my men, 'Go!' and he goes; to another,
'Come!' and he comes; to my servant, 'Do this!' and he does it."

Listening to him, Jesus was struck with admiration and said to those
around him, "Actually, let me tell you, I have not found such faith as this
in Israel! That is why I declare to you that many will come from the East
and from the West to sit down at table with Abraham and Isaac and Jacob
in the kingdom of heaven, while the natural heirs of the kingdom will be
thrown out into the darkness, where there will be tears and gnashing of
teeth."

Then he told the centurion, "Go. What you have asked of me with faith,
I grant you!"

At that very moment his servant was healed.

OFFERTORY ANTIPHON *Ps. 117:16, 17*

The right hand of the Lord has struck with power: the right hand
of the Lord has exalted me. I shall not die, but live, and declare the
works of the Lord.

Prayer over the Offerings

Hæc hóstia, Dómine, quǽsumus, emúndet nostra delícta: et
ad sacrifícium celebrándum, subditórum tibi córpora mentésque
sanctíficet. Per Dóminum.

May this victim, Lord, purify us
from our sins, and may it dispose the
bodies and souls of your children to
celebrate this sacrifice in a holy manner. This we ask of you through our
Lord.

COMMUNION ANTIPHON *Luke 4:22*

All marvelled at the words that came from the mouth of God.

Prayer after the Communion

Quos tantis, Dómine, largíris uti mystériis: quæsumus; ut efféctibus nos eórum veráciter aptáre dignéris. Per Dóminum.

Lord, you grant us the favor of participating in such great mysteries! Please make us capable also of receiving their full effects. This we ask of you through our Lord.

FOURTH SUNDAY AFTER EPIPHANY

ENTRANCE ANTIPHON *Ps. 96:7-8, 1*

Adore God, all you his angels: Sion hears and is glad, and the cities of Juda rejoice.

Ps. The Lord is king; let the earth rejoice; let the many isles be glad.

Glory be to the Father and to the Son and to the Holy Spirit. As it was in the beginning, is now and ever shall be world without end. Amen. Adore God . . .

Prayer over the Assembly

Deus, qui nos in tantis perículis constitútos pro humána scis fragilitáte non posse subsístere: da nobis salútem mentis et córporis; ut ea, quæ pro peccátis nostris pátimur, te adiuvánte vincámus. Per Dóminum.

Lord, you know that in our human weakness we cannot stand fast in the midst of the dangers that surround us. Give us a hardiness of soul and body, and with your help we shall overcome the trials that have come upon us because of our sins. This we ask of you through our Lord.

EPISTLE   Romans 13:8-10

God has saved us out of pure love. We shall never be free of debt in his regard. He has willed that we pay our debt to him by loving our brethren. This love sums up the whole law of God.

A reading from the letter of the apostle Paul to the Christians of Rome

Brethren,

There is one debt you will never finish paying, the debt of brotherly love: to love your neighbor is to fulfill the whole law [of God].

For the commandments "You shall not commit adultery, you shall not kill, you shall not steal, you shall not be a false witness, you shall not have evil desires" [1] and any other commandment there may be — all are summed up in this one: "You shall love your neighbor as yourself."

Where there is love of neighbor, there can be no evil. To love, therefore, is to fulfill the whole law.

[1] Exodus 20:13-17; Leviticus 19:18.

Gradual Ps. 101:16-17

The nations shall revere your name, O Lord, and all the kings of the earth your glory. For the Lord has rebuilt Sion, and he shall appear in his glory.

Alleluia Ps. 96:1

Alleluia, alleluia. The Lord is king; let the earth rejoice; let the many isles be glad. Alleluia.

GOSPEL   Matthew 8:23-27

The miracle of the tempest calmed confirms our faith in the power of Christ the Savior.

A reading from the holy Gospel according to Matthew

At that time Jesus got into a boat with his disciples [to cross the lake]. After they were under way, a storm broke. Huge waves were rising up to engulf the boat.

Jesus meanwhile had fallen asleep. The apostles came to wake him up. "Help, Lord!" they shouted. "We'll drown!"

"Men of little faith," he answered, "why are you afraid?" Then, getting up, he commanded the wind and the sea; and at once there was a great calm.

All those who witnessed the event were amazed. "What kind of man is this," they said, "that the wind and the sea obey him?"

OFFERTORY ANTIPHON *Ps. 117:16, 17*

The right hand of the Lord has struck with power: the right hand of the Lord has exalted me. I shall not die, but live, and declare the works of the Lord.

Prayer over the Offerings

Concéde, quǽsumus, omnípotens Deus: ut huius sacrifícii munus oblátum, fragilitátem nostram ab omni malo purget semper, et múniat. Per Dóminum.

God all-powerful, may the offering of this sacrifice make our sinful souls purer and stronger. This we ask of you through our Lord.

COMMUNION ANTIPHON *Luke 4:22*

All marvelled at the words that came from the mouth of God.

Prayer after the Communion

Múnera tua nos, Deus, a delectatiónibus terrénis expéciant: et cæléstibus semper instáurent aliméntis. Per Dóminum.

May your gifts, O Lord, detach us from the seductions of the world, and may our souls find their strength in the bread of heaven. This we ask of you through our Lord.

FIFTH SUNDAY AFTER EPIPHANY

ENTRANCE ANTIPHON *Ps. 96:7-8, 1*

Adore God, all you his angels: Sion hears and is glad, and the cities of Juda rejoice.

Ps. The Lord is king; let the earth rejoice; let the many isles be glad.

Glory be to the Father and to the Son and to the Holy Spirit. As it was in the beginning, is now and ever shall be world without end. Amen. Adore God . . .

Prayer over the Assembly

Famíliam tuam, quǽsumus, Dómine, contínua pietáte custódi: ut, quæ in sola spe grátiæ cælésti innítitur, tua semper protectióne muniátur. Per Dóminum.

We are your family, Lord; in your goodness preserve us. And, since we place all our hope in the assistance offered us by your divine grace, may it protect us always! This we ask of you through our Lord.

EPISTLE   Colossians 3:12-17

Being called to form but one body, the very Body of Christ, which is animated by the Holy Spirit, Christians are to bind themselves to one another by a perfect charity. In this way they will keep proclaiming the message of salvation among their contemporaries.

A reading from the letter of the apostle Paul to the Christians of Colossae

Brethren,

Since God has chosen you, since he has made you his saints and his beloved, have nothing in your hearts but mercy, tenderness, humility, kindness and patience. Bear with one another and forgive one another for any wrongs that may be committed. The Lord has forgiven you. Do as he has done.

Above all, have charity; it is the bond of all the virtues. And let the peace of Christ reign in your hearts, that peace to which God calls you to make you all one Body! Live in a state of thanksgiving.

May Christ's word dwell in your soul with all its riches! Study it, and encourage one another in your efforts toward perfection. With all your hearts, sing: let your thanks rise up to God in psalms, hymns and canticles! And whatever you do or say, let it be in the name of the Lord Jesus; let it be in thanksgiving, through him, to God the Father.

Gradual Ps. 101:16-17

The nations shall revere your name, O Lord, and all the kings of the earth your glory. For the Lord has rebuilt Sion, and he shall appear in his glory.

Alleluia Ps. 96:1

Alleluia, alleluia. The Lord is king; let the earth rejoice; let the many isles be glad. Alleluia.

GOSPEL Matthew 13:24-30

While passing through the ordeals imposed by the forces of evil, God's kingdom must grow slowly. Its manifestation will not be complete until the last day.

A reading from the holy Gospel according to Matthew

At that time Jesus told the crowds this parable: "The kingdom of heaven may be compared to a man who had sown good grain in his field. But, while everyone was sleeping, his enemy came and sowed weeds among the wheat, and made off.

"The blades sprang up and formed their heads; then the weeds appeared also. The hired hands went to find the householder and asked him, 'Sir, wasn't it good grain that you sowed in your field? Where did the weeds come from?'

" 'This is the work of an enemy,' he answered.

" 'Do you want us to go and pull up the weeds?' asked the workmen.

" 'No,' he replied. 'In getting the weeds out, you would run the risk of uprooting the wheat too. Let them grow side by side until the harvest. When the harvest time comes, I will tell the reapers, "Gather up the weeds first, and tie them in bundles to be burned. Then store the wheat in my granary." ' "

OFFERTORY ANTIPHON Ps. 117:16, 17

The right hand of the Lord has struck with power: the right hand of the Lord has exalted me. I shall not die, but live, and declare the works of the Lord.

Prayer over the Offerings

Hóstias tibi, Dómine, placatiónis offérimus: ut et delícta nostra miserátus absólvas, et nutántia corda tu dírigas. Per Dóminum.

It is to obtain your pardon, Lord, that we bring these offerings. In your mercy absolve us from our sins and bring our inconstant hearts under control. This we ask of you through our Lord.

COMMUNION ANTIPHON Luke 4:22

All marvelled at the words that came from the mouth of God.

Prayer after the Communion

Quǽsumus, omnípotens Deus: ut illíus salutáris capiámus efféctum, cuius per hæc mystéria pignus accépimus. Per Dóminum.

God all-powerful, grant us the eternal salvation of which this sacrament has given us the pledge. This we ask of you through our Lord.

SIXTH SUNDAY AFTER EPIPHANY

ENTRANCE ANTIPHON *Ps. 96:7-8, 1*

Adore God, all you his angels: Sion hears and is glad, and the cities of Juda rejoice.

Ps. The Lord is king; let the earth rejoice; let the many isles be glad.

Glory be to the Father and to the Son and to the Holy Spirit. As it was in the beginning, is now and ever shall be world without end. Amen. Adore God . . .

Prayer over the Assembly

Præsta, quæsumus, omnípotens Deus: ut, semper rationabília meditántes, quæ tibi sunt plácita, et dictis exsequámur, et factis. Per Dóminum.

Lord all-powerful, keep our thoughts fixed always on spiritual realities, and we shall be able to please you both in our words and in our actions. This we ask of you through our Lord.

EPISTLE   1 Thessalonians 1:2-10

By presenting the case of the Christians of Thessalonica, the Epistle shows how God's action unfolds in a Christian community which lives on faith, hope and charity.

A reading from the first letter of the apostle Paul to the Christians of Thessalonica

Brethren,

I keep thinking of you in my prayers, and this makes me give thanks to God; for I cannot forget, in the presence of our God and Father, your active faith, or your charity always at work, or your unshakable hope in the return of our Lord Jesus Christ. And I am very sure, my brethren, that God loves you and that he has chosen you in a special way. I have the proof of this in the manner in which the gospel was brought to you. There was not only my word; there were miracles, there was the intervention of the Holy Spirit, which gave me a perfect assurance. Just recall the good that was done during my stay among you. You weighed my conduct and decided to model yourselves on me and on Christ himself. Despite all the difficulties placed in your way, you welcomed his word with a joy that could come only from the Holy Spirit.

Thus all the nearby Christian communities have been able, in their turn, to take you as a model. Not only have you spread the word of God in Macedonia and Achaia, but your faith has become renowned throughout the Church; I need not speak of it. They are telling everywhere how well you received me, how you abandoned your idols to serve the true and ever-living God and to wait for the return of his Son Jesus, the Son whom he has raised from the dead and who saves us from the terrors of the judgment.

Gradual Ps. 101:16-17

The nations shall revere your name, O Lord, and all the kings of the earth your glory. For the Lord has rebuilt Sion, and he shall appear in his glory.

Alleluia Ps. 96:1

Alleluia, alleluia. The Lord is king; let the earth rejoice; let the many isles be glad. Alleluia.

GOSPEL   Matthew 13:31-35

The parable of the grain of mustard seed and that of the leaven mixed in the dough bring out the progressive and dynamic aspect of the kingdom of God. Jesus is the seed put into the ground, whose development is now seen in the Church.

A reading from the holy Gospel according to Matthew

At that time Jesus suggested this parable to the crowds: "The kingdom of heaven resembles a grain of mustard seed which a man sowed in his field. This is indeed the smallest of all the seeds, but it grows up taller than any garden herb and becomes a tree large enough to shelter the birds from the sky in its branches."

Jesus proposed another parable to them: "The kingdom of heaven resembles the leaven that a housewife mixes with three measures of flour; its fermentation makes the whole dough rise."

All this teaching Jesus imparted to the crowds in parables; in no other way did he speak to them, that the saying of the prophet might be fulfilled: "I will speak to them in parables; I will reveal secrets to them that have remained undisclosed since the creation of the world." [1]

OFFERTORY ANTIPHON *Ps. 117:16, 17*

The right hand fothe Lord has struck with power: the right hand of the Lord has exalted me. I shall not die, but live, and declare the works of the Lord.

Prayer over the Offerings

Hæc nos oblátio, Deus, mundet, quǽsumus, et rénovet, gubérnet, et prótegat. Per Dóminum.

Lord, may this Mass purify us and renew us, put us on the right path and protect us. This we ask of you through our Lord.

COMMUNION ANTIPHON *Luke 4:22*

All marvelled at the words that came from the mouth of God.

Prayer after the Communion

Cæléstibus, Dómine, pasti delíciis: quǽsumus; ut semper éadem,

Lord, we have tasted the heavenly sweetness of your Eucharist; make us

[1] Psalm 77:2.

per quæ veráciter vívimus, appetá-
mus. Per Dóminum.

desire always this food which gives us
the true life. This we ask of you
through our Lord.

SEPTUAGESIMA SUNDAY

ENTRANCE ANTIPHON *Ps. 17:5, 6, 7, 2-3*

The terrors of death surged round about me, the cords of the nether
world enmeshed me. In my distress I called upon the Lord; from his
holy temple he heard my voice.

Ps. I love you, O Lord, my strength, O Lord, my rock, my fortress,
my deliverer.

Glory be to the Father and to the Son and to the Holy Spirit. As it
was in the beginning, is now and ever shall be, world without end.
Amen. The terrors . . .

Prayer over the Assembly

Preces pópuli tui, quǽsumus,
Dómine, cleménter exáudi: ut, qui
iuste pro peccátis nostris afflígimur, pro tui nóminis glória miseri-
córditer liberémur. Per Dóminum.

Your people are praying to you,
Lord; listen to them in your goodness.
In all justice we suffer for our sins;
may your mercy deliver us for the
glory of your name. This we ask of
you through our Lord.

EPISTLE   1 Corinthians 9:24-27; 10:1-5

*Although they had been freed from Egyptian bondage, the Hebrews
were detained in the desert for 40 years, exposed to all kinds of struggles
and temptations. In the same way the Church, which is made up of those
who have been renewed by the water of baptism, continues the long journey of Exodus on earth. In order not to slow down that journey, each
Christian must exert all his energies, like an athlete in competition.*

A reading from the first letter of the apostle Paul to the Christians
of Corinth

From the race courses you have learned that of all those who run, only
one wins the prize. Apply the lesson, then, and run so as to be a winner.
In preparing for competition, the athlete imposes all sorts of privations on
himself. He does this for a transient glory, while we are concerned with a
glory that lasts forever!

As for me, if I run, it is not without a goal; if I strike, I am not lashing
out in a void. I gain mastery over my body to make it a good servant.
After having encouraged others, I do not want to be disqualified myself.

Brethren, remember this too: [after going out of Egypt] our ancestors
all followed Moses across the Red Sea and under the luminous cloud. All
bathed, as if being baptized, in that water and in that light. All ate the same

mysterious bread [the manna]. All drank at the same mysterious spring (the spring gushing from that symbolic rock which was accompanying them, that rock which was the image of Christ). Yet most of them were unworthy of God's friendship.

Gradual *Ps. 9:10-11, 19-20*

A stronghold in times of distress; they trust in you who cherish you; for you forsake not those who seek you, O Lord. For the needy shall not always be forgotten; nor shall the hope of the afflicted forever perish; rise, O Lord, let not man prevail.

Tract *Ps. 129:1-4*

Out of the depths I cry to you, O Lord; Lord, hear my voice! Let your ears be attentive to the prayer of your servant. If you, O Lord, mark iniquities, Lord, who can stand it? But with you is forgiveness, and by reason of your law I have waited for you, O Lord.

GOSPEL   Matthew 20:1-16

The successive hours of the day suggest the various "ages" of history. God has kept calling men to come and work with him. The gentiles were the last ones invited, and these "last are the first" to understand the Father's plan. We in our turn are hired for the Lord's vineyard. The alliance that binds us to God, an alliance due entirely to his gratuitous kindness, associates us with his work in the world.

A reading from the holy Gospel according to Matthew

At that time Jesus told the crowds this parable: "The kingdom of heaven is like a land owner who went out early in the morning to hire workers for his vineyard. He made an agreement with them to pay one denarius for the day, and sent them to their work.

"He went out again about nine o'clock and saw other workmen standing around in the market place, doing nothing. 'You too,' he said, 'go to work in my vineyard; I will pay you what is right.' And they went.

"He went out again about noon, and about three hours after noon, and did the same.

"One hour before nightfall, he found others standing idle and said to them, 'Why do you stay there all day, doing nothing?'

" 'Because no one has hired us,' they answered.

" 'You too go into my vineyard.' he told them.

"At nightfall the owner said to his steward, 'Call the workmen together and pay them, beginning with those who came last.'

"Those who had worked only one hour got in line, and each received a denarius.

"When the earliest comers had their turn, they were expecting to receive more; but they too received only one denarius. As they took their pay, they grumbled at the land owner. 'These latecomers,' they complained, 'have worked only one hour, and you've put them on the same footing with us, who have borne the burden of the day and of the heat!'

" 'Friend,' replied the owner to one of them, 'I am doing you no wrong. Did we not agree on one denarius? Take your money, then, and go! It is my pleasure to give this latecomer as much as I give you. Have I not the right to do what I please with my property? Or must you scowl at me because I am good?' "

So the first will be last, and the last will be first. For many are called, but few are chosen.

OFFERTORY ANTIPHON *Ps. 91:2*

It is good to give thanks to the Lord, and to sing praise to your name, Most High.

Prayer over the Offerings

Munéribus nostris, quǽsumus, Dómine, precibúsque suscéptis: et cæléstibus nos munda mystériis, et cleménter exáudi. Per Dóminum.	Be pleased to accept our offerings and our prayers and in your kindness purify us, Lord, through this holy sacrifice. This we ask of you through our Lord.

COMMUNION ANTIPHON *Ps. 30:17-18*

Let your face shine upon your servant; save me in your kindness. O Lord, let me not be put to shame, for I call upon you.

Prayer after the Communion

Fidéles tui, Deus, per tua dona firméntur: ut éadem et percipiéndo requírant, et quæréndo sine fine percípiant. Per Dóminum.	May your children, Lord, be strengthened by the gifts that come to them in your Eucharist. Even while receiving these gifts may they keep seeking them; and in seeking them, may they receive them for eternity. This we ask of you through our Lord.

SEXAGESIMA SUNDAY

ENTRANCE ANTIPHON *Ps. 43:23-26, 2*

Awake! Why are you asleep, O Lord? Arise! Cast us not off forever! Why do you hide your face, forgetting our oppression? Our bodies are pressed to the earth. Arise, O Lord, help us, and deliver us.

Ps. O God, our ears have heard, our fathers have declared to us.

Glory be to the Father and to the Son and to the Holy Spirit. As it was in the beginning, is now and ever shall be, world without end. Amen. Awake! Why . . .

Prayer over the Assembly

Deus, qui cónspicis quia ex nulla nostra actióne confídimus: concéde propítius; ut contra advérsa ómnia Doctóris géntium protectióne muniámur. Per Dóminum.

Lord, you know well that we can put no trust in any of our own achievements. Under the protection of St. Paul, apostle of the pagan countries, grant us in your goodness the strength to meet every adversity. This we ask of you through our Lord.

EPISTLE   2 Corinthians 11:19-33; 12:1-9

In a profoundly stirring passage, the apostle Paul recalls his achievements for Christ and the sufferings he has undergone. But he also vigorously affirms his own weakness, and concludes that God's strength is displayed when man is powerless.

A reading from the second letter of the apostle Paul to the Christians of Corinth

You think you are full of wisdom, and you put up with the foolishness [of our adversaries]. Yes, you let them enslave you, devour you, steal from you, insult you, slap you in the face. I say it to our shame: it is to be presumed that we have shown ourselves too weak. Yet, look at the things they boast of; can I not boast of them just as well? Are they Hebrews? So am I. Descendants of Israel? So am I. Sons of Abraham? So am I. Servants of Christ? (I am a fool to say this): Much more am I!

I have undergone more difficulties, more imprisonments, suffered more blows, been more often in danger of death. Five times I have received the thirty-nine lashes from the Jews, three times I have been beaten with rods, once stoned, three times shipwrecked: I was even adrift a day and a night on the high seas. There have been journeys without number, dangers in crossing rivers, dangers from robbers, from my own countrymen, from the pagans, dangers of the city, of the desert, of the sea, dangers from false brethren. Toil and fatigue there have been, frequent vigils, hunger and thirst, repeated fasts, cold and nakedness. Not to mention the rest: my daily burden, the care of all the Churches. Who is sick, wthout my being sick until I can help? Who is in danger of falling, without my being aroused?

Ah, if boasting is the order of the day, it is of my weaknesses that I shall boast! God, the Father of our Lord Jesus Christ (may he be blessed forever!) knows that I am not lying.

At Damascus, the governor appointed by King Aretas had put the city in a state of siege in order to arrest me. But I was let out of a window, in a basket, along the wall, and that is how I escaped him.

If I must boast (this little is enough, however), I shall come to the visions and revelations from the Lord.

I know a disciple of Christ who, fourteen years ago (was it with his body, was it without his body? I do not know; God knows), but I know that this man was lifted up to the third heaven. And that man (with his body or without it, I do not know; God knows), I know that he was lifted up to paradise and that he heard mysterious words which no man may repeat. For that man I might boast, but for myself I will not boast except of my infirmities. If I wanted to boast about myself, I could do so without folly: I would only have to tell the truth. But I will not do so, for fear that someone may form a better judgment of me than my actions or my teaching would warrant.

Moreover, to keep my head from being turned by such revelations, I was given a thorn in my flesh: an envoy of Satan charged with humiliating me.[1]

Three times I asked the Lord that it be taken away from me, but he answered me, "My grace is sufficient for you, for it is in [man's] weakness that my strength shines forth."

I shall be glad to boast of my infirmities, therefore, that Christ's power may reign in me!

Gradual *Ps. 82:19, 14*

Let the nations know that God is your name; you alone are the Most High over all the earth. O my God, make them like leaves in a whirlwind, like chaff before the wind.

Tract *Ps. 59:4, 6*

You have rocked the country, O Lord, and split it open. Repair the cracks in it, for it is tottering. That they may flee out of bowshot; that your loved ones may escape.

GOSPEL   Luke 8:4-15

The evangelization of the world, begun by Christ, continued by the apostles and now by the Church, encounters the sins of men and the machinations of Satan. The work will seem endless; the word of God will bear fruit in the measure in which each one welcomes it with faith and docility.

A reading from the holy Gospel according to Luke

At that time, when an immense crowd, assembled from several cities, were flocking after Jesus, he told them this parable: "A sower went out to sow his seed. And while he was sowing, some of the seed fell along the edge of the road; it was trampled by the passersby, and the birds flew down and ate it. Another part fell on stony ground; hardly had it sprung up when it withered, for want of moisture. Another part fell among thorns; and the thorns, growing up at the same time, smothered it. Another part fell on good ground; it developed and produced a hundred for one." And Jesus cried out, "He who has ears for hearing, let him hear!"

His disciples asked him the meaning of this parable. "To you," he replied, "is granted the privilege of knowing the secrets of God's kingdom. To the rest, only comparisons are given, so that they look without seeing and hear without understanding. Here is the meaning of this parable, then.

"The seed is the word of God. 'The edge of the road' refers to those who

---

[1] Probably a chronic ailment.

hear, but the devil comes to snatch the word out of their hearts, to keep them from believing and being saved. The 'stony ground' refers to those who welcome the word joyfully; but, not having depth enough for it to take root, they believe only for a time; at the first difficulty, they give up. The soil that is full of thorns: these are those who have heard the word, but who let it be smothered by the cares of life, by money and pleasures, so that it cannot bear its fruit in them. Finally, the 'good ground' means those who hear the word and keep it in a well-disposed, generous heart; they bear fruit, thanks to their perseverance."

OFFERTORY ANTIPHON *Ps. 16:5, 6-7*

Make my steps steadfast in your paths, that my feet may not falter. Incline your ear to me; hear my word. Show your wondrous kindness, O Lord, savior of those who trust in you.

Prayer over the Offerings

Oblátum tibi, Dómine, sacrifícium, vivíficet nos semper, et múniat. Per Dóminum.

Lord, may the offering of this sacrifice always obtain life and strength for us! This we ask of you through our Lord.

COMMUNION ANTIPHON *Ps. 42:4*

I will go in to the altar of God, the God of my gladness and joy.

Prayer after the Communion

Súpplices te rogámus, omnípotens Deus: ut, quos tuis réficis sacraméntis, tibi étiam plácitis móribus dignánter deservíre concédas. Per Dóminum.

We beseech you, all-powerful God, give those whom you nourish by your sacrament the grace to serve you by conduct that conforms to your will. This we ask of you through our Lord.

QUINQUAGESIMA SUNDAY

ENTRANCE ANTIPHON *Ps. 30:3-4, 2*

Be my rock of refuge, O God, a stronghold to give me safety. You are my rock and my fortress; for your name's sake you will lead and guide me.

Ps. In you, O Lord, I take refuge; let me never be put to shame. In your justice rescue me and deliver me.

Glory be to the Father and to the Son and to the Holy Spirit. As it was in the beginning, is now and ever shall be, world without end. Amen. Be my rock . . .

Prayer over the Assembly

Preces nostras, quǽsumus, Dómine, cleménter exáudi: atque, a peccatórum vínculis absolútos, ab

God of mercy, hear our prayers and, after delivering us from the bonds of our sins, keep us from every omni nos adversitáte custódi. Per Dóminum.

evil. This we ask of you through our Lord.

EPISTLE   1 Corinthians 13:1-13

If God requisitions your heart, it is to transform it, and to teach it how to love. True power is the power of love.

A reading from the first letter of the apostle Paul to the Christians of Corinth

No matter whether I speak miraculously all languages, those of men and those of angels, if I have not charity, I am no more than the blare of brass or the clash of cymbals.

No matter whether I possess the gift of prophecy and penetrate all mysteries and all science, no matter whether I have enough faith to transport mountains, if I have not charity, I am nothing.

No matter whether I distribute all my goods to the poor and let myself be burned alive, if I have not charity, none of that does me any good.

He who loves is patient, he is kind, he is not envious, he takes care not to offend, he is not conceited. He is not rude and does not seek his own interest; he is not irritable, he has no evil intentions. He is not pleased by injustice: his only joy is [the triumph of] truth. He excuses everything, believes everything, hopes everything, puts up with everything.

Charity will never end. The gift of prophecy will one day lose its reason for being; the gift of tongues will cease, the gift of knowledge will disappear. For our knowledge is imperfect, and so is our prophecy; and when the time of perfection comes, everything that is imperfect will disappear. Just so, when I was a child, I spoke like a child, I thought and I reasoned like a child; but when I became a man, I put off all those childish ways.

Here below we do not see [the things of God] well, we have only a mysterious reflection of them, as in a crude kind of mirror. Later, we shall see face to face. Here below, my knowledge is only fragmentary. But then I shall know God as he knows me.

Here below there remain these three virtues: faith, hope, charity. But the greatest of the three is charity.

Gradual *Ps. 76:15, 16*

You are the God who alone works wonders; among the peoples you have made known your power. With your strong arm you delivered your people, the sons of Israel and Joseph.

Tract *Ps. 99:2-3*

Sing joyfully to God, all you lands; serve the Lord with gladness. Come before him with joyful song; know that the Lord is God. He made us, his we are; his people, the flock he tends.

GOSPEL   Luke 18:31-43

As Lent approaches, the prophecy made by Jesus reminds us that we are on the march toward Easter: by his death, the proof of a love that knows

no limits, Christ will save the world. The cure of the blind man of Jericho shows God's love at work among men.

A reading from the holy Gospel according to Luke

At that time Jesus took the twelve apostles aside and said to them, "We are going up to Jerusalem now, and all that the prophets wrote about the Son of Man is going to be fulfilled. He will be delivered to the pagans; they will make sport of him, mistreat him, spit on him; and, after scourging him, they will put him to death. But on the third day he will rise again."

The apostles understood not a word of all this; it was a hidden language to them; they did not grasp what he meant.

As they were drawing near Jericho, they met a blind man sitting at the roadside to beg. Hearing the crowd, he asked what it was all about. They told him that Jesus of Nazareth was passing. Then he cried out, "Jesus, Son of David, have pity on me!" The people who came first in the crowd reproved him and tried to make him be quiet. But he only cried out the louder, "Son of David, have pity on me!"

Jesus stopped and had the man brought to him. "What do you want me to do for you?" He asked.

"Lord, make me see!"

"See, then!" said Jesus. "Your faith has saved you."

At that very moment the blind man gained his sight, and, glorifying God, he followed Jesus. Observing this, the people too began to sing God's praises.

OFFERTORY ANTIPHON *Ps. 118:12-13*

Blessed are you, O Lord; teach me your statutes. With my lips I declare all the ordinances of your mouth.

Prayer over the Offerings

Hæc hóstia, Dómine, quæsumus, emúndet nostra delícta: et ad sacrifícium celebrándum, subditórum tibi córpora, mentésque sanctíficet. Per Dóminum.

May these offerings, Lord purify us from our sins. May they dispose the bodies and souls of your children to celebrate this sacrifice in a holy manner. This we ask of you through our Lord.

COMMUNION ANTIPHON *Ps. 77:29-30*

They ate and were wholly surfeited; the Lord had brought them what they craved: they were not defrauded of that which they craved.

Prayer after the Communion

Quǽsumus, omnípotens Deus: ut, qui cæléstia aliménta percépimus, per hæc contra ómnia advérsa muniámur. Per Dóminum.

We have received your Eucharist; may it strengthen us, Lord, in all the trials of life. This we ask of you through our Lord.

FIRST SUNDAY OF LENT

ENTRANCE ANTIPHON *Ps. 90:15, 16, 1*

He shall call upon me, and I will answer him; I will deliver him and glorify him; with length of days I will gratify him.

Ps. You who dwell in the shelter of the Most High, shall abide in the shadow of the Almighty.

Glory be to the Father and to the Son and to the Holy Spirit. As it was in the beginning, is now and ever shall be, world without end. Amen. He shall call . . .

Prayer over the Assembly

Deus, qui Ecclésiam tuam ánnua quadragesimáli observatióne puríficas: præsta famíliæ tuæ; ut, quod a te obtinére abstinéndo nítitur, hoc bonis opéribus exsequátur. Per Dóminum.

Through the observance of Lent, O Lord, you purify your Church every year. See to it that your children lead a better life and so obtain the graces they are striving to acquire by doing penance. This we ask of you through our Lord.

EPISTLE   2 Corinthians 6:1-10

St. Paul reminds us of the conditions under which the apostle lives. Subjected to all kinds of difficulties, persecuted, despised, he has no riches except his poverty. The world rejects the spirit to which Christ's disciple wants to bear witness. We in our turn are involved in this contradiction. Let us bear in mind that we have entered the age of grace and that God is laboring to save us through the Cross.

A reading from the second letter of the apostle Paul to the Christians of Corinth

I call on you not to let the grace that God gives you be lost. He once said, "At the time of grace I will hear your prayers; on the day of salvation I will help you." [1] And here we are now in the time of grace, here we are on the day of salvation.

Let us not scandalize anyone, in order that nothing in our actions may lay us open to criticism. On the contrary, in every circumstance let us show what God's servants are: valiant in enduring difficulties, privations, stresses; courageous under beatings, imprisonment, hostile demonstrations; steadfast in hard labors, nights without sleep, hunger and thirst. Let us show it by our chaste life, our enlightened faith, our patience, our kindness, our docility to the Holy Spirit, our genuine charity, the sincerity of our speech. Let us rely on the power of God, let us attack and defend only with the arms of justice. Whether we are honored or despised, whether we are praised or defamed, let us conduct ourselves always in this way.

People take us for liars, whereas we are spreading the truth. They pretend not to know us, whereas they know us well. They say that we are

[1] Isaiah 49:8.

dying, and actually we are living. They strike us, but they do not succeed in killing us. They think we are sad — we who are always rejoicing! They treat us like paupers — us who are enriching the rest! They say that we have nothing, yet it is we who possess everything!

Gradual *Ps. 90:11-12*

To his angels God has given command about you, that they guard you in all your ways. Upon their hands they shall bear you up, lest you dash your foot against a stone.

Tract *Ps. 90:1-7, 11-16*

You who dwell in the shelter of the Most High, shall abide in the shadow of the Almighty. Say to the Lord, "My refuge and my fortess, my God, in whom I trust." For he will rescue you from the snare of the fowler, from the destroying pestilence. With his pinions he will cover you, and under his wings you shall take refuge. His faithfulness is a buckler and a shield; you shall not fear the terror of the night. Nor the arrow that flies by day; nor the pestilence that roams in darkness; nor the devastating plague at noon. Though a thousand fall at your side, ten thousand at your right side, near you it shall not come. For to his angels he has given command about you, that they may guard you in all your ways. Upon their hands they shall bear you up lest you dash your foot against a stone. You shall tread upon the asp and the viper; you shall trample down the lion and the dragon. Because he clings to me, I will deliver him; I will set him on high because he acknowledges my name. He shall call upon me, and I will answer him; I will be with him in distress. I will deliver him and glorify him; with length of days I will gratify him and will show him my salvation.

GOSPEL
Matthew 4:1-11

In their journey through the desert the Hebrew people had often suc-cumbed to Satan's temptations. Jesus in the desert took up the same fight again and defeated the enemy. He remained faithful to his mission, which was to save the world not by human triumphs but through sufferings and through love. It is in us, the baptized, the members of Christ, that the fight is continued. Like Jesus, let us seek help only in God.

A reading from the holy Gospel according to Matthew

At that time Jesus was led by the Holy Spirit into the desert, to be tempted by the devil.

After forty days and forty nights of fasting, he was hungry. The tempter approached and said to him, "If you are the Son of God, give orders that these stones become loaves of bread."

Jesus answered, "It is written: Man does not live by bread alone, but by every word that comes out of the mouth of God." [1]

[1] Deuteronomy 8:3.

Then the devil carried him up to the temple in the holy city, set him on the edge of the terrace and said, "If you are the Son of God, throw yourself down. For it is written: God orders his angels to hold you up in their hands, that your foot may not hit against the stones." [1]

Jesus replied, "It is written again: You shall not provoke the Lord your God [to do miracles]." [2]

Finally the devil took him up on a very high mountain and showed him all the kingdoms of the world in their splendor. "All this," he said, "I will give you, if you fall at my feet and adore me."

Jesus answered, "Away, Satan! For it is written: The Lord your God you shall adore; him only shall you serve!" [3]

Then the devil left him; and with that the angels approached and began to serve him.

OFFERTORY ANTIPHON *Ps. 90:4-5*

With his pinions the Lord will cover you, and under his wings you shall take refuge; his faithfulness is a buckler and a shield.

Prayer over the Offerings

Sacrifícium quadragesimális inítii solémniter immolámus, te, Dómine, deprecántes: ut, cum epulárum restrictióne carnálium, a nóxiis quoque voluptátibus temperémus. Per Dóminum.

In offering you this sacrifice at the beginning of Lent, we ask you, Lord, that as we impose restrictions on our eating, we may also renounce all dangerous pleasures. This we ask of you through our Lord.

COMMUNION ANTIPHON *Ps. 90:4-5*

With his pinions the Lord will cover you, and under his wings you shall take refuge; his faithfulness is a buckler and a shield.

Prayer after the Communion

Tui nos, Dómine, sacraménti libátio sancta restáuret: et a vetustáte purgátos, in mystérii salutáris fáciat transíre consórtium. Per Dóminum.

We have taken part, O Lord, in your sacrifice. May this communion repair our strength; may it purify our old sinful nature and give us a share in the grace of your redemption. This we ask of you through our Lord.

SECOND SUNDAY OF LENT

ENTRANCE ANTIPHON *Ps. 24:6, 3, 22, 1-2*

Remember that your compassion, O Lord, and your kindness are from of old; let not our enemies exult over us; deliver us, O God of Israel, from all our tribulations.

[1] Psalm 90:11-12.　　[2] Deuteronomy 6:16.　　[3] Deuteronomy 6:13.

Ps. To you I lift up my soul, O Lord; in you, O my God, I trust; let me not be put to shame.

Glory be to the Father and to the Son and to the Holy Spirit. As it was in the beginning, is now and ever shall be, world without end. Amen. Remember . . .

Prayer over the Assembly

Deus, qui cónspicis omni nos virtúte destítui: intérius exteriúsque custódi; ut ab ómnibus adversitátibus muniámur in córpore, et a pravis cogitatiónibus mundémur in mente. Per Dóminum.

Lord, you see how weak we are. Guard us within, guard us without; protect our bodies against the dangers of life and keep all rebellious thoughts out of our minds. This we ask of you through our Lord.

EPISTLE   1 Thessalonians 4:1-7

Christians are called to live in holiness in the midst of a world that ignores God and yields to all the passions. They must fight against themselves and against the bad influences coming from the outside.

A reading from the first letter of the apostle Paul
to the Christians of Thessalonica

Brethren,

We have taught you how you must live to please God, and that is how you are living. But now you must make new progress; this we ask of you, we beseech you by the Lord Jesus.

You have not forgotten the instructions we gave you in his name: what God wants is to make you saints; he wants you to avoid impurity; he wants each one of you to know how to treat his body with a religious respect instead of giving in to the passions, like the pagans who do not know God. On this point, let no one cause his brother to fall through violence or through seduction; for the Lord takes it upon himself to avenge any such thing, as we have already told you and proved to you. It is not to impurity that God has called us; it is to holiness, in Christ Jesus our Lord.

Gradual *Ps. 24:17-18*

Relieve the troubles of my heart and bring me out of my distress, O Lord. Put an end to my affliction and my suffering, and take away all my sins.

Tract *Ps. 105:1-4*

Give thanks to the Lord, for he is good, for his kindness endures forever. Who can tell the mighty deeds of the Lord, or proclaim all his praises? Happy are they who observe what is right, who do always what is just. Remember us, O Lord, as you favor your people; visit us with your saving help.

GOSPEL   Matthew 17:1-9

After exhorting us to fight, the liturgy gives us a glimpse of the glory of the resurrection by having us contemplate Christ transfigured. Victory is promised; Easter is announced.

A reading from the holy Gospel according to Matthew

At that time Jesus took with him Peter, James and his brother John and led them aside, onto a high mountain. There he was transfigured before them. His face became as radiant as the sun, and his clothes dazzling white, like snow. And Moses and Elijah appeared to them too, conversing with Jesus.

Peter spoke up and said to Jesus, "What a good thing it is that we are here, Lord! Do you want us to put up three tents here, one for you, one for Moses and one for Elijah?"

He was still speaking when a luminous cloud enveloped them in its shadow, and from within the cloud a voice was heard: "This is my beloved Son in whom I am well pleased; listen to him!" At the sound of this voice the apostles fell with their faces to the ground, awe-struck.

But Jesus approached them, touched them and said, "Get up! No need to be afraid!" Raising their eyes then, they saw no one but Jesus.

While they were coming down from the mountain, Jesus gave them this order: "Tell no one about this vision until the Son of Man has risen from the dead."

OFFERTORY ANTIPHON *Ps. 118:47, 48*

I will delight in your commands, which I love exceedingly; and I will lift up my hands to your commands, which I love.

Prayer over the Offerings

Sacrifíciis præséntibus, Dómine, quǽsumus, inténde placátus: ut et devotióni nostræ profíciant, et salúti. Per Dóminum.

Lord, here are the offerings for the sacrifice. Look favorably on them, we implore you; may they increase our fervor and obtain salvation for us. This we ask of you through our Lord.

COMMUNION ANTIPHON *Ps. 5:2-4*

Attend to my sighing; heed my call for help, my king and my God! To you I pray, O Lord.

Prayer after the Communion

Súpplices te rogámus, omnípotens Deus: ut, quos tuis réficis sacraméntis, tibi étiam plácitis móribus dignánter deservíre concédas. Per Dóminum.

We beseech you, all-powerful God, give those whom you nourish by your sacrament the grace to serve you by conduct that conforms to your will. This we ask of you through our Lord.

THIRD SUNDAY OF LENT

ENTRANCE ANTIPHON *Ps. 24:15-16, 1-2*

My eyes are ever toward the Lord, for he will free my feet from the snare. Look toward me, and have pity on me, for I am alone and afflicted.

Ps. To you I lift up my soul, O Lord. In you, O my God, I trust; let me not be put to shame.

Glory be to the Father and to the Son and to the Holy Spirit. As it was in the beginning, is now and ever shall be, world without end. Amen. My eyes . . .

Prayer over the Assembly

Quǽsumus, omnípotens Deus, vota humílium réspice: atque, ad defensiónem nostram, déxteram tuæ maiestátis exténde. Per Dóminum.

Lord, God all-powerful, accept our poor prayers and stretch out your powerful hand to defend us. This we ask of you through our Lord.

EPISTLE   Ephesians 5:1-9

Having once been darkness and now being light, Christians must live according to the example set by Christ and destroy all the forces of sin in themselves.

A reading from the letter of the apostle Paul
to the Christians of Ephesus

Brethren,

Take God himself for a model, since you are his beloved children.

Let love pervade your lives, after the example of Christ, who loved us so much that he delivered himself for us, offering himself to God as a perfect sacrifice.

As for debauchery, all forms of impurity, and greed too, there should not even be any question of these things among you: they are not befitting to Christians. Let there be no unbecoming speech on your lips — questionable conversations, vulgarities, stupid pleasantries — but rather words of thanksgiving.

For you may be sure of this: no debauchee, so sensualist, no greedy person — worshipper of idols! — has any share in the kingdom of Christ and of God.

Whatever anyone may say to deceive you, do not let him succeed. That is the kind of thing that brings down God's anger on people without faith.

Do not be one of them! For, if at one time you were darkness, now, in the Lord, you have become light. Live as children of light, therefore; in this light you will bear no fruits but those of goodness, justice and truth.

Gradual Ps. 9:20, 4

Rise, O Lord, let not man prevail; let the nations be judged in your presence. Because my enemies are turned back, overthrown and destroyed before you.

Tract Ps. 122:1-3

To you I lift up my eyes, who are enthroned in heaven. Behold, as the eyes of servants are on the hands of their masters, as the eyes of a maid are on the hands of her mistress, so are our eyes on the Lord our God, till he have pity on us. Have pity on us, O Lord, have pity on us.

GOSPEL   Luke 11:14-28

Driven out by exorcisms, the devil will keep right on attacking us. We must expect a battle without quarter, therefore: the service of Christ requires a total engagement.

A reading from the holy Gospel according to Luke

At that time Jesus was driving out [from a possessed person] a devil who was making him dumb. As soon as the devil had gone out of him, the dumb man began to speak, and the crowd was carried away with admiration.

There were some among them, however, who objected, "It is by the authority of Beelzebub, prince of the devils, that he casts out devils." Others, to provoke him, demanded of him a sign from heaven.

Jesus, seeing what was at the back of their minds, said to them, "Any kingdom divided against itself is brought to ruin, one house attacking another. If Satan, then, is divided against himself — since you say that it is by Beelzebub that I cast out devils — how is his kingdom going to last?

"And if *I* cast out devils by Beelzebub, what about *your* exorcists — by whom do they cast them out? Their success is a condemnation of you. But if it is really by the finger of God that I cast out devils, then the kingdom of God has arrived among you.

"When a strong, armed man guards his house, all his possessions are undisturbed. But if someone stronger than he attacks him and defeats him, he will take away the weapons on which he was depending and make a distribution of spoils.

"He who is not with me is against me; and he who does not hoard up with me is making himself poor.

"When the impure spirit goes out of a man, it wanders in the desert, looking for a place to rest. Not finding any, it says to itself, 'I will go back to the home that I left.' But on arriving there it finds the place swept and decorated. Then it goes to look for seven other spirits more evil than itself; in they go and establish themselves; and that man is worse off in the end than he was before."

While he was speaking in this way, a woman raised her voice from the middle of the crowd: "How happy the mother must be who carried you in her womb and nursed you at her breasts!"

But Jesus answered, "Say rather: Happy are those who hear the word of God and put it into practice!"

OFFERTORY ANTIPHON *Ps. 18:9, 10, 11, 12*

The precepts of the Lord are right, rejoicing the heart, and his ordinances are sweeter than syrup or honey from the comb; therefore your servant is careful of them.

Prayer over the Offerings

Hæc hóstia, Dómine, quǽsumus, emúndet nostra delícta: et ad sacrifícium celebrándum, subditórum tibi córpora, mentésque sanctíficet. Per Dóminum.

May these offerings, Lord, purify us from our sins, and may they dispose the bodies and souls of your children to celebrate this sacrifice in a holy manner. This we ask of you through our Lord.

COMMUNION ANTIPHON *Ps. 83:4-5*

The sparrow finds a home, and the swallow a nest in which she puts her young: your altars, O Lord of hosts, my king and my God! Happy they who dwell in your house! continually they praise you.

Prayer after the Communion

A cunctis nos, quǽsumus, Dómine, reátibus et perículis propitiátus absólve: quos tanti mystérii tríbuis esse partícipes. Per Dóminum.

From all sin, O Lord, from all danger deliver your children whom you invite to take part in the grandeur of this mystery. This we ask of you through our Lord.

FOURTH SUNDAY OF LENT

ENTRANCE ANTIPHON *Is. 66:10, 11; Ps. 121:1*

Rejoice, O Jerusalem, and come together, all you who love her. Rejoice with joy, you who have been in sorrow: that you may exult, and be filled from the breasts of your consolation.

Ps. I rejoiced because they said to me, "We will go up to the house of the Lord."

Glory be to the Father and to the Son and to the Holy Spirit. As it was in the beginning, is now and ever shall be, world without end. Amen. Rejoice, O Jerusalem . . .

Prayer over the Assembly

Concéde, quǽsumus, omnípotens Deus: ut, qui ex mérito no-

Listen to us, all-powerful God; in justice we are stifled under the weight

stræ actiónis afflígimur, tuæ grá- / of our sins; may your grace console
tiæ consolatióne respirémus. Per / us and let us breathe again in joy.
Dóminum. / This we ask of you through our Lord.

EPISTLE   Galatians 4:22-31

*The "Jerusalem here below" has come to the end of its time. The old
covenant, which made the Jews servants of God, has given way to the new
covenant, which allows all men to become children of God. From now on,
it is the time of the "Jerusalem on high."*

A reading from the letter of the apostle Paul to the Christians of Galatia

*The Christians of Galatia were exposed to persecutions, or at least to
pressures, which were aimed at bringing them, or bringing them back, to
the practice of the laws of the Jewish religion.*

Brethren,

It is written [in the Bible] that Abraham had two sons, one from a slave
woman, the other from a free woman. But the son of the slave was born
only of the flesh; that of the free woman [Isaac] was born in virtue of the
divine promises.

In this there is symbolism. These two women are the two covenants [of
God with men]. The first, the alliance made at Sinai [with the Hebrew
people], results only in slaves: this is Agar (in Arabia, moreover, the word
Agar designates Mount Sinai). It represents the Jerusalem here below,
who is in slavery along with her children.

But the Jerusalem on high [the Church] is free, and it is she who is our
mother, she of whom it is written:

"Shout for joy, barren woman who did not give birth! Break into joyful
song, you who have no child; for your children, O deserted wife, shall be
more numerous than the children of her who has a husband!" [1]

We too, brethren, are therefore, like Isaac, the children of the divine
promise.

And just as, in those days, the child of the flesh persecuted the child of
the spirit, that is still what happens today.

But what does the Scripture say? "Put them out, the slave and her son,
for the son of the slave cannot share the heritage that falls to the free
woman's son." [2]

And so, brethren, we are not children of the slave, we are children of
the free woman; and Christ has made us free in order that we may remain
so.

Gradual Ps. 121:1, 7

I rejoiced because they said to me, "We will go up to the house
of the Lord." May peace be within your walls, prosperity in your
buildings.

[1] Isaiah 54:1.   [2] Genesis 21:10.

Tract Ps. 124:1-2

They who trust in the Lord are like Mount Sion, which is immovable, which forever stands. Mountains are round about Jerusalem; so the Lord is round about his people, both now and forever.

GOSPEL   John 6:1-15

As "the Passover is near," the liturgy is concerned henceforth with preparing the catechumens directly for the sacraments (baptism, confirmation and Eucharist) which they will receive at this solemn time, and which will constitute their Christian initiation. The multiplication of the loaves is an awe-inspiring forecast of the Eucharistic bread.

A reading from the holy Gospel according to John

At that time Jesus crossed to the other side of the Sea of Galilee (or the Lake of Tiberias). A great crowd followed him, attracted by the miraculous cures he had worked. Jesus climbed up the hillside and sat down among his disciples. The Passover, the great feast of the Jews, was near.

Raising his eyes and seeing what a huge crowd was coming toward him, Jesus said to Philip, "Where could we buy bread for all these people to eat?" He asked this question to test Philip; he himself knew what he was going to do.

Philip answered him, "Two hundred denarii worth of bread would not be enough so that each one might get a piece."

Another apostle, Andrew, the brother of Simon Peter, said to him, "There is a boy here who has five barley loaves and two fishes. But what is that for so many people?"

Then Jesus said to them, "Have them all sit down." It was quite a grassy place. They sat down, therefore; about five thousand there were.

Jesus took the five loaves and, after giving thanks, had them distributed to those who were seated — and the same with the fish — as much as they wanted. When all had satisfied their hunger, Jesus said to his disciples, "Gather up the pieces that are left over, so that nothing will be lost." They gathered them up. The pieces that were left over from the five barley loaves after everyone had eaten filled twelve baskets.

Seeing the miracle Jesus had just performed, the people were saying, "This is really the one, the Prophet who is to come into the world." But Jesus, knowing that they were going to come and carry him off to proclaim him king, retired into the hill country again, all by himself.

OFFERTORY ANTIPHON Ps. 134:3, 6

Praise the Lord, for he is good; sing praise to his name, for he is sweet; all that he wills he does in heaven and on earth.

Prayer over the Offerings

Sacrifíciis præséntibus, Dómine, quǽsumus, inténde placátus: Here are the offerings for the sacrifice, Lord. Look favorably on them,

ut et devotióni nostræ profíciant, et salúti. Per Dóminum.

we implore you; may they increase our fervor and be useful for our salvation. This we ask of you through our Lord.

COMMUNION ANTIPHON *Ps. 121:3-4*

Jerusalem, built as a city, with compact unity: to it the tribes go up, the tribes of the Lord, to give thanks to your name, O Lord.

Prayer after the Communion

Da nobis, quǽsumus, miséricors Deus: ut sancta tua, quibus incessánter explémur, sincéris tractémus obséquiis, et fidéli semper mente sumámus. Per Dóminum.

Give us the grace, O God of mercy, to surround with deepest respect the holy Eucharist which is our constant nourishment; grant that we may receive it always into a soul filled with faith. This we ask of you through our Lord.

FIRST SUNDAY OF PASSIONTIDE

In all ferial Masses of Passiontide the Glory be to the Father *is omitted in the Entrance Antiphon and the* Sprinkle me. Glory be to the Father *is said, however, on any feasts that may occur during this time.*

ENTRANCE ANTIPHON *Ps. 42:1-2, 3*

Do me justice, O God, and fight my fight against a faithless people; from the deceitful and impious man rescue me. For you are my God and my strength.

Ps. Send forth your light and your fidelity; they shall lead me on and bring me to your holy mountain, to your dwelling-place. Do me justice . . .

Prayer over the Assembly

Quǽsumus, omnípotens Deus, famíliam tuam propítius réspice: ut, te largiénte, regátur in córpore; et, te servánte, custodiátur in mente. Per Dóminum.

God all-powerful, look upon your family with kindness: may your generous bounty take care of our bodies and your solicitude watch over our souls. This we ask of you through our Lord.

EPISTLE   Hebrews 9:11-15

The sacrifices of the old law were a sort of substitute and a foreshadowing of the redemptive sacrifice of Christ. By the blood of bulls, Moses at the foot of Sinai had signified the covenant which united Yahweh and Israel. Later, the high priest of the temple of Jerusalem was not to go into the sanctuary, where he entered alone in God's presence, until he had poured out the blood of the animals offered in sacrifice for the sins of the people. Before entering heaven in the name of all of us. Christ had to consent to the bloody sacrifice of the Cross. By his Blood Christ seals the new and definitive covenant between God and men.

A reading from the letter of the apostle Paul to the Hebrews

Brethren,

Christ has come as the high priest of the future kingdom.

Having ingress to a temple greater and more perfect [than that of Jerusalem], a temple which is not built by the hands of men and is not of this world, he entered once for all into the sanctuary [of heaven], not with blood of goats or of calves, but covered with his own blood, the blood that paid the price of our deliverance for eternity.

If the blood of goats and of bull calves and the ashes of a heifer, with which those [among the Jews] who have been defiled are sprinkled, sanctify them by obtaining purity of body for them, how much more must the blood of Christ — who, prompted by the Holy Spirit, offered himself to God as a victim all-pure — purify our soul of all sin and make us true adorers of the living God!

It is he who has concluded the new covenant between God and men. It is his death that has destroyed sin, that sin which remained under the former covenant. It is his death that puts us in possession of the eternal inheritance, to which God is calling us in Jesus Christ our Lord.

Gradual Ps. 142:9, 10; Ps. 17:48-49

Rescue me from my enemies, O Lord; teach me to do your will. O Lord, my deliverer from the angry nations, truly above my adversaries you exalt me and from the violent man you have rescued me.

Tract Ps. 128:1-4

Much have they oppressed me from my youth. Let Israel say: Much have they oppressed me from my youth. Yet they have not prevailed against me; upon my back the plowers plowed. Long did they make their furrows. But the just Lord has severed the cords of the wicked.

GOSPEL John 8:46-59

The Son is eternal like the Father, but he became flesh in order that human nature, in him, might honor God with an absolute love. Those who follow his example by doing the will of the Father will know, beyond death, the life that does not end.

A reading from the holy Gospel according to John

At that time Jesus said to the Jews, "Which of you can prove that I have committed any sin? If it is the truth that I tell, why do you not believe me? He who is from God welcomes the word of God. That, to be sure, is the reason you do not welcome it: your heart does not belong to God."

The Jews protested, "Are we not right in saying that you are a Samaritan and possessed by a devil?"

Jesus replied, "No, I am not possessed. I honor my Father, whereas you dishonor me. That matters little, however: I am not pursuing my own glory; there is one who does pursue it and who will see justice done. It is a solemn truth that I tell you: if anyone obeys my word, he shall never see death."

The Jews interrupted him: "This time we can see well enough that you are possessed. Abraham is dead, and the prophets too; and now you come and tell us, 'If anyone obeys my word, he shall never see death'! Do you think you are greater than our father Abraham, who is nonetheless dead, or than the prophets, who are dead also? Who are you pretending to be?"

Jesus answered, "If I glorify myself, my glory is without value. It is my Father who glorifies me, he of whom you say that he is your God, whereas you do not know him. I do know him, and if I were to say that I did not know him, I should be like you: a liar. But I know him, and I obey his word. You should know, then, that Abraham, your father, thrilled with the hope of seeing my day. He saw it, and that was his joy."

The Jews said to him then, "You, not yet fifty years old, you have seen Abraham?"

Jesus replied, "This is a solemn truth that I tell you: before Abraham was born, I AM."

They picked up stones to throw at him, but Jesus slipped away from them and went out of the temple.

OFFERTORY ANTIPHON *Ps. 118:17, 107*

I praise you, O Lord, with all my heart; be good to your servant, that I may live and keep your words. O Lord, give me life according to your word.

Prayer over the Offerings

Hæc múnera, quǽsumus, Dómine, et víncula nostræ pravitátis absólvant, et tuæ nobis misericórdiæ dona concílient. Per Dóminum.

May these offerings, Lord, free us from the bonds of our sins and obtain for us the benefits of your mercy. This we ask of you through our Lord.

COMMUNION ANTIPHON *1 Cor. 11:24, 25*

"This is my body, which shall be given up for you: this is the cup of the new covenant in my blood," says the Lord. "Do this as often as you receive it, in remembrance of me."

Prayer after the Communion

Adésto nobis, Dómine Deus noster: et quos tuis mystériis recreásti, perpétuis defénde subsídiis. Per Dóminum.

Stay near us, Lord our God. You have renewed us with your Eucharist; continue to help us always. This we ask of you through our Lord.

SECOND SUNDAY OF PASSIONTIDE
PALM SUNDAY

The Solemn Procession of Palms in Honor of Christ the King
The Blessing of the Palms

When the celebrant approaches the place where the branches are to be blessed, the choir sings the following antiphon.

Hosanna to the Son of David! Blessed is he who comes in the name of the Lord. O king of Israel: hosanna in the highest.

The celebrant blesses the branches with this prayer:

Priest: Dóminus vobíscum.

All: Et cum spíritu tuo.

Priest: Orémus. Béne † dic, quǽsumus, Dómine, hos palmárum (seu olivárum aut aliarum arborum) ramos: et præsta; ut, quod pópulus tuus in tui veneratiónem hodiérno die corporáliter agit, hoc spirituáliter summa devotióne perfíciat, de hoste victóriam reportándo et opus misericórdiæ summópere diligéndo. Per Christum Dóminum nostrum.

All: Amen.

The Lord be with you.

And with your spirit.

Let us pray. Lord, please † bless these branches of palm (or olive or other trees). What your people are celebrating today by an outward worship in your honor, grant that they may perfect in their inmost souls by winning a victory over the devil and by attaching themselves with all their hearts to the salvation that comes from your mercy. Through Christ our Lord. Amen.

The Distribution of the Palms

When the celebrant begins to distribute the blessed branches, the choir sings the following antiphons and psalms.

I Antiphon. The children of the Hebrews, bearing olive branches, went to meet the Lord, crying aloud and saying, "Hosanna in the highest."

Psalm 23. The Lord's are the earth and its fullness; the world and those who dwell in it.

2. For he founded it upon the seas and established it upon the rivers.

I Antiphon. The children of the Hebrews, bearing olive branches, went to meet the Lord, crying aloud and saying, "Hosanna in the highest."

7. Lift up, O gates, your lintels; reach up, you ancient portals, that the king of glory may come in!

8. "Who is this king of glory?" "The Lord, strong and mighty, the Lord, mighty in battle."

I Antiphon. The children of the Hebrews, bearing olive branches, went to meet the Lord, crying aloud and saying, "Hosanna in the highest."

9. Lift up, O gates, your lintels; reach up, you ancient portals, that the king of glory may come in!

10. "Who is this king of glory?" "The Lord of hosts; he is the king of glory."

I Antiphon. The children of the Hebrews, bearing olive branches, went to meet the Lord, crying aloud and saying, "Hosanna in the highest."

Glory be to the Father and to the Son and to the Holy Spirit. As it was in the beginning, is now and ever shall be, world without end. Amen.

I Antiphon. The children of the Hebrews, bearing olive branches, went to meet the Lord, crying aloud and saying, "Hosanna in the highest."

II Antiphon. The Hebrew children spread their garments in the way, and shouted, saying: "Hosanna to the Son of David: blessed is he who comes in the name of the Lord."

Psalm 46. All you peoples, clap your hands, shout to God with cries of gladness.

2. For the Lord, the Most High, the awesome, is the great king over all the earth.

II Antiphon. The Hebrew children spread their garments in the way, and shouted, saying, "Hosanna to the Son of David: blessed is he who comes in the name of the Lord."

3. He brings peoples under us; nations under our feet.

4. He chooses for us our inheritance, the glory of Jacob, whom he loves.

II Antiphon. The Hebrew children spread their garments in the way, and shouted, saying, "Hosanna to the Son of David: blessed is he who comes in the name of the Lord."

5. God mounts his throne amid shouts of joy; the Lord, amid trumpet blasts.

6. Sing praise to God, sing praise; sing praise to our king, sing praise.

II Antiphon. The Hebrew children spread their garments in the way, and shouted, saying, "Hosanna to the Son of David: blessed is he who comes in the name of the Lord."

7. For king of all the earth is God; sing hymns of praise.

8. God reigns over the nations, God sits upon his holy throne.

II Antiphon. The Hebrew children spread their garments in the way, and shouted, saying, "Hosanna to the Son of David: blessed is he who comes in the name of the Lord."

9. The princes of the peoples are gathered together with the people of the God of Abraham. For God's are the guardians of the earth; he is supreme.

II Antiphon. The Hebrew children spread their garments in the way, and shouted, saying, "Hosanna to the Son of David: blessed is he who comes in the name of the Lord."

Glory be to the Father and to the Son and to the Holy Spirit. As it was in the beginning, is now and ever shall be, world without end. Amen.

II Antiphon. The Hebrew children spread their garments in the way, and shouted, saying, "Hosanna to the Son of David: blessed is he who comes in the name of the Lord."

THE READING OF THE GOSPEL

Priest: **The Lord be with you.**

All: **And with your spirit.**

Priest: **A reading from the holy Gospel according to Matthew (21:1-9).**

All: **Glory to you, O Lord.**

At that time, as Jesus was approaching Jerusalem and found himself within view of Bethphage on the Mount of Olives, he sent two of his disciples ahead of him. "Go to the village that is facing you," he told them. "At once you will find an ass tethered there, and her foal with her. Untie them and bring them to me. If anyone says anything to you, you shall answer, 'The Lord has need of them, but he will send them back as soon as he is through with them.' "

All this was done in order that the word of the prophet might be fulfilled: "Say to [Jerusalem] the daughter of Sion: Here is your king coming to you, humble, riding on an ass, on a colt, the foal of a beast of burden."

The disciples went, therefore, and did as Jesus had ordered them. They brought the ass and the foal, placed their cloaks on them and had Jesus sit on these.

And many among the crowd spread their cloaks on the road; others were cutting branches off the trees and strewing the way with them; and the crowds preceding him and those following him kept shouting, "Hosanna to the Son of David! Blessed is he who comes in the name of the Lord!"

The Procession with the Blessed Branches

When the ministers are ready to begin the procession, the celebrant (or deacon, if one is present) sings:

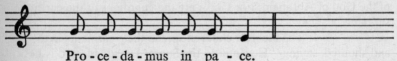

Pro - ce - da - mus in pa - ce.
Let us go forward in peace.

All present reply:

In no - mi - ne Chri - sti. A - men.
In the name of Christ. Amen.

During the procession, the choir sings some or all of the following antiphons, psalm, and/or hymn. The hymn, **All Glory, Laud, and Honor,** *or any other hymn in honor of Christ the King may be sung.*

I Antiphon. With flowers and palms the multitudes run to meet the redeemer, and they give becoming honors to the triumphant victor; the nations utter the praises of the Son of God, and their voices thunder through the clouds in praise of Christ: "Hosanna."

II Antiphon. With the angels and the children, let us be found faithful, acclaiming him who triumphs over death: "Hosanna in the highest."

III Antiphon. The great crowd gathered for the feastday acclaimed the Lord: "Blessed is he who comes in the name of the Lord: "Hosanna in the highest."

IV Antiphon. The whole company of those descending began to rejoice and to praise God with a loud voice for all the miracles that they had seen, saying, "Blessed is he who comes as king, in the name of the Lord! Peace on earth, and glory in the highest!"

V Antiphon. All join together in praising your name, and saying: "Blessed is he who comes in the name of the Lord: hosanna in the highest.

Psalm 147. Glorify the Lord, O Jerusalem; praise your God, O Sion.

2. For he has strengthened the bars of your gates; he has blessed your children within you.

3. He has granted peace in your borders; with the best of wheat he fills you.

4. He sends forth his command to the earth; swiftly runs his word!

5. He spreads snow like wool; frost he strews like ashes.

6. He scatters his hail like crumbs; before his cold the waters freeze.

7. He sends his word and melts them; he lets his breeze blow and the waters run.

8. He has proclaimed his word to Jacob, his statutes and his ordinances to Israel.

9. He has not done thus for any other nation; his ordinances he has not made known to them.

10. Glory be to the Father and to the Son and to the Holy Spirit.

11. As it was in the beginning, is now and ever shall be, world without end. Amen.

V Antiphon. All join together in praising your name, and saying: "Blessed is he who comes in the name of the Lord: hosanna in the highest."

VI Antiphon. Like splendid palm branches we are strewn in the Lord's path: let us all go to meet him with hymns and canticles, glorifying him and saying: "Blessed is the Lord."

VII Antiphon. Hail, our king, the Son of David, redeemer of the world, whom the prophets foretold as the savior to come to the house of Israel. For you the Father sent into the world as the saving victim whom all the saints awaited from the beginning of the world even unto the present: "Hosanna to the Son of David. Blessed is he who comes in the name of the Lord. Hosanna in the highest."

When the celebrant enters the door of the church, the following antiphon is sung:

When the Lord entered the holy city, the children of the Hebrews, foretelling the resurrection of life,

Carrying palm branches, cried out, "Hosanna in the highest."

When the populace had heard that Jesus was coming to Jerusalem, they went out to meet him.

Carrying palm branches, they cried, "Hosanna in the highest."

Arrived at the altar, the priest sings a Collect. It encourages us to take our blessed "palm" home, as a constant reminder of the loyalty we pledged to Christ today, and as a sacramental to be kept in the home — laudably until next Ash Wednesday, when we burn it to ashes.

COLLECT

Priest: Dóminus vobíscum.

The Lord be with you.

All: Et cum spíritu tuo.

And with your spirit.

Priest: Orémus. Dómine Iesu Christe, Rex ac Redémptor noster, in cuius honórem, hos ramos

Let us pray. Lord Jesus Christ, our King, our Redeemer, in your honor we have carried these branches

gestántes, solémnes laudes decantávimus: concéde propítius; ut, quocúmque hi rami deportáti fúerint, ibi tuæ benedictiónis grátia descéndat, et, quavis dæmonum iniquitáte vel illusióne profligáta, déxtera tua prótegat, quos redémit. Qui vivis et regnas in sæcula sæculórum.

All: Amen.

and sung solemn praises. In your kindness make the grace of your blessing descend wherever these branches are taken; and may your hand, by thwarting the devil's wickedness and his tricks, protect those whom it has redeemed. This we ask of you who live and reign forever.

Amen.

THE MASS

ENTRANCE ANTIPHON *Ps. 21:20, 22, 2*

O Lord, be not far from me: O my help, hasten to aid me. Save me from the lion's mouth; from the horns of the wild bulls, my wretched life.

Ps. My God, my God, look upon me, why have you forsaken me? Far from my salvation are the words of my sins. O Lord . . .

Prayer over the Assembly

Omnípotens sempitérne Deus, qui humáno géneri, ad imitándum humilitátis exémplum, Salvatórem nostrum carnem súmere et crucem subíre fecísti: concéde propítius; ut et patiéntiæ ipsíus habére documénta et resurrectiónis consórtia mereámur. Per eúndem Dóminum nostrum Iesum Christum Fílium tuum, qui tecum vivit et regnat in unitáte Spíritus Sancti, Deus, per ómnia sæcula sæculórum.

All-powerful, eternal God, you have chosen to give mankind a model of humility: our Savior took on our flesh and subjected himself to the Cross. Grant us the grace to preserve faithfully the lessons he has given us in his passion and to have a share in his resurrection. This we ask of you through the same Jesus Christ, our Lord and your Son, who lives and reigns with you in the unity of the Holy Spirit, God, forever.

EPISTLE

Philippians 2:5-11

St. Paul stresses the fact that the Passion derives its redemptive force from the obedience shown by Jesus. Jesus obeyed his Father perfectly, subjecting himself to all the servitudes of his human condition, including death; and it was this submission which was necessary if the price was to be paid for Adam's disobedience.

A reading from the letter of the apostle Paul to the Christians of Philippi

Brethren,

Let your sentiments be the same as those of Christ Jesus. Divine though he was, he did not want to take advantage of his equality with God, but he emptied himself by taking on the condition of a slave, becoming similar to men; he had all the outward appearance of a man. Debasing himself still further, he became obedient to the point of death — even death on a cross.

That is why God has exalted him to the highest degree and given him the name that is above all other names. That is why, at the name of Jesus, every knee bends in heaven, on earth and in hell. That is why every tongue should proclaim, to the glory of God the Father, that Jesus Christ is the Lord!

Gradual Ps. 72:24, 1-3

You have hold of my right hand; with your counsel you guide me; in the end you will receive me in glory. How good God is to Israel, to those who are clean of heart! But, as for me, I almost lost my balance; my feet all but slipped, because I was envious of sinners when I saw them prosper though they were wicked.

Tract Ps. 21:2-9, 18, 19, 22, 24, 32

My God, my God, look upon me: why have you forsaken me? Far from my salvation are the words of my sins. O my God, I cry out by day and you answer not; by night, and there is no relief. But you are enthroned in the holy place, O glory of Israel! In you our fathers trusted: they trusted and you delivered them. To you they cried, and they escaped; in you they trusted, and they were not put to shame. But I am a worm, not a man: the scorn of men, despised by the people. All who see me, scoff at me; they mock me with parted lips, they wag their heads. "He relied on the Lord; let him deliver him, let him rescue him, if he loves him." But they look on and gloat over me; they divide my garments among them, and for my vesture they cast lots. Save me from the lion's mouth; from the horns of the wild bulls, my wretched life. You who fear the Lord, praise him: all you descendants of Jacob, give glory to him. There shall be declared to the Lord a generation to come: and the heavens shall show forth his justice — to a people that shall be born, which the Lord has made.

If the priest has celebrated another Mass, in which he has already read the Passion, he may read merely the following passage as a gospel:

GOSPEL Matthew 27:45-52

A reading from the holy Gospel according to Matthew

After they had crucified Jesus, * starting at noon . . . and what follows, page 88, up to bodies of many of the saints rose **.

PASSION Matthew 26:36-75; 27:1-60

St. Matthew, who addresses himself especially to the Christians of Jewish origin, strives to show, by recalling the psalms and the oracles of the prophets, that Jesus is indeed the Messiah announced by the Old Testament: his Passion, which was foreseen, puts an end to the old covenant. Thanks to Christ's sacrifice, all men can henceforth become the people of God.

To recite the Passion as a dialogue in English, it will be well to have 5 persons:

> ✝ Jesus
> R Reader
> D Disciples (and friends)
> C the crowd
> A other adversaries

If need be, one person could take both D and C.

The Reader's passages printed in smaller type could be skipped in the public reading in dialogue form.

The Passion of our Lord Jesus Christ
according to Matthew

26:36-46   THE AGONY

R   At that time Jesus came with his disciples to a country place called Gethsemane. He said to the disciples:

> ✝ Stay here, while I go to pray over there.

R He took Peter, James and John with him, and he began to be over-whelmed with sorrow and anguish.

Then he said to them:

> ✝ I am sad, to the point of death. Stay here and watch with me.

R Taking a few steps and falling with his face to the ground, he begged:

> ✝ Father, if it is possible, let this cup pass away from me. But no! not my will, but yours!

R He came back to his disciples and found them sleeping. He said to Peter:

> ✝ So, you could not watch for one hour with me! Watch and pray, so as not to succumb to temptation. The spirit is eager, but the flesh is weak.

R For the second time he withdrew; he prayed:

> ✝ Father, if it is not possible that this cup pass without my drinking it, may your will be done!

R On his return he found them sleeping again, for their eyes were heavy with drowsiness.

He left them once more and went off to pray a third time, repeating the same words. Then he came back to his disciples and said,

> ✝ Sleep now and take your rest. . . .
> Look, the hour has arrived, and the Son of Man is going to be de-livered into the hands of sinners!
> On your feet! Let us go! The one who is handing me over is there!

26:47-56   THE ARREST

R He was still speaking when along came Judas, one of the twelve, and with him a numerous throng, armed with swords and clubs, sent by the chief priests and the elders of the people. Judas, who was betraying him, had given them a sign:

> A The one I kiss will be your man! Arrest him.

R He went up to Jesus immediately, saying:
  A Good evening, Rabbi! [1]
R And he kissed him.

Jesus said to him:

  ✠ My friend, why are you here?

R The others approached, took hold of Jesus and arrested him. At that moment one of those who were with Jesus drew his sword and struck the servant of the high priest; he cut off his ear.

Then Jesus said to him:

  ✠ Put your sword back in its place. All those who use the sword will die by the sword. Do you think that I cannot appeal to my Father? He would send me immediately a dozen armies of angels. But then how would the words of the Scripture be fulfilled which announce that this is to happen just so?

R At this time Jesus said to the crowd:

  ✠ Have you come with swords and clubs, then, to take me like a bandit? Yet day after day I was sitting in the temple to teach, and you did not arrest me.

R All this took place to fulfill the predictions of the prophets. Then the disciples abandoned him and fled, all of them.

THE TRIAL BEFORE THE JEWS

26:57–27:10   *The interrogation before the high priest*

R Those who had arrested Jesus led Him to Caiphas, the high priest, where the scribes and the elders had assembled. Peter had followed at a distance, as far as the high priest's courtyard. He had entered and was sitting with the guards, to see how the matter would end.

The chief priests and the whole council were looking for false testimony against Jesus, in order to put him to death. But they were finding nothing, despite the many false witnesses who were testifying.

Finally, two false witnesses came forward and declared:

  C This man said, "I can destroy the temple of God and rebuild it in three days." [2]

R The high priest stood up:

  A You have nothing to answer to these depositions?

R Jesus remained silent. The high priest said to him:

  A I adjure you, in the name of the living God, to tell us whether you are the Messiah, the Son of God.

R Jesus answered him:

  ✠ Yes, you have said it. And I for my part declare to you: in the future you shall see the Son of Man sitting at the right hand of the Almighty and coming on the clouds in the sky. [3]

---

[1] Aramaic for "Master."
[2] John 2:19.
[3] Allusion to Psalm 109 (Sunday Vespers) and to the vision of Daniel 7:13: "On the clouds in the sky comes one like a Son of Man; dominion and kingship have been given him."

R Then the high priest tore his garments:

    A He has blasphemed! No need now to look for witnesses! Now you have heard the blasphemy! What do you think of it?

R They answered:

    C He deserves death!

The outrages

R Then they spit in his face, and punched him and slapped him, saying:

    C Play the prophet, Messiah! Tell us who hit you!

Peter's denial

R Now Peter was sitting outside, in the courtyard. A servant girl came up to him:

    A You too, you were with Jesus the Galilean!

R But he protested before them all:

    D I don't know what you mean!

R As he was passing under the portico to go out, another girl noticed him and said to those around:

    A And that one, he was with Jesus of Nazareth!

R He protested a second time with an oath:

    D That man — why, I don't even know him!

R A while later, the people who were standing at the gate said to Peter:

    A There's no doubt about it, you're one of them too. Why, anyone can tell by your accent!

R But he began cursing, and swearing that he did not know him. Just then a rooster crowed. With that, Peter remembered what Jesus had said: "Before the cock crows, you will have disowned me three times." He went away, his eyes smarting with tears.

Jesus handed over to Pilate

R When morning came, all the chief priests and the elders of the people laid plans against Jesus to put him to death. Then he was bound and led out to be handed over to Pontius Pilate, the Roman governor.

Despair of Judas

R When Judas, the one who had betrayed him, saw that he had been condemned, he was stricken with remorse and brought back his thirty pieces of silver to the chief priests and the elders.

    A I have sinned, betraying an innocent man!

R They answered him:

    C What difference does that make to us? That's your affair!

R He threw the money down in the temple and left. Then he went away and hanged himself.

    Gathering up the silver pieces, the chief priests said:

    C They may not be put into the treasury, because they are the price of blood.

R They decided, therefore, to use this money for buying the "Potter's Field" as a burial place for strangers. Hence the name of this tract: to our day it is still called "Haceldama," that is, "Field of Blood." Thus was fulfilled what the prophet Jeremias had said: "They took thirty pieces of silver, the price of a man who was sold, for some of the sons of Israel had calculated his price; and with the money they bought the Potter's Field, as the Lord had commanded me."

THE TRIAL BEFORE THE ROMANS

27:11-31 *The interrogation by Pilate*

R Jesus meanwhile was haled before the governor, who questioned him:

    A You are the King of the Jews, are you?

R Jesus answered:

    ✠ Yes, you are right.

R The chief priests and the elders were accusing him. But he did not answer. Then Pilate said to him:

    A Don't you hear all these depositions they're making against you?

R Jesus did not answer any of his questions, so that the governor was much surprised.

Now every year at the Passover the governor had the custom of granting the crowd the liberation of a prisoner, whatever one they wanted. That year there was a notorious prisoner named Barabbas. As they were assembled, therefore, Pilate asked them:

    A Whom do you want me to release to you: Barabbas? or Jesus who is called the Messiah?

R For he knew that it was out of jealousy that they handed him over. Besides, while he was sitting at the tribunal, his wife had sent him a message:

    D Do not get involved in the affair of that good man; last night I had a very troublesome dream on account of him.

R But the chief priests and the elders persuaded the crowd to ask for Barabbas and to have Jesus killed. When the governor asked them, therefore:

    A Which of the two do you want me to release to you?

R They answered:

    C Barabbas!

R But Pilate replied:

    A What am I going to do, then, about Jesus, who is called the Messiah?

R They all cried:

    C Have him crucified!

R He protested:

    A But what evil has he done?

R And they cried louder:

    C Have him crucified!

The condemnation by Pilate

R Seeing that this served no purpose, unless to increase the uproar, Pilate took water and washed his hands in front of the crowd, saying:

    A I am innocent of the blood of this just man! It is your affair!

R And all the people answered him:

    C His blood be upon us and upon our children!

R Then he released Barabbas to them. As for Jesus, after having him scourged, he turned him over to the soldiers to be crucified.

The crowning with thorns

R The soldiers of the governor took Jesus to the praetorium. They had assembled the whole company around Him. They took away his clothes and put a scarlet cloak on him. Then they plaited a crown of thorns, which they placed on his head, and they put a reed in his right hand. Then, going down on their knees before him, they made fun of him:

C Greetings, King of the Jews!

R They kept spitting on him, and taking the reed and hitting him over the head with it.
When they were through making fun of him, they took off the cloak and put his own clothes on him again. Then they led him away to crucify him.

27:32-34   THE WAY OF THE CROSS

R As they were going out, they met a man from Cyrene, named Simon; they commandeered him to carry the cross.
Having arrived at the place called "Golgotha," that is, "Place of the Skull" (or Calvary), they gave him wine mixed with gall. He tasted it, but would not drink it.

27:35-44   JESUS ON THE CROSS

R After crucifying him, they divided his clothes among them by drawing lots. (This action fulfilled the prophet's prediction: "They distributed my clothes among them, and for my garment they cast lots." [1] Then they sat down to guard him. Over his head an inscription had been placed with the reason for his condemnation: "This is Jesus, the King of the Jews." Then two bandits were crucified with him, one on his right and the other on his left.
The passersby kept insulting him,[2] shaking their heads:

C Ha! You that destroy the temple and build it up again in three days, save yourself! If you're the Son of God, come down from the cross!

R In the same way the chief priests kept mocking him, together with the scribes and the elders:

A He saved others, but he cannot save himself! The King of Israel! Let him come down from the Cross, and we'll believe in him! He put his trust in God; let God get him out of this, if he loves him! After all, he said, "I am the Son of God."

R The bandits who had been crucified with him were abusing him in the same way.

27:45-50   LAST MOMENTS AND DEATH

R * Starting at noon, the whole country was plunged into darkness until three o'clock.
Around three o'clock Jesus gave a loud cry:

[1] Psalm 21:19.
[2] Psalm 21:8.

✠ Eli, Eli, lema sabachthani?

R That is to say:

✠ My God, my God, why have you abandoned me? [1]

R Hearing this, some people said:

C He is calling Elijah!

R Immediately one of them ran to get a sponge, which he dipped in the vinegar, affixed to the end of a reed and started offering to Jesus for a drink. But the others said:

A Wait! Let's see whether Elijah comes to set him free!

R Then Jesus gave a great cry again and yielded up his spirit.

All kneel in silence for a little while.

27:51-56   AFTER THE DEATH

R And with that the curtain of the temple was torn in two, from top to bottom, the earth trembled, the rocks split, the tombs opened and the bodies of many of the saints rose **: they left their tombs after the resurrection of Jesus and went into the holy city, where many of the people could see them.

The centurion and those who were guarding Jesus with him, witnessing the earthquake and everything that was happening, were very much afraid, and they said:

C He really was the Son of God!

R There were many women there looking on from a distance. They were the ones who had followed Jesus since he left Galilee and had put themselves at his service. Among others, there were Mary Magdalene, Mary the mother of James and Joseph, and the mother of [James and John] the sons of Zebedee.

27:57-60   THE BURIAL

R When evening came, there arrived a rich man from Arimathea, named Joseph, who himself was also a disciple of Jesus. He sought an audience with Pilate and claimed the body of Jesus. Pilate had the body consigned to him.

Taking the body, Joseph wrapped it in a white shroud and placed it in his own tomb, a new tomb which he had had hollowed out in a rock. Then he rolled a great stone to the entrance of the tomb and went away.

OFFERTORY ANTIPHON *Ps. 68:21-22*

Insult has broken my heart, and I am weak; I looked for sympathy, but there was none; for comforters, and I found none. Rather they put gall in my food and in my thirst they gave me vinegar to drink.

Prayer over the Offerings

Concéde, quǽsumus, Dómine: ut óculis tuæ maiestátis munus oblátum, et grátiam nobis devotiónis

We bring our offerings before your majesty, Lord; may they obtain for us the grace of a more fervent piety

---

[1] First verse of Psalm 21, which must be read in its entirety for a good understanding of Jesus's cry.

obtíneat, et efféctum beátæ perennitátis acquírat. Per Dóminum.

and ensure us an eternity of happiness. This we ask of you through our Lord.

COMMUNION ANTIPHON *Matthew 26:42*

Father, if this cup cannot pass away, unless I drink it, your will be done.

Prayer after the Communion

Per huius, Dómine, operatiónem mystérii: et vítia nostra purgéntur, et iusta desidéria compleántur. Per Dóminum.

Lord, by the working of this mystery purify us from our vices and fulfill our desires. This we ask of you through our Lord.

EASTER SUNDAY

ENTRANCE ANTIPHON *Ps. 138:18, 5, 6, 1-2*

I arose, and am still with you, alleluia; you rest your hand upon me, alleluia. Your knowledge is too wonderful, alleluia, alleluia.

Ps. O Lord, you have probed me and you know me; you know when I sit and when I stand.

Glory be to the Father and to the Son and to the Holy Spirit. As it was in the beginning, is now and ever shall be, world without end. Amen. I arose . . .

Prayer over the Assembly

Deus, qui hodiérna die per Unigénitum tuum, æternitátis nobis áditum, devícta morte, reserásti: vota nostra, quæ præveniéndo aspíras, étiam adiuvándo proséquere. Per eúndem Dóminum nostrum Iesum Christum, Fílium tuum, qui tecum vivit et regnat in unitáte Spíritus Sancti, Deus, per ómnia sǽcula sæculórum.

Today, Lord, through your only-begotten Son, the conqueror of death, you reopen the way to heaven for us. May your grace inspire rightful desires in us and help us also in their fulfillment. This we ask of you through the same Jesus Christ, our Lord and your Son, who lives and reigns with you in the unity of the Holy Spirit, God, forever.

EPISTLE   1 Corinthians 5:7-8

During the Passover celebrations, to recall their hurried departure for the promised land the Jews ate only unleavened bread, that is to say, bread which had not had time to rise. But a change in food is not enough: we must make our life a dough that is purified of all bad yeast.

A reading from the first letter of the apostle Paul
to the Christians of Corinth

Brethren,

Let there be no trace in you of the old leaven! Be a brand new dough, so as to be [as at the Passover meal] unleavened bread.

For our paschal lamb — Christ — has been sacrificed.

Let us make our feast, therefore, not with the old leaven — the leaven of malice and wickedness — but with the unleavened bread of sincerity and truth.

Gradual Ps. 117:24, 1

This is the day the Lord has made; let us be glad and rejoice in it. Give thanks to the Lord, for he is good, for his mercy endures forever.

Alleluia 1 Cor. 5:7

Alleluia, alleluia. Christ, our passover, has been sacrificed.

Sequence

Christians, to the paschal victim offer your thankful praises! A lamb the sheep redeemeth: Christ, who only is sinless, reconcileth sinners to the Father. Death and life have contended in that combat stupendous; the Prince of life, who died, reigns immortal.

Speak, Mary, declaring what thou sawest wayfaring. "The tomb of Christ, who is living, the glory of Jesus' resurrection; bright angels attesting, the shroud and napkin resting. Yea, Christ my hope is arisen: to Galilee he goes before you."

Christ indeed from death is risen, our new life obtaining. Have mercy, victor King, ever reigning! Amen. Alleluia.

GOSPEL   Mark 16:1-7
"If Christ is not risen, our faith is vain," says St. Paul; but our faith rests on the testimony of those who found the empty tomb and who saw the Lord again.

A reading from the holy Gospel according to Mark

At that time [as soon as the sabbath rest was ended, at sunset], Mary Magdalene, Mary the mother of James, and Salome bought perfumes for embalming the body of Jesus.

And very early in the morning on the first day of the week [Sunday], they went to the tomb, just at sunrise. They were asking one another, "Whom can we get to roll back the stone that blocks the entrance to the tomb?"

But when they looked, they saw that the stone, which was very large, had been rolled aside. On entering the tomb they saw a young man clothed in a white robe, sitting at the right side; and they were awestruck. But he said to them, "Do not be frightened. You are looking for Jesus of Nazareth, the crucified. He has risen; he is no longer here. Look, this is the place where they laid him. Go, therefore, and tell his disciples, and especially Peter, that he is going to Galilee ahead of you. There you will see him, as he told you."

OFFERTORY ANTIPHON Ps. 75:9-10

The earth feared and was silent when God arose for judgment. Alleluia.

Prayer over the Offerings

Súscipe, quǽsumus, Dómine, preces pópuli tui cum oblatiónibus hostiárum: ut paschálibus initiáta mystériis, ad æternitátis nobis medélam, te operánte, profíciant. Per Dóminum.

Lord, please accept the prayers and the offerings of your people. With the help of your grace may the sacrifice inaugurated by the paschal mysteries serve as an everlasting remedy for us. This we ask of you through our Lord.

COMMUNION ANTIPHON *1 Cor. 5:7-8*

Christ, our passover, has been sacrificed, alleluia. Therefore let us keep festival with the unleavened bread of sincerity and truth, alleluia, alleluia, alleluia.

Prayer after the Communion

Spíritum nobis, Dómine, tuæ caritátis infúnde: ut, quos sacraméntis paschálibus satiásti, tua fácias pietáte concórdes. Per Dóminum nostrum Iesum Christum Fílium tuum, qui tecum vivit et regnat in unitáte eiúsdem Spíritus Sancti, Deus, per ómnia sǽcula sæculórum.

Pour out on us, Lord, the Spirit of your charity. We have just taken part in the paschal communion; keep us united in your love. This we ask of you through our Lord Jesus Christ, your Son, who lives and reigns with you in the unity of the same Holy Spirit, God, forever.

LOW SUNDAY

ENTRANCE ANTIPHON *1 Peter 2, 2; Ps. 80:2*

Crave as newborn babes, alleluia: pure spiritual milk: alleluia, alleluia, alleluia.

Ps. Sing joyfully to God our strength; acclaim the God of Jacob.

Glory be to the Father and to the Son and to the Holy Spirit. As it was in the beginning, is now and ever shall be, world without end. Amen. Crave as newborn babes . . .

Prayer over the Assembly

Præsta, quǽsumus, omnípotens Deus: ut, qui paschália festa perégimus, hæc, te largiénte, móribus et vita teneámus. Per Dóminum.

God all-powerful, we have just celebrated the paschal festivals; grant by your grace that we may preserve the spirit of them in our way of life. This we ask of you through our Lord.

EPISTLE   1 John 5:4-10

Through their faith, Christians are associated in the victory which Christ won over the world by dying on the Cross. Faith is the welcome we give the word of the Father; it is filial submission to the Father with Christ;

it is interior docility to the Holy Spirit. Faith is given us by baptism; it is strengthened by confirmation; it is nourished by the Eucharist, which brings us the blood of the new covenant.

A reading from the first letter of the apostle John to the Christians

Beloved brethren,

Whoever is born of God is victor over the world, and this victory which conquers the world is our faith.

Who is it that overpowers the world, if not he who believes that Jesus is the Son of God? It is he, Jesus Christ, who came through water and through blood, not just by water, but by water and by blood.[1]

And there is the Holy Spirit too, who bears witness to the truth of Christ.

You have on earth, then, three testimonies on behalf of Christ: the Holy Spirit, the water and the blood; and these three are in agreement.

(Just as there are three in heaven to give testimony: the Father, the Son and the Holy Spirit, and these three form but one.)

We do put trust in the testimony of men. The testimony of God has a much greater value! And such is the witness that God has borne to his Son.

He who believes that Jesus is the Son of God bears within himself the testimony of God.

AFTER THE EPISTLE *Matt. 28:7; John 20:26*

Alleluia, alleluia. "On the day of my resurrection," says the Lord, "I will go before you into Galilee." Alleluia. After eight days, the doors being closed, Jesus stood in the midst of his disciples, and said, "Peace be to you!" Alleluia.

GOSPEL   John 20:19-31

At the end of his account of Jesus' apparitions, St. John himself draws the lesson from them: we must believe that Jesus is the Son of God if we are to have life in his name.

A reading from the holy Gospel according to John

At that time, on the same day [Easter], the first of the week, when evening had come and when, in fear of the Jews, the disciples had closed the doors of the quarters where they were staying, Jesus came. He stood in their midst and said, "Peace be with you!" and immediately after this greeting he showed them his hands and his side. The disciples were filled with joy when they saw the Lord.

Then Jesus said to them a second time, "Peace be with you! Just as the Father sent me, I also send you." With this he breathed on them and added, "Receive the Holy Spirit. If you forgive anyone's sins, they shall be forgiven; if you hold anyone's sins back, they shall be held back."

Now Thomas, one of the twelve, the one called the Twin, was not with them when Jesus came. The disciples told him, "We have seen the Lord." But he answered, "Unless I see in his hands the wounds from the nails,

[1] Water of baptism in the Jordan and blood of the Passion; water and blood which flow from the side opened by the lance; baptismal water and eucharistic blood.

and put my finger into the place of the nails, and my hand into his side, I will not believe."

Eight days later, the disciples were in the house again, and this time Thomas was with them. Although the doors were closed, Jesus came; he stood in their midst and said to them, "Peace be with you!" Then, addressing Thomas, "Put your finger here," he said, "and see my hands. Bring your hand here: put it into my side. And from now on, do not be incredulous, but believe."

"My Lord and my God!" cried Thomas.

"Because you have seen me, Thomas, you have believed," replied Jesus. "Blessed are those who believe without having had to see!"

Jesus did many other miracles in the presence of his disciples, which are not reported in this book. These have been put into writing in order that you may believe that Jesus is the Christ and the Son of God, and that through this faith you may have life in his name.

OFFERTORY ANTIPHON *Matt. 28:2, 5, 6*

An angel of the Lord came down from heaven, and said to the women: "He whom you seek has risen even as he said," alleluia.

Prayer over the Offerings

Súscipe múnera, Dómine, quǽsumus, exsultántis Ecclésiæ: et cui causam tanti gáudii præstitísti, perpétuæ fructum concéde lætítiæ. Per Dóminum.

Your Church, exultant, brings you her offerings, Lord. You have brought about this happiness by the resurrection; bestow on the Church the gift of eternal joy. This we ask of you through our Lord.

COMMUNION ANTIPHON *John 20:27*

Put in your hand, and know the place of the nails, alleluia. And be not unbelieving, but believing, alleluia, alleluia.

Prayer after the Communion

Quǽsumus, Dómine Deus noster: ut sacrosáncta mystéria, quæ pro reparatiónis nostræ munímine contulísti; et præsens nobis remédium esse fácias, et futúrum. Per Dóminum.

Lord, our God, to ensure our salvation you have us participate in your holy mysteries. Make them beneficial for our present life and for the life to come. This we ask of you through our Lord.

SECOND SUNDAY AFTER EASTER

ENTRANCE ANTIPHON *Ps. 32:5, 6, 1*

Of the kindness of the Lord the earth is full, alleluia; by the word of the Lord the heavens were made, alleluia, alleluia.

Ps. Exult, you just, in the Lord; praise from the upright is fitting.

Glory be to the Father and to the Son and to the Holy Spirit. As it was in the beginning, is now and ever shall be, world without end. Amen. Of the kindness . . .

Prayer over the Assembly

Deus, qui in Fílii tui humilitáte iacéntem mundum erexísti: fidélibus tuis perpétuam concéde lætítiam; ut, quos perpétuæ mortis eripuísti cásibus, gáudiis fácias pérfrui sempitérnis. Per eúndem Dóminum nostrum Iesum Christum Fílium tuum, qui tecum vivit et regnat in unitáte Spíritus Sancti, Deus, per ómnia sǽcula sæculórum.

Lord, by the humiliation of your Son you have lifted up our fallen world; grant that your children may live in joy. You have rescued them from falling to eternal death: lead them always toward eternal happiness. This we ask of you through the same Jesus Christ, our Lord and your Son, who lives and reigns with you in the unity of the Holy Spirit, God, forever.

EPISTLE 1 Peter 2:21-25

St. Peter, who was commissioned by Christ to pasture the lambs and the sheep of his flock, reminds us that Christ, like a good shepherd, died in order that we might have life.

A reading from the first letter of the apostle Peter to the Christians
Beloved brethren,

Christ suffered for us. Follow the example he has given you, "He [as the prophet Isaias says] who has committed no sin, he whose lips are not soiled by any lie";[1] he who did not curse those who wronged him, who did not threaten those who were tormenting him, but entrusted himself to the just judge; he who was burdened with our sins and bore them in his body on the wood [of the Cross], that we might be dead to sin and might live in holiness; "he whose wounds have healed you!"[2]

You were once "lost sheep," wandering at random. Now you have been gathered around the shepherd and the guardian of your souls.

AFTER THE EPISTLE *Luke 24:35; John 10:14*

Alleluia, alleluia. The disciples recognized the Lord Jesus in the breaking of the bread. Alleluia. I am the good shepherd: and I know my sheep, and mine know me. Alleluia.

GOSPEL John 10:11-16

In stating that he is the good shepherd, Jesus is stating that he is the redeemer announced by Ezekiel. He reveals moreover his plan to save all men by gathering them into the sheepfold of God.

A reading from the holy Gospel according to John

At that time Jesus said to the pharisees, "I am the good shepherd. The good shepherd sacrifices his life for his sheep; but the hired man,[3] who is

---

[1] Isaiah 53:9.   [2] Isaiah 53:4-5.   [3] If he has the soul of a mercenary.

not the real shepherd and who does not own the sheep, if he sees the wolf coming, abandons the sheep and runs away; and the wolf carries off the sheep and scatters them. The hired man runs away because, being a mercenary, he does not have the welfare of the sheep at heart.

"I am the good shepherd; I know my sheep, and my sheep know me — just as my Father knows me and I know my Father — and I sacrifice my life for my sheep.

"I have still other sheep who are not of this fold; I must put myself at the head of them also; they will hear my voice. Then there will be but one flock and one shepherd."

OFFERTORY ANTIPHON *Ps. 62:2, 5*

O God, my God, to you do I watch at break of day, and in your name I will lift up my hands, alleluia.

Prayer over the Offerings

Benedictiónem nobis, Dómine, cónferat salutárem sacra semper oblátio: ut, quod agit mystério, virtúte perfíciat. Per Dóminum.

Lord, may this sacred offering draw down your blessing on us; and, just as it will be transformed in the mystery of this Mass, so may it succeed by its power in transforming our souls. This we ask of you through our Lord.

COMMUNION ANTIPHON *John 10:14*

I am the good shepherd, alleluia: and I know my sheep, and mine know me, alleluia, alleluia.

Prayer after the Communion

Præsta nobis, quǽsumus, omnípotens Deus: ut vivificatiónis tuæ grátiam consequéntes, in tuo semper múnere gloriémur. Per Dóminum.

God all-powerful, we have received from you the grace of a new life; grant that this sacred gift may always be the source of our joy. This we ask of you through our Lord.

THIRD SUNDAY AFTER EASTER

ENTRANCE ANTIPHON *Ps. 65:1, 2, 3*

Shout joyfully to God, all you on earth, alleluia; sing praise to the glory of his name, alleluia. Proclaim his glorious praise, alleluia, alleluia, alleluia.

Ps. Say to God, "How tremendous are your deeds, O Lord! For your great strength your enemies fawn upon you."

Glory be to the Father and to the Son and to the Holy Spirit. As it was in the beginning, is now and ever shall be, world without end. Amen. Shout joyfully . . .

Prayer over the Assembly

Deus, qui errántibus, ut in viam possint redíre iustítiæ, veritátis tuæ lumen osténdis: da cunctis, qui christiána professióne censéntur, et illa respúere, quæ huic inimíca sunt nómini; et ea, quæ sunt apta, sectári. Per Dóminum.

O Lord, to bring back to the right way those who are in error, you show them the light of your truth. To those who have been baptized grant the grace of adhering faithfully to that which makes them worthy to be called Christians and of rejecting everything that is incompatible with that title. This we ask of you through our Lord.

EPISTLE   1 Peter 2:11-19

Christians are citizens of heaven: on earth they are only travelers. St. Peter reminds them that their behavior must make manifest in the sight of men the divine life with which they are invested.

A reading from the first letter of the apostle Peter to the Christians
Beloved brethren,

Since you are only strangers and transients here below, do not yield, I entreat you, to the desires of the body which war against the soul.

In the midst of the pagans, conduct yourselves in an irreproachable manner, that in the very points on which they slander you and treat you as evildoers they may glorify God, being impressed by your good actions, when they finally do turn to him.

For love of God, be submissive to every human authority, to the ruler who has charge of the country and to the magistrates delegated by him for the maintenance of order. It is God's will that, by your exemplary behavior, you silence the criticism of yourselves that is based on ignorance.

Be submissive, but as free men who are slaves only of God, not like those hypocrites who see freedom merely as another opportunity for doing evil. Respect all men, love your brethren, fear God, honor the one who holds power.

Servants, obey your masters and respect them, not only if they are kind and understanding, but even if they are difficult.

For all this is grace, in Christ Jesus our Lord.

AFTER THE EPISTLE *Ps. 110:9; Luke 24:46*

Alleluia, alleluia. The Lord has sent deliverance to his people. Alleluia. It behooved Christ to suffer and to rise again from the dead, and so to enter into his glory. Alleluia.

GOSPEL   John 16:16-22

Until Pentecost, the liturgy has us reread the discourse which Jesus addressed to his apostles after he had instituted the Eucharist. This long conversation reveals the Lord's most hidden secrets: it makes us penetrate as deeply as possible into the divine. Today it gives us a glimpse, beyond the apparitions of Christ, into his return on the last day.

A reading from the holy Gospel according to John

At that time Jesus said to his disciples, "A little while, and you will no longer see me; then a little while again, and you will see me; for I am returning to my Father."

Certain of his disciples asked one another, "What does this mean that he is telling us: 'A little while, and you will no longer see me; then a little while again, and you will see me'? and these words also: 'For I am returning to my Father'?" They kept saying, therefore, "What does he understand by 'a little while'? We don't know what he means."

Jesus knew that they wanted to question him, and he said, "You ask one another the meaning of my words, 'A little while, and you will no longer see me; then a little while again, and you will see me.' Be assured of this: you will weep, you will be in tears, while the world is rejoicing. Yes, you will be sad, but your sadness will be turned into joy. When a woman is giving birth, she is in pain, because her time has come; but as soon as the infant is born, she forgets her anguish, in the joy of having brought a person into the world. You, too, are now in sorrow; but I shall see you again, and your heart will be overflowing with joy, and this joy no one can take from you."

OFFERTORY ANTIPHON *Ps. 145:2*

Praise the Lord, O my soul; I will praise the Lord all my life; I will sing praise to my God while I live. Alleluia.

Prayer over the Offerings

His nobis, Dómine, mystériis conferátur, quo terréna desidéria mitigántes, discémus amáre cæléstia. Per Dóminum.

Lord, may this Mass cool the ardor of our earthly desires and teach us to love the joys of heaven. This we ask of You through our Lord.

COMMUNION ANTIPHON *John 16:16*

A little while, and you shall not see me, alleluia: and again a little while, and you shall see me: because I go to the Father. Alleluia, alleluia.

Prayer after the Communion

Sacraménta quæ súmpsimus, quǽsumus, Dómine: et spirituálibus nos instáurent aliméntis, et corporálibus tueántur auxíliis. Per Dóminum.

May this communion, Lord, be the food of our spiritual life and help us even in our material concerns. This we ask of you through our Lord.

FOURTH SUNDAY AFTER EASTER

ENTRANCE ANTIPHON *Ps. 97:1, 2, 1*

Sing to the Lord a new song, alleluia; for the Lord has done wondrous deeds, alleluia; in the sight of the nations he has revealed his justice: alleluia, alleluia, alleluia.

Ps. His right hand has won victory for him, his holy arm.

Glory be to the Father and to the Son and to the Holy Spirit. As it was in the beginning, is now and ever shall be, world without end. Amen. Sing to the Lord . . .

Prayer over the Assembly

Deus, qui fidélium mentes ι níus éfficis voluntátis: da pópulis tuis id amáre quod præcipis, id desideráre quod promíttis; ut inter mundánas varietátes ibi nostra fixa sint corda, ubi vera sunt gáudia. Per Dóminum.

Lord, you have made your faithful to be of one heart and one soul. Grant that they love what you command and aspire to the happiness which you promise; then, amid the constantly changing allurements of this world, our hearts will be set on that place where true joys reside. This we ask of you through our Lord.

EPISTLE   James 1:17-21

We cannot change ourselves; but to us Christians the Holy Spirit is given, and he makes us the beginning of a new world.

A reading from the letter of the apostle James to the Christians
Beloved brethren,

Every choice grace and every perfect gift comes from above, from the Father of lights, in whom there is no change, no shadow caused by movement.

Of his own will he has called us to life by his word of truth, to make of us the beginning of a new world.

You know, beloved brethren, everyone must be quick to listen, but reflect before speaking and know how to restrain his anger, for man's anger does not do the work of God.

Cast away, therefore, all uncleanness and all malice, to welcome the word [of God] with docility: it is rooted in your souls and has the power to save them.

AFTER THE EPISTLE *Ps. 117:16; Rom. 6:9*

Alleluia, alleluia. The right hand of the Lord has struck with power; the right hand of the Lord has exalted me. Alleluia. Christ, having risen from the dead, dies now no more; death shall no longer have dominion over him. Alleluia.

GOSPEL   John 16:5-14

Beyond his Ascension, which is to occur soon, Christ gives us a glimpse of the coming of the Holy Spirit. It is well for us to have the presence of God become more interior.

A reading from the holy Gospel according to John
At that time Jesus said to his disciples, "I am going to him who sent me, and none of you asks me where I am going. But at the news of my imminent departure, sadness fills your hearts. I tell you the truth, however:

your welfare requires that I go. If I did not go away, the Spirit who is to assist you would not come to you. But if I go, I will send him to you.

"And when he comes he will show the world, beyond dispute, where sin is, and holiness, and judgment. Where sin is: for the world did not believe in me. Where holiness is: for if I am no longer seen, it will be because I am at the Father's side. Where judgment is: for Satan, prince of this world, is already condemned.

"I would still have many things to tell you, but you are not yet able to bear them. When he comes, the Spirit of truth, he will guide you toward the full truth. What he tells you will not be drawn from his own resources: he will repeat to you what he has heard, and will announce to you what is to come. He will enhance my glory, because whatever he tells you, he will have received from me."

OFFERTORY ANTIPHON *Ps. 65:1, 2, 16*

Shout joyfully to God, all you on earth, sing praise to the glory of his name. Hear now, all you who fear God, while I declare what the Lord has done for me. Alleluia.

Prayer over the Offerings

Deus, qui nos per huius sacrifícii veneránda commércia, uníus summæ divinitátis partícipes effecísti: præsta, quæsumus; ut, sicut tuam cognóscimus veritátem, sic eam dignis móribus assequámur. Per Dóminum.

O Lord, in the sacred exchange which takes place in this mystery you give us a share in your divine life. Since we know your truth, give us the grace to come to you through conduct that is worthy of you. This we ask of you through our Lord.

COMMUNION ANTIPHON *John 16:8*

When the Paraclete has come, the Spirit of truth, he will convict the world of sin, and of justice, and of judgment, alleluia, alleluia.

Prayer after the Communion

Adésto nobis, Dómine Deus noster: ut per hæc, quæ fidéliter súmpsimus, et purgémur a vítiis, et a perículis ómnibus eruámur. Per Dóminum.

Be near us, Lord our God: We have received your sacrament with faith; may it purify us of our evil inclinations and shelter us from all danger. This we ask of you through our Lord.

FIFTH SUNDAY AFTER EASTER

ENTRANCE ANTIPHON *Is. 48:20; Ps. 65:1-2*

Declare the word of joy, and let it be heard, alleluia; declare it even to the ends of the earth. The Lord has delivered his people: alleluia, alleluia.

Ps. Shout joyfully to God, all you on earth, sing praise to the glory of his name; proclaim his glorious praise.

Glory be to the Father and to the Son and to the Holy Spirit. As it was in the beginning, is now and ever shall be, world without end. Amen. Declare the word . . .

Prayer over the Assembly

Deus, a quo bona cuncta procédunt, largíre supplícibus tuis: ut cogitémus, te inspiránte, quæ recta sunt; et, te gubernánte, éadem faciámus. Per Dóminum.

Lord, all that is good comes from you. Listen to our prayers: inspire rightful ideas in us and direct us to act in accordance with them. This we ask of you through our Lord.

EPISTLE   James 1:22-27

To contemplate is to listen to the word of God. But this word must transform our lives. Baptism, which has made us citizens of heaven, requires of us on earth a behavior in conformity with the law of God.

A reading from the letter of the apostle James to the Christians

Beloved brethren,

Put the word of God into practice, and do not be content with listening to it: that would be self-deception. He who listens to the word and does not conform his life to it is like a man who looks at his face in a mirror: he has looked at himself and walked away, and he no longer knows what he looked like!

By contrast, he who applies himself to acquiring a good knowledge of Christ's law, the perfect law, the law of freedom; he who is not content to listen to it and then forget it but who really puts it into practice — *he* will find happiness in the fulfillment of the law.

If anyone supposes that he is a religious man and does not know how to hold his tongue, he is deceiving himself: his religion is worth nothing. Religion pure and undefiled in the eyes of God our Father is this: to go to the aid of orphans and widows in their distress, and to keep oneself pure in the midst of a world that is not pure.

AFTER THE EPISTLE *John 16:28*

Alleluia, alleluia. Christ is risen, and has shone upon us, whom he redeemed with his blood. Alleluia. I came forth from the Father, and have come into the world. Again I leave the world, and go to the Father. Alleluia.

GOSPEL   John 16:23-30

Through faith, we take part in the intimate dialogue between the Father and the Son: we believe that Christ came forth from the Father and we welcome the gift of God, we believe that Christ is returning to the Father and, joyfully, we live with him.

A reading from the holy Gospel according to John

At that time Jesus said to his disciples, "This I promise you: anything you ask of the Father he will grant you for my sake. Up to now, you have not yet asked for anything in my name. Ask, therefore, and you shall receive; and you will have perfect joy.

"Up to the present, I have used parables to impart my teaching to you. The hour is approaching when I shall no longer speak to you in parables: it will be in plain language that I speak to you of my Father.

"When that day comes, you will address your petitions to him in my name; and I do not tell you that I will petition the Father for you: [that would be unnecessary], the Father himself loves you, because you love me and believe that I came forth from God.

"I went forth from the Father to come into the world; now I am leaving the world and going back to the Father."

His disciples said to him, "Yes, Lord, now you are speaking in plain language, without recourse to any parable. We know now that you know all things, and that you do not even need to have questions put to you. Because of this, we believe that you have come forth from God."

OFFERTORY ANTIPHON *Ps. 65:8-9, 20*

Bless the Lord our God, you peoples, loudly sound his praise; he has given life to my soul, and has not let my feet slip. Blessed be the Lord, who refused me not my prayer, or his kindness. Alleluia.

Prayer over the Offerings

Súscipe, Dómine, fidélium preces cum oblatiónibus hostiárum: ut per hæc piæ devotiónis offícia, ad cæléstem glóriam transeámus. Per Dóminum.

Lord, please accept the prayers and the offerings of your faithful. May these services of our filial piety bring us some day to the glory of heaven! This we ask of you through our Lord.

COMMUNION ANTIPHON *Ps. 95:2*

Sing to the Lord, alleluia; sing to the Lord; bless his name; announce his salvation day after day, alleluia, alleluia.

Prayer after the Communion

Tríbue nobis, Dómine, cæléstis mensæ virtúte satiátis: et desideráre quæ recta sunt, et desideráta percípere. Per Dóminum.

Lord, at your table you have filled us with the bread of the strong; grant that we may desire what is good and may see our desires fulfilled. This we ask of you through our Lord.

THE ASCENSION OF OUR LORD

ENTRANCE ANTIPHON *Acts 1:11; Ps. 46:2*

Men of Galilee, why do you stand looking up to heaven? Alleluia. He shall come in the same way as you have seen him going up to heaven: alleluia, alleluia, alleluia.

Ps. All you peoples, clap your hands, shout to God with cries of gladness.

Glory be to the Father and to the Son and to the Holy Spirit. As it was in the beginning, is now and ever shall be, world without end. Amen. Men of Galilee . . .

Prayer over the Assembly

Concéde, quǽsumus, omnípotens Deus: ut, qui hodiérna die Unigénitum tuum Redemptórem nostrum ad cælos ascendísse crédimus; ipsi quoque mente in cæléstibus habitémus. Per eúndem Dóminum nostrum Iesum Christum Fílium tuum, qui tecum vivit et regnat in unitáte Spíritus Sancti, Deus, per ómnia sǽcula sæculórum.

God all-powerful, we believe that your only-begotten Son, our Redeemer, ascended on this day to the glory of heaven. Grant us the grace to make our hearts dwell with him in heaven. This we ask of you through the same Jesus Christ, our Lord and your Son, who lives and reigns with you in the unity of the Holy Spirit, God, forever.

EPISTLE   Acts 1:1-11

St. Luke reminds us that between Christ's departure and his return, the Church under the guidance of the Holy Spirit is to continue the work of salvation.

A reading from the Acts of the Apostles

I have already told,[1] dear Theophilus, all that Jesus did and taught from the beginning until the day when, after giving his last instructions through the Holy Spirit to the apostles whom he had chosen, he was taken up to heaven.

It was to these apostles that he showed himself alive after his passion, giving them many proofs of his resurrection, appearing to them during a forty-day period and talking about the kingdom of God.

Now one day while he was eating with them, he ordered them not to leave Jerusalem, but to wait there for the Holy Spirit whom the Father had promised. "I myself," he said, "have told you: John baptized with water, but you, a few days from now, will be baptized in the Holy Spirit."

Those who were gathered together asked him, "Lord, is it now that you are going to reestablish the kingdom in Israel?"

"It is not for you," he answered, "to know the times and the dates which the Father has fixed in his omnipotence. But the Holy Spirit will come upon you, and you will receive his power and become witnesses to me at Jerusalem, throughout Judea and Samaria, and even to the farthest parts of the earth."

When he had said this, they saw him lifted up, and soon a cloud took him out of their sight.

And as they remained staring up at the sky, watching him go away, two men clothed in white appeared to them and said, "Men of Galilee, why

[1] In the Gospel according to St. Luke.

do you stand here looking up at the sky? This Jesus, who has been taken away from you to go to heaven, will return in the same way that you have seen him going up."

AFTER THE EPISTLE *Ps. 46:6; Ps. 67:18-19*

Alleluia, alleluia. God mounts his throne amid shouts of joy; the Lord, amid trumpet blasts. Alleluia. The Lord advances from Sinai to the sanctuary; ascending on high, he has led captivity captive. Alleluia.

GOSPEL   Mark 16:14-20

St. Mark makes the point that Christ is at work in his Church even though he can no longer be seen.

A reading from the holy Gospel according to Mark

At that time, while the eleven were at table, Jesus appeared to them. He reproached them for their lack of faith and their hardness of heart; for they had not believed those who had seen him in his risen state.

He also said to them, "Go out into the whole world and preach the Gospel to every creature. He who believes and is baptized will be saved; he who refuses to believe will be condemned. The conversion of those who believe will be followed by miracles: in my name they will cast out devils; they will speak new languages; they will pick up serpents and, if they drink a deadly poison, they will feel no ill effect from it; they will lay their hands on the sick, and the sick will be healed."

After he had given them his last instructions, the Lord Jesus was taken up to heaven, where he took possession of his throne at the right hand of God. The apostles, for their part, set out to preach the Gospel in every country. The Lord was working with them and lending support to their words by the miracles that accompanied their preaching.

After the singing of the gospel the paschal candle is extinguished, as a reminder of Christ's departure.

OFFERTORY ANTIPHON *Ps. 46:6*

God mounts his throne amid shouts of joy; the Lord, amid trumpet blasts. Alleluia.

Prayer over the Offerings

Súscipe, Dómine, múnera, quæ pro Fílii tui gloriósa Ascensióne deférimus: et concéde propítius; ut a præséntibus perículis liberémur, et ad vitam perveniámus ætérnam. Per eúndem Dóminum nostrum Iesum Christum Fílium tuum, qui tecum vivit et regnat in unitáte Spíritus Sancti, Deus, per ómnia sæcula sæculórum.

On this day of the glorious ascension of your Son, receive our offerings, Lord; keep us free from dangers during this life and bring us to life eternal. This we ask of you through the same Jesus Christ, our Lord and your Son, who lives and reigns with you in the unity of the Holy Spirit, God, forever.

COMMUNION ANTIPHON *Ps. 67:33-34*

Chant praise to the Lord, who rises on the heights of the heavens to the east. Alleluia.

Prayer after the Communion

Præsta nobis, quǽsumus, omnípotens et miséricors Deus: ut, quæ visibílibus mystériis suménda percépimus, invisíbili consequámur efféctu. Per Dóminum.

All-powerful and merciful God, we have communicated under the visible sign of the sacrament; bestow on our souls the graces hidden in this mystery. This we ask of you through our Lord.

SUNDAY AFTER THE ASCENSION

ENTRANCE ANTIPHON *Ps. 26:7, 8, 9, 1*

Hear, O Lord, the sound of my call, alleluia; to you my heart speaks. Your glance I seek; your presence, O Lord, I seek. Hide not your face from me, alleluia, alleluia.

Ps. The Lord is my light and my salvation; whom should I fear?

Glory be to the Father and to the Son and to the Holy Spirit. As it was in the beginning, is now and ever shall be, world without end. Amen. Hear, O Lord . . .

Prayer over the Assembly

Omnípotens sempitérne Deus: fac nos tibi semper et devótam gérere voluntátem; et maiestáti tuæ sincéro corde servíre. Per Dóminum.

All-powerful, eternal God, give us the grace to consecrate permanently to your service the devoted loyalty of our will and the sincerity of our heart. This we ask of you through our Lord.

EPISTLE   1 Peter 4:7-11

It is around Peter that the apostles are grouped after the departure of Jesus. Peter here reminds us that Christ's disciples must form a community animated by charity; only this fraternal love makes it possible for us to receive the Spirit.

A reading from the first letter of the apostle Peter to the Christians

Beloved brethren,

Keep yourselves in the state of watchfulness and attention necessary for prayer. But above all, never stop loving one another, for "charity covers a multitude of sins."

Know how to offer hospitality cheerfully.

Let each one of you put the gift he has received at the service of the rest; in this way you will be good stewards of the divine grace, which is not the same in everyone. If anyone is a speaker, let him transmit the word of

God to others. If another's role is service, let him fulfill the service with the strength that God gives him. In all things may God be glorified through Jesus Christ our Lord!

AFTER THE EPISTLE *Ps. 46:9; John 14:18*

Alleluia, alleluia. The Lord reigns over all the nations, God sits upon his holy throne. Alleluia. I will not leave you orphans: I go away and I come to you, and your heart shall rejoice. Alleluia.

GOSPEL
John 15:26-27; 16:1-4

Charged with continuing the work of Christ on earth, the apostles, and after them all Christians, will experience persecution and struggle, but they are assured of having a protector in the person of the Holy Spirit.

A reading from the holy Gospel according to John

At that time Jesus said to his disciples, "When the Paraclete [the Protector] comes, whom I shall send you from my place at the Father's side, the Spirit of truth who proceeds from the Father, *he* will bear witness concerning me; and you also will bear witness to me, since you have been with me from the beginning.

"I am warning you of this, to forestall any wavering on your part: you will be driven out of the synagogues; what is more, a time will come when those who put you to death will think they are serving God's honor. They will act in that way because they do not know my Father, any more than they have known me. I am warning you of this; when the time comes, remember that I told you about it."

OFFERTORY ANTIPHON *Ps. 46:6*

God mounts his throne amid shouts of joy; the Lord, amid trumpet blasts. Alleluia.

Prayer over the Offerings

Sacrifícia nos, Dómine, immaculáta puríficent: et méntibus nostris supérnæ grátiæ dent vigórem. Per Dóminum.

May the unspotted victim of this Mass purify us, Lord, and give our souls the vigor of supernatural life. This we ask of you through our Lord.

COMMUNION ANTIPHON *John 17:12-13, 15*

Father, while I was with them, I kept them whom you have given me, alleluia; but now I am coming to you: I do not pray that you take them out of the world, but that you keep them from evil, alleluia, alleluia.

Prayer after the Communion

Repléti, Dómine, munéribus sacris: da, quǽsumus; ut in gratiárum semper actióne maneámus. Per Dóminum.

We have received your Eucharist, Lord; give us the grace to remain always in a state of thanksgiving. This we ask of you through our Lord.

PENTECOST

ENTRANCE ANTIPHON *Wis. 1:7; Ps. 67:2*

The spirit of the Lord fills the world, alleluia, is all-embracing, and knows man's utterance, alleluia, alleluia, alleluia.

Ps. God arises; his enemies are scattered, and those who hate him flee before him.

Glory be to the Father and to the Son and to the Holy Spirit. As it was in the beginning, is now and ever shall be, world without end. Amen. The spirit . . .

Prayer over the Assembly

Deus, qui hodiérna die corda fidélium Sancti Spíritus illustratióne docuísti: da nobis in eódem Spíritu recta sápere; et de eius semper consolatióne gaudére. Per Dóminum nostrum Iesum Christum Fílium tuum, qui tecum vivit et regnat in unitáte eiúsdem Spíritus Sancti, Deus, per ómnia sǽcula sæculórum.

On this day, Lord, you have instructed the hearts of your faithful by the brilliant light of the Holy Spirit. Give us the grace, under his divine inspiration, to have a sense of the true and a taste for the good, and always to find our consolation and our joy in him. This we ask of you through our Lord Jesus Christ, your Son, who lives and reigns with you in the unity of the same Holy Spirit, God, forever.

EPISTLE   Acts 2:1-11

As Yahweh showed himself to Moses in the form of fire, so it was under the form of fire that the Holy Spirit manifested himself to the apostles. Fire is light, power, heat. Transformed at once by the Holy Spirit, the apostles "tell of the marvels of God" to men who have come from all the nations of the earth.

A reading from the Acts of the Apostles

When the feast of Pentecost came, the disciples were all gathered in the same house. Suddenly there came from the sky a great noise, like that of a violent wind, and the whole house was filled with it.

What appeared to them then was like tongues of fire separating to take their places over each of them. At the same time they were all filled with the Holy Spirit, and they began to speak various tongues, according to the inspiration they received from the Spirit.

Now on these festival days there were at Jerusalem devout Jews, who had come [on pilgrimage] from every nation under heaven. Attracted by the noise, a crowd of them gathered and stood there amazed, for each one of them heard the apostles speaking his own language.

In their astonishment and wonder they were saying, "These people who are speaking are all Galileans! Then how does it happen that each one of us hears them speaking his own native language? Whether we are Parthians, Medes or Elamites, whether we live in Mesopotamia, Judea or Cappadocia, on the shores of the Black Sea or in Asia, whether we come from Phrygia, Pamphylia, Egypt or Cyrenaic Libya, whether we are visitors from Rome, Jews, converts to Judaism, Cretans, Arabians — we hear them telling in our own languages of the great things God has done!"

AFTER THE EPISTLE *Ps. 103:30*

Alleluia, alleluia. Send forth your spirit, and they shall be created; and you shall renew the face of the earth. Alleluia. Come, Holy Spirit, fill the hearts of your faithful: and kindle in them the fire of your love.

Sequence

Come, thou Holy Spirit, come!
And from thy celestial home
   Shed a ray of light divine!
Come, thou Father of the poor!
Come, thou source of all our store!
   Come, within our bosoms shine!
Thou, of comforters the best;
Thou, the soul's most welcome guest;
   Sweet refreshment here below;
In our labor, rest most sweet;
Grateful coolness in the heat;
   Solace in the midst of woe.
O most blessed Light divine,
Shine within these hearts of thine,
   And our inmost being fill!
Where thou art not, man hath naught,
Nothing good in deed or thought,
   Nothing free from taint of ill.
Heal our wounds, our strength renew;
On our dryness pour thy dew;
   Wash the stains of guilt away:
Bend the stubborn heart and will;
Melt the frozen, warm the chill;
   Guide the steps that go astray.
On the faithful, who adore
And confess thee, evermore
   In thy sev'nfold gift descend;
Give them virtue's sure reward;
Give them thy salvation, Lord;
   Give them joys that never end.
Amen, Alleluia.

GOSPEL   John 14:23-31

The new law, Christ's word, is not written on tablets of stone, but engraved in our hearts. It is the Holy Spirit working within us who makes us understand the full import of the Gospel and reveals to us all the demands of charity.

A reading from the holy Gospel according to John

At that time Jesus said to his disciples, "He who loves me obeys my word, and my Father will love him, and we shall come to him and dwell within him. He who does not love me does not obey my word. Moreover, this word that you hear from me is not mine; it is the word of my Father, who sent me. I address it to you, this word, as long as I am with you. But it is the Defender, the Holy Spirit whom the Father will send in my name, who will finish instructing you, at the same time that he reminds you of all that I have told you.

"Peace I bequeath to you; my peace I give you. I do not give it to you as the world does. Let your heart stop being troubled and fearful, then! You have just heard me say, 'I am going away, but I shall come back to you.' If you loved me, you would be happy that I am going to the Father, for the Father is greater than I.

"I have given you fair warning, therefore, before the events, in order that, when they happen, you may believe.

"I shall not have much more conversation with you, for the prince of this world is soon going to act. He has no rights over me; but the world must know that I love the Father and that I do what the Father has commanded me."

OFFERTORY ANTIPHON *Ps. 67:29-30*

Confirm, O God, what you have wrought in us; from your temple, which is in Jerusalem, kings shall offer gifts to you, alleluia.

Prayer over the Offerings

Múnera, quǽsumus, Dómine, obláta sanctífica: et corda nostra Sancti Spíritus illustratióne emúnda. Per Dóminum nostrum Iesum Christum Fílium tuum, qui tecum vivit et regnat in unitáte eiúsdem Spíritus Sancti, Deus, per ómnia sǽcula sæculórum.

Lord, please sanctify our offerings and purify our hearts by the enlightenment of the Holy Spirit. This we ask of you through our Lord Jesus Christ, your Son, who lives and reigns with you in the unity of the same Holy Spirit, God, forever.

COMMUNION ANTIPHON *Acts 2:2, 4*

Suddenly there came a sound from heaven, as of a violent wind blowing, where they were sitting, alleluia. And they were all filled with the Holy Spirit, speaking of the wonderful works of God, alleluia, alleluia.

Prayer after the Communion

Sancti Spíritus, Dómine, corda nostra mundet infúsio: et sui roris íntima aspersióne fecúndet. Per Dóminum nostrum Iesum Christum Fílium tuum, qui tecum vivit et regnat in unitáte eiúsdem Spíritus Sancti, Deus, per ómnia sǽcula sæculórum.

Lord, you have poured out upon us the gifts of the Holy Spirit; may our hearts be purified by them, and may the dew of his grace make them fruitful in good works. This we ask of you through our Lord Jesus Christ, your Son, who lives and reigns with you in the unity of the same Holy Spirit, God, forever.

FEAST OF THE MOST HOLY TRINITY

ENTRANCE ANTIPHON *Tob. 12:6, Ps. 8:2*

Blessed be the Holy Trinity and undivided Unity: we will give glory to him, because he has shown his mercy to us.

Ps. O Lord, our Lord, how glorious is your name over all the earth!

Glory be to the Father and to the Son and to the Holy Spirit. As it was in the beginning, is now and ever shall be, world without end. Amen. Blessed be . . .

Prayer over the Assembly

Omnípotens sempitérne Deus, qui dedísti fámulis tuis, in confessióne veræ fídei, ætérnæ Trinitátis glóriam agnóscere, et in poténtia maiestátis adoráre Unitátem: quǽsumus; ut, eiúsdem fídei firmitáte, ab ómnibus semper muniámur advérsis. Per Dóminum.

All-powerful, eternal God, you have given your children the true faith: they adore you in the glory of your Trinity and in the grandeur of your Unity; may the firmness of this belief strengthen us in the face of life's difficulties. This we ask of you through our Lord.

EPISTLE   Romans 11:33-36

The existence and the names of the three divine Persons allow us to surmise that God is Love. The history of our salvation is the manifestation of the divine love. After having shown how God's mercy wanted to save all men, whether Jews or pagans, St. Paul concludes with an exclamation filled with gratitude.

A reading from the letter of the apostle Paul to the Christians of Rome

What a boundless wealth there is in God's knowledge and wisdom! How impenetrable his designs are, and how far beyond our understanding are his ways of doing things! It is written, "Who can boast that he knows the mind of the Lord, who can boast that he has given him advice? He has received nothing from anyone, and he owes nothing to anyone."

For everything comes from him, everything exists through him, everything is going toward him. To him be glory forever! Amen.

Gradual Dan. 3:55-56

Blessed are you, O Lord, who look into the depths from your throne upon the Cherubim. Blessed are you, O Lord, in the firmament of heaven, and praiseworthy forever.

Alleluia Dan. 3:52

Alleluia, alleluia. Blessed are you, O Lord, the God of our fathers, and praiseworthy forever. Alleluia.

GOSPEL
Matthew 28:18-20

Christ's last words to his apostles, at the time of his Ascension, sum up his whole teaching, revealing clearly the existence of three Persons in God and specifying that it is they who together communicate the divine life to us.

A reading from the holy Gospel according to Matthew

At that time Jesus said to his disciples, "I have received full powers in heaven and on earth. Go, therefore! Make all the nations my disciples, baptizing them in the name of the Father and of the Son and of the Holy Spirit, and teaching them to observe all that I have commanded you. And be assured that I shall be with you in all the days to come, to the end of time."

OFFERTORY ANTIPHON Tob. 12:6

Blessed be God the Father, and the only-begotten Son of God, and also the Holy Spirit: because he has shown his mercy to us.

Prayer over the Offerings

Sanctífica, quǽsumus, Dómine Deus noster, per tui sancti nóminis invocatiónem, huius oblatiónis hóstiam: et per eam nosmetípsos tibi pérfice munus ætérnum. Per Dóminum.

Lord, by our invocation of your holy name please consecrate this victim which is offered to you and make it the means by which our life itself becomes an eternal offering to you. This we ask of you through our Lord.

COMMUNION ANTIPHON Tob. 12:6

We bless the God of heaven, and before all living we will praise him; because he has shown his mercy to us.

Prayer after the Communion

Profíciat nobis ad salútem córporis et ánimæ, Dómine Deus noster, huius sacraménti suscéptio: et sempitérnæ sanctæ Trinitátis, eiusdémque indivíduæ Unitátis conféssio. Per Dóminum.

May this communion, Lord, our God, and our faith in the indivisible unity of your eternal, holy Trinity ensure the salvation of our soul and body. This we ask of you through our Lord.

SECOND SUNDAY AFTER PENTECOST

ENTRANCE ANTIPHON *Ps. 17:19, 20, 2-3*

The Lord came to my support. He set me free in the open, and rescued me, because he loves me.

Ps. I love you, O Lord, my strength, O Lord, my rock, my fortress, my deliverer.

Glory be to the Father and to the Son and to the Holy Spirit. As it was in the beginning, is now and ever shall be, world without end. Amen. The Lord came . . .

Prayer over the Assembly

Sancti nóminis tui, Dómine, timórem páriter et amórem fac nos habére perpétuum: quia numquam tua gubernatióne destítuis, quos in soliditáte tuæ dilectiónis instítuis. Per Dóminum.

Lord, make us fear you and love you always, for your providence never fails those whom you establish firmly in their love for you. This we ask of you through our Lord.

EPISTLE   1 John 3:13-18

To communicate is to receive into ourselves the life of God, who is love. Taking part in the Eucharist would be a lie on our part if we did not love our brethren "in action and in truth."

A reading from the first letter of the apostle John to the Christians

Beloved brethren,

Do not be surprised if the world hates you. We know that we ourselves have passed from death to life, because we love our brethren. But he who does not love remains dead. Whoever hates his brother is a murderer, and you know that no murderer has a hold on eternal life.

How have we known God's love? By this, that he gave his life for us. That is why we also should give our life for our brethren.

Suppose that a person owned some of the good things of this world and saw his brother in need, and yet closed his heart against the needy brother; how do you suppose that the love of God could dwell in such a person? My dear children, let us not love merely in words, in idle talk; let us love in action and in truth.

Gradual Ps. 119:1-2

In my distress, I called to the Lord, and he answered me. O Lord, deliver me from lying lip, from treacherous tongue.

Alleluia Ps. 7:2

Alleluia, alleluia. O Lord my God, in you I take refuge; save me from all my pursuers and rescue me. Alleluia.

GOSPEL   Luke 14:16-24

This parable of the banquet was told by Christ to indicate that the pagans would answer the Lord's call more readily than the Jews. And the Father "wants his house to be filled."

A reading from the holy Gospel according to Luke

At that time, addressing the pharisees, Jesus proposed this parable: "A man gave a great dinner, to which he invited many people. When the time for the banquet arrived, he sent his servant to tell those invited, 'Come; everything is ready now.'

"But a chorus of excuses went up from all of them. The first one said, 'I have just bought an estate, and I must go and see it. Please excuse me.' The second answered, 'I have bought five teams of oxen, and I am on my way to try them out. Please excuse me.' Still another said, 'I have just got married. You understand that I cannot come.'

"On his return the servant made his report. The master, annoyed at the excuses, gave new orders: 'Make a quick circuit of the public squares and the streets of the city, and bring here the poor, the crippled, the blind and the lame.'

"The servant was soon back. 'Sir,' he reported, 'your orders have been carried out, but there is still room.'

"Then the master commanded, 'Go out along the highways and the hedgerows, and make people come in. I want my house to be full. And let me tell you, not one of those persons whom I had invited will get a taste of my banquet.' "

OFFERTORY ANTIPHON *Ps. 6:5*

Return, O Lord, save my life; rescue me because of your kindness.

Prayer over the Offerings

Oblátio nos, Dómine, tuo nómini dicánda puríficet: et de die in diem ad cæléstis vitæ tránsferat actiónem. Per Dóminum.

Here are our offerings, Lord; raised to the divine level by their consecration to you, may they purify us and transform us so that we may live more and more a heavenly life. This we ask of you through our Lord.

COMMUNION ANTIPHON *Ps. 12:6*

I will sing of the Lord, "He has been good to me"; and I will sing to the name of the Lord the Most High.

Prayer after the Communion

Sumptis munéribus sacris, quæsumus, Dómine: ut cum frequentatióne mystérii, crescat nostræ salútis efféctus. Per Dóminum.

We have received your holy Eucharist, Lord; may our frequent communions bring about an increase of your saving grace in us. This we ask of you through our Lord.

THIRD SUNDAY AFTER PENTECOST

ENTRANCE ANTIPHON *Ps. 24:16, 18, 1-2*

Look toward me, and have pity on me, O Lord, for I am alone and afflicted; put an end to my affliction and my suffering, and take away all my sins, O my God.

Ps. To you, I lift up my soul, O Lord. In you, O my God, I trust; let me not be put to shame.

Glory be to the Father and to the Son and to the Holy Spirit. As it was in the beginning, is now and ever shall be, world without end. Amen. Look toward me . . .

Prayer over the Assembly

Protéctor in te sperántium, Deus, sine quo nihil est válidum, nihil sanctum: multíplica super nos misericórdiam tuam; ut, te rectóre, te duce, sic transeámus per bona temporália, ut non amittámus ætérna. Per Dóminum.

You protect those who hope in you, Lord; without you there is no strength, no holiness. Extend your mercy to us more and more, that, drawn on by you, we may use the good things of this world only in passing, and not lose the treasures of heaven. This we ask of you through our Lord.

EPISTLE   1 Peter 5:6-11

As the sheep, alone in the desert, is in danger from the lion, so we are exposed to the assaults of the devil. Let us not rely only on ourselves to escape this danger.

A reading from the first letter of the apostle Peter to the Christians

Beloved brethren,

Be humble under God's powerful hand, that he may lift you up in his own time. Cast all your cares on him, for he has your concerns at heart.

Be sober and watchful, because the devil, your enemy, prowls about like a roaring lion, looking for someone to devour. Resist him with an unshakable faith, knowing that all your brethren scattered throughout the world are undergoing the same sufferings.

After these brief sufferings, the God of all goodness, who is calling you to his eternal glory in Christ Jesus, will himself complete his work; he will strengthen you and make you invincible.

To him be glory and power for ever and ever! Amen.

Gradual *Ps. 54:23, 17, 19*

Cast your care upon the Lord, and he will support you. When I called upon the Lord, he heard my voice and freed me from those who war against me.

Alleluia Ps. 7:12

Alleluia, alleluia. A just judge is God, strong and patient; is he angry every day? Alleluia.

GOSPEL   Luke 15:1-10

The parable of the good shepherd said to the primitive Church what the image of the Sacred Heart says to modern Christians: God loves us, and he has done everything in his power to save us.

A reading from the holy Gospel according to Luke

At that time the pharisees and the scribes were criticizing Jesus because he was letting publicans and sinners approach him, and they were crowding around in great numbers to hear him. "He welcomes sinners," they complained, "and dines at their table."

Jesus therefore proposed this parable to them:

"What man among you, if he owns a hundred sheep and loses one of them, does not leave the other ninety-nine in the desert and run after the one that is lost, until he finds it? And when he has found it, he joyfully puts it on his shoulders and brings it home. Then he calls together all his friends and neighbors. 'Come and be happy with me,' he says. 'I have found my sheep, the one that was lost!' So it will be in heaven, I tell you: there will be greater joy over one sinner who repents than over ninety-nine of the just who have no need of repentance.

"In the same way, what woman who has ten pieces of money and loses one of them does not light the lamp, sweep the house and look in every corner until she finds it? And when she has found it, she calls together her friends and neighbors. 'Come and rejoice with me,' she says. 'I have found the money, the piece I had lost!'

"In the same way, I tell you, there is joy among the angels of God, every time a sinner repents."

OFFERTORY ANTIPHON *Ps. 9:11-12, 13*

They trust in you who cherish your name, O Lord, for you forsake not those who seek you. Sing praise to the Lord enthroned in Sion, for he has not forgotten the cry of the afflicted.

Prayer over the Offerings

Réspice, Dómine, múnera supplicántis Ecclésiæ: et salúti credéntium perpétua sanctificatióne suménda concéde. Per Dóminum.

Your Church is praying to you, Lord; look down upon her offerings. Grant that your faithful may always receive them in a state of grace, that their communion may be profitable for their salvation. This we ask of you through our Lord.

COMMUNION ANTIPHON *Luke 15:10*

I say to you: there is joy among the angels of God over one sinner who repents.

Prayer after the Communion

Sancta tua nos, Dómine, sumpta vivíficent: et misericórdiæ sempitérnæ prǽparent expiátos. Per Dóminum.

Lord, may your sacrament give us life, purify our souls and make them worthy of your eternal love. This we ask of you through our Lord.

FOURTH SUNDAY AFTER PENTECOST

ENTRANCE ANTIPHON *Ps. 26:1, 2, 3*

The Lord is my light and my salvation; whom should I fear? The Lord is my life's refuge; of whom should I be afraid? My enemies that trouble me, themselves stumble and fall.

Ps. Though an army encamp against me, my heart will not fear.

Glory be to the Father and to the Son and to the Holy Spirit. As it was in the beginning, is now and ever shall be, world without end. Amen. The Lord . . .

Prayer over the Assembly

Da nobis, quǽsumus, Dómine: ut et mundi cursus pacífice nobis tuo órdine dirigátur; et Ecclésia tua tranquílla devotióne lætétur. Per Dóminum.

Lord, grant that we may see the course of events proceed peacefully by the observance of your divine order, and grant that your Church may know the joy of serving you without disturbance. This we ask of you through our Lord.

EPISTLE　　　　　　　　　　　　　　　Romans 8:18-23

The entire universe, for which man is responsible, is to live the paschal mystery: to pass from the state of oppression to the radiant freedom of grace. This passage will be fully achieved at the end of the world, when the redemption will be completed.

A reading from the letter of the apostle Paul to the Christians of Rome
Brethren,
In my estimation, the sufferings of the present life are nothing compared to the glory with which we shall one day shine.

All creation is tense with expectation. It is waiting for this glory of the sons of God to be revealed. For, if creation is placed at the service of evil, this is not by its own choice; it is because God has subjected creation to man.

But it has kept up its hope: for creation itself is to be freed from corruption in order to share the glorious freedom of God's children. Until that day comes, all creation is groaning, as we know; but these are the pains of childbirth.

But it is not alone: we ourselves who have already begun to receive the

Spirit of God are groaning inwardly: we are looking forward to the day when we shall be fully sons of God, when our body itself will experience its liberation in Christ Jesus our Lord.

Gradual Ps. 78:9, 10

Pardon our sins, O Lord; why should the nations say, "Where is their God?" Help us, O God our savior; because of the glory of your name, O Lord, deliver us.

Alleluia Ps. 9:5, 10

Alleluia, alleluia. O God, seated on your throne, judging justly: be a stronghold for the oppressed in times of distress. Alleluia.

GOSPEL   Luke 5:1-11

It is the Church that continues Christ's mission. "Fishers of men," after Peter and the apostles, are the pope and the bishops, the priests and the laymen who take part in the apostolate of the hierarchy. They must drag men up from the depths of the sea (where, according to the biblical tradition, the sinister power of the devil holds sway).

A reading from the holy Gospel according to Luke

At that time Jesus was standing on the shore of Lake Genesareth, and the people were crowding around him to hear the word of God.

Seeing two boats drawn up on the beach while the fishermen had gone ashore to clean their nets, Jesus went aboard one of them and asked Simon Peter, to whom it belonged, to pull away a little from the shore. Then he sat down and began to teach the crowd from the boat.

When he was through speaking to them, he said to Simon, "Push out to the deep water, and let down your nets for a catch."

"Master," replied Simon, "we have labored the whole night without catching anything; but, since you tell me to, I will let down the nets."

When they had done so, they caught so many fish that the nets were beginning to break. They gestured to their companions in the other boat, therefore, to come and help them. The latter came, and the two boats were filled with fish until they were on the point of sinking.

Seeing this, Peter threw himself down at Jesus' knees, saying, "Stay away from this sinner, Lord!" For this catch of fish they had just made had filled them with awe — Peter, that is, and all those who were with him, as well as James and John, the sons of Zebedee, his companions.

But Jesus said to Simon, "Have no fear. From now on, you will be catching men."

They pulled their boats up on land and followed him, leaving everything.

OFFERTORY ANTIPHON *Ps. 12:4-5*

Give light to my eyes that I may never sleep in death, lest my enemy say, "I have overcome him."

Prayer over the Offerings

Oblatiónibus nostris, quǽsumus, Dómine, placáre suscéptis: et ad te nostras étiam rebélles compélle propítius voluntátes. Per Dóminum.

Let your heart be touched, O Lord, by our offerings. Our wills resist your grace; Lord, bring them back to yourself! This we ask of you through our Lord.

COMMUNION ANTIPHON *Ps. 17:3*

O Lord, my rock, my fortress, my deliverer: my God, my rock of refuge!

Prayer after the Communion

Mystéria nos, Dómine, quǽsumus, sumpta puríficent: et suo múnere tueántur. Per Dóminum.

May this communion, Lord, purify our souls and give them its protective grace. This we ask of you through our Lord.

FIFTH SUNDAY AFTER PENTECOST

ENTRANCE ANTIPHON *Ps. 26:7, 9, 1*

Hear, O Lord, the sound of my call; be my helper: forsake me not: despise me not, O God my savior.

Ps. The Lord is my light and my salvation; whom should I fear?

Glory be to the Father and to the Son and to the Holy Spirit. As it was in the beginning, is now and ever shall be, world without end. Amen. Hear, O Lord . . .

Prayer over the Assembly

Deus, qui diligéntibus te bona invisibília præparásti: infúnde córdibus nostris tui amóris afféctum; ut, te in ómnibus et super ómnia diligéntes, promissiónes tuas, quæ omne desidérium súperant, consequámur. Per Dóminum.

For those who love you, Lord, you have prepared good things that no eye has seen. Fill our hearts with fervent love for you; then, seeing you in every creature and preferring you above every creature, we shall attain to those good things you have promised us, which surpass all desire. This we ask of you through our Lord.

EPISTLE   1 Peter 3:8-15

St. Peter, whose feast is celebrated at this season, describes for us the concrete forms which our brotherly love must take.

A reading from the first letter of the apostle Peter to the Christians
Beloved brethren,
Be of one heart in prayer; take part in the sufferings of others, love one another like brothers, be merciful, gentle and humble. Do not return evil

for evil, nor injury for injury. On the contrary, if anyone curses you, bless him, since it is your vocation to bless, that you yourselves may receive God's blessing.

For, as the psalm says, "What kind of man loves life and wants to know happiness? Let him keep his tongue from evil and his lips from lying! Let him turn away from evil to do good, let him be untiring in his search for peace! For God looks on his servants with love, and inclines his ear to their prayer. But he stands opposed to those who do evil." [1]

And who can do any real evil to you if the good is what you love?

If it happens that you must suffer for justice, the Lord proclaims you blessed.

Have no fear of their threats, then, and do not let yourselves be troubled, but put the Lord Christ above everything else in your hearts.

Gradual *Ps. 83:10, 9*

Behold, O God, our protector, and look on your servants. O Lord God of hosts, hear the prayers of your servants.

Alleluia Ps. 20:1

Alleluia, alleluia. O Lord, in your strength the king is glad; in your victory how greatly he rejoices! Alleluia.

GOSPEL   Matthew 5:20-24

The Mass ought to be the occasion for Christians to renew and increase their mutual love. The kiss of peace which the officiating ministers exchange during the solemn Mass is the reminder of this duty.

A reading from the holy Gospel according to Matthew

At that time Jesus said to his disciples, "If your conscience is not more delicate than that of the scribes and the pharisees, you will not get into the kingdom of heaven.

"You have heard that it was said to the ancients,[2] 'You shall not kill! If anyone kills, he shall be condemned by the tribunal.' Well, I tell you: He who abandons himself to anger against his brother deserves to be condemned by the tribunal; he who insults his brother deserves to be condemned by the Sanhedrin; he who treats him as a renegade deserves to be condemned to the fire of hell.

"If, therefore, you are presenting your offering at the altar, and just then you remember that your brother has something against you, leave your offering before the altar and go to be reconciled with your brother. After that, you shall return and present your offering."

OFFERTORY ANTIPHON *Ps. 15:7-8*

I bless the Lord who counsels me; I set God ever before me; with him at my right hand I shall not be disturbed.

---

[1] Psalm 33:13-17.   [2] Exodus 20:13.

Prayer over the Offerings

Propitiáre, Dómine, supplicatió-nibus nostris: et has oblatiónes famulórum famularúmque tuárum benígnus assúme; ut, quod sínguli obtulérunt ad honórem nóminis tui, cunctis profíciat ad salútem. Per Dóminum.

Let your heart be touched, Lord, by our prayers and, in your goodness, please accept the offerings of your faithful; thus what each one brings to honor you will contribute to the salvation of all. This we ask of you through our Lord.

COMMUNION ANTIPHON *Ps. 26:4*

One thing I ask of the Lord; this I seek: to dwell in the house of the Lord all the days of my life.

Prayer after the Communion

Quos cælésti, Dómine, dono satiásti: præsta, quǽsumus; ut a nostris mundémur occúltis, et ab hóstium liberémur insídiis. Per Dóminum.

We have just received the heavenly gift of your sacrament, Lord; may it cleanse us from our hidden sins and free us from the traps set by our enemies. This we ask of you through our Lord.

SIXTH SUNDAY AFTER PENTECOST

ENTRANCE ANTIPHON *Ps. 27:8-9, 1*

The Lord is the strength of his people, the saving refuge of his anointed. Save your people, O Lord, and bless your inheritance: and rule them forever!

Ps. To you, O Lord, I call; O my God, be not deaf to me, lest, if you heed me not, I become one of those going down into the pit.

Glory be to the Father and to the Son and to the Holy Spirit. As it was in the beginning, is now and ever shall be, world without end. Amen. The Lord . . .

Prayer over the Assembly

Deus virtútum, cuius est totum quod est óptimum: ínsere pectóribus nostris amórem tui nóminis, et præsta in nobis religiónis augméntum; ut, quæ sunt bona, nútrias, ac pietátis stúdio, quæ sunt nutríta, custódias. Per Dóminum.

From you alone, O God of strength, comes all that is good! Fill our hearts with love for you and draw tight the bond that ties us to you; thus will you strengthen what there is of good in us and guard it with fatherly care. This we ask of you through our Lord.

EPISTLE   Romans 6:3-11

Through baptism we have agreed to die to ourselves in order to live with the divine life. Through the Mass we renew our communion with Christ's death and resurrection.

A reading from the letter of the apostle Paul to the Christians of Rome
Brethren,
All of us who have been baptized in Christ Jesus have been baptized into
his death. Going down into the waters of baptism, as he went down into
the tomb, we have been plunged with him into death. But, just as he was
raised from the dead by the glory of the Father, so we too are now living
with a new life. If we have been bound to Jesus in his death, we shall be
bound to him also in his resurrection.

We know that our old sinful nature was crucified with him so as to be
destroyed, that sin might no longer have authority over us: sin can do
nothing further against a dead person.

But, if we have died with Christ, we believe that with him we shall live;
we know that the Christ who has risen from the dead does not die any
more. Death no longer has any power over him. He died for sin — once
and for all — ; but he is living now, and it is for God that he lives.

In the same way, you too: be dead to sin. But live for God; live in Christ
Jesus our Lord!

Gradual *Ps. 89:13, 1*

Return, O Lord! How long? Have pity on your servants! O Lord,
you have been our refuge through all generations.

Alleluia Ps. 30:2-3

Alleluia, alleluia. In you, O Lord, I take refuge; let me never be put
to shame. In your justice rescue me and release me, incline your ear to
me, make haste to deliver me! Alleluia.

GOSPEL   Mark 8:1-9

*Just as Christ fed the crowd in the desert, so the Church gives her faithful
the bread that makes them live.*

A reading from the holy Gospel according to Mark

At that time, as the large crowd which had followed him had nothing
to eat, Jesus called his disciples together and told them, "I have pity on this
crowd. They have had the perseverance to pass three days with me. There
is nothing left for them to eat; and, if I send them home fasting, their
strength is going to fail them on the way, for some of them have come a
long way."

The disciples answered him, "Where will anyone find the means, here
in a desert place, of giving them bread and letting them eat their fill?"

"How many loaves have you?" Jesus asked them.

"Seven," they answered.

Jesus ordered the crowd to sit down on the ground. He took the seven
loaves of bread and, after giving thanks, broke them and gave them to the
disciples to distribute to the crowd. They had some little fish also. Jesus
blessed them too and had them distributed.

When they had all eaten their fill and the disciples had gathered up the bits that were left over — they filled seven baskets with them, and the number who had eaten were about four thousand — Jesus dismissed them.

OFFERTORY ANTIPHON *Ps. 16:5, 6-7*

Make my steps steadfast in your paths, that my feet may not falter. Incline your ear to me; hear my word. Show your wondrous kindness, O Lord, O savior of those who trust in you.

Prayer over the Offerings

Propitiáre, Dómine, supplicatiónibus nostris, et has pópuli tui oblatiónes benígnus assúme: et ut nullíus sit írritum votum, nullíus vácua postulátio, præsta; ut, quod fidéliter pétimus, efficáciter consequámur. Per Dóminum.

Let your heart be touched, Lord, by our prayers and, in your goodness, please accept the offerings of your people, that no desire of ours may be in vain, no prayer unanswered. What we ask of you with loyal trust, grant that we may obtain without fail. This we ask of you through our Lord.

COMMUNION ANTIPHON *Ps. 26:6*

I will go round and offer in his tent sacrifices with shouts of gladness; I will sing and chant praise to the Lord.

Prayer after the Communion

Repléti sumus, Dómine, munéribus tuis: tríbue quæsumus; ut eórum et mundémur efféctu, et muniámur auxílio. Per Dóminum.

We have received your Eucharist, Lord; may your sacrament purify us and make us stronger. This we ask of you through our Lord.

SEVENTH SUNDAY AFTER PENTECOST

ENTRANCE ANTIPHON *Ps. 46:2, 3*

All you peoples, clap your hands, shout to God with cries of gladness.

Ps. For the Lord, the Most High, the awesome, is the great king over all the earth.

Glory be to the Father and to the Son and to the Holy Spirit. As it was in the beginning, is now and ever shall be, world without end. Amen. All you peoples . . .

Prayer over the Assembly

Deus, cuius providéntia in sui dispositióne non fállitur: te súpplices exorámus; ut nóxia cuncta

O God, whose providence disposes all things without any error, remove far from us anything that might hurt

submóveas, et ómnia nobis profu-
túra concédas. Per Dóminum.

us, and make everything work for our good. This we ask of you through our Lord.

EPISTLE
Romans 6:19-23

It is God who delivers us from evil and rescues us from the slavery of sin, as in former times he rescued the Hebrews from the oppression of Egypt. If we observe the law he gives us, we shall obtain eternal life.

A reading from the letter of the apostle Paul to the Christians of Rome
Brethren,

I am going to use a very human way of speaking, but that is because of your imperfection:

Formerly, you delivered your bodies to the slavery of uncleanness and of evil, and evil was what you found by doing this. Similarly, now, deliver your bodies to the slavery of the good; in doing this you will find holiness.

When you were slaves of evil and freed from the good, what fruit did you gather? You blush to think of it now: the end of all that is death. But now that you are freed from sin and have become slaves of God, your harvest is holiness and, at the end, life eternal.

For the wage paid by sin is death. But the gift of God is eternal life in Christ Jesus our Lord.

Gradual *Ps. 33:12, 6*

Come, children, hear me; I will teach you the fear of the Lord. Look to him that you may be radiant with joy, and your faces may not blush with shame.

Alleluia *Ps. 46:2*

Alleluia, alleluia. All you peoples, clap your hands, shout to God with cries of gladness. Alleluia.

GOSPEL
Matthew 7:15-21

To love God is to do his will. Our faith is not just a matter of vague sentiments. It must bear good fruits.

A reading from the holy Gospel according to Matthew

At that time Jesus said to his dsciples, "Be on your guard against the false prophets; they come to you disguised as sheep, but actually they are ferocious wolves. You will recognize them [as one recognizes a tree] by their fruits. Does anyone gather grapes from thorn bushes, or figs from thistles? The fact is that a good tree produces good fruits, and an evil tree produces evil fruits. The good tree cannot bear bad fruit, nor can the bad tree bear good fruit. The tree that does not bear good fruit will be cut down and thrown into the fire. It is by their fruits, therefore, that you will recognize them.

"Not everyone who says to Me, 'Lord, Lord!' will get into the kingdom of heaven. He who does the will of My Father who is in heaven — *that* is the one who will get into the kingdom of heaven."

OFFERTORY ANTIPHON *Dan. 3:40*

As though it were holocausts of rams and bullocks, or thousands of fat lambs, so let our sacrifice be in your presence today, that it may please you; for those who trust in you cannot be put to shame, O Lord.

Prayer over the Offerings

Deus, qui legálium differéntiam hostiárum uníus sacrifícii perfectióne sanxísti: áccipe sacrifícium a devótis tibi fámulis, et pari benedictióne, sicut múnera Abel, sanctífica; ut, quod sínguli obtulérunt ad maiestátis tuæ honórem, cunctis profíciat ad salútem. Per Dóminum.

O Lord, in the sacrifice of the Mass all the ancient sacrifices find their fulfillment. You blessed the offerings of Abel; bless in the same way the offerings of your children. Thus, what each one brings to you will contribute to the salvation of all. This we ask of you through our Lord.

COMMUNION ANTIPHON *Ps. 30:3*

Incline your ear to me, make haste to deliver me.

Prayer after the Communion

Tua nos, Dómine, medicinális operátio, et a nostris perversitátibus cleménter expédiat, et ad ea quæ sunt recta, perdúcat. Per Dóminum.

God of mercy, may the purifying action of your grace free us from our evil inclinations and lead us along the path of duty. This we ask of you through our Lord.

EIGHTH SUNDAY AFTER PENTECOST

ENTRANCE ANTIPHON *Ps. 47:10-11, 2*

O God, we ponder your kindness within your temple. As your name, O God, so also your praise reaches to the ends of the earth. Of justice your right hand is full.

Ps. Great is the Lord and wholly to be praised in the city of our God, his holy mountain.

Glory be to the Father and to the Son and to the Holy Spirit. As it was in the beginning, is now and ever shall be, world without end. Amen. O God . . .

Prayer over the Assembly

Largíre nobis, quæsumus, Dómine, semper spíritum cogitándi quæ recta sunt, propítius et agéndi: ut, qui sine te esse non póssumus, secúndum te vívere valeámus. Per Dóminum.

Lord, we cannot exist without you; grant us the grace always to think and act according to your truth. This we ask of you through our Lord.

EPISTLE   Romans 8:12-17

In the language of St. Paul, the flesh designates our human nature with its egoistic tendencies which close us in upon ourselves; the Spirit designates the grace that acts in us, the Holy Spirit who communicates the divine life to us and opens us up to the love of God and of our neighbor.

A reading from the letter of the apostle Paul to the Christians of Rome

Brethren,

[Since we have received the the Spirit of God], we no longer owe anything to the flesh. It is not for the flesh to direct our life. But if you do live according to the flesh, you are heading for death. If, on the contrary, the Spirit is directing you, you are condemning to death the tendencies of your flesh, but you are headed for life!

All those who allow themselves to be led by the Spirit of God are the sons of God.

For the Spirit whom you have received makes you no longer slaves obeying out of fear. He makes you sons whom God adopts, and he makes us cry out to God, "Abba!" [that is to say:] "Father!"

It is the Spirit himself who makes our spirit certain of this: to God, we are sons. Being sons, we are heirs, the heirs of God, sharing the heritage of Christ.

Gradual *Ps. 30:3; Ps. 70:1*

Be my rock of refuge, O God, a stronghold to give me safety. In you, O God, I take refuge; O Lord, let me never be put to shame.

Alleluia *Ps. 47:2*

Alleluia, alleluia. Great is the Lord and wholly to be praised in the city of our God, his holy mountain. Alleluia.

GOSPEL   Luke 16:1-9

The unfaithful manager is a model, not by reason of his fraud, but by reason of his prudence and the activity he displays in assuring his earthly future. In order to enter the eternal dwelling place, one must know how to look ahead and to take pains.

A reading from the holy Gospel according to Luke

At that time, addressing his disciples, Jesus proposed this parable: "A rich man had a manager for his property, and the complaint reached him that the manager was squandering his possessions. He summoned the manager, therefore, and said to him, 'What is this that I hear about you? You are to give me an accounting of your management, for it is impossible that you continue in this position any longer.'

"The manager said to himself, 'What is to become of me now that my master is taking the management of his property away from me? Shall I work a piece of land? I am not capable of it. Beg? I would be ashamed to. . . . I know what I shall do, so that when I am deprived of my position as manager, other people will be pleased to give me a home.'

"One after another, therefore, he had all those who owed anything to his master come before him. 'How much do you owe?' he asked the first.

" 'A hundred barrels of oil,' [1] he replied.

" 'Here, I am giving you back your note. Hurry, sit down and sign a note for fifty.'

"Going on to the next: 'How much do you owe?' he asked.

" 'A hundred measures of wheat,' [2] was the answer.

" 'Here, I am giving you back your note. Make me one for eighty.'

"And the master could not help admiring the cleverness of this unprincipled manager.

"For it must be acknowledged: the children of this world are cleverer with their own kind than are the children of light.

"This is what I have to tell you, then: Use money, which is otherwise worthless, to make friends for yourselves! And when the day comes that you have nothing, they will be there to welcome you into the everlasting dwelling places."

OFFERTORY ANTIPHON *Ps. 17:28, 32*

Lowly people you save, O Lord, but haughty eyes you bring low; for who is God except you, O Lord?

Prayer over the Offerings

Súscipe, quǽsumus, Dómine, múnera, quæ tibi de tua largitáte deférimus: ut hæc sacrosáncta mystéria, grátiæ tuæ operánte virtúte, et præséntis vitæ nos conversatióne sanctíficent, et ad gáudia sempitérna perdúcant. Per Dóminum.

It was from you, Lord, that we received this bread and this wine. Now we offer them to you. Please accept them; and, under the powerful operation of your grace, this Mass will make our life more Christian and lead us toward heavenly joys. This we ask of you through our Lord.

COMMUNION ANTIPHON *Ps. 33:9*

Taste and see how good the Lord is; happy the man who takes refuge in him.

Prayer after the Communion

Sit nobis, Dómine, reparátio mentis et córporis cæléste mystérium: ut, cuius exséquimur cultum, sentiámus efféctum. Per Dóminum.

O Lord, we have taken part in this Mass; make us feel its benefits; may it renew the forces of our soul and our body. This we ask of you through our Lord.

---

[1] 44.6 quarts to the barrel.

[2] About 1400 bushels.

NINTH SUNDAY AFTER PENTECOST

ENTRANCE ANTIPHON *Ps. 53:6-7, 3*

Behold, God is my helper, the Lord sustains my life. Turn back the evil upon my foes; in your faithfulness destroy them, O Lord, my protector.

Ps. O God, by your name save me, and by your might deliver me.

Glory be to the Father and to the Son and to the Holy Spirit. As it was in the beginning, is now and ever shall be, world without end. Amen. Behold . . .

Prayer over the Assembly

Páteant aures misericórdiæ tuæ, Dómine, précibus supplicántium: et, ut peténtibus desideráta concédas; fac eos, quæ tibi sunt plácita, postuláre. Per Dóminum.

In your mercy, Lord, listen to our entreaties. Since you are most willing to give us that for which we petition, make us ask for that which pleases you. This we ask of you through our Lord.

EPISTLE   1 Corinthians 10:6-13

After the crossing of the Red Sea, the Hebrews, delivered from the Egyptians, remained subject to their evil tendencies: often during their long march to the promised land, they rebelled against God. After our baptism, on the march to heaven, we too must battle the temptations that assail us.

A reading from the first letter of the apostle Paul
to the Christians of Corinth

Brethren,

Let us not abandon ourselves to evil inclinations, as [our fathers] did. Let us not be idolators, as were some of them, of whom it is written, "The people sat down to eat and drink, and got up only to amuse themselves." [1] Let us not give ourselves over to impurity, either, as some of them did: in a single day twenty-three thousand of them died. Let us not provoke the Lord, as some of them provoked Him: they died as victims of serpents. Let us not murmur against God as some of them murmured: they were killed by the exterminator.

Everything that happened to them is a lesson for us, and it is written down to instruct us, who have come to the last age of the world. If anyone thinks his footing is well established, then, he should watch out that he does not fall!

None of the trials and temptations that assail you is beyond human strength. God protects you faithfully: he will not let you be tempted beyond your strength, but with the temptation he will give you the grace that enables you to overcome it.

[1] Exodus 32:6.

Gradual Ps. 8:2

O Lord, our Lord, how glorious is your name over all the earth! You have elevated your majesty above the heavens.

Alleluia Ps. 58:2

Alleluia, alleluia. Rescue me from my enemies, O my God; from my adversaries defend me. Alleluia.

GOSPEL   Luke 19:41-47

This text can be understood in two senses:
— *historically, the city of Jerusalem, which did not recognize in Jesus the ambassador of God, was destroyed;*
— *spiritually, Jerusalem, the holy city, is the image of the Church surrounded by the forces of evil.*
The Church is also this temple, this house of God, which we profane by our sins.

A reading from the holy Gospel according to Luke

At that time, when Jesus had arrived at the outskirts of Jerusalem and the panorama of the city was unfolded before his eyes, he could not hold back his tears. "If only, in this day that is left to you," he said, "you too could understand the message of peace! But no, it remains hidden from your eyes! And now the days are coming upon you when your enemies will encircle you with trenches; they will lay siege to you and hem you in from all sides. They will crush you to the ground, you and the children who live within your walls. They will not leave a stone of you upon a stone, because you have not been aware when [God] was visiting you."

When he had gone into the temple, Jesus began to drive out those who were selling and buying there. "It is written," He said, " 'My house is a house of prayer. And *you* have made it a den of thieves' " [1]

And every day after that, he was teaching in the temple.

OFFERTORY ANTIPHON Ps. 18:9, 10, 11, 12

The precepts of the Lord are right, rejoicing the heart, and his ordinances sweeter than syrup or honey from the comb; therefore your servant is careful of them.

Prayer over the Offerings

Concéde nobis, quǽsumus, Dómine, hæc digne frequentáre mystéria: quia, quóties huius hóstiæ commemorátio celebrátur, opus nostræ redemptiónis exercétur. Per Dóminum.

We entreat you, Lord, grant that we may participate worthily in this Mass, for Christ's redemption is fulfilled in us every time we celebrate this sacrifice in memory of him. This we ask of you through our Lord.

[1] Isaiah 56:7; Jeremiah 7:11.

COMMUNION ANTIPHON *John 6:57*

"He who eats my flesh, and drinks my blood, abides in me, and I in him," says the Lord.

Prayer after the Communion

Tui nobis quæsumus, Dómine, commúnio sacraménti, et purificatiónem cónferat, et tríbuat unitátem. Per Dóminum.

Lord, may our communion in your sacrament purify our souls and give them the bond of charity. This we ask of you through our Lord.

TENTH SUNDAY AFTER PENTECOST

ENTRANCE ANTIPHON *Ps. 54:17, 18, 20, 23, 2-3*

When I called upon the Lord, he heard my voice and freed me from those who war against me; and he humbled them, he who is before all ages, and remains forever. Cast your care upon the Lord, and he will support you.

Ps. Hearken, O God, to my prayer; turn not away from my pleading; give heed to me, and answer me.

Glory be to the Father and to the Son and to the Holy Spirit. As it was in the beginning, is now and ever shall be, world without end. Amen. When I called . . .

Prayer over the Assembly

Deus, qui omnipoténtiam tuam parcéndo máxime et miserándo maniféstas: multíplica super nos misericórdiam tuam; ut, ad tua promíssa curréntes, cæléstium bonórum fácias esse consórtes. Per Dóminum.

O God, it is above all in forgiving us and showing us mercy that you show your omnipotence. Pour out abundant graces on us, and we shall advance joyfully toward the things you have promised, to share one day the treasures of heaven. This we ask of you through our Lord.

EPISTLE   1 Corinthians 12:2-11

Every Christian has received from the Holy Spirit, especially at confirmation, special graces which enable him to be an active member in the Church. These gifts do not take on a miraculous form, as they did in the time of the apostles, but they are none the less real, and fraught with obligations for us.

A reading from the first letter of the apostle Paul
to the Christians of Corinth

Brethren,

Remember the days when you were pagans: you were following the current that carried you along toward the dumb idols. [In the same way, now, let yourselves be carried along by the Holy Spirit]. For, under the influence of the Spirit of God, no one will say, "Cursed be Jesus!" Nor can anyone say, "Jesus is the Lord!" unless the Holy Spirit is breathing on him.

There is variety in our aptitudes, but it is the same Spirit who awakens them in each of us. There is variety in our vocations, but it is the same Master who calls us. There is variety in our activities, but it is the same God who does all things in everyone.

The Spirit manifests himself differently in each one, with a view to the greatest good of all. The same Spirit will make this one capable of speaking of the mysteries of God, that one capable of explaining; he will fill another with an outstanding faith.

From this one Spirit, one person has received the grace of effecting cures, another the gift of miracles, still others the gift of speaking, the discernment of spirits, the gift of tongues or the gift of interpreting them.

But all this is the work of one and the same Spirit, who distributes his gifts to each one as he pleases.

Gradual *Ps. 16:8, 2*

Keep me, O Lord, as the apple of your eye; hide me in the shadow of your wings. From you let judgment come; your eyes behold what is right.

Alleluia *Ps. 64:2*

Alleluia, alleluia. To you we owe our hymn of praise, O God, in Sion; to you must vows be fulfilled in Jerusalem. Alleluia.

GOSPEL   Luke 18:9-14

"No one without the Holy Spirit can say, 'Jesus is the Lord.'" No one without the Holy Spirit can be just in the eyes of God.

A reading from the holy Gospel according to Luke

At that time, aiming His remarks at certain persons who were satisfied with their own virtues and contemptuous of others, Jesus proposed this parable:

"Two men went up to the temple to pray. One of them was a pharisee and the other a publican.

"The pharisee, holding his head high, prayed thus in his heart: 'O God, I give you thanks that I am not like the rest of men, who are robbers, unjust, adulterers, nor even like that publican. I fast twice a week, and I am very exact in making an offering of a tenth of my income.'

"As for the publican, he did not dare to come forward or even to raise his eyes toward heaven, but he kept striking his breast and saying, 'God, have pity on me; I am nothing but a sinner.'

"I tell you, when the publican set out again for his home, he had become, in God's eyes, more just than the other.

"For 'whoever exalts himself will be humbled; whoever humbles himself will be raised up.' "

OFFERTORY ANTIPHON *Ps. 24:1-3*

To you I lift up my soul, O Lord! In you, O my God, I trust; let me not be put to shame, let not my enemies exult over me. No one who waits for you shall be put to shame.

Prayer over the Offerings

Tibi, Dómine, sacrifícia dicáta reddántur: quæ sic ad honórem nóminis tui deferénda tribuísti, ut éadem remédia fíeri nostra præstáres. Per Dóminum.

To you, Lord, may the homage of our offerings be rendered. You have given us the grace of presenting them for the honor of your name, and have granted that they may also be a remedy to heal our souls. This we ask of you through our Lord.

COMMUNION ANTIPHON *Ps. 50:21*

You shall be pleased with due sacrifices, burnt offerings and holocausts on your altar, O Lord.

Prayer after the Communion

Quæsumus, Dómine Deus noster: ut, quos divínis reparáre non désinis sacraméntis, tuis non destítuas benígnus auxíliis. Per Dóminum.

O Lord, you keep restoring our souls by your Eucharist; please, in your goodness, never deprive them of your help. This we ask of you through our Lord.

ELEVENTH SUNDAY AFTER PENTECOST

ENTRANCE ANTIPHON *Ps. 67:6-7, 36, 2*

God is in his holy dwelling, God who makes men of one mind to dwell in a house; he shall give power and strength to his people.

Ps. God arises; his enemies are scattered, and those who hate him flee before him.

Glory be to the Father and to the Son and to the Holy Spirit. As it was in the beginning, is now and ever shall be, world without end. Amen. God is in . . .

Prayer over the Assembly

Omnípotens sempitérne Deus, qui, abundántia pietátis tuæ, et mérita súpplicum excédis et vota: effúnde super nos misericórdiam tuam; ut dimíttas quæ consciéntia métuit, et adícias quod orátio non præsúmit. Per Dóminum.

All-powerful, eternal God, your infinite goodness surpasses anything we might deserve and even that which we desire. Pour out your mercy on us, forgiving the sins that trouble our conscience and giving us, moreover, the graces we dare not ask you for. This we ask of you through our Lord.

EPISTLE   1 Corinthians 15:1-10

The death and the resurrection of Jesus are the central mystery of our faith. We are saved if we participate in Christ's Pasch. Every Sunday, moreover, is a reminder of it.

A reading from the first letter of the apostle Paul
to the Christians of Corinth

Brethren,

I recall to your minds the Gospel, that good news which I brought you, which you welcomed and to which you have remained faithful. It will bring you salvation, provided you keep it faithfully just as I have taught it to you. Otherwise, what good would it do you to have believed?

The fundamental teaching which I have handed on to you after having received it myself is that Christ died for our sins (in agreement with the Scriptures); then, that he was buried and that he rose the third day (always in agreement with the Scriptures); that he was seen by Peter, then by the eleven, then by more than five hundred of our brethren at one time (some of them have died, but most of them are still living), then by James and again by all the apostles, finally by me. I, the last of all, brought forth suddenly like an abortive child — I saw him.

I myself saw him; but I am really the last of the apostles, and I do not even deserve the name of apostle, because I persecuted the Church of God. It is only God's grace that has made me what I am now. And this grace has indeed worked a transformation in me.

Gradual Ps. 27:7, 1

In God my heart trusts, and I find help; then my heart exults, and with my song I give him thanks. To you, O Lord, I call; O my God, be not deaf to me; depart not from me.

Alleluia Ps. 80:2-3

Alleluia, alleluia. Sing joyfully to God our strength; acclaim the God of Jacob. Take up a pleasant psalm with the harp. Alleluia.

GOSPEL   Mark 7:31-37

In the ceremonies of baptism, one of the exorcisms repeats the gesture and the word with which Christ delivered the deaf mute from his affliction.

A reading from the holy Gospel according to Mark

At that time Jesus left the country of Tyre and came, by way of Sidon, to the sea of Galilee. Within the Decapolis territory they brought him a deaf mute and begged him to lay his hands on the person. Jesus took him aside and, when they were away from the crowd, put his fingers into his ears and put some saliva on his tongue. Then, raising his eyes to heaven, he let out a sigh and said to him, "Ephpheta," which means, "Open." At once his ears were opened, his tongue was able to move normally, and he began to speak correctly.

Jesus forbade the few witnesses of this miracle to speak of it to anyone; but the more he forbade them, the more they talked about it; and the crowd, carried away in admiration, kept exclaiming, "Everything he does is wonderful: he makes the deaf hear and the dumb speak!"

OFFERTORY ANTIPHON *Ps. 29:2-3*

I will extol you, O Lord, for you drew me clear and did not let my enemies rejoice over me. O Lord, I cried out to you and you healed me.

Prayer over the Offerings

Réspice, Dómine, quǽsumus, nostram propítius servitútem: ut, quod offérimus, sit tibi munus accéptum, et sit nostræ fragilitátis subsídium. Per Dóminum.

Look graciously, Lord, upon the homage rendered by our ministry. May our offering be acceptable to you, and may this Mass support us in our weakness. This we ask of you through our Lord.

COMMUNION ANTIPHON *Prov. 3:9-10*

Honor the Lord with your wealth, with first fruits of all your produce. Then will your barns be filled with grain, with new wine your vats will overflow.

Prayer after the Communion

Sentiámus, quǽsumus, Dómine, tui perceptióne sacraménti, subsídium mentis et córporis: ut in utróque salváti, cæléstis remédii plenitúdine gloriémur. Per Dóminum.

We have received your Eucharist, Lord; please allow us to feel its effects in our soul and in our body, that our whole being may one day enjoy it to the full in the glory of your heaven. This we ask of you through our Lord.

TWELFTH SUNDAY AFTER PENTECOST

ENTRANCE ANTIPHON *Ps. 69:2-3, 4*

Deign, O God, to rescue me; O Lord, make haste to help me. Let them be put to shame and confounded who seek my life.

Ps. Let them be turned back in disgrace, who desire my ruin.

Glory be to the Father and to the Son and to the Holy Spirit. As it was in the beginning, is now and ever shall be, world without end. Amen. Deign, O God . . .

Prayer over the Assembly

Omnípotens et miséricors Deus, de cuius múnere venit, ut tibi a

God of power and of mercy, the gift of your grace enables us to honor

fidélibus tuis digne et laudabíliter serviátur: tríbue, quǽsumus, nobis; ut ad promissiónes tuas sine offensióne currámus. Per Dóminum.

and serve you worthily; grant that we may advance without faltering toward the good things you have promised us. This we ask of you through our Lord.

EPISTLE   2 Corinthians 3:4-9

The Church has the task of bringing all men into alliance with God. All the baptized should consider themselves activators of the new alliance. To that end, let them be most faithful to the action of the Spirit, that the presence of God may be made manifest in them as it once was in Moses.

A reading from the second letter of the apostle Paul
to the Christians of Corinth

Brethren,

If we have such assurance before God, this we owe to Christ. Not that, by ourselves, we are capable of anything that really comes from ourselves. No, it is God who makes us capable, by making us the proper activators of his work, the activators of the new alliance, which is no longer the alliance of the letter but the alliance of the Spirit: the letter kills, while the Spirit gives life.

Now Moses, activator of the alliance of death engraved on the tables of the law, shone with such glory (a passing glory, however) that the Israelites were dazzled by it and could not look at his face. What will be the glory, then, with which the activators of the alliance of the Spirit will shine!

For if so much splendor surrounded the one who was bringing words of condemnation to men, imagine the splendor that will be ours, since we are bringing them holiness!

Gradual Ps. 33:2-3

I will bless the Lord at all times; his praise shall be ever in my mouth. Let my soul glory in the Lord; the lowly will hear and be glad.

Alleluia Ps. 87:2

Alleluia, alleluia. O Lord, the God of my salvation, by day I cry out, at night I clamor in your presence. Alleluia.

GOSPEL   Luke 10:23-37

The alliance between God and his people is an alliance of love. The Law already required the Jews to love God and their neighbor. The Law remains, but the Holy Spirit makes us see new requirements in it. Henceforth the neighbor will no longer be only the men of our own nation, but everyone, even our enemies. And furthermore, Christians must love after the manner of Christ, the true "good Samaritan" who has come to the aid of a distressed mankind.

A reading from the holy Gospel according to Luke

At that time Jesus said to his disciples, "What a blessing for you to see what you are seeing! For, I tell you, many prophets and kings desired to see what you are seeing, but did not see it, and to hear what you are hearing, but did not hear it."

Then a doctor of the law stood up and put this question to him, to see what he would answer: "Master, what must I do to possess eternal life?"

"What is written in the law?" Jesus asked him. "What teaching do you find there?"

The doctor recited the law's prescription: "You shall love the Lord your God with your whole heart, with your whole soul, with all your strength and with your whole mind; and your neighbor as yourself." [1]

"You have answered well," said Jesus. "Do that, and you will live."

Then, to justify his question, the doctor asked, "But who exactly is my neighbor?"

Jesus answered in this way: "A man was going down from Jerusalem to Jericho. He fell into the hands of robbers, who stripped him, beat him savagely and left him half dead. It happened that a priest went down by the same road; he took a look at the unfortunate man, and went on his way. A levite, too, came near the place, looked at him and continued on his way.

"A Samaritan, however, journeying that way, came upon him and, seeing his plight, felt sorry for him. He approached, poured oil and wine over his injuries and bandaged his wounds. Then he lifted him onto his own mount and took him to an inn, where he continued to take care of him. The next day he took two denarii from his purse and gave them to the innkeeper, saying, 'Take care of him, and I will reimburse you on my return for whatever you may spend beyond this.'

"Which of the three seems to you to have been the neighbor of the man who had fallen into the robbers' hands?"

"The one who took pity on him," answered the doctor.

"Go," said Jesus in conclusion, "and do as he did."

OFFERTORY ANTIPHON *Ex. 32:11, 13-14*

Moses prayed in the sight of the Lord his God and said, "Why, O Lord, is your indignation enkindled against your people? Let the anger of your mind cease; remember Abraham, Isaac, and Jacob, to whom you swore to give a land flowing with milk and honey."

And the Lord was appeased from doing the evil which he had spoken of doing against his people.

Prayer over the Offerings

Hóstias, quǽsumus, Dómine, propítius inténde, quas sacris altáribus exhibémus: ut nobis indul-

Look down with favor, Lord, upon the offerings which we present at your holy altar: may they win for-

[1] Deuteronomy 6:5; Leviticus 19:18.

géntiam largiéndo, tuo nómini dent honórem. Per Dóminum.

giveness for us and give glory to you. This we ask of you through our Lord.

COMMUNION ANTIPHON *Ps. 103, 13-15*

The earth is replete with the fruit of your works, O Lord; you produce bread from the earth, and wine to gladden men's hearts, so that their faces gleam with oil, and bread fortifies the hearts of men.

Prayer after the Communion

Vivíficet nos, quæsumus, Dómine, huius participátio sancta mystérii: et páriter nobis expiatiónem tríbuat, et munímen. Per Dóminum.

O Lord, may our holy communion give life to our soul, and may it bestow on us at the same time your forgiveness of our sins and your protection. This we ask of you through our Lord.

THIRTEENTH SUNDAY AFTER PENTECOST

ENTRANCE ANTIPHON *Ps. 73:20, 19, 23, 1*

Look to your covenant, O Lord, forsake not forever the lives of your afflicted ones. Arise, O Lord, defend your cause; be not unmindful of the voices of those who ask you.

Ps. Why, O God, have you cast us off forever? Why does your anger smolder against the sheep of your pasture?

Glory be to the Father and to the Son and to the Holy Spirit. As it was in the beginning, is now and ever shall be, world without end. Amen. Look to . . .

Prayer over the Assembly

Omnípotens sempitérne Deus, da nobis fídei, spei et caritátis augméntum: et, ut mereámur ássequi quod promíttis, fac nos amáre quod præcipis. Per Dóminum.

All-powerful, eternal God, give us an increase of faith, hope and charity; and, that we may one day attain the good things you have promised, make us love your commandments. This we ask of you through our Lord.

EPISTLE   Galatians 3:16-22

The alliance involves, on God's part, the promise to save us; and, on the part of men, faith, that is to say, the welcome acceptance of God's gift. But everything rests on the initiative and the goodness of God.

A reading from the letter of the apostle Paul to the Christians of Galatia
Brethren,
God has promised to save us. He made this promise solemnly to Abraham and to his offspring. [The Bible] does not say "to his descendants"

in the plural, but "to his offspring" in the singular, as if there were only one descendant, Christ.

This is what I say, then: Since God bound himself formally in this way, [the Jewish religion, which is called] "the law," and which did not come until four hundred and thirty years later, cannot annul this engagement and make God's promise void. Now if it were the observance of the [Jewish] law that saved us, it would no longer be God's promise; and it was really by a wholly gratuitous promise that God bound himself with regard to Abraham.

What purpose did the law serve, then? It served to make sin conspicuous, until [Christ] should come, that "descendant" of Abraham for whom the promise was meant. It was a sort of contract promulgated by the angels with the help of an intermediary [Moses]. Now there is no intermediary when one is alone [in being bound], and God is alone [with regard to his promise of salvation].

In giving the law, is God going against his promises? Certainly not. If that law were capable of making us live, we would really be saved by the observance of the law.

But [far from bringing us out of sin], that written law encloses us within it, in order that the promised salvation may be achieved in the believers only by the faith they have in Jesus Christ.

Gradual *Ps. 73:20, 19, 22*

Look to your covenant, O Lord, be not unmindful of the lives of your afflicted ones. Arise, O Lord, defend your cause; remember the reproach of your servants.

Alleluia *Ps. 89:1*

Alleluia, alleluia. O Lord, you have been our refuge through all generations. Alleluia.

GOSPEL Luke 17:11-19

As Christ in former times healed the sick, the Church today purifies by baptism and by penance all those who present themselves to her. Let us not forget to express our thanks to the Lord.

A reading from the holy Gospel according to Luke

At that time, on his way to Jerusalem, Jesus was following the route that lies along the frontier between Samaria and Galilee. At the entrance to a village ten lepers came before him. Not daring to come nearer than they were supposed to, they raised their voices to say, "Jesus, our master, have pity on us!"

As soon as Jesus saw that they were lepers, he said to them, "Go and show yourselves to the priests." They set out, therefore, to show themselves to the priests; and, on the way, they were cured.

One of them, as soon as he became aware of his cure, retraced his steps, proclaiming aloud the glory of God. He lay with his face to the ground at the feet of Jesus, giving him thanks. And this was a Samaritan.

"Were not the ten healed?" said Jesus. "And where are the other nine? Is there no one found but this foreigner to come back and give glory to God?" And Jesus said to the leper, "Get up and go on your way; your faith has saved you."

OFFERTORY ANTIPHON *Ps. 30:15-16*

My trust is in you, O Lord; I say, "You are my God." In your hands is my destiny.

Prayer over the Offerings

Propitiáre, Dómine, pópulo tuo, propitiáre munéribus: ut hac oblatióne placátus, et indulgéntiam nobis tríbuas, et postuláta concédas. Per Dóminum.

With love, O Lord, look upon your people and their offerings; may this Mass make you still more favorably inclined to grant us forgiveness and to answer our prayers. This we ask of you through our Lord.

COMMUNION ANTIPHON *Wis. 16:20*

You have given us, O Lord, bread from heaven, endowed with all delights and the sweetness of every taste.

Prayer after the Communion

Sumptis, Dómine, cæléstibus sacraméntis: ad redemptiónis ætérnæ, quǽsumus, profíciá.nus augméntum. Per Dóminum.

We have received the bread of heaven; be pleased, O Lord, to make the work of your eternal redemption increase in us. This we ask of you through our Lord.

FOURTEENTH SUNDAY AFTER PENTECOST

ENTRANCE ANTIPHON *Ps. 83, 10-11, 2-3*

Behold, O God, our protector, and look upon the face of your anointed. Better is one day in your courts than a thousand elsewhere. *Ps.* How lovely is your dwelling place, O Lord of hosts! My soul yearns and pines for the courts of the Lord.

Glory be to the Father and to the Son and to the Holy Spirit. As it was in the beginning, is now and ever shall be, world without end. Amen. Behold, O God . . .

Prayer over the Assembly

Custódi, Dómine, quǽsumus, Ecclésiam tuam propitiatióne per-

O Lord, in your goodness, guard your Church always. Without you,

pétua: et quia sine te lábitur humána mortálitas; tuis semper auxíliis et abstrahátur a nóxiis, et ad
salutária dirigátur. Per Dóminum.

our human nature cannot help falling: help us avoid what is harmful,
and direct our steps toward that which
furthers our salvation. This we ask of
you through our Lord.

EPISTLE   Galatians 5:16-24

*The life of the children of God is not subject to an arbitrary law of
morality. But it is governed by docility to the Holy Spirit, who himself
associates us to God's life and effects our sanctity little by little.*

A reading from the letter of the apostle Paul to the Christians of Galatia

Brethren,

Be tractable to the Spirit, and you will not yield to your evil inclinations.
For there is in you a creature of flesh, whose desires go against those of
the Spirit; and there is the Spirit, whose aspirations go against those of the
flesh. That is why you do not do all that you would like to do. But if the Spirit leads you, you are no longer subject to the prescriptions of the [Jewish]
law.

Everyone knows the things into which the flesh drags us: evil conduct,
impurity and debauchery; irreligion and superstition; grudges, contentions,
jealousies, anger, rivalries, divisions, sectarianism, ill will and murders;
drunkenness, orgies and sins of that kind. Once more I tell you: those
who live in that way will not possess the kingdom of God.

What the Spirit gives, on the contrary, is charity, joy, peace, patience,
affability, goodness, forbearance, gentleness, fidelity, moderation, self-
control and purity. Where such things prevail, the law does not exist. But
those who belong to Christ in this way have crucified their flesh with its
passions and its evil desires.

Gradual *Ps. 117:8-9*

It is better to take refuge in the Lord than to trust in men. It is better to take refuge in the Lord than to trust in princes.

Alleluia *Ps. 94:1*

Alleluia, alleluia. Come, let us sing joyfully to the Lord; let us acclaim the God of our salvation. Alleluia.

GOSPEL   Matthew 6:24-33

*To die with Christ is to "crucify our flesh." To live with Christ is to look
on God as a Father, to be concerned only with his kingdom and to trust
ourselves entirely to him.*

A reading from the holy Gospel according to Matthew

At that time Jesus said to his disciples, "It is impossible to serve two
masters. He who tries to do so, soon comes to detest one and love the

other, or he becomes attached to one and has no use for the other. You cannot serve God and money.

"That is why I tell you:

"Do not be anxious about your life, asking yourselves what you are going to eat; nor about your body, asking yourselves what you are going to wear. Is not the life more than the food, and the body more than the clothing?

"Consider the birds that fly in the sky. They neither sow nor reap; they do not lay up provisions in granaries. But your heavenly Father feeds them. Do you think that you would not be worth more than they in his eyes? Or do you think that your anxiety could add to the length of your life?

"As for clothing, why be worried about it? Look at the field lilies. How do they grow? They neither work nor spin; but, I assure you, Solomon himself, at the height of his glory, was never clothed like one of them. But if God takes care to clothe in this way the grass in the fields, which is alive today, and tomorrow will be thrown into the furnace, what will he not do for you, men of little faith?

"Do not be disturbed, therefore, about these questions: 'What are we going to eat? What are we going to drink? What are we going to wear?' Those are the things the pagans are concerned about; but you should know that your heavenly Father is aware of your needs! Be concerned first of all with his kingdom and the perfection it demands; all the rest will be given you besides."

OFFERTORY ANTIPHON *Ps. 33:8-9*

The angel of the Lord encamps around those who fear him, and delivers them. Taste and see how good the Lord is.

Prayer over the Offerings

Concéde nobis, Dómine, quæsumus, ut hæc hóstia salutáris, et nostrórum fiat purgátio delictórum, et tuæ propitiátio potestátis. Per Dóminum.

Lord, may this saving victim purify us from our sins and obtain for us the help of your majestic power. This we ask of you through our Lord.

COMMUNION ANTIPHON *Matt. 6:33*

"Seek first the kingdom of God; and all things shall be given you besides," says the Lord.

Prayer after the Communion

Puríficent semper et múniant tua sacraménta nos, Deus: et ad perpétuæ ducant salvatiónis efféctum. Per Dóminum.

May your sacrament, Lord, make our souls pure; and, strengthened by this sacrament, may they advance in the way of eternal salvation. This we ask of you through our Lord.

FIFTEENTH SUNDAY AFTER PENTECOST

ENTRANCE ANTIPHON *Ps. 85:1, 2-3, 4*

Incline your ear, O Lord; answer me; save your servant, O my God, who trusts in you. Have pity on me, O Lord, for to you I call all the day.

Ps. Gladden the soul of your servant, for to you, O Lord, I lift up my soul.

Glory be to the Father and to the Son and to the Holy Spirit. As it was in the beginning, is now and ever shall be, world without end. Amen. Incline your ear . . .

Prayer over the Assembly

Ecclésiam tuam, Dómine, miserátio continuáta mundet et múniat: et quia sine te non potest salva consístere; tuo semper múnere gubernétur. Per Dóminum.

Lord, have pity on your Church: strengthen her, purify her always; and, since she cannot live without you, may your grace never cease to guide her. This we ask of you through our Lord.

EPISTLE

Galatians 5:25-26; 6:1-10

The Holy Spirit, who has been the principle of life in us since our baptism, causes us to participate in the relations of love uniting the three divine Persons to one another. Hence there is within us a demand of brotherly love.

A reading from the letter of the apostle Paul to the Christians of Galatia

Brethren,

If it is the Spirit who gives us life, let us conduct ourselves according to the Spirit.

Let us be on our guard against the desire of seeming superior to others: let there be no rivalries among us, no jealousies!

Brethren, if anyone happens to do wrong, set him right without being harsh to him, you who want to live according to the Spirit. And be careful: you yourself may be tempted. Carry one another's burdens; in that way you will fulfill the law of Christ.

If you think that you are something, whereas in reality you are nothing, you deceive yourself. Let each one examine his own behavior. If he has reason to be satisfied with it, so much the better! But let him not seek to justify himself by comparing himself with others. It is up to each one to carry his own burden.

Let him who is being instructed in the word of God help satisfy the needs of the one who is instructing him, as far as he is able.

Make no mistake: God is not mocked. A person will reap what he sows. He who sows according to the flesh will reap his harvest from the flesh: a perishable harvest. He who sows according to the Spirit will reap his harvest from the Spirit: eternal life. There is good to be done; let us not fail to do it. When the time comes, we shall reap, if we do not give up. So therefore, while there is time, let us be good to all, and especially to our brethren in the faith.

Gradual Ps. 91:2-3

It is good to give thanks to the Lord, to sing to your name, Most High. To proclaim your kindness at dawn and your faithfulness throughout the night.

Alleluia Ps. 94:3

Alleluia, alleluia. For the Lord is a great God, and a great king over all the earth. Alleluia.

GOSPEL   Luke 7:11-16

The resurrections performed by Christ during his earthly life showed that he had come to bring life to the world. The Church continues Christ's work: she gives men life through baptism.

A reading from the holy Gospel according to Luke

At that time Jesus was going to a city called Naïm; His disciples, as well as a large crowd of people, were going along with him.

They were just approaching the city gate when they met a funeral procession coming out. The funeral was that of a young man. A great number of people were following with the mother, who was a widow and had no other child.

When he saw her, Jesus had pity on her. "Dry your tears!" he said, and he stepped forward and touched the stretcher. The bearers stopped.

"Young man," he said, "I tell you: get up!" The dead man sat up and began to speak. And Jesus gave him back to his mother.

They were all awestruck, and they began to give glory to God in these words: "A great prophet has risen among us, and God has visited his people."

OFFERTORY ANTIPHON *Ps. 39:2, 3, 4*

I have waited, waited for the Lord, and he stooped toward me, and heard my cry; and he put a new song into my mouth, a hymn to our God.

Prayer over the Offerings

Tua nos, Dómine, sacraménta custódiant: et contra diabólicos semper tueántur incúrsus. Per Dóminum.

Lord, may the grace of this Mass protect your children and defend them always against the assaults of the devil. This we ask of you through our Lord.

COMMUNION ANTIPHON *John 6:52*

The bread that I will give is my flesh for the life of the world.

Prayer after the Communion

Mentes nostras, et córpora possídeat, quǽsumus, Dómine, doni cæléstis operátio: ut non noster sensus in nobis, sed iúgiter eius prævéniat efféctus. Per Dóminum.

Lord, may the power of the Eucharist take possession of our souls and our bodies, that it may no longer be our own will but the grace of the sacrament which acts in us. This we ask of you through our Lord.

SIXTEENTH SUNDAY AFTER PENTECOST

ENTRANCE ANTIPHON *Ps. 85:3, 5, 1*

Have pity on me, O Lord, for to you I call all the day. For you, O Lord, are good and forgiving, abounding in kindness to all who call upon you.

Ps. Incline your ear, O Lord, answer me, for I am afflicted and poor.

Glory be to the Father and to the Son and to the Holy Spirit. As it was in the beginning, is now and ever shall be, world without end. Amen. Have pity . . .

Prayer over the Assembly

Tua nos, quǽsumus, Dómine, grátia semper et prævéniat et sequátur: ac bonis opéribus iúgiter præstet esse inténtos. Per Dóminum.

Lord, may your grace go before us. May it always accompany us and make us constantly intent upon doing good. This we ask of you through our Lord.

EPISTLE   Ephesians 3:13-21

By meditating on the way in which God directs our lives, on the destiny of his Church and the salvation of the world, we can get some idea of the boundless love with which we are loved.

A reading from the letter of the apostle Paul to the Christians of Ephesus
Brethren,
Please, do not be discouraged by the trials I am undergoing for you; rather, be proud of them.

When I think of God's designs, I fall on my knees to ask the Father of our Lord Jesus Christ, the source and model of all fatherhood in heaven and on earth, to grant, in his glorious generosity, that you be strengthened by the energy of the Holy Spirit in such a way as to foster the growth of the interior man in you. May Christ, through faith, dwell in your hearts! Be rooted, be grounded in charity, that you may succeed in understanding, with all the Christians, what is the breadth and the height and the depth and the immensity [of the divine plan], and that you may know Christ's love, that love which surpasses all human experience. Thus you will be filled with the very riches of God.

To him whose power is active in us, and who can do all things — infinitely more than we ask or imagine — to him be glory in the Church and in Christ Jesus, throughout the ages and into eternity! Amen!

Gradual *Ps. 101:16-17*

The nations shall revere your name, O Lord, and all the kings of the earth your glory. For the Lord has rebuilt Sion, and he shall appear in his glory.

Alleluia *Ps. 97:1*

Alleluia, alleluia. Sing to the Lord a new song, for the Lord has done wondrous deeds. Alleluia.

GOSPEL   Luke 14:1-11

Christ, whose work the Church is now continuing on earth, came to heal that which was sick, to save that which was lost. The more aware we are of our weakness and our sinfulness, the more we shall draw down the divine mercy on ourselves, and the more likely we shall be to take part in the heavenly banquet.

A reading from the holy Gospel according to Luke

At that time Jesus entered the home of one of the principal pharisees to take his meal there; it was the sabbath day. All the pharisees present were watching him. Suddenly there before him was a man afflicted with dropsy.

Jesus asked the doctors of the law and the pharisees, "Is it permissible or not, during the sabbath rest, to perform a cure?" No one answered. Taking the sick man's hand, therefore, Jesus cured him and dismissed him. Then he said to them, "Which of you, if he had an ass or an ox that fell into a pit, would not pull him out at once, despite the sabbath rest?" They could find no reply to make to this.

Noticing with what haste the guests were appropriating the first places, he then told them this parable: "When someone invites you to a wedding banquet, do not install yourself in the place of honor. It may happen that a person more important than you has also been invited. Then the one who invited you both will say to you, 'Make room for this guest,' and you will have to start moving down, to your great embarrassment, toward the lowest place.

"Rather, when you are invited, put yourself in the last place; and the one who invited you will come and tell you, 'Move up, my friend.' This time the honor will be yours, in front of all the guests. For 'whoever exalts himself will be humbled; whoever humbles himself will be exalted.' "

OFFERTORY ANTIPHON *Ps. 39:14, 15*

Deign, O Lord, to rescue me; let all be put to shame and confusion who seek to snatch away my life. Deign, O Lord, to rescue me.

Prayer over the Offerings

Munda nos, quǽsumus, Dómine, sacrifícii præséntis efféctu: et

Purify us, Lord, by the grace of this Mass, and in your mercy allow

pérfice miserátus in nobis; ut eius mereámur esse partícipes. Per Dóminum.

us to take part in the sacrifice. This we ask of you through our Lord.

COMMUNION ANTIPHON *Ps. 70:16-17, 18*

O Lord, I will tell of your singular justice; O God, you have taught me from my youth; and now that I am old and gray, O God, forsake me not.

Prayer after the Communion

Purífica, quǽsumus, Dómine, mentes nostras benígnus, et rénova cæléstibus sacraméntis: ut consequénter et córporum præsens páriter, et futúrum capiámus auxílium. Per Dóminum.

In your kindness, Lord, purify and renew our souls in holy communion; and may that purification benefit our bodies too, both now and in the future. This we ask of you through our Lord.

SEVENTEENTH SUNDAY AFTER PENTECOST

ENTRANCE ANTIPHON *Ps. 118:137, 124, 1*

You are just, O Lord, and your ordinance is right. Deal with your servant according to your kindness.

Ps. Happy are they whose way is blameless, who walk in the law of the Lord.

Glory be to the Father and to the Son and to the Holy Spirit. As it was in the beginning, is now and ever shall be, world without end. Amen. You are just . . .

Prayer over the Assembly

Da, quǽsumus, Dómine, pópulo tuo diabólica vitáre contágia: et te solum Deum pura mente sectári. Per Dóminum.

Lord, give your people the grace to avoid the contagious errors of the devil and to follow you, our only God, in sincerity of heart. This we ask of you through our Lord.

EPISTLE   Ephesians 4:1-6

We are all called to constitute the whole body of Christ. The first demand of our Christian vocation, therefore, is unity.

A reading from the letter of the apostle Paul to the Christians of Ephesus Brethren,

I, a prisoner for Christ, entreat you to conduct yourselves in a manner worthy of the vocation to which [God] is calling you. Practice humility, gentleness, patience among one another, supporting one another by love, being careful to preserve that peace which unites you to one another, that you may be one in the Spirit.

All together you are but one body, but one spirit, as you have but one hope — that [of the same heaven] to which you are all called — one Lord, Christ, one faith, one baptism, one God, who is the Father of us all, who is above all, who acts in all and who is in all.

Blessed is he for ever and ever! Amen!

Gradual Ps. 32:12, 6

Happy the nation whose God is the Lord, the people the Lord has chosen for his own inheritance. By the word of the Lord the heavens were made; by the breath of his mouth all their host.

Alleluia Ps. 101:2

Alleluia, alleluia. O Lord, hear my prayer, and let my cry come to you. Alleluia.

GOSPEL   Matthew 22:34-46

The first part of this text recalls to us the great law of love which sums up all the commandments of God. The second part proposes for our contemplation Christ, Son of David, in his glory.

A reading from the holy Gospel according to Matthew

At that time the pharisees approached Jesus, and one of them, a doctor of the law, posed this question to see what he would answer: "Master, what is the greatest commandment in the law?"

Jesus said to him, "You shall love the Lord your God with your whole heart, with your whole soul and with your whole mind;[1] that is the greatest and the first commandment. But the second is like it: You shall love your neighbor as yourself.[2] On these two commandments rest the whole law and the prophets."

Since the pharisees were gathered together, Jesus took advantage of the occasion to question them: "What is your opinion about the Messiah? Whose son is he?"

"David's," they replied.

"Then how is it," asked Jesus, "that David, speaking under divine inspiration, gives him the title of 'Lord'? For he says in the psalm, 'The Lord said to my Lord, "Sit at my right hand until I put your enemies under your feet like a footstool." '[3] How can the one whom David calls 'Lord' be his son?"

None of them knew what answer to make; and, from that day on, no one dared question Him.

OFFERTORY ANTIPHON Dan. 9:17, 18, 19

I, Daniel, prayed to my God, saying, "Hear, O Lord, the prayers of your servant; show your face upon your sanctuary, and favorably look down upon this people, upon whom your name is invoked, O God."

[1] Deuteronomy 6.   [2] Leviticus 19:18.   [3] Psalm 109:1.

Prayer over the Offerings

Maiestátem tuam, Dómine, supplíciter deprecámur: ut hæc sancta, quæ gérimus, et a prætéritis nos delíctis éxuant, et futúris. Per Dóminum.

O Lord, as we take part in this Mass, we ask your majesty that, while delivering us from our past sins, you also give us the strength to keep from falling into sin again in the future. This we ask of you through our Lord.

COMMUNION ANTIPHON *Ps. 75:12-13*

Make vows to the Lord, your God, and fulfill them; let all round about him bring gifts to the terrible Lord who checks the pride of princes, who is terrible to the kings of the earth.

Prayer after the Communion

Sanctificatiónibus tuis, omnípotens Deus, et vítia nostra curéntur, et remédia nobis ætérna provéniant. Per Dóminum.

By this sacrament which makes saints, God all-powerful, heal our vices and give us remedies that are salutary for all eternity. This we ask of you through our Lord.

EIGHTEENTH SUNDAY AFTER PENTECOST

ENTRANCE ANTIPHON *Sir. 36:18; Ps. 121:1*

Give peace, O Lord, to those who have hoped in you, and let your prophets be proved true. Hear the prayers of your servant, and of your people Israel.

Ps. I rejoiced because they said to me, "We will go up to the house of the Lord."

Glory be to the Father and to the Son and to the Holy Spirit. As it was in the beginning, is now and ever shall be, world without end. Amen. Give peace . . .

Prayer over the Assembly

Dírigat corda nostra, quǽsumus, Dómine, tuæ miseratiónis operátio: quia tibi sine te placére non póssumus. Per Dóminum.

Let the working of your mercy, Lord, direct our hearts, for without your help we cannot do anything that will be acceptable to you. This we ask of you through our Lord.

EPISTLE 1 Corinthians 1:4-8

As members of the Church we are already rich with all the graces of Christ; but we still have to wait for all these riches to be displayed in glory, at the end of the world.

A reading from the first letter of the apostle Paul
to the Christians of Corinth

Brethren,

I keep thanking God for the divine grace he has given you in Christ Jesus. Through your union with him you have been enriched in every way, with all the riches of eloquence and all those of knowledge, in the same measure in which you have borne firm witness to Christ. You are not lacking any spiritual gift. You have only to wait for the manifestation of our Lord Jesus Christ. May God keep you faithful and without sin, until the day when our Lord Jesus Christ returns!

Gradual *Ps. 121:1, 7*

I rejoiced because they said to me, "We will go up to the house of the Lord." May peace be within your walls, prosperity in your buildings.

Alleluia *Ps. 101:16*

Alleluia, alleluia. The nations shall revere your name, O Lord, and all the kings of the earth your glory. Alleluia.

GOSPEL   Matthew 9:1-8

The cure of the paralytic is the symbol of the spiritual health which has been granted us. It is by baptism that Christ has overwhelmed us with riches and has put us on the march toward the new Jerusalem.

A reading from the holy Gospel according to Matthew

At that time, Jesus, getting into a boat, crossed the lake and came back to his own city [Capharnaum]. And just then a paralyzed man was brought to him, lying on a stretcher. Seeing the faith of those who were carrying him, and that of the sick man, Jesus said to him, "Take courage, my son, your sins are forgiven!"

Several scribes who were present said to themselves, "This man is blaspheming!"

Reading their minds at once, Jesus said to them, "Why these spiteful thoughts in your inmost hearts? Which is easier to say, 'Your sins are forgiven' or 'Get up and walk'? Well, that you may know that the Son of Man has the power on earth to forgive sins" — addressing the paralytic, he commanded, "Get up, pick up your stretcher and go home." At once the paralytic got up and returned home.

At this spectacle the crowd was seized with a religious fear and began to glorify God, who had given such power to men.

OFFERTORY ANTIPHON *Ex. 24:4, 5*

Moses consecrated an altar to the Lord, offering upon it holocausts, and sacrificing victims. He made an evening sacrifice to the Lord God for an odor of sweetness, in the sight of the Israelites.

Prayer over the Offerings

Deus, qui nos per huius sacrifícii veneránda commércia, uníus summæ divinitátis partícipes éfficis: præsta, quæsumus; ut, sicut tuam cognóscimus veritátem, sic eam dignis móribus assequámur. Per Dóminum.

O Lord, in the sacred exchange which takes place in this mystery, you give us a share in your divine life. Since we know your truth, give us the grace to put it into practice by conduct that is worthy of you. This we ask of you through our Lord.

COMMUNION ANTIPHON *Ps. 95:8-9*

Bring gifts and enter his courts; worship the Lord in his holy court.

Prayer after the Communion

Grátias tibi reférimus, Dómine, sacro múnere vegetáti: tuam misericórdiam deprecántes; ut dignos nos eius participatióne perfícias. Per Dóminum.

We thank you, Lord, for having nourished us on your Eucharist, and we entreat your mercy to make us worthy of participating in this mystery. This we ask of you through our Lord.

NINETEENTH SUNDAY AFTER PENTECOST

ENTRANCE ANTIPHON *Ps. 77:1*

"I am the salvation of the people," says the Lord; "in whatever tribulation they shall cry to me, I will hear them; and I will be their Lord forever."

Ps. Hearken, my people, to my teaching; incline your ears to the words of my mouth.

Glory be to the Father and to the Son and to the Holy Spirit. As it was in the beginning, is now and ever shall be, world without end. Amen. "I am the salvation . . .

Prayer over the Assembly

Omnípotens et miséricors Deus, univérsa nobis adversántia propitiátus exclúde: ut, mente et córpore páriter expedíti, quæ tua sunt, líberis méntibus exsequámur. Per Dóminum.

God of mercy and of power, in your goodness remove the obstacles from our path, that without hindrance to soul or body we may freely serve you. This we ask of you through our Lord.

EPISTLE Ephesians 4:23-28

The white garment put on at baptism is the sign of that transformation by which we have become a new man, living with Christ's life. This interior renewal must be expressed in our everyday behavior.

A reading from the letter of the apostle Paul to the Christians of Ephesus

Brethren,

Renew yourselves to the very depths of your soul: put on the new man whom God has created to his image in true justice and true charity.

Be done with lying, therefore: let each one of you speak the truth to his neighbor, since we are members of one another. If something makes you angry, do not yield to sin: do not let the sun set upon your anger; do not give the devil a hold on you.

If anyone used to steal, let him steal no more, but rather work honestly with his hands, that he may have something to give to one who is poorer than he!

Gradual *Ps. 140:2*

Let my prayer come like incense before you, O Lord, the lifting up of my hands, like the evening sacrifice.

Alleluia *Ps. 104:1*

Alleluia, alleluia. Give thanks to the Lord, invoke his name; make known among the nations his deeds. Alleluia.

GOSPEL   Matthew 22:1-14

The father of the family is God. His son is Christ, who is marrying mankind. The first ones invited are the many Jews who have not answered the call. Those who participate in the banquet, clothed in the white garment of the nuptials, are those who keep the robe of their baptism without spot.

A reading from the holy Gospel according to Matthew

At that time, addressing the chief priests and the pharisees, Jesus proposed this parable:

"The kingdom of heaven can be compared to a king who was celebrating his son's wedding. He sent his servants to summon those who were invited, but they refused to come. Then he sent other servants to say, "Look, I have prepared my feast. The bullocks and the fattened animals are killed. Everything is ready. Come to the wedding feast." But those who had been invited paid no attention to these overtures. Off they went, one to his farm, another to his shop. Some of them even seized some of the servants, abused them and killed them.

"When the king got word of this, he was enraged. He sent his troops to put those murderers to death and burn their city.

"Then he said to his servants, 'The wedding feast is ready, but those who were invited were not worthy of it. Go station yourselves at the crossroads, and invite everyone you meet to the wedding.' The servants took to the roads, therefore, and brought in everyone they found, the bad as well as the good; and the wedding hall was filled with guests.

"The king came in to see those who were at table; he noticed a man who was not wearing the white wedding garment. 'My friend,' he said, 'how is it that you have come in here without putting on the white wedding garment?' The man had nothing to say for himself. The king said to his servants, 'Bind him hand and foot, and throw him out in the dark, where there is weeping and grinding of teeth.' For 'many are called, but few are chosen.' " [1]

OFFERTORY ANTIPHON *Ps. 137:7*

Though I walk amid distress, you preserve me, O Lord; against the anger of my enemies you raise your hand; your right hand saves me.

Prayer over the Offerings

Hæc múnera, quæsumus, Dómine, quæ óculis tuæ maiestátis offérimus, salutária nobis esse concéde. Per Dóminum.

In the sight of your majesty, Lord, we bring our offerings; make them profitable for our salvation. This we ask of you through our Lord.

COMMUNION ANTIPHON *Ps. 118:4-5*

You have commanded that your precepts be diligently kept. Oh, that I might be firm in the ways of keeping your statutes!

Prayer after the Communion

Tua nos, Dómine, medicinális operátio, et a nostris perversitátibus cleménter expédiat, et tuis semper fáciat inhærére mandátis. Per Dóminum.

God of mercy, may the purifying action of your grace free us from our evil inclinations and make us adhere always to your will. This we ask of you through our Lord.

TWENTIETH SUNDAY AFTER PENTECOST

ENTRANCE ANTIPHON *Dan. 3:31, 29, 35; Ps. 118:1*

All that you have done to us, O Lord, you have done in true judgment, because we have sinned against you, and we have not obeyed your commandments; but give glory to your name, and deal with us according to the multitude of your mercy.

Ps. Happy are they whose way is blameless, who walk in the law of the Lord.

Glory be to the Father and to the Son and to the Holy Spirit. As it was in the beginning, is now and ever shall be, world without end. Amen. All that you . . .

Prayer over the Assembly

Largíre, quæsumus, Dómine, fidélibus tuis indulgéntiam placátus et pacem: ut páriter ab ómni-

Let your heart be touched, Lord: grant forgiveness and peace to your faithful. Purified of all their sins,

---

[1] The parable suggests an opposite conclusion, as far as numbers are concerned; but the point to be noticed is the urgent appeal not to refuse entrance into the kingdom of God.

bus mundéntur offénsis, et secúra tibi mente desérviant. Per Dóminum.

they will be able to serve you with a tranquil heart. This we ask of you through our Lord.

EPISTLE   Ephesians 5:15-21

We must make the best possible use of the time given us on earth; and, by our docility to the Holy Spirit, we must live even here on earth as citizens of the heavenly city.

A reading from the letter of the apostle Paul to the Christians of Ephesus
Brethren,

Be careful of your behavior: do not live as thoughtless people do, but rather like those who are thoughtful. Make the best possible use of the time allotted you, for we are passing through evil days.

It is not enough just to live along heedlessly; you must understand what is the will of God.

Do not drink too much wine; it leads to debauchery.

Fill yourselves rather with the Holy Spirit. In your assemblies, speak to God by means of psalms, hymns and canticles; with all your heart, sing to the Lord and praise him. Whatever happens, always give thanks to God our Father for it, in the name of our Lord Jesus Christ.

Let each one place himself at the service of the rest, out of love for Christ!

Gradual Ps. 144:15-16

The eyes of all look hopefully to you, O Lord, and you give them their food in due season. You open your hand and satisfy the desire of every living thing.

Alleluia Ps. 107:2

Alleluia, alleluia. My heart is steadfast, O God; my heart is steadfast; I will sing and chant praise to you, my glory. Alleluia.

GOSPEL   John 4:46-53

Following in Christ's footsteps, the Church is at work in the world to save men from death. It is through faith that we obtain eternal life.

A reading from the holy Gospel according to John

At that time, having learned that Jesus on his return from Judea was in Galilee [and was staying at Cana], an official of the royal court came to see him and asked him to make the trip to Capharnaum and heal his sick son, who was at the point of death.

"Unless you see signs and miracles," Jesus said to him, "you will not believe!"

"Lord," he replied, "come down, or my boy will die!"

"Return home," said Jesus. "Your son is alive and well."

The man believed what Jesus said, and went back. On the way, he met his servants, who were coming to tell him that his son was alive and well. He asked them, therefore, at just what time the boy had taken a turn for the better. "Yesterday," they told him, "one hour after noon, the fever left him." And the father recognized that this was the exact hour when Jesus had told him, "Your son is alive and well." He became a believer, and his whole household with him.

OFFERTORY ANTIPHON *Ps. 136:1*

By the streams of Babylon we sat and wept when we remembered you, O Sion.

Prayer over the Offerings

Cæléstem nobis præbeant hæc mystéria, quæsumus, Dómine, medicínam: et vítia nostri cordis expúrgent. Per Dóminum.

May this mystery bring us a heavenly remedy, Lord, and purge our heart of its vices. This we ask of you through our Lord.

COMMUNION ANTIPHON *Ps. 118:49-50*

Remember your word to your servant, O Lord, since you have given me hope. This is my comfort in my affliction.

Prayer after the Communion

Ut sacris, Dómine, reddámur digni munéribus: fac nos, quæsumus, tuis semper obedíre mandátis. Per Dóminum.

To make us more worthy of taking part in the holy Mass, teach us, Lord, always to obey Your commandments. This we ask of you through our Lord.

TWENTY-FIRST SUNDAY AFTER PENTECOST

ENTRANCE ANTIPHON *Esther 13:9, 10-11; Ps. 118:1*

In your will are all things, O Lord, and there is none that can resist your will; for you have made all things, heaven and earth, and all things that are under the cope of heaven. You are Lord of all.

Ps. Happy are they whose way is blameless, who walk in the law of the Lord.

Glory be to the Father and to the Son and to the Holy Spirit. As it was in the beginning, is now and ever shall be, world without end. Amen. In your will . . .

Prayer over the Assembly

Famíliam tuam, quæsumus, Dómine, contínua pietáte custódi: ut a cunctis adversitátibus, te protegénte, sit líbera; et in bonis áctibus

We are your children, Lord; in your goodness preserve us always. Under your protection we shall be delivered from all evil and shall serve

tuo nómini sit devóta. Per Dóminum.

your glory by doing good. This we
ask of you through our Lord.

EPISTLE   Ephesians 6:10-17

*To prepare ourselves for God's judgment, we must carry on an unremit-
ting warfare against Satan. Only Christ can supply us with the arms we
need.*

A reading from the letter of the apostle Paul to the Christians of Ephesus
Brethren,

Draw your strength from the Lord, from the omnipotent strength that is
his. To stand fast against the devil's tricks, put on the armor of God. For
our real enemies are not human powers; they are the lords and rulers, the
masters of this dark world, the spirits of evil who infest our atmosphere.

Put on the armor of God, therefore, that you may stand fast in the evil
days and hold your ground securely.

On your feet, then! To protect yourself, take truth as your sword-belt,
justice as your breastplate, with your feet shod, ready to march for the
Gospel of peace. Always take faith in hand as your shield: it will quench
the fiery missiles of the evil one. For a helmet take your hope of salvation;
for a sword, that which the Holy Spirit provides for us, namely the word
of God.

Gradual Ps. 89:1-2

O Lord, you have been our refuge through all generations. Before
the mountains were begotten and the earth and the world were brought
forth, from everlasting to everlasting you are God.

Alleluia Ps. 113:1

Alleluia, alleluia. When Israel came forth from Egypt, the house of
Jacob from a people of alien tongue. Alleluia.

GOSPEL   Matthew 18:23-35

*To prepare ourselves for God's judgment, what we must do above all is
to forgive those who have offended us and thereby bring down the Lord's
mercy on ourselves.*

A reading from the holy Gospel according to Matthew

At that time, addressing his disciples, Jesus proposed this parable: "The
kingdom of heaven may be compared to a king who wanted to settle his
accounts with his officials. One of the first to appear before him was found
to be ten thousand talents [1] in his debt. As the official had no means of
paying the debt, the master ordered that he be sold, together with his wife,
his children and all his possessions, in compensation. Then this official,
falling on his knees at his master's feet, begged him, 'Grant me a postpone-

[1] About 12 million dollars.

ment, and I will pay you everything.' The king's heart was touched; he gave the man back his freedom and even forgave him his debt.

"Well, scarcely had this official left his master's presence when he met one of his fellow officials who owed him a hundred denarii.[1] He seized him by the throat started to choke him, saying, 'Pay what you owe!'

"The other official, falling at his feet, begged him, 'Grant me a postponement, and I will pay you everything.' But he would not hear of it; he had the man put into prison until the debt should be paid.

"This conduct made the king's other officials very indignant, and they told him about the affair. The king had the official recalled. 'Heartless servant,' he said, 'I made you a gift of the whole amount you owed me, on the basis of a simple appeal to my bounty. Should you not have had pity on your fellow servant, as I had pity on you?' And in his indignation the master turned him over to the torturers, until he should pay everything that he owed.

"That is how my Father in heaven will treat you if you do not forgive your brethren from the bottom of your heart."

OFFERTORY ANTIPHON *Job 1*

There was a man in the land of Hus, whose name was Job, simple, and upright, and fearing God, whom Satan besought that he might tempt; and power was given him from the Lord over his possessions and his flesh. And he destroyed all his substance and his children, and wounded his flesh also with a grievous ulcer.

Prayer over the Offerings

Súscipe, Dómine, propítius hóstias: quibus et te placári voluísti, et nobis salútem poténti pietáte restítui. Per Dóminum.

Receive favorably, Lord, the offerings of this Mass, which has to appease your justice; and, since you are so good and so powerful, may this Mass help us to save our souls. This we ask of you through our Lord.

COMMUNION ANTIPHON *Ps. 118:81, 84, 86*

My soul pines for your salvation; I hope in your word. When will you do judgment on my persecutors? The wicked persecuted me wrongfully; help me, O Lord my God!

Prayer after the Communion

Immortalitátis alimóniam consecúti, quǽsumus, Dómine: ut, quod ore percépimus, pura mente sectémur. Per Dóminum.

Nourished by the bread that gives immortality, may we keep in a pure soul, O Lord, the host that our lips have received. This we ask of you through our Lord.

---

[1] About 17 dollars.

TWENTY-SECOND SUNDAY AFTER PENTECOST

ENTRANCE ANTIPHON *Ps. 129:3-4, 1-2*

If you, O Lord, mark iniquities, Lord, who can stand? But with you is forgiveness, O God of Israel.

Ps. Out of the depths I cry to you, O Lord; Lord, hear my voice!

Glory be to the Father and to the Son and to the Holy Spirit. As it was in the beginning, is now and ever shall be, world without end. Amen. If you, O Lord . . .

Prayer over the Assembly

Deus, refúgium nostrum et virtus: adésto piis Ecclésiæ tuæ précibus, auctor ipse pietátis, et præsta; ut, quod fidéliter pétimus, efficáciter consequámur. Per Dóminum.

O God, our refuge and our strength, listen to your Church; with love she prays to you, and you are the one who can teach her to love. What we ask of you with loyal hearts, therefore, grant that we may obtain without fail. This we ask of you through our Lord.

EPISTLE   Philippians 1:6-11

It is not enough to wait for Christ's return if we want to be found without sin on judgment day. We must let charity grow in us.

A reading from the letter of the apostle Paul to the Christians of Philippi

Brethren,

The Lord has begun a good work in you; I am sure that he will continue bringing it to perfection until the day when Christ Jesus returns.

It is only right that I should have this confidence with regard to all of you. For I carry you in my heart, all of you who share the grace that has been given me, in this captivity as well as in my work of defending and confirming the Gospel. God knows that I love you all tenderly, with the heart of Christ Jesus himself!

What I ask him is that your charity grow more and more in knowledge and in perfect insight, that you may be able to discern what is best. Thus on the day when Christ returns, you will be found pure and without sin, and you will be filled with that holiness which is given us by Jesus Christ, to the glory and the praise of God.

Gradual Ps. 132:1-2

Behold how good it is, and how pleasant where brethren dwell as one! It is as when the precious ointment upon the head runs down over the beard, the beard of Aaron.

Alleluia Ps. 113:11

Alleluia, alleluia. Those who fear the Lord trust in the Lord; he is their help and their shield. Alleluia.

GOSPEL   Matthew 22:15-21

Christ establishes forcefully the fact that the Christian belongs both to the city of the earth and to the city of God. Our legitimate concern about the former should not make us forget the supremacy of the latter.

A reading from the holy Gospel according to Matthew

At that time the pharisees held a consultation to find a means of catching Jesus in a trap by leading him to make compromising statements.

They sent some of their disciples to him, therefore, with partisans of Herod. These emissaries addressed Jesus in these terms: "Master, we know that you speak the truth, and that you teach the ways of God in all sincerity, without letting yourself be influenced by anyone; for it matters little to you whether you please or displease men. Give us your opinion, therefore: Is it permissible to pay the tribute to Caesar, or should one refuse it?"

Knowing what their evil intention was, Jesus said to them, "Why are you setting a trap for me, hypocrites? Show me the money that is used to pay the tax." They brought him a denarius. "Whose image and inscription are these?" he asked.

"Caesar's," they said.

"Then give back to Caesar what belongs to Caesar, and to God what belongs to God."

OFFERTORY ANTIPHON *Esther 14:12, 13*

Remember me, O Lord, you who rule above all power: and give a well-ordered speech in my mouth, that my words may be pleasing in the sight of the prince.

Prayer over the Offerings

Da, miséricors Deus: ut hæc salutáris oblátio et a própriis nos reátibus indesinénter expédiat, et ab ómnibus tueátur advérsis. Per Dóminum.

God of mercy, grant that this Mass may keep us free from sin and protect us from all adversity. This we ask of you through our Lord.

COMMUNION ANTIPHON *Ps. 16:6*

I call upon you, for you will answer me, O God; incline your ear to me; hear my word.

Prayer after the Communion

Súmpsimus, Dómine, sacri dona mystérii, humíliter deprecántes: ut quæ in tui commemoratiónem nos fácere præcepísti, in nostræ profíciant infirmitátis auxílium: Qui vivis et regnas cum Deo Patre in unitáte Spíritus Sancti, Deus, per ómnia sǽcula sæculórum.

We have just received the sacred gift of your Eucharist; we entreat you humbly, Lord, that this sacrifice offered in memory of you may become a support for us in our weakness. This we ask of you, Lord Jesus, living and reigning with the Father in the unity of the Holy Spirit, God, forever.

TWENTY-THIRD SUNDAY AFTER PENTECOST

ENTRANCE ANTIPHON *Jer. 29:11, 12, 14; Ps. 84:2*

The Lord says: "I think thoughts of peace, and not of affliction. You shall call upon me, and I will hear you; and I will bring back your captivity from all places."

Ps. You have favored, O Lord, your land; you have restored the well-being of Jacob.

Glory be to the Father and to the Son and to the Holy Spirit. As it was in the beginning, is now and ever shall be, world without end. Amen. The Lord says . . .

Prayer over the Assembly

Absólve, quǽsumus, Dómine, tuórum delícta populórum: ut a peccatórum néxibus, quæ pro nostra fragilitáte contráximus, tua benignitáte liberémur. Per Dóminum.

O Lord, forgive the sins your children have committed by reason of their weakness; and may your kindness set us free from the bonds of sin. This we ask of you through our Lord.

EPISTLE   Philippians 3:17–4:3

It is Christ who saves men. But Christ continues his work through his apostles and his disciples. We also should labor to bring the Gospel to the world.

A reading from the letter of the apostle Paul to the Christians of Philippi

Brethren,

Imitate me, and notice those who follow my example.

For there are many — I have told you this often, but, I am sorry to say, I must tell you again today—there are many who behave like enemies of the Cross of Christ. They are heading for death: their god is their stomach. They are proud of that which should make them blush. Their taste is all for the things of earth.

But as for us, our proper environment is heaven. It is to heaven that we look for the return of our Savior, the Lord Jesus Christ, who will transform our wretched body even to the point of making it like his glorious body; for all things obey him, the all-powerful Master.

That is why you must stand fast in your fidelity to the Lord, my cherished brethren, my dearly beloved brethren, my pride and my joy.

I beg Evodia, I implore Syntyche to live on good terms with each other, in the Lord. And you, my loyal comrade, please help them; for they have done good work with me for the sake of the Gospel, as have Clement and my other companions whose names are inscribed in the book of life.

Gradual *Ps. 43:8-9*

You saved us, O Lord, from our foes, and those who hated us you put to shame. In God we gloried day by day; your name we praised always.

Alleluia Ps. 129:1-2

Alleluia, alleluia. Out of the depths I cry to you, O Lord; Lord, hear my prayer! Alleluia.

GOSPEL   Matthew 9:18-26

The sick woman, the dead girl, represent all mankind subjected to the powers of evil and of death. Christ brings life to mankind.

A reading from the holy Gospel according to Matthew

At that time Jesus was speaking to the crowd when the head of a synagogue approached and bowed low before him. "Lord," he said, "my daughter has just died; but come and lay your hand on her, and she will come to life." Jesus got up and followed him with his disciples.

Just then a woman who had been afflicted with hemorrhages for twelve years slipped up behind him and touched the edge of his cloak. She was saying to herself, "If I can only get to touch the edge of his cloak, I shall be cured!"

Turning and catching her in the act, Jesus said, "Take heart, my daughter, your faith has made you well!" And at that moment the woman was cured.

At length Jesus reached the house of the head of the synagogue. When he saw the flute players and the crowd who had already begun the usual lamentations, he gave them orders to leave. "The girl is not dead," he explained, "she has only fallen asleep." But they started to laugh at him.

When the crowd had finally been put out, he entered the room. He took the girl by the hand, and she got up.

This miracle caused a great stir throughout the region.

OFFERTORY ANTIPHON *Ps. 129:1-2*

Out of the depths I cry to you, O Lord; Lord, hear my prayer! Out of the depths I cry to you, O Lord.

Prayer over the Offerings

Pro nostræ servitútis augménto sacrifícium tibi, Dómine, laudis offérimus: ut, quod imméritis contulísti, propítius exsequáris. Per Dóminum.

Lord, in offering you this sacrifice of praise, we ask you to increase our priestly fervor. This office you conferred on us through no merit on our part; but in your goodness bring this grace to perfection, that it may bear its full fruits. This we ask of you through our Lord.

COMMUNION ANTIPHON *Mark 11:24*

Amen I say to you, all things whatever you ask for in prayer, believe that you shall receive, and it shall be done to you.

Prayer after the Communion

Quǽsumus, omnípotens Deus: ut, quos divína tríbuis participatióne gaudére, humánis non sinas subiacére perículis. Per Dóminum.	God all-powerful, you have given us the joy of sharing the bread of heaven; do not let us succumb to the evils of this earth. This we ask of you through our Lord.

THE LAST SUNDAYS AFTER PENTECOST

The Entrance Antiphon, Gradual, Alleluia, Offertory Antiphon, Communion Antiphon remain the same for the remaining Sundays after Pentecost. The text is as follows:

ENTRANCE ANTIPHON *Jer. 29:11, 12, 14; Ps. 84:2*

The Lord says: "I think thoughts of peace, and not of affliction. You shall call upon me, and I will hear you; and I will bring back your captivity from all places."

Ps. You have favored, O Lord, your land; you have restored the well-being of Jacob.

Glory be to the Father and to the Son and to the Holy Spirit. As it was in the beginning, is now and ever shall be, world without end. Amen. The Lord says . . .

AFTER THE EPISTLE

Gradual Ps. 43:8-9

You saved us, O Lord, from our foes, and those who hated us you put to shame. In God we gloried day by day; your name we praised always.

Alleluia Ps. 129:1-2

Alleluia, alleluia. Out of the depths I cry to you, O Lord; Lord, hear my prayer! Alleluia.

OFFERTORY ANTIPHON *Ps. 129:1-2*

Out of the depths I cry to you, O Lord; Lord, hear my prayer! Out of the depths I cry to you, O Lord.

COMMUNION ANTIPHON *Mark 11:24*

Amen I say to you, all things whatever you ask for in prayer, believe that you shall receive, and it shall be done to you.

If there are exactly 24 Sundays after Pentecost, the Mass for the 24th Sunday is that of the Last Sunday after Pentecost given below. This formulary is always used on the final Sunday of the Pentecost season, the Sunday immediately preceding the first Sunday of Advent.

If there are more than 24 Sundays in the Pentecost season, the Masses used between the twenty-third and final Sunday of the season are as follows, excluding the parts printed above:

if 25, the 24th is that of the 6th Sunday after Epiphany, page 54.

if 26, the 24th is that of the 5th Sunday after Epiphany, page 52.
the 25th is that of the 6th Sunday after Epiphany, page 54.

if 27, the 24th is that of the 4th Sunday after Epiphany, page 50.
the 25th is that of the 5th Sunday after Epiphany, page 52.
the 26th is that of the 6th Sunday after Epiphany, page 54.

if 28, the 24th is the feast of Christ the King
the 25th is that of the 4th Sunday after Epiphany, page 50.
the 26th is that of the 5th Sunday after Epiphany, page 52.
the 27th is that of the 6th Sunday after Epiphany, page 54.

LAST SUNDAY AFTER PENTECOST

ENTRANCE ANTIPHON *Jer. 29:11, 12, 14; Ps. 84:2*

The Lord says: "I think thoughts of peace, and not of affliction. You shall call upon me, and I will hear you; and I will bring back your captivity from all places."

Ps. You have favored, O Lord, your land; you have restored the well-being of Jacob.

Glory be to the Father and to the Son and to the Holy Spirit. As it was in the beginning, is now, and ever shall be, world without end. Amen. The Lord says . . .

Prayer over the Assembly

Excita, quæsumus, Dómine, tuórum fidélium voluntátes: ut, divíni óperis fructum propénsius exsequéntes; pietátis tuæ remédia maióra percípiant. Per Dóminum.

Incite the wills of those who believe in you, Lord! As they work harder to make their corner of the divine vineyard more fruitful, may they obtain greater proofs of your healing mercy. This we ask of you through our Lord.

EPISTLE　　　　　　　　　　　　　　　Colossians 1:9-14

The Christian should live in hope. He is waiting for Christ's kingdom to be established in glory. But he knows that he has already been introduced into that kingdom. He lives, therefore, "in patience, courage and joy."

A reading from the letter of the apostle Paul to the Christians of Colossae

Brethren,

We never stop praying for you, that God may let you understand his will perfectly, and that he may give you in abundance the spirit of wisdom and of understanding. Thus you will be able to lead a life worthy of the Lord and to please him in all things.

May he cause you to perform good works of all kinds and to increase in the knowledge of God! Strengthened in every way by his glorious power, you will live lives of patience and courage.

With joy you will give thanks to the Father, who has enabled us to share the lot of the saints in the kingdom of light, who has rescued us from the [devil], prince of darkness, to transport us into the kingdom of his beloved Son, whose blood redeems us and cleanses us of our sins.

Gradual *Ps. 43:8-9*

You saved us, O Lord, from our foes, and those who hated us you put to shame. In God we gloried day by day; your name we praised always.

Alleluia *Ps. 129:1-2*

Alleluia, alleluia. Out of the depths I cry to you, O Lord; Lord, hear my prayer! Alleluia.

GOSPEL   Matthew 24:15-35

In biblical language, which Jesus uses in this discourse, God's "judgments" designate the interventions of the Lord in history. The destruction of Jerusalem was one of those judgments; it put an end to the privileged role of the people of Israel. The end of the world will be the supreme intervention of God in history: it will mark the end of the Church's earthly mission.

A reading from the holy Gospel according to Matthew

At that time Jesus said to his disciples, "When you see 'the abomination of desolation,' [1] which the prophet Daniel foretold, installed in the holy place — let him who knows the Scripture understand! — then those who are in Judea should flee to the mountains, he who is on the roof should not go down into the house to get anything, he who is in the fields should not go back to get his cloak. How unhappy it will be for women who are pregnant or nursing in those days! Pray that your flight may not take place in winter or on the sabbath.

"For at that time a great catastrophe will occur, such as has not occurred since the beginning of the world and will not happen again. And if those days were not to be cut short, no one's life would be safe; but for the sake of the elect those days will be cut short. Then if anyone tells you, 'Here is the Messiah' or 'There he is,' do not believe him. For false messiahs and false prophets will make their appearance; they will produce false miracles and great prodigies, capable of deceiving even the elect, if that were possible. See, I have forewarned you!

"If anyone says to you, therefore, 'Look, the Messiah is in the desert,'

[1] This expression indicates a terrifying and sacrilegious act. The perspectives of the two "judgments" are continually mixed: the destruction of Jerusalem is the prophetic announcement of the last judgment.

do not go out. If anyone says, 'Look, he is hiding in the caves,' do not believe it. For, sudden and swift as the lightning which starts in the east and flashes across to the west, so will the coming of the Son of Man be. 'Where the corpse is [says the proverb], there will the vultures gather.' [1]

"Immediately after the catastrophe of those days, the sun will be obscured, the moon will no longer give her light, the stars will fall from the sky, the heavenly bodies will be shaken. Then the sign of the Son of Man will appear in the sky; then all the nations of the earth will beat their breast, and they will see the Son of Man coming on the clouds of the sky, in the glory of his power and his majesty. He will send his angels, and their trumpet blast will summon the elect from all directions, from one end of the heavens to the other.

"Let a comparison borrowed from the fig tree teach you a lesson. When its branches have become more tender and put forth leaves, you know that summer is near. In the same way, when you see all these signs, know that HE is near, at your door.

"It is a solemn truth that I tell you: this generation shall not pass till all these things have happened. The sky and the earth will pass away, but my words shall not." [2]

OFFERTORY ANTIPHON *Ps. 129:1-2*

Out of the depths I cry to you, O Lord; Lord, hear my prayer! Out of the depths I cry to you, O Lord.

Prayer over the Offerings

Propítius esto, Dómine, supplicatiónibus nostris: et pópuli tui oblatiónibus, precibúsque suscéptis, ómnium nostrum ad te corda convérte; ut a terrénis cupiditátibus liberáti, ad cæléstia desidéria transeámus. Per Dóminum.

In your kindness, Lord, accept our prayers and our offerings; turn the hearts of all of us toward yourself, that we may be delivered from material desires and turn to the heavenly instead. This we ask of you through our Lord.

COMMUNION ANTIPHON *Mark 11:24*

Amen I say to you, all things whatever you ask for in prayer, believe that you shall receive, and it shall be done to you.

Prayer after the Communion

Concéde nobis, quǽsumus, Dómine: ut per hæc sacraménta quæ súmpsimus, quidquid in nostra mente vitiósum est, ipsórum medicatiónis dono curétur. Per Dóminum.

Lord, by the grace of the sacrament we have just received, heal whatever is wrong in our souls. This we ask of you through our Lord.

---

[1] Where the Son of Man appears, the elect will immediately be gathered.

[2] "As to that day and hour, no one knows it, not even the angels in heaven, not even the Son; only the Father knows" (*ibid.*, v. 36).

PROPER OF THE SAINTS

THE IMMACULATE CONCEPTION OF THE
BLESSED VIRGIN MARY

ENTRANCE ANTIPHON *Is. 61:10; Ps. 29:2*

I will heartily rejoice in the Lord, in my God is the joy of my soul; for he has clothed me with a robe of salvation, and wrapped me in a mantle of justice, like a bride bedecked with her jewels.

Ps. I will extol you O Lord, for you drew me clear and did not let my enemies rejoice over me.

Glory be to the Father and to the Son and to the Holy Spirit. As it was in the beginning, is now and ever shall be, world without end. Amen. I will . . .

Prayer over the Assembly

Deus, qui per immaculátam Vírginis Conceptiónem dignum Fílio tuo habitáculum præparásti: quæsumus; ut, qui ex morte eiúsdem Fílii tui prævísa eam ab omni labe præservásti, nos quoque mundos eius intercessióne ad te perveníre concédas. Per eúndem Dóminum nostrum Iesum Christum Fílium tuum, qui tecum vivit et regnat in unitáte Spíritus Sancti, Deus, per ómnia sǽcula sæculórum.

Through the Immaculate Conception of the Virgin, O Lord, you prepared a worthy dwelling-place for your Son; you preserved the Virgin from all stain by letting her benefit in advance from the sacrifice of the Cross. We entreat you: may her intercession purify our souls and help us to come into your presence. This we ask of you through the same Jesus Christ, our Lord and your Son, who lives and reigns with you in the unity of the Holy Spirit, God, forever.

EPISTLE   Proverbs 8:22-35

This text can be understood in two ways. It designates directly the Wisdom of God, that eternal Word which presided at the creation of the world and which, out of love for men, was to become flesh within the Virgin Mary.

In an allegorical sense, it can be understood of Mary herself, of whom God has been thinking from all eternity and whose perfect holiness is the Father's joy.

A reading from the book of Wisdom

The Lord was thinking of me even as he began his work, from the very start, before he made anything at all. He was thinking of me from all eternity, long before the world existed. Before boundless space was created, his mind had conceived me.

The fountains had not gushed forth, the huge mass of the mountains had not yet risen up, the hills had not been born, when I already existed in him; he had not yet made the earth, or the rivers, or the first elements of the globe.

I was there when he flung out the vault of the skies, when he encircled the universe, when he gave the clouds their place and opened the fountains, when he marked out the limits of the sea and gave orders to the waters not to overflow their banks; I was there when he laid the foundations of the earth.

I was at his side in all his work, enjoying myself day after day, playing always in his presence, playing in the whole creation; and it was my joy to be with the children of men.

And now, children, listen to me; if you want true happiness, follow my path; listen to my counsels if you would be filled with wisdom; do not reject them!

Happy is the man who listens to me and who watches, day by day, before my door! In finding me he has found life; from this well, he will draw the salvation that comes to us from the Lord.

Gradual *Judith 13:23; 15:10*

Blessed are you, O Virgin Mary, by the Lord the most high God, above all women upon the earth. You are the glory of Jerusalem, you are the joy of Israel, you are the honor of our people.

Alleluia *Cant. 4:7*

Alleluia, alleluia. You are all-beautiful, O Mary, and there is in you no stain of original sin. Alleluia.

GOSPEL Luke 1:26-28

Gabriel's greeting to Mary, "You are full of grace," reveals the privilege of her immaculate conception.

A reading from the holy Gospel according to Luke

At that time the angel Gabriel was sent by God into a town of Galilee, called Nazareth, to a virgin engaged to a man of the house of David, called Joseph. The name of the virgin was Mary.

The angel entered her home and said to her, "I greet you, who are full of grace; the Lord is with you; you are blessed among all women."

OFFERTORY ANTIPHON *Luke 1:28*

Hail, Mary, full of grace, the Lord is with you; blessed are you among women, alleluia.

Prayer over the Offerings

Salutárem hóstiam, quam in solemnitáte immaculátæ Conceptiónis beátæ Vírginis Maríæ tibi, Dómine, offérimus, súscipe et præsta: ut, sicut illam tua grátia prævéniénte ab omni labe immúnem profitémur; ita eius intercessióne a culpis ómnibus liberémur. Per Dóminum.

For our salvation, Lord, we offer you this victim on the feast of the Immaculate Conception of the Blessed Virgin Mary. We believe that even before the sacrifice of your Son your grace preserved her from all stain; may her prayers deliver us from all sin. This we ask of you through our Lord.

COMMUNION ANTIPHON

Glorious things are said of you, O Mary, because he who is mighty has done great things for you.

Prayer after the Communion

Sacraménta quæ súmpsimus, Dómine Deus noster: illíus in nobis culpæ vúlnera réparent; a qua immaculátam beátæ Maríæ Conceptiónem singuláriter præservásti. Per Dóminum.

May this communion, Lord, our God, heal the wound made in us by original sin, from which, by a unique privilege, you preserved the immaculate Virgin. This we ask of you through our Lord.

DECEMBER 26

COMMEMORATION OF ST. STEPHEN, PROTOMARTYR

Prayer over the Assembly

Da nobis, quǽsumus, Dómine, imitári quod cólimus: ut discámus et inimícos dilígere; quia eius natalítia celebrámus, qui novit étiam pro persecutóribus exoráre Dóminum nostrum Iesum Christum, Fílium tuum: Qui tecum vivit et regnat in unitáte Spíritus Sancti, Deus, per ómnia sǽcula sæculórum.

Give us the grace, Lord, to imitate St. Stephen, whom we are honoring. We shall learn to love even our enemies as we celebrate the birth into heaven of him who was even willing to plead for his persecutors with Christ Jesus, your Son and our Lord, who lives and reigns with you in the unity of the Holy Spirit, God, forever.

Prayer over the Offerings

Súscipe, Dómine, múnera pro tuórum commemoratióne Sanctórum: ut, sicut illos pássio gloriósos effécit; ita nos devótio reddat innócuos. Per Dóminum.

Receive our offerings, Lord, in memory of your saints. Just as they won the crown of glory by uniting themselves through their martyrdom to Christ's passion, may we regain our innocence by participating in his sacrifice. This we ask of you through our Lord.

Prayer after the Communion

Auxiliéntur nobis, Dómine, sumpta mystéria: et, intercedénte beáto Stéphano Mártyre tuo, sempitérna protectióne confírment. Per Dóminum.

May our communion be helpful to us, Lord, and, by the intercession of your martyr St. Stephen, may it keep us always under your protection. This we ask of you through our Lord.

DECEMBER 27

COMMEMORATION OF ST. JOHN, APOSTLE AND EVANGELIST

Prayer over the Assembly

Ecclésiam tuam, Dómine, benígnus illústra: ut, beáti Ioánnis Apóstoli tui et Evangelístæ illumináta doctrínis, ad dona pervéniat sempitérna. Per Dóminum.

Lord, in your goodness enlighten your Church: in the light of the teachings of St. John the evangelist, your apostle, may she come into possession of the everlasting treasures. This we ask of you through our Lord.

Prayer over the Offerings

Súscipe, Dómine, múnera, quæ in eius tibi solemnitáte deférimus, cuius nos confídimus patrocínio liberári. Per Dóminum.

Receive our offerings, Lord; in presenting them to you, we celebrate the feast of the holy apostle to whom we confidently look for protection and deliverance. This we ask of you through our Lord.

Prayer after the Communion

Refécti cibo potúque cælésti, Deus noster, te súpplices deprecámur: ut, in cuius hæc commemoratióne percépimus, eius muniámur et précibus. Per Dóminum.

Strengthened by the nourishment of the Eucharist, we entreat you, our God: may this communion on the feast day of your apostle win for us the protection of his prayers. This we ask of you through our Lord.

DECEMBER 28

COMMEMORATION OF THE HOLY INNOCENTS, MARTYRS

Prayer over the Assembly

Deus, cuius hodiérna die præcónium Innocéntes Mártyres non loquéndo, sed moriéndo conféssi

Lord our God, the Holy Innocents, martyrs, did not proclaim your glory in words, but only bore witness to it

sunt: ómnia in nobis vitiórum mala mortífica; ut fidem tuam, quam lingua nostra lóquitur, étiam móribus vita fateátur. Per Dóminum.

by their death. Put to death the wickedness of sin in us: may the Christian faith which we express in words be revealed also in the virtuous character of our lives. This we ask of you through our Lord.

Prayer over the Offerings

Sanctórum tuórum, Dómine, nobis pia non desit orátio: quæ et múnera nostra concíliet, et tuam nobis indulgéntiam semper obtíneat. Per Dóminum.

Lord, may the fervent prayer of your saints never fail us; may it make our offerings acceptable to you and always obtain your pardon for us. This we ask of you through our Lord.

Prayer after the Communion

Votíva, Dómine, dona percépimus: quæ Sanctórum nobis précibus, et præséntis, quæsumus, vitæ páriter et ætérnæ tríbue conférre subsídium. Per Dóminum.

May this communion, Lord, obtain for us, through the prayers of your saints, the help necessary for our present life as well as for life eternal. This we ask of you through our Lord.

FEBRUARY 2

THE FEAST OF THE PURIFICATION OF THE BLESSED VIRGIN MARY

AT THE BLESSING OF THE CANDLES

Priest: Dóminus vobíscum.   The Lord be with you.
All: Et cum spíritu tuo.   And with your spirit.

The celebrant will select one of the following five prayers:

Prayer

Orémus. Dómine sancte, Pater omnípotens, ætérne Deus, qui ómnia ex níhilo creásti, et iussu tuo per ópera apum, hunc liquórem ad perfectiónem cérei veníre fecísti: et qui hodiérna die petitiónem iusti Simeónis implésti: te humíliter deprecámur; ut has candélas ad usus hóminum, et sanitátem córporum et animárum, sive in terra, sive in aquis, per invocatiónem tui sanctíssimi nóminis, et per intercessiónem beátæ Maríæ semper Vírginis, cuius hódie festa devóte

Let us pray. Lord, holy Father, God eternal and all-powerful, you created the world out of nothing; you ordered the bees to transform the perfumes of the flowers into wax; and on this day you fulfilled the good Simeon's desires by showing him your Son. We humbly beseech you, by our invocation of your most holy name, by the intercession of the Blessed Virgin Mary, whose feast we celebrate today, and by the prayers of all your saints, to ✠ bless and ✠ sanctify these candles, that they may obtain for us

celebrántur, et per preces ómnium Sanctórum tuórum, bene ✠ dícere, et sancti ✠ ficáre dignéris: et huius plebis tuæ, quæ illas honorífice in mánibus desíderat portáre, teque cantándo laudáre, exáudias voces de cælo sancto tuo, et de sede maiestátis tuæ: et propítius sis ómnibus clamántibus ad te, quos redemísti pretióso sánguine Fílii tui: Qui tecum vivit et regnat in sǽcula sæculórum. ℟. Amen.

health of body and of soul, on land and on sea. Your people desire to carry them reverently in their hands and to sing your praises. From heaven, where your majesty is enthroned, hear our voices and bestow your fatherly blessing on all these prayerful Christians, whom you have redeemed by the precious Blood of your Son, who lives and reigns with you forever. ℟. Amen.

Prayer

Orémus. Omnípotens sempitérne Deus, qui hodiérna die Unigénitum tuum ulnis sancti Simeónis in templo sancto tuo suscipiéndum præsentásti: tuam súpplices deprecámur clementiam; ut has candélas, quas nos fámuli tui, in tui nóminis magnificéntiam suscipiéntes, gestáre cúpimus luce accénsas, bene ✠ dícere, et sancti ✠ ficáre, atque lúmine supérnæ benedictiónis accéndere dignéris: quátenus eas tibi Dómino Deo nostro offeréndo digni, et sancto igne dulcíssimæ caritátis tuæ succénsi, in templo sancto glóriæ tuæ repræsentári mereámur. Per eúndem Christum Dóminum nostrum. ℟. Amen.

Let us pray. All-powerful, eternal God, you had your Son brought to the temple on this day that Simeon might receive him into his arms. We, your servants, are about to receive these candles and carry them, lighted, for the glory of your name. We entreat you, therefore, in your goodness to ✠ bless them, ✠ sanctify them and light them with the light of your heavenly blessing. Then, when we offer them to you, we shall burn with the fire of your love and we too shall deserve to be presented to you in the holy temple of your heavenly glory. Through the same Christ our Lord. ℟. Amen.

Prayer

Orémus. Dómine Iesu Christe, lux vera, quæ illúminas omnem hóminem veniéntem in hunc mundum: effúnde bene ✠ dictiónem tuam super hos céreos, et sanctí ✠ fica eos lúmine grátiæ tuæ, et concéde propítius; ut, sicut hæc lumináría igne visíbili accénsa noctúrnas depéllunt ténebras; ita corda nostra invisíbili igne, id est, Sancti Spíritus splendóre illustráta ómnium vitiórum cæcitáte cáreant: ut,

Let us pray. Lord Jesus Christ, you are the true light who enlightens every man that comes into this world. Pour out your ✠ blessing, therefore, on these candles, sanctify ✠ them by the light of your grace and answer our prayer. Our candles, which burn with a visible flame, dispel the darkness of the night. Like them, may our hearts, illumined by invisible fire, the splendor of the Holy Spirit, be freed of the vices that blind them! With the

purgáto mentis óculo, ea cérnere possímus, quæ tibi sunt plácita, et nostræ salúti utília; quátenus post huius sǽculi caliginósa discrímina, ad lucem indeficiéntem perveníre mereámur. Per te, Christe Iesu, Salvátor mundi, qui in Trinitáte perfécta vivis et regnas Deus, in sǽcula sæculórum. ℟. Amen.

eyes of our soul purified, we shall see clearly what is pleasing to you and what is useful for our salvation. Thus, after the dangerous obscurities of this life, we shall deserve to enter into the eternal light of your heaven. Through you, Christ Jesus, Savior of the world, who live and reign in the perfect Trinity, God, forever. ℟. Amen.

Prayer

Orémus. Omnípotens sempitérne Deus, qui per Móysen fámulum tuum puríssimum ólei liquórem ad luminária ante conspéctum tuum iúgiter concinnánda præparári iussísti: bene ✠ dictiónis tuæ grátiam super hos céreos benígnus infúnde; quátenus sic adminístrent lumen extérius, ut, te donánte, lumen Spíritus tui nostris non desit méntibus intérius. Per Christum Dóminum nostrum. ℟. Amen.

Let us pray. All-powerful, eternal God, you ordered Moses to supply with purest oil the lamps that burned continually before your altar. Bless ✠ our candles, therefore; and, while they give light for our eyes, the Holy Spirit will let his light shine in our souls. Through Christ our Lord. ℟. Amen.

Prayer

Orémus. Dómine Iesu Christe, qui hodiérna die in nostræ carnis substántia inter hómines appárens, a paréntibus in templo es præsentátus: quem Símeon venerábilis senex, lúmine Spíritus tui irradiátus, agnóvit, suscépit, et benedíxit: præsta propítius; ut eiúsdem Spíritus Sancti grátia illumináti, atque edócti, te veráciter agnoscámus, et fidéliter diligámus: Qui vivis et regnas in sǽcula sæculórum. ℟. Amen.

Let us pray. Lord Jesus Christ, on this day when your parents presented you in the temple, you showed yourself to men with your human nature; and the venerable old man, Simeon, enlightened by your Spirit, recognized you, received you and blessed you. Enlighten our hearts and our minds also, that we may know you truly and love you faithfully, you who live and reign forever. ℟. Amen.

During the distribution of the blessed candles the following antiphon is sung to the verses of the Canticle of Simeon (Luke 2:29-32). The melody here given is one of several that may be used:

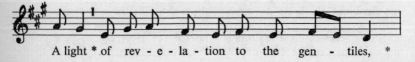

A light * of rev - e - la - tion to the gen - tiles, *

and a glo - ry for your peo - ple Is - ra - el.

Now you dis - miss your serv - ant, O Lord, *

ac - cord - ing to your word, in peace.

Repeat A light.
Because my EYES have seen * *your* salvation.
Repeat A light.
Which you HAVE prepared * before the face *of* all peoples.
Repeat A light.
Glory be to the Father and TO the Son * and to the *Ho*-ly Spirit.
Repeat A light.
As it was in the beginning, is now and ever SHALL be, * world with-*out* end. Amen.
Repeat A light.

Priest: **Dóminus vobíscum.**
All: **Et cum spíritu tuo.**
Priest: **Orémus. Exáudi, quǽsumus, Dómine, plebem tuam: et, quæ extrínsecus ánnua tríbuis devotióne venerári, intérius ássequi grátiæ tuæ luce concéde. Per Christum Dóminum nostrum.**
All: **Amen.**

The Lord be with you.
And with your spirit.
Let us pray. Be pleased, O Lord, to listen to your people; and, by the light of your grace, grant that we may understand inwardly the mystery which we celebrate every year with devotion. Through Christ our Lord.
Amen.

Then the deacon (or celebrant) intones the following versicle; all respond, and the procession begins.

Pro - ce - da - mus in pa - ce.
Let us go for-ward in peace.

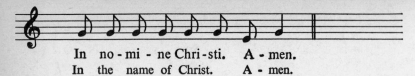

In no - mi - ne Chri - sti. A - men.
In the name of Christ. A - men.

During the procession, the following two antiphons are sung:

ANTIPHON I

Adorn your bridal chamber, Sion, and welcome Christ the King; embrace Mary, who is the gate of heaven, for she carries the glorious King of the new light. She remains a virgin, bearing in her hands the Son begotten before the day-star. Holding him in his arms, Simeon proclaimed to the peoples, "He is the Lord of life and death and the Savior of the world."

ANTIPHON II *Luke 2:26, 27, 28-29*

It had been revealed to Simeon by the Holy Spirit that he should not see death before he had seen the Christ of the Lord, and when they brought the child into the temple, he received him into his arms and blessed God, saying: "Now you dismiss your servant, O Lord, in peace." When his parents brought in the child Jesus, to do for him according to the custom of the Law, he received him into his arms.

When the procession re-enters the church, the following response is sung:

They offered for him to the Lord a pair of turtledoves or two young pigeons, as it is written in the law of the Lord. After the days of Mary's purification were fulfilled, according to the law of Moses, they took Jesus up to Jerusalem to present him to the Lord. As it is written in the law of the Lord. Glory be to the Father, and to the Son, and to the Holy Spirit. As it is written in the law of the Lord.

THE MASS

ENTRANCE ANTIPHON *Ps. 47:10-11, 2*

O God, we ponder your kindness within your temple. As your name, O God, so also your praise reaches to the ends of the earth. Of justice your right hand is full.

Ps. Great is the Lord, and wholly to be praised in the city of our God, his holy mountain.

Glory be to the Father and to the Son and to the Holy Spirit. As it was in the beginning, is now and ever shall be, world without end. Amen. O God . . .

Prayer over the Assembly

Omnípotens sempitérne Deus, maiestátem tuam súpplices exorámus: ut, sicut unigénitus Fílius tuus hodiérna die cum nostræ carnis substántia in templo est præsentátus; ita nos fácias purificátis tibi méntibus præsentári. Per eúndem Dóminum nostrum Iesum Christum Fílium tuum, qui tecum vivit et regnat in unitáte Spíritus Sancti, Deus, per ómnia sǽcula sæculórum.

All-powerful, eternal God, we humbly implore your majesty: your only-begotten Son, clothed in our flesh, was presented to you on this day in the temple; grant that we may likewise be presented to you with purified souls. This we ask of you through the same Jesus Christ, our Lord and your Son, who lives and reigns with you in the unity of the Holy Spirit, God, forever.

EPISTLE
Malachi 3:1-4

The last of the prophets, Malachi, had emphasized the priestly role of the Messiah. Christ, by his total love of the Father and his complete obedience to the Father's will, does away with any further need for the blood of victims on the altars of the temple. Through the eucharistic rite the Church will continue to offer a spiritual sacrifice: the unique love of the Son for the Father.

A reading from the book of the prophet Malachi

Word of the Lord God: "Behold, I am sending my messenger to prepare the way for me. And suddenly into his temple will come the Lord for whom you are looking, the messenger of the covenant whom you desire."

"See, he is coming," says the Lord all-powerful. "Who will be able to endure the day of his coming, and who will be able to remain standing before his face? Like the refiner's fire [which purifies the gold], like the lye that bleaches [the linens], he will consume every impurity. He will sit refining and purifying silver, he will purify the priests of the temple and make them as pure as gold and silver. Then they will be able to present to the Lord a holy offering. And the offering of Juda and of Jerusalem will be pleasing to the Lord, as it was in the early days, as it was in ancient times." Word of the Lord all-powerful.

After Septuagesima Sunday, the Alleluia *with its verse is omitted and the Tract is said.*

Gradual *Ps. 47:10-11, 9*

O God, we ponder your kindness within your temple. As your name, O God, so also your praise reaches to the ends of the earth. As we have heard, so have we seen, in the city of our God, in his holy mountain.

Alleluia

Alleluia, alleluia. The old man carried the Child: but the Child governed the old man. Alleluia.

Tract Luke 2:29-32

Now you dismiss your servant, O Lord, according to your word, in peace, because my eyes have seen your salvation which you have prepared before the face of all peoples, a light of revelation to the Gentiles, and a glory for your people Israel.

GOSPEL   Luke 2:22-32

The Gospel simply reports the historical event, the mystery of which is unfolded by this whole feast.

A reading from the holy Gospel according to Luke

At that time, when the [forty] days prescribed by the law of Moses for purification were over, Mary and Joseph carried the child Jesus to Jerusalem to present him to the Lord — complying with what is written in the law of the Lord: "Every first-born boy shall be consecrated to the Lord" — and to offer in sacrifice — according to a further prescription of the law of the Lord — a pair of turtle doves or two young pigeons.

Now there was living in Jerusalem a man named Simeon, who was observing the law of the Lord with precision and with fervor and was awaiting the consolation of Israel. The Holy Spirit rested on him; and it had even been revealed to him by the Holy Spirit that he would not see death until he had looked upon the Messiah of the Lord. He came to the temple, prompted by the Spirit, just when Mary and Joseph, carrying the child Jesus, were coming to fulfill what the law prescribed with regard to him; he received him into his arms and blessed God with these words:

"Now, O sovereign Master,
you may let your servant go
in peace, according to your word;
for my eyes have seen your salvation,
which you are preparing in the sight of all the peoples;
a light to enlighten the pagans
and the glory of Israel, your people!"

OFFERTORY ANTIPHON *Ps. 44:3*

Grace is poured out upon your lips; thus God has blessed you forever and ever.

Prayer over the Offerings

Exáudi, Dómine, preces nostras: et, ut digna sint múnera, quæ óculis tuæ maiestátis offérimus, subsídium nobis tuæ pietátis impénde. Per Dóminum.

Lord, hear our prayers! We should like to present offerings that are worthy of you; grant us the aid of your fatherly goodness. This we ask of you through our Lord.

COMMUNION ANTIPHON *Luke 2:26*

It was revealed to Simeon by the Holy Spirit that he should not see death before he had seen the Christ of the Lord.

Prayer after the Communion

Quǽsumus, Dómine Deus noster: ut sacrosáncta mystéria, quæ pro reparatiónis nostræ munímine contulísti, intercedénte beáta María semper Vírgine, et præsens nobis remédium esse fácias, et futúrum. Per Dóminum.

Lord, our God, to ensure our salvation you have us participate in your holy mysteries. Through the intercession of the blessed Mary, ever virgin, make them beneficial for our present life and for the life to come. This we ask of you through our Lord.

FEBRUARY 22

COMMEMORATION OF THE CHAIR OF ST. PETER, APOSTLE

Prayer over the Assembly

Deus, qui beáto Petro Apóstolo tuo, collátis clávibus regni cæléstis, ligándi atque solvéndi pontifícium tradidísti: concéde; ut, intercessiónis eius auxílio, a peccatórum nostrórum néxibus liberémur.

O Lord, you entrusted to your apostle St. Peter the keys of the kingdom of heaven and the pontifical power of binding and loosing. Grant that by his prayers we may be freed from the bonds of our sins.

A commemoration is made of St. Paul, Apostle, by means of prayer under a single conclusion.

Deus, qui multitúdinem géntium beáti Pauli Apóstoli prædicatióne docuísti: da nobis, quǽsumus; ut, cuius commemoratiónem cólimus, eius apud te patrocínia sentiámus. Per Dóminum.

O Lord, you instructed the pagan world through the preaching of the apostle St. Paul. We honor his memory today; make us feel his protection. This we ask of you through our Lord.

Prayer over the Offerings

Ecclésiæ tuæ, quǽsumus, Dómine, preces et hóstias beáti Petri Apóstoli comméndet orátio: ut, quod pro illíus glória celebrámus, nobis prosit ad véniam.

Lord, may the prayer of your apostle St. Peter commend to you the entreaties and the offerings of your Church, and this sacrifice celebrated in his honor will win forgiveness for us.

A commemoration is made of St. Paul, Apostle, by means of prayer under a single conclusion.

Apóstoli tui Pauli précibus, Dómine, plebis tuæ dona sanctífica: ut, quæ tibi tuo grata sunt institúto,

Through the prayer of your apostle St. Paul sanctify the offerings of your people, Lord; and this sacrifice,

gratióra fiant patrocínio supplicántis. Per Dóminum.

which pleases you because you instituted it, will be more pleasing to you as presented by St. Paul when he intercedes for us. This we ask of you through our Lord.

Prayer after the Communion

Lætíficet nos, Dómine, munus oblátum: ut, sicut in Apóstolo tuo Petro te mirábilem prædicámus; sic per illum tuæ sumámus indulgéntiæ largitátem.

Lord, may the offering of this sacrifice fill us with joy! We proclaim that you have worked great wonders in your apostle St. Peter; may we obtain through him, therefore, the generous gift of your forgiveness.

A commemoration is made of St. Paul, Apostle, by means of prayer under a single conclusion.

Sanctificáti, Dómine, salutári mystério: quæsumus; ut nobis eius non desit orátio, cuius nos donásti patrocínio gubernári. Per Dóminum.

We have been sanctified, Lord, by your redemptive mystery. You have given us St. Paul to guide us and protect us; may his prayer never fail us. This we ask of you through our Lord.

February 24 or 25 in Leap Year

COMMEMORATION OF ST. MATTHIAS, APOSTLE

Prayer over the Assembly

Deus, qui beátum Matthíam Apostolórum tuórum collégio sociásti: tríbue, quæsumus; ut, eius interventióne, tuæ circa nos pietátis semper víscera sentiámus. Per Dóminum.

Lord, you added St. Matthias to the company of your apostles. Grant that we, thanks to his prayer, may feel ourselves surrounded always by the kind attentions of your fatherly concern. This we ask of you through our Lord.

Prayer over the Offerings

Hóstias tibi, Dómine, quas nómini tuo sacrándas offérimus, sancti Matthíæ Apóstoli tui prosequátur orátio: per quam nos expiári fácias, et deféndi. Per Dóminum.

Lord, may the prayer of the apostle Matthias accompany the offerings which are to be consecrated to your glory. May his intercession purify us and protect us. This we ask of you through our Lord.

Prayer after the Communion

Præsta, quæsumus, omnípotens Deus: ut per hæc sancta, quæ

God all-powerful, we have just received your holy mysteries. Through

súmpsimus, interveniénte beáto Matthía Apóstolo tuo, véniam consequámur, et pacem. Per Dóminum.

the prayers of your apostle St. Matthias, may they obtain forgiveness and peace for us. This we ask of you through our Lord.

APRIL 25

COMMEMORATION OF ST. MARK, EVANGELIST

Prayer over the Assembly

Deus, qui beátum Marcum Evangelístam tuum evangélicæ prædicatiónis grátia sublimásti: tríbue, quǽsumus; eius nos semper et eruditióne profícere, et oratióne deféndi. Per Dóminum.

To St. Mark, your evangelist, you have given the honor and the grace, O Lord, of preaching the Gospel. Grant that we may always be instructed by his teaching and protected by his prayers. This we ask of you through our Lord.

Prayer over the Offerings

Beáti Marci Evangelístæ tui solemnitáte, tibi múnera deferéntes, quǽsumus, Dómine: ut, sicut illum prædicátio evangélica fecit gloriósum; ita nos eius intercéssio et verbo, et ópere tibi reddat accéptos. Per Dóminum.

On this solemnity of your evangelist St. Mark, we bring you our offerings, Lord. His preaching of the Gospel earned glory for him; may his intercession make our words and our deeds acceptable to you. This we ask of you through our Lord.

Prayer after the Communion

Tríbuant nobis, quǽsumus, Dómine, contínuum tua sancta præsídium: quo, beáti Marci Evangelístæ tui précibus, nos ab ómnibus semper tueántur advérsis. Per Dóminum.

May your holy mysteries, Lord, be for us a continual means of sustenance; and, through the prayers of your evangelist St. Mark, may they protect us against all adversity. This we ask of you through our Lord.

MAY 1

ST. JOSEPH THE WORKMAN, SPOUSE OF THE BLESSED VIRGIN MARY

ENTRANCE ANTIPHON *Wis. 10:17; Ps. 126:1*
Wisdom gave the holy ones the recompense of their labors, and conducted them by a wondrous road, and became a shelter for them by day and a starry flame by night. Alleluia, alleluia.
Ps. Unless the Lord build the house, they labor in vain who build it.

Glory be to the Father and to the Son and to the Holy Spirit. As it was in the beginning, is now and ever shall be, world without end. Amen. Wisdom gave . . .

Prayer over the Assembly

Rerum cónditor Deus, qui legem labóris humáno géneri statuísti: concéde propítius; ut, sancti Ioseph exémplo et patrocínio, ópera perficiámus quæ præcipis, et præmia consequámur quæ promíttis. Per Dóminum.

O God, Creator of the world, you have established for mankind the law of work. Following the example of St. Joseph and under his protection, may we be enabled, by your mercy, to do all the work you require of us and to obtain for it the reward you have promised. This we ask of you through our Lord.

EPISTLE   Colossians 3:14-15, 17, 23-24

By the work of his hands Joseph was directly serving Christ, the Son of God, whose daily bread he had to provide. Our occupational work is a means of serving our brethren and expressing our love for them. Performed in this spirit and in union with Christ, who himself worked in the shop at Nazareth, our labor becomes a prayer agreeable to the Father.

A reading from the letter of the apostle Paul to the Christians of Colossae
Brethren,

Have charity; it is the bond of all the virtues. And let the peace of Christ reign in your hearts, that peace to which you are called, assembled into one body. Live in a state of thanksgiving.

Whatever you do, every word and every labor, let everything be in the name of the Lord Jesus Christ; let it be in thanksgiving, through him, to God the Father.

Whatever you do, work with your whole heart, as working for the Lord and not for men. You know the compensation you will receive from the Lord: his inheritance. It is the Lord Christ whom you are to serve.

AFTER THE EPISTLE

Alleluia, alleluia. In whatever trouble they shall call upon me, I will hear them, and I will always be their protector. Alleluia. Obtain for us grace to lead an innocent life, O Joseph; and may it ever be secure under your protection. Alleluia.

GOSPEL   Matthew 13:54-58

Christ, the Son of God, at the risk of disconcerting his fellow countrymen, wished to lead the plain, laborious life of a village craftsman.

A reading from the holy Gospel according to Matthew

At that time Jesus came back to his own country and began to teach in the synagogues. There was general amazement. "Where did he get this knowledge and these powers?" people were saying. "Isn't this the carpenter's son? Isn't his mother the one called Mary? Aren't James, Joseph, Simon and Jude his relatives? And his female relatives, aren't they all our neighbors? Where did he go, then, to find all that?" And they could not get over this.

Jesus answered them, "A prophet is not without success except in his own country and in his own family." And he performed hardly any miracles among them because of their unbelief.

OFFERTORY ANTIPHON *Ps. 89:17*

May the gracious care of the Lord our God be ours; prosper the work of our hands for us! Prosper the work of our hands! Alleluia.

Prayer over the Offerings

Quas tibi, Dómine, de opéribus mánuum nostrárum offérimus hóstias, sancti Ioseph interpósito suffrágio, pignus fácias nobis unitátis et pacis. Per Dóminum.

These offerings which we present to you, Lord, come from the labor of our hands. Through the intercession of St. Joseph may they ensure unity and peace for us. This we ask of you through our Lord.

COMMUNION ANTIPHON *Matt. 13:54-55*

Where did he get this wisdom and these miracles? Is not this the carpenter's son? Is not his mother called Mary? Alleluia.

Prayer after the Communion

Hæc sancta quæ súmpsimus, Dómine: per intercessiónem beáti Ioseph; et operatiónem nostram cómpleant, et præmia confírment. Per Dóminum.

Lord, we have received your sacrament. Through the intercession of St. Joseph may this sacrament give our work its full value and guarantee us the reward you have promised. This we ask of you through our Lord.

MASS OUTSIDE THE EASTER SEASON

For Labor Day

ENTRANCE ANTIPHON *Wis. 10:17; Ps. 126:1*

Wisdom gave the holy ones the recompense of their labors, and conducted them by a wondrous road, and became a shelter for them by day and a starry flame by night.

Ps. Unless the Lord build the house, they labor in vain who build it.

Glory be to the Father and to the Son and to the Holy Spirit. As it was in the beginning, is now and ever shall be, world without end. Amen. Wisdom gave . . .

Collects, Epistle and Gospel as above, page 178.

Gradual *Ps. 127:1-2*

Happy are you who fear the Lord, who walk in his ways! You shall eat the fruit of your handiwork and you shall be favored.

Alleluia

Alleluia, alleluia. Obtain for us grace to lead an innocent life, O Joseph; and may it ever be secure under your protection. Alleluia.

OFFERTORY ANTIPHON *Ps. 89:17*

May the gracious care of the Lord our God be ours; prosper the work of our hands for us! Prosper the work of our hands!

COMMUNION ANTIPHON *Matt. 13:54-55*

Where did he get this wisdom and these miracles? Is not this the carpenter's son? Is not his mother called Mary?

MAY 11

COMMEMORATION OF STS. PHILIP AND JAMES, APOSTLES

Prayer over the Assembly

Deus, qui nos ánnua Apostoló-rum tuórum Philíppi et Iacóbi so-lemnitáte lætíficas: præsta, quǽ-sumus; ut, quorum gaudémus mé-ritis, instruámur exémplis. Per Dó-minum.

Every year, Lord, you give us the joy of celebrating the feast of your apostles St. Philip and St. James. We rejoice in their merits; in your good-ness please inflame our hearts with their example. This we ask of you through our Lord.

Prayer over the Offerings

Múnera, Dómine, quæ pro Apostolórum tuórum Philíppi et Iacóbi solemnitáte deférimus, pro-pítius súscipe: et mala ómnia, quæ merémur, avérte. Per Dóminum.

Lord, in your kindness, receive the gifts offered to you on the solemnity of your apostles Philip and James, and ward off all the evils we deserve. This we ask of you through our Lord.

Prayer after the Communion

Quǽsumus, Dómine, salutáribus repléti mystériis: ut, quorum so-

Nourished by your redemptive sac-raments, we implore you, Lord, that

lémnia celebrámus, eórum orátiónibus adiuvémur. Per Dóminum.

your holy apostles whose feast we are celebrating may help us by their prayers. This we ask of you through our Lord.

MAY 31

COMMEMORATION OF BLESSED VIRGIN MARY, QUEEN

Prayer over the Assembly

Concéde nobis, quǽsumus, Dómine: ut, qui solemnitátem beátæ Maríæ Vírginis Regínæ nostræ celebrámus; eius muníti præsídio, pacem in præsénti et glóriam in futúro cónsequi mereámur. Per Dóminum.

We celebrate the solemnity of our Queen, the Blessed Virgin Mary. Grant, O Lord, that under her protection we may obtain peace and glory in heaven. This we ask of you through our Lord.

Prayer over the Offerings

Accipe, quǽsumus, Dómine, múnera lætántis Ecclésiæ, et beátæ Vírginis Maríæ Regínæ suffragántibus méritis, ad nostræ salútis auxílium proveníre concéde. Per Dóminum.

Your Church rejoices, Lord. Please accept the gifts she offers you; and, by the merits of our Queen, the Blessed Virgin Mary, grant that this offering may become a help toward our salvation. This we ask of you through our Lord.

Prayer after the Communion

Celebrátis solémniis, Dómine, quæ pro sanctæ Maríæ, Regínæ nostræ, festivitáte perégimus: eius, quǽsumus, nobis intercessióne fiant salutária; in cuius honóre sunt exsultánter impléta. Per Dóminum.

On this feast of our Queen, the Virgin Mary, we have celebrated a solemn sacrifice, Lord. It is in her honor that we have offered it with joy; grant therefore, by her intercession, that it may be useful for our salvation. This we ask of you through our Lord.

JUNE 24

THE BIRTH OF ST. JOHN THE BAPTIST

ENTRANCE ANTIPHON *Is. 49:1, 2; Ps. 91:2*

From my mother's womb the Lord called me by my name, and made my mouth a sharp-edged sword. He concealed me in the shadow of his hand, and made me a chosen arrow.

Ps. It is good to give thanks to the Lord, to sing praise to your name, Most High.

Glory be to the Father and to the Son and to the Holy Spirit. As it was in the beginning, is now and ever shall be, world without end. Amen. From my mother's womb . . .

Prayer over the Assembly

Deus, qui præséntem diem honorábilem nobis in beáti Ioánnis nativitáte fecísti: da pópulis tuis spirituálium grátiam gaudiórum; et ómnium fidélium mentes dírige in viam salútis ætérnæ. Per Dóminum.

Lord, this is a festive day for us, the birthday of St. John the Baptist. Grant your Christian people the grace to know spiritual joys, and lead the souls of your faithful along the way of eternal salvation. This we ask of you through our Lord.

EPISTLE   Isaiah 49:1-3, 6-7

The liturgy here places on the lips of John the Baptist the words of an anonymous prophet whose writings were added to the book of Isaias and whom God had raised up at Babylon, during the exile, to proclaim the universal aspect of salvation.

A reading from the book of the prophet Isaiah

Peoples of all the continents and of the distant islands, listen:
Even before my birth the Lord called me; while I was still in my mother's womb, he knew my name.
He made my speech as penetrating as a sword. He protected me in the shadow of his hand, he made me a choice arrow, reserved in his quiver. And he said to me, "You are at my service, and you will be my glory."
Now the Lord, who formed me to his service from my mother's womb, says to me again, "I am going to make you the light of the nations, that the whole world may receive my salvation. The kings and the great ones of the earth will rise up to adore the Lord most holy, who has chosen you."

Gradual *Jer. 1:5, 9*

Before I formed you in the womb, I knew you, and before you were born, I dedicated you. The Lord extended his hand, and touched my mouth, and said to me.

Alleluia *Luke 1:76*

Alleluia, alleluia. You, child, shall be called the prophet of the Most High; you shall go before the Lord to prepare his ways. Alleluia.

GOSPEL   Luke 1:57-68

The events surrounding the birth of John showed that God had chosen him to play a role in the history of his people.

A reading from the holy Gospel according to Luke

The time arrived for Elizabeth to give birth, and she brought a son into the world. Learning that the Lord had conferred on her this special mark of his bounty, her neighbors and her relatives congratulated her. On the eighth day they came for the circumcision of the child. They wanted to call him Zachary after his father, but his mother opposed this. "No," she said, "he is to be called John."

"There is no one by that name among your relatives," they objected, and by way of signs they asked his father [who had been mute since the apparition of the angel] what name he wanted to give him.

Zachary took a writing-tablet and wrote, "John is his name." Everyone was astonished. And at that very moment Zachary's mouth was opened, his tongue was released, and he began to speak, blessing God.

The whole neighborhood experienced a feeling of religious fear, and the event was recounted throughout the hill country of Judea. Those who learned of it impressed the memory of it on their hearts, saying within themselves, "What do you suppose this child will be?" And really, the hand of the Lord was with him.

Zachary, his father, was filled with the Holy Spirit, and he said, prophesying, "Blessed be the Lord, the God of Israel, for he has come to visit and redeem his people. . . ."

OFFERTORY ANTIPHON *Ps. 91:13*

The just man shall flourish like the palm tree; like a cedar of Lebanon shall he grow.

Prayer over the Offerings

Tua, Dómine, munéribus altária cumulámus: illíus nativitátem honóre débito celebrántes, qui Salvatórem mundi et cécinit adfutúrum, et adésse monstrávit, Dóminum nostrum Iesum Christum Fílium tuum: Qui tecum vivit et regnat in unitáte Spíritus Sancti, Deus, per ómnia sǽcula sæculórum.

O Lord, we cover your altars with offerings; may they help us to celebrate worthily the birth of him who announced the coming and showed the presence of the Savior of the world, our Lord Jesus Christ, your Son, who lives and reigns with you in the unity of the Holy Spirit, God, forever.

COMMUNION ANTIPHON *Luke 1:76*

You, child, shall be called the prophet of the Most High; for you shall go before the face of the Lord to prepare his ways.

Prayer after the Communion

Sumat Ecclésia tua, Deus, beáti Ioánnis Baptístæ generatióne lætítiam: per quem suæ regeneratiónis cognóvit auctórem, Dóminum nostrum Iesum Christum Fílium tuum: Qui tecum vivit et regnat in unitáte Spíritus Sancti, Deus, per ómnia sǽcula sæculórum.

May your Church, O Lord, find joy in celebrating the birth of St. John the Baptist. Through him she knew the Savior who caused us to be reborn to the life of grace, our Lord Jesus Christ, your Son, who lives and reigns with you in the unity of the Holy Spirit, God, forever.

JUNE 29

STS. PETER AND PAUL, APOSTLES

ENTRANCE ANTIPHON *Acts 12:11; Ps. 138:1-2*

Now I know for certain that the Lord has sent his angel and rescued me from the power of Herod and from all that the Jewish people were expecting.

Ps. O Lord, you have probed me and you know me; you know when I sit and when I stand.

Glory be to the Father and to the Son and to the Holy Spirit. As it was in the beginning, is now and ever shall be, world without end. Amen. Now I know . . .

Prayer over the Assembly

Deus, qui hodiérnam diem Apostolórum tuórum Petri et Pauli martýrio consecrásti: da Ecclésiæ tuæ, eórum in ómnibus sequi præcéptum; per quos religiónis sumpsit exórdium. Per Dóminum.

O Lord, on this day which you have sanctified by the martyrdom of St. Peter and of St. Paul, give your Church the grace to follow in all things the teachings of these apostles from whom Christianity first began to spread. This we ask of you through our Lord.

EPISTLE   Acts 12:1-11

A reading from the Acts of the Apostles

In those days King Herod had some members of the Church arrested to do them violence. He had James, the brother of John, beheaded. Seeing that this pleased the Jews, he decided to arrest Peter. It was during the festival days of the Passover.

Peter was arrested and thrown into prison under a strong guard: four groups of four soldiers each, taking turns. Herod's intention was to have him appear before the people after the festival days. During this time the Church kept praying to God constantly on Peter's behalf.

The night before he was to be judged, Peter was sleeping between two soldiers, bound by two chains; sentinels were guarding the door.

All at once a light shone in the cell and the angel of the Lord appeared beside the prisoner. He shook Peter and woke him up. "Quick! On your feet!" he told him, and at the same instant the chains fell from his hands. The angel continued, "Tie your girdle and put on your sandals." Peter obeyed, and the angel then told him, "Wrap your cloak around you and follow me."

Peter went out after the angel; he did not think that all this was real, but supposed that it was a vision. Passing the first sentinel's station and then the second, they arrived at the iron gate that led to the city, and it opened by itself before them. They passed through it and started down a street, and suddenly the angel disappeared.

Coming to himself then, Peter said, "Now I know that it's true! The Lord has really sent me his angel and rescued me from the hands of Herod and from the penalty the Jewish people had in store for me!"

Gradual *Ps. 44:17-18*

You shall make them princes through all the land; they shall remember your name, O Lord. The place of your fathers your sons shall have; therefore shall nations praise you.

Alleluia *Matt. 16:18*

Alleluia, alleluia. You are Peter, and upon this rock I will build my Church. Alleluia.

GOSPEL   Matthew 16:13-19

A reading from the holy Gospel according to Matthew

At that time, having come to the region of Caesarea Philippi, Jesus asked his disciples, "What do people say about the Son of Man? Who do they say that I am?"

They answered, "Some say you are John the Baptist; others say you are Elijah; still others, that you are Jeremiah or one of the prophets."

"But you, who do you say that I am?"

Simon Peter answered, "You are the Christ, the Son of the living God."

Jesus said to him, "Blessed are you, Simon, son of Jona, for it was not the eyes of the flesh that were able to reveal this to you, but only my Father who is in heaven. And I in turn tell you this: You are 'Peter' ['the Rock'], and upon this rock I will build my Church, and the powers of hell shall not be able to overthrow it. I will give you the keys to the kingdom of heaven: whatever you bind on earth shall be bound in heaven, and whatever you unbind on earth shall be unbound in heaven."

OFFERTORY ANTIPHON *Ps. 44:17-18*

You shall make them princes through all the land; they shall remember your name, O Lord, through all generations.

Prayer over the Offerings

Hóstias, Dómine, quas nómini tuo sacrándas offérimus, apostólica prosequátur orátio: per quam nos expiári tríbuas, et deféndi. Per Dóminum.

Lord, may the prayers of your apostles accompany the offerings which are to be consecrated to your glory. May their intercession purify us and protect us. This we ask of you through our Lord.

COMMUNION ANTIPHON *Matt. 16:18*

You are Peter, and upon this rock I will build my Church.

Prayer after the Communion

Quos cælésti, Dómine, aliménto satiásti: apostólicis intercessiónibus ab omni adversitáte custódi. Per Dóminum.

Lord, may the intercession of your apostles keep from any adversity those whom you have nourished with your Eucharist. This we ask of you through our Lord.

JULY 1

THE FEAST OF THE MOST PRECIOUS BLOOD OF OUR LORD JESUS CHRIST

ENTRANCE ANTIPHON *Apoc. 5:9-10; Ps. 88:2*

You have redeemed us, O Lord, with your blood, out of every tribe and tongue and people and nation, and have made us for our God a kingdom.

Ps. The favors of the Lord I will sing forever; through all generations my mouth shall proclaim your faithfulness.

Glory be to the Father and to the Son and to the Holy Spirit. As it was in the beginning, is now and ever shall be, world without end. Amen. You have redeemed us . . .

Prayer over the Assembly

Omnípotens sempitérne Deus, qui unigénitum Fílium tuum mundi Redemptórem constituísti, ac eius Sánguine placári voluísti: concéde, quǽsumus, salútis nostræ prétium solémni cultu ita venerári, atque a præséntis vitæ malis eius virtúte deféndi in terris; ut fructu perpétuo lætémur in cælis. Per eúndem Dóminum nostrum Iesum Christum Fílium tuum, qui tecum vivit et regnat in unitáte Spíritus Sancti, Deus, per ómnia sǽcula sæculórum.

All-powerful, eternal God, you made your Son the Redeemer of the world, and your justice was appeased by his blood. Each year on this feast we adore that blood, which is the price of our salvation; may its power defend us against all the evils of this life on earth and prepare us for the eternal joy of heaven. This we ask of you through the same Jesus Christ, our Lord and your Son, who lives and reigns with you in the unity of the Holy Spirit, God, forever.

EPISTLE   Hebrews 9:11-15

Christ by his blood has sealed the new covenant of God and mankind.

A reading from the letter of the apostle Paul to the Hebrews

Brethren,

Christ has come as the high priest of the future kingdom. Having ingress to a temple greater and more perfect [than that of Jerusalem], a temple which is not built by the hands of men and is not of this world, he entered once for all into the sanctuary [of heaven], not with blood of goats or of calves, but covered with his own blood, the blood that paid the price of our deliverance for eternity.

If the blood of goats and of bull calves and the ashes of a heifer, with which those [among the Jews] who have been defiled are sprinkled, sanctify them by obtaining purity of body for them, how much more must the blood of Christ — who, prompted by the Holy Spirit, offered himself to God as a victim all-pure — purify our soul of all sin and make us true adorers of the living God!

It is he who has concluded the new covenant between God and men. It is his death that has destroyed sin, that sin which remained under the former covenant. It is his death that puts us in possession of the eternal inheritance, to which God is calling us in Jesus Christ our Lord.

Gradual *1 John 5:6, 7-8*

This is he who came in water and in blood, Jesus Christ; not in the water only, but in the water and in the blood. There are three that bear witness in heaven: the Father, the Word, and the Holy Spirit; and these three are one. And there are three that bear witness on earth: the Spirit, the water, and the blood; and these three are one.

Alleluia *1 John 5:9*

Alleluia, alleluia. If we receive the testimony of men, the testimony of God is greater. Alleluia.

GOSPEL   John 19:30-35

To show his love for men, Christ shed the very last drop of his blood. His opened side is a reminder of the birth of Eve, who was taken from the side of Adam as he slept. While Christ "sleeps" on the Cross, the Church is born. The water and the blood suggest the sacraments of baptism and the Eucharist, which prolong the life of Christ among men.

A reading from the holy Gospel according to John

At that time, after taking the vinegar, Jesus said, "All is accomplished." And, bowing his head, he gave up his spirit.

It was the day on which the preparations were being made for the Passover. Not wanting the bodies to remain on the cross the next day, which was the sabbath — especially since this sabbath was a great feast day — the Jews asked Pilate to have the legs of the crucified men broken, so that they could be taken away.

The soldiers came, therefore. They broke the legs of the first, then of the second of the two who were crucified with Jesus. Finally they came to Jesus himself. Seeing that he was already dead, they did not break his legs; but one of the soldiers opened his side with the thrust of a lance, and blood and water flowed out immediately. He who saw this bears witness to it, and his testimony is true.

OFFERTORY ANTIPHON *1 Cor. 10:16*

The cup of blessing that we bless, is it not the sharing of the blood of Christ? And the bread that we break, is it not the partaking of the body of the Lord?

Prayer over the Offerings

Per hæc divína mystéria, ad novi, quǽsumus, testaménti mediatórem Iesum accedámus: et super altária tua, Dómine virtútum, aspersiónem sánguinis mélius loquéntem, quam Abel, innovémus. Per eúndem Dóminum nostrum Iesum Christum Fílium tuum, qui tecum vivit et regnat in unitáte Spíritus Sancti, Deus, per ómnia sǽcula sæculórum.

May this Mass unite us to Jesus, Mediator of the new alliance, and may we renew on your altar, Lord, the offering of a blood which cries out to you even more than that of Abel. This we ask of you through the same Jesus Christ, our Lord and your Son, who lives and reigns with you in the unity of the Holy Spirit, God, forever.

COMMUNION ANTIPHON *Heb. 9:28*

Christ was offered once to take away the sins of many; the second time he will appear with no part in sin to those who wait for him unto salvation.

Prayer after the Communion

Ad sacram, Dómine, mensam admíssi, háusimus aquas in gáudio de fóntibus Salvatóris: sanguis eius fiat nobis, quǽsumus, fons aquæ in vitam ætérnam saliéntis: Qui tecum vivit et regnat in unitáte Spíritus Sancti, Deus, per ómnia sǽcula sæculórum.

Admitted to the holy table, Lord, we have drawn water with joy at the fountain of salvation. May the Savior's blood become in us a fountain of water springing up unto life everlasting. This we ask of you through him, who lives and reigns with you in the unity of the Holy Spirit, God, forever.

JULY 2

COMMEMORATION OF THE VISITATION OF THE BLESSED VIRGIN MARY

Prayer over the Assembly

Fámulis tuis, quǽsumus, Dómine, cæléstis grátiæ munus impertíre: ut, quibus beátæ Vírginis partus éxstitit salútis exórdium; Visitatiónis eius votíva solémnitas pacis tríbuat increméntum. Per Dóminum.

We are your children, Lord; grant us the favor of your divine grace. The motherhood of the Virgin was the beginning of our salvation; may the feast of her Visitation give us a greater abundance of your grace. This we ask of you through our Lord.

Prayer over the Offerings

Unigéniti tui, Dómine, nobis succúrrat humánitas: ut, qui natus de Vírgine, matris integritátem non mínuit, sed sacrávit; in Visitatiónis eius solémniis, nostris nos piáculis éxuens, oblatiónem nostram tibi fáciat accéptam Iesus Christus Dóminus noster: Qui tecum vivit et regnat in unitáte Spíritus Sancti, Deus, per ómnia sǽcula sæculórum.

Let your incarnate Son come to our aid, O Lord! In being born of the Virgin he did not impair, but consecrated, his mother's virginity. May he deliver us from our sins and make our offering acceptable to you on this feast of her Visitation. This we ask of you through him, who lives and reigns with you in the unity of the Holy Spirit, God, forever.

Prayer after the Communion

Súmpsimus, Dómine, celebritátis ánnuæ votíva sacraménta: præsta, quǽsumus; ut et temporális vitæ nobis remédia prǽbeant, et ætérnæ. Per Dóminum.

On this great yearly feast, Lord, we have received the sacred gifts of your Eucharist; may they obtain your grace for our daily life and for life eternal. This we ask of you through our Lord.

JULY 25

COMMEMORATION OF ST. JAMES, APOSTLE

Prayer over the Assembly

Esto, Dómine, plebi tuæ sanctificátor et custos: ut, Apóstoli tui Iacóbi muníta præsídiis, et conversatióne tibi pláceat, et secúra mente desérviat. Per Dóminum.

O Lord, sanctify and guard your people; assure them of the protection of your apostle St. James. Then they will be able to please you by their conduct and serve you with a tranquil soul. This we ask of you through our Lord.

Prayer over the Offerings

Oblatiónes pópuli tui, quǽsumus, Dómine, beáti Iacóbi Apóstoli pássio beáta concíliet: et quæ nostris non aptæ sunt méritis, fiant tibi plácitæ eius deprecatióne. Per Dóminum.

May the glorious martyrdom of the apostle St. James induce you, Lord, to accept the offerings of your people. Our merits do not make them worthy of being presented to you; may his prayers make them pleasing to you. This we ask of you through our Lord.

Prayer after the Communion

Beáti Apóstoli tui Iacóbi, quǽsumus, Dómine, intercessióne nos

Help us, Lord, at the intercession of your apostle St. James; to cele-

ádiuva: pro cuius festivitáte percépimus tua sancta lætántes. Per Dóminum.

brate his feast, we have joyfully received your holy Eucharist. This we ask of you through our Lord.

JULY 26

COMMEMORATION OF ST. ANNE

Prayer over the Assembly

Deus, qui beátæ Annæ grátiam conférre dignátus es, ut Genetrícis Unigéniti Fílii tui mater éffici mererétur: concéde propítius; ut, cuius solémnia celebrámus, eius apud te patrocíniis adiuvémur. Per eúndem Dóminum nostrum Iesum Christum Fílium tuum, qui tecum vivit et regnat in unitáte Spíritus Sancti, Deus, per ómnia sǽcula sæculórum.

O Lord, you reserved to St. Anne the grace of giving birth to the Mother of your Son. Grant that we may be helped through the intercession of her whose feast we celebrate today. This we ask of you through the same Jesus Christ, our Lord and your Son, who lives and reigns with you in the unity of the Holy Spirit, God, forever.

Prayer over the Offerings

Sacrifíciis præséntibus, quǽsumus, Dómine, placátus inténde: ut per intercessiónem beátæ Annæ, quæ Genetrícis Fílii tui Dómini nostri Iesu Christi mater éxstitit, et devotióni nostræ profíciant, et salúti. Per eúndem Dóminum nostrum Iesum Christum Fílium tuum, qui tecum vivit et regnat in unitáte Spíritus Sancti, Deus, per ómnia sǽcula sæculórum.

Look favorably, Lord, on this sacrifice. Through the intercession of St. Anne, who brought into the world the Mother of your Son, our Lord Jesus Christ, may it increase our love and be useful for our salvation. This we ask of you through the same Jesus Christ, our Lord and your Son, who lives and reigns with you in the unity of the Holy Spirit, God, forever.

Prayer after the Communion

Cæléstibus sacraméntis vegetáti, quǽsumus, Dómine Deus noster: ut, intercessióne beátæ Annæ, quam Genetrícis Fílii tui matrem esse voluísti, ad ætérnam salútem perveníre mereámur. Per eúndem Dóminum nostrum Iesum Christum Fílium tuum, qui tecum vivit et regnat in unitáte Spíritus Sancti, Deus, per ómnia sǽcula sæculórum.

Nourished on the bread of heaven, we entreat you, Lord, our God: may the intercession of St. Anne, chosen to bring into the world the Mother of your Son, win entrance for us into eternal salvation. This we ask of you through the same Jesus Christ, our Lord and your Son, who lives and reigns with you in the unity of the Holy Spirit, God, forever.

AUGUST 6

THE TRANSFIGURATION
OF OUR LORD JESUS CHRIST

ENTRANCE ANTIPHON *Ps. 76:19; 83:2-3*

Your lightning illumined the world: the earth quivered and quaked.

Ps. How lovely is your dwelling place, O Lord of hosts! My soul yearns and pines for the courts of the Lord.

Glory be to the Father and to the Son and to the Holy Spirit. As it was in the beginning, is now and ever shall be, world without end. Amen. Your lightning . . .

Prayer over the Assembly

Deus, qui fídei sacraménta in Unigéniti tui gloriósa Transfiguratióne patrum testimónio roborásti, et adoptiónem filiórum perféctam, voce delápsa in nube lúcida, mirabíliter præsignásti: concéde propítius; ut ipsíus Regis glóriæ nos coherédes effícias, et eiúsdem glóriæ tríbuas esse consórtes. Per eúndem Dóminum nostrum Iesum Christum Fílium tuum, qui tecum vivit et regnat in unitáte Spíritus Sancti, Deus, per ómnia sǽcula sæculórum.

Lord, at the Transfiguration of your only-begotten Son the witness borne by the prophets confirmed the mysteries of our faith, and your voice, speaking in the luminous cloud, by a miracle of love foretold that we would be your children. In your mercy grant that we may be heirs of the kingdom of glory and may share with your Son the glory of heaven. This we ask of you through the same Jesus Christ, our Lord and your Son, who lives and reigns with you in the unity of the Holy Spirit, God, forever.

EPISTLE   2 Peter 1:16-19

A witness of the transfiguration of Jesus on Thabor, St. Peter recalls this event as one of the most obvious proofs of the divinity of Christ.

A reading from the second letter of the apostle Peter to the Christians

Beloved brethren,

When I made known to you the power and the coming of our Lord Jesus Christ, it was not just a clever story that I was telling you: we saw with our own eyes his [divine] majesty.

It was God the Father himself who gave him honor and glory, when he made his voice heard from the depths of his majestic glory: "This is my beloved Son in whom I am well pleased; listen to him!" That voice from heaven we ourselves heard, the day that we were with him on the holy mountain.

Thus was the word of the prophets confirmed for us. Keep your eyes fixed on that word, as on a lamp that shines in the night, until the day begins to dawn and the morning star [Christ] rises in your hearts.

Gradual Ps. 44:3, 2

Fairer in beauty are you than the sons of men; grace is poured out upon your lips. My heart overflows with a goodly theme; as I sing my ode to the king.

Alleluia Wis. 7:26

Alleluia, alleluia. He is the refulgence of eternal light, the spotless mirror, and the image of his goodness. Alleluia.

GOSPEL   Matthew 17:1-9

The presence and the action of God are perceptible to us only in faith. Glory is for a later time. The Transfiguration lasted only a few brief moments, being permitted in order to establish more solidly the faith of the apostles.

A reading from the holy Gospel according to Matthew

At that time Jesus took with him Peter, James and his brother John and led them aside, onto a high mountain. There he was transfigured before them. His face became as radiant as the sun, and his clothes dazzling white, like snow. And Moses and Elijah appeared to them too, conversing with Jesus.

Peter spoke up and said to Jesus, "What a good thing it is that we are here, Lord! Do you want us to put up three tents here, one for you, one for Moses and one for Elijah?"

He was still speaking when a luminous cloud enveloped them, and from within the cloud a voice was heard: "This is my beloved Son in whom I am well pleased; listen to him!" At the sound of this voice the apostles fell with their faces to the ground, awe-struck.

But Jesus approached them, touched them and said, "Get up! No need to be afraid!" Raising their eyes then, they saw no one but Jesus.

While they were coming down from the mountain, Jesus gave them this order: "Do not tell anyone about this vision until the Son of Man has risen from the dead."

OFFERTORY ANTIPHON Ps. 111:3

Glory and wealth are in his house; his generosity shall endure forever. Alleluia.

Prayer over the Offerings

Obláta, quǽsumus, Dómine, múnera gloriósa Unigéniti tui Transfiguratióne sanctífica: nosque a peccatórum máculis, splendóribus ipsíus illustratiónis emúnda. Per eúndem Dóminum nostrum Iesum Christum Fílium tu-

Consecrate our offerings, Lord, in this Mass of the Transfiguration of your Son, and purify us from the stains of our sins in the splendor of his light. This we ask of you through the same Jesus Christ, our Lord and your Son, who lives and reigns with

um, qui tecum vivit et regnat in
unitáte Spíritus Sancti, Deus, per
ómnia sǽcula sæculórum.

you in the unity of the Holy Spirit,
God, forever.

COMMUNION ANTIPHON *Matt. 17:9*

Tell the vision you have seen to no one, till the Son of Man has risen
from the dead.

Prayer after the Communion

Præsta, quǽsumus, omnípotens
Deus: ut sacrosáncta Fílii tui
Transfiguratiónis mystéria, quæ solémni celebrámus offício, purificátæ mentis intellegéntia consequámur. Per eúndem Dóminum nostrum Iesum Christum Fílium tuum, qui tecum vivit et regnat in
unitáte Spíritus Sancti, Deus, per
ómnia sǽcula sæculórum.

Enable us, all-powerful God, in the
clarity of our purified souls to understand the lessons of the Transfiguration of your Son, which we celebrate
each year on this solemn feast day.
This we ask of you through the same
Jesus Christ, our Lord and your Son,
who lives and reigns with you in the
unity of the Holy Spirit, God, forever.

AUGUST 10

COMMEMORATION OF ST. LAWRENCE, MARTYR

Prayer over the Assembly

Da nobis, quǽsumus, omnípotens Deus, vitiórum nostrórum
flammas exstínguere: qui beáto
Lauréntio tribuísti tormentórum
suórum incéndia superáre. Per Dóminum.

Give us the grace, Lord, to ex-
tinguish the fires of our evil passions,
as you gave St. Lawrence the strength
to triumph over the flames of his cruel
torture. This we ask of you through
our Lord.

Prayer over the Offerings

Accipe, quǽsumus, Dómine,
múnera dignánter obláta: et beáti
Lauréntii suffragántibus méritis,
ad nostræ salútis auxílium proveníre concéde. Per Dóminum.

Please accept our offerings, Lord;
and, through the merits of St. Lawrence, may they help toward our salvation. This we ask of you through
our Lord.

Prayer after the Communion

Sacro múnere satiáti, súpplices
te, Dómine, deprecámur: ut, quod
débitæ servitútis celebrámus offício, intercedénte beáto Lauréntio
Mártyre tuo, salvatiónis tuæ sentiámus augméntum. Per Dóminum.

Nourished on your Eucharist, we
recognize your sovereignty and we
entreat you, Lord, through the intercession of your martyr St. Lawrence,
to make the fruits of your redemption
increase in us. This we ask of you
through our Lord.

<small>AUGUST 15</small>

THE ASSUMPTION OF THE BLESSED VIRGIN MARY

ENTRANCE ANTIPHON *Apoc. 12:1; Ps. 97:1*

A great sign appeared in heaven: a woman clothed with the sun and the moon was under her feet, and upon her head a crown of twelve stars.

Ps. Sing to the Lord a new song, for he has done wondrous deeds.

Glory be to the Father and to the Son and to the Holy Spirit. As it was in the beginning, is now and ever shall be, world without end. Amen. A great sign . . .

Prayer over the Assembly

Omnípotens sempitérne Deus, immaculátam Vírginem Maríam, Fílii tui Genetrícem, córpore et ánima ad cæléstem glóriam assumpsísti: concéde, quǽsumus; ut, ad supérna semper inténti, ipsíus glóriæ mereámur esse consórtes. Per eúndem Dóminum nostrum Iesum Christum Fílium tuum, qui tecum vivit et regnat in unitáte Spíritus Sancti, Deus, per ómnia sǽcula sæculórum.

All-powerful, eternal God, you took up to the glory of heaven the body and soul of Mary, the immaculate Virgin, Mother of your Son. Grant us the grace always to keep our souls intent on supernatural goods, and thus to obtain a share in the glory of her assumption. This we ask of you through the same Jesus Christ, our Lord and your Son, who lives and reigns with you in the unity of the Holy Spirit, God, forever.

EPISTLE   Judith 13:22-25; 15:10

The victory won by Judith over Holofernes, enemy of God's people, was a forecast of the victory which Mary, by her fidelity to the Lord, won over Satan.

A reading from the book of Judith

The Lord, in all his power, has blessed you. Through you he has crushed our enemies.

My daughter, you are blessed by the most high God among all the women of the earth.

Let us bless the Lord, the Creator of heaven and earth! He made use of you to cut off the head of our mortal enemy. On this day he has given you such glory that your praises will always be on the lips of men, who will remember the power of the Lord forever.

Faced with the sufferings and the distress of your people, you gave no thought to your own life, but you saved us from destruction under the eyes of God.

You are the glory of Jerusalem, you are the joy of Israel, you are the honor of our people!

Gradual Ps. 44:11-12, 14

Hear, O daughter, and see; turn your ear; for the king shall desire your beauty. All glorious is the king's daughter as she enters; her raiment is threaded with spun gold.

Alleluia

Alleluia, alleluia. Mary has been taken up into heaven; the choirs of the angels rejoice. Alleluia.

GOSPEL   Luke 1:41-50

The proclamations of the dogmas of the Immaculate Conception and of the Assumption have fulfilled what Mary herself had prophesied: "All generations shall call me blessed."

A reading from the holy Gospel according to Luke

Now it came about that, when Elizabeth heard Mary's greeting, her infant leaped in her womb. Elizabeth was filled with the Holy Spirit, and cried out with a loud voice:

"Blessed are you among women, and blessed is the fruit of your womb! And why should I enjoy the happiness of having the mother of my Lord come to me? Yes, hardly had the sound of your voice reached my ears when the infant in my womb leaped for joy. Blessed is she who has believed that the words spoken to her by the Lord would be fulfilled!"

And Mary answered, "My soul glorifies the Lord; and my spirit leaps for joy because of God my Savior!

"For he has looked favorably on his lowly servant, and henceforth all generations shall call me blessed.

"For he, the All-Powerful, has done great things in me! Holy is his name.

"His mercy extends from age to age on all those who fear him."

OFFERTORY ANTIPHON Gen. 3:15

I will put enmity between you and the woman, between your seed and her seed.

Prayer over the Offerings

Ascéndat ad te, Dómine, nostræ devotiónis oblátio: et, beatíssima Vírgine María in cælum assúmpta intercedénte, corda nostra, caritátis igne succénsa, ad te iúgiter adspírent. Per Dóminum.

May the offering of our sacrifice rise up into your presence, Lord! Through the intercession of the Blessed Virgin Mary, taken up into heaven, may our hearts, on fire with love, keep longing for you. This we ask of you through our Lord.

COMMUNION ANTIPHON Luke 1:48-49

All generations shall call me blessed; because he who is mighty has done great things for me.

Prayer after the Communion

Sumptis, Dómine, salutáribus sacraméntis: da, quǽsumus; ut, méritis et intercessióne beátæ Vírginis Maríæ in cælum assúmptæ, ad resurrectiónis glóriam perducámur. Per Dóminum.

We have just received the sacrament of the Eucharist, Lord. By the merits of the Virgin Mary, taken up into heaven, and at her intercession, grant that we may rise one day in glory. This we ask of you through our Lord.

AUGUST 16

COMMEMORATION OF ST. JOACHIM

Prayer over the Assembly

Deus, qui præ ómnibus Sanctis tuis beátum Ióachim Genetrícis Fílii tu patrem esse voluísti: concéde, quǽsumus; ut, cuius festa venerámur, eius quoque perpétuo patrocínia sentiámus. Per eúndem Dóminum nostrum Iesum Christum Fílium tuum, qui tecum vivit et regnat in unitáte Spíritus Sancti, Deus, per ómnia sǽcula sæculórum.

Among all the saints, Lord, you chose St. Joachim to be the father of her who was to give birth to your Son. Grant that we may always be under the protection of him whose feast we celebrate today. This we ask of you through the same Jesus Christ, our Lord and your Son, who lives and reigns with you in the unity of the Holy Spirit, God, forever.

Prayer over the Offerings

Súscipe, clementíssime Deus, sacrifícium in honórem sancti Patriárchæ Ióachim, patris Maríæ Vírginis, maiestáti tuæ oblátum: ut, ipso cum cóniuge sua, et beatíssima prole intercedénte, perféctam cónsequi mereámur remissiónem peccatórum, et glóriam sempitérnam. Per Dóminum.

Lord, God of mercy, receive this sacrifice offered to your majesty in honor of St. Joachim, father of the Virgin Mary. May this holy patriarch, with his wife and their blessed child, win for us the pardon of our sins and glory everlasting! This we ask of you through our Lord.

Prayer after the Communion

Quǽsumus, omnípotens Deus: ut per hæc sacraménta, quæ súmpsimus, intercedéntibus méritis et précibus beáti Ióachim patris Genetrícis dilécti Fílii tui Dómini nostri Iesu Christi, tuæ grátiæ in præsénti, et ætérnæ glóriæ in fu-

May this communion, Lord, obtain for us a share of your grace in this world and of your glory in heaven, through the merits and the prayers of St. Joachim, father of her who gave birth to your beloved Son, our Lord Jesus Christ, who lives and reigns with

túro partícipes esse mereámur. Per eúndem Dóminum nostrum Iesum Christum Fílium tuum, qui tecum vivit et regnat in unitáte Spíritus Sancti, Deus, per ómnia sǽcula sæculórum.

you in the unity of the Holy Spirit, God, forever.

AUGUST 22

COMMEMORATION OF THE IMMACULATE HEART OF MARY

Prayer over the Assembly

Omnípotens sempitérne Deus, qui in Corde beátæ Maríæ Vírginis dignum Spíritus Sancti habitáculum præparásti: concéde propítius; ut, eiúsdem immaculáti Cordis festivitátem devóta mente recoléntes, secúndum Cor tuum vívere valeámus. Per Dóminum nostrum Iesum Christum Fílium tuum, qui tecum vivit et regnat in unitáte eiúsdem Spíritus Sancti, Deus, per ómnia sǽcula sæculórum.

All-powerful, eternal God, in the heart of the Blessed Virgin Mary you prepared a dwelling-place worthy of the Holy Spirit. Grant that, after celebrating with love the feast of her immaculate heart, we may live according to your heart. This we ask of you through our Lord Jesus Christ, your Son, who lives and reigns with you in the unity of the same Holy Spirit, God, forever.

Prayer over the Offerings

Maiestáti tuæ, Dómine, Agnum immaculátum offeréntes, quǽsumus: ut corda nostra ignis ille divínus accéndat, qui Cor beátæ Maríæ Vírginis ineffabíliter inflammávit. Per eúndem Dóminum nostrum Iesum Christum Fílium tuum, qui tecum vivit et regnat in unitáte Spíritus Sancti, Deus, per ómnia sǽcula sæculórum.

Before your majesty, Lord, we present the Lamb without blemish; through him, may the fire of divine love which consumed the immaculate heart of the Blessed Virgin Mary be kindled also in our hearts. This we ask of you through the same Jesus Christ, our Lord and your Son, who lives and reigns with you in the unity of the Holy Spirit, God, forever.

Prayer after the Communion

Divínis refécti munéribus te, Dómine, supplíciter exorámus: ut beátæ Maríæ Vírginis intercessióne, cuius immaculáti Cordis solémnia venerándo égimus, a præséntibus perículis liberáti, ætérnæ vitæ

Strengthened by the sacrament of your Eucharist, we entreat you, Lord: may the intercession of the Blessed Virgin Mary, whose immaculate heart we honor in this yearly feast, deliver us from the dangers of the

gáudia consequámur. Per Dóminum.

present life and lead us to the joys of
life eternal. This we ask of you
through our Lord.

COMMEMORATION OF ST. BARTHOLOMEW, APOSTLE

Prayer over the Assembly

Omnípotens sempitérne Deus,
qui huius diéi venerándam sanc-
támque lætítiam in beáti Apóstoli
tui Bartholomǽi festivitáte tribuísti: da Ecclésiæ tuæ, quǽsumus; et
amáre quod crédidit, et prædicáre
quod dócuit. Per Dóminum.

All-powerful, eternal God, today
you give us a holy joy, full of reverence, in celebrating the feast of your
apostle St. Bartholomew. Grant that
your Church may love what he believed and preach what he taught.
This we ask of you through our Lord.

Prayer over the Offerings

Beáti Apóstoli tui Bartholomǽi
solémnia recenséntes, quǽsumus,
Dómine: ut eius auxílio tua benefícia capiámus, pro quo tibi laudis
hóstias immolámus. Per Dóminum.

We celebrate the solemnity of your
apostle St. Bartholomew by offering
this Mass to your glory, Lord; may
he help us obtain your favors. This
we ask of you through our Lord.

Prayer after the Communion

Sumptum, Dómine, pignus redemptiónis ætérnæ: sit nobis, quǽsumus; interveniénte beáto Bartho-
lomǽo Apóstolo tuo, vitæ præséntis auxílium páriter et futúræ. Per
Dóminum.

We have received, O Lord, the
pledge of our eternal redemption.
Through the interecession of your
apostle St. Bartholomew, may it be
helpful to us both in the present life
and for the life to come. This we ask
of you through our Lord.

*In the United States the Mass of St. Joseph the Workman may be
said on Labor Day, the first Monday of September (see page 179).*

COMMEMORATION OF THE BIRTHDAY
OF THE BLESSED VIRGIN MARY

Prayer over the Assembly

Fámulis tuis, quǽsumus, Dómine, cæléstis grátiæ munus impertíre: ut, quibus beátæ Vírginis partus éxstitit salútis exórdium; Nativitátis eius votíva solémnitas pacis
tríbuat increméntum. Per Dóminum.

We are your children, Lord; grant
us the favor of your divine grace. The
motherhood of the Virgin was the beginning of our salvation; may the
feast of her nativity give us a greater
abundance of your peace. This we ask
of you through our Lord.

Prayer over the Offerings

Unigéniti tui, Dómine, nobis succúrrat humánitas: ut, qui natus de Vírgine, matris integritátem non mínuit, sed sacrávit; in Nativitátis eius solémniis, nostris nos piáculis éxuens, oblatiónem nostram tibi fáciat accéptam Iesus Christus Dóminus noster: Qui tecum vivit et regnat in unitáte Spíritus Sancti, Deus, per ómnia sǽcula sæculórum.

Let your incarnate Son come to our aid, O Lord! In being born of the Virgin he did not impair, but consecrated, his Mother's virginity. May he deliver us from our sins and make our offering acceptable to you on this feast of her nativity. This we ask of you through him, who lives and reigns with you in the unity of the Holy Spirit, God, forever.

Prayer after the Communion

Súmpsimus, Dómine, celebritátis ánnuæ votíva sacraménta: præsta, quǽsumus; ut et temporális vitæ nobis remédia prǽbeant, et ætérnæ. Per Dóminum.

On this great yearly feast, Lord, we have received the sacred gifts of your Eucharist; may they obtain your grace for our daily life and for life eternal. This we ask of you through our Lord.

SEPTEMBER 14

THE EXALTATION OF THE HOLY CROSS

ENTRANCE ANTIPHON *Gal. 6:14; Ps. 66:2*

But it behooves us to glory in the cross of our Lord Jesus Christ, in whom is our salvation, life, and resurrection; by whom we are saved and delivered.

Ps. May God have pity on us and bless us; may he let his face shine upon us; and may he have pity on us.

Glory be to the Father and to the Son and to the Holy Spirit. As it was in the beginning, is now and ever shall be, world without end. Amen. But it behooves . . .

Prayer over the Assembly

Deus, qui nos hodiérna die Exaltatiónis sanctæ Crucis ánnua solemnitáte lætíficas: præsta, quǽsumus; ut, cuius mystérium in terra cognóvimus, eius redemptiónis prǽmia in cælo mereámur. Per eúndem Dóminum nostrum Iesum Christum Fílium tuum, qui tecum

With joy, O Lord, we celebrate today the exaltation of the holy Cross. We have learned to know, here on earth, the mystery of a Savior God; grant that we may obtain, in heaven, the fruit of his redemption. This we ask of you through the same Jesus Christ, our Lord and your Son, who

vivit et regnat in unitáte Spíritus Sancti, Deus, per ómnia sǽcula sæculórum.

lives and reigns with you in the unity of the Holy Spirit, God, forever.

EPISTLE   Philippians 2:5-11

St. Paul stresses the fact that Christ deserved to enter into glory by reason of his total obedience to the Father.

A reading from the letter of the apostle Paul to the Christians of Philippi

Brethren,

Let your sentiments be the same as those of Christ Jesus. Divine though he was, he did not want to take advantage of his equality with God, but he emptied himself by taking on the condition of a slave, becoming similar to men; he had all the outward appearance of a man. Debasing himself still further, he became obedient to the point of death — even death on a cross.

That is why God has exalted him to the highest degree and given him the name that is above all other names. That is why, at the name of Jesus, every knee bends in heaven, on earth and in hell. That is why every tongue should proclaim, to the glory of God the Father, that Jesus Christ is the Lord!

Gradual *Phil. 2:8-9*

Christ became obedient for us to death, even to death on a cross. Therefore God also has exalted him and has bestowed upon him the name that is above every name.

Alleluia

Alleluia, alleluia. Sweet the wood, sweet the nails, sweet the load that hangs on you! You alone were worthy to bear up the King and Lord of heaven. Alleluia.

GOSPEL   John 12:31-36

It is by his death, as we know, that Christ has saved the whole world; but the death of the Son of God remains an impenetrable mystery.

A reading from the holy Gospel according to John

At that time [1] Jesus said to the Jewish crowd, "Now begins the judgment of this world; now the prince of this world is going to be cast out. As for me, when I have been raised up above the earth, I will draw everything to myself."

By these words Jesus was indicating clearly the kind of death he was going to die. The crowd replied to him, "The law teaches us that the Christ remains forever. How can you say, then, 'The Son of Man must be lifted up above the earth'? Who is this Son of Man anyway?"

Jesus said to them, "The light still shines among you for a little while.

[1] The evening of Palm Sunday.

Walk while the light is shining, for fear that you may be surprised by darkness; he who walks in darkness does not know where he is going. Yes, while the light is still shining, believe in the light, that it may illumine your life."

OFFERTORY ANTIPHON

Protect your people, O Lord, through the sign of the Holy Cross, from the snares of their enemies, that we may pay you a pleasing service, and our sacrifice may be acceptable to you. Alleluia.

Prayer over the Offerings

Iesu Christi Dómini nostri córpore et sánguine saginándi, per quem Crucis est sanctificátum vexíllum: quǽsumus, Dómine Deus noster; ut, sicut illud adoráre merúimus, ita perénniter eius glóriæ salutáris potiámur efféctu. Per eúndem Dóminum nostrum Iesum Christum Fílium tuum, qui tecum vivit et regnat in unitáte Spíritus Sancti, Deus, per ómnia sǽcula sæculórum.

We are preparing to receive the body and blood of Jesus Christ, which have made sacred the standard of the Cross. You have permitted us to adore that Cross of the Savior; O Lord, grant that we may enjoy its glory forever in heaven. This we ask of you through the same Jesus Christ, our Lord and your Son, who lives and reigns with you in the unity of the Holy Spirit, God, forever.

COMMUNION ANTIPHON

O our God, through the sign of the Cross, deliver us from our enemies.

Prayer after the Communion

Adésto nobis, Dómine Deus noster: et quos sanctæ Crucis lætári facis honóre, eius quoque perpétuis defénde subsídiis. Per Dóminum.

Stay near us, Lord our God. We are happy in the honor given the holy Cross: may it always be our defense and our help! This we ask of you through our Lord.

SEPTEMBER 15

COMMEMORATION OF THE SEVEN SORROWS OF THE BLESSED VIRGIN MARY

Prayer over the Assembly

Deus, in cuius passióne, secúndum Simeónis prophetíam, dulcíssimam ánimam gloriósæ Vírginis et Matris Maríæ dolóris gládius pertransívit: concéde propítius; ut, qui dolóres eius venerándo recólimus, passiónis tuæ efféctum felí-

Your passion, Lord, plunged into the soul of the Virgin Mary, your Mother, the sword of sorrow foretold by Simeon. We reverently call her sufferings to mind; grant that we may profit by the happy effects of your redemption. This we ask of you, Lord

cem consequámur: Qui vivis et regnas cum Deo Patre in unitáte Spíritus Sancti, Deus, per ómnia sǽcula sæculórum.

Jesus, living and reigning with the Father in the unity of the Holy Spirit, God, forever.

Prayer over the Offerings

Offérimus tibi preces et hóstias, Dómine Iesu Christe, humíliter supplicántes: ut, qui Transfixiónem dulcíssimi spíritus beátæ Maríæ Matris tuæ précibus recensémus; suo, suorúmque sub Cruce Sanctórum consórtium multiplicáto piíssimo intervéntu, méritis mortis tuæ, méritum cum beátis habeámus: Qui vivis et regnas cum Deo Patre in unitáte Spíritus Sancti, Deus, per ómnia sǽcula sæculórum.

Lord Jesus Christ, here are our offerings and our humble prayers. This Mass recalls to us how the most gentle soul of your Mother was pierced with sorrow. Grant therefore, that, through her faithful intercession, through the saints who have suffered with her at the foot of the Cross and through the merits of your death, we may one day share the happiness of the elect. This we ask of you, Lord Jesus, living and reigning with the Father in the unity of the Holy Spirit, God, forever.

Prayer after the Communion

Sacrifícia, quæ súmpsimus, Dómine Iesu Christe, Transfixiónem Matris tuæ et Vírginis devóte celebrántes: nobis ímpetrent apud cleméntiam tuam omnis boni salutáris efféctum: Qui vivis et regnas cum Deo Patre in unitáte Spíritus Sancti, Deus, per ómnia sǽcula sæculórum.

Lord Jesus Christ, we have taken part in your sacrifice while celebrating with fervor the seven sorrows of your Mother. In your goodness grant us all the graces that will help toward our salvation. This we ask of you, Lord Jesus, living and reigning with the Father in the unity of the Holy Spirit, God, forever.

SEPTEMBER 21

COMMEMORATION OF ST. MATTHEW, APOSTLE

Prayer over the Assembly

Beáti Apóstoli et Evangelístæ Matthǽi, Dómine, précibus adiuvémur: ut, quod possibílitas nostra non óbtinet, eius nobis intercessióne donétur. Per Dóminum.

May St. Matthew, apostle and evangelist, be our aid! Of ourselves, Lord, we cannot obtain your grace; please grant it to us through his merits. This we ask of you through our Lord.

Prayer over the Offerings

Supplicatiónibus beáti Matthǽi Apóstoli et Evangelístæ, quǽsu-

Lord, may the suppliant prayers of the apostle and evangelist St. Matthew mus, Dómine, Ecclésiæ tuæ commendétur oblátio: cuius magníficis prædicatiónibus erudítur. Per Dóminum.

recommend to you the offerings of your Church, which has been taught by his magnificent preaching of the Gospel. This we ask of you through our Lord.

Prayer after the Communion

Percéptis, Dómine, sacraméntis, beáto Matthǽo Apóstolo tuo et Evangelísta interveniénte, deprecámur: ut, quæ pro eius celebráta sunt glória, nobis profíciant ad medélam. Per Dóminum.

We have just received your sacrament; grant, Lord, that this Mass in which we honor your apostle and evangelist St. Matthew may serve by his intercession to heal our souls. This we ask of you through our Lord.

SEPTEMBER 29

THE DEDICATION OF ST. MICHAEL THE ARCHANGEL

ENTRANCE ANTIPHON *Ps. 102:20, 1*

Bless the Lord, all you his angels, you mighty in strength, who do his bidding, obeying his spoken word.

Ps. Bless the Lord, O my soul; and, all my being, bless his holy name.

Glory be to the Father and to the Son and to the Holy Spirit. As it was in the beginning, is now and ever shall be, world without end. Amen. Bless the Lord . . .

Prayer over the Assembly

Deus, qui, miro órdine, Angelórum ministéria hominúmque dispénsas: concéde propítius; ut, a quibus tibi ministrántibus in cælo semper assístitur, ab his in terra vita nostra muniátur. Per Dóminum.

Lord, by an arrangement that commands our admiration you establish the different functions of angels and of men. The angels are always serving you in heaven; grant that at the same time they may protect our life on earth. This we ask of you through our Lord.

EPISTLE   Apocalypse 1:1-5

The angels — as the meaning of the Greek word indicates — are God's messengers to men.

A reading from the book of the Revelations of the apostle John

In those days, to reveal the events that must soon happen, God sent his angel to his servant John. And John has told all that he saw: the word of God and the testimony of Jesus Christ!

Blessed is he who reads and blessed are those who hear the words of this prophecy, if they observe what is written herein; for the time is near!

John to the seven Churches of Asia: Grace and peace be given you by him who is, who was, and who is coming; and by the seven spirits who are before his throne; and by Jesus Christ, who is the faithful witness, the first risen from the dead and the Prince of the kings of earth, who loves us and has delivered us from our sins by his Blood!

Gradual *Ps. 102:20, 1*

Bless the Lord, all you his angels, you mighty in strength, who do his bidding. Bless the Lord, O my soul; and, all my being, bless his holy name.

Alleluia

Alleluia, alleluia. Saint Michael the Archangel, defend us in battle, that we may not perish in the dreadful judgment. Alleluia.

GOSPEL   Matthew 18:1-10

The angels in heaven always see the face of God; but their greatness derives from their humility: before the Lord they are like little children.

A reading from the holy Gospel according to Matthew

At that time the disciples approached Jesus and put this question to him: "Who is the greatest in the kingdom of heaven?"

Jesus called a little child to him. Placing him in their midst, he said to them, "Let me tell you: if you do not change, so as to make your soul like that of a child, you shall not enter the kingdom of heaven. The one who makes himself little like this child, that one will be the greatest in the kingdom of heaven.

"Whoever, in my name, welcomes one of these children with kindness, is really welcoming me. But whoever would lead into sin one of these little ones who believe in me, would be better off if someone tied a millstone around his neck and dropped him to the bottom of the sea.

"Too bad for the world that there are scandals! It is impossible to prevent scandals from coming to be; but it is too bad for that man by whom the scandal is given!

"If your hand or your foot leads you into sin, therefore, cut it off and throw it away from you. It is better for you to enter into life one-handed or lame than to be thrown into the eternal fire with both your hands and both your feet. And if it is your eye that leads you into sin, tear it out and throw it away from you. It is better for you to enter into life with only one eye than to be thrown into the eternal fire with both your eyes.

"See to it, then, that you do not consider any of these little ones as beneath your notice; for I tell you that their angels in heaven never stop contemplating the face of my Father who is in heaven."

OFFERTORY ANTIPHON *Apoc. 8:3, 4*

An angel stood before the altar of the temple, having a golden censer in his hand; and there was given to him much incense; and the smoke of the spices ascended before God. Alleluia.

Prayer over the Offerings

Hóstias tibi, Dómine, laudis offérimus, supplíciter deprecántes: ut eásdem, angélico pro nobis interveniénte suffrágio, et placátus accípias, et ad salútem nostram proveníre concédas. Per Dóminum.

With a fervent prayer we offer this sacrifice, Lord, to your glory; may your holy angels present it to you. In your goodness, please accept it and make it serve toward our salvation. This we ask of you through our Lord.

COMMUNION ANTIPHON *Dan. 3:58*

All you angels of the Lord, bless the Lord, sing a hymn, and exalt him above all forever.

Prayer after the Communion

Beáti Archángeli tui Michaélis intercessióne suffúlti: súpplices te, Dómine, deprecámur; ut, quod ore proséquimur, contingámus et mente. Per Dóminum.

Supported by the intercession of your archangel St. Michael, we entreat you, Lord, that we may receive into our inmost souls the sacrament that has passed our lips. This we ask of you through our Lord.

OCTOBER 7

COMMEMORATION OF BLESSED VIRGIN MARY OF THE ROSARY

Prayer over the Assembly

Deus, cuius Unigénitus per vitam, mortem et resurrectiónem suam nobis salútis ætérnæ præmia comparávit: concéde, quæsumus; ut, hæc mystéria sacratíssimo beátæ Maríæ Vírginis Rosário recoléntes, et imitémur quod cóntinent, et quod promíttunt, assequámur. Per eúndem Dóminum nostrum Iesum Christum Fílium tuum, qui tecum vivit et regnat in unitáte Spíritus Sancti, Deus, per ómnia sæcula sæculórum.

Lord God, your only-begotten Son, by his life, his death and his resurrection, won salvation for us. In the rosary of the Blessed Virgin Mary we relive these mysteries; give us the grace to follow the examples they set before us and to obtain the rewards they promise. This we ask of you through the same Jesus Christ, our Lord and your Son, who lives and reigns with you in the unity of the Holy Spirit, God, forever.

Prayer over the Offerings

Fac nos, quæsumus, Dómine, his munéribus offeréndis conveniénter aptári: et per sacratíssimi Rosárii mystéria sic vitam, passiónem et glóriam Unigéniti tui recólere; ut eius digni promissiónibus efficiámur: Qui tecum vivit et regnat in unitáte Spíritus Sancti, Deus, per ómnia sǽcula sæculórum.

Enable us, Lord, worthily to offer you this sacrifice. Through the mysteries of the rosary make us live again the life, the passion and the glory of your Son and make us worthy of his promises. This we ask of you through him, who lives and reigns with you in the unity of the Holy Spirit, God, forever.

Prayer after the Communion

Sanctíssimæ Genetrícis tuæ, cuius Rosárium celebrámus, quǽsumus, Dómine, précibus adiuvémur: ut et mysteriórum, quæ cólimus, virtus percipiátur; et sacramentórum, quæ súmpsimus, obtineátur efféctus: Qui vivis et regnas cum Deo Patre in unitáte Spíritus Sancti, Deus, per ómnia sǽcula sæculórum.

May your most holy Mother, whose rosary we celebrate, help us, O Lord, by her prayers. Then we shall obtain the fruit of the mysteries we meditate and the effect of the sacraments we have received. This we ask of you, Lord Jesus, living and reigning with the Father in the unity of the Holy Spirit, God, forever.

OCTOBER 11

COMMEMORATION OF THE MOTHERHOOD OF THE BLESSED VIRGIN MARY

Prayer over the Assembly

Deus, qui de beátæ Maríæ Vírginis útero Verbum tuum, Angelo nuntiánte, carnem suscípere voluísti: præsta supplícibus tuis; ut, qui vere eam Genetrícem Dei crédimus, eius apud te intercessiónibus adiuvémur. Per eúndem Dóminum nostrum Iesum Christum Fílium tuum, qui tecum vivit et regnat in unitáte Spíritus Sancti, Deus, per ómnia sǽcula sæculórum.

It was your will, O Lord, that your divine Word should become flesh in the womb of the Blessed Virgin Mary when the angel made his announcement. Grant that your faithful who believe in this divine motherhood may have their prayers heard through Mary's intercession. This we ask of you through the same Jesus Christ, our Lord and your Son, who lives and reigns with you in the unity of the Holy Spirit, God, forever.

Prayer over the Offerings

Tua, Dómine, propitiatióne, et beátæ Maríæ semper Vírginis,

You are kind to us, Lord; and the Blessed Virgin Mary, Mother of your

Unigéniti tui Matris, intercessióne, ad perpétuam atque præséntem hæc oblátio nobis profíciat prosperitátem et pacem. Per eúndem Dóminum nostrum Iesum Christum Fílium tuum, qui tecum vivit et regnat in unitáte Spíritus Sancti, Deus, per ómnia sǽcula sæculórum.

only-begotten Son, intercedes with you. May this offering obtain happiness and peace for us now and forever. This we ask of you through the same Jesus Christ, our Lord and your Son, who lives and reigns with you in the unity of the Holy Spirit, God, forever.

Prayer after the Communion

Hæc nos commúnio, Dómine, purget a crímine: et, intercedénte beáta Vírgine Dei Genetríce María, cæléstis remédii fáciat esse consórtes. Per eúndem Dóminum nostrum Iesum Christum Fílium tuum, qui tecum vivit et regnat in unitáte Spíritus Sancti, Deus, per ómnia sǽcula sæculórum.

May this communion, Lord, cleanse us of our sins; through the intercession of the Blessed Virgin Mary, Mother of God, may it heal our souls and make them share in the happiness of heaven. This we ask of you through the same Jesus Christ, our Lord and your Son, who lives and reigns with you in the unity of the Holy Spirit, God, forever.

OCTOBER 28

COMMEMORATION OF STS. SIMON AND JUDE, APOSTLES

Prayer over the Assembly

Deus, qui nos per beátos Apóstolos tuos Simónem et Iudam ad agnitiónem tui nóminis veníre tribuísti: da nobis eórum glóriam sempitérnam et proficiéndo celebráre, et celebrándo profícere. Per Dóminum.

Through your apostles, St. Simon and St. Jude, you have allowed us, Lord, to learn about yourself. Grant that we may celebrate their everlasting glory by advancing more and more towards the good, and grant that this celebration itself may help us advance in virtue. This we ask of you through our Lord.

Prayer over the Offerings

Glóriam, Dómine, sanctórum Apostolórum tuórum Simónis et Iudæ perpétuam venerántes: quæsumus; ut eam, sacris mystériis expiáti, dígnius celebrémus. Per Dóminum.

Lord, we are honoring your holy apostles Simon and Jude. Purify us by this Mass, and we shall be able more fitly to celebrate their eternal glory. This we ask of you through our Lord.

Prayer after the Communion

Percéptis, Dómine, sacraméntis, supplíciter exorámus: ut, intercedéntibus beátis Apóstolis tuis Simóne et Iuda, quæ pro illórum veneránda gérimus passióne, nobis profíciant ad medélam. Per Dóminum.

We have just received your sacrament; grant, Lord, that this Mass in which we honor the martyrdom of your holy apostles Simon and Jude may serve by their intercession to heal our souls. This we ask of you through our Lord.

THE LAST SUNDAY IN OCTOBER

THE FEAST OF CHRIST THE KING

ENTRANCE ANTIPHON *Apoc. 5:12; 1:6; Ps. 71:1*

Worthy is the Lamb who was slain to receive power, and divinity, and wisdom, and strength, and honor; to him belong glory and dominion forever and ever.

Ps. O God, with your judgment endow the king, and with your justice, the king's son.

Glory be to the Father and to the Son and to the Holy Spirit. As it was in the beginning, is now and ever shall be, world without end. Amen. Worthy is the Lamb . . .

Prayer over the Assembly

Omnípotens sempitérne Deus, qui in dilécto Fílio tuo, universórum Rege, ómnia instauráre voluísti: concéde propítius; ut cunctæ famíliæ géntium, peccáti vúlnere disgregátæ, eius suavíssimo subdántur império: Qui tecum vivit et regnat in unitáte Spíritus Sancti, Deus, per ómnia sǽcula sæculórum.

All-powerful, eternal God, you willed the restoration of all things in Christ, our King. Grant that the family of nations, torn apart by the wound of sin, may submit to the soothing action of his supreme authority. This we ask of you through him, who lives and reigns with you in the unity of the Holy Spirit, God, forever.

EPISTLE   Colossians 1:12-20

In this magnificent text St. Paul reveals to us the mysterious design of the Father: to gather all things together in Christ. The raison d'être of creation is to become the Body of the only and well-beloved Son.

A reading from the letter of the apostle Paul to the Christians of Colossae

Brethren,

We give thanks to God the Father, who has enabled us to share the lot of the saints in the kingdom of light, who has rescued us from the [devil], prince of darkness, to transport us into the kingdom of his beloved Son, whose blood redeems us and cleanses us of our sins.

This Son is the visible image of the invisible God; he is the elder brother of all creation, for it is in him that everything was created, in heaven and on earth, bodies and spirits, even the angels, thrones, dominations, principalities and powers. Everything was created by him and for him; and he himself exists before all things, and everything subsists only in him.

It is he who is the head of the body, that is to say of the Church, he who is the source of life and the first risen from the dead, in order that he may have the first place in all things. In him God has been pleased to gather together all things and, through him, to reconcile his whole creation to himself; for peace has been restored everywhere, on earth and in heaven, through the Blood which our Lord Jesus Christ shed on the Cross.

Gradual *Ps. 71:8, 11*

He shall rule from sea to sea, and from the river to the ends of the earth. All kings shall pay him homage, all nations shall serve him.

Alleluia *Dan. 7:14*

Alleluia, alleluia. His dominion is an everlasting dominion that shall not be taken away, and his kingdom shall not be destroyed. Alleluia.

GOSPEL John 18:33-37

Even while affirming that he is a king, Jesus specifies that his kingdom is of a spiritual order. It is established by faith.

A reading from the holy Gospel according to John

At that time Pilate said to Jesus, "You are the King of the Jews, are you?"

Jesus answered, "Is this something you thought of saying by yourself, or are you repeating what others have said to you about me?"

"Am I a Jew?" Pilate retorted. "Your own people and their high priests have delivered you into my hands. What have you done?"

"My kingship does not come to me from this world," replied Jesus. "If my kingship came from this world, my partisans would have fought to prevent my falling into the hands of the Jews. But my kingship does not have its origin here below."

"Then you are a king?" Pilate concluded.

"Yes, you are right, I am a king. The reason for my being born and for my coming into the world is to bear witness to the truth. Whoever is on the side of truth listens to my word."

OFFERTORY ANTIPHON *Ps. 2:8*

Ask of me and I will give you the nations for an inheritance and the ends of the earth for your possession.

Prayer over the Offerings

Hóstiam tibi, Dómine, humánæ reconciliatiónis offérimus: præsta, quæsumus; ut quem sacrifíciis præséntibus immolámus, ipse cunctis géntibus unitátis et pacis dona concédat, Iesus Christus Fílius tuus Dóminus noster: Qui tecum vivit et regnat in unitáte Spíritus Sancti, Deus, per ómnia sǽcula sæculórum.

We offer you, Lord, the victim who has reconciled mankind to you. May all nations be granted the gifts of unity and peace by him who is immolated in this sacrifice, Jesus Christ, your Son, our Lord, who lives and reigns with you in the unity of the Holy Spirit, God, forever.

COMMUNION ANTIPHON *Ps. 28:10, 11*

The Lord is enthroned as king forever; may the Lord bless his people with peace!

Prayer after the Communion

Immortalitátis alimóniam consecúti, quæsumus, Dómine: ut, qui sub Christi Regis vexíllis militáre gloriámur, cum ipso, in cælésti sede, iúgiter regnáre possímus: Qui tecum vivit et regnat in unitáte Spíritus Sancti, Deus, per ómnia sǽcula sæculórum.

We have received the bread of immortality. Grant, O Lord, to the Christians who glory in fighting under the standard of Christ the King that they may one day reign with him in his heavenly kingdom. This we ask of you through him who lives and reigns with you in the unity of the Holy Spirit, God, forever.

November 1

THE FEAST OF ALL SAINTS

ENTRANCE ANTIPHON *Ps. 32:1*

Let us all rejoice in the Lord, celebrating a feast-day in honor of all the saints, on whose solemnity the angels rejoice, and join in praising the Son of God.

Ps. Exult, you just, in the Lord; praise from the upright is fitting.

Glory be to the Father and to the Son and to the Holy Spirit. As it was in the beginning, is now and ever shall be, world without end. Amen. Let us all rejoice . . .

Prayer over the Assembly

Omnípotens sempitérne Deus, qui nos ómnium Sanctórum tuórum mérita sub una tribuísti cele-

All-powerful, eternal God, you have made it possible for us to honor in this one solemnity the merits of all

britáte venerári: quǽsumus; ut desiderátam nobis tuæ propitiatiónis abundántiam, multiplicátis intercessóribus, largiáris. Per Dóminum.

your saints. Since there are so many pleading for us, give us more abundantly the pardon we desire. This we ask of you through our Lord.

EPISTLE   Apocalypse 7:2-12

The people of Israel numbered 12 tribes. Christ chose to found his Church on the twelve apostles. The number 12 multiplied by itself is the biblical symbol of the totality of the people of God, the sign of the innumerable multitude of the elect.

A reading from the book of the Revelations of the apostle John

In those days I, John, saw an angel ascending from the side where the sun rises, holding in his hand the seal of the living God. In a loud voice he cried to the four angels who had been commissioned to afflict the earth and the sea, "Do not afflict the earth or the sea or the trees, until we have marked the servants of our God on their foreheads!"

And I heard the number of those who had received the impress [of the seal of God].

There were a hundred and forty-four thousand of them, from all the tribes of the people of Israel: the tribes of Juda, Ruben, Gad, Aser, Nephthali, Manasses, Simeon, Levi, Issachar, Zabulon, Joseph and Benjamin; twelve thousand chosen in each one, and each marked with the seal of God.[1]

After that, I saw a crowd so numerous that no one could count them, a crowd from all nations, races, peoples and tongues.

They were all standing before the throne and before the Lamb, clothed in white robes and holding palms in their hands.

They were crying out with all their strength, "Salvation comes from our God who sits upon the throne, and from the Lamb!"

All the angels were standing around the throne, with the elders and the four living creatures;[2] they prostrated themselves before the throne, face downward; and they adored God, while singing:

"Amen! Praise and glory to our God! Wisdom and thanksgiving, honor, power and strength to our God, for ever and ever! Amen!"

Gradual *Ps. 33:10, 11*

Fear the Lord, all you his holy ones, for nought is lacking to those who fear him. But those who seek the Lord want for no good thing.

Alleluia *Matt. 11:28*

Alleluia, alleluia. Come to me, all you who labor and are burdened, and I will give you rest. Alleluia.

[1] The text is here simplified to avoid the repetition of these phrases after the name of each tribe.
[2] Angels who preside at God's creation.

GOSPEL   Matthew 5:1-12

To be members of Christ, we must live according to his spirit. The spirit of Christ sets us in contradiction to the judgment and behavior of the world.

A reading from the holy Gospel according to Matthew

At that time, seeing the crowd who were coming to him, Jesus went up on the mountain and sat down; his disciples gathered around him, and he proceeded to instruct them in these words:

"Blessed are those who have the soul of a poor man! The kingdom of heaven belongs to them.

"Blessed are the meek! They shall possess the land.

"Blessed are those who weep! They shall be consoled.

"Blessed are those who have a hunger and a thirst for perfection! They shall have their fill.

"Blessed are those who know how to show mercy! Mercy will be shown to them.

"Blessed are those who have a pure heart! They shall see God.

"Blessed are the peace-makers! They are the children of God.

"Blessed are those who suffer persecution for the sake of that which is good! The kingdom of heaven belongs to them.

"Blessed are you if people insult you, if they persecute you, if they falsely say all sorts of evil things about you because of me! Be glad, thrill with joy: your reward is great in heaven."

OFFERTORY ANTIPHON *Wis. 3:1-2, 3*

The souls of the just are in the hand of God, and no torment shall touch them; they seemed, in view of the foolish, to be dead; but they are in peace. Alleluia.

Prayer over the Offerings

Múnera tibi, Dómine, nostræ devotiónis offérimus: quæ et pro cunctórum tibi grata sint honóre iustórum, et nobis salutária, te miseránte, reddántur. Per Dóminum.

With love, O Lord, we present our offerings to you. Please accept them as honoring all your saints, and in your mercy make them profitable for our salvation. This we ask of you through our Lord.

COMMUNION ANTIPHON *Matt. 5:8-10*

Blessed are the pure of heart, for they shall see God. Blessed are the peacemakers, for they shall be called children of God. Blessed are they who suffer persecution for justice' sake, for theirs is the kingdom of heaven.

Prayer after the Communion

Da, quǽsumus, Dómine, fidélibus pópulis ómnium Sanctórum semper veneratióne lætári: et eórum perpétua supplicatióne muníri. Per Dóminum.

Grant, O Lord, to your faithful people the continuing joy of honoring all the saints and of being strengthened by their constant intercession. This we ask of you through our Lord.

NOVEMBER 9

DEDICATION OF THE ARCHBASILICA
OF THE MOST HOLY SAVIOR

ENTRANCE ANTIPHON *Gen. 28:17; Ps. 83:2-3*

How awesome is this place! This is none other than the house of God; this is the gate of heaven; and it shall be called the court of God.

Ps. How lovely is your dwelling place, O Lord of hosts! My soul yearns and pines for the courts of the Lord.

Glory be to the Father and to the Son and to the Holy Spirit. As it was in the beginning, is now and ever shall be, world without end. Amen. How awesome . . .

Prayer over the Assembly

Deus, qui nobis per síngulos annos huius sancti templi tui consecratiónis réparas diem, et sacris semper mystériis repræséntas incólumes: exáudi preces pópuli tui, et præsta; ut, quisquis hoc templum benefícia petitúrus ingréditur, cuncta se impetrásse lætétur. Per Dóminum.

O Lord, you recall to us each year the day on which this church was consecrated to you, and you still permit us to celebrate your mysteries in it in good health. To all those who enter this church to implore your favors, grant the joy of seeing all their requests fulfilled. This we ask of you through our Lord.

EPISTLE   Apocalypse 21:2-5

In the Church the presence of God among men is already mysteriously achieved. Every church is an image and an anticipation of the heavenly Jerusalem.

A reading from the book of the Revelations of the apostle John

In those days I saw the holy city, the new Jerusalem, coming down from heaven, from the throne of God, beautiful as a bride adorned for her husband on the wedding day. And I heard a great voice coming from the throne, which said, "Here is God's home with men. Here he will live with them; they shall be his people, and he shall be their God, living with them. He will wipe away every tear from their eyes, and no longer will there be any death; no longer will there be mourning or outcries or suffering, for the former state of the world has disappeared!"

And [God] who was sitting on his throne said, "You see, I am making a new world."

Gradual

This place was made by God, a priceless mystery; it is without reproof. O God, before whom stands the choir of angels, hear the prayers of your servants.

Alleluia Ps. 137:2

Alleluia, alleluia. I will worship at your holy temple and give thanks to your name. Alleluia.

GOSPEL   Luke 19:1-10

Christ went down to the house of the publican least worthy to receive him. Thus has he chosen to live among men, in his Church which is open to all.

It is by imitating Zacchaeus, with the same impatience, the same haste, the same joy, that we are to get inside of God's house to share in his sacrifice.

A reading from the holy Gospel according to Luke

At that time Jesus was passing through the city of Jericho. Now there was a man named Zacchaeus there, head of the publicans and very rich; and he was trying to see who Jesus was. But the crowd blocked his view, as he was a short man. So he ran ahead and climbed a sycamore from which he could see him when he passed. On arriving at this spot, Jesus raised his eyes and said to him, "Zacchaeus, come down quickly; I must stay in your house today." Zacchaeus hurried down and received him with joy.

On seeing this everyone began to murmur, "From a sinner he asks hospitality."

But Zacchaeus, standing before the Lord, said, "Lord, I am going to give half of my possessions to the poor; and, if I have done wrong to anyone, I will give him back four times the amount."

"Today," said Jesus, "salvation has come for this house; for here also is a son of Abraham. The Son of Man has come to seek what was lost and save it."

OFFERTORY ANTIPHON *1 Par. 29:17, 18*

O Lord God, in the simplicity of my heart I have joyfully offered all these things; and I have seen with great joy your people which is here present; O God of Israel, keep this will. Alleluia.

Prayer over the Offerings

Annue, quǽsumus, Dómine, précibus nostris: ut, dum hæc vota præséntia réddimus, ad ætérna prǽmia, te adiuvánte, pervenire mereámur. Per Dóminum.

O Lord, listen favorably to our prayers; may these offerings enable us to obtain the eternal reward. This we ask of you through our Lord.

COMMUNION ANTIPHON *Matt. 21:13*

"My house shall be called a house of prayer," says the Lord; "in it everyone who asks receives; and he who seeks finds, and to him who knocks, it shall be opened."

Prayer after the Communion

Deus, qui de vivis et eléctis lapídibus ætérnum maiestáti tuæ præparas habitáculum: auxiliáre pópulo tuo supplicánti; ut, quod Ecclésiæ tuæ corporálibus próficit spátiis, spirituálibus amplificétur augméntis. Per Dóminum.

O Lord, to build your heavenly temple you choose the living stones of souls. Help your suppliant people: grant that the consecration of new churches on earth may bring your Church a spiritual enrichment. This we ask of you through our Lord.

NOVEMBER 30

COMMEMORATION OF ST. ANDREW, APOSTLE

Prayer over the Assembly

Maiestátem tuam, Dómine, supplíciter exorámus: ut, sicut Ecclésiæ tuæ beátus Andréas Apóstolus éxstitit prædicátor et rector; ita apud te sit pro nobis perpétuus intercéssor. Per Dóminum.

We entreat your majesty, Lord: the apostle St. Andrew taught and directed your Church; may he keep interceding with you on our behalf. This we ask of you through our Lord.

Prayer over the Offerings

Sacrifícium nostrum tibi, Dómine, quǽsumus, beáti Andréæ Apóstoli precátio sancta concíliet: ut, in cuius honóre solémniter exhibétur, eius méritis efficiátur accéptum. Per Dóminum.

Lord, may the prayers and the merits of your apostle St. Andrew make this Mass which we are celebrating in his honor acceptable to you. This we ask of you through our Lord.

Prayer after the Communion

Súmpsimus, Dómine, divína mystéria, beáti Andréæ Apóstoli festivitáte lætántes: quæ, sicut tuis Sanctis ad glóriam, ita nobis, quǽsumus, ad véniam prodésse perfícias. Per Dóminum.

In the joy of this feast of the apostle St. Andrew we have received your divine sacraments, O Lord. To your saints they bring glory; for us may they win forgiveness. This we ask of you through our Lord.

VOTIVE MASS OF THE MOST HOLY SACRAMENT OF THE EUCHARIST

ENTRANCE ANTIPHON *Ps. 80:17, 2*

He fed them with the best of wheat, and filled them with honey from the rock (P.T. alleluia, alleluia).

Ps. Sing joyfully to God our strength; acclaim the God of Jacob.

Glory be to the Father and to the Son and to the Holy Spirit. As it was in the beginning, is now and ever shall be, world without end. Amen. He fed them . . .

Prayer over the Assembly

Deus, qui nobis sub Sacraménto mirábili passiónis tuæ memóriam reliquísti: tríbue, quǽsumus, ita nos Córporis et Sánguinis tui sacra mystéria venerári; ut redemptiónis tuæ fructum in nobis iúgiter sentiámus: Qui vivis et regnas cum Deo Patre in unitáte Spíritus Sancti, Deus, per ómnia sǽcula sæculórum.

Lord Jesus, in a wonderful sacrament you have left us the memorial of your passion. Grant us the grace to adore the hidden presence of your body and blood with such faith that we may always feel within ourselves the effects of your redemption. This we ask of you, Lord Jesus, living and reigning with the Father in the unity of the Holy Spirit, God, forever.

EPISTLE   1 Corinthians 11:23-29

St. Paul's teaching emphasizes the fact that the Mass, or the Lord's supper, sums up the whole mystery of redemption which is being achieved in the history of the world and which the Church makes us relive in the course of every liturgical year. For it is through the Mass that the new alliance is proclaimed, which has been sealed in the blood of Christ and which will be made manifest when the Lord returns in his glory.

A reading from the first letter of the apostle Paul
to the Christians of Corinth

Brethren,

As for me, I have taught you what I myself learned as coming from the Lord. On the night when he was betrayed, the Lord Jesus took bread and, after giving thanks, broke it and said, "Take some of this and eat it. This is my Body, which is going to be sacrificed for you. Do this in remembrance of me." Similarly, at the end of the meal, he took the cup of wine, saying, "This chalice is the new alliance [concluded between God and men] in my Blood. Whenever you drink it, do so in remembrance of me."

Every time you eat this bread and drink this chalice, therefore, you are proclaiming the death of the Lord; and this you will do until he comes again. That is why anyone who eats the bread and drinks the chalice of the Lord in an unworthy manner will have to answer for the way he has mistreated the Lord's Body and Blood.

Let each one examine himself, then, before eating this bread and drinking this chalice. For he who eats and drinks as if there were no question of the Lord's Body, eats and drinks to his own damnation.

Gradual *Ps. 144:15-16*

The eyes of all look hopefully to you, O Lord; and you give them their food in due season. You open your hand; and satisfy the desire of every living thing.

Alleluia John 6:56-57

Alleluia, alleluia. My flesh is food indeed, and my blood is drink indeed. He who eats my flesh, and drinks my blood, abides in me and I in him. Alleluia.

After Septuagesima the **Alleluia** *and following verse are omitted; in their place is said:*

Tract *Mal. 1:11; Prov. 9:5*

From the rising of the sun, even to its setting, my name is great among the nations and everywhere they bring sacrifice to my name, and a pure offering; for great is my name among the nations. Come, eat of my bread, and drink of the wine I have mixed for you.

During Easter season the following is said:

AFTER THE EPISTLE *Luke 24:35; John 6:56-57*

Alleluia, alleluia. The disciples recognized the Lord Jesus in the breaking of the bread. Alleluia. My flesh is food indeed, and my blood is drink indeed. He who eats my flesh, and drinks my blood, abides in me and I in him. Alleluia.

GOSPEL   John 6:56-59

It was after multiplying the loaves in the desert that Jesus announced the Eucharist. By this sequence of acts he was underscoring the fact that his Body and his Blood would be given us to appease our hunger for God and to sustain us in our journey through the desert of this life.

A reading from the holy Gospel according to John

At that time Jesus said to the Jewish throng, "My flesh is a true food, and my blood is a true drink. He who eats my flesh and drinks my blood dwells in me, and I dwell in him.

"The Father, the living God, has sent me, and it is he who makes me live. Similarly, when someone eats me, it is I who make him live. This is the bread that has come down from heaven. It is not like the manna which your fathers ate: they died [none the less]. He who eats this bread will live forever."

OFFERTORY ANTIPHON *Lev. 21:6*

The priests of the Lord offer incense and loaves to God, and therefore they shall be sacred to their God and shall not profane his name (P.T. alleluia).

Prayer over the Offerings

Ecclésiæ tuæ, quǽsumus, Dómine, unitátis et pacis propítius dona concéde: quæ sub oblátis munéri-	To your Church, Lord, please grant the peace and the unity which are signified mystically by the gifts offered

bus mýstice designántur. Per Dóminum.

for your Eucharist. This we ask of you through our Lord.

COMMUNION ANTIPHON *1 Cor. 11:26-27*

As often as you shall eat this bread and drink the cup, you proclaim the death of the Lord, until he comes. Therefore whoever eats this bread or drinks the cup of the Lord unworthily will be guilty of the body and the blood of the Lord (P.T. alleluia).

Prayer after the Communion

Fac nos, quǽsumus, Dómine, divinitátis tuæ sempitérna fruitióne repléri: quam pretiósi Córporis et Sánguinis tui temporális percéptio præfigúrat: Qui vivis et regnas cum Deo Patre in unitáte Spíritus Sancti, Deus, per ómnia sǽcula sæculórum.

Grant us, Lord, in the life to come, the full enjoyment of your divinity, an enjoyment of which we now find the pledge in the reception of your precious body and blood. This we ask of you, Lord Jesus, living and reigning with the Father in the unity of the Holy Spirit, God, forever.

VOTIVE MASS FOR A BRIDE AND GROOM

ENTRANCE ANTIPHON *Tob. 7:15; 8:19; Ps. 127:1*

May the God of Israel join you together; and may he be with you, who was merciful to two only children: and now, O Lord, make them bless you more fully (P.T. alleluia, alleluia).

Ps. Blessed are all who fear the Lord, who walk in his ways.

Glory be to the Father and to the Son and to the Holy Spirit. As it was in the beginning, is now and ever shall be, world without end. Amen. May the God . . .

Prayer over the Assembly

Exáudi nos, omnípotens et miséricors Deus: ut, quod nostro ministrátur offício, tua benedictióne pótius impleátur. Per Dóminum.

Listen to our petition, O almighty and merciful God, so that what is posited by our action here may come to full flower through your blessing. This we ask of you through our Lord.

EPISTLE   Ephesians 5:22-33

The Christian home is to be a manifestation in the world of the love of Christ and his Church. That is why the husband will love his wife as Christ loves the Church, and the wife will love her husband as the Church loves Christ.

A reading from the letter of the apostle Paul to the Christians of Ephesus Brethren,

The wife should be subject to her husband as to the Lord, because for the wife the husband is the head, just as for the Church it is Christ who is the head, the head of that Church which is his Body and which he has saved. Therefore, just as the Church is subject to Christ, the wife must be subject in all things to her husband.

Husbands, love your wives as Christ loves his Church: for her he gave his life in order to make her holy, purifying her by the baptism of water with the accompanying words; for he wants to unite with himself a Church resplendent with beauty, having no blemish or wrinkle or anything of the kind, but all holy and pure.

It is in this way that a man must love his wife: love her as his own body. He who loves his wife is loving himself. No one hates his own body; rather, he nourishes it and takes care of it. That is what Christ does for his Church, [for us] since we are the members of his Body, we are of his flesh and his bones.

Therefore [as the Scripture says], "a man shall leave his father and his mother and stand by his wife; and the two of them shall become one." [1] This is a great mystery; I mean in so far as it signifies [the union of] Christ and his Church. That is why each one of you ought to love his wife as himself, and the wife ought to have a deep respect for her husband.

Gradual *Ps. 127:3*

Your wife shall be like a fruitful vine in the recesses of your home, your children like olive plants around your table.

Alleluia *Ps. 19:3*

Alleluia, alleluia. May the Lord send you help from the sanctuary, from Sion may he sustain you. Alleluia.

After Septuagesima the **Alleluia** *and following verse are omitted; in their place is said:*

Tract *Ps. 127:4-6*

Behold, thus is the man blessed who fears the Lord. The Lord bless you from Sion: may you see the prosperity of Jerusalem all the days of your life. May you see your chiidren's children. Peace be upon Israel!

During Easter season the following is said:

AFTER THE EPISTLE *Ps. 19:3; Ps. 133:3*

Alleluia, alleluia. May the Lord send you help from the sanctuary, from Sion may he sustain you. Alleluia. May the Lord bless you from Sion, the maker of heaven and earth. Alleluia.

GOSPEL   Matthew 19:3-6

The Church, the spouse of Christ, is by that very fact his own body. Christian marriage is indissoluble; in this respect it is the image of the alliance of Christ and the Church.

[1] Genesis 2:24.

A reading from the holy Gospel according to Matthew

At that time some pharisees approached Jesus and posed this question to put him to the test: "Is there any reason at all for which a man is permitted to divorce his wife?"

Jesus answered them, "Do you not know that in the beginning the Creator made them man and woman, and said, 'Thus a man shall leave his father and his mother and stand by his wife; and the two of them shall become one.' [1] As a result, they are no longer two, but only one.

"Man is not to separate, therefore, what God has united!"

OFFERTORY ANTIPHON *Ps. 30:15-16*

My trust is in you, O Lord; I say, "You are my God." In your hands is my destiny (P. T. alleluia).

Prayer over the Offerings

Súscipe, quǽsumus, Dómine, pro sacra connúbii lege munus oblátum: et, cuius largítor es óperis, esto dispósitor. Per Dóminum.

We beseech you, O Lord, accept the sacrifice now being offered for the sacred purposes of marriage; bring to a blessed conclusion this union which you arranged. This we ask of you through our Lord.

COMMUNION ANTIPHON *Ps. 127:4, 6*

Behold, thus is the man blessed who fears the Lord; may you see your children's children. Peace be upon Israel! (P. T. alleluia).

Prayer after the Communion

Quǽsumus, omnípotens Deus: instítúta providéntiæ tuæ pio favóre comitáre; ut, quos legítima societáte connéctis, longǽva pace custódias. Per Dóminum.

With kindly favor accompany this expression of your Providence, we beg of you, almighty God; keep permanently in peace those whom you have united in lawful union. This we ask of you through our Lord.

VOTIVE MASS OF THE HOLY SPIRIT

ENTRANCE ANTIPHON *Wis. 1:7; Ps. 67:2*

The spirit of the Lord fills the world, is all-embracing, and knows man's utterance (P.T. alleluia, alleluia).

Ps. God arises; his enemies are scattered, and those who hate him flee before him.

Glory be to the Father and to the Son and to the Holy Spirit. As it was in the beginning, is now and ever shall be, world without end. Amen. The spirit . . .

[1] Genesis 2:24.

Prayer over the Assembly

Deus, qui corda fidélium Sancti Spíritus illustratióne docuísti: da nobis in eódem Spíritu recta sápere; et de eius semper consolatióne gaudére. Per Dóminum nostrum Iesum Christum Fílium tuum, qui tecum vivit et regnat in unitáte eiúsdem Spíritus Sancti, Deus, per ómnia sǽcula sæculórum.

O Lord, you have instructed the hearts of your faithful by the brilliant light of the Holy Spirit. Give us the grace, under his divine inspiration, to have a sense of the true and a taste for the good, and always to find our consolation and our joy in him. This we ask of you through our Lord Jesus Christ, your Son, who lives and reigns with you in the unity of the same Holy Spirit, God, forever.

EPISTLE   Acts 8:14-17

It is by the sacrament of confirmation that the Holy Spirit is communicated to the Christians in a special way.

A reading from the Acts of the Apostles

In those days the apostles who had remained at Jerusalem learned that the people of Samaria had welcomed the word of God. They therefore sent Peter and John to them.

The two apostles on their arrival prayed for the new believers, that the Holy Spirit might be given them; for he had not yet come down upon any of them: they had only received baptism in the name of the Lord Jesus. Then Peter and John laid their hands on them, and they received the Holy Spirit.

Gradual *Ps. 32:12, 6*

Happy the nation whose God is the Lord, the people he has chosen for his own inheritance. By the word of the Lord the heavens were made; by the breath of his mouth all their hosts.

Alleluia

Alleluia, alleluia. Come, O Holy Spirit, fill the hearts of your faithful; and kindle in them the fire of your love. Alleluia.

After Septuagesima the **Alleluia** *and following verse are omitted; in their place is said:*

Tract Ps. 103:30

Send forth your spirit, and they shall be created; and you shall renew the face of the earth.

O Lord, how good and sweet is your spirit within us! Come, O Holy Spirit, fill the hearts of your faithful; and kindle in them the fire of your love.

During the Easter season the following is said:

AFTER THE EPISTLE *Ps. 103:30*

Alleluia, alleluia. Send forth your spirit, and they shall be created; and you shall renew the face of the earth. Alleluia. Come, O Holy Spirit, fill the hearts of your faithful; and kindle in them the fire of your love. Alleluia.

GOSPEL   John 14:23-31

The new law, Christ's word, is not written on tablets of stone, but engraved in our hearts. It is the Holy Spirit working within us who makes us understand the full import of the Gospel and reveals to us all the demands of charity.

A reading from the holy Gospel according to John

At that time Jesus said to his disciples, "He who loves me obeys my word, and my Father will love him, and we shall come to him and dwell within him. He who does not love me does not obey my word. Moreover, this word that you hear from me is not mine; it is the word of my Father, who sent me. I address it to you, this word, as long as I am with you. But it is the Defender, the Holy Spirit whom the Father will send in my name, who will finish instructing you, at the same time that he reminds you of all that I have told you.

"Peace I bequeath to you; my peace I give you. I do not give it to you as the world does. Let your heart stop being troubled and fearful, then! You have just heard me say, 'I am going away, but I shall come back to you.' If you loved me, you would be happy that I am going to the Father, for the Father is greater than I.

"I have given you fair warning, therefore, before the events, in order that, when they happen, you may believe.

"I shall not have much more conversation with you, for the prince of this world is soon going to act. He has no rights over me; but the world must know that I love the Father and that I do what the Father has commanded me."

OFFERTORY ANTIPHON *Ps. 67:29-30*

Confirm, O God, what you have wrought in us; from your temple, which is in Jerusalem, kings shall offer gifts to you (alleluia).

Prayer over the Offerings

Múnera, quǽsumus, Dómine, obláta sanctífica: et corda nostra Sancti Spíritus illustratióne emúnda. Per Dóminum nostrum Iesum Christum Fílium tuum, qui tecum

Lord, please sanctify our offerings and purify our hearts by the enlightenment of the Holy Spirit. This we ask of you through our Lord Jesus Christ, your Son, who lives and reigns

vivit et regnat in unitáte eiúsdem Spíritus Sancti, Deus, per ómnia sǽcula sæculórum.

with you in the unity of the same Holy Spirit, God, forever.

COMMUNION ANTIPHON *Acts 2:2, 4*

Suddenly there came a sound from heaven, as of a violent wind blowing, where they were sitting. And they were all filled with the Holy Spirit, speaking of the wonderful works of God (alleluia).

Prayer after the Communion

Sancti Spíritus, Dómine, corda nostra mundet infúsio: et sui roris íntima aspersióne fecúndet. Per Dóminum nostrum Iesum Christum Fílium tuum, qui tecum vivit et regnat in unitáte eiúsdem Spíritus Sancti, Deus, per ómnia sǽcula sæculórum.

Lord, you have poured out upon us the gifts of the Holy Spirit; may our hearts be purified by them, and may the dew of his grace make them fruitful in good works. This we ask of you through our Lord Jesus Christ, your Son, who lives and reigns with you in the unity of the same Holy Spirit, God, forever.

VOTIVE MASS OF THANKSGIVING

The Mass of the Most Holy Trinity is said, or of the Holy Spirit, or of the Blessed Virgin Mary, or of any canonized saint listed in the Roman Martyrology, with the following prayers added under a single conclusion:

Prayer over the Assembly

Deus, cuius misericórdiæ non est númerus, et bonitátis infinítus est thesáurus: piíssimæ maiestáti tuæ pro collátis donis grátias ágimus, tuam semper cleméntiam exorántes; ut, qui peténtibus postuláta concédis, eósdem non déserens, ad prǽmia futúra dispónas. Per Dóminum.

O Lord, your mercy is infinite and your goodness is an inexhaustible treasure. For the benefits we have received, we give thanks to your most gracious majesty; and we keep imploring your kindness not to abandon the petitioners whose wishes you have already granted, but to prepare them for receiving your eternal gifts. This we ask of you through our Lord.

Prayer over the Offerings

Odórem, Dómine, sacrifícii huius cum gratiárum actiónibus súscipe, et præsta: ut, quos exaudíre, et incólumes serváre dignátus es,

Accept, O Lord, with our thanksgiving, the perfume of this sacrifice. You have seen fit to listen to us and to keep us safe and sound; guard us

ab omni in pósterum adversitáte custódias; et in tuo servítio, et amóre concréscant. Per Dóminum.

against any adversity in the future, and make us increase in serving and loving you. This we ask of you through our Lord.

Prayer after the Communion

Deus, qui néminem, in te sperántem, nímium afflígi permíttis, sed pium précibus præstas audítum: pro postulatiónibus nostris votísque suscéptis grátias ágimus, te piíssime deprecántes; ut per hæc quæ súmpsimus, a cunctis éripi mereámur advérsis. Per Dóminum.

O Lord, you do not allow those who trust in you to be afflicted with trials too heavy to bear, but you listen to their prayers with kindness. We give you thanks for having heard our supplications and our requests, and we fervently implore that we may be preserved from all adversity by reason of the sacrament we have received. This we ask of you through our Lord.

VOTIVE MASS OF THE MOST HOLY TRINITY

(The Usual Mass for Thanksgiving)

DURING THE YEAR

The choir parts and Collects are as on page 110.

EPISTLE   2 Corinthians 13:11, 13
A reading from the second letter of the apostle Paul
to the Christians of Corinth

Brethren,

Be joyful, seek perfection, encourage one another, have only one heart, live in peace, and the God of peace and love will be with you.

May the grace of our Lord Jesus Christ, the love of God and the communion of the Holy Spirit be with all of you! Amen.

After Septuagesima, **the** **Alleluia** *with its verse is omitted and the following Tract is said:*

Tract

With all our hearts we confess you, we praise you, we bless you, God the Father unbegotten, the only-begotten Son, the Holy Spirit, the Consoler, holy and undivided Trinity; for you are great and do wonderful things; you alone are God. To you be praise, to you glory, to you thanksgiving for eternal ages, O blessed Trinity.

GOSPEL *(same as on the Sunday after the Ascension, page 106).*

DURING THE EASTER SEASON

ENTRANCE ANTIPHON *Tob. 12:6; Ps. 8:2*

Blessed be the holy Trinity and undivided Unity: we will give glory to him, because he has shown his mercy to us. Alleluia, alleluia.

Ps. O Lord, our Lord, how glorious is your name over all the earth!

Glory be to the Father and to the Son and to the Holy Spirit. As it was in the beginning, is now and ever shall be, world without end. Amen. Blessed be . . .

AFTER THE EPISTLE *Dan. 3:52*

Alleluia, alleluia. Blessed are you, O Lord, the God of our fathers, and praiseworthy forever. Alleluia. Let us bless the Father and the Son with the Holy Spirit. Alleluia.

OFFERTORY ANTIPHON *Tob. 12:6*

Blessed be God the Father, and the only-begotten Son of God, and also the Holy Spirit, because he has shown his mercy to us. Alleluia.

COMMUNION ANTIPHON *Tob. 12:6*

We bless the God of heaven, and before all living we will praise him, because he has shown his mercy to us. Alleluia.

VOTIVE MASS FOR PEACE

ENTRANCE ANTIPHON *Sir. 36:18; Ps. 121:1*

Give peace, O Lord, to those who have hoped in you, and let your prophets be proved true. Hear the prayers of your servant, and of your people Israel (P.T. alleluia, alleluia).

Ps. I rejoiced because they said to me, "We will go up to the house of the Lord."

Glory be to the Father and to the Son and to the Holy Spirit. As it was in the beginning, is now and ever shall be, world without end. Amen. Give peace . . .

Prayer over the Assembly

Deus, a quo sancta desidéria, recta consília et iusta sunt ópera: da servis tuis illam, quam mundus dare non potest, pacem; ut et corda nostra mandátis tuis dédita, et, hóstiam subláta formídine, témpora sint, tua protectióne, tranquílla. Per Dóminum.

From you, Lord, comes holiness in our desires, right thinking in our plans and justice in our actions. Grant your children that peace which the world cannot give; then our hearts will be devoted to your laws, we shall be delivered from the terrors of war and, under your protection, we shall be able to live in tranquillity. This we ask of you through our Lord.

EPISTLE   2 Machabees 1:1-5

The text which the liturgy has us read as the Epistle of this Mass is a letter written by the Jews of Palestine to the Jewish communities of Egypt to show them that, despite the persecutions afflicting their people, God is not forgetting his promises and is protecting his faithful. This passage stresses the fact that peace is a divine gift, that it resides primarily in our reconciliation with God and that it demands the opening of our soul to the word of the Lord.

A reading from the book of the Machabees

A letter from the Jews who live in Jerusalem and the region of Judea, to the Jews their brethren who live in Egypt: Greetings and true peace!

May God be good to you, and may he remember the covenant he made with his faithful servants Abraham, Isaac and Jacob.

May he give you all a generous heart that you may adore him and do his will with enthusiasm and docility. May he open your heart to his law and his commandments, and may he establish you in peace. May he listen to your prayers, may he be reconciled with you, and may he not abandon you in time of adversity — he who is the Lord our God.

Gradual Ps. 121:6-7

Pray for the peace of Jerusalem! May those who love you prosper. May peace be within your walls, prosperity in your buildings.

Alleluia Ps. 147:12

Alleluia, alleluia. Glorify the Lord, O Jerusalem; praise your God, O Sion. Alleluia.

After Septuagesima the **Alleluia** *and following verse are omitted; in their place is said:*

Tract Ps. 75:2-4

God is renowned in Juda; in Israel great is his name. In the city of peace is his abode; his dwelling is in Sion. There he shattered the flashing shafts of the bow, shield and sword, and weapons of war.

During Easter season the following is said:

AFTER THE EPISTLE *Ps. 147:12, 14*

Alleluia, alleluia. Glorify the Lord, O Jerusalem; praise your God, O Sion. Alleluia. He has granted peace in your borders; with the best of wheat he fills you. Alleluia.

GOSPEL   John 20:19-23

It is the evening of Easter day. Jesus proclaims peace to his apostles as the first fruit of the Redemption. He sends them to bring to the world that peace which results from the forgiveness of sins.

A reading from the holy Gospel according to John

At that time, on the same day [Easter], the first of the week, when evening had come and when, in fear of the Jews, the disciples had closed the doors of the quarters where they were staying, Jesus came. He stood in their midst and said, "Peace be with you!" and immediately after this greeting he showed them his hands and his side. The disciples were filled with joy when they saw the Lord.

Then Jesus said to them a second time, "Peace be with you! Just as the Father sent me, I also send you." With this he breathed on them and added, "Receive the Holy Spirit. If you forgive anyone's sins, they shall be forgiven; if you hold anyone's sins back, they shall be held back."

OFFERTORY ANTIPHON *Ps. 134:3, 6*

Praise the Lord, for he is good; sing to his name, for it is sweet. All that he wills he does in heaven and on earth (P.T. alleluia).

Prayer over the Offerings

Deus, qui credéntes in te pópulos nullis sinis cóncuti terróribus: dignáre preces et hóstias dicátæ tibi plebis suscípere; ut pax a tua pietáte concéssa, christianórum fines ab omni hoste fáciat esse secúros. Per Dóminum.

O Lord, you do not allow the nations who put their trust in you to live in fear. Please accept the prayers and the offerings of your Church, and in your kindness grant us peace, that our country may be safe from all enemies. This we ask of you through our Lord.

COMMUNION ANTIPHON *John 14:27*

"Peace I leave with you, my peace I give to you," says the Lord (P.T. alleluia).

Prayer after the Communion

Deus, auctor pacis et amátor, quem nosse vívere, cui servíre regnáre est: prótege ab ómnibus impugnatiónibus súpplices tuos; ut, qui in defensióne tua confídimus, nullíus hostilitátis arma timeámus. Per Dóminum.

O God, source and lover of peace, to know you is to live, and to serve you is to reign. Preserve your faithful from war. They know that you can defend them; do not let them fear the assaults of any foe. This we ask of you through our Lord.

VOTIVE MASS OF THE ANGELS

ENTRANCE ANTIPHON *Ps. 102: 20, 1*

Bless the Lord, all you his angels, you mighty in strength, who do his bidding, obeying his spoken word (P.T. alleluia, alleluia).

Ps. Bless the Lord, O my soul; and, all my being, bless his holy name.

Glory be to the Father and to the Son and to the Holy Spirit. As it was in the beginning, is now and ever shall be, world without end. Amen. Bless the Lord . . .

Prayer over the Assembly

Deus, qui, miro órdine, Angelórum ministéria hominúmque dispénsas: concéde propítius; ut, a quibus tibi ministrántibus in cælo semper assístitur, ab his in terra vita nostra muniátur. Per Dóminum.

Lord, by an arrangement that commands our admiration, you establish the different functions of angels and of men. The angels are always serving you in heaven; grant that at the same time they may protect our life on earth. This we ask of you through our Lord.

EPISTLE   Apocalypse 5:11-14

A reading from the book of the Revelations of the apostle John

In those days I heard the sound of a multitude of angels, encircling the throne, and of the living creatures and the elders. They numbered into the thousands of thousands, and they were crying in a loud voice:

"He is worthy, the Lamb who was crucified, to receive power and adoration; wisdom, honor and strength; and glory and blessing!"

And all creation that is in heaven and on earth and under the earth and in the sea — all the beings that are found anywhere — I heard them saying:

"To him who sits on the throne and to the Lamb: praise, honor, glory and power for ever and ever!"

And the four living creatures were saying, "Amen!" And the twenty-four elders fell face downward, and they adored him who lives for ever and ever.

Gradual *Ps. 148:1-2*

Praise the Lord from the heavens, praise him in the heights. Praise him, all you his angels, praise him, all you his hosts.

Alleluia *Ps. 137:1-2*

Alleluia, alleluia. In the presence of the angels I will sing your praise; I will worship at your holy temple and give thanks to your name. Alleluia.

After Septuagesima the **Alleluia** *and following verse are omitted; in their place is said:*

Tract *Ps. 102:20, 21-22*

Bless the Lord, all you his angels, you mighty in strength who do his bidding. Bless the Lord, all you his hosts, his ministers, who do his will. Bless the Lord, all his works, everywhere in his domain. Bless the Lord, O my soul!

During Easter season the following is said:

AFTER THE EPISTLE *Ps. 137:1-2; Matt. 28:2*

Alleluia, alleluia. In the presence of the angels I will sing your praise; I will worship at your holy temple and give thanks to your name. Alleluia. An angel of the Lord came down from heaven, and drawing near rolled back the stone, and sat upon it. Alleluia.

GOSPEL   John 1:47-51

A reading from the holy Gospel according to John

At that time, seeing Nathanael coming to meet him, Jesus said, "Here is a true son of Israel, a man without subterfuge."

"How do you know me?" asked Nathanael.

"Before Philip called you, when you were under the fig tree, I saw you."

"Rabbi," cried Nathanael, "you are the Son of God! You are the King of Israel!"

Jesus answered, "Because I said to you, 'I saw you under the fig tree,' you believe in me. You will see something greater than that! This is a solemn truth I am telling you: you will see heaven wide open, and the angels of God going up and coming down upon the Son of Man."

OFFERTORY ANTIPHON *Apoc. 8:3, 4*

An angel stood near the altar of the temple, having a golden censer in his hand. And there was given to him much incense: and the smoke of the perfumes ascended before God (P.T. alleluia).

Prayer over the Offerings

Hóstias tibi, Dómine, laudis offérimus, supplíciter deprecántes: ut eásdem, angélico pro nobis interveniénte suffrágio, et placátus accípias, et ad salútem nostram proveníre concédas. Per Dóminum.

With a fervent prayer we offer this sacrifice, Lord, to your glory; may your holy angels present it to you. In your goodness, please accept it and make it serve toward our salvation. This we ask of you through our Lord.

COMMUNION ANTIPHON

Angels, archangels, thrones and dominations, principalities, and powers, the virtues of heaven, cherubim and seraphim, bless the Lord forever (P.T. alleluia).

Prayer after the Communion

Repléti, Dómine, benedictióne cælésti, supplíciter implorámus: ut, quod frágili celebrámus of-

Filled, through the Eucharist, with your heavenly blessing, we humbly entreat you, Lord, that, with the help

fício, sanctórum Angelórum atque Archangelórum nobis prodésse sentiámus auxílio. Per Dóminum.

of the angels and the archangels, we may be able to feel the good effects of the sacrifice which we frail mortals have celebrated. This we ask of you through our Lord.

MASS ON THE DAY OF BURIAL

The Mass on the day of burial is given on page 307.

MASS FOR THE DEAD

ENTRANCE ANTIPHON *4 Esdras 2:34, 35; Ps. 64:2-3*

Eternal rest grant unto them, O Lord: and let perpetual light shine upon them.

Ps. To you we owe our hymn of praise, O God, in Sion; to you must vows be fulfilled in Jerusalem. Hear my prayer; to you all flesh must come. Eternal rest . . .

Prayer over the Assembly

Inclína, Dómine, aurem tuam ad preces nostras, quibus misericórdiam tuam súpplices deprecámur: ut ánimam fámuli tui N., quam de hoc sǽculo migráre iussísti; in pacis ac lucis regióne constítuas, et Sanctórum tuórum iúbeas esse consórtem. Per Dóminum.

O Lord, hear our prayers, in which we humbly ask of your mercy that you would give your servant, N., whom you have commanded to leave this world, a place in the land of light and peace, and bid that he be made a companion of your saints. This we ask of you through our Lord.

EPISTLE   Apocalypse 14:13

It is in connection with the martyrs that St. John promises happiness to those who die in the Lord. But all those who have lived for Christ are assured of the same reward.

A reading from the book of the Revelations of the apostle John

In those days I heard a voice from heaven saying to me, "Write this: Blessed are the dead who die in the Lord! Yes, says the Spirit, from now on, let them rest from their troubles. For the good that they have done is going along with them."

Gradual 4 Esdras 2:34, 35; Ps. 111:7

Eternal rest grant unto them, O Lord: and let perpetual light shine upon them. The just man shall be in everlasting remembrance; an evil report he shall not fear.

Tract

Absolve, O Lord, the souls of all the faithful departed from every bond of sin, and by the help of your grace may they deserve to escape the judgment of vengeance and to enjoy the blessedness of light eternal.

GOSPEL   John 6:51-55

The Eucharist renews in us every day the eternal life received at baptism. And the communion in Christ's Body is, moreover, like a pledge of the resurrection of our body.

A reading from the holy Gospel according to John

At that time Jesus said to the Jewish crowd, "I am the living bread that comes down from heaven. If anyone eats some of this bread, he will live for eternity. And the bread that I shall give is my flesh, delivered up for the life of the world."

The Jews then quarreled among themselves. "How can this man give us his flesh to eat?" they were saying.

Jesus said to them, therefore, "This is the solemn truth: If you do not eat the flesh of the Son of Man and if you do not drink His blood, you shall not have life in you. But he who eats my flesh and drinks my blood possesses life eternal; and I myself will raise him up on the last day."

OFFERTORY RESPONSE

Lord Jesus Christ, King of glory, deliver the souls of all the faithful departed from the pains of hell and the deep pit; deliver them from the lion's mouth; may hell not swallow them up, nor may they fall into darkness, but may Michael, the holy standard-bearer, bring them into the holy light which you once promised to Abraham and to his seed. We offer you, O Lord, sacrifices and prayers of praise; receive them for the souls whom we remember this day. Grant, O Lord, that they may pass from death to life, which you once promised to Abraham and to his seed.

Prayer over the Offerings

Annue nobis, quǽsumus, Dómine, ut ánimæ fámuli tui N., hæc prosit oblátio: quam immolándo, totíus mundi tribuísti relaxári delícta. Per Dóminum.

Listen, Lord, as we plead that this offering be beneficial to the soul of your servant, N.; for at its immolation you deigned to forgive the sins of the entire world. This we ask of you through our Lord.

COMMUNION ANTIPHON *4 Esdras 2:35, 34*

May light eternal shine upon them, O Lord, with your saints forever, for you are merciful. Eternal rest grant unto them, O Lord; and let perpetual light shine upon them, with your saints forever, for you are merciful.

Prayer after the Communion

Absólve, quǽsumus, Dómine, ánimam fámuli tui N. ab omni vínculo delictórum: ut in resurrectiónis glória inter Sanctos et eléctos tuos resuscitátus respíret. Per Dóminum.

Lord, please remove every hindrance of sin from the soul of your servant, N., in order that he may live anew in the glory of your holy elect. This we ask of you through our Lord.

MASS ON THE ANNIVERSARY OF THE DAY OF BURIAL

The prayers are the same as in the preceding Mass for the Dead except for the following:

Prayer over the Assembly

Deus, indulgentiárum Dómine: da ánimæ fámuli tui N. (fámulæ tuæ N. vel animábus famulórum, famularúmque tuárum) cuius (quorum) anniversárium depositiónis diem commemorámus, refrigérii sedem, quiétis beatitúdinem, et lúminis claritátem. Per Dóminum nostrum.

Lord God most kind, bestow upon the soul of your servant, N., the anniversary of whose burial we are commemorating, refreshment, beatitude, and the light of glory. This we ask of you through our Lord.

EPISTLE   2 Machabees 12:43-46

At the period of the Machabees, in the course of the persecutions they had to undergo, the Jews, inspired by God, proclaimed their faith in the immortality of the soul and the resurrection of bodies.

It is this belief, confirmed by Christ's teaching, that gives meaning to our prayer for the departed.

A reading from the book of Machabees

In those days [after the battle], the valiant Judas Machabeus, having made a collection, sent two thousand drachmas of silver to Jerusalem, that a sacrifice might be offered in expiation for the sins of the dead; a fine, noble thought, inspired by his belief in the resurrection.

For, if he had not believed that those who had fallen would rise again, it would have been useless and superfluous to pray for the dead. But it was his considered opinion that great mercy is in store for those who have fallen asleep with the love of God.

It is a holy and pious thought, therefore, to pray for the dead, that they may be freed from their sins.

GOSPEL   John 6:37-40

The will of the Father is to associate all men in his happy, eternal life by adopting them as sons in Christ Jesus, his only-begotten Son.

A reading from the holy Gospel according to John

At that time Jesus said to the Jewish crowd, "All those whom my Father gives me will come to me; and those who come to me I will not cast out. For it was not to do my will that I came down from heaven, but to do the will of him who sent me. Now the will of him who sent me, the will of the Father, is that I should not lose any of those whom he gives me, but that I should raise them up on the last day. Yes, the will of my Father who sent me is that whoever sees the Son and believes in him should have eternal life; and I myself will raise him upon the last day."

Prayer over the Offerings

Propitiáre, Dómine, supplicatiónibus nostris, pro ánima fámuli tui N. (fámulæ tuæ N., vel animábus famulórum, famularúmque tuárum), cuius (quorum) hódie ánnua dies ágitur: pro qua (quibus) tibi offérimus sacrifícium laudis; ut eam (eas) sanctórum tuórum consórtio sociáre dignéris. Per Dóminum.

O Lord, be mercifully disposed toward our supplications in favor of your servant, N., whose anniversary of death occurs today; for him do we offer this sacrifice of praise to you that you may number him among your holy ones. This we ask of you through our Lord.

Prayer after the Communion

Præsta, quæsumus, Dómine: ut ánima fámuli tui N. (fámulæ tuæ N., vel ánimæ famulórum, famularúmque tuárum), cuius (quorum) anniversárium depositiónis diem commemorámus; his purgáta (purgátæ) sacrifíciis, indulgéntiam páriter et réquiem cápiat (cápiant) sempitérnam. Per Dóminum.

Answer our petition, Lord; may the soul of your servant, N., the anniversary of whose burial we are commemorating, become purified by this sacrifice and obtain forgiveness and eternal rest. This we ask of you through our Lord.

APPROVED TEXT FOR THE ORDINARY PARTS OF THE MASS PERTAINING TO THE PEOPLE

THE LITURGY OF THE WORD OF GOD

Entrance Rite

KYRIE

Priest: Lord, have mercy.

All: Lord, have mercy.

Priest: Lord, have mercy.

All: Christ, have mercy.

Priest: Christ, have mercy.

All: Christ, have mercy.

Priest: Lord, have mercy.

All: Lord, have mercy.

Priest: Lord, have mercy.

GLORIA

Priest: Glory to God in the highest.

All: And on earth peace to men of good will. *
We praise you. We bless you.
   We worship you. We glorify you. *
We give you thanks for your great glory. *
Lord God, heavenly King, God the Father almighty. *
Lord Jesus Christ, the only-begotten Son. *
Lord God, Lamb of God, Son of the Father. *
You, who take away the sins of the world, *
   have mercy on us. *
You, who take away the sins of the world, *
   receive our prayer. *
You, who sit at the right hand of the Father, *
   have mercy on us. *
For you alone are holy. * You alone are Lord. *
You alone, O Jesus Christ, are most high, * With the
   Holy Spirit, in the glory of God the Father. Amen.

THE PRAYER (COLLECT)

Priest: Dominus vobiscum.

All: Et cum spiritu tuo.

Priest: Oremus . . .
per omnia saecula saeculorum. All: Amen.

234

The Word of God

EPISTLE

GOSPEL

Deacon (or Priest): The Lord be with you.

All: And with your spirit.

Deacon (or Priest): † A reading from the holy Gospel
according to (Matthew) . . .

All: Glory to you, O Lord.

CREED

Priest: I believe in one God.

All: The Father almighty, maker of heaven and earth, *
and of all things visible and invisible. *
And I believe in one Lord, Jesus Christ, *
the only-begotten Son of God. *
Born of the Father before all ages. *
God of God, Light of Light, true God of true God. *
Begotten, not made, * of one substance with the Father. *
By whom all things were made. *
Who for us men and for our salvation
came down from heaven. *
And he became flesh by the Holy Spirit
of the Virgin Mary: * and was made man. *
He was also crucified for us, *
suffered under Pontius Pilate, and was buried. *
And on the third day he rose again,
according to the Scriptures. *
He ascended into heaven
and sits at the right hand of the Father. *
He will come again in glory
to judge the living and the dead. *
And of his kingdom there will be no end. *
And I believe in the Holy Spirit,
the Lord and Giver of life, *
who proceeds from the Father and the Son. *
Who together with the Father and the Son
is adored and glorified, *
and who spoke through the prophets. *
And one holy, Catholic, and Apostolic Church. *
I confess one baptism for the forgiveness of sins. *
And I await the resurrection of the dead. *
And the life of the world to come. Amen.

THE LITURGY OF THE EUCHARIST

The Preparation of the Gifts

OFFERTORY

Priest: The Lord be with you.

All: And with your spirit.

Priest: Let us pray.

PRAYER OVER THE GIFTS (SECRET)

Priest: . . . per omnia saecula saeculorum.

All: Amen.

The Eucharistic Prayer

PREFACE

Priest: Dominus vobiscum.

All: Et cum spiritu tuo.

Priest: Sursum corda.

All: Habemus ad Dominum.

Priest: Gratias agamus Domino Deo nostro.

All: Dignum et iustum est.

SANCTUS

All: Holy, holy, holy Lord God of hosts. *
Heaven and earth are filled with your glory. *
Hosanna in the highest. *
Blessed is he who comes in the name of the Lord. *
Hosanna in the highest.

CONCLUSION OF CANON

Priest: . . . per omnia saecula saeculorum.

All: Amen.

The Eucharistic Banquet

THE LORD'S PRAYER

Priest: Let us pray. Taught by our Savior's command
and formed by the word of God, we dare to say:

All: Our Father, who art in heaven, *
hallowed be thy name; *
thy kingdom come; *
thy will be done on earth as it is in heaven. *
Give us this day our daily bread; *
and forgive us our trespasses *
as we forgive those who trespass against us; *
and lead us not into temptation, *
but deliver us from evil.

PRAYER FOR PEACE

Priest: . . . per omnia saecula saeculorum.

All: Amen.

Priest: Pax Domini sit semper vobiscum.

All: Et cum spiritu tuo.

AGNUS DEI

All: Lamb of God, who take away the sins of the world, *
have mercy on us. *

All: Lamb of God, who take away the sins of the world, *
have mercy on us. *

All: Lamb of God, who take away the sins of the world, *
grant us peace.

(In Requiem Masses: . . . grant them rest . . . grant them rest . . .
grant them eternal rest.)

COMMUNION OF THE FAITHFUL

Priest: Behold the Lamb of God, * behold him who takes away the
sins of the world.

All (three times): Lord, I am not worthy that you should come
under my roof. *
Speak but the word and my soul will be healed.

Priest: The Body of Christ.

Communicant: Amen.

POSTCOMMUNION PRAYER

Priest: Dominus vobiscum.

All: Et cum spiritu tuo.

Priest: Oremus . . . per omnia saecula saeculorum.

All: Amen.

DISMISSAL

Priest: The Lord be with you.

All: And with your spirit.

Deacon (or Priest): Go, the Mass is ended.

All: Thanks be to God.

(In Requiem Masses: May they rest in peace.

All: Amen.)

BLESSING

Priest: May almighty God bless you, the Father, and the Son, † and
the Holy Spirit.

All: Amen.

THE ORDINARY OF THE MASS

THE LITURGY OF THE WORD

The complete text of the Ordinary of the Mass is here
given. It may well serve as a **constant** providing the form
upon which variations may be made according to circumstances and degrees of solemnity. Although the parts are
assigned to **Priest** and **All**, the specific application is now
so diverse that the rubrics locally intended for a given
Mass provide the guide for the distribution of parts.
The parts of the Mass proper to each Sunday and greater
feast are given on pages 15 to 233.

Entrance Rite

We greet Christ in the person of the priest as he approaches the altar to renew the great Sacrifice of redemption.

STAND

Entrance hymn from Nos. 35-50, or other hymn as directed.

KNEEL

PRAYERS AT THE FOOT OF THE ALTAR

Priest: In nómine Patris † et Fílii et Spíritus Sancti. Amen.

In the Name of the Father †
and of the Son and of the Holy
Spirit. Amen.

Introíbo ad altáre Dei.
All: Ad Deum qui lætíficat
iuventútem meam.

I am come to the altar of God.
To God who makes me young
and joyful.

Priest: Adiutórium nostrum in
nómine Dómini.
All: Qui fecit cælum et ter-
ram.

Our help is in the Name of the
Lord,
who made heaven and earth.

Priest: Confíteor Deo omnipoténti . . . oráre pro me ad Dóminum Deum nostrum.

I confess to almighty God,
etc.

238

All: Misereátur tui omnípotens Deus, / et dimíssis peccátis tuis, perdúcat te ad vitam ætérnam.
Priest: Amen.

May almighty God have mercy on you. Having forgiven you your sins, may he guide you to eternal life.
Amen.

The Confiteor is the Church's Act of Contrition. To the whole Communion of Saints, in heaven and on earth, we publicly acknowledge ourselves as sinners, and with repentant hearts implore their intercession and God's forgiveness.

All: Confíteor Deo omnipoténti, / beátæ Maríæ semper Vírgini, / beáto Michaéli Archángelo, / beáto Ioánni Baptístæ, / sanctis Apóstolis Petro et Paulo, / ómnibus Sanctis, et tibi, Pater, / quia peccávi nimis / cogitatióne, verbo et ópere,

I confess to almighty God, to blessed Mary, ever Virgin, to blessed Michael the Archangel, to blessed John the Baptist, to the holy Apostles Peter and Paul, to all the Saints, and to you, Father, that I have sinned exceedingly in thought, word and deed,

(strike the breast three times as a sign of contrition),

mea culpa, / mea culpa, / mea máxima culpa. / Ideo precor beátam Maríam semper Vírginem, / beátum Michaélem Archángelum, / beátum Ioánnem Baptístam, / sanctos Apóstolos Petrum et Paulum, / omnes Sanctos, et te, Pater, / oráre pro me ad Dóminum Deum nostrum.
Priest: Misereátur vestri omnípotens Deus, et dimíssis peccátis vestris, perdúcat vos ad vitam ætérnam.
All: Amen.

through my fault, through my fault, through my most grievous fault. Therefore I beseech blessed Mary, ever Virgin, blessed Michael the Archangel, blessed John the Baptist, the holy Apostles Peter and Paul, all the Saints and you, Father, to pray to the Lord our God for me.
May almighty God have mercy on you. Having forgiven you your sins, may he guide you to eternal life.
Amen.

We continue with invocations expressing our confidence in God's mercy.

Priest: Indulgéntiam, † absolutiónem, et remissiónem peccatórum nostrórum, tríbuat nobis omnípotens et miséricors Dóminus.
All: Amen.

May the almighty and merciful Lord grant us pardon, † absolution and remission of our sins.

Amen.

Priest: Deus, tu convérsus vivifi-
cábis nos.

Be concerned, Lord, and confer your life upon us,

All: Et plebs tua lætábitur in
te.

that your people may share
your joy.

Priest: Osténde nobis, Dómine,
misericórdiam tuam.

Favor us, O Lord,

All: Et salutáre tuum da nobis.

by granting us your saving
grace.

Priest: Dómine, exáudi orlatió-
nem meam.

Listen to my plea, O Lord,

All: Et clamor meus ad te
véniat.

and give my prayer a hearing.

Priest: Dóminus vobíscum.

The Lord be with you.

All: Et cum spíritu tuo.

And with your spirit.

As the priest ascends the altar, he says silently:

Orémus. Aufer a nobis, quæsumus, Dómine, iniquitátes nostras:
ut ad Sancta sanctórum puris mereámur méntibus introíre. Per
Christum Dóminum nostrum.
Amen.

Let us pray. Lord, we beg you
to efface our sins, for only with
purified hearts may we enter this
holiest sanctuary. Through Christ
our Lord. Amen.

*The altar (Christ) is greeted with a kiss while the priest
continues:*

Orámus te, Dómine, per mérita
Sanctórum tuórum, quorum relí-
quiæ hic sunt, et ómnium Sanctórum: ut indulgére dignéris ómnia
peccáta mea. Amen.

Through the merits of all your
saints, particularly of those whose
relics are honored here, we beg
you, Lord, to pardon all my sins.
Amen.

ENTRANCE ANTIPHON

STAND

*The text of the Entrance Antiphon and other prayers for
Sundays, greater feasts and other parochial occasions
are given on pages 15 to 233.*

*The Entrance Antiphon, which in most instances sets the
mood and spirit for a given Mass, is followed by our
repeated cry for divine mercy (for melodies, see page
266; 347-422*

KYRIE

Priest: Lord, have mercy.
All: Lord, have mercy.

Priest: Lord, have mercy.
All: Christ, have mercy.

Priest: Christ, have mercy.
All: Christ, have mercy.

Priest: Lord, have mercy.
All: Lord, have mercy.

Priest: Lord, have mercy.

Continuing the angels' song on Christmas night, we voice our praise and gratitude to the Father, Son, and Holy Spirit in the

GLORIA

Priest: Glory to God in the highest.
All: And on earth peace to men of good will. *
We praise you. We bless you.
We worship you. We glorify you. *
We give you thanks for your great glory. *
Lord God, heavenly King, God the Father almighty. *
Lord Jesus Christ, the only-begotten Son. *
Lord God, Lamb of God, Son of the Father. *
You, who take away the sins of the world, *
have mercy on us. *
You, who take away the sins of the world, *
receive our prayer. *
You, who sit at the right hand of the Father, *
have mercy on us. *
For you alone are holy. * You alone are Lord. *
You alone, O Jesus Christ, are most high, *
With the Holy Spirit, in the glory of God the
Father. Amen.

Priest: Dóminus vobíscum.   The Lord be with you.
All: Et cum spíritu tuo.   And with your spirit.

Representing all of us who are gathered around the altar, the priest addresses our petitions to the Father,

through the Son, in the Holy Spirit. With an animated
AMEN we put our seal to his prayer, the

COLLECT

Priest: Orémus . . . per ómnia   Let us pray . . . for ever and
sǽcula sæculórum.   ever.
   All: Amen.   Amen.

We have raised our hearts to God in petition and in
praise; God now answers us with words that enlighten
our minds and direct our wills according to his holy
wisdom. He speaks to us through his prophets (Epistle),
through his Son (Gospel), and through the Church (sermon). We listen attentively, gratefully.

The Word of God

EPISTLE

SIT

While the Epistle is read, listen attentively; if you have
difficulty understanding the reader, follow along in your
missal or with the text as given on pages 15 to 233.

Optional. If there is singing, it would not be inappropri-
ate to voice our gratitude for God's message in a
GRADUAL RESPONSORY as given on pages 15 to 233.

The priest prepares for the proclamation of the Gospel
by reciting:

Munda cor meum, ac lábia mea,   Purify my heart and my lips, al-
omnípotens Deus, qui lábia Isaíæ   mighty God. Just as you purified
Prophétæ cálculo mundásti igní-   the lips of the prophet Isaiah
to: ita me tua grata miseratióne   with a burning coal, so purify me
dignáre mundáre, ut sanctum   now through your generous mer-
Evangélium tuum digne váleam   cy in order that I may compe-
nuntiáre. Per Christum Dómi-   tently proclaim your holy Gos-
num nostrum. Amen.   pel. Through Christ our Lord.
   Amen.

Iube, Dómine, benedícere.   Give a blessing, Lord.
Dóminus sit in corde meo, et in   May the Lord be present in my
lábiis meis: ut digne et competén-   heart and upon my lips, enabling
ter annúntiem Evangélium suum.   me to retell his Gospel in a com-
Amen.   petent and truthful manner.
   Amen.

As if Christ himself were personally speaking, we listen to the

STAND

GOSPEL

Deacon (or Priest): The Lord be with you.
All: And with your spirit.
Deacon (or Priest): † A reading from the holy Gospel according to (Matthew) . . .
All: Glory to you, O Lord.

Kissing the Gospel book, the priest adds:

Per evangélica dicta deleántur nostra delícta.

By the Gospel message may our sins be blotted out.

SIT

The Church, the voice of the Holy Spirit, now addresses us through the priest as he applies directly and personally the content of the Readings in a sermon or homily. We give our willing response in the

STAND

CREED

Priest: I believe in one God.
All: The Father almighty, maker of heaven and earth, *
and of all things visible and invisible. *
And I believe in one Lord, Jesus Christ, *
the only-begotten Son of God. *
Born of the Father before all ages. *
God of God, Light of Light, true God of true God. *
Begotten, not made, *
of one substance with the Father. *
By whom all things were made. *
Who for us men and for our salvation
came down from heaven. *
And he became flesh by the Holy Spirit
of the Virgin Mary: * and was made man. *
He was also crucified for us, *
suffered under Pontius Pilate, and was buried. *
And on the third day he rose again,
according to the Scriptures. *
He ascended into heaven
and sits at the right hand of the Father. *

He will come again in glory
   to judge the living and the dead. *
And of his kingdom there will be no end. *
And I believe in the Holy Spirit,
   the Lord and Giver of life, *
   who proceeds from the Father and the Son. *
Who together with the Father and the Son
   is adored and glorified, *
   and who spoke through the prophets. *
And one holy, Catholic, and Apostolic Church. *
I confess one baptism for the forgiveness of sins. *
And I await the resurrection of the dead. *
And the life of the world to come. Amen.

> With this public profession of faith, the liturgy of the
> word comes to an end. In ancient times the catechumens
> were dismissed at this point, because they were not yet
> baptized and therefore unable to share in the Eucharistic
> liturgy that follows. This is why it was sometimes called
> the Mass of the Catechumens, and the remaining portion,
> the Mass of the Faithful.

THE LITURGY OF THE EUCHARIST

Preparation of the Gifts — Eucharistic Sacrifice — Communion Banquet

> Three actions are proper to the liturgy of the Eucha-
> rist: a) bread and wine are readied for the sacrifice; b)
> these gifts are made holy, consecrated, becoming the
> Body and Blood of the Lord; c) we receive back from
> God our gifts as Eucharistic food.
>
> The priest opens the Preparation of the Gifts with the
> greeting:

OFFERTORY

Priest: The Lord be with you.
   All: And with your spirit.
Priest: Let us pray.

> If the PRAYERS OF THE FAITHFUL are to be said at this
> point, suggested forms for text and melody may be found
> on page 272; 281.

OFFERTORY ANTIPHON

For the text of the Offertory Antiphon, see pages 15 to 233.

Offertory hymn from Nos. 51-60 or other hymn as directed.

In gifts of bread and wine we offer ourselves and all our activity in union with Christ to the heavenly Father. At the altar the priest offers the bread, saying:

Súscipe, sancte Pater, omnípotens ætérne Deus, hanc immaculátam hóstiam, quam ego indígnus fámulus tuus óffero tibi Deo meo vivo et vero, pro innumerabílibus peccátis, et offensiónibus, et neglegéntiis meis, et pro ómnibus circumstántibus, sed et pro ómnibus fidélibus christiánis vivis atque defúnctis: ut mihi, et illis profíciat ad salútem in vitam ætérnam. Amen.

Holy Father, almighty and eternal God, accept this immaculate host that I, your unworthy servant, am offering to you, my true and living God. It is an offering for my own countless sins, sins of commission and sins of omission; an offering likewise for the failings of all here present as well as for all who have the faith, Christians alive or dead. May it prove spiritually beneficial to me and to them, a means of gaining eternal life. Amen.

The priest blesses the water and adds a few drops to the wine as he prays:

Deus, qui humánæ substántiæ dignitátem mirabíliter condidísti, et mirabílius reformásti: da nobis per huius aquæ et vini mystérium, eius divinitátis esse consórtes, qui humanitátis nostræ fíeri dignátus est párticeps, Iesus Christus, Fílius tuus, Dóminus noster: Qui tecum vivit et regnat in unitáte Spíritus Sancti Deus: per ómnia sǽcula sæculórum. Amen.

O God, marvellous was the manner in which you created human nature in all its dignity, but still more marvellous was the way in which you renewed it. Through the mystical union of this water with wine bring us to union with the divine nature of him who graciously willed to share our human nature, Jesus Christ, your Son and our Lord. Being God, he lives and exercises kingship with you in oneness with the Holy Spirit, age after age. Amen.

Offering the chalice

Offérimus tibi, Dómine, cálicem salutáris, tuam deprecántes cleméntiam: ut in conspéctu divínæ maiestátis tuæ, pro nostra et totíus mundi salúte, cum odóre suavitátis ascéndat. Amen.

We offer you, O Lord, this saving chalice, imploring your goodness to make it ascend as sweetest fragrance into your divine presence, there to effect our salvation and that of all the world. Amen.

In spíritu humilitátis et in ánimo contríto suscipiámur a te, Dómine: et sic fiat sacrifícium nostrum in conspéctu tuo hódie, ut pláceat tibi, Dómine Deus.

Because of our humble attitude and repentant spirit take us into your embrace, O Lord. Then will our Sacrifice offered in your presence today become pleasing in your eyes, Lord God.

Invocation of the Holy Spirit

Veni, sanctificátor omnípotens ætérne Deus: et béne † dic hoc sacrifícium, tuo sancto nómini præparátum.

Come, O sanctifying Spirit, God almighty and eternal, come and † bless this Sacrifice readied to glorify your holy Name.

In a High Mass, the priest now censes the offered gifts and the altar. Then he washes his hands, an action that once was functional when material gifts of various kinds were brought to and divided at the altar; it now takes on symbolic meaning well expressed in the accompanying psalm:

Lavábo inter innocéntes manus meas: et circúmdabo altáre tuum, Dómine:

Among innocent men I wash my hands; I stay close to your altars, Lord.

Ut áudiam vocem laudis, et enárrem univérsa mirabília tua.

For I want to voice your praises, and openly tell your countless wonders.

Dómine, diléxi decórem domus tuæ et locum habitátionis glóriæ tuæ.

Lord, I love the beauty of your house, that glorious place where you dwell.

Ne perdas cum ímpiis, Deus, ánimam meam, et cum viris sánguinum vitam meam:

O God, do not allow me to perish with the wicked; do not destroy my life with sinners

In quorum mánibus iniquitátes sunt: déxtera eórum repléta est munéribus.

whose hands are foul with crime, and heavily-weighted with bribes.

Ego autem in innocéntia mea ingréssus sum: rédime me et miserére mei.

Pes meus stetit in dirécto: in ecclésiis benedícam te, Dómine.

Glória Patri, et Fílio, et Spirítui Sancto.

Sicut erat in princípio, et nunc, et semper: et in sǽcula sæculórum. Amen.

But I, I try to live virtuously; have pity and save me.

Firmly my foot is planted in the proper path; in the presence of the whole church I will bless you, Lord.

Glory be to the Father and to the Son and to the Holy Spirit.

As it was in the beginning, is now, and ever shall be, world without end. Amen.

Our gifts are offered to the Blessed Trinity:

Súscipe, sancta Trínitas, hanc oblatiónem, quam tibi offérimus ob memóriam passiónis, resurrectiónis, et ascensiónis Iesu Christi, Dómini nostri: et in honórem beátæ Maríæ semper Vírginis, et beáti Ioánnis Baptístæ, et sanctórum Apostolórum Petri et Pauli, et istórum et ómnium Sanctórum: ut illis profíciat ad honórem, nobis autem ad salútem: et illi pro nobis intercédere dignéntur in cælis, quorum memóriam ágimus in terris. Per eúndem Christum Dóminum nostrum. Amen.

Holy Trinity, accept this offering that we are presenting to you as a memorial of the passion, resurrection, and ascension of Christ Jesus, our Lord. It is also made in honor of blessed Mary ever Virgin, of St. John the Baptist, of the apostle saints, Peter and Paul, of the saints whose relics are here enshrined and of all the saints. For them may it mean greater honor, for us greater assurance of salvation; and may they, in heaven, intercede for us who keep them in mind upon earth. Through the same Christ our Lord. Amen.

The priest appeals for our help:

Priest: Oráte, fratres: ut meum ac vestrum sacrifícium acceptábile fiat apud Deum Patrem omnipoténtem.

All: Suscípiat Dóminus sacrifícium de mánibus tuis / ad laudem et glóriam nóminis sui, / ad utilitátem quoque nostram, / totiúsque Ecclésiæ suæ sanctæ.

Pray, brethren, so that my Sacrifice — and it is yours likewise — may prove acceptable to God, our almighty Father.

May the Lord accept the Sacrifice from your hands unto his own praise and glory, for our benefit, and for the good of all his holy Church.

PRAYER OVER THE GIFTS (SECRET)

The Secret prayer, given on pages 15-233, is the final prayer over the sacrificial offering. As in the Collect, the priest summarizes our thoughts and intentions, and we add our approval with a sincere and ringing AMEN.

Priest: . . . per ómnia sǽcula sæculórum.   . . . for ever and ever.

All: Amen.   Amen.

The Canon of the Mass is introduced by a Preface, a solemn thanksgiving song for the privilege of sharing in the supreme act of worship. A spirited dialog between priest and people begins the sacred action.

The Eucharistic Prayer

PREFACE

Priest: Dóminus vobíscum.   The Lord be with you.

All: Et cum spíritu tuo.   And with your spirit.

Priest: Sursum corda.   Turn your hearts heavenwards.

All: Habémus ad Dóminum.   We are facing the Lord.

Priest: Grátias agámus Dómino Deo nostro.   Let us be grateful to the Lord, our God.

All: Dignum et iustum est.   That is fitting and proper.

On most Sundays of the year the following Preface in honor of the Blessed Trinity is said (Prefaces proper to feasts and seasons, pages 260-264).

Priest: Vere dignum et iustum est, æquum et salutáre, nos tibi semper et ubíque grátias ágere: Dómine, sancte Pater, omnípotens ætérne Deus: Qui cum unigénito Fílio tuo et Spíritu Sancto unus es Deus, unus es Dóminus: non in uníus singularitáte persónæ, sed in uníus Trinitáte substántiæ. Quod enim de tua glória, revelánte te, crédimus, hoc de Fílio tuo, hoc de Spíritu Sancto sine differéntia discretiónis sentímus. Ut in confessióne veræ

It is truly right and necessary, it is our duty and our salvation always and everywhere to give thanks to you, O Lord, holy Father, all-powerful and eternal God.

With your only Son and the Holy Spirit you are but one God, one Lord, not in the individuality of a single person, but in a Trinity of one essence. What the faith teaches us about your greatness, that we believe also about your Son and the Holy Spirit, who can-

sempiternǽque Deitátis et in persónis propríetas et in esséntia únitas et in maiestáte adorétur æquálitas.

Quam laudant Angeli atque Archángeli, Chérubim quoque ac Séraphim: qui non cessant clamáre cotídie, una voce dicéntes:

not be separated from you. In acknowledging you as the true, eternal God, we worship your three distinct persons, their one essence and their equal majesty.

Your praise the angels and the archangels, the cherubim and the seraphim sing, their daily hymn rising up, constant, never-ending:

SANCTUS

All: Holy, holy, holy Lord God of hosts,*
Heaven and earth are filled with your glory. *
Hosanna in the highest. *
Blessed is he who comes in the name of the Lord. *
Hosanna in the highest.

KNEEL

It is with heightened reverential awe that we begin the most sacred part of the Mass mystery, the Canon. This is the great consecratory prayer; beginning here it continues on to the "Amen" before the Lord's Prayer, as Christ through the priest offers himself as a Victim to the Father, intercedes in behalf of his mystical Body, and commends all our needs and petitions to God most High.

THE CANON

Te ígitur, clementíssime Pater, per Iesum Christum, Fílium tuum, Dóminum nostrum, súpplices rogámus, ac pétimus, uti accépta hábeas et benedícas, hæc ✠ dona, hæc ✠ múnera, hæc ✠ sancta sacrifícia illibáta,

Kindest Father, humbly we now ask and beg you through Jesus Christ, your Son and our Lord, to accept and bless these gifts, these presents, these offerings so holy and so pure.

This Mass is offered for the Church, Pope, Bishops.

in primis, quæ tibi offérimus pro Ecclésia tua sancta cathólica: quam pacificáre, custodíre, adunáre et régere dignéris toto orbe terrárum: una cum fámulo tuo Papa nostro N. et Antístite no-

First of all we offer them to you in behalf of your holy, catholic Church (graciously give her peace, protect her, bring her together in unity and guide her in every part of the world) and your

stro N. et ómnibus orthodóxis, atque cathólicæ et apostólicæ fídei cultóribus.

servant, N., our Pope, N., our Bishop, as well as for all others who, cherishing true doctrine, guard the faith that is catholic and apostolic.

This Mass is offered for our parents, friends, relatives.

Meménto, Dómine, famulórum famularúmque tuárum N. et N.

Lovingly keep in mind, O Lord, all your servants, N . . . , N . . . ,

Pause and silently pray for those whom you wish to remember in a special manner.

et ómnium circumstántium, quorum tibi fides cógnita est et nota devótio, pro quibus tibi offérimus: vel qui tibi ófferunt hoc sacrifícium laudis, pro se suísque ómnibus: pro redemptióne animárum suárum, pro spe salútis et incolumitátis suæ: tibíque reddunt vota sua ætérno Deo, vivo et vero.

even as those here assembled whose faith and fidelity you know. For them do we offer this sacrifice of praise to you — they themselves offer it to you likewise — and for all their loved ones, to obtain the redemption of their souls and the security and salvation they hope for. To you, eternal God, living and true, do they now direct their petitions.

We pray in union with our forefathers now in heaven.

Communicántes, et memóriam venerántes, in primis gloriósæ semper Vírginis Maríæ, Genitrícis Dei et Dómini nostri Iesu Christi: sed et beáti Ioseph, eiúsdem Vírginis Sponsi, et beatórum Apostolórum ac Mártyrum tuórum,

United together through the communion of saints, we first bring reverently to mind Mary, the everglorious Virgin Mother of our Lord and God, Jesus Christ; then blessed Joseph, the Virgin's husband; and your holy apostles and martyrs:

Petri et Pauli,
Andréæ, Iacóbi, Ioánnis,
Thomæ, Iacóbi, Philíppi,
Bartholomǽi, Matthǽi,
Simónis et Thaddǽi:
Lini,
Cleti,
Cleméntis,
Xysti,

Peter and Paul,			
Andrew, James, John,			
Thomas, James, Philip,			
Bartholomew, Matthew,			
Simon and Thaddeus,			apostles
Linus,	2nd pope,	martyred c.	79
Cletus,	3rd "	"	90
Clement,	4th "	"	97
Sixtus,	"	"	258

Cornélii,
Cypriáni,
Lauréntii,
Chrysógoni,
Ioánnis et Pauli,
Cosmæ et Damiáni:
et ómnium Sanctórum tuórum;
quorum méritis precibúsque con-
cédas, ut in ómnibus protectiónis
tuæ muniámur auxílio. Per eún-
dem Christum Dóminum nostrum.
Amen.

and all your saints.

Through their merits and prayers favor us at all times with your powerful help and protection. Through Christ our Lord. Amen.

Holding his hands over the chalice as a sign of placing upon it all our petitions, the priest continues:

Hanc ígitur oblatiónem servitútis nostræ, sed et cunctæ famíliæ
tuæ, quæsumus, Dómine, ut placátus accípias: diésque nostros in
tua pace dispónas, atque ab ætérna damnatióne nos éripi, et in
electórum tuórum iúbeas grege
numerári. Per Christum Dóminum
nostrum. Amen.

Here, then, is the offering that we, your servants, and together with us your whole household, present to you. Graciously accept it, Lord. May each day of our lives be spent in your peace. Intervene to save us from eternal damnation, and put us in the flock of your chosen ones. Through Christ our Lord. Amen.

Quam oblatiónem tu, Deus, in
ómnibus, quæsumus, bene ✠ díc-
tam, adscríp ✠ tam, ra ✠ tam,
rationábilem, acceptabilémque fácere dignéris: ut nobis Cor ✠ pus,
et San ✠ guis fiat dilectíssimi
Fílii tui, Dómini nostri Iesu Christi.

We beg you, O God, conde-scend to bless this offering. Accept it, accord it your fullest favor, make it perfect, pleasing to your-self in every way, so that it may become for us the Body and Blood of your dearly beloved Son, Christ Jesus our Lord.

Our bread becomes Christ's Body.

Qui prídie quam paterétur, accé-
pit panem in sanctas ac venerábiles manus suas, et elevátis óculis

On the evening before his pas-sion, he took bread into his holy and adorable hands. Then, with

in cælum ad te Deum, Patrem suum omnipoténtem, tibi grátias agens, bene ✠ díxit, fregit, dedítque discípulis suis, dicens: Accípite, et manducáte ex hoc omnes.

HOC EST ENIM
CORPUS MEUM.

eyes lifted heavenwards to you, O God, his almighty Father, he gave thanks to you as he blessed the bread, broke and gave it to his disciples with the words: Take and eat this, all of you.

FOR THIS IS MY BODY.

Our wine becomes Christ's Blood.

Símili modo postquam cenátum est, accípiens et hunc præclárum cálicem in sanctas ac venerábiles manus suas: item tibi grátias agens, bene ✠ díxit, dedítque discípulis suis, dicens: Accípite, et bíbite ex eo omnes.

HIC EST ENIM CALIX SANGUINIS MEI, NOVI ET ÆTERNI TESTAMENTI: MYSTERIUM FIDEI: QUI PRO VOBIS ET PRO MULTIS EFFUNDETUR IN REMISSIONEM PECCATORUM.

In a similar manner, after the meal was over, he took that most precious chalice into his holy and adorable hands. Again he gave thanks to you as he blessed it and gave it to his disciples with the words: Take and drink this, all of you.

FOR THIS IS THE CHALICE OF MY BLOOD, THE BLOOD OF THE NEW AND NEVER-ENDING COVENANT (THE MYSTERY OF THE FAITH) THAT WILL BE SHED FOR YOU AND FOR ALL MEN TO EFFECT THE FORGIVENESS OF SINS.

Hæc quotiescúmque fecéritis, in mei memóriam faciétis.

Every time you do this, you will do it in memory of me.

Silently, humbly we adore the Body and Blood of Christ. In compliance with our Savior's bidding to do this "in memory of me," the priest continues:

Unde et mémores, Dómine, nos servi tui, sed et plebs tua sancta, eiúsdem Christi Fílii tui, Dómini nostri, tam beátæ passiónis, nec non et ab ínferis resurrectiónis, sed et in cælos gloriósæ ascensiónis: offérimus præcláræ maiestáti tuæ de tuis donis ac datis, hóstiam ✠ puram, hóstiam ✠ sanctam, hóstiam ✠ immaculátam,

In memory, then, O God, of the sacred passion of Christ, your Son and our Lord, as also of his resurrection from sheol[1] and of his glorious ascension into heaven, do we your ministers and with us, your holy people, present to your sovereign Majesty this offering chosen from the blessings you have given us — a Victim

[1] The abode of the dead according to the Old Testament.

Panem ✠ sanctum vitæ ætérnæ, et Cálicem ✠ salútis perpétuæ.

all-perfect, a Victim holy and unblemished: the sacred Bread that gives unending life and the chalice that confers lasting salvation.

Supra quæ propítio ac seréno vultu respícere dignéris: et accépta habére, sícuti accépta habére dignátus es múnera púeri tui iusti Abel, et sacrifícium Patriárchæ nostri Abrahæ: et quod tibi óbtulit summus sacérdos tuus Melchísedech, sanctum sacrifícium, immaculátam hóstiam.

Upon this offering please condescend to look kindly, favorably. Accept it as you accepted the oblation of your holy servant Abel, or the sacrifice of Abraham our father, or that sacred offering, that spotless sacrifice presented to you by your great priest Melchisedech.

May our Sacrifice be taken to the heavenly altar and bring us every blessing.

Súpplices te rogámus, omnípotens Deus: iube hæc perférri per manus sancti Angeli tui in sublíme altáre tuum, in conspéctu divínæ maiestátis tuæ: ut, quotquot ex hac altáris participatióne sacrosánctum Fílii tui Cor ✠ pus, et Sán ✠ guinem sumpsérimus, omni benedictióne cælésti et grátia repleámur. Per eúndem Christum Dóminum nostrum. Amen.

Almighty God, humbly we beg you to have this sacrifice carried by the hands of your holy angel to your heavenly altar, into the presence of your divine Majesty. Every one who then takes part in the sacrifice at this altar here below and receives the infinitely holy Body and Blood of your Son will be filled with all the blessings and grace of heaven. Through the same Christ our Lord. Amen.

We pray for those who have died.

Meménto étiam, Dómine, famulórum famularúmque tuárum N. et N., qui nos præcessérunt cum signo fídei, et dórmiunt in somno pacis.

Lovingly keep in mind, O Lord, all your servants, N . . . , N . . . , who have preceded us with the indelible mark of baptism and are now resting in peaceful sleep.

Here we may add the names of those for whom we wish to pray in particular.

Ipsis, Dómine, et ómnibus in Christo quiescéntibus locum refrigérii, lucis et pacis ut indúlgeas, depre-

To these and to all who rest in Christ, we entreat you, Lord, to grant heavenly happiness, light,

cámur. Per eúndem Christum Dóminum nostrum. Amen.

and peace. Through the same Christ our Lord. Amen.

We ask to be united with God's saints.

Nobis quoque peccatóribus, fámulis tuis, de multitúdine miseratiónum tuárum sperántibus, partem áliquam et societátem donáre dignéris, cum tuis sanctis Apóstolis et Martýribus: cum

Also to us sinners, still your servants who trust in your boundless mercies, be pleased to grant a share in the heavenly community of your holy apostles and martyrs,

Ióanne,	John,	the Baptist
Stéphano,	Stephen,	first martyr
Matthía,	Matthias,	apostle
Bárnaba,	Barnabas,	Paul's companion
Ignátio,	Ignatius,	bishop of Antioch, martyred 107
Alexándro,	Alexander,	pope, martyred 119
Marcellíno,	Marcellinus,	martyred 304
Petro,	Peter,	martyred 304
Felicitáte,	Felicitas,	martyr at Carthage
Perpétua,	Perpetua,	martyr at Carthage
Agatha,	Agatha,	virgin, martyr
Lúcia,	Lucy,	virgin, martyr
Agnéte,	Agnes,	virgin, martyr
Cæcília,	Cecilia,	virgin, martyr

Anastásia, et ómnibus Sanctis tuis: intra quorum nos consórtium, non æstimátor mériti, sed véniæ, quæsumus, largítor admítte. Per Christum Dóminum nostrum.

Anastasia, and all your other saints. Into their company admit us. We beg this of you, not by reason of our own merits but through your gracious pardon. Through Christ our Lord.

Per quem hæc ómnia, Dómine, semper bona creas, sanctí ✠ ficas, viví ✠ ficas, bene ✠ dícis et præstas nobis.

It is through him, O God, that you continue to provide all these good gifts, sanctifying them, endowing them with life, and blessing them before you bestow them upon us.

The Canon ends with a solemn doxology. Through Christ supreme glory and honor are given to the Father by the Church united in the Holy Spirit. To the entire most sacred action we, Christ's members, add our sincerest AMEN.

Priest: Per ipsum, et cum ipso, et in ipso, est tibi Deo Patri omnipoténti, in unitáte Spíritus Sancti, omnis honor et glória, per ómnia sǽcula sæculórum.

All: AMEN.

Through him, with him, in him there is given to you, almighty God and Father, in the unity of the Holy Spirit, all honor and glory for ever and ever.

AMEN.

STAND

The Eucharistic Banquet

The final portion of the Eucharistic liturgy centers around the Communion Banquet. The "Our Father" is our table prayer. As children we honor our Father and ask for bread; as brothers we beg mutual forgiveness while saying aloud with the priest the

OUR FATHER

Priest: Let us pray. Taught by our Savior's command and formed by the word of God, we dare to say:

All: Our Father, who art in heaven, *
hallowed be thy name; *
thy kingdom come; *
thy will be done on earth as it is in heaven. *
Give us this day our daily bread; *
and forgive us our trespasses *
as we forgive those who trespass against us; *
and lead us not into temptation, *
but deliver us from evil.

The last petition of the Lord's Prayer is amplified as the priest continues:

Líbera nos, quǽsumus, Dómine, ab ómnibus malis, prætéritis, præséntibus et futúris: et intercedénte beáta et gloriósa semper Vírgine Dei Genitríce María, cum beátis Apóstolis tuis Petro et Paulo, atque Andréa, et ómnibus Sanctis, da propítius pacem in diébus nostris: ut, ope misericórdiæ tuæ adiúti, et a peccáto simus semper líberi et ab omni perturbatióne secúri. Per eúndem Dóminum no-

Deliver us, Lord, from all evils, whether of the past, present, or future. In response to the intercession of blessed Mary, the ever-glorious Virgin Mother of God, of your apostle-saints Peter and Paul, of Andrew too, and of all the saints, be merciful and favor us with peace throughout our lifetime. For with your compassion and help we will always be both free of sin and safely sheltered

strum Iesum Christum Fílium tuum: Qui tecum vivit et regnat in unitáte Spíritus Sancti Deus, per ómnia sǽcula sæculórum.

All: Amen.

Priest: Pax † Dómini sit † semper vobís † cum.

All: Et cum spíritu tuo.

from every type of trouble. Through Jesus Christ, our Lord and your Son. Being God, he lives and exercises kingship with you in oneness with the Holy Spirit, for ever and ever.

Amen.

May the peace of the Lord be always with you.

And with your spirit.

Consecrated Bread is mixed with consecrated wine — another sign of Eucharistic unity. Formerly the action brought together the liturgy of the previous day or from adjacent churches, symbolizing the harmony and love between Christian communities.

Priest: Hæc commíxtio, et consecrátio Córporis et Sánguinis Dómini nostri Iesu Christi, fiat accipiéntibus nobis in vitam ætérnam. Amen.

May this sacred commingling of the Body and Blood of Christ Jesus our Lord mean eternal life to us who are about to receive it. Amen.

We beg mercy and peace in the Mass' first petitions addressed directly to Christ. The same spirit continues in the three prayers that follow the "Agnus Dei."

Agnus Dei

All: Lamb of God, who take away the sins of the world, *
    have mercy on us. *
Lamb of God, who take away the sins of the world, *
    have mercy on us. *
Lamb of God, who take away the sins of the world, *
    grant us peace.
(In Requiem Masses: . . . grant them rest . . . grant them rest . . . grant them eternal rest.)

KNEEL

Three prayers follow, which constitute the priest's immediate preparation for holy Communion.

Dómine Iesu Christe, qui dixísti Apóstolis tuis: Pacem relínquo vobis, pacem meam do vobis: ne respícias peccáta mea, sed fidem Ecclésiæ tuæ; eámque secúndum

Lord Jesus Christ, you said to your apostles: Peace I bequeath to you. My peace I give to you. Take no note of my sins, but see the faith of your Church. Grant

voluntátem tuam pacificáre et coadunáre dignéris: Qui vivis et regnas Deus per ómnia sǽcula sæculórum. Amen.

Dómine Iesu Christe, Fili Dei vivi, qui ex voluntáte Patris, cooperánte Spíritu Sancto, per mortem tuam mundum vivificásti: líbera me per hoc sacrosánctum Corpus et Sánguinem tuum ab ómnibus iniquitátibus meis, et univérsis malis: et fac me tuis semper inhærére mandátis, et a te numquam separári permíttas: Qui cum eódem Deo Patre et Spíritu Sancto vivis et regnas Deus in sǽcula sæculórum. Amen.

Percéptio Córporis tui, Dómine Iesu Christe, quod ego indígnus súmere præsúmo, non mihi provéniat in iudícium et condemnatiónem: sed pro tua pietáte prosit mihi ad tutaméntum mentis et córporis, et ad medélam percipiéndam: Qui vivis et regnas cum Deo Patre in unitáte Spíritus Sancti Deus, per ómnia sǽcula sæculórum. Amen.

her the peace that you have willed, and make her harmoniously one, for you are God, living and exercising kingship in every age. Amen.

Lord Jesus Christ, Son of the living God, through your death you gave life to the world in accord with the Father's will and with the cooperation of the Holy Spirit. Through this, your infinitely holy Body and Blood, free me from all my sins and from every evil. Make me cling to your commandments always; never allow me to be separated from you, for you are God, living and exercising kingship with the Father and the Holy Spirit, from age to age. Amen.

Lord Jesus Christ, in spite of my unworthiness I purpose to receive your Body. Do not let it mean judgment and condemnation for me. But because of your loving kindness, may it prove beneficial, a protection and a means unto health for soul and body, O God, living and exercising kingship with the Father in oneness with the Holy Spirit, through all the passing ages. Amen.

Before communicating, the priest acknowledges his unworthiness.

Panem cæléstem accípiam, et nomen Dómini invocábo.

Dómine, non sum dignus, ut intres sub tectum meum: sed tan-

I will take the Bread of heaven and beseech the Lord.

Lord, I am not worthy that you should come under my roof.

tum dic verbo, et sanábitur ánima mea (repeated three times).

Speak but the word and my soul will be healed (repeated three times).

Corpus Dómini nostri Iesu Christi custódiat ánimam meam in vitam ætérnam. Amen.

May the Body of our Lord Jesus Christ keep my soul alive forever. Amen.

The priest drinks the sacred Blood after saying:

Quid retríbuam Dómino pro ómnibus, quæ retríbuit mihi?

Cálicem salutáris accípiam, et nomen Dómini invocábo. Laudans invocábo Dóminum, et ab inimícis meis salvus ero.

Sanguis Dómini nostri Iesu Christi custódiat ánimam meam in vitam ætérnam. Amen.

What can I give the Lord for all he has given me!

I will take the chalice of salvation and beseech the Lord. With praise I will beseech the Lord, and I will be freed of my enemies.

May the Blood of our Lord Jesus Christ keep my soul alive forever. Amen.

COMMUNION OF THE FAITHFUL

Our participation in the Mass attains its fullness through the reception of holy Communion. The priest, holding the ciborium containing the consecrated Bread, addresses those about to receive with the words:

Priest: Behold the Lamb of God, * behold him who takes away the sins of the world.

All: (three times): Lord, I am not worthy that you should come under my roof. * Speak but the word and my soul will be healed.

Priest: The Body of Christ. Communicant: Amen.

After distributing holy Communion the priest purifies the chalice, saying:

Quod ore súmpsimus, Dómine, pura mente capiámus: et de múnere temporáli fiat nobis remédium sempitérnum.

What we have taken after the manner of bodily food, O Lord, may we treasure in a pure heart. And may the gift we have received in this life be our provision for eternity.

Corpus tuum, Dómine, quod sumpsi, et Sanguis, quem potávi, adhǽreat viscéribus meis: et præ-

May your Body, Lord, that I have eaten and your Blood that I have drunk, affect me to the

sta; ut in me non remáneat scéle-
rum mácula, quem pura et sancta
refecérunt sacraménta: Qui vivis
et regnas in sǽcula sæculórum.
Amen.

depths of my being. Grant that no
trace of sin be left in me, whom
these pure and holy mysteries
have renewed. O God, you live
and reign for ever and ever.
Amen.

COMMUNION ANTIPHON:

The Communion Antiphon (see pages 15-233) may be
said or sung during the reception of holy Communion;
other hymns or psalms may likewise be used (see Nos.
61-82).

After reading the Communion Antiphon the priest
again greets us:

STAND

Priest: Dóminus vobíscum.

All: Et cum spíritu tuo.

The Lord be with you.

And with your spirit.

The final prayer usually implores for each the full fruits
of the Mass liturgy by reminding us to "live out" its message and grace.

THE POSTCOMMUNION

Priest: Orémus . . . per ómnia
sǽcula sæculórum.

All: Amen.

Let us pray . . . for ever and
ever.

Amen.

It is now time for the dismissal. The priest "commissions"
us to go and "live the Mass," and thereby to make our
daily living a sacrifice pleasing to God.

DISMISSAL

Priest: The Lord be with you.

All: And with your spirit.

Deacon (or Priest): Go, the Mass is ended.

All: Thanks be to God.

(In Requiem Masses): May they rest in peace.

All: Amen.

KNEEL

PRAYER TO THE BLESSED TRINITY

Pláceat tibi, sancta Trínitas, ob-
séquium servitútis meæ: et præsta; ut sacrifícium, quod óculis
tuæ maiestátis indígnus óbtuli, tibi sit acceptábile, mihíque et ómnibus, pro quibus illud óbtuli, sit,

May the homage of my service be
pleasing to you, O holy Trinity.
Grant that the sacrifice which I,
though unworthy, have offered in
the presence of your Majesty, be
acceptable to you. Through your

te miseránte, propitiábile. Per Christum, Dóminum nostrum. Amen.

mercy may it obtain forgiveness for me and all those for whom I have offered it. Through Christ our Lord. Amen.

FINAL BLESSING

Priest: May almighty God bless you, the Father, and the Son, † and the Holy Spirit.

All: Amen.

RECESSIONAL HYMN: a song of praise and thanksgiving for the privilege of sharing in the great Sacrifice of redemption (see Nos. 83-97, or other hymn as directed).

PREFACE OF CHRISTMAS

It is truly right and necessary, it is our duty and our salvation always and everywhere to give thanks to you, O Lord, holy Father, all-powerful and eternal God.

For, by becoming man in his mysterious incarnation, your Son has made his glory shine with the most vivid light before the eyes of our soul. From now on, we can know God visibly, and this knowledge will make us love what remains invisible.

Therefore, with the angels and the archangels, with the thrones and the dominations and with the whole army of heavenly spirits, we sing your glory in ceaseless praise:

PREFACE OF EPIPHANY

It is truly right and necessary, it is our duty and our salvation always and everywhere to give thanks to you, O Lord, holy Father, all-powerful and eternal God.

For, in coming to manifest himself in our mortal nature, your only Son has restored it by the new splendor of his immortality.

Therefore, with the angels and the archangels, with the thrones and the dominations and with the whole army of heavenly spirits, we sing your glory in ceaseless praise:

PREFACE OF LENT

It is truly right and necessary, it is our duty and our salvation always and everywhere to give thanks to you, O Lord, holy Father, all-powerful and eternal God.

Through the bodily privations that you ask of us, you hold our vices in check, you lift up our minds, you grant us power and merit, through Christ our Lord.

He it is who presents to your divine majesty the song of the angels, the worship of the dominations, the reverence of the powers and the unanimous praise of the heavens, the heavenly virtues and the blessed seraphim. To their chants we beg you to let us join our voices so that we may proclaim in humble praise:

PREFACE OF THE HOLY CROSS

It is truly right and necessary, it is our duty and our salvation always and everywhere to give thanks to you, O Lord, holy Father, all-powerful and eternal God.

This was your decree: that men be saved by the wood of the Cross; a tree was the source of death, let another tree be the source of life; the devil used the tree of paradise to make his conquest, let him be conquered in turn by the tree of the Cross, through Christ our Lord.

He it is who presents to your divine majesty the song of the angels, the worship of the dominations, the reverence of the powers and the unanimous praise of the heavens, the heavenly virtues and the blessed seraphim. To their chants we beg you to let us join our voices so that we may proclaim in humble praise:

PREFACE OF THE EASTER SEASON

It is truly right and necessary, it is our duty and our salvation to praise you at every season, O Lord. But we acclaim you even more joyously on this day (during this season) when Christ, our Passover, was immolated. He is the true paschal Lamb, who by his sacrifice took away the sins of the world. By his death he destroyed death in us, and by his resurrection he restored life to us.

Therefore, with the angels and the archangels, with the thrones and the dominations and with the whole army of heavenly spirits, we sing your glory in ceaseless praise:

PREFACE OF ASCENSION

It is truly right and necessary, it is our duty and our salvation always and everywhere to give thanks to you, O Lord, holy Father, all-powerful and eternal God, through Christ our Lord.

After his resurrection he made himself clearly visible to his disciples, and before their eyes he rose up to heaven, in order to give us a share in his divinity.

Therefore, with the angels and the archangels, with the thrones and the dominations and with the whole army of heavenly spirits, we sing your glory in ceaseless praise:

PREFACE OF CHRIST THE KING

It is truly right and necessary, it is our duty and our salvation always and everywhere to give thanks to you, O Lord, holy Father, all-powerful and eternal God.

By your holy anointing you consecrated our Lord Jesus Christ, your Son, as eternal Priest and King of the universe. To make our peace with you, he then offered himself as a spotless victim on the altar of the Cross, achieving the mysterious redemption of mankind. By bringing all creatures under his authority, he has permitted your infinite majesty to reign forever over the universe, to reign through truth and life, to reign through holiness and grace, to reign through justice, love and peace.

Therefore, with the angels and the archangels, with the thrones and the dominations and with the whole army of heavenly spirits, we sing your glory in ceaseless praise:

PREFACE OF THE HOLY SPIRIT

It is truly right and necessary, it is our duty and our salvation always and everywhere to give thanks to you, O Lord, holy Father, all-powerful and eternal God, through Christ our Lord.

After his ascension into heaven, seated at your right hand, he sent down (during the octave: this day) upon your adopted sons the Holy Spirit whom he had promised them.

Therefore the whole world exults with overflowing joy, while the heavenly virtues and the angelic powers sing your glory in ceaseless praise:

PREFACE OF THE TRINITY

It is truly right and necessary, it is our duty and our salvation always and everywhere to give thanks to you, O Lord, holy Father, all-powerful and eternal God.

With your only Son and the Holy Spirit you are but one God, one Lord, not in the individuality of a single person, but in a Trinity of one essence. What the faith teaches us about your greatness, that we believe also about your Son and the Holy Spirit, who cannot be separated from you. In acknowledging you as the true, eternal God, we worship your three distinct persons, their one essence and their equal majesty.

Your praise the angels and the archangels, the cherubim and the seraphim sing, their daily hymn rising up, constant, never-ending:

PREFACE OF THE BLESSED VIRGIN

It is truly right and necessary, it is our duty and our salvation always and everywhere to give thanks to you, O Lord, holy Father, all-powerful and eternal God.

We praise you, we bless you and we extol you on this feast (add the name) of the Blessed Virgin Mary. By the overshadowing of the Holy Spirit she conceived your only Son, and without losing her glorious virginity she brought into the world the eternal light, Jesus Christ our Lord.

He it is who presents to your divine majesty the song of the angels, the worship of the dominations, the reverence of the powers and the unanimous praise of the heavens, the heavenly virtues and the blessed seraphim. To their chants we beg you to let us join our voices so that we may proclaim in humble praise:

PREFACE OF ST. JOSEPH

It is truly right and necessary, it is our duty and our salvation always and everywhere to give thanks to you, O Lord, holy Father, all-powerful and eternal God.

We proclaim your greatness, we bless you and we extol you on this feast of (in votive Mass: in this Mass commemorating) St. Joseph. He is the just man whom you gave as a spouse to the Virgin Mother of God; he is the faithful and prudent servant whom you made the head of your family, to watch with fatherly care over your only Son, conceived by the overshadowing of the Holy Spirit.

It is that Son, Jesus Christ our Lord, who presents to your divine majesty the song of the angels, the worship of the dominations, the reverence of the powers and the unanimous praise of the heavens, the heavenly virtues and the blessed seraphim. To their chants we beg you to let us join our voices so that we may proclaim in humble praise:

PREFACE OF APOSTLES

It is truly right and necessary, it is our duty and our salvation humbly to beg you, O Lord, eternal Shepherd, not to abandon your flock but to keep it under your constant protection through your holy apostles; for you appointed them as shepherds in your place to carry on the work of governing your flock.

Therefore, with the angels and the archangels, with the thrones and the dominations and with the whole army of heavenly spirits, we sing your glory in ceaseless praise:

COMMON PREFACE

It is truly right and necessary, it is our duty and our salvation always and everywhere to give thanks to you, O Lord, holy Father, all-powerful and eternal God, through Christ our Lord.

He it is who presents to your divine majesty the song of the angels, the worship of the dominations, the reverence of the powers and the unanimous praise of the heavens, the heavenly virtues and the blessed seraphim. To their chants we beg you to let us join our voices so that we may proclaim in humble praise:

PREFACE OF THE DEAD

It is truly right and necessary, it is our duty and our salvation always and everywhere to give thanks to you, O Lord, holy Father, all-powerful and eternal God, through Christ our Lord.

In him is the source of our bright hope for a blessed resurrection, for his promise of immortality in the world to come dispels the gloom cast over us by the knowledge that we must die. Actually, to those who have faith in you, Lord, life does not cease — it merely changes! And when our earthly dwelling falls to ruins, we find an eternal home in heaven.

Therefore, with the angels and the archangels, with the thrones and the dominations, and with the whole army of heavenly spirits, we sing your glory in ceaseless praise:

THE SUNG MASS

For purposes of convenience, text and melody for hymns and the Ordinary parts of a sung Mass are here given in sequence; this will prove very helpful for beginners or for occasions on which little or no preparation is possible. Alternate selections are, of course, always in order. To pray the Ordinary of the Mass, turn to page **238**; for the Proper parts of the day's Mass, turn to pages **15-233**.

ENTRANCE HYMN (or alternate from Nos. 35–50, or other hymn as directed)

1. COME, THOU ALMIGHTY KING

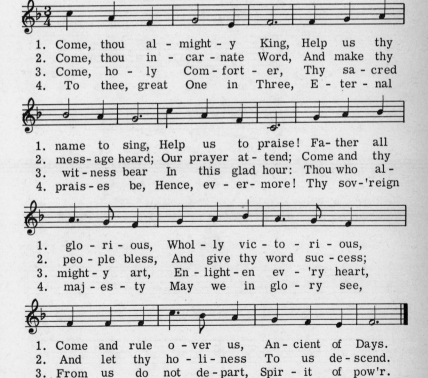

1. Come, thou al - might - y King, Help us thy
2. Come, thou in - car - nate Word, And make thy
3. Come, ho - ly Com - fort - er, Thy sa - cred
4. To thee, great One in Three, E - ter - nal

1. name to sing, Help us to praise! Fa - ther all
2. mess - age heard; Our prayer at - tend; Come and thy
3. wit - ness bear In this glad hour: Thou who al -
4. prais - es be, Hence, ev - er - more! Thy sov - 'reign

1. glo - ri - ous, Whol - ly vic - to - ri - ous,
2. peo - ple bless, And give thy word suc - cess;
3. might - y art, En - light - en ev - 'ry heart,
4. maj - es - ty May we in glo - ry see,

1. Come and rule o - ver us, An - cient of Days.
2. And let thy ho - li - ness To us de - scend.
3. From us do not de - part, Spir - it of pow'r.
4. And to e - ter - ni - ty Love and a - dore.

For the SPRINKLE ME, O LORD, WITH HYSSOP or I SAW WATER COMING FORTH, turn to page 345.

The Entrance, Gradual, Offertory and Communion antiphons given in the Proper may be extended by the addition of verses from the seasonal or other psalms, page 464ff.

2. PEOPLE'S SUNG MASS

LORD, HAVE MERCY

GLORY TO GOD IN THE HIGHEST

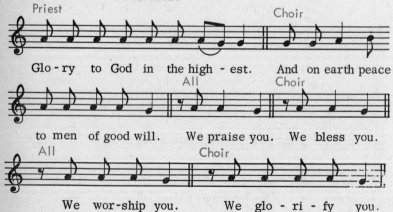

All
We give you thanks for your great glo - ry.

Choir   All
Lord, God, heav-en-ly King, God the Fa-ther al-might-y.

Choir
Lord Je-sus Christ,   the on - ly -

All
be - got - ten Son.   Lord, God, Lamb of God, Son of the

Choir
Fa-ther. You, who take a-way the sins   of the world,

All   Choir
have mer-cy on us. You, who take a-way the sins

All   Choir
of the world, re-ceive our prayer. You, who sit at

All
the right hand of the Fa - ther, have mer-cy on us.

Choir   All
For you a - lone are ho - ly. You a-lone are Lord.

Choir
You a - lone, O Je - sus Christ, are most high.

All
With the Ho - ly Spir - it, in the glo - ry of God

the Fa - ther. A - men.

PRAYER OVER THE ASSEMBLY

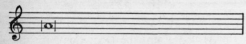

Do - mi - nus vo - bis - cum.
The Lord be with you.

Et cum spi - ri - tu tu - o.
And with your spirit.

Priest: Orémus . . . per ómnia   Let us pray . . . for ever and
sǽcula sæculórum.   ever.

A - men.

MEDITATION CHANTS

After the Epistle, the Gradual and Alleluia verse may be
read or sung according to chant melodies. The Gospel is
then read.

I BELIEVE IN ONE GOD

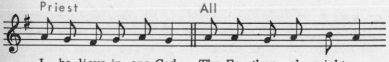

Priest   All

I be-lieve in one God. The Fa - ther al - might-y,

ma - ker of heav - en and earth, and of all

things vis - i - ble and in - vis - i - ble.

Choir

And I be - lieve in one Lord, Je - sus Christ,

the on - ly - be - got - ten Son of God.

All

Born of the Fa - ther be - fore all a - ges.

Choir

God of God , Light of Light, true God of true God.

All

Be - got - ten, not made, of one sub - stance

Choir

with the Fa - ther. By whom all things were made.

All

Who for us men and for our sal - va - tion

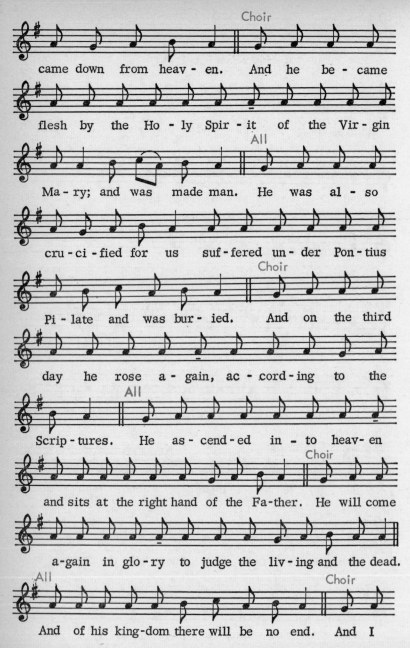

came down from heav - en. And he be - came
flesh by the Ho - ly Spir - it of the Vir - gin
Ma - ry; and was made man. He was al - so
cru - ci - fied for us suf - fered un - der Pon - tius
Pi - late and was bur - ied. And on the third
day he rose a - gain, ac - cord - ing to the
Scrip - tures. He as - cend - ed in - to heav - en
and sits at the right hand of the Fa - ther. He will come
a - gain in glo - ry to judge the liv - ing and the dead.
And of his king - dom there will be no end. And I

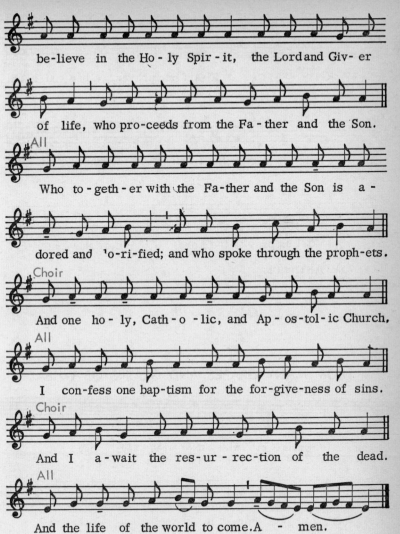

be-lieve in the Ho-ly Spir-it, the Lord and Giv-er

of life, who pro-ceeds from the Fa-ther and the Son.

All

Who to-geth-er with the Fa-ther and the Son is a-

dored and 'o-ri-fied; and who spoke through the proph-ets.

Choir

And one ho-ly, Cath-o-lic, and Ap-os-tol-ic Church,

All

I con-fess one bap-tism for the for-give-ness of sins.

Choir

And I a-wait the res-ur-rec-tion of the dead.

All

And the life of the world to come. A - men.

PRAYER OF THE FAITHFUL

There is no rigid form into which the Prayers of the Faithful must be cast and the method of expression normally used will be that of recitation. Under circumstances in which singing is feasible, the following melodies for the people's response may prove helpful (see also page 281):

3. PRAYER OF THE FAITHFUL RESPONSE

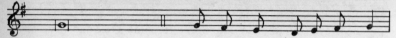

Leader: - - - - - -:   All: Grant our prayer, we beg you, Lord.

First alternate:

Leader: - - - let us pray to the Lord: All: Lord, have mer-cy!

Second alternate:

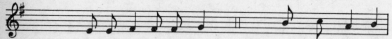

Leader: - - - let us pray to the Lord: All: Lord, have mer-cy!

OFFERTORY ANTIPHON

The Offertory antiphon may be read or chanted according to a psalm tone. While the celebrant readies the bread and wine for the sacrifice and prays the prescribed prayers, an Offertory hymn is appropriate (for alternates, Nos. 51-60).

4. FROM MANY GRAPES AND GRAINS OF WHEAT

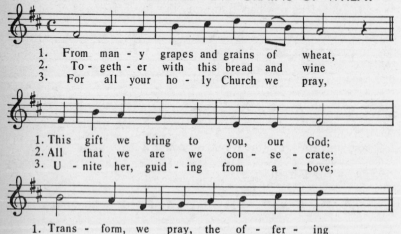

1. From man - y grapes and grains of wheat,
2. To - geth - er with this bread and wine
3. For all your ho - ly Church we pray,

1. This gift we bring to you, our God;
2. All that we are we con - se - crate;
3. U - nite her, guid - ing from a - bove;

1. Trans - form, we pray, the of - fer - ing
2. Im - part to us the life di - vine
3. Then shall we all one bod - y be

1. To Christ's own pre - cious flesh and blood.
2. Of him who did our na - ture take.
3. In Christ's un - bound - ed peace and love.

PRAYER OVER THE OFFERINGS

In chanting the Prayer over the Offerings, the celebrant uses one of the prescribed melodies concluding with the familiar:

Per o - mni - a sae - cu - la sae - cu - lo - rum.

A - men.

Do - mi - nus vo - bis - cum.

Et cum spi - ri - tu tu - o.

Sur - sum cor - da.

Ha - be - mus ad Do - mi - num.

Gra - ti - as a - ga - mus Do - mi - no De - o no - stro.

Di - gnum et iu - stum est.

HOLY, HOLY, HOLY

Ho - ly, ho - ly, ho - ly Lord God of hosts. Heav - en and earth are filled with your glo - ry. Ho - san - na in the high - est. Bless - ed is he who comes in the name of the Lord. Ho - san - na in the high - est.

A spirit of deepest silence and reverence comes over all assembled during the Canon, the most sacred part of the holy Sacrifice. Follow this sublime prayer as given on page 249, and at its close with the solemn doxology be ready to add your fervent AMEN.

Priest: . . . per ómnia sæcula . . . for ever and ever. sæculórum.

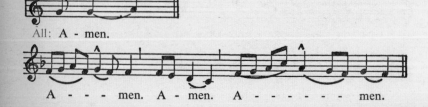

All: A - men.

A - - - men. A - men. A - - - - - men.

THE LORD'S PRAYER

With the "Pater Noster," the Lord's Prayer, begins the final portion of the Mass, the Communion Banquet. It is Christ's Eucharistic table prayer and the traditional melody has been adapted to vernacular settings.

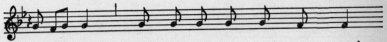

Let us pray. Taught by our Sav - ior's com - mand

and formed by the word of God, we dare to say:

Our Fa-ther, who art in heav-en, hal-low'd be thy name; thy

king-dom come; thy will be done on earth as it is in heav-en.

Give us this day our dai-ly bread; and for-give us our tres-

pass-es as we for-give those who tres-pass a-gainst us; and

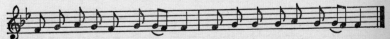

lead us not in-to temp-ta-tion, but de-liv-er us from e-vil.

EMBOLISM UPON THE LORD'S PRAYER

> According to prescribed form the priest continues with the prayer developing the final petition of the Lord's Prayer, ending with the usual:

Priest: . . . per ómnia sǽcula . . . for ever and ever.
sæculórum.

All: A - men.

Priest: Pax Dómini sit semper vobíscum.

May the peace of the Lord be always with you.

All: Et cum spi-ri-tu tu -o.

LAMB OF GOD

Choir

Lamb of God, who take a - way the sins of

All

the world, have mer - cy on us. Lamb of God,

Choir

who take a - way the sins of the world, have mer -

All

cy on us. Lamb of God, who take a - way

Choir

the sins of the world, grant us peace

All

COMMUNION ANTIPHON

The Communion Antiphon serves as the principal song during the distribution of the holy Eucharist. It may serve as a refrain to verses chanted from a seasonal psalm (page 464) or may be chanted according to a psalm-tone and followed by a hymn. Alternates to the one given here are Nos. 61-82.

5. O JESUS, WE ADORE THEE

1. O Je - sus, we a - dore thee, Who in thy love di -
2. O Je - sus, we a - dore thee, Our Vic - tim and our
3. O Je - sus, we a - dore thee, Our Sav - ior and our
4. O Je - sus, we a - dore thee; Come, live in us, we
5. O come, all you who la - bor In sor - row and in

1. vine, Con - ceal thy might - y God - head In
2. Priest, whose pre - cious blood and bod - y Be -
3. King, And with the saints and an - gels A
4. pray, That all our thoughts and ac - tions Be
5. pain; Come, eat this bread from heav - en, Your

Refrain

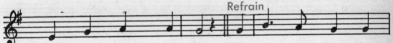

1. forms of bread and wine. O Sac - ra - ment most
2. come our sa - cred feast.
3. hum - ble hom - age bring.
4. thine a - lone to - day.
5. peace and strength re - gain.

ho - ly, O Sac - ra - ment di - vine, All praise and all thanks-

giv - ing Be ev - 'ry mo - ment thine!

DISMISSAL

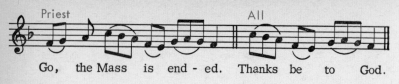

Go, the Mass is end-ed. Thanks be to God.

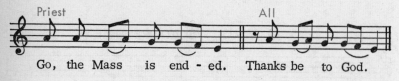

Go, the Mass is end-ed. Thanks be to God.

For the recessional, choice may be made from Nos. 83 to 97, or from other appropriate numbers in the hymn section of this book.

6. LORD, DISMISS US WITH YOUR BLESSING

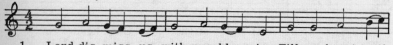

1. Lord, dis-miss us with your bless-ing; Fill our hearts with
2. Thanks we give and ad - o - ra-tion For your gos-pel's
3. So that when your love shall call us, Sav-ior, from the

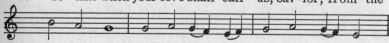

1. joy and peace; Let us each, your love pos - sess-ing,
2. joy-ful sound: May the fruits of this Com-mun-ion
3. world a - way, Let no fear of death up - set us,

1. Tri - umph in re - deem-ing grace: O re-fresh us,
2. In our hearts and lives a-bound: Ev - er faith - ful,
3. Glad your sum- mons to o - bey: May we ev - er,

1. O re-fresh us, As we work to keep a - pace.
2. Ev- er faith-ful To the truth may we be found.
3. May we ev - er In your lov - ing pres-ence stay. A-men.

Melodic unity characterizes the following sequence of hymns.[1] Any of the English sung Masses may be selected for the Ordinary.

7. WITH JOYFUL HEARTS WE ENTER

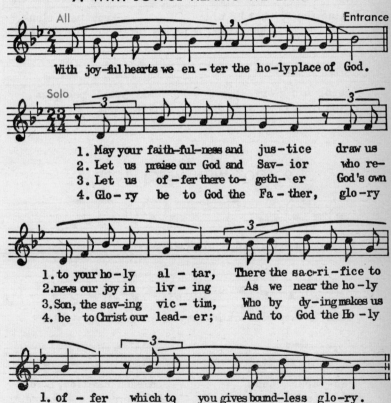

All   Entrance

With joy—ful hearts we en – ter the ho—ly place of God.

Solo

1. May your faith–ful–ness and   jus – tice   draw us
2. Let us praise our God and   Sav– ior   who re-
3. Let us of – fer there to– geth– er   God's own
4. Glo – ry   be to God the Fa – ther,   glo –ry

1. to your ho – ly   al – tar, There the sac–ri – fice to
2. news our joy in   liv – ing   As we near the ho–ly
3. Son, the sav–ing vic– tim, Who by dy–ing makes us
4. be to Christ our lead– er; And to God the Ho – ly

1. of – fer   which to   you gives bound–less glo–ry.
2. moun–tain   where God gives his life to save us.
3. shar–ers   in his   light and life e – ter–nal.
4. Spir–it   praise be giv–en with–out end–ing.

[1] These compositions are taken from *The Eucharistic Liturgy in Song and Dialog* by E. Arrondo and A. Danoz, a booklet that has proved very practical for parish worship (available from: The Liturgical Press, Collegeville, Minnesota).

8. ALLELUIA — PRAISE THE LORD

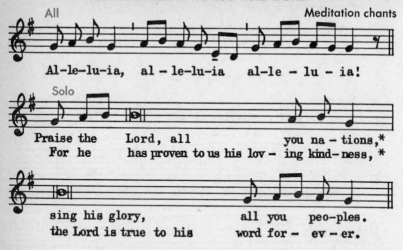

All

Meditation chants

Al-le-lu-ia, al-le-lu-ia al-le-lu-ia!

Solo

Praise the   Lord, all   you na-tions,*
For he   has proven to us his lov-ing kind-ness, *

sing his glory,   all you   peo-ples.
the Lord is true to his   word for-ev-er.

During the season of Lent, No. 9 is used in place of No. 8:

9. LOOK WITH MERCY, LORD

All

Look with mer-cy, Lord,   look with mer-cy on your peo-ple:

turn a-way your wrath from your sin-ful peo-ple.

Solo

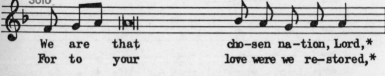

We are that   cho-sen na-tion, Lord,*
For to your   love were we re-stored,*

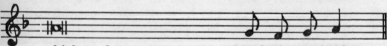

which you have pur-   chased at great price:
by Christ's redeem-   ing sac-ri-fice.

10. WE BESEECH YOU, O LORD

We be-seech you, O Lord, hear the plead-ing of your peo - ple!

1. For the holy Church of Christ * spread over the face of the earth.

2 For our Holy Father, THE Pope, * that he ever may be guided by the light of your SPIRit —
All: We beseech you, O Lord, hear the pleading of your people.

3 For the bishops, priests and ministers of YOUR Church * that they may increase in holiness and JUStice —
All: We beseech you, O Lord, hear the pleading of your people.

4 For the apostles who announce your GOSpel * that they may sow the seeds of your KINGdom —
All: We beseech you, O Lord, hear the pleading of your people.

5 For your consecrated reLIgious * that they may persevere in their CALLing —
All: We beseech you, O Lord, hear the pleading of your people.

6 For those who direct the destinies of NAtions * that they may love peace and JUStice —
All: We beseech you, O Lord, hear the pleading of your people.

7 For our separated BRETHren * that they may come into the fold of YOUR Church —
All: We beseech you, O Lord, hear the pleading of your people.

8 For non-Christians throughout THE world * that they may come to the light of your GOSpel —
All: We beseech you, O Lord, hear the pleading of your people.

9 For all those *here* PRESent * whose faith and de*votion* YOU
know —

All: We beseech you, O Lord, hear the pleading of your people.

10 For all our sins and *of*FENses * that we may obtain your *pardon*
AND grace —

All: We beseech you, O Lord, hear the pleading of your people.

11 For the blessing of *good* WEATHer * that we may have a boun-
tiful HARvest —

All: We beseech you, O Lord, hear the pleading of your people.

12 For all the faithful *de*PARTed * that they may be granted *eter-*
NAL rest —

All: We beseech you, O Lord, hear the pleading of your people.

The above petitions may be recited instead of being sung.

11. GOD, OUR FATHER

Offertory

1. God, our Fa - ther ev - er - last-ing, please ac-
2. Thank-ful hearts and joy-ful voic - es, we ap-
3. To you, Fa - ther, now we of -fer with the

1. cept the gifts we of - fer: take our
2. proach your ho- ly al - tar. Bear-ing
3. host and with the chal - ice, all we

1. bread up - on the al - tar and our
2. gifts of your cre - a - tion, we re-
3. have, and all our be - ing in this

1. wine that fills the chal - ice.
2. turn what you have giv - en.
3. sac - ri - fice most ho - ly.

12. AS RUNS THE THIRSTING DEER

Communion

1. As runs the thirst-ing deer to find where cool-ing wa—ters flow,———— so rush the wish—es of my heart to come be—fore you, Lord.————

Lord, come, make our hearts your dwell-ing. For you we are long—ing. Come, O Lord!——

2 The Lord, the God of heaven, is the thirsting of my heart. * When will this lowly servant see your face, O mighty Lord?

All: Lord, come, make our hearts your dwelling. For you we are longing. Come, O Lord!

3 With songs in praise of you upon my lips and in my heart, * I joyfully approach the banquet table of the Lord.

All: Lord, come . . .

4 The splendor of the altar beckons for us to approach: * we all have been invited to the table of the Lord.

All: Lord, come . . .

5 We eat this bread in holy and fraternal unity, * this bread made for us by the hands of Jesus Christ our Lord.

All: Lord, come . . .

6 We drink there of the chalice which salvation overflows; * till then we will be singing songs in praise of Christ our Lord.

All: Lord, come . . .

7 We find there bread to give us life, there wine to fire our love. * It is the Blood of God's own Lamb, the Body of our Lord.

All: Lord, come . . .

8 May all our lives be sanctified by living unity * with Body, Blood, with Soul and Godhead of our saving Lord.

All: Lord, come . . .

9 Well, Lord, we are your creatures, take us, do your will in us; * may we be only yours both now and always, mighty Lord.

All: Lord, come . . .

13. ACCEPT NOW OUR ACT OF WORSHIP

1. Ac - cept now our act of wor - ship, O Most Ho - ly Trin - i - ty, that we have pre-sent-ed to you, in the name of Christ our Lord.

2. Ac - cept it, O God, we ask you, for the
3. For you give our ac- tions mean - ing and the

2. u – ni – ver – sal   Church: for
3. warmth of   ho – ly   love.   Please

2. those who in you   are   seek – ing   lives of
3. grant us   a Fa – ther's   bless – ing   and be–

2. ho – li – ness and   truth.
3. stow on   us   your   peace.

THE RITE FOR MARRIAGE
and
THE NUPTIAL MASS

The sanctity of Christian marriage has become more universally understood during the past few decades. The divine exemplar upon which husband and wife are to base their union is the existing union of Christ and his bride, the Church. This foundation for marriage is explicitly stated in the excerpt serving as the Epistle of the Nuptial Mass.

The Mass follows the regular form, see page **238**; the proper parts and the sacramental rite for marriage are given below together with four hymns that may be used if alternates are not chosen. Any of the Mass melodies may serve for the ordinary sung parts of the Mass.

14. WE ALL HAVE GATHERED HERE IN JOY

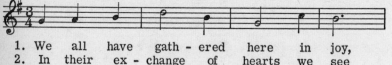

1. We all have gath - ered here in joy,
2. In their ex - change of hearts we see
3. To God the Fa - ther, through the Son,

1. To pray with our two friends, Who will to-day be
2. How mar-riage is the sign Of Christ's own love for
3. We pray this ho-ly day: That in the Spir-it

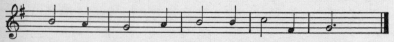

1. joined in Christ By love that nev - er ends.
2. us, his Church, In cov - e - nant di - vine.
3. their love mean What words can nev - er say.

ENTRANCE ANTIPHON Tob. 7:15; 8:19; Ps. 127:1

May the God of Israel join you together; and may he be with you who was merciful to two only children: and now, O Lord, make them bless you more fully.

Ps. Blessed are all who fear the Lord, who walk in his ways.

Glory be to the Father and to the Son and to the Holy Spirit. As it was in the beginning, is now and ever shall be, world without end. Amen. May the God . . .

PRAYER OVER THE ASSEMBLY

Let us pray. Listen to our petition, O almighty and merciful God, so that what is posited by our action here may come to full flower through your blessing. Through our Lord Jesus Christ, your Son, who lives and reigns with you in the unity of the Holy Spirit, God, for ever and ever.

All: **Amen.**

EPISTLE Ephesians 5:22-23

> The Christian home is to be a manifestation in the world of the love of Christ and his Church. That is why the husband will love his wife as Christ loves the Church, and the wife will love her husband as the Church loves Christ.

A reading from the letter of the apostle Paul
to the Christians of Ephesus

Brethren,

The wife should be subject to her husband as to the Lord, because for the wife the husband is the head, just as for the Church it is Christ who is the head, the head of that Church which is his body and which he has served. Therefore, just as the Church is subject to Christ, the wife must be subject in all things to her husband.

Husbands, love your wives as Christ loves his Church: for her he gave his life in order to make her holy, purifying her by the baptism of water with the accompanying words; for he wants to unite with himself a Church resplendent with beauty, having no blemish or wrinkle or anything of the kind, but all holy and pure.

It is in this way that a man must love his wife: love her as his own body. He who loves his wife is loving himself. No one hates his own body; rather, he nourishes it and takes care of it. That is what Christ does for his Church, [for us] since we are the members of his body, we are of his flesh and his bones.

Therefore [as the Scripture says], "a man shall leave his father and his mother and stand by his wife; and the two of them shall become one." [1] This is a great mystery; I mean in so far as it signifies [the union of] Christ and his Church. That is why each one of you ought to love his wife as himself, and the wife ought to have a deep respect for her husband.

REFLECTION CHANTS Ps. 127:3; Ps. 19:3

Your wife shall be like a fruitful vine in the recesses of your home. Your children like olive plants around your table.

Alleluia, alleluia. May the Lord send you help from the sanctuary, from Sion may he sustain you. Alleluia.

Instead of the Alleluia and Versicle given above, the following Tract is said after Septuagesima:

Behold, thus is the man blessed who fears the Lord. The Lord bless you from Sion: may you see the prosperity of Jerusalem all the days of your life. May you see your children's children. Peace be upon Israel!

During Eastertide the following is said:

Alleluia, alleluia. May the Lord send you help from the sanctuary, from Sion may he sustain you, alleluia. May the Lord bless you from Sion, the maker of heaven and earth, alleluia.

GOSPEL Matthew 19:3-6

The Church, the spouse of Christ, is by that very fact his own body. Christian marriage is indissoluble; in this respect it is the image of the alliance of Christ and the Church.

A reading from the holy Gospel according to Matthew

At that time some pharisees approached Jesus and posed this question to put him to the test: "Is there any reason at all for which a man is permitted to divorce his wife?"

Jesus answered him, "Do you not know that in the beginning the Creator made them man and woman, and said, 'Thus a man shall leave his father and his mother and stand by his wife; and the two of them shall become one.' [1] As a result, they are no longer two, but only one.

"Man is not to separate, therefore, what God has united!"

[1] Genesis 2:24.

THE RITE FOR THE
SACRAMENT OF MATRIMONY

After the Gospel, the priest may give a homily or he may
read and develop the following in whole or in part.

Dear friends in Christ: As you know, you are about to enter into a union which is most sacred and most serious, a union which was established by God himself. By it, he gave to man a share in the greatest work of creation, the work of the continuation of the human race. And in this way he sanctified human love and enabled man and woman to help each other live as children of God, by sharing a common life under his fatherly care.

Because God himself is thus its author, marriage is of its very nature a holy institution, requiring of those who enter into it a complete and unreserved giving of self. But Christ our Lord added to the holiness of marriage an even deeper meaning and a higher beauty. He referred to the love of marriage to describe his own love for his Church, that is, for the people of God whom he redeemed by his own blood.

And so he gave to Christians a new vision of what married life ought to be, a life of self-sacrificing love like his own. It is for this reason that his apostle, St. Paul, clearly states that marriage is now and for all time to be considered a great mystery, intimately bound up with the supernatural union of Christ and the Church, which union is also to be its pattern.

This union then is most serious, because it will bind you together for life in a relationship so close and so intimate that it will profoundly influence your whole future. That future, with its hopes and disappointments, its successes and its failures, its pleasures and its pains, its joys and its sorrows, is hidden from your eyes. You know that these elements are mingled in every life and are to be expected in your own. And so, not knowing what is before you, you take each other for better or for worse, for richer or for poorer, in sickness and in health, until death.

Truly, then, these words are most serious. It is a beautiful tribute to your undoubted faith in each other, that, recognizing their full import, you are nevertheless so willing and ready to pronounce them. And because these words involve such solemn obligations, it is most fitting that you rest the security of your wedded life upon the great principle of self-sacrifice. And so you begin your married life by the voluntary and complete surrender of your individual lives in the interest of that deeper and wider life which you are to have in common.

Henceforth you belong entirely to each other; you will be one in mind, one in heart, and one in affections. And whatever sacrifices you may hereafter be required to make to preserve this common life, always make them generously. Sacrifice is usually difficult and irksome. Only love can make it easy; and perfect love can make it a joy. We are willing to give in proportion as we love. And when love is perfect, the sacrifice is complete. God so loved the world that he gave his only-begotten Son, and the Son so loved us that he gave himself for our salvation. "Greater love than this no one has, that one lay down his life for his friends."

No greater blessing can come to your married life than pure conjugal love, loyal and true to the end. May, then, this love with which you join your hands and hearts today never fail, but grow deeper and stronger as the years go on. And if true love and the unselfish spirit of perfect sacrifice guide your every action, you can expect the greatest measure of earthly happiness that may be allotted to man in this vale of tears. The rest is in the hands of God. Nor will God be wanting to your needs; he will pledge you the lifelong support of his graces in the holy sacrament which you are now going to receive.

SEALING OF THE MARRIAGE BOND

Bridegroom and bride are now asked individually by the officiating priest to express their willingness to marry the partner present.

First the priest asks the bridegroom:

N., do you take N., here present, for your lawful wife according to the rite of our holy mother, the Church?

The bridegroom replies:

I do.

Then the priest asks the bride:

N., do you take N., here present, for your lawful husband according to the rite of our holy mother, the Church?

The bride replies:

I do.

After the mutual consent of the contractants has been given, the priest directs them:

Now join your right hands and say after me:

Groom: I, N.N., take you, N.N., for my lawful wife, to have and to hold, from this day forward, for better, for worse, for richer, for poorer, in sickness and in health, until death do us part.

Bride: I, N.N., take you, N.N., for my lawful husband, to have and to hold, from this day forward, for better, for worse, for richer, for poorer, in sickness and in health, until death do us part.

CONFIRMATION OF THE MARRIAGE BOND

The priest solemnly joins them together in the Name of the Most Holy Trinity:

By the authority of the Church I ratify and bless the bond of marriage you have contracted. In the name of the Father, and of the Son, † and of the Holy Spirit.

All: Amen.

The priest continues:

I call upon all of you here present to be witnesses of this holy union which I have now blessed. "Man must not separate what God has joined together."

Then he sprinkles them with holy water.

BLESSING OF THE WEDDING RING, OR RINGS

Next the priest blesses the ring or rings on a plate held by a server:

Priest: Our help is in the name of the Lord.
All: Who made heaven and earth.
Priest: O Lord, hear my prayer.
All: And let my cry come to you.
Priest: The Lord be with you.
All: And with your spirit.

Prayer (for two rings)

Let us pray. Bless, † O Lord, these rings, which we are blessing † in your name, so that they who wear them, keeping faith with each other in unbroken loyalty, may ever remain at peace with you according to your will, and may live together always in mutual love. Through Christ our Lord.

All: Amen.

Prayer (for one ring)

Let us pray. Bless, † O Lord, this ring, which we are blessing † in your name, so that she who wears it, keeping faith with her husband in unbroken loyalty, may ever remain at peace with you according to your

will, and may live with him always in mutual love. Through Christ our
Lord.

All: Amen.

Then he sprinkles the ring or rings with holy water.

GIVING THE RING, OR RINGS

The priest addresses the bridal couple:

Now that you have sealed a truly Christian marriage, give these wedding rings to each other (this wedding ring to your bride) saying after me:

The groom takes the bride's ring from the priest and
places it on the bride's ring finger, saying after the priest:

In the name of the Father and of the Son and of the Holy Spirit.
Take and wear this ring as a sign of our marriage vows.

The bride takes the groom's ring from the priest and
places it on the groom's ring finger, saying after the
priest:

In the name of the Father and of the Son and of the Holy Spirit.
Take and wear this ring as a sign of our marriage vows.

Priest: In the name of the Father and of the Son † and of the Holy
Spirit. Amen.

Then the priest adds:

Priest: Strengthen, O God, what you have wrought in us.
All: From your holy temple, which is in Jerusalem.
Priest: Lord, have mercy.
Christ, have mercy.
Lord, have mercy.
Our Father (silently as far as:)
Priest: And lead us not into temptation.
All: But deliver us from evil.
Priest: Save your servants.
All: Who trust in you, my God.
Priest: Send them help, O Lord, from your sanctuary.
All: And sustain them from Sion.
Priest: Be a tower of strength for them, O Lord.
All: Against the attack of the enemy.
Priest: O Lord, hear my prayer.
All: And let my cry come to you.
Priest: The Lord be with you.
All: And with your spirit.

Prayer

Let us pray. We beg you, Lord, to look on these your servants, and graciously to uphold the institution of marriage established by you for the continuation of the human race, so that they who have been joined together by your authority may remain faithful together by your help. Through Christ our Lord.

All: **Amen.**

BLESSING

Next, with his hands elevated and extended above the spouses to bless them (the server holding the book), the priest says:

May almighty God bless you by the Word of his mouth, and unite your hearts in the enduring bond of pure love.

All: **Amen.**

The following blessing may be omitted when bridegroom and bride are quite advanced in years:

May you be blessed in your children, and may the love that you lavish on them be returned a hundredfold.

All: **Amen.**

The rite closes with the following three prayers:

May the peace of Christ dwell always in your hearts and in your home; may you have true friends to stand by you, both in joy and in sorrow. May you be ready with help and consolation for all those who come to you in need; and may the blessings promised to the compassionate descend in abundance on your house.

All: **Amen.**

May you be blessed in your work and enjoy its fruits. May cares never cause you distress, nor the desire for earthly possessions lead you astray; but may your hearts' concern be always for the treasures laid up for you in the life of heaven.

All: **Amen.**

May the Lord grant you fullness of years so that you may reap the harvest of a good life, and, after you have served him with loyalty in his kingdom on earth, may he take you up into his eternal dominions in heaven. Joining his hands together, the priest concludes: Through our Lord Jesus Christ, his Son, who lives and reigns with him in the unity of the Holy Spirit, God, for ever and ever.

All: **Amen.**

294 THE NUPTIAL MASS

The married couple and the witnesses return to their places. After the **Our Father** they come to the altar step for the first part of the solemn Nuptial Blessing, the text for which is given on page **296.** They receive Holy Communion before anyone else present, and, just before the Last Blessing of the Mass, they again come to the altar for the second part of the Nuptial Blessing. The text for this is on page **298.**

The priest begins the Offertory with a salutation to the faithful:

Priest: **The Lord be with you.**
All: **And with your spirit.**
Priest: **Let us pray.**

If the **Prayers of the Faithful** are to be said, the following may serve in whole or in part as a model:

Now that we have invoked God's blessing on the union of N.N. and N.N., let us pray for our parish community and for the Church everywhere, that we may be faithful to the love of Christ:

For holy Church, beloved bride of Christ, blemished with our sins, adorned with the holiness of the saints, let us pray.

All: Lord, have mercy.

For Pope Paul, our Bishop _____, and all his priests, devoted servants of God's people, let us pray.

For the sanctity of Christian marriage, school of perfection and sign of Christ's redeeming love, let us pray.

For all our married couples, that God give them comfort and strength in each other and joy in their children, let us pray.

For those preparing for marriage, that God dispose them for the grace of the holy sacrament, let us pray.

For housewives and all homemakers, that their devotion inspire us to all forms of Christian service, let us pray.

For all gathered together here today, that the Eucharist may be for us a foretaste of the eternal banquet of God's love, let us pray.

Be merciful, almighty God, and hear our prayers; strengthen the bonds of holy matrimony in your Church as a source of great blessing for society and as a saving sign of the new and eternal covenant. Through Christ our Lord. Amen.

OFFERTORY HYMN

Lord, I put my trust in you! I say: You are my God, and in your hands lies my future.

In gifts of bread and wine we offer ourselves and all our activity in union with Christ to the heavenly Father; for bridegroom and bride it is their gift of self to each other and themselves together in the oneness of married life that is presented to God.

The Mass continues as in the Ordinary, page 245.

15. WE JOIN THE BRIDEGROOM AND THE BRIDE

1. We join the bride - groom and the bride
2. As man and wife they pledge their lives
3. O Christ, be - hold your Bride, the Church.

1. In of - f'ring now this bread and wine;
2. To self - do - na - tion by God's grace;
3. Ac - cept this pre - cious gift we give:

1. By these two gifts: two hearts u - nite,
2. Let this be their re - hears - al for
3. To love all men as you love us,

1. That in one Lord one love may shine.
2. A love that shall the world em - brace.
3. And for the Fa - ther's praise to live.

PRAYER OVER THE GIFTS

Let us pray. We beseech you, O Lord, accept the sacrifice now being offered for the sacred purposes of marriage; bring to a blessed conclusion this union which you arranged. Through our Lord Jesus Christ, your Son, who lives and reigns with you in the unity of the Holy Spirit, God, for ever and ever.

NUPTIAL BLESSING

*After the **Our Father**, bridegroom and bride approach the altar and kneel for receiving the first part of the Nuptial Blessing. Facing the couple, the priest prays over them as follows:*

Let us pray. Listen with favor, O Lord, to our prayers, and graciously uphold the institution of marriage established by you for the continuation of the human race, so that they who have been joined together by your authority may remain faithful together by your help. Through our Lord Jesus Christ, your Son, who lives and reigns with you in the unity of the Holy Spirit, God, for ever and ever.

All: Amen.

Let us pray. O God, by your mighty power you made all things where before there was nothing; you put in order the beginnings of the universe and formed for man, made to your image, an inseparable helpmate, woman. You gave woman's body its origin from man's flesh, to teach that it is never right to separate her from the one being from whom it has pleased you to take her.

O God, you consecrated the union of marriage, making it a sign so profound as to prefigure in the marriage covenant the mystery of Christ and the Church.

O God, you join woman to man and give to that society, the first to be established, the blessing which alone was not taken away in punishment for original sin or in the doom of the Flood:

Look with kindness on this your servant who is to be joined to her husband in the companionship of marriage and who seeks to be made secure by your protection.

May this yoke that she is taking on herself be one of love and peace. May she be faithful and chaste, marrying in Christ, and may she always imitate the holy women: may she be the beloved of her husband, as was Rachel; wise, as was Rebecca; long-lived and loyal, as was Sara.

May the author of sin have no mastery over her because of her acts. May she hold firm to the faith and the commandments. Faithful to one embrace, may she flee from unlawful companionship. By firm discipline may she fortify herself against her weakness. May she be grave in her modesty, honorable in her chastity, learned in the teachings of heaven.

May she be rich in children, may she prove worthy and blameless, and may she attain in the end to the peace of the blessed, the kingdom of heaven.

May she and her husband together see their children's children to the third and fourth generation and enjoy the long life that will fulfill their desires. Through the same Jesus Christ, your Son, our Lord, who lives and reigns with you in the unity of the Holy Spirit, God, for ever and ever.

All: Amen.

The newly-wed couple return to their places, while the priest continues with the Mass, page 255.

Where the practice of receiving the holy Eucharist under both Species has been introduced, the rite as approved by the bishop is observed; in other instances the usual form is followed.

The laudable custom of all present receiving holy Communion at a Nuptial Mass is constantly growing; there is no reason why full participation in the Eucharistic sacrifice should not be part of our response at a time when we seek God's blessings upon the couple just beginning married life.

For reflection or song at this point in the Eucharistic service, the Nuptial Mass provides this

COMMUNION VERSE

Behold, thus is the man blessed who fears the Lord. May you see your children's children! Peace be upon Israel (P.T. Alleluia).

16. GLADLY NOW WE SHARE COMMUNION

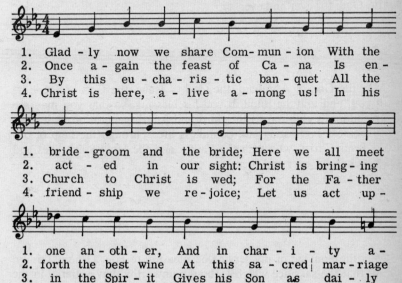

1. Glad-ly now we share Com-mun-ion With the bride-groom and the bride; Here we all meet one an-oth-er, And in char-i-ty a-
2. Once a-gain the feast of Ca-na Is en-act-ed in our sight: Christ is bring-ing forth the best wine At this sa-cred mar-riage
3. By this eu-cha-ris-tic ban-quet All the Church to Christ is wed; For the Fa-ther in the Spir-it Gives his Son as dai-ly
4. Christ is here, a-live a-mong us! In his friend-ship we re-joice; Let us act up-on our un-ion, For his love leaves us no

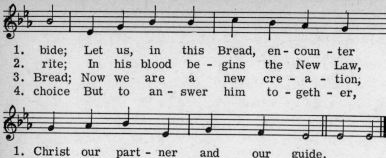

1. bide; Let us, in this Bread, en - coun - ter
2. rite; In his blood be - gins the New Law,
3. Bread; Now we are a new cre - a - tion,
4. choice But to an - swer him to - geth - er,

1. Christ our part - ner and our guide.
2. And all men with God u - nite.
3. And to God's own heart are led.
4. When we hear the Bride - groom's voice. A-men.

POSTCOMMUNION PRAYER

At the missal the priest addresses a final prayer to God, begging the continuance of his mercy upon bridegroom and bride.

Let us pray. With kindly favor accompany this expression of your Providence, we beg of you, almighty God; keep permanently in peace those whom you have united in lawful union. Through our Lord Jesus Christ, your Son, who lives and reigns with you in the unity of the Holy Spirit, God, for ever and ever.

If customary, the bride and groom come to the altar step to receive the second part of the Nuptial Blessing; otherwise they remain at their places. Facing them, the priest says:

May the God of Abraham, the God of Isaac, the God of Jacob be with you, and may he fulfill in you his blessing, so that you may see your children's children to the third and fourth generation and afterward possess everlasting and boundless life. Through the help of our Lord Jesus Christ, who with the Father and the Holy Spirit lives and reigns, God, for ever and ever.

All: Amen.

The priest may add a few words of exhortation; he then sprinkles bride and groom with holy water. Facing the altar again, he says the final prayer to the Blessed Trinity:

May the homage of my service be pleasing to you, O holy Trinity. Grant that the sacrifice which I, though unworthy, have offered in the presence of your Majesty, be acceptable to you. Through your mercy may it obtain forgiveness for me and all those for whom I have offered it. Through Christ our Lord. Amen.

THE LAST BLESSING

All kneel as the priest gives the final blessing:

May almighty God bless you, the Father, and the Son, † and the Holy Spirit.

All: **Amen.**

After some few moments of personal prayer, the newly-married couple rise, genuflect and precede all others out of church.

17. NOW MAY THE GOD OF ALL

1. Now may the God of all, Of A - bra - ham, and
2. May we be - hold in you The acts of God a -

1. I - saac, The God of Is - ra - el: En -
2. mong us: All his cre - a - tive love, All

1. fold you with his bless - ing. May you be filled with
2. his re - demp - tive pur - pose. May ev - 'ry - thing you

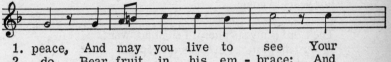

1. peace, And may you live to see Your
2. do Bear fruit in his em - brace; And

1. chil - dren's chil - dren, here And in e - ter - ni - ty.
2. may your whole life be: A ju - bi - lee of grace!

PRAYERS FOR RECITATION AT A WAKE
ADAPTED FROM THE OFFICE FOR THE DEAD

Making the sign of the Cross, the priest or leader begins:

STAND

Come, † let us adore the King of life.

All: Come, let us adore the King of life.

Leader: Come, let us sing joyfully to the Lord;
let us acclaim the Rock of our salvation.
Let us greet him with thanksgiving;
let us joyfully sing psalms to him.

All: Come, let us adore the King of life.

Leader: For the Lord is a great God,
and a great king above all gods;
In his hands are the depths of the earth,
and the tops of the mountains are his.

All: Come, let us adore the King of life.

Leader: His is the sea, for he has made it,
and the dry land, which his hands have formed.
Come, let us bow down in worship;
let us kneel before the Lord who made us.
For he is our God,
and we are the people he shepherds, the flock he guides.

All: Come, let us adore the King of life.

Leader: Eternal rest grant unto him (her), O Lord;
and let perpetual light shine upon him (her).

All: Come, let us adore the King of life.

Psalm 22

Leader: I shall dwell in the house of the Lord.

All: For years to come.

SIT

Leader: The Lord is my shepherd; I shall not want.

All: In verdant pastures he gives me repose;

This and the following psalms may be prayed in either of
two ways: (1) all present pray the entire text, or (2) two
sides are formed, with those on the right side reciting
lines preceded by number one, and those on the left
reciting lines preceded by number two.

1 Beside restful waters he leads me;
   he refreshes my soul.
2 He guides me in right paths
   for his name's sake.
1 Even though I walk in the dark valley
   I fear no evil; for you are at my side
2 With your rod and your staff
   that give me courage.
1 You spread the table before me
   in the sight of my foes;
2 You anoint my head with oil;
   my cup overflows.
1 Only goodness and kindness follow me
   all the days of my life;
2 And I shall dwell in the house of the Lord
   for years to come.

All: Eternal rest grant unto him (her), O Lord;
      and let perpetual light shine upon him (her).
      I shall dwell in the house of the Lord
      for years to come.

The leader continues with a reading from the Old Testament (2 Machabees 12:43-46). All listen to the word of God.

Then did Judas Machabeus take up a collection that amounted to two thousand drachmas of silver; this he sent to Jerusalem to provide a sin offering — an excellent and praiseworthy act in view of the resurrection. For if he had not hoped that the fallen soldiers would rise again, it would have been superfluous and foolish to pray for the dead. But if he believed that a very splendid recompense is in store for those who fall asleep in godliness, such thought is indeed holy and pious. See, then, why he arranged that atonement sacrifice for the dead: it was for the purpose of freeing them from their sin.

All: Thanks be to God.

STAND

Leader: Most loving Lord Jesus Christ, you who have redeemed us by your most precious Blood, take pity on the soul of this your servant, N.; open to him (her) the gates of life and cause him (her) to rejoice with your saints in everlasting glory. Lead him (her) into the lovely places of paradise that are forever green, so that he (she) may live with you in undivided love, never to be separated from you and from those whom you have chosen.

All: For to those who have faith in you, Lord,
    life does not cease —
    it merely changes!
  And when our earthly dwelling falls to ruins,
    we find an eternal home in heaven.

Psalm 26

Leader: I believe that I shall see the goodness of the Lord.
All: In the land of the living.

SIT

Leader: The Lord is my light and my salvation; whom should I fear?
All: The Lord is my life's refuge;
    of whom should I be afraid?
1 Though an army encamp against me,
    my heart will not fear;
2 Though war be waged upon me,
    even then will I trust.
1 One thing I ask of the Lord;
    this I seek:
2 To dwell in the house of the Lord
    all the days of my life,
1 That I may gaze on the loveliness of the Lord
    and contemplate his temple.
2 For he will hide me in his abode
    in the day of trouble;
1 He will conceal me in the shelter of his tent,
    he will set me high upon a rock.
2 Even now my head is held high
    above my enemies on every side.
1 Hear, O Lord, the sound of my call;
    have pity on me, and answer me.
2 Of you my heart speaks; you my glance seeks;
    your presence, O Lord, I seek.
1 Hide not your face from me;
    do not in anger repel your servant.
2 You are my helper: cast me not off;
    forsake me not, O God my savior.
1 Though my father and mother forsake me,
    yet will the Lord receive me.
2 Show me, O Lord, your way,
    and lead me on a level path.

1 I believe that I shall see the goodness of the Lord
   in the land of the living.

2 Wait for the Lord with courage;
   be stouthearted, and wait for the Lord.

All: Eternal rest grant unto him (her), O Lord;
   and let perpetual light shine upon him (her).
   I believe that I shall see the goodness of the Lord
   in the land of the living.

Again all listen as the leader reads a message taken from St. Augustine, one of the great Fathers of the Church.

From a funeral sermon of St. Augustine. The arrangements for a funeral, the place of interment, the externals proper to the obsequies, serve more as consolation to the living than as aid for the dead. Nevertheless, the bodies of our deceased must not be treated lightly or disregarded, particularly the bodies of the faithful or of virtuous men; for these bodies were used by their souls in a holy manner as instruments and agents for the performance of all their good works.

A father's clothing, his ring or some similar object is treasured more highly by one who loves his father more dearly. In no case, therefore, may our mortal bodies be contemned, for we are joined to them more intimately than to any external apparel. The body belongs to man's very nature; it is not an ornament or some secondary adjunct. For this reason virtuous men in ages past were given reverent burial and their obsequies piously celebrated.

Now if they who do not believe in the resurrection of the flesh are so anxious about the care of the physical body, how much greater should be our concern, we who do believe! May our tender care for the body of our deceased, which is destined, as we know, for an eternal resurrection, be, then, a manifestation of the faith and love within us.

All: Thanks be to God.

STAND

Leader: Come to his (her) aid, O saints of God; come forth to meet him (her), angels of the Lord, receiving his (her) soul, presenting it to the Most High. May Christ, who has called you, now receive you, and may the angels bring you to Abraham's bosom.

All: For to those who have faith in you, Lord,
   life does not cease —
   it merely changes!
  And when our earthly dwelling falls to ruins,
   we find an eternal home in heaven.

Psalm 129

Leader: If you, O Lord, mark iniquities,
All: Lord, who can stand?

SIT

Leader: Out of the depths I cry to you, O Lord;
      Lord, hear my voice!
All: Let your ears be attentive
      to my voice in supplication:
  1 If you, O Lord, mark iniquities,
      Lord, who can stand?
  2 But with you is forgiveness,
      that you may be revered.
  1 I trust in the Lord;
      my soul trusts in his word.
  2 My soul waits for the Lord
      more than sentinels wait for the dawn.
  1 More than sentinels wait for the dawn,
      let Israel wait for the Lord,
  2 For with the Lord is kindness
      and with him is plenteous redemption;
  1 And he will redeem Israel
      from all their iniquities.
All: Eternal rest grant unto him (her), O Lord;
      and let perpetual light shine upon him (her).
    If you, O Lord, mark iniquities,
    Lord, who can stand?

The final reading is from the holy Gospel, words of comfort spoken by Jesus to all in sorrow (John 5:24-29). All stand and listen reverently as the leader reads:

STAND

Then Jesus said to the crowds of Jews: "Amen, amen, I say to you, he who hears my word, and believes him who sent me, has life everlasting, and does not come to judgment, but has passed from death to life.

"Amen, amen, I say to you, the hour is coming, and now is here (in a very real sense), when the dead shall hear the voice of the Son of God, and those who hear shall live. For as the Father has life in himself, even so he has given to the Son also to have life in himself; and he has granted him power to render judgment, because he is Son of Man. Do not wonder at this, for the hour is coming in which all who are in the tombs shall hear the voice of the Son of God. And they who have done good shall come forth unto resurrection of life; but they who have done evil unto resurrection of judgment."

All: Praise to you, O Christ.

Leader: May the angels lead him (her) into paradise. At his (her) coming may the martyrs receive him (her) and accompany him (her) into the holy city Jerusalem. May choirs of angels receive him (her), and with once poor Lazarus may he (she) have rest everlasting.

All: For to those who have faith in you, Lord,
      life does not cease —
      it merely changes!
And when our earthly dwelling falls to ruins,
      we find an eternal home in heaven.

Leader: I am the resurrection and the life;
All: He who believes in me, even if he die, shall live;
      and whoever lives and believes in me, shall never die.

The Canticle of Zachary (Luke 1:68-79)

Leader: Blessed be the Lord, the God of Israel,
      because he has visited and wrought redemption
        for his people,

All: And has raised up a horn of salvation for us,
      in the house of David his servant,

1   As he promised through the mouth of his holy ones,
      the prophets from of old;

2   Salvation from our enemies,
      and from the hand of all who hate us,

1   To show mercy to our forefathers
      and to be mindful of his holy covenant,

2   Of the oath that he swore to Abraham our father,
      that he would grant us,

1   That, delivered from the hand of our enemies,
      we should serve him without fear,

2   In holiness and justice before him all our days.

1   And thou, child, shalt be called the prophet of the Most High,
      for thou shalt go before the face of the Lord
        to prepare his ways,

2   To give to his people knowledge of salvation
      through forgiveness of their sins,

1   Because of the loving-kindness of our God,
      wherewith the Orient from on high has visited us,

 2 To shine on those who sit in darkness and in the
         shadow of death,
       to guide our feet into the way of peace.

All: Eternal rest grant unto him (her), O Lord;
       and let perpetual light shine upon him (her).
     I am the resurrection and the life;
       he who believes in me, even if he die, shall live;
     and whoever lives and believes in me,
         shall never die.

Leader: Lord, have mercy.
All: Christ, have mercy. Lord, have mercy.
Leader: Our Father, etc.
All: Give us this day, etc.
Leader: O Lord, hear my prayer.
All: And let my cry come unto you.
Leader: Let us pray. O God, Creator and Redeemer of all the faithful, hear our supplications and through your infinite love and mercy graciously grant to the soul of your servant, N., whom you have called forth out of this life, the remission of all sins by which he (she) may have deserved the severity of divine justice and punishment in the world to come. Be pleased to grant him (her) grace and mercy before your tribunal, and let him (her) attain to everlasting rest and happiness through the infinite merits of Jesus Christ.

Grant, O Lord, that as we lament the departure of our brother (sister), your servant, out of this life, we may bear in mind that we are most certainly to follow him (her). Give us grace to make ready for that last hour by a devout and holy life, and protect us against a sudden and unprovided death. Teach us how to watch and pray that when your summons comes, we may go forth to meet the Bridegroom and enter with him into life everlasting. Through Christ our Lord.

All: Amen.
Leader: Eternal rest grant unto him (her), O Lord.
All: And let perpetual light shine upon him (her).
Leader: May his (her) soul and the souls of all the faithful departed through the mercy of God rest in peace.
All: Amen.

18. PEOPLE'S SUNG MASS

THE LITURGY FOR CHRISTIAN BURIAL

I. THE BODY IS BROUGHT INTO CHURCH

If the priest cannot go to the house of the deceased, he meets the body in the vestibule of the church, or at its entrance. He is accompanied by a cross-bearer and acolytes with lighted candles and holy water. The body is sprinkled with holy water — a sacramental symbolic of purification from the stains of sin. The following antiphon and psalm begin the service.

PSALM 129

Ant. If you, O Lord, mark in-iq - ui-ties, O Lord, who can stand?

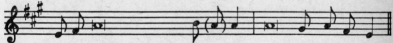

1. Out of the depths I cry to YOU, O Lord; * . . . *Lord,* hear my voice!
2. Let your ears be at-TEN-tive * to my voice in *sup*-plication.
3. If you, O Lord, mark in-IQ-uities, * . . . *Lord,* who can stand?
4. But with you is for-GIVE-ness, * that you *may* be revered.
5. I trust in the LORD; * my soul *trusts* in his word.
6. My soul waits for the LORD * more than sentinels *wait* for the dawn.
7. More than sentinels wait for the DAWN, * let Israel *wait* for the Lord.
8. For with the Lord is KIND-ness * and with him is plente-*ous* redemption.
9. And he will redeem IS-rael * from all *their* iniquities.
10. Eternal rest grant unto HIM (HER), O Lord. * And let perpetual light *shine* upon him (her).

If you, O Lord, mark in-iq- ui-ties, O Lord, who can stand?

307

Priest: **The Lord be with you.**
All: **And with your spirit.**

Let us pray. O Lord, we commend to you the soul of your servant, N., that, having departed from this world, he may live with you. And by the grace of your merciful love, wash away the sins that in human frailty he has committed in the conduct of his life. Through Christ our Lord.
All: **Amen.**

The Lord be with you.
And with your spirit.

Let us pray. O Lord, we commend to you the soul of your servant, N., that, having departed from this world, she may live with you. And by the grace of your merciful love, wash away the sins that in human frailty she has committed in the conduct of her life. Through Christ our Lord.
All: **Amen.**

PROCESSION TO THE CHURCH

The body of the deceased is then carried into church. The cross-bearer precedes. The crucifix at the head of the procession is an admonition that Jesus is the Way and the Truth and the Life (John 14:6), and that death was vanquished by the death of Jesus on the Cross (1 Cor. 15:54-58). Psalm 50, "Have mercy on me, O God," is a prayer not only for pardon but also for spiritual rebirth. The psalm is introduced and concluded with a consolatory antiphon:

PSALM 50

Ant. They shall re-joice in the Lord, the bones that are brought low in the dust.

1. Have mer - cy on me, O God, in your good - ness;

1. in the greatness of
   your compassion wipe out my of- fense.

2. Thoroughly	wash	me	from	my	guilt
3. For I ac-	knowl-	edge	my	of-	fense
4. "Against you	on-	ly	have	I	sinned,
5. That you may be justified in	your	sen-			tence,
6. Indeed, in	guilt	was	I		born,
7. Behold, you are pleased with sin-	cer-	i-	ty	of	heart,
8. Cleanse me of sin with hyssop, that I	may be	pu-	ri-		fied;
9. Let me hear the sounds of joy	and	glad-			ness;
10. Turn away your	face	from	my		sins,
11. A clean heart cre-	ate	for	me,	O	God,
12. Cast me not	out	from	your	pres-	ence,
13. Give me back the joy	of your	sal-	va-		tion,
14. I will teach trans-	gres-	sors	your		ways,
15. Free me from blood guilt, O	God,	my	sav-	ing	God;
16. O Lord,	o-	pen	my		lips,
17. For you are not	pleased	with	sac-ri-	fic-	es;
18. My sacrifice, O God, is a	con-	trite	spir-		it;
19. Be bountiful, O Lord, to	Si-	on in	your	kind-	ness
20. Then shall you be pleased with due sacrifices, burnt	of-	fer-ings and hol-	o-		causts;
21. Eternal rest	grant	un-to	him,	O	Lord.
		(her,)			

2. and of	my	sin	cleanse		me.
3. and my sin	is	be-	fore	me	al-ways.
4. and done what is	e-	vil	in	your	sight"—
5. vindicat-	ed	when you	con-		demn.
6. and in sin my moth-	er	con-ceived			me.
7. and in my inmost be-	ing	you	teach	me	wis-dom.
8. wash me, and I	shall be	whiter	than	snow.
9. the bones you	have crushed shall	re-		joice.
10. and	blot	out	all	my	guilt.
11. and a steadfast spirit re-	new	with- in			me.

12. and your holy spir- it take not from me.
13. and a willing spir- it sus- tain in me.
14. and sinners shall re- turn to you.
15. then my tongue shall rev- el in your jus - tice.
16. and my mouth shall pro- claim your praise.
17. should I offer you a
holocaust you would not ac- cept it.
18. a heart contrite and
humbled, O God, you will not spurn.
19. by rebuilding the walls of Je- ru- sa- lem;
20. then shall they offer up bull- ocks on your al - tar.
21. And let perpetual light shine up- on him(her).

Repeat antiphon: They shall rejoice.

The body of the deceased is placed in the middle of the church with lighted candles to signify the eternal light that will shine for the departed. The following responsory is said after having entered the church:

COME TO HIS AID

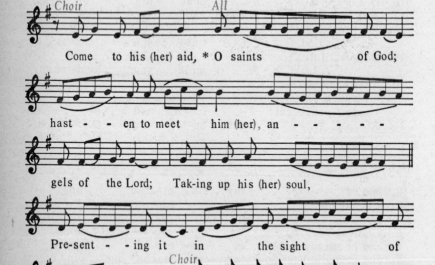

Come to his (her) aid, * O saints of God;
hast - - en to meet him (her), an - - - - - gels of the Lord; Tak-ing up his (her) soul, Pre-sent - - ing it in the sight of the Most High. ℣. May you be re-ceived by Christ,

who has called you:

and may the an - gels bring you in-to the bos - -

All

- - om of A - bra - ham. ℟. Tak-ing up his (her) soul,

Pre-sent - ing it in the

Choir

sight of the Most High. ℣. E - ter-nal

rest grant un - to him (her),

O Lord: and let per-pet-u- al light shine up -

All

on him (her). ℟. Pre-sent - ing his (her) soul

in the sight of the Most High.

COME TO HIS AID (alternate melody)

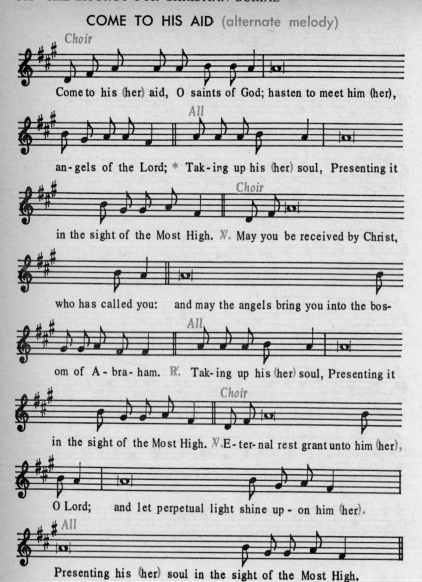

Choir

Come to his (her) aid, O saints of God; hasten to meet him (her),

All

an-gels of the Lord; * Tak-ing up his (her) soul, Presenting it

Choir

in the sight of the Most High. ℣. May you be received by Christ,

who has called you: and may the angels bring you into the bos-

All

om of A-bra-ham. ℟. Tak-ing up his (her) soul, Presenting it

Choir

in the sight of the Most High. ℣.E-ter-nal rest grant unto him (her),

O Lord; and let perpetual light shine up-on him (her).

All

Presenting his (her) soul in the sight of the Most High.

If the Office of the Dead is to be recited, it follows now. At the end of the Office the holy sacrifice of the Mass is offered for the departed.

II. THE MASS OF REQUIEM

A. The Liturgy of the Word of God

PRELIMINARY PRAYERS

At a Requiem Mass which is not a funeral Mass the priest begins with the usual prayers at the foot of the altar (see page **238**). Otherwise the service continues with the chanting of the

ENTRANCE ANTIPHON

Choir Eternal rest grant unto them, O Lord: * and let perpetual light All shine upon them. Choir To you we owe our hymn of praise, O God, in Sion; to All you must vows be fulfilled in Jerusalem. Hear my prayer: to you all flesh must come. All Eternal rest grant unto them, O Lord: and let perpetual light shine upon them.

Life on earth knows no rest; trials, sufferings, dangers, misery and death are the lot of man. And at times, man's heart is uneasy until it rests in God. Therefore "weep but a little for the dead, for he is at rest" (Eccli. 22:11). And let perpetual light shine upon them! Heaven is the kingdom of light; God is light (John 1:5). Man in baptism received the light, but it is only in heaven, the abode of eternal light, that he is intimately united with Light itself.

LORD, HAVE MERCY

After the usual greeting, the officiating priest recites the **Prayer over the Assembly.** The text of this prayer varies according to the rank or status of the deceased; the one given here would be the usual one in a parish service.

Priest: **Dóminus vobíscum.**
All: **Et cum spíritu tuo.**

The Lord be with you.
And with your spirit.

For a deceased man.

Let us pray. O God, it is your very nature to show mercy always and to spare. Humbly, then, do we plead with you in behalf of your servant N., whom you have called out of this world today; do not deliver him into the hands of the enemy nor forget him forever, but command the holy angels to take

For a deceased woman.

Let us pray. O God, it is your very nature to show mercy always and to spare. Humbly, then, do we plead with you in behalf of your servant N., whom you have called out of this world today; do not deliver her into the hands of the enemy nor forget her forever, but command the holy angels to take

him and lead him to the home of paradise. Because he put his hope and trust in you, may he escape the pains of hell and come to the possession of eternal joys. This we ask of you through our Lord Jesus Christ, your Son, who lives and reigns with you in the unity of the Holy Spirit, God, forever.
All: **Amen.**

her and lead her to the home of paradise. Because she put her hope and trust in you, may she escape the pains of hell and come to the possession of eternal joys. This we ask of you through our Lord Jesus Christ, your Son, who lives and reigns with you in the unity of the Holy Spirit, God, forever.
All: **Amen.**

God's mercy spares all (Wis. 11:27). Therefore the Church prays for mercy at the hour of death. She prays for mitigation of the punishment, for union with the blessed in the home of paradise, and participation in the joys of the blessed.

EPISTLE 1 Thessalonians 4:13-18

Our faith in the final resurrection depends on our faith in the resurrection of Christ. Through baptism we have become one with Christ: we shall rise with him and rise as he did.

A reading from the letter of the apostle Paul to the Christians of Thessalonica

Brethren,

I want you to know the truth about your dead, in order that you may not grieve as others do, who have no hope.

The fact is, if we know that Jesus died and rose again, then we should believe that those who have fallen asleep in the love of Jesus will be brought by God with his Son.

What I am going to say to you is in accordance with the words of the Lord: when the Lord comes back on earth, the living, the survivors, will not get ahead of those who died before them. For the Lord himself, at the given signal, at the voice of the archangel, at the sound of the divine trumpet, will come down from heaven; and those who have died in [the love of] Christ will be the first to rise. Then the living, the survivors, united with those who have risen, will be taken up with them into the air, to meet Christ. And from then on, forever, we shall be with the Lord.

May these words help you console one another!

A world of comfort lies in these words for those who believe and hope in Christ!

GRADUAL

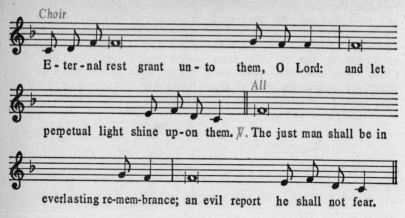

E-ter-nal rest grant un-to them, O Lord: and let perpetual light shine up-on them. ℣. The just man shall be in everlasting re-mem-brance; an evil report he shall not fear.

TRACT

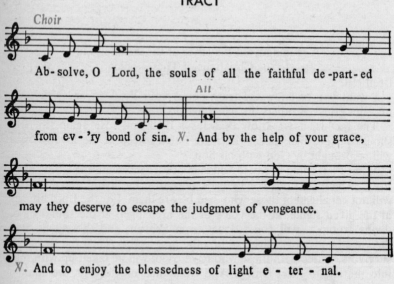

Ab-solve, O Lord, the souls of all the faithful de-part-ed from ev-'ry bond of sin. ℣. And by the help of your grace, may they deserve to escape the judgment of vengeance.

℣. And to enjoy the blessedness of light e-ter-nal.

SEQUENCE

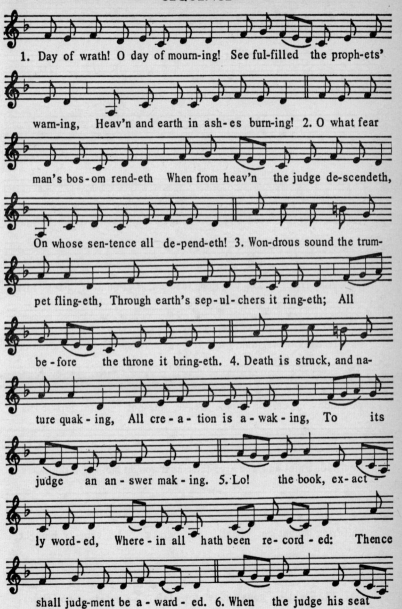

1. Day of wrath! O day of mourn-ing! See ful-filled the proph-ets' warn-ing, Heav'n and earth in ash-es burn-ing! 2. O what fear man's bos-om rend-eth When from heav'n the judge de-scendeth, On whose sen-tence all de-pend-eth! 3. Won-drous sound the trum-pet fling-eth, Through earth's sep-ul-chers it ring-eth; All be-fore the throne it bring-eth. 4. Death is struck, and na-ture quak-ing, All cre-a-tion is a-wak-ing, To its judge an an-swer mak-ing. 5. Lo! the book, ex-act-ly word-ed, Where-in all hath been re-cord-ed: Thence shall judg-ment be a-ward-ed. 6. When the judge his seat

at - tain - eth And each hid - den deed ar - raign - eth, Noth-

ing un - a - venged re - main - eth. 7. What shall I, frail man, be

plead-ing? Who for me be in - ter - ced - ing, When the

just are mer - cy need-ing? 8. King of maj - es - ty tre - men - dous,

Who dost free sal - va - tion send us, Fount of pit - y, then

be - friend us! 9. Think, good Je - sus, my sal - va - tion Cost thy

won-drous in - car - na - tion; Leave me not to rep - ro - ba-

tion! 10. Faint and wea - ry, thou hast sought me, On the cross of

suff'-ring bought me. Shall such grace be vain - ly brought

me? 11. Right - eous judge! for sin's pol - lu - tion Grant

thy gift   of ab - so - lu - tion,   Ere the day of ret - ri - bu -

tion. 12. Guilt - y, now I pour   my moan - ing,   All   my

shame   with an - guish own - ing;   Spare, O God, thy sup -

pliant groan - ing. 13. Thou the sin - ful wom- an sav-edst;   Thou

the dy -   ing thief for-gav-est;   And to me a hope vouch -

saf - est.   14. Worth-less are my prayers and sigh-ing,   Yet, good

Lord,   in grace com - ply - ing,   Res-cue me from fires un -

dy - ing! 15. With thy fa - vored sheep O place me Nor a - mong the

goats a - base me, But   to thy   right hand up - raise me.

16. While the wick- ed are con-found-ed,   Doomed to flames of woe

un-bound-ed, Call me with thy saints sur-round-ed.

17. Low I kneel with heart sub-mis-sion: See, like ash-es, my con-tri-tion; Help me in my last con-di-tion.

18. Ah! that day of tears and mourn-ing! From the dust of earth re-turn-ing. 19. Man for judg-ment must pre-pare him! Spare, O God, in mer-cy spare him! 20. Lord, all pit-y-ing, Je-sus blest, Grant them thine e-ter-nal rest.

A - - - men.

A non-Catholic has described this magnificent hymn as "solitary in its excellence. The secret of its irresistible power lies in the awful grandeur of the theme, the intense earnestness and pathos of the poet, the simple majesty and solemn music of its language, the stately metre, the triple rhyme — all combining to produce an overwhelming effect, as if we heard the final crash of the universe, the commotion of the opening of graves, the trumpet of the Archangel summoning the quick and the dead, and saw the King 'of tremendous majesty' seated on the throne of justice and mercy, and ready to dispense 'everlasting life or everlasting woe.' "

The priest prepares himself to announce the holy Gospel with the following prayer; then he greets the assembled people and gives the reading from the fourth evangelist.

Purify my heart and my lips, almighty God. Just as you purified the lips of the prophet Isaiah with a burning coal, so purify me now through your generous mercy in order that I may competently proclaim your holy Gospel. Through Christ our Lord. Amen.

GOSPEL John 11:21-27

On several occasions during his public life, Jesus raised the dead to life. In this way he showed that he was the master of life and death, and he foretold the resurrection which we shall all experience some day, thanks to him.

Priest: The Lord be with you.
All: And with your spirit.
Priest: A reading from the holy Gospel according to John
All: Glory to you, O Lord.

At that time Martha said to Jesus, "Lord, if you had been there, my brother would not be dead. But even now, I know, whatever you ask of God, God will grant you."

Jesus answered, "Your brother will rise again."

"I know," she said, "that he will rise again at the resurrection, on the last day."

Jesus said to her, "I myself am the resurrection and the life. He who believes in me, even if he dies, shall live. And he who lives and believes in me shall not die forever. Do you believe that?"

"Yes, Lord," she replied, "I believe that you are the Christ [the Messiah], the Son of the living God, the one who was to come into the world!"

As a joyful song of victory the words of Christ resound: "I am the resurrection and the life." Faith in him is the pledge of future glory. "He who believes in me, even if he dies, shall live; and he who lives and believes in me, shall not die forever."

B. The Liturgy of the Eucharist

THE OFFERING OF THE GIFTS

The priest begins the Offertory with a salutation to the faithful:

Priest: The Lord be with you.
   All: And with your spirit.
Priest: Let us pray.

OFFERTORY ANTIPHON

TWO VERSIONS

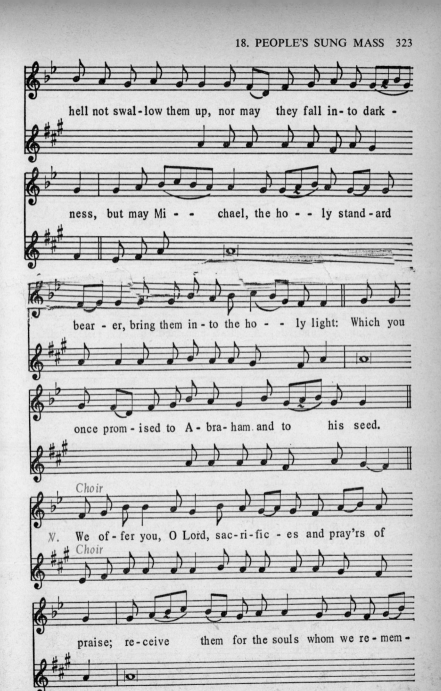

hell not swal-low them up, nor may   they fall in- to dark -

ness, but may Mi - - chael, the ho - - ly stand -ard

bear - er, bring them in - to the ho - - ly light: Which you

once prom - ised to A - bra - ham.and to   his seed.

Choir

℣. We of- fer you, O Lord, sac- ri- fic - es and pray'rs of

Choir

praise; re - ceive   them for the souls whom we re - mem -

ber this day.   Grant, O Lord,   that they may pass from

death   to   life.   Which you once

prom - ised to A - bra - ham and to   his seed.

The prayers ordinarily said during the Offertory are given on page **245.**

The **Prayer over the Offerings** or **Secret** is usually the following:

O Lord, we beg you to be merciful to the soul of your servant, N. For him (her) do we offer you this sacrifice of praise, humbly beseeching your Majesty that by these holy peace offerings he (she) may be found worthy to win everlasting rest. This we ask of you through our Lord Jesus Christ, your Son, who lives and reigns with you in the unity of the Holy Spirit, God,

The priest concludes:

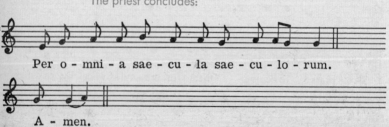

Per o - mni - a sae - cu - la sae - cu - lo - rum.

A - men.

Do - mi - nus vo - bis - cum.

Et cum spi - ri - tu tu - o.

Sur - sum cor - da.

Ha - be - mus ad Do - mi - num.

Gra - ti - as a - ga - mus Do - mi - no De - o no - stro.

Di - gnum et iu - stum est.

It is indeed fitting and proper, and a duty necessary for salvation, to be grateful at all times and places to you, holy Lord, almighty Father, eternal God: through Christ our Lord.

In him the hope of a blessed resurrection has been shown to us: that they who are saddened by the certain necessity of dying be comforted by the promise of eternal life to come.

For to those who have faith in you, Lord, life does not cease — it merely changes! And when our earthly dwelling falls to ruins, we find an eternal home in heaven.

Therefore with the Angels and Archangels, the Thrones and Dominions, and the whole host of the heavenly army do we hymn your glory, singing continuously:

HOLY, HOLY, HOLY

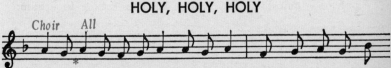

Ho - ly, ho - ly, ho - ly Lord God of hosts. Heav'n and earth are filled

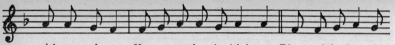

with your glo-ry. Ho-san-na in the high-est. Bless-ed is he who

comes in the name of the Lord. Ho-san-na in the high-est.

We may imagine that the departed is now chanting with the angels, archangels, and the whole host of the heavenly army: "Holy, holy, holy is the Lord, God over the heavenly hosts."

THE CANON

Custom and a decision of the Church (Sept. 3, 1958), as also respect and reverence for the approaching Godhead during this most solemn part of the Mass, demand that we pray in silence until the beginning of the "Our Father." This part of the Mass is given on page 249.

The Canon concludes with a solemn doxology:

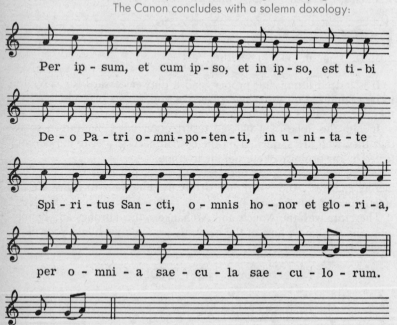

Per ip - sum, et cum ip - so, et in ip - so, est ti - bi

De - o Pa - tri o - mni - po - ten - ti, in u - ni - ta - te

Spi - ri - tus San - cti, o - mnis ho - nor et glo - ri - a,

per o - mni - a sae - cu - la sae - cu - lo - rum.

A - men.

THE EUCHARISTIC BANQUET

The "Our Father" is the most perfect prayer of praise of God and petition for our needs. It is all the more powerful in that it is not so much our prayer as Christ's, who taught it to his disciples. If we pray rightly and becomingly, we never say but what is found expressed in this prayer of the Lord, for it is the summary of all prayer.

THE LORD'S PRAYER

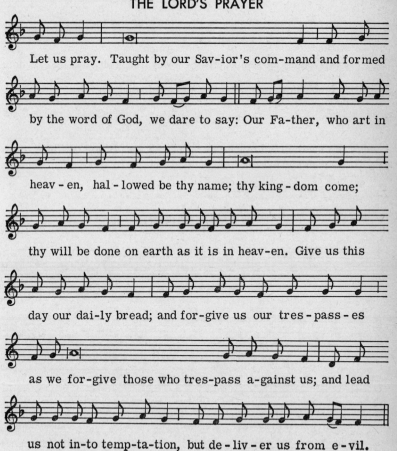

Let us pray. Taught by our Sav-ior's com-mand and formed by the word of God, we dare to say: Our Fa-ther, who art in heav-en, hal-lowed be thy name; thy king-dom come; thy will be done on earth as it is in heav-en. Give us this day our dai-ly bread; and for-give us our tres-pass-es as we for-give those who tres-pass a-gainst us; and lead us not in-to temp-ta-tion, but de-liv-er us from e-vil.

The priest continues, enlarging upon the last petition of the Our Father:

Deliver us, Lord, from all evils, whether of the past, present, or future. In response to the intercession of blessed Mary, the ever-glorious Virgin Mother of God, of your apostle-saints Peter and Paul, of Andrew too, and of all the saints, be merciful and favor us with peace throughout our lifetime. For with your compassion and help we will always be both free of sin and safely sheltered from every type of trouble. Through Jesus Christ, our Lord and your Son. Being God, he lives and exercises kingship with you in oneness with the Holy Spirit,

Priest: . . . per ómnia sǽcula sæculórum.
    All: Amen.
Priest: Pax Dómini sit semper vobíscum.
    All: Et cum spíritu tuo.

for ever and ever.

Amen.

May the peace of the Lord be always with you.

And with your spirit.

Dropping a particle of the Sacred Host, which he has just broken, into the chalice, the priest continues silently:

May this sacred commingling of the Body and Blood of Christ Jesus our Lord mean eternal life to us who are about to receive it. Amen.

Priest and people say or sing:

LAMB OF GOD

Lamb of God,* who take a-way the sins of the world, grant them rest. Lamb of God,* who take a-way the sins of the world, grant them rest. Lamb of God,* who take a-way the sins of the world, grant them e-ter-nal rest.

PREPARATORY PRAYERS FOR HOLY COMMUNION

Lord Jesus Christ, Son of the living God, through your death you gave life to the world in accord with the Father's will and with the co-operation of the Holy Spirit. Through this, your infinitely holy Body and Blood, free me from all my sins and from every evil. Make me cling to your commandments always; never allow me to be separated from you, for you are God, living and exercising kingship with the Father and the Holy Spirit, from age to age. Amen.

Lord Jesus Christ, in spite of my unworthiness I purpose to receive your Body. Do not let it mean judgment and condemnation for me. But because of your loving kindness, may it prove beneficial, a protection and a means unto health for soul and body, O God, living and exercising kingship with the Father in oneness with the Holy Spirit, through all the passing ages. Amen.

I will take the Bread of heaven, and beseech the Lord.

Holding the Sacred Host in his left hand, the priest then devoutly and humbly says three times:

Lord, I am not worthy that you should come under my roof. Speak but the word, and my soul will be healed.

COMMUNION OF THE PRIEST

He then signs himself with the Sacred Host saying:

May the Body of our Lord Jesus Christ keep my soul alive forever. Amen.

Having received the Host, the priest prays:

What can I give the Lord for all he has given me! I will take the chalice of salvation and beseech the Lord. With praise I will beseech the Lord, and I will be freed from my enemies.

He now receives the Precious Blood saying:

May the Blood of our Lord Jesus Christ keep my soul alive forever. Amen.

The laudable custom of receiving holy Communion at a Mass of Requiem is constantly growing; there is no reason why a full participation in the Eucharistic sacrifice should not be part of our devotion at a time when we need God's consolation most both for ourselves and for our beloved deceased.

Facing the people with the ciborium of consecrated Bread, the priest exclaims:

Priest: **Behold the Lamb of God, / behold him who takes away the sins of the world.**

All (three times): **Lord, I am not worthy that you should come under my roof. / Speak but the word, and my soul will be healed.**

Priest: **The Body of Christ.**

Communicant: **Amen.**

COMMUNION ANTIPHON

May light e - ter - nal * shine up - on   them, O Lord: With your

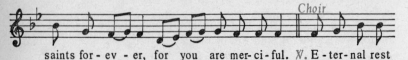

saints for - ev - er, for you are mer - ci - ful. ℣. E - ter - nal rest

grant un - to them, O Lord; and let per - pet - u - al light shine up - on

them. With your saints for - ev - er, for you are mer - ci - ful.

Psalm 129, "Out of the Depths," page 307, may be used here for the Communion psalm.

A petition for eternal light and eternal rest in heaven, based on the infinite mercy of God. The Mass having been offered for the departed, the Church now prays with greater confidence, as is evident from the more buoyant strain in the melody of the chant. In the eyes of the Church this is a precious moment, and she therefore admonishes the Christian to include in his Communion prayers a petition for the departed.

AFTER COMMUNION

The priest purifies the chalice with wine and water while saying the two following prayers:

What we have taken after the manner of bodily food, O Lord, may we treasure in a pure heart. And may the gift we have received in this life be our provision for eternity.

May your Body, Lord, that I have eaten and your Blood that I have drunk affect me to the depths of my being. Grant that no trace of sin be left in me, whom these pure and holy mysteries have renewed. O God, you live and reign for ever and ever. Amen.

CONCLUDING PRAYERS

From the middle of the altar the priest again salutes the faithful:

Priest: Dóminus vobíscum.   The Lord be with you.
All: Et cum spíritu tuo.   And with your spirit.

Let us pray. Almighty God, this do we beg of you: may the soul of your servant N., who today has departed out of this world be cleansed by this sacrifice; being freed from sins, may he (she) receive forgiveness and everlasting rest. This we ask of you through our Lord Jesus Christ, your Son, who lives and reigns with you in the unity of the Holy Spirit, God, forever.

All: Amen.

Another petition for the departed soul, but also an exhortation to the survivors to practice the virtue of charity, and remember the soul which has passed into eternity. From the middle of the altar the priest salutes the faithful.

Priest: The Lord be with you.
All: And with your spirit.
Priest: May they rest in peace!
All: Amen.

The words are earnest, and well so, for the word "peace" is indicative of all happiness and blessing. What greater happiness can we wish the departed, we who are living in a world that knows no peace. True peace is with God, as in God. May the departed enjoy that peace, and may it also be our portion when the end comes!

Bowing, the priest says the final prayer to the Blessed Trinity:

May the homage of my service be pleasing to you, O Holy Trinity. Grant that the sacrifice which I, though unworthy, have offered in the presence of your Majesty, be acceptable to you. Through your mercy may it obtain forgiveness for me and all those for whom I have offered it. Through Christ our Lord. Amen.

III. BLESSING OF THE BODY AND BURIAL

Prayer

O Lord, do not bring your servant to trial, for no man becomes holy in your sight unless you grant him forgiveness of all his sins. We implore you, therefore, do not let the verdict of your judgment go against him, whom the loyal prayer of Christian faith is commending to your mercy. Rather, by the help of your grace, may he escape the sentence which he deserves, for during his earthly life, he was signed with the seal of the Holy Trinity. You who live and reign for ever and ever.

All: Amen.

O Lord, do not bring your servant to trial, for no man becomes holy in your sight unless you grant him forgiveness of all his sins. We implore you, therefore, do not let the verdict of your judgment go against her, whom the loyal prayer of Christian faith is commending to your mercy. Rather, by the help of your grace, may she escape the sentence which she deserves, for during her earthly life, she was signed with the seal of the Holy Trinity. You who live and reign for ever and ever.

All: Amen.

A wonderful prayer in its simplicity and confidence. The departed has indeed been a sinner, because he was human; but he was sealed with the seal of the Holy Trinity in baptism. He believed in the triune God, and therefore the Church confidently hopes for mercy from this same God.

DELIVER ME, O LORD

shak - - en. As you come to judge

the world by fire. ℣. I am in

fear and trem - - bling at the judg - ment and the

wrath that is to come. When the heav - ens and the

earth will be shak - - en. ℣. That day will be

a day of wrath, of mis - er - y, and of ru - in: a day

of gran - deur and great hor - ror: As you

come to judge the

world by fire. ℣. E - ter - nal rest grant un - to them, O

Lord, and   let per-pet - u - al light shine up - on   them.

All
De - liv - er me, O   Lord, from   ev - er -

last - ing death on   that day   of ter - - ror:

When the heav - ens and   the earth   will   be

shak - - en. As you   come   to

judge   the   world by   fire.

DELIVER ME, O LORD (ALTERNATE MELODY)

Choir
De - liv-er me, O Lord, from ev - er - last - ing death on that day

All
of ter - ror. When the heavens and the earth will be shak - en.

Choir
As you come to judge the world by fire. ℣. I am in fear and

trem - bling at the judgment and the wrath that is to come. When

the heavens and the earth will be shak-en. ℣. That day will be

a day of wrath, of mis - er - y, and of ru - in: a day of grandeur

and great hor - ror: As you come to judge the world by fire.

℣. E - ter - nal rest grant un - to them, O Lord, and let perpetual light

shine up - on them. De-liv - er me, O Lord, from ev - er - last -

ing death on that day of ter - ror: When the heavens and the

earth will be shak - en. As you come to judge the world by fire.

Lord, have mer - cy. Christ have mer - cy. Lord,

have mer - - cy. Priest; Our Fa - ther.

While the priest recites the **Lord's Prayer**, he goes around the bier and sprinkles it with holy water thrice on each side. Then, in the same way, he incenses it. Holy water and incense, becoming efficacious sacramentals through the prayer and blessing of the Church, are again employed because the soul of the departed benefits by their application, and because the body of the departed was a temple of the Holy Spirit which will be rebuilt at the final resurrection. As the clouds of incense ascend, so let our prayers ascend to the throne of God to plead for mercy and eternal rest.

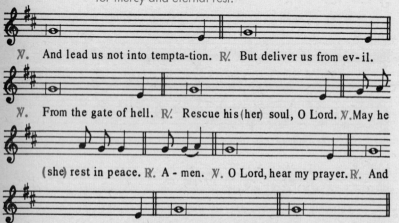

℣. And lead us not into tempta-tion. ℟. But deliver us from ev-il. ℣. From the gate of hell. ℟. Rescue his (her) soul, O Lord. ℣. May he (she) rest in peace. ℟. A - men. ℣. O Lord, hear my prayer. ℟. And let my cry come to you. ℣. The Lord be with you. ℟. And with your spirit.

Let us pray. O God, who alone are ever merciful and sparing of punishment, humbly we pray you in behalf of the soul of your servant, N., whom you have commanded to go forth today from this world. Do not hand him over to the power of the enemy and do not forget him forever; but command that this soul be taken up by the holy angels and brought home to paradise, so that, since he hoped and believed in you, he may not undergo the punishments of hell, but rather possess everlasting joys. Through Christ our Lord.

All: Amen.

Let us pray. O God, who alone are ever merciful and sparing of punishment, humbly we pray you in behalf of the soul of your servant, N., whom you have commanded to go forth today from this world. Do not hand her over to the power of the enemy and do not forget her forever; but command that this soul be taken up by the holy angels and brought home to paradise, so that, since she hoped and believed in you, she may not undergo the punishments of hell, but rather possess everlasting joys. Through Christ our Lord.

All: Amen.

Before conveying the body from the church to its narrow cell in the cemetery, the Church recalls the last day when the dead shall rise and be hailed before the just Judge. It is a terrible thing to fall into his hands. But Christ has now been offered for the departed, and in the beautiful words and melody of the following antiphon the Church anticipates the entrance of the soul into paradise eternal.

CARRYING THE BODY FROM CHURCH

As the body is carried out of the church the choir sings or the priest recites the following:

MAY THE ANGELS TAKE YOU INTO PARADISE

May the an-gels * take you in-to par-a-dise: may the mar-tyrs come to wel-come you on your way, and lead you in-to the ho-ly cit-y, Je-ru-sa-lem. May the choir of an-gels wel - - - come you, and with Laz-a-rus who once was poor may you have ev-er-last-ing rest.

PSALM 114

1. I love the Lord be-cause he has heard

2. Because he has in-   clined his   ear to   me
3. The cords of death
    encompassed me;the
    snares of the nether
                    world seized up-   on   me;
4. And I called upon the   name of   the   Lord,
5. Gracious   is   the   Lord and   just;
6. The   Lord   keeps the lit-   tle   ones;
7. Return, O my soul, to   your   tran-   quil- i-   ty,
8. For he has   freed   my   soul from death,
9. I shall   walk   be-   fore   the   Lord,
10. Eternal rest   grant un-   to   him, O   Lord.
                    (her,)

1. my   voice   in   sup- pli-   ca-   tion.
2. - - - -   the   day   I   called.
3. I fell in-   to   dis-   tress and   sor- row.
4. "O   Lord,   save   my   life!"
5. yes, our   God   is   mer- ci-   ful.
6. I was brought   low   and   he   saved me.
7. for the   Lord   has been   good to   you.
8. my eyes from   tears, my   feet   from stum-bling.
9. in the   lands   of   the   liv- ing.
10. And let perpetual   light   shine   up- on   him.
                    (her.)

Repeat Antiphon: May the angels . . .

ON THE WAY TO THE CEMETERY

The thoughts which Mother Church would have us keep
in mind while proceeding to the cemetery are contained
in the following antiphon and canticle:

I AM THE RESURRECTION AND THE LIFE

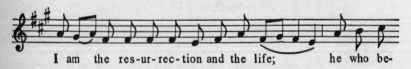

I am   the res-ur-rec-tion and the life;   he who be-

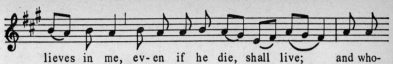

lieves in me, ev - en if he die, shall live; and who-

ev - er lives and be-lieves in me, shall nev - - er die.

CANTICLE OF ZACHARY

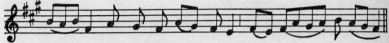

1. Bless- ed   be the Lord, the God of   Is-   .ra- el,
2. And   has   raised up a horn of
                    salvation   for   us
3. As   he   promised through the
                    mouths of his   ho-   ly   ones.
4. Sal-   va-   tion from our   en-   e-   mies.
5. He   has   fulfilled his kindness to our fa-   thers,
6. In   the   oath to Abraham our   fa-   ther,
7. That,   de-   livered from the hands
                    of our   en-   e-   mies,
8. In   ho-   liness and justice be-   fore   him
9. And   you,   O child, shall be called
                    the prophet of the Most   High;
10. To   grant   his people knowledge of sal-va-   tion
11. Be-   cause   of the compassionate
                    kindness of   our   God
12. To   shine   on those who sit in
                    darkness and the
                    shadow of   death,
13. E-   ter-   nal rest grant unto   him,   O   Lord.
                                                (her,)

1. because he has visited and
       wrought redemption for   his   peo- ple,
2. in the house of Da-   vid   his   serv- ant.
3. the prophets   from   of   old:
4. and from the hands of   all   our   foes.
5. and been mindful of his ho-   ly   cov-   e- nant.
6. by which he   swore to   grant us

7. we should serve him	with-	out		fear.
8. - - - -	all	our		days.
9. for you shall go before the				
Lord to pre-	pare	his		ways.
10. through forgiveness	of	their		sins.
11. with which the Orient from				
on high	will	vis-	it	us.
12. to guide our feet into the	way	of		peace.
13. And let perpetual light	shine	up-	on	him.
				(her.)

Repeat Antiphon: I am . . .

IN THE CEMETERY

In the cemetery the priest blesses the grave, unless the entire cemetery is already consecrated or solemnly blessed.

Let us pray. O God, by whose mercy rest is given to the souls of the faithful, in your kindness bless † this grave. Entrust it to the care of your holy angel, and set free from all the chains of sin the soul of him whose body is buried here, so that with all your saints he may rejoice in you forever. Through Christ our Lord.

All: Amen.

Let us pray. O God, by whose mercy rest is given to the souls of the faithful, in your kindness bless † this grave. Entrust it to the care of your holy angel, and set free from all the chains of sin the soul of her whose body is buried here, so that with all your saints she may rejoice in you forever. Through Christ our Lord.

All: Amen.

With holy water and sacred incense the priest sanctifies the body and the grave in the name of the Blessed Trinity. The dignity of the bodies of Christians demands such respect for them and their last resting place. Their bodies, consecrated temples of the Holy Spirit in baptism, should rest in consecrated soil, from whence, on the last day, the omnipotent summons of God will call them to praise and glorify him for all eternity. The bodies are buried facing the east, because the departed place their hopes in Christ, who is the light of the soul.

Priest: Dearest brothers, let us faithfully and lovingly remember our brother, whom God has taken to himself from the trials of this world.

Dearest brothers, let us faithfully and lovingly remember our sister, whom God has taken to himself from the trials of this world.

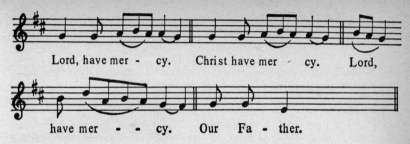

Lord, have mer - cy. Christ have mer - cy. Lord, have mer - - cy. Our Fa - ther.

The body is sprinkled with holy water.

℣. And lead us not into tempta-tion. ℟. But deliver us from ev-il.

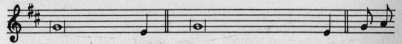

℣. From the gate of heH. ℟. Rescue his (her) soul, O Lord. ℣. May he

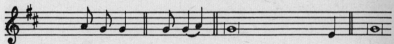

(she) rest in peace. ℟. A - men. ℣. O Lord, hear my prayer. ℟. And

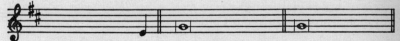

let my cry come to you. ℣. The Lord be with you. ℟. And with your spirit.

Let us pray. O Lord, we implore you to grant this mercy to your dead servant, that he who held fast to your will by his intentions, may not receive punishment in return for his deeds; so that, as the true faith united him with the throng of the faithful on earth, your mercy may unite him with the company of the choirs of angels in heaven. Through Christ our Lord.

All: Amen.

Let us pray. O Lord, we implore you to grant this mercy to your dead servant, that she who held fast to your will by her intentions, may not receive punishment in return for her deeds; so that, as the true faith united her with the throng of the faithful on earth, your mercy may unite her with the company of the choirs of angels in heaven. Through Christ our Lord.

All: Amen.

Then the celebrant, making the sign of the Cross with his right hand over the coffin, says:

Priest: **Eternal rest grant unto him, O Lord.**

Eternal rest grant unto her, O Lord.

All: **And let perpetual light shine upon him.**

And let perpetual light shine upon her.

Chanters: **May he rest in peace.**

Chanters: **May she rest in peace.**

All: **Amen.**

Amen.

Priest: **May his soul and the souls of all the faithful departed through the mercy of God rest in peace.**

May her soul and the souls of all the faithful departed through the mercy of God rest in peace.

All: **Amen.**

Amen.

PRAYERS AT THE GRAVE

In some places the following prayers are added before leaving the cemetery:

For a Man

Let us pray. O Lord, hear our prayers, in which we humbly ask of your mercy that you would give your servant, N., whom you have commanded to leave this world, a place in the land of light and peace, and bid that he be made a companion of your saints. Through Christ our Lord.

All: **Amen.**

For a Woman

Let us pray. O Lord, we implore you in your fatherly love, have mercy on the soul of your servant, N., and grant that, freed from the stains of her mortal life, she may receive her inheritance of eternal salvation. Through Christ our Lord.

All: **Amen.**

For Those Resting in the Cemetery

Let us pray. O God, by whose mercy rest is given to the souls of the faithful, in your kindness grant forgiveness of sins to your servants and to all those who rest in Christ here and everywhere else; so that, set free from all sin, they may be happy with you forever. Through Christ our Lord.

All: **Amen.**

For All the Faithful Departed

Let us pray. Almighty God, Creator and Redeemer of all the faithful, grant to the souls of your servants the forgiveness of all their sins, so that, by the prayers which we offer in affection, they may receive the pardon which they have always desired. Through Christ our Lord.

All: **Amen.**

In many places the priest recites the following or a similar prayer at the grave or after the Mass.

Let us pray. O God, the Creator and Redeemer of all the faithful, hear our supplications and through your infinite love and mercy graciously grant to the soul of your servant departed the remission of all his sins, by which he may have deserved the severity of your justice and punishments in the world to come. Grant to him grace and mercy before your tribunal, and let him attain to everlasting rest and happiness through the infinite merits of Jesus Christ.

All: Amen.

Let us pray. O God, the Creator and Redeemer of all the faithful, hear our supplications and through your infinite love and mercy graciously grant to the soul of your servant departed the remission of all her sins, by which she may have deserved the severity of your justice and punishments in the world to come. Grant to her grace and mercy before your tribunal, and let her attain to everlasting rest and happiness through the infinite merits of Jesus Christ.

All: Amen.

O God, great and omnipotent Judge of the living and the dead, before whom we are all to appear after this short life, to render an account of our works, let our hearts, we pray you, be deeply moved at this sight of death, and while we consign the body of the deceased to the earth, let us be mindful of our own frailty and mortality, that walking always in your fear and in the ways of your commandments, we may, after our departure from this world, experience a merciful judgment and rejoice in everlasting happiness. Through Christ our Lord.

All: Amen.

Prayers for the Bystanders at the Grave

Let us pray. Grant, O Lord, we pray you, that while we lament the departure of our brother, your servant, out of this life, we may bear in mind that we are most certainly to follow him. Give us the grace to make ready for that last hour by a devout and holy life, and protect us against a sudden and unprovided death. Teach us how to watch and pray that when your summons comes, we may go forth to meet the Bridegroom and enter with him into life everlasting. Through Christ our Lord.

All: Amen.

Let us pray. Grant, O Lord, we pray you, that while we lament the departure of our sister, your servant, out of this life, we may bear in mind that we are most certainly to follow her. Give us the grace to make ready for that last hour by a devout and holy life, and protect us against a sudden and unprovided death. Teach us how to watch and pray that when your summons comes, we may go forth to meet the Bridegroom and enter with him into life everlasting. Through Christ our Lord.

All: Amen.

Let us pray. Almighty and most merciful Father, you know the weakness of our nature. Bow down your ear in pity to your servants, upon whom you have laid the heavy burden of sorrow. Take away out of their hearts the spirit of rebellion, and teach them to see your good and gracious purpose working in all the trials which you send upon them. Grant that they may not languish in fruitless and unavailing grief, nor sorrow as those who have no hope, but through their tears look meekly up to you, the God of all consolation. Through Christ our Lord.

Ali: Amen.

Priest: Eternal rest grant unto him, O Lord.

All: And let perpetual light shine upon him.

Priest: May he rest in peace.

All: Amen.

Priest: May his soul and the souls of all the faithful departed through the mercy of God rest in peace.

All: Amen.

Eternal rest grant unto her, O Lord.

And let perpetual light shine upon her.

May she rest in peace.

Amen.

May her soul and the souls of all the faithful departed through the mercy of God rest in peace.

Amen.

19. AT OUR LIFE'S LAST MOMENT FLEETING

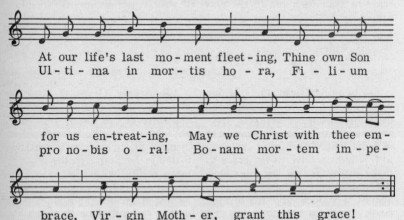

At our life's last mo - ment fleet - ing, Thine own Son
Ul - ti - ma in mor - tis ho - ra, Fi - li - um

for us en-treat-ing, May we Christ with thee em-
pro no - bis o - ra! Bo - nam mor - tem im - pe-

brace, Vir - gin Moth - er, grant this grace!
tra, Vir - go Ma - ter Do - mi - na!

SPRINKLE ME, O LORD, WITH HYSSOP

Every Sunday is a "little Easter." And Easter is the day of resurrection through the waters of holy baptism. Since only the pure of heart may share in the Eucharist, the Church repeats our baptismal purification through a sacramental each Sunday in the rite called

20. SPRINKLE ME, O LORD, WITH HYSSOP

Sprin-kle me, O Lord, with hys-sop, *and I shall be pu-ri-

fied; wash me and I shall be whit-er than snow. Ps. 50:3

Have mer-cy on me, O God, in your good-ness.

V. Glo-ry be to the Father and to the Son / and to the Holy

Spir-it. R. As it was in the beginning, is now and ever

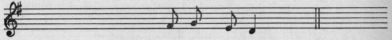

shall be, / world with-out end. A-men.

The antiphon, "Sprinkle me," is repeated; on Passion Sunday and on Palm Sunday, the "Glory be to the Father" is not said, but immediately after the psalm the antiphon is repeated.

Priest: Show us, O Lord, your mercy.

All: And grant us your salvation.

Priest: O Lord, hear my prayer.

All: And let my cry come to you.

Priest: The Lord be with you.

All: And with your spirit.

Priest: Let us pray. Hear us, Lord, holy Father, almighty and eternal God, and graciously send your holy angel from heaven to watch over, to cherish, to protect, to abide with, and to defend all who dwell in this house. Through Christ our Lord.

All: Amen.

21. I SAW WATER COMING FORTH

From Easter to Pentecost "I Saw Water Coming Forth" is sung in place of the above. Originally this was the song chanted as the newly-baptized proceeded to take part for the first time in the holy Eucharist during the Easter Vigil Service.

I saw wa - ter * com - ing forth from the tem - ple, from the

right side, al - le - lu - ia: and all those were saved to whom

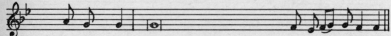

that wa - ter came, and they shall say: al - le - lu - ia, al - le - lu - ia.

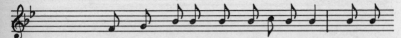

Ps. 117:1 Give thanks to the Lord, for he is good, * for his

mer - cy en - dures for-ev-er. ℣. Glo - ry be to the Father and

to the Son/ and to the Holy Spir-it. ℟. As it was in the begin-

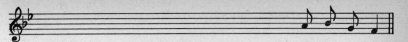

ning, is now and ev-er shall be, / world with-out end. A-men.

The antiphon I saw water is repeated.

Priest: **Show us, O Lord, your mercy, alleluia.**
All: **And grant us your salvation, alleluia.**
Priest: **O Lord, hear my prayer.**
All: **And let my cry come to you.**
Priest: **The Lord be with you.**
All: **And with your spirit.**
Priest: **Let us pray. Hear us, Lord, holy Father, almighty and eternal God, and graciously send your holy angel from heaven to watch over, to cherish, to protect, to abide with, and to defend all who dwell in this house. Through Christ our Lord.**
All: **Amen.**

22. PEOPLE'S SUNG MASS

LORD, HAVE MERCY
Adapted from Mass XVII

Lord, have mer - cy. Lord, have mer - cy. Lord, have mer - cy. Christ, have mer-cy. Christ, have mer - cy. Christ, have mer-cy. Lord, have mer- cy. Lord, have mer - cy. Lord, have mer - cy.

HOLY, HOLY, HOLY

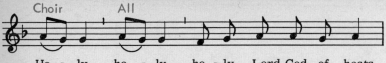

Ho - ly,   ho - ly,   ho - ly   Lord God of   hosts.

Heav-en and earth are filled with your glo - ry. Ho-san - na

in   the high - est. Bless-ed is   he who comes in the name

of   the Lord.   Ho - san - na   in   the high - est.

LAMB OF GOD

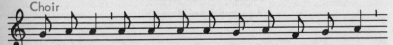

Lamb of God, who take a - way   the   sins   of   the world,

have mer-cy   on   us.   Lamb of God, who take a - way

the   sins   of the world,   grant   us peace.

GO, THE MASS IS ENDED

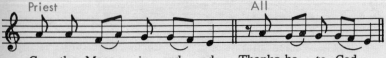

Go,   the   Mass   is   end - ed.   Thanks be   to God.

23. PEOPLE'S SUNG MASS

LORD, HAVE MERCY
Adapted from Mass XVI

Lord, have mer-cy *iij.* Christ, have mer-cy *iij.* Lord,

have mer-cy *ij.* Lord, have mer - cy.

HOLY, HOLY, HOLY

Choir   All

Ho - ly, ho - ly, ho - ly Lord God of hosts.

Heav - en and earth are filled with your glo - ry.

Choir

Ho - san - na in the high - est. Bless - ed

is he who comes in the name of the

All

Lord. Ho - san - na in the high - est.

LAMB OF GOD

Choir

Lamb of God, who take a - way the sins

of the world, have mer - cy on us. Lamb
of God, who take a - way the sins of the world,
have mer - cy on us. Lamb of
God, who take a - way the sins of
the world, grant us peace

GO, THE MASS IS ENDED

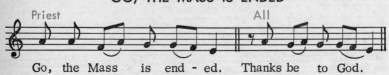

Go, the Mass is end - ed. Thanks be to God.

I BELIEVE IN ONE GOD
Adapted from Credo II

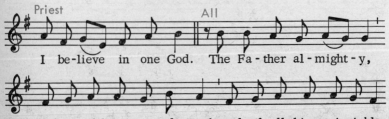

I be-lieve in one God. The Fa - ther al - might - y,

mak-er of heav-en and earth, and of all things vis-i-ble

Choir
and in - vis - i - ble. And I be - lieve in one Lord,

Je - sus Christ, the on - ly - be - got - ten Son of God.

All
Born of the Fa - ther be - fore all a - ges.

Choir
God of God, Light of Light, true God

All
of true God. Be - got - ten, not made, of one sub - stance

Choir
with the Fa - ther. By whom all things were made.

All
Who for us men and for our sal - va - tion

Choir
came down from heav - en. And he be - came flesh by the

Ho - ly Spir - it of the Vir - gin Ma - ry:

All
and was made man. He was al - so cru - ci - fied

for us, suf-fered un - der Pon - tius Pi - late,

Choir
and was bur - ied.   And on the third day he

rose a - gain, ac - cord-ing to the Scrip - tures.

All
He as - cend - ed in - to heav - en and sits

Choir
at the right hand of the Fa - ther.   He will

come a-gain in glo - ry to judge the liv - ing

All
and the dead. And of his king - dom there will

Choir
be no end. And I be - lieve in the Ho - ly

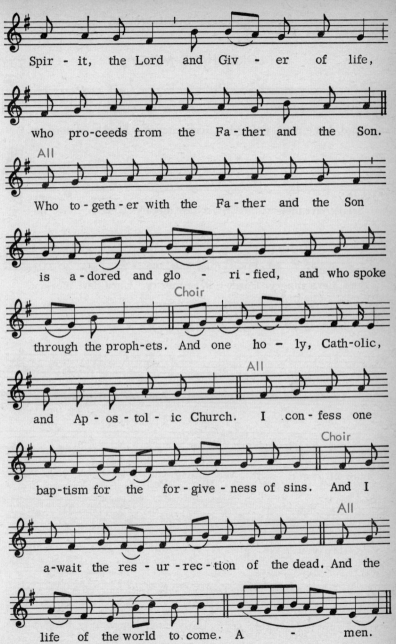

Spir - it, the Lord and Giv - er of life,

who pro-ceeds from the Fa - ther and the Son.

All

Who to-geth-er with the Fa - ther and the Son

is a-dored and glo - ri-fied, and who spoke

Choir

through the proph-ets. And one ho - ly, Cath-olic,

All

and Ap - os - tol - ic Church. I con-fess one

Choir

bap-tism for the for-give-ness of sins. And I

All

a-wait the res - ur -rec-tion of the dead. And the

life of the world to.come. A - men.

24. PEOPLE'S SUNG MASS

LORD, HAVE MERCY

Lord, have mer-cy. Lord, have mer-cy. Lord, have mer- cy.

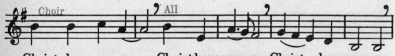

Christ, have mer-cy.   Christ, have mer-cy. Christ, have mer-cy.

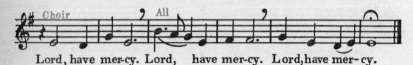

Lord, have mer-cy. Lord, have mer-cy. Lord, have mer- cy.

GLORY TO GOD

Glo-ry to God in the high-est. And on earth peace   to

men of   good   will. We praise you. We bless you. We

wor-ship you. We glo-ri-fy   you. We give you thanks

for your great glo - ry. Lord God, heav-en-ly King, God

the Fa-ther al-might-y.   Lord   Je-sus Christ,   the

on-ly-be-got-ten Son. Lord God, Lamb of God, Son of the

Fa - ther.   You, who take a-way the sins of the

world, have mer-cy on us. You, who take a-way the sins of the

world, re-ceive our prayer.   You, who sit at the right hand of the

Fa-ther, have mer-cy on us.   For you a-lone are

ho - ly. You a-lone are Lord. You   a-lone, O

Je-sus Christ, are most high, With the Ho-ly Spir-it,

in the glo-ry of God the Fa-ther. A - men.

I BELIEVE IN ONE GOD

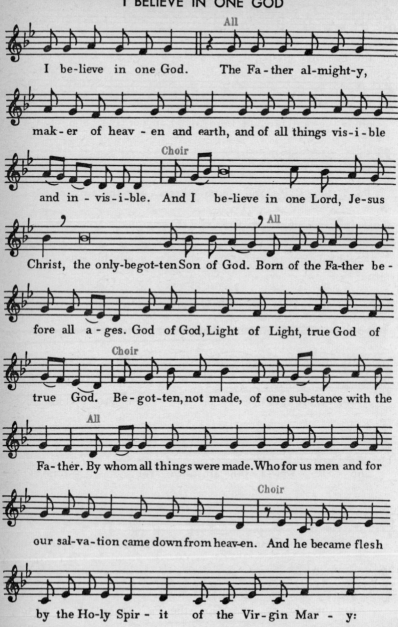

I be-lieve in one God.   The Fa-ther al-might-y,

mak-er of heav-en and earth, and of all things vis-i-ble

and in-vis-i-ble. And I   be-lieve in one Lord, Je-sus

Christ, the only-begot-ten Son of God. Born of the Fa-ther be-

fore all a-ges. God of God, Light of Light, true God of

true God.   Be-got-ten, not made, of one sub-stance with the

Fa-ther. By whom all things were made. Who for us men and for

our sal-va-tion came down from heav-en.   And he became flesh

by the Ho-ly Spir-it   of the Vir-gin Mar-y:

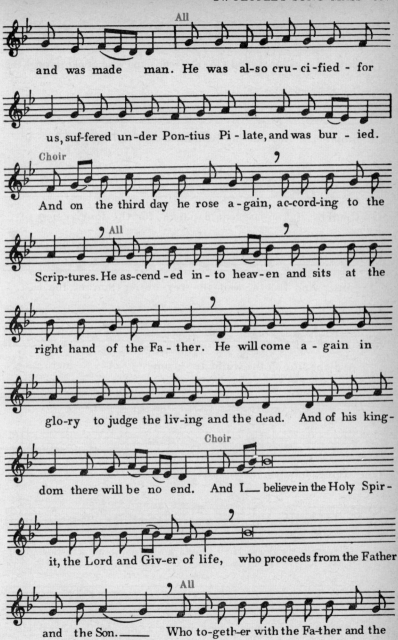

All
and was made man. He was al-so cru-ci-fied - for

us, suf-fered un-der Pon-tius Pi-late, and was bur - ied.

Choir
And on the third day he rose a-gain, ac-cord-ing to the

All
Scrip-tures. He as-cend-ed in-to heav-en and sits at the

right hand of the Fa-ther. He will come a-gain in

glo-ry to judge the liv-ing and the dead. And of his king-

Choir
dom there will be no end. And I— believe in the Holy Spir-

it, the Lord and Giv-er of life, who proceeds from the Father

All
and the Son.___ Who to-geth-er with the Fa-ther and the

Son is a-dored and glo-ri-fied, and who spoke through the

Choir

proph-ets. And one ho-ly, Cath-o-lic, and Ap-os-tol-ic

Church. I con-fess one bap-tism for the for-give-ness of

sins. And I   a-wait the res-ur-rec-tion of the dead.

All

And the life of the world to   come.   A - men.__

HOLY, HOLY, HOLY

All

Ho-ly, ho-ly, ho-ly Lord God of hosts. Heaven and earth are

filled with your glory. Ho - san-na, ho-san-na, hosanna in the highest.

All

Bless-ed is he who comes in the name of the Lord. Ho-

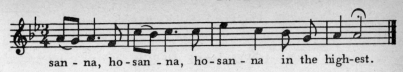

san - na, ho - san - na, ho - san - na in the high-est.

LAMB OF GOD

Choir   All

Lamb of God, who take a-way the sins of the world, have
Lamb of God, who take a-way the sins of the world,

Choir   All

mer - cy on us.   Lamb of God, who take a-way the
grant___ them rest.   Lamb of God, who take a-way the

Choir   All

sins of the world, have mer - cy on us.   Lamb of God, who
sins of the world,   grant___ them rest.   Lamb of God, who

take a-way the sins of the world,   grant___ us ___ peace.
take a-way the sins of the world, grant them e-ter-nal rest.

RESPONSES

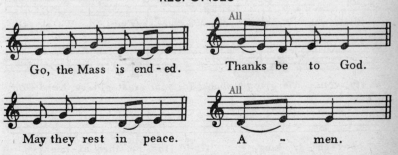

Go, the Mass is end-ed.

All

Thanks be to God.

May they rest in peace.

All

A — men.

25. PEOPLE'S SUNG MASS

LORD, HAVE MERCY

CHOIR

Lord, have mer cy. Lord, have mer - cy.

ALL

Lord, have mer - cy. Christ, have mer - cy. Christ, have

CHOIR

mer - cy. Christ, have mer - cy. Lord, have mer -

ALL

cy. Lord, have mer - cy. Lord, have mer - cy.

GLORY TO GOD

PRIEST

Glo - ry to God in the high - est.

CHOIR   ALL

And on earth peace to men of good will. We

praise you. We bless you. We wor-ship you. We glo-ri-

CHOIR   ALL

fy you. We give you thanks for your great glo-ry. Lord God,

heav-en-ly king,   God   the Fa-ther al-might-y.

CHOIR
Lord Je-sus Christ, the on - ly - be-got - ten son.

ALL
Lord God, Lamb of God, Son of the Fa-ther. You who

take a - way the sins of the world, have mer-cy on us.

CHOIR
You, who take a - way the sins of the world, re-

ALL
ceive our pray - er. You who sit at the

right hand of the Fa - ther, have mer - cy on us.

CHOIR
For you a - lone are ho - ly. You a-

ALL
lone are Lord. You a - lone, O Je - sus

Christ, are most high. With the Ho - ly Spir - it,

in the glo - ry of God the Fa-ther. A - men.

I BELIEVE IN ONE GOD

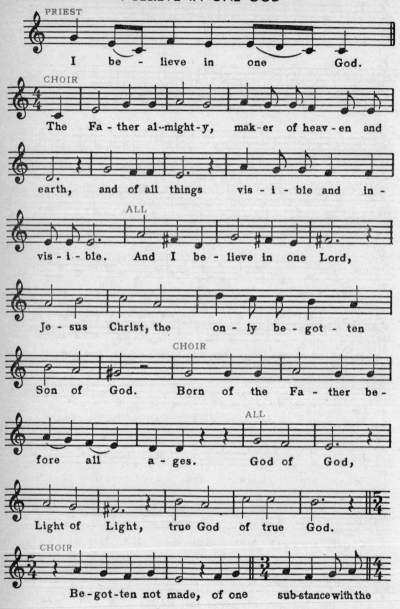

PRIEST: I be - lieve in one God.

CHOIR: The Fa - ther al - might-y, mak-er of heav-en and earth, and of all things vis - i - ble and in - vis - i - ble.

ALL: And I be - lieve in one Lord, Je - sus Christ, the on - ly be - got - ten Son of God.

CHOIR: Born of the Fa - ther be - fore all a - ges.

ALL: God of God, Light of Light, true God of true God.

CHOIR: Be - got-ten not made, of one sub-stance with the

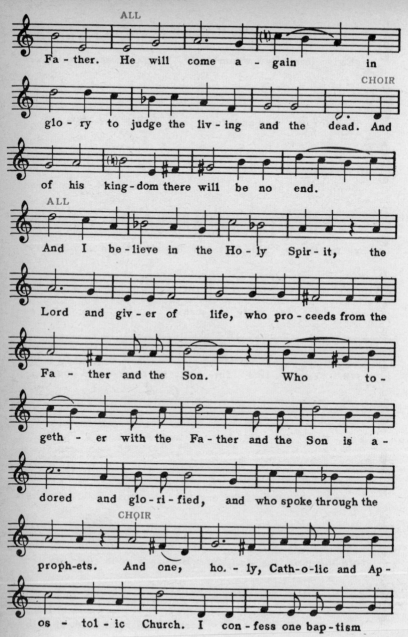

ALL
Fa - ther. He will come a - gain in

CHOIR
glo - ry to judge the liv - ing and the dead. And

of his king-dom there will be no end.

ALL
And I be - lieve in the Ho - ly Spir - it, the

Lord and giv - er of life, who pro - ceeds from the

Fa - ther and the Son. Who to -

geth - er with the Fa - ther and the Son is a -

dored and glo - ri - fied, and who spoke through the

CHOIR
proph-ets. And one, ho. - ly, Cath-o-lic and Ap -

os - tol - ic Church. I con - fess one bap - tism

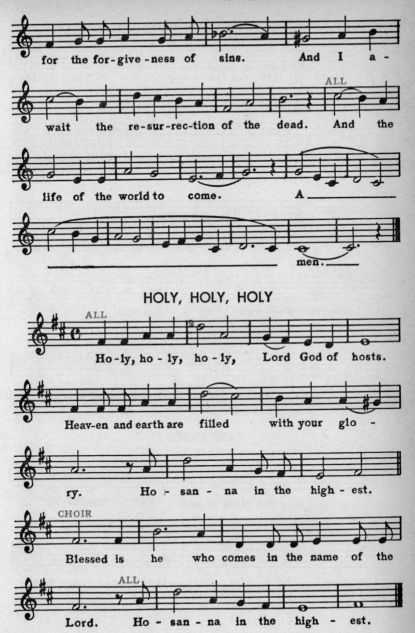

for the for-give-ness of sins. And I a-wait the re-sur-rec-tion of the dead. And the life of the world to come. A—— men.

HOLY, HOLY, HOLY

ALL

Ho-ly, ho-ly, ho-ly, Lord God of hosts. Heav-en and earth are filled with your glo-ry. Ho-san-na in the high-est.

CHOIR

Blessed is he who comes in the name of the Lord.

ALL

Ho-san-na in the high-est.

LAMB OF GOD

CHOIR

Lamb of God who take a-way the sins of the world,
in Requiem Masses :→

ALL

have mer - cy on us.
grant them _____ rest.

CHOIR

Lamb of God, who take a-way the sins of the world, have mer - cy on us.
grant them _____ rest.

ALL

CHOIR

Lamb of God, who take a - way the sins of the

ALL

world, grant us _____ peace.
grant them e - ter - nal rest.

RESPONSES

ALL

Go, the Mass is end - ed. Thanks be to

ALL

God. May they rest in peace, A - men.

26. PEOPLE'S SUNG MASS

LORD, HAVE MERCY

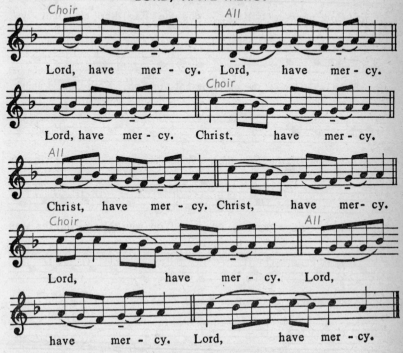

Lord, have mer - cy. Lord, have mer - cy.

Lord, have mer - cy. Christ, have mer - cy.

Christ, have mer - cy. Christ, have mer - cy.

Lord, have mer - cy. Lord,

have mer - cy. Lord, have mer - cy.

GLORY TO GOD

Glo - ry to God in the high-est. And on earth peace to men of

good will. We praise you. We bless you. We wor-ship you.

We glo - ri - fy you. We give you thanks for your great glo - ry.

Lord, God, heav-en-ly King,   God the Fa-ther al-might-y.

Lord Je-sus Christ, the on-ly be-got-ten Son. Lord God, Lamb

of God, Son of the Fa-ther. You, who take a-way the sins of

the world,   have mer-cy on us. You, who take a-way the sins

of the world,   re-ceive our prayer.   You, who sit at the right

hand of the Fa-ther, have mer-cy on   us.   For you a-

lone are ho-ly. You a-lone are Lord. You a-lone, O

Je-sus Christ, are most high, With the Ho-ly Spir-it, in

the glo-ry of God the Fa - - ther. A - - men.

I BELIEVE IN ONE GOD
Adapted from Credo I

Priest I be-lieve in one God. *All* The Fa - ther al-might- y,

ma - ker of heav-en and earth, and of all things vis-i-ble

Choir and in- vis - i- ble. And I be-lieve in one Lord, Je -

sus Christ, the on-ly-be-got-ten Son of God. *All* Born of

Choir the Fa - ther be-fore all a - ges. God of God, Light

of Light, *All* true God of true God. Be-got - ten,

not made, of one sub-stance with the Fa- ther. *Choir* By

All whom all things were made. Who for us men and for

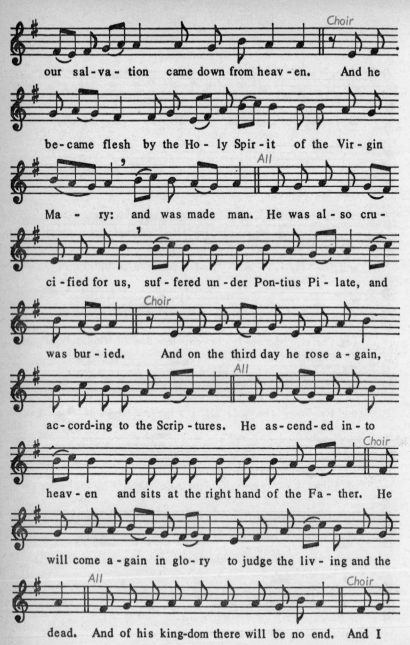

our sal-va-tion came down from heav-en.   And he

be-came flesh by the Ho-ly Spir-it   of the Vir-gin

Ma - ry: and was made man. He was al-so cru-

ci-fied for us,   suf-fered un-der Pon-tius Pi-late, and

was bur-ied.   And on the third day he rose a-gain,

ac-cord-ing to the Scrip-tures. He as-cend-ed in-to

heav-en   and sits at the right hand of the Fa-ther. He

will come a-gain in glo-ry   to judge the liv-ing and the

dead. And of his king-dom there will be no end. And I

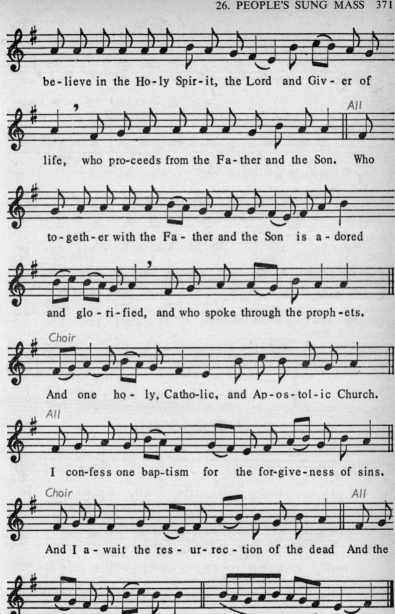

be-lieve in the Ho-ly Spir-it, the Lord and Giv-er of

life, who pro-ceeds from the Fa-ther and the Son. *All* Who

to-geth-er with the Fa-ther and the Son is a-dored

and glo-ri-fied, and who spoke through the proph-ets.

Choir And one ho-ly, Catho-lic, and Ap-os-tol-ic Church.

All I con-fess one bap-tism for the for-give-ness of sins.

Choir And I a-wait the res-ur-rec-tion of the dead *All* And the

life of the world to come. A - - men.

HOLY, HOLY, HOLY

Ho - ly, ho - ly, ho - ly Lord God of hosts. Heav-
en and earth are filled with your glo - ry. Ho - -
san - na in the high-est. Bless - ed is
he who comes in the name of the Lord. Ho - -
san - na in the high - est.

LAMB OF GOD

Lamb of God, who take a - way the sins of the
world, have mer - - cy on us. Lamb of God, who
take a - way the sins of the world, have mer -

cy   on   us.   Lamb   of   God,   who   take a-way

the sins   of the world,   grant   us   peace.

GO, THE MASS IS ENDED

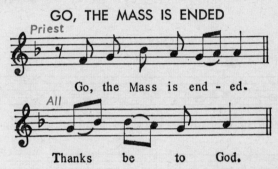

Go,   the   Mass   is   end - ed.

Thanks   be   to   God.

27. PEOPLE'S SUNG MASS

LORD, HAVE MERCY

Lord,   have mer - cy.   Lord,   have

mer - cy.   Lord,   have mer - cy.   Christ,

have mer - cy.   Christ,   have mer - cy. Christ,

have mer - cy. Lord, have mer - cy.

Lord, have mer - cy. Lord, have mer - cy.

GLORY TO GOD

Glory to God in the high-est. And on earth peace to

men of good will. We praise you. We bless you. We

worship you. We glo-ri-fy you. We give you thanks for

your great glory. Lord God, heav-en-ly King, God the

Father al-migh-ty. Lord Jesus Christ, the only be-got-

CHOIR

ten Son. Lord God, Lamb of God, Son of the Father.

ALL

You, who take away the sins of the world, have mercy

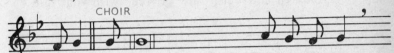

CHOIR

on us. You, who take away the sins of the world,

ALL

receive our prayer. You, who sit at the right hand of

CHOIR

the Father, have mercy on us. For you alone are ho-

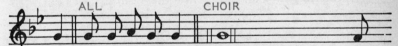

ALL   CHOIR

ly. You alone are Lord. You alone, O Jesus Christ,

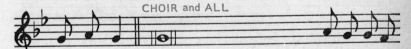

CHOIR and ALL

are most high. With the Holy Spirit, in the glory of God

the Father.   A - men.

HOLY, HOLY, HOLY

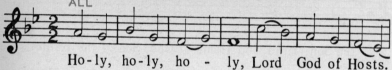

Ho-ly, ho-ly, ho - ly, Lord God of Hosts.

Heav-en and earth are filled with your glo-

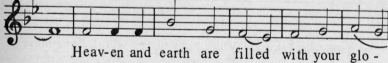

- - - ry. Ho - san-na in the high - est.

Bles-sed is he who comes in the name of the

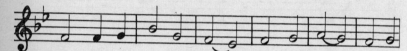

Lord. Ho - san-na in the high - est.

LAMB OF GOD

Lamb of God, who take a - way the sins of the
in Requiem

world, have mer - cy on us. Lamb of God, who
Masses: grant - - - them peace.

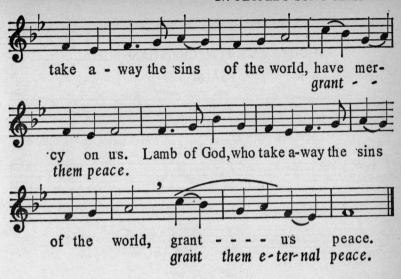

take a - way the sins   of the world, have mer-
                        grant - -

·cy   on us.   Lamb of God, who take a-way the sins
them peace.

of the world,   grant - - - - us   peace.
                grant   them e - ter - nal peace.

RESPONSES

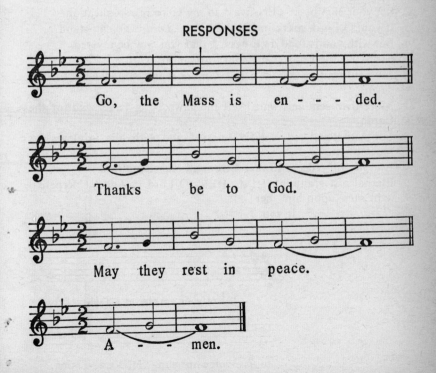

Go,   the   Mass is   en - - - ded.

Thanks   be   to   God.

May   they   rest   in   peace.

A - - - men.

28. PEOPLE'S SUNG MASS

THE LITURGY FOR CHRISTIAN BURIAL
PSALM 129

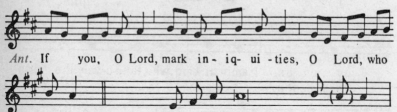

Ant. If   you, O Lord, mark in - iq- ui -ties, O Lord, who

can stand? *Ps.* 129 1. Out of the depths I cry to you, O Lord; *

Lord, hear my   voice.

2. Let your ears be at-TEN-tive * to my voice in *sup*-plication.
3. If you, O Lord, mark in-IQ-uities, * ...*Lord*, who can stand?
4. But with you is for-GIVE-ness, * that you *may* be revered.
5. I trust IN the Lord; * my soul *trusts* in his word.
6. My soul waits FOR the Lord * more than sentinels *wait* for the dawn.
7. More than sentinels wait FOR the dawn, * let Israel *wait* for the Lord.
8. For with the Lord is KIND-ness * and with him is plente-*ous* redemption.
9. And he will redeem IS-rael * from all *their* iniquities.
10. Eternal rest grant unto HIM (HER), O Lord. * And let perpetual light *shine* upon him (her).
 Repeat Antiphon: If you...

An optional setting of verses 2 - 4 - 6 - 8 - 10.

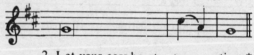

2. Let your ears be at - ten - tive *

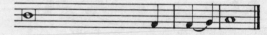

to my voice in sup- pli - ca - tion.

4. But with you is for-GIVE-ness, * that you *may* be revered.

6. My soul WAITS for the Lord * more than sentinels *wait* for the dawn.

8. For with the Lord is KIND-ness * and with him is plenteous *re*-demption.

10. Eternal rest grant unto HIM (HER), O Lord. * And let perpetual light shine *up*-on him (her).

Repeat Antiphon: **If you...**

PSALM 50

Ant. They shall re-joice in the Lord * the bones that are brought low

in the dust. *Ps. 50* Have mer - cy on me, O God , in your good-ness;

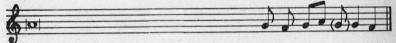

* in the greatness of your compassion wipe out my of - - fense.

2. Thoroughly WASH me from my guilt * and of *my* sin cleanse me.

3. For I ac-KNOWL-edge my offense, * and my sin is be-*fore* me always:

4. "Against you ON-ly have I sinned, * and done what is e-*vil* in your sight."

5. That you may be justified IN your sentence, * vindicated *when* you condemn.

6. Indeed, in GUILT was I born, * and in sin my moth-*er* conceived me.

7. Behold, you are pleased with sin-CER-ity of heart, * and in my inmost being you *teach* me wisdom.

8. Cleanse me of sin with hyssop, that I may be purified; * wash me, and I shall be *whit*-er than snow.

9. Let me hear the sounds of JOY and gladness; * the bones you *have* crushed shall rejoice.

10. Turn away your FACE from my sins, * and *blot* out all my guilt.

11. A clean heart cre-ATE for me, O God, * and a steadfast spirit re-*new* within me.

12. Cast me not OUT from your presence, * and your holy spirit *take* not from me.

13. Give me back the joy of YOUR salvation, * and a willing spir-*it* sustain in me.

14. I will teach trans-GRES-sors your ways, * and sinners *shall* return to you.

15. Free me from blood guilt, o GOD, my saving God; * then my tongue shall revel *in* your justice.

16. O Lord, O-pen my lips, * and my mouth *shall* proclaim your praise.

17. For you are not pleased with SAC-rifices; * should I offer you a holocaust, you would *not* accept it.

18. My sacrifice, O God, is a CON-trite spirit; * a heart contrite and humbled, O God, *you* will not spurn.

19. Be bountiful, O Lord, to Sion IN your kindness * by rebuilding the walls *of* Jerusalem.

20. Then shall you be pleased with due sacrifices, burnt offer-INGS and holocausts; * then shall they offer up bullocks *on* your altar.

21. Eternal rest grant UN-to him (her), O Lord. * And let perpetual light *shine* upon him (her).

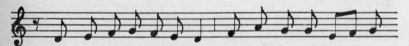

Ant. They shall re-joice in the Lord * the bones that are brought low

in the dust.

COME TO HIS AID

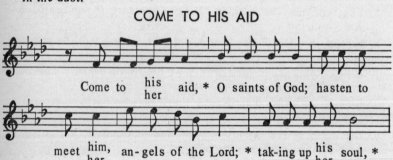

Come to his/her aid, * O saints of God; hasten to

meet him,/her, an-gels of the Lord; * tak-ing up his/her soul, *

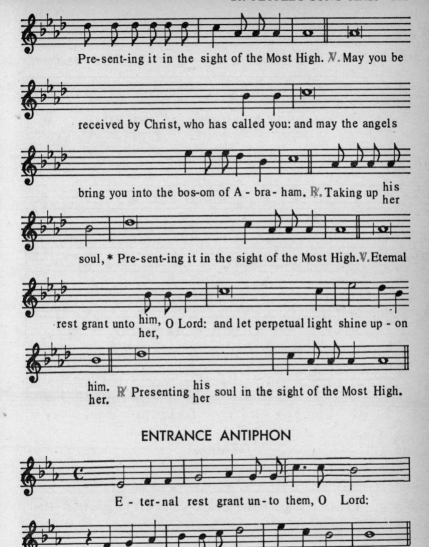

Pre-sent-ing it in the sight of the Most High. ℣. May you be

received by Christ, who has called you: and may the angels

bring you into the bos-om of A - bra - ham. ℟. Taking up his/her

soul, * Pre-sent-ing it in the sight of the Most High. ℣. Eternal

rest grant unto him/her, O Lord: and let perpetual light shine up - on

him./her. ℟ Presenting his/her soul in the sight of the Most High.

ENTRANCE ANTIPHON

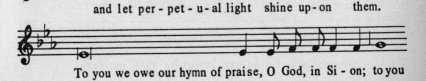

E - ter-nal rest grant un-to them, O Lord:

and let per - pet - u - al light shine up-on them.

To you we owe our hymn of praise, O God, in Si - on; to you

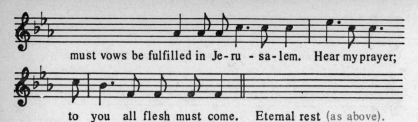

must vows be fulfilled in Je - ru - sa - lem. Hear my prayer;

to you all flesh must come. Eternal rest (as above).

LORD, HAVE MERCY

Lord, have mer - cy. Lord, have mer - cy. Lord,

have mer - cy. Christ, have mer - cy. Christ, have

mer - cy. Christ, have mer - cy. Lord, have mer -

cy. Lord, have mer - cy. Lord, have mer - - cy.

GRADUAL

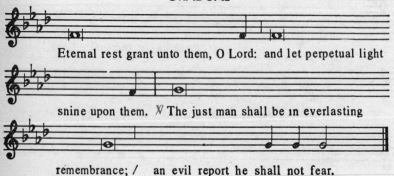

Eternal rest grant unto them, O Lord: and let perpetual light

snine upon them. The just man shall be in everlasting

remembrance; / an evil report he shall not fear.

TRACT

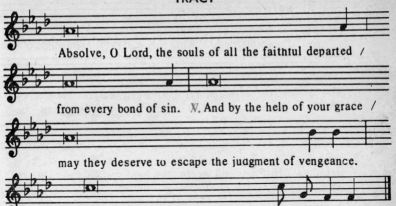

Absolve, O Lord, the souls of all the faithful departed /

from every bond of sin. ℣. And by the help of your grace /

may they deserve to escape the judgment of vengeance.

℣. And to enjoy the blessedness of light e - ter - nal.

SEQUENCE

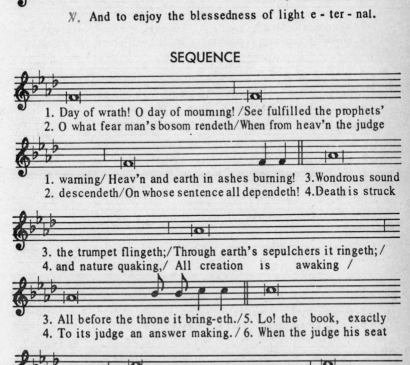

1. Day of wrath! O day of mourning! /See fulfilled the prophets'
2. O what fear man's bosom rendeth/When from heav'n the judge

1. warning/ Heav'n and earth in ashes burning! 3.Wondrous sound
2. descendeth/On whose sentence all dependeth! 4.Death is struck

3. the trumpet flingeth;/Through earth's sepulchers it ringeth; /
4. and nature quaking,/ All creation is awaking /

3. All before the throne it bring-eth./5. Lo! the book, exactly
4. To its judge an answer making. / 6. When the judge his seat

5. worded, / Wherein all hath been recorded: / Thence shall
6. attaineth/ And each hidden deed arraigneth,/Nothing unavenged

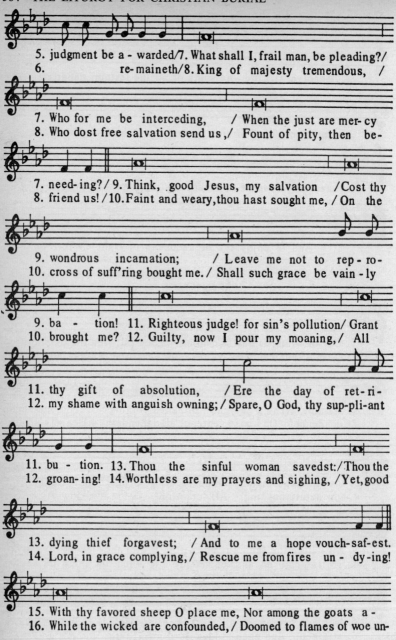

5. judgment be a - warded/7. What shall I, frail man, be pleading?/
6.   re - maineth/8. King of majesty tremendous, /

7. Who for me be interceding,   / When the just are mer - cy
8. Who dost free salvation send us,/ Fount of pity, then be-

7. need - ing?/9. Think, good Jesus, my salvation /Cost thy
8. friend us!/10. Faint and weary, thou hast sought me, / On the

9. wondrous incarnation;   / Leave me not to rep - ro-
10. cross of suff'ring bought me./ Shall such grace be vain - ly

9. ba - tion! 11. Righteous judge! for sin's pollution/ Grant
10. brought me? 12. Guilty, now I pour my moaning,/ All

11. thy gift of absolution,   / Ere the day of ret - ri-
12. my shame with anguish owning;/ Spare, O God, thy sup-pli-ant

11. bu - tion. 13. Thou the sinful woman savedst:/ Thou the
12. groan - ing! 14. Worthless are my prayers and sighing, / Yet, good

13. dying thief forgavest; / And to me a hope vouch-saf-est.
14. Lord, in grace complying, / Rescue me from fires un - dy-ing!

15. With thy favored sheep O place me, Nor among the goats a-
16. While the wicked are confounded,/ Doomed to flames of woe un-

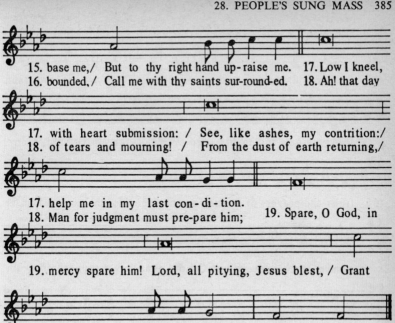

15. base me,/ But to thy right hand up-raise me.   17. Low I kneel,
16. bounded,/ Call me with thy saints sur-round-ed.   18. Ah! that day

17. with heart submission: / See, like ashes, my contrition:/
18. of tears and mourning! /   From the dust of earth returning,/

17. help me in my last con-di-tion.
18. Man for judgment must pre-pare him;   19. Spare, O God, in

19. mercy spare him! Lord, all pitying, Jesus blest, / Grant

19. them thine e - ter - nal rest.   A -   men.

OFFERTORY ANTIPHON

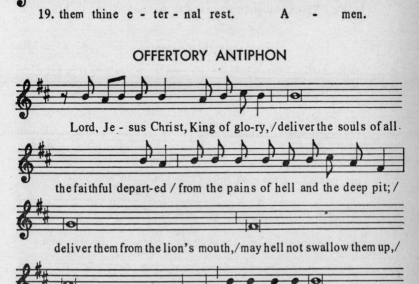

Lord, Je - sus Christ, King of glo-ry, /deliver the souls of all.

the faithful depart-ed / from the pains of hell and the deep pit; /

deliver them from the lion's mouth,/may hell not swallow them up,/

nor may they fall into darkness, but may Michael, the holy standard-

bearer, bring them in-to the ho-ly light:*Which you once promised

to A-bra-ham and to his seed. ℣. We of-fer you, O Lord, sacri-

fices and prayers of praise;/ receive them for the souls whom we

re-mem-ber this day. Grant, O Lord, that they may pass from death

to life./ Which you once promised to A-bra-ham and to his seed.

HOLY, HOLY, HOLY

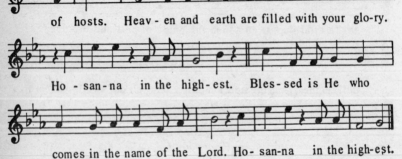

Ho - ly, ho - ly, ho - ly, Lord God

of hosts. Heav - en and earth are filled with your glo-ry.

Ho - san-na in the high-est. Bles-sed is He who

comes in the name of the Lord. Ho-san-na in the high-est.

LAMB OF GOD

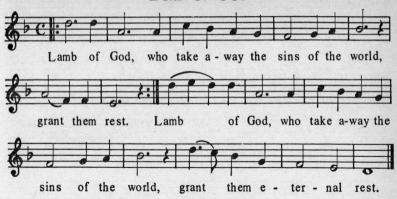

Lamb of God, who take a - way the sins of the world,

grant them rest.   Lamb   of God, who take a-way the

sins of the world, grant   them e - ter - nal rest.

COMMUNION ANTIPHON

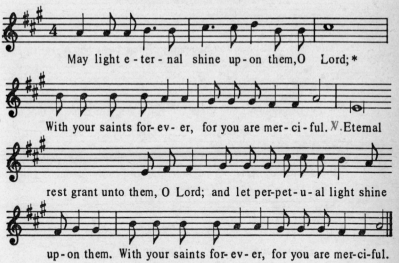

May light e - ter - nal shine up - on them, O   Lord; *

With your saints for- ev- er, for you are mer - ci - ful. ℣. Eternal

rest grant unto them, O Lord; and let per-pet- u - al light shine

up- on them. With your saints for- ev- er, for you are mer-ci-ful.

DELIVER ME, O LORD

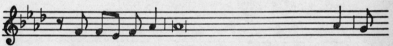

De - liv - er me, O Lord, from ev-er-last-ing death on

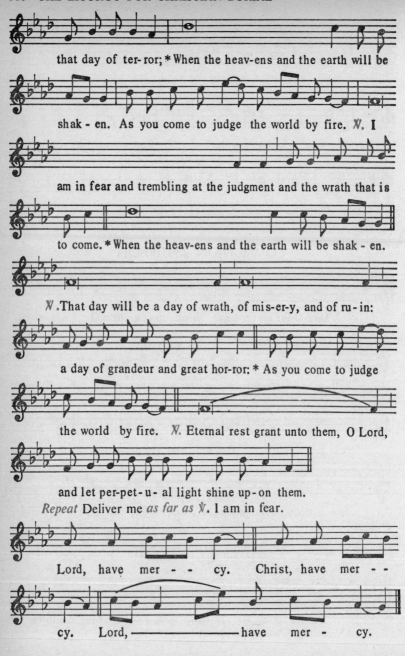

that day of ter-ror; * When the heav-ens and the earth will be

shak - en. As you come to judge the world by fire. ℣. I

am in fear and trembling at the judgment and the wrath that is

to come. * When the heav-ens and the earth will be shak - en.

℣. That day will be a day of wrath, of mis-er-y, and of ru-in:

a day of grandeur and great hor-ror: * As you come to judge

the world by fire. ℣. Eternal rest grant unto them, O Lord,

and let per-pet-u-al light shine up-on them.
Repeat Deliver me *as far as* ℣. I am in fear.

Lord, have mer - - cy. Christ, have mer - -

cy. Lord, —————————— have mer - cy.

Priest: Our Father...

℣. And lead us not into temptation.

℞. But deliver us from evil.

℣. From the gate of hell.

℞. Rescue his (her) soul, O Lord.

℣. May he (she) rest in peace.

℞. Amen.

℣. O Lord, hear my prayer.

℞. And let my cry come to you.

℣. The Lord be with you.

℞. And with your spirit.

Let us pray...

℞. Amen.

MAY THE ANGELS TAKE YOU INTO PARADISE

May the an-gels*take you in-to par-a-dise: may the mar-

tyrs come to wel-come you on your way, and lead you in-to

the ho-ly cit-y, Je-ru-sa-lem. May the choir of an-

gels wel - - come you, and with Laz-a-rus who

once was poor may you have ev - er-last-ing rest.

or the above put more simply:

ev-er-last-ing rest.

PSALM 114

I love the Lord be-cause he has heard * my voice in

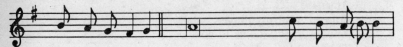

sup-pli-ca-tion. 2. Because he has in-clined his ear to me:

* the day I called.

3. The cords of death encompassed *me*; † the snares of the nether world SEIZED upon me: * I fell into dis-TRESS and sorrow.

4. And I called upon the NAME of the Lord, * "o LORD, save my life!"

5. Gracious IS the Lord and just; * yes, our GOD is merciful.

6. The Lord KEEPS the little ones; * I was brought low AND he saved me.

7. Return, O my soul, to YOUR tranquility, * for the Lord has BEEN good to you.

8. For he has FREED my soul from death, * my eyes from tears, my FEET from stumbling.

9. I shall WALK before the Lord, * in the LANDS of the living.

10. Eternal rest GRANT unto him (her), O Lord. * And let perpetual LIGHT shine upon him (her).

Repeat Antiphon: **May the angels...**

I AM THE RESURRECTION AND THE LIFE

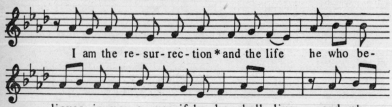

I am the re-sur-rec-tion * and the life he who be-

lieves in me, e-ven if he die, shall live; and who-

e - ver lives and be-lieves in me   shall nev - er   die.

CANTICLE OF ZACHARY

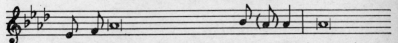

Bless-ed be the Lord, the God of Is- ra - el * because he

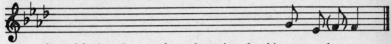

has visited and wrought redemption for his peo - ple.

2. And has raised up a horn of salvation FOR us * in the house of David *his* servant.
3. As he promised through the mouths of his HO-ly ones, * the proph-*ets* from of old:
4. Salvation from our EN-emies * and from the hands *of* all our foes.
5. He has fulfilled his kindness to our FA-thers, * and been mindful of his ho-*ly* covenant.
6. In the oath to Abraham our FA-ther, * by which he swore *to* grant us
7. That, delivered from the hands of our EN-emies, * we should serve *him* without fear.
8. In holiness and justice be-FORE him * ... *all* our days.
9. And you, O child, shall be called the prophet of the MOST High; * for you shall go before the Lord to *pre*-pare his ways.
10. To grant his people knowledge of sal-VA-tion * through forgive-*ness* of their sins.
11. Because of the compassionate kindness of OUR God * with which the Orient from on high *will* visit us.
12. To shine on those who sit in darkness and the shadow OF death, * to guide our feet into *the* way of peace.
13. ... e-TER-nal rest * grant un-TO him (her), O Lord.
14. And let per-PET-ual light * ... shine *up*-on him (her).
Repeat Antiphon: I am...

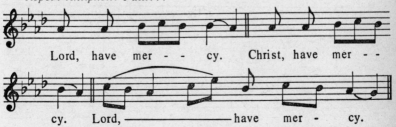

Lord, have mer - - cy.   Christ, have mer - -

cy.   Lord, ————— have mer - cy.

Priest: **Our Father...**

℣. And lead us not into temptation.

℟. But deliver us from evil.

℣. From the gate of hell.

℟. Rescue his (her) soul, O Lord.

℣. May he (she) rest in peace.

℟. Amen.

℣. O Lord, hear my prayer.

℟. And let my cry come to you.

℣. The Lord be with you.

℟. And with your spirit.

Let us pray...

℟. Amen.

℣. Eternal rest grant unto him (her), O Lord.

℟. And let perpetual light shine upon him (her).

℣. May he (she) rest in peace.

℟. Amen.

29. PEOPLE'S SUNG MASS

LORD, HAVE MERCY

Choir: Lord, have mer-cy. All: Lord, have mer-cy. Lord, have mer-cy.

Choir: Christ, have mer-cy. All: Christ, have mer-cy. Christ, have mer-cy.

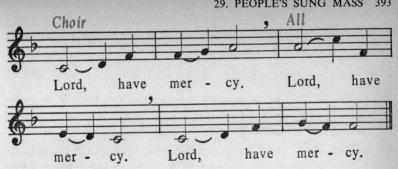

Choir ... *All*

Lord, have mer - cy. Lord, have

mer - cy. Lord, have mer - cy.

GLORY TO GOD

Choir

Glo - ry to God in the high - est. And on earth

All

peace to men of good will. We praise you. We

bless you. We wor - ship you. We glo - ri - fy

Choir

you. We give you thanks for your great glo - ry.

Lord God, heav'n - ly King, God the Fa - ther al -

All

might - y. Lord Je - sus Christ, the on - ly

be - got - ten Son.   Lord God, Lamb of God, Son

Choir

of the Fa - ther.   You, who take a - way the

sins of the world,   have mer - cy   on us.

All

You, who take a - way the sins of the world,

Choir

re - ceive   our   prayer.   You, who sit at the

All

right hand of the Fa - ther,   have mer - cy

Choir

on   us.   For you a - lone are ho - ly. You

a - lone are Lord.   You a - lone, O Je - sus

All

Christ,   are   most high,   With the Ho - ly

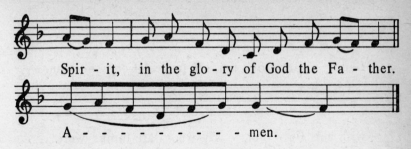

Spir - it,   in the glo - ry of God the Fa - ther.

A - - - - - - - - - men.

I BELIEVE IN ONE GOD

Choir

I be - lieve in one God.   The Father almighty, /

mak - er of heaven and earth,   and of all things

All

visible and in - vis - i - ble.   And I be - lieve

in one Lord, Jesus Christ, /the only - begot - ten Son

of God.   Born of the Father be - fore all a - ges.

Choir

God of God, Light of   Light,   true God of true

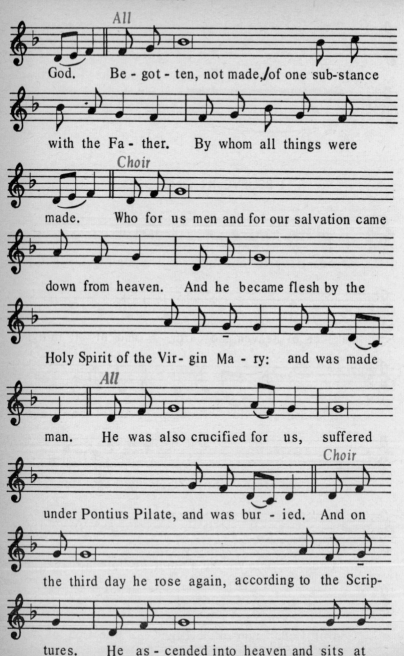

All
God. Be - got - ten, not made, / of one sub-stance

with the Fa - ther. By whom all things were

Choir
made. Who for us men and for our salvation came

down from heaven. And he became flesh by the

Holy Spirit of the Vir - gin Ma - ry: and was made

All
man. He was also crucified for us, suffered

Choir
under Pontius Pilate, and was bur - ied. And on

the third day he rose again, according to the Scrip-

tures. He as - cended into heaven and sits at

the right hand of the Fa - ther. He will come

again in glory to judge the living and the dead.

And of his kingdom there will be no end. And I

believe in the Holy Spirit,/the Lord and Giver of

life, who pro - ceeds from the Fa - ther and the

Son. Who to - gether with the Father and the Son

is adored and glo - ri - fied, and who spoke through

the pro - phets. And one holy, Catholic and

Ap - os - tol - ic Church. I con - fess one baptism

for the for-give-ness of sins. And I await

the resurrec-tion of the dead. And the life of

the world to come. A - - men.

HOLY, HOLY, HOLY

Choir

Ho - ly, ho - ly, ho - - - - ly

All

Lord God of hosts. Heav - en and

earth are filled with your glo - ry.

Ho - san - na in the high - est.

Choir

Bless - ed is he who comes in the

All

name   of   the   Lord.   Ho - san - na

in   the   high - est.

LAMB OF GOD

Choir

Lamb   of   God,   who   take a - way the

All

sins   of   the   world,   have   mer - - cy

Choir

on   us.   Lamb   of   God,   who   take a - way the

All

sins   of   the   world,   have   mer - - cy   on   us.

Choir

Lamb   of   God,   who   take a - way   the   sins

All

of   the   world,   grant   us   peace. ——

GO, THE MASS IS ENDED

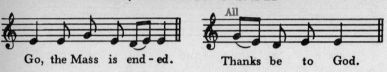

Go, the Mass is end-ed.   Thanks be to God.

30. PEOPLE'S SUNG MASS

LORD, HAVE MERCY

Lord, have mer - cy. Lord, have mer - cy. Lord,
have mer - cy. Christ, have mer - cy. Christ, have
mer - cy. Christ, have mer - cy. Lord, have mer - cy.
Lord, have mer - cy. Lord, have mer - cy.

GLORY TO GOD

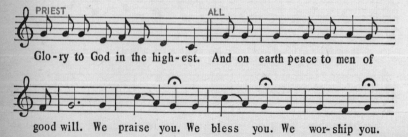

Glo-ry to God in the high-est. And on earth peace to men of
good will. We praise you. We bless you. We wor-ship you.

CHOIR

We glo - ri - fy you. We give you thanks for your

great glo - ry. Lord God, heavenly King, God the Father al -

ALL

might - y. Lord Je - sus Christ, the on - ly be - got - ten Son.

CHOIR

Lord God, Lamb of God, Son of the Fa - ther. You, who take

ALL   CHOIR

away the sins of the world, have mer - cy on us. You, who take

ALL

away the sins of the world, re - ceive our prayer. You, who sit

CHOIR

at the right hand of the Fa - ther, have mer - cy on us. For

ALL

you a - lone are ho - ly. You a - lone are Lord. You a - lone, O

Je - sus Christ are most high, With the Ho - ly Spir - it, in the

glo - ry of God, the Fa - ther. A - - - men.

HOLY, HOLY, HOLY

ALL
Ho - ly, ho - ly, ho - ly Lord God of hosts.

CHOIR / ALL
Heav - en and earth are filled with your glo - ry. Ho - san - na in

CHOIR
the high - est. Bles - sed is he who comes in the name of

ALL
the Lord. Ho - san - na in the high - est.

LAMB OF GOD

CHOIR / ALL
Lamb of God, who take a - way the sins of the world, have

CHOIR
mer - cy on us. Lamb of God, who take a - way the sins of

ALL / CHOIR
the world, have mer - cy on us. Lamb of God, who take a -

ALL
way the sins of the world, grant us peace.

31. PEOPLE'S SUNG MASS

LORD, HAVE MERCY

Lord,——— have mer - cy. (3 times)   Christ,———

have mer - cy. (3 times)   Lord, ——— have mer -

cy. (twice)   Lord,——— have mer - cy.

GLORY TO GOD

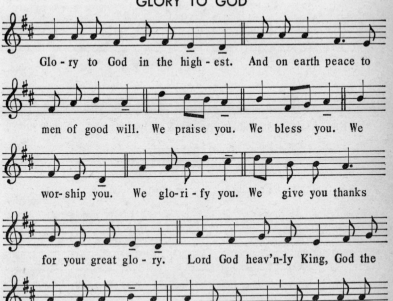

Glo - ry to God in the high - est.   And on earth peace to

men of good will. We praise you. We bless you. We

wor - ship you.   We glo - ri - fy you. We   give you thanks

for your great glo - ry.   Lord God heav'n-ly King, God the

Fa - ther al - might- y.   Lord Je - sus Christ, the on - ly - be -

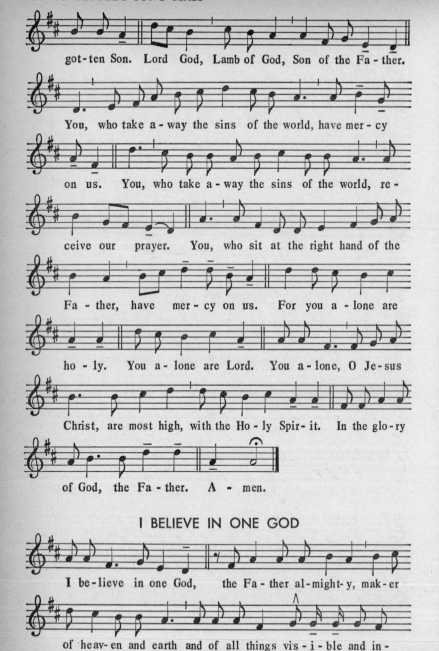

got-ten Son. Lord God, Lamb of God, Son of the Fa - ther.

You, who take a - way the sins of the world, have mer - cy

on us. You, who take a - way the sins of the world, re -

ceive our prayer. You, who sit at the right hand of the

Fa - ther, have mer - cy on us. For you a - lone are

ho - ly. You a - lone are Lord. You a - lone, O Je - sus

Christ, are most high, with the Ho - ly Spir - it. In the glo - ry

of God, the Fa - ther. A - men.

I BELIEVE IN ONE GOD

I be - lieve in one God, the Fa - ther al - might - y, mak - er

of heav - en and earth and of all things vis - i - ble and in -

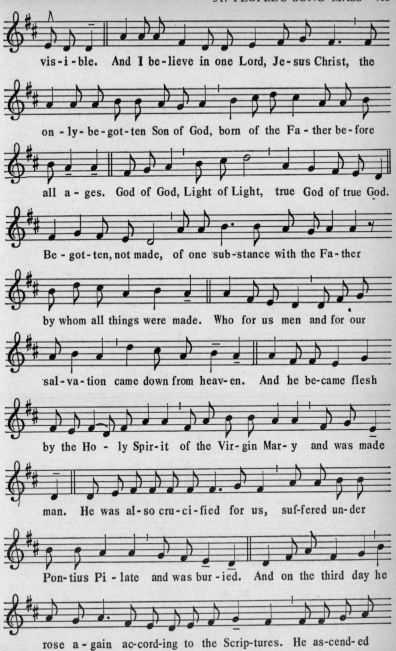

vis-i-ble. And I be-lieve in one Lord, Je-sus Christ, the

on-ly-be-got-ten Son of God, born of the Fa-ther be-fore

all a-ges. God of God, Light of Light, true God of true God.

Be-got-ten, not made, of one sub-stance with the Fa-ther

by whom all things were made. Who for us men and for our

sal-va-tion came down from heav-en. And he be-came flesh

by the Ho-ly Spir-it of the Vir-gin Mar-y and was made

man. He was al-so cru-ci-fied for us, suf-fered un-der

Pon-tius Pi-late and was bur-ied. And on the third day he

rose a-gain ac-cord-ing to the Scrip-tures. He as-cend-ed

in-to heav-en   and sits at the right hand of the Fa - ther.

He will come a - gain in glo-ry   to judge the liv-ing and

the dead, and of his king-dom there will be no end. And I

be-lieve in the Ho-ly Spir-it,   the Lord and Giv-er of life,

who pro-ceeds from the Fa- ther and the Son.   Who to-geth-er

with the Fa-ther and the Son   is a -dored and glo-ri-fied and

who spoke through the proph-ets.   And one   ho - ly, Cath-o-

lic and ap-os-to- lic Church. I con-fess one bap-tis-m

for the for-give-ness of sins. And I a-wait the re - sur-rec-

tion of the dead, and the life of the world to come. A - - men.

HOLY, HOLY, HOLY

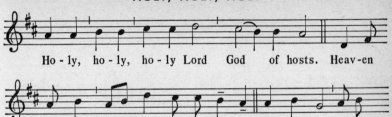

Ho - ly, ho - ly, ho - ly Lord God of hosts. Heav-en

and earth are filled with your glo - ry. Ho - san - na in the

high - est. Bless-ed is he who comes in the name of the

Lord. Ho - san - na in the high - est.

LAMB OF GOD

Lamb of God, who take a - way the sins of the world, have

mer - cy on us. Lamb of God, who take a - way the sins of

the world, have mer - cy on us. Lamb of God, who take a - way

the sins of the world, grant us peace.

32. PEOPLE'S SUNG MASS

LORD, HAVE MERCY

Choir

All

Lord,   have mer - cy. Lord, have mer - cy. Lord,

Choir

All

have mer - cy. Christ,   have mer - cy. Christ,   have mer - cy.

Choir

Christ,   have   mer - cy. Lord,   have mer - cy.

All

Lord,   have mer - cy. Lord,   have   mer - cy.

GLORY TO GOD

Choir

All

And on earth peace to men   of good will.   We praise

Choir

All

Choir

you.   We bless   you.   We wor - ship you.   We

All

glo - - ri - fy you.   We give you thanks for your great glo - ry.

Choir

Lord God, heav-en-ly King,   God   the Fa-ther al -might - y.

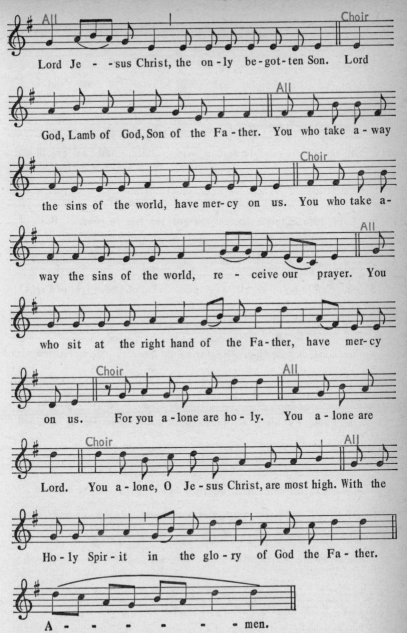

All
Lord Je - -sus Christ, the on - ly be - got - ten Son. Lord
Choir

God, Lamb of God, Son of the Fa - ther. You who take a - way
All

the sins of the world, have mer - cy on us. You who take a -
Choir

way the sins of the world, re - ceive our prayer. You
All

who sit at the right hand of the Fa - ther, have mer - cy

on us. For you a - lone are ho - ly. You a - lone are
Choir   All

Lord. You a - lone, O Je - sus Christ, are most high. With the
Choir   All

Ho - ly Spir - it in the glo - ry of God the Fa - ther.

A - - - - - - men.

I BELIEVE IN ONE GOD

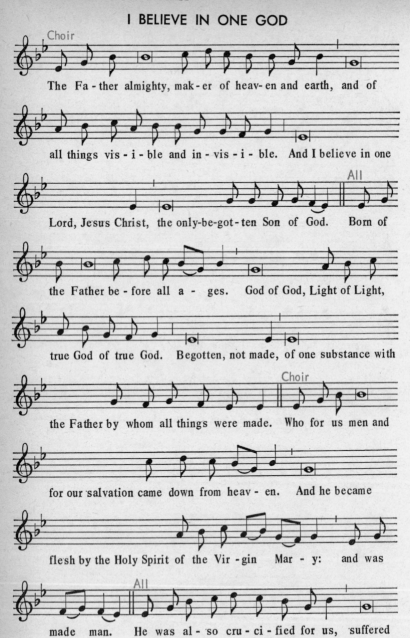

Choir

The Fa - ther almighty, mak - er of heav- en and earth, and of

all things vis - i - ble and in - vis - i - ble.   And I believe in one

Lord, Jesus Christ, the only-be-got-ten Son of God.   All   Born of

the Father be - fore all a - ges.   God of God, Light of Light,

true God of true God.   Begotten, not made, of one substance with

the Father by whom all things were made.   Choir   Who for us men and

for our salvation came down from heav - en.   And he became

flesh by the Holy Spirit of the Vir - gin   Mar - y: and was

made man.   All   He was al - so cru - ci - fied for us,   suffered

under Pon - tius Pi - late, and was bur - ied.   And on the third

Choir

day he rose again, ac - cord - ing to the Scrip-tures.   He as -

cend -ed into heaven and sits at the right hand of the Fa - ther.

He will come again in glory to judge the liv - ing and the dead.

All

And of his kingdom there will be no end.   And I be - lieve in

the Holy Spirit, the Lord and Giv - er of life,   who proceeds from

the Father and the Son.   Who together with the Father and the Son

is a - dored and glo - ri - fied;   and who spoke through the proph-

ets.   And one, holy, Catholic, and ap - os - tol - ic Church, I

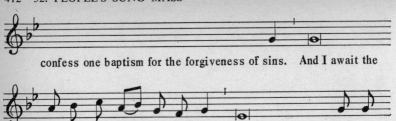

confess one baptism for the forgiveness of sins.   And I await the

res - ur - rec - tion   of the dead.   And the life of the world to

come.   A - men.

HOLY, HOLY, HOLY

Ho - ly, ho - ly, ho - ly Lord God of hosts.   Heav-en

and earth are filled   with your   glo-ry.   Ho - san-na in

the high-est.   Bless-ed is he   who comes in the name of the

Lord.   Ho - - san-na in   the high-est.

LAMB OF GOD

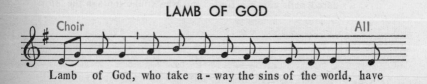

Lamb   of God, who take a - way the sins of the world, have

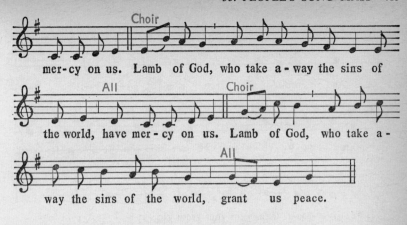

mer-cy on us. Lamb of God, who take a-way the sins of

the world, have mer-cy on us. Lamb of God, who take a-

way the sins of the world, grant us peace.

33. PEOPLE'S SUNG MASS

LORD HAVE MERCY

Lord, have mer - cy. Lord, have mer - cy.

Lord, have mer - - cy.   Christ, have mer- cy.

Christ, have mer - cy. Christ, have mer - - cy.

Lord, have mer- cy.   Lord, have mer- cy.

have mer - - - cy.

Lord, have mer - cy, have have mer - - cy.

GLORY TO GOD

ther, have mer - cy on us.   For you a-lone are

ho - ly. You a-lone are Lord. You a - lone, O Je-sus Christ,

are most high. With the Ho- ly Spir- it,   in the glo-ry of

God the Fa-ther,   in the glo-ry of   God the Fa - ther.

A - - men.

HOLY, HOLY, HOLY

ho - - ly

Ho - - - -ly, ho - - - ly, ho - ly,

ho - - - - -ly.

ho - - - ly Lord God of hosts, of   hosts.

Heav - en and earth   are filled with your glo - ry.

Ho-san-na, ho-san-na, ho-san-na in the high--est.

Bless-ed is he who comes in the name of the Lord.

Ho-san-na, ho-san-na, ho-san-na in the high--est.

LAMB OF GOD

Lamb of God, who take a-way the sins of the world,

have mer-cy on us. Lamb of God, who take a-way the

sins of the world, have mer-cy on us Lamb of God,

who take a-way the sins of the world, grant us peace,

grant us peace, grant us peace.

34. PEOPLE'S SUNG MASS

LORD, HAVE MERCY

Lord, have mer-cy. Lord, have mer-cy. Lord, have mer-cy.

Christ, have mer-cy. Christ, have mer-cy. Christ, have mer-cy.

Lord, have mer-cy. Lord, have mer-cy. Lord, have mer-cy.

GLORY TO GOD

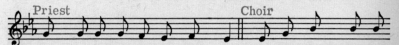

Glo - ry to God in the high - est. And on earth peace to

men of good will. We praise you. We bless you. We

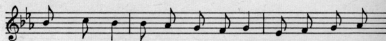

wor - ship you. We glo - ri - fy you. We give you thanks

for your great glo - ry. Lord God, heav - en - ly King,

God the Fa - ther al - might - y, Lord Je - sus Christ,

the on - ly - be - got - ten Son. Lord God, Lamb of God,

Son of the Fa - ther. You, who take a - way the sins of

the world, have mer - cy on us. You, who take a - way

the sins of the world, re - ceive our prayer. You, who

sit at the right hand of the Fa - ther, have mer - cy on

us. For you a - lone are ho - ly. You a - lone are Lord.

You a - lone, O Je - sus Christ, are most high. With the

Ho - ly Spir - it in the glo - ry of God the Fa - ther. A - men.

I BELIEVE IN ONE GOD

I be - lieve in one God. The Fa - ther al - might - y,

mak - er of heav - en and earth, and of all things vis -

i - ble and in - vis - i - ble. And I be - lieve in one Lord,

Je - sus Christ, the on - ly - be - got - ten Son of God.

Born of the Fa - ther be - fore all a - ges. God of God,

Light of Light, true God of true God. Be - got - ten,

not made, of one sub - stance with the Fa - ther, by

whom all things were made. Who for us men and for

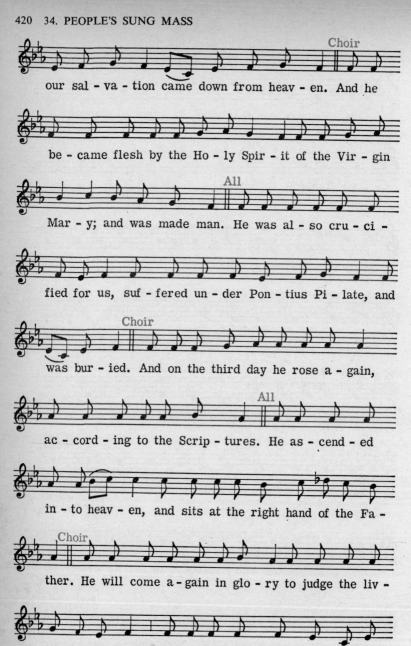

Choir
our sal - va - tion came down from heav - en. And he

be - came flesh by the Ho - ly Spir - it of the Vir - gin

All
Mar - y; and was made man. He was al - so cru - ci -

fied for us, suf - fered un - der Pon - tius Pi - late, and

Choir
was bur - ied. And on the third day he rose a - gain,

All
ac - cord - ing to the Scrip - tures. He as - cend - ed

in - to heav - en, and sits at the right hand of the Fa -

Choir
ther. He will come a - gain in glo - ry to judge the liv -

ing and the dead. And of his king - dom there will be

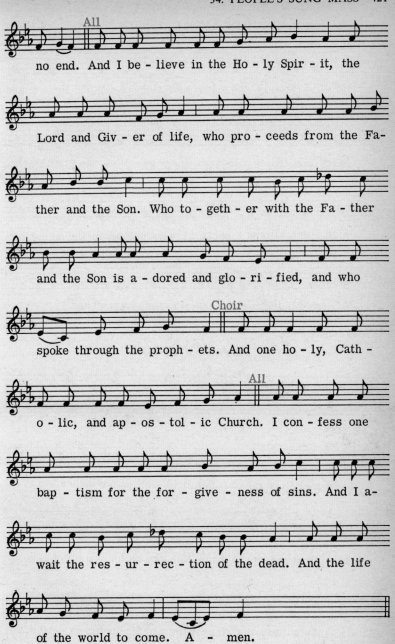

no end. And I be - lieve in the Ho - ly Spir - it, the

Lord and Giv - er of life, who pro - ceeds from the Fa-

ther and the Son. Who to - geth - er with the Fa - ther

and the Son is a - dored and glo - ri - fied, and who

spoke through the proph - ets. And one ho - ly, Cath -

o - lic, and ap - os - tol - ic Church. I con - fess one

bap - tism for the for - give - ness of sins. And I a-

wait the res - ur - rec - tion of the dead. And the life

of the world to come. A - men.

HOLY, HOLY, HOLY

Choir All

Ho - ly, ho - ly, ho - ly Lord God of hosts. Heav'n and

earth are filled with your glo - ry. Ho - san - na in the

high - est. Bless - ed is he who comes in the name of

the Lord. Ho - san - na in the high - est.

LAMB OF GOD

Choir All

Lamb of God, who take a - way the sins of the world,

Choir All

have mer - cy on us. Lamb of God, who take a - way

Choir

the sins of the world, have mer - cy on us. Lamb of God,

All

who take a - way the sins of the world, grant us peace.

HYMNS FOR HOLY MASS

At four points in the Eucharistic liturgy hymns have proven to be suitable means for group participation whether sung by a choir, by all assembled, or by both choir and people.

The following selection by no means implies that hymns for the various seasons or occasions given later in this book are not to be used. Nor is there any implication that a given hymn would not serve equally well in a category different from that to which it is assigned.

For the convenience of beginners the following classification is offered:

Nos. 35—50 Entrance hymns
     51—60 Offertory hymns
     61—82 Communion hymns
     83—97 Recessional hymns

35. PRAISE TO THE LORD

1. Praise to the Lord, the Al-might-y, the King of cre-a-tion!
2. Praise to the Lord, let us of-fer our gifts at the al-tar.
3. Praise to the Lord, O let all that is in us a-dore him.

1. O my soul, praise him for he is our health and sal-
2. Let not our sins and of-fens-es now cause us to
3. All that has life and breath come now re-joic-ing be-

1. va-tion. All you who hear now to his pres-
2. fal-ter. Christ, the High Priest, bids us all join
3. fore him. Let the A-men sound from his peo-

1. ence draw near; Join in pro-found ad-o-ra-tion.
2. in his feast, Vic-tims with him on the al-tar.
3. ple a-gain, As we here wor-ship be-fore him.

36. AT THE LAMB'S HIGH FEAST

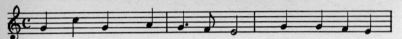

1. At   the Lamb's high feast we sing   Praise to our vic-
2. Where the pas - chal blood is poured, Death's dark an - gel

1. to - rious King. He has cleansed us in the tide
2. sheathes his sword; God's tri - um - phant peo - ple go

1. Flow - ing from his   o - pen side; Praise to him whose
2. Through the sea that drowns the foe. Praise to Christ whose

1. love di - vine, Gives his sa - cred blood for wine, Gives his
2. blood was shed, Christ our vic - tim, Christ our bread, Let us

1. bod - y for the feast, Christ e - ter - nal vic - tim - priest!
2. feast with faith and love   On this man - na from a - bove!

37. HAIL, REDEEMER, KING DIVINE

1. Hail, Re - deem - er, King di - vine! Priest and Lamb,
2. With your truth our minds im - bue, Guide our wills,
3. King most ho - ly, King of hope, Show the way

1. the throne is thine; King whose reign shall nev - er
2. our hearts re - new, Till in peace each na - tion
3. to all who grope; Christ, thou King of glo - ry

1. cease, Prince of ev - er - last - ing peace.
2. rings With thy prais - es, King of kings.
3. bright, Be to us e - ter - nal light.

Refrain:

An - gels, saints, and na - tions sing: "Praised be

Je - sus Christ, our King; Lord of life, earth,

sky and sea, King of love on Cal - va - ry."

38. COME, LET US SING JOYFULLY TO THE LORD

Choir

Come, let us sing joy - ful - ly to the Lord; he is our God,

All

he is our shep - herd. Come, let us sing joy - ful - ly

to the Lord; he is our God, he is our shep - herd.

Choir

Let us ac - claim the Rock of our sal - va - tion;

let us greet him with thanks - giv - ing.

All repeat the refrain, Come, let us sing . . .

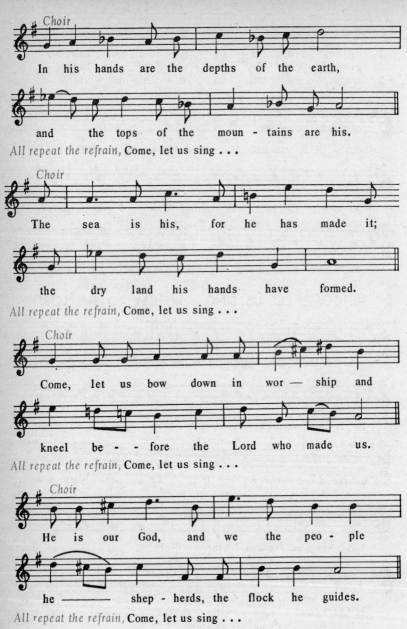

Choir

In his hands are the depths of the earth,

and the tops of the moun - tains are his.

All repeat the refrain, Come, let us sing . . .

Choir

The sea is his, for he has made it;

the dry land his hands have formed.

All repeat the refrain, Come, let us sing . . .

Choir

Come, let us bow down in wor — ship and

kneel be - - fore the Lord who made us.

All repeat the refrain, Come, let us sing . . .

Choir

He is our God, and we the peo - ple

he ——— shep - herds, the flock he guides.

All repeat the refrain, Come, let us sing . . .

Choir

Oh, that to - day you would hear his voice:

"Hard - en not your hearts as in the des - ert!"

Choir (ad lib)

Come, let us sing ——— to the Lord;

All

Come, let us sing ——— joy - ful - ly to the Lord;

he is our God, —— he is our shep - herd.

he is our God, —— he is our shep - herd.

39. TO HEAVEN'S SOVEREIGN LORD

1. To heav -en's sov-'reign Lord give hon - or praise and
2. To the E - ter - nal Word give hom-age ev - 'ry

1. glo - ry, Who in his love for us did
2. na - tion, Who through his end - less love chose

1. write cre - a -tion's sto- ry. He fash - ioned all the
2. death for our sal - va-tion. The price he gavefor

1. earth, on her his im - age lies; Sing prais-es to his
2. us he now re-news each day; His pas - sion pleads for

1. Name, as earth his glo - ry cries.
2. us as in his Name we pray.

40. ALL HAIL THE POWER OF JESUS' NAME

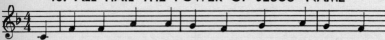

All hail the pow'r of Je - sus' name! Let an - gels

pros - trate fall; Bring forth the roy - al di - a - dem, And

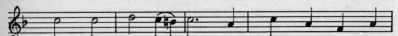

crown him Lord of all; Bring forth the roy - al

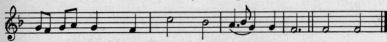

di - a - dem, And crown him Lord of all! A - men.

41. HOSANNA TO THE LIVING LORD

1. Ho - san - na to the liv - ing Lord! Ho - san - na
2. Ho - san - na, Lord! your an - gels cry; Ho - san - na,
3. O Sav - ior, with pro - tect - ing care A - bide in

1. to the in - car- nate Word! To Christ, Cre - a - tor,
2. Lord, your saints re - ply; A - bove, be - neath us,
3. this your house of prayer, Where we your East-er

1. Sav - ior, King, Let earth, let heav'n ho - san - na
2. and a - round, The dead and liv - ing swell the
3. prom -ise claim, As - sem - bled in your sa - cred

1. sing! Ho - san - na, Lord! Ho - san - na in the high - est!
2. sound; Ho - san - na, Lord! Ho - san - na in the high - est!
3. name. Ho - san - na, Lord! Ho - san - na in the high - est!

42. O GOD OF HOSTS

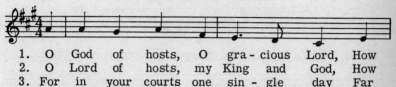

1. O God of hosts, O gra - cious Lord, How
2. O Lord of hosts, my King and God, How
3. For in your courts one sin - gle day Far
4. For God, who is our Sun and Shield, Will

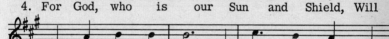

1. love - ly is the place En-throned in glo - ry
2. high- ly blest are they Who in your pres-ence
3. bet - ter to at - tend, Than, Lord, in an - y
4. grace and glo - ry give; And no good thing will

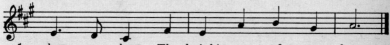

1. where you show The bright-ness of your face.
2. choose to dwell, And serve you day by day.
3. oth - er place A thou - sand days to spend.
4. he with- hold If we his law do live.

43. CHRIST IS MADE THE SURE FOUNDATION

1. Christ is made the sure Foun-da-tion, Christ the Head and
2. To us gath-ered here to - geth-er, Come, O Lord of
3. Laud and hon - or to the Fa-ther, Laud and hon - or

1. Cor - ner-stone, Cho-sen of the Lord and pre-cious,
2. hosts, to - day: With a fa-ther's lov-ing-kind-ness
3. to the Son, Laud and hon - or to the Spir - it,

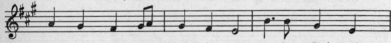

1. Bind - ing all the Church in one; Ho-ly Si - on's
2. Hear your peo - ple as we pray; All the need - ed
3. Ev - er Three and ev - er One, One in might, and

1. help for - ev - er, And her con-fi-dence a - lone.
2. grace and bless-ing Give to us a - long life's way.
3. One in glo - ry, While un-end-ing a - ges run.

44. FROM ALL WHO DWELL BENEATH THE SKIES

1. From all who dwell be-neath the skies Let praise to
2. E - ter-nal are your mer-cies, Lord; E - ter - nal

1. our Cre - a - tor rise: Al - le - lu - ia! Al - le - lu - ia!
2. truth at-tends your word: Al - le - lu - ia! Al - le - lu - ia!

1. Let our Re - deem-er's name be sung Through
2. Your praise shall sound from shore to shore, Till

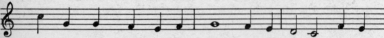

1. ev-'ry land, by ev-'ry tongue. Al - le - lu - ia! Al - le-
2. sun and moon shall be no more. Al - le - lu - ia! Al - le-

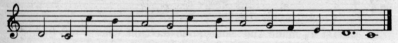

1. lu - ia! Al - le - lu - ia! Al - le - lu - ia! Al - le - lu - ia!
2. lu - ia! Al - le - lu - ia! Al - le - lu - ia! Al - le - lu - ia!

45. O COME, LET US SING TO THE LORD

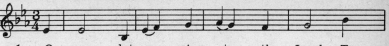

1. O come, let us sing to the Lord, To
2. Let us be-fore his pres-ence come; A-
3. To him the spa-cious sea be-longs, For
4. O come, and let us wor-ship him, Ask

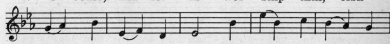

1. him our voic-es raise; With joy-ous shout let
2. bove all gods he is. The depths of earth are
3. he the same did make; The dry land al-so
4. en-trance to his rest, And on our knees be-

1. us the Rock Of our sal-va-tion praise.
2. in his hand; The heights of hills are his.
3. from his hands Its form at first did take.
4. fore the Lord, Our faith in him at-test.

46. COME, HOLY GHOST, CREATOR BLEST

1. Come, Ho-ly Ghost, Cre-a-tor blest, And deign
2. To thee, the Com-fort-er, we cry, To thee,
3. Make thou to us the Fa-ther known, Through thee
4. To God the Fa-ther let us sing, To God

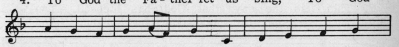

1. with-in our souls to rest; Come with thy grace and
2. the gift of God Most High; The fount of life, the
3. his Son in faith be shown; Be this our nev-er-
4. the Son our ris-en King, And e-qual-ly let

1. heav'n-ly aid And fill the hearts which thou hast made.
2. fire of love, The soul's a-noint-ing from a-bove.
3. chang-ing creed: That thou dost from them both pro-ceed.
4. us a-dore The Spir-it, God for ev-er-more.

47. HOLY, HOLY, HOLY

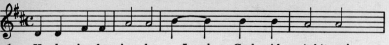

1. Ho-ly, ho-ly, ho-ly, Lord God Al - might - y!
2. Ho-ly, ho-ly, ho-ly, an - gel hosts a - dore thee,
3. Ho-ly, ho-ly, ho-ly, though the dark-ness hide thee,

1. Bowed in ad - o - ra - tion now we lift our hearts to
2. Veil their gaze in deep-est awe be-fore thy maj - es -
3. Though the eye of mor-tal man thy glo-ry may not

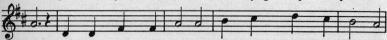

1. thee. Ho - ly, ho - ly ho-ly, mer - ci - ful and might-y!
2. ty. All the saints in glo-ry lay their crowns be-fore thee.
3. see; Thou art God most ho-ly, none there is be-side thee.

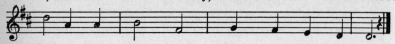

God in three Per - sons, Bless - ed Trin - i - ty!

48. COME, LET US JOIN WITH ONE ACCORD

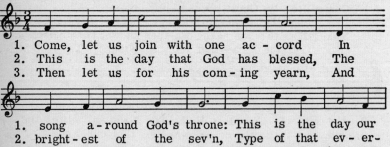

1. Come, let us join with one ac - cord In
2. This is the day that God has blessed, The
3. Then let us for his com - ing yearn, And

1. song a - round God's throne: This is the day our
2. bright - est of the sev'n, Type of that ev - er -
3. for that day pre - pare When our Re - deem - er

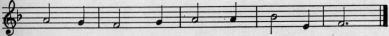

1. ris - ing Lord Did make and call his own.
2. last - ing rest The saints en - joy in heav'n.
3. shall re - turn, His glo - ry full to share.

49. ON THIS DAY, THE FIRST OF DAYS

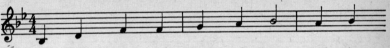

1. On this day, the first of days, God the
2. On this day th'e - ter - nal Son O - ver
3. Fa - ther, you cre - at - ed me Im - age

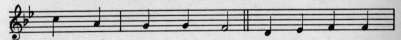

1. Fa - ther's name we praise, Who, cre - a - tion's
2. death his tri - umph won. On this day the
3. of your - self to be; Fill me with your

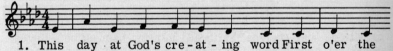

1. Lord and spring, Did the world from dark-ness bring.
2. Spir - it came With his gifts of liv - ing flame.
3. love di - vine, And my acts to good con - fine.

50. THIS DAY AT GOD'S CREATING WORD

1. This day at God's cre - at - ing word First o'er the
2. This day the Lord for sin - ners slain In might vic-
3. This day the Ho - ly Spir - it came With fi - ery
4. All praise to God the Fa - ther be, All praise, e-

1. earth the light was poured: O Lord, this day up-
2. to - rious rose a - gain: O Je - sus, may we
3. tongues of part - ed flame: O Spir - it, fill our
4. ter - nal Son, to thee, Whom, with the Spir - it,

1. on us shine And fill our souls with light di - vine.
2. res - cued be From death of sin to life in thee!
3. hearts this day With grace to hear and grace to pray.
4. we a - dore For ev - er and for ev - er-more.

51. WONDROUS GIFT
52. HE WHO ONCE TO DIE A VICTIM

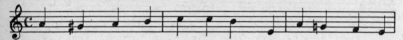

1. Won - drous gift! The Word who fash-ioned All things by his

As an Entrance hymn, verses 2 and 3

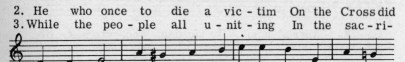

2. He who once to die a vic - tim On the Cross did
3. While the peo - ple all u - nit - ing In the sac - ri -

1. might di - vine, Bread in - to his bod-y chang-es, In - to
2. not re - fuse, Day by day up-on our al - tars, That same
3. fice sub - lime, Of- fer Christ to his high Fa - ther, Of - fer

1. his own blood the wine. What though sense no
2. sac - ri - fice re - news, Through his ho - ly
3. up them - selves with him; Then, to - geth - er

1. change per - ceives? Faith ad - mires, a - dores, be - lieves.
2. priest-hood's hands, Faith-ful to his last com-mands.
3. with the priest, On the liv - ing vic - tim feast.

53. ALL MAN'S LABOR CAN PRODUCE

1. All man's la - bor can pro -duce You have giv - en
2. On this gift of bread and wine, Of our sac - ri -
3. May this food which strength im-parts, Bring re-fresh-ment

1. for our use: Take, O Lord, our of - fer - ing!
2. fice a sign, Fa - ther, look with fa - vor now!
3. to our hearts, And a taste of joy to come!

Refrain

May this low-ly bread and wine Be the sac-ri-fice di-vine

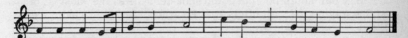

Of our Sav-ior Je-sus Christ! Of our Sav-ior Je-sus Christ!

54. ACCEPT, ALMIGHTY FATHER

1. Ac - cept, al - might - y Fa - ther, These gifts of
2. O   God, by   this com - min - gling Of   wa - ter

1. wine and bread Now of - fered at the al - tar To
2. and of wine, May he   who took our na - ture Give

1. you through Christ our head In   hum - ble rep -
2. us   his   life di - vine. Come, then, and make

1. a - ra - tion For sins and fail - ings dread To gain
2. us ho - ly, Re - ceive this sac - ri - fice; In - to

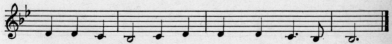

1. life ev - er - last - ing For liv - ing and for dead.
2. your fa - vor take us; In Christ may we a - rise.

55. LORD, ACCEPT THE GIFTS

1. Lord, ac-cept the gifts we of - fer   At this eu - cha-
2. May our souls be pure and spot-less   As the host of
3. Take our gifts, al-might- y Fa -ther, Liv -ing God,   e -

1. ris -tic feast. Bread and wine   to   be trans-formed now
2. wheat so fine, May all stain   of   sin be crushed out,
3. ter - nal, true, Which we give through Christ, our   Sav - ior,

1. Through the ac - tion of   thy priest. Take us, too, O
2. Like   the grape that forms the wine,   As we, too, be-
3. Plead - ing here for   us   a - new. Grant sal -va- tion

1. Lord, trans-form us; Be thy grace in   us in -creased.
2. come   par - tak - ers   In this sac - ri -fice di - vine.
3. to   all   pres- ent And our faith and love re - new.

56. SEND FORTH, O LORD, THY LIGHT

1. Send forth, O Lord, thy light and thy re -deem-ing
2. With con - trite lov - ing hearts we come be -fore thy

1. grac-es; That they may lead us now with thee to take our
2. al -tar; Pre-pared for sac-ri-fice with Christ we do not

1. plac - es. O God, thou art our strength, our
2. fal - ter. The ho - ly bread and wine   the

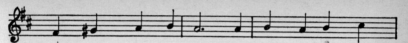

1. Mas -ter, Lord and King; Thy al -tar we ap -
2. priest now lifts on high; To these we join our -

1. proach to join thee in this feast, In which, O Lord, our
2. selves, we of - fer all to thee. We sing in praise to

1. God, thou art the Vic - tim -priest.
2. God, the Bless -ed Trin - i - ty.

57. O KING OF MIGHT AND SPLENDOR

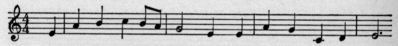

1. O King of might and splen-dor, Cre- a - tor most a - dored,
2. Thy bod-y thou hast giv - en, thy blood thou hast out-poured

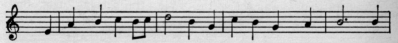

1. This sac - ri - fice we ren-der To thee as sov'-reign Lord. May
2. That sin might be for-giv-en, O Je-sus, lov - ing Lord. As

1. these our-gifts be pleas-ing Un - to thy Maj-es-ty, Man-
2. now with love most ten - der Thy death we cel - e-brate, Our

1. kind from sin re - leas-ing Who have of-fend-ed thee.
2. lives in self - sur - ren - der To thee we con-se-crate.

58. O LORD, FROM ALL YOUR CHURCH

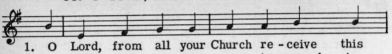

1. O Lord, from all your Church re-ceive this
2. A drop of wa-ter now is poured in-
3. Cre-a-tor of hu-man-i-ty, man's

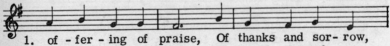

1. of-fer-ing of praise, Of thanks and sor-row,
2. to the cup of wine, Re-quest-ing of your
3. life you have re-stored, And in this ho-ly

1. prayer for need, with host our hearts we raise.
2. Maj-es-ty, to share your life di-vine.
3. sac-ri-fice our faith re-ceives re-ward.

59. ACCEPT FROM HUMAN HANDS ANOINTED

1. Ac-cept from hu-man hands a-noint-ed Cre-
2. The Cross was once the Vic-tim's meas-ure, Un-

1. at-ed gifts of bread and wine. And haste the time
2. dy-ing proof of end-less love. The al-tar now

1. which Christ ap-point-ed 'Til al-tar
2. con-tains the treas-ure, Christ's pre-cious

Refrain

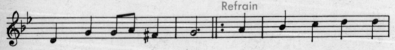

1. holds the gifts di-vine.
2. bod-y and his blood.

In-crease our faith, that

we may see   The depths   of   this   great   mys - ter - y.

60. THIRSTING FOR THE LIVING FOUNTAIN

1. Thirst - ing   for   the   liv - ing   foun - tain   Stream - ing
2. Bread   and   wine   from   dai - ly   liv - ing   Are   the

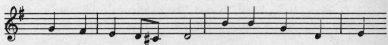

1. from   the   Sav - ior's   side,   We   as - cend   God's   ho -
2. low - ly   gifts   we   bear;   At   the   al - tar   priest -

1. ly   moun - tain   Where   for   love   of   us   he   died.
2. ly   giv - ing   Makes   us   in   Christ's   life   to   share.

1. Once   a - gain   Christ's   sa - cred   pas - sion   In
2. In   this   ban - quet   where   the   Fa - ther   Gives

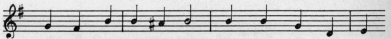

1. this   ho - ly   sac - ri - fice   Par - don   and   new   grace
2. as   food   his   on - ly   Son,   There   the   sanc - ti - fy -

1. will   fash - ion,   Off - 'ring   our   re - demp - tion's   price.
2. ing   Spir - it   Is   the   love   that   makes   us   one.

61. AT THAT FIRST EUCHARIST

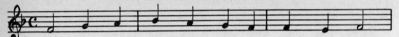

1. At that first Eu - cha - rist be - fore you died,
2. For all your Church, O Lord, we in - ter - cede;
3. We pray for those who wan - der from the fold;
4. So, Lord, at length when sac - ra - ments shall cease,

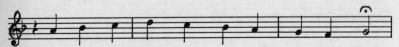

1. O Lord, you prayed that all be one in you;
2. O make our lack of char - i - ty to cease;
3. O bring them back, Good Shep - herd of the sheep,
4. May we be one with all your Church a - bove,

1. At this our Eu - cha - rist a - gain pre - side,
2. Draw us the near - er each to each, we plead,
3. Back to the faith which saints be - lieved of old,
4. One with your saints in one un - end - ing peace,

1. And in our hearts your law of love re - new.
2. By draw-ing all to you, O Prince of peace.
3. Back to the Church which still that faith does keep.
4. One with your saints in one un - bound - ed love.

Refrain

Thus may we all one bread, one bod - y be,

Through this blest sac - ra - ment of u - ni - ty.

62. AT THAT FIRST EUCHARIST

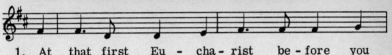

1. At that first Eu - cha - rist be - fore you
2. For all your Church, O Lord, we in - ter -
3. We pray for those who wan - der from the
4. So, Lord, at length when sac - ra - ments shall

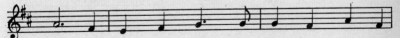

1. died, O Lord, you prayed that all be one in
2. cede; O make our lack of char - i - ty to
3. fold; O bring them back, Good Shep-herd of the
4. cease, May we be one with all your Church a-

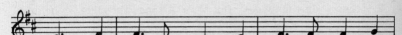

1. you; At this our Eu - cha - rist a - gain pre -
2. cease; Draw us the near - er each to each, we
3. sheep, Back to the faith which saints be-lieved of
4. bove, One with your saints in one un - end - ing

1. side, And in our hearts your law of love re-
2. plead, By draw-ing all to you, O Prince of
3. old, Back to the Church which still that faith does
4. peace, One with your saints in one un - bound - ed

Refrain

1. new. Thus may we all one Bread, one Bod - y
2. peace.
3. keep.
4. love.

be, Through this blest Sac - ra - ment of u - ni - ty.

63. DEVOUTLY, HIDDEN GODHEAD

1. De - vout - ly, hid - den   God - head, thee I
2. Sight and touch   and   taste   are each in
3. On the Cross   was   hid - den thy di -
4. Thom - as   saw   the wounds which I   yet a -
5. O what won - drous   sym - bol   of the
6. Lov - ing Sav - ior, thou with love now my
7. Je - sus, here   I   gaze up - on thy face

1. now   a - dore,   Un - der cho - sen   sym -
2. thee de - ceived;   But   a - lone through   hear -
3. vin - i - ty,   Here   is   al - so   hid -
4. wait to see,   Still I firm - ly   thee con -
5. Sav - ior's death!   Liv - ing Bread for   soul of
6. heart dost flood; Cleanse my un - clean   soul,
7. veiled from me.   Deign to quench the   thirst with

1. bols, bread and wine   no more; Thee while con -
2. ing   safe - ly   art   be - lieved. All that thou
3. den   thy   hu - man - i - ty;   Yet in   both
4. fess   my   true God to   be! Make me   al -
5. man   giv - ing life and breath! Be thou food
6. Lord, by   thy   pre - cious blood,   One mere drop
7. which my heart longs for   thee! Lift the   veil

1. tem - plat - ing, sens - es fail to   see, Hence my
2. hast   said,   Lord, I do firm - ly   hold, Tru - er
3. be - liev - ing, Lord, I thee pro - fess; What the
4. ways more and more deep - en faith in   thee, Hope in
5. of   my poor soul so that I may live! Be its
6. of   which for   poor sin - ners could free All man -
7. that hides thy face from my mor - tal   sight. Bless me

1. soul com - plete - ly I sub - mit to thee.
2. word of truth than thine nev - er has been told.
3. Good Thief begged thee I the same ex - press.
4. thee and love thee as thou lov - est me.
5. con - stant sweet - ness which is thine to give.
6. kind from sin and turn the whole world to thee.
7. with the vi - sion of thy glo - ry bright.

64. SING WITH JOY THE SAVIOR'S GLORY

1. Sing with joy the Sav - ior's glo - ry, Of his flesh the
2. On the night of his last sup - per, Seat - ed with his
3. While we bow in ad - o - ra - tion, Let our hearts his

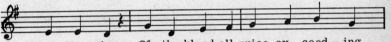

1. mys - t'ry sing; Of the blood all price ex - ceed - ing,
2. cho - sen band, He as food to all his breth - ren
3. gift re - vere; Faith, its aid to vi - sion lend - ing,

Refrain

1. Shed by our im - mor - tal King. Men and an - gels,
2. Gave him - self with his own hand.
3. Tells that he, un - seen, is here.

sing in cho - rus, And a - dor - ing bend the knee! Praise our

God whom here be - fore us In the sa - cred host we see.

65. WE LONG FOR YOU, O LORD

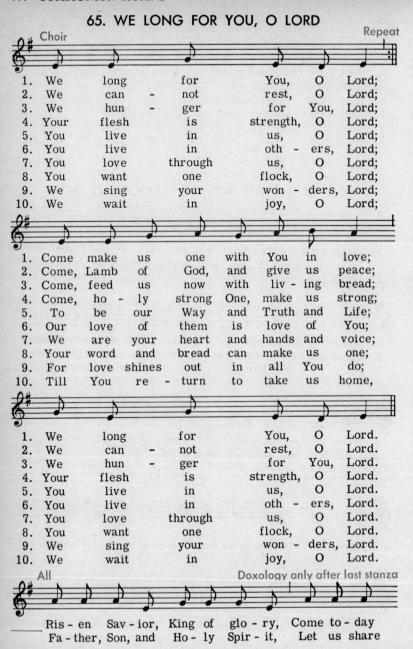

Choir   Repeat

1. We long for You, O Lord;
2. We can - not rest, O Lord;
3. We hun - ger for You, Lord;
4. Your flesh is strength, O Lord;
5. You live in us, O Lord;
6. You live in oth - ers, Lord;
7. You love through us, O Lord;
8. You want one flock, O Lord;
9. We sing your won - ders, Lord;
10. We wait in joy, O Lord;

1. Come make us one with You in love;
2. Come, Lamb of God, and give us peace;
3. Come, feed us now with liv - ing bread;
4. Come, ho - ly strong One, make us strong;
5. To be our Way and Truth and Life;
6. Our love of them is love of You;
7. We are your heart and hands and voice;
8. Your word and bread can make us one;
9. For love shines out in all You do;
10. Till You re - turn to take us home,

1. We long for You, O Lord.
2. We can - not rest, O Lord.
3. We hun - ger for You, Lord.
4. Your flesh is strength, O Lord.
5. You live in us, O Lord.
6. You live in oth - ers, Lord.
7. You love through us, O Lord.
8. You want one flock, O Lord.
9. We sing your won - ders, Lord.
10. We wait in joy, O Lord.

All   Doxology only after last stanza

Ris - en Sav - ior, King of glo - ry, Come to - day
Fa - ther, Son, and Ho - ly Spir - it, Let us share

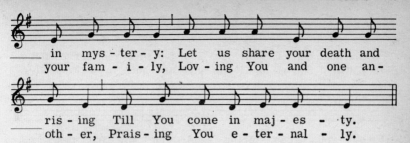

_____ in mys - ter - y: Let us share your death and
your fam - i - ly, Lov - ing You and one an-

ris - ing Till You come in maj - es - ty.
oth - er, Prais - ing You e - ter - nal - ly.

66. THERE'S A WIDENESS IN GOD'S MERCY

1. There's a wide-ness in God's mer - cy, Like the wide -
2. For the love of God is broad-er Than the meas -

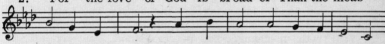

1. ness of the sea; There's a kind-ness in his jus-tice,
2. ure of man's mind; And the heart of the E-ter-nal

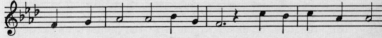

1. Which is more than lib-er-ty. There is wel-come for
2. Is most won-der-ful-ly kind. There is plen-ti-ful

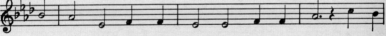

1. the sin - ner, And more bless-ings for the good; There is
2. re-demp-tion In the blood that has been shed; There is

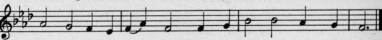

1. mer-cy with the Sav - ior; There is heal-ing in his blood.
2. joy for all the mem-bers Now at one with Christ our Head.

67. MERCIFUL SAVIOR

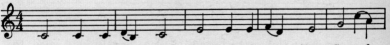

1. Mer - ci - ful Sav - ior, Lord of cre - a - tion, Son of
2. Mer - ci - ful Sav - ior, King of the na - tions, Son of

1. God and Son of Man! Je - sus, we love you, serve and o-
2. God and Son of Man! Glo - ry and hon - or, Praise, ad - o-

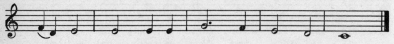

1. bey you, Light of the soul, our joy and peace.
2. ra - tion, Ev - er be yours from all man - kind!

68. O JESUS, JOY OF LOVING HEARTS

1. O Je - sus, joy of lov - ing hearts, The fount of
2. We taste and eat, O liv - ing Bread, And long to
3. Your truth un - changed has ev - er stood, You save all

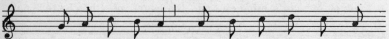

1. life, the light of men, From all the pleas - ures earth
2. feast up - on you still; We drink of you, the foun-
3. those who on you call; To them that seek, you are

1. im - parts, We turn, un - filled, to you a - gain.
2. tain - head, Our thirst - ing souls a - gain you fill.
3. all good, To them that find, you are their all.

69. SING, MY TONGUE, THE SAVIOR'S GLORY, OF HIS FLESH

1. Sing, my tongue, the Sav - ior's glo - ry, Of his flesh the
2. Word made flesh, the bread of na - ture By his word to
3. To the ev - er - last - ing Fa - ther And the Son who

1. mys-t'ry sing;   Of the blood all price ex-ceed-ing
2. flesh he turns, Wine in-to his blood he chang-es
3. reigns on high, With the Ho-ly Ghost pro-ceed-ing

1. Shed by   our im-mor-tal King, Des-tined for the
2. What though sense no change dis-cerns! On-ly be the
3. Forth from each e-ter-nal-ly, Be sal-va-tion,

1. world's re-demp-tion From a no-ble womb to spring.
2. heart in ear-nest, Faith her les-son quick-ly learns.
3. hon-or, bless-ing, Might and end-less maj-es-ty.

70. O SACRAMENT MOST HOLY

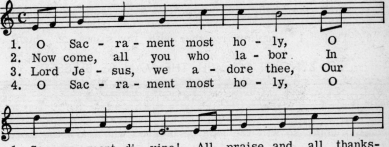

1. O   Sac-ra-ment most ho-ly, O
2. Now come, all you who la-bor. In
3. Lord Je-sus, we a-dore thee, Our
4. O   Sac-ra-ment most ho-ly, O

1. Sac-ra-ment di-vine! All praise and all thanks-
2. sor-row and in pain, Come, eat this bread from
3. Vic-tim and our Priest, Whose pre-cious blood and
4. Sac-ra-ment di-vine! All praise and all thanks-

1. giv-ing Be ev-'ry   mo-ment thine.
2. heav-en; Thy peace and strength re-gain.
3. bod-y Be-come our sa-cred feast.
4. giv-ing Be ev-'ry   mo-ment thine.

71. SOUL OF MY SAVIOR

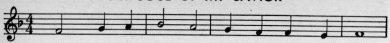

1. Soul   of   my Sav - ior, sanc - ti - fy   my breast;
2. Strength and pro - tec - tion may thy pas - sion be;
3. Guard   and de - fend me from the wick - ed foe;

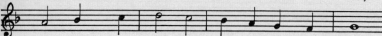

1. Bod - y   of Christ, be   thou my sav - ing   guest;
2. O   bless - ed   Je - sus, hear and an - swer   me;
3. In death's dread mo - ments on - ly thee   to   know;

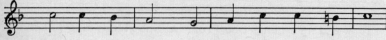

1. Blood of   my   Sav - ior, bathe me   in   thy tide,
2. Deep in   thy wounds, Lord, hide and shel - ter   me;
3. Call me, and   bid   me   to   thy throne draw nigh

1. Wash me   with   wa - ter flow - ing from thy side.
2. So   shall I   nev - er, nev - er part from thee.
3. That   I   may praise thee with thy saints on   high.

72. BEHOLD! SO WILL THE MAN BE BLESSED

All

Be - hold! so will the man be blessed who fears the Lord.

7c²   Choir

1. I will bless the LORD at all times; *
   his praise shall be EV-er in my mouth.
2. Let my soul GLO-ry in the Lord; *
   the lowly will HEAR me and be glad.
3. I sought the LORD, and he answered me *
   and delivered ME from all my fears.
4. Look to him that you may be RA-diant with joy, *
   and your faces MAY not blush with shame.
5. Taste and see how GOOD the Lord is; *
   happy the man who takes REF-uge in him.

6. Fear the LORD, you his holy ones, *
   for naught is lacking to THOSE who fear him.
7. The great grow POOR and hungry; *
   but those who seek the Lord WANT for no good thing.

73. GIVE THANKS TO GOD

All

Give thanks to God; praise the Lord our God.

Choir

1. Adore   God, all you his   an -   gels;
2. The Lord   is king; let the   earth re - joice,
3. The heavens   declare   his   jus -   tice;
4. For you,   O Lord, are   en - throned on high,
5. Clouds and   darkness are a - round   him,
6. Light   dawns for   the   up -   right,
7. Glory   to God   the   Fa -   ther,
8. As it   was in the   be - gin -   ning,

1. Sion   hears and is   glad,
2. let the many   is - lands be   glad;
3. all the   world sees his glo - ry,
4. above   all   of   the   earth,
5. justice and judgement   sit   in   his   throne;
6. gladness for the   truth - ful of   heart;
7. glory   be   to   the   Son,
8. is now and   ev - er   shall   be,

1. and   the   cit - ies of   Ju - da   re - joice.
2. in   his   name let   the   whole world ex - ult.
3. and   the   na - tions pro- claim the Lord's name.
4. and   ex - alt - ed   be - yond all false gods.
5. moun - tains melt like wax be - fore our God.
6. O   give glo - ry   and thanks to   the Lord.
7. glo - ry   be   to   the Spir - it   of   God.
8. for - ev - er   world with - out end. A - men.

450 COMMUNION HYMNS

Antiphons Nos. 74—77 may be sung with the psalm following No. 77; antiphons Nos. 78, 79 with the psalm following No. 79, etc.

74. THIS IS THE BREAD COME DOWN FROM HEAVEN

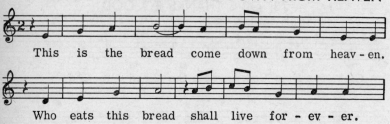

This is the bread come down from heav-en.
Who eats this bread shall live for-ev-er.

75. O CARRY ONE ANOTHER'S BURDENS

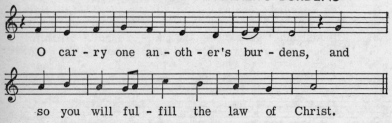

O car-ry one an-oth-er's bur-dens, and
so you will ful-fill the law of Christ.

76. BY THIS SHALL ALL MEN KNOW

By this shall all men know that we are his dis-ci-ples:

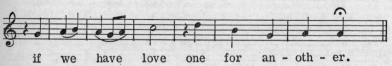

if we have love one for an-oth-er.

77. HE WHO DRINKS OF THE WATER

He who drinks of the wa-ter that I will give him, says the

Lord, shall find in him - self a foun - tain of

wa - ter spring - ing up in - to ev - er - last - ing life.

1.	O God, you are my God! For	you	I	long;
2.	My body	de-	sires	you
3.	For your love is bet-	ter	than	life;
4.	I will bless you	all	my	days
5.	My soul shall be filled as	with	a ban-	quet,
6.	My soul	clings to		you;
7.	Those who seek to de-	stroy	my	life
8.	They shall be put under the power	of	the	sword,
9.	Praise the Father, the Son and Ho-	ly	Spir-	it,
10.	The God who is, who was	and	who will	be

1.	for you my	soul	is reach-	ing.
2.	like arid land	with-	out wa-	ter.
3.	my lips shall	speak	your	praise.
4.	in your name I will lift	up	my	hands.
5.	my mouth shall praise	you	with	joy.
6.	your right hand	holds	me	fast.
7.	shall go down to the depths	of	the	earth;
8.	and left as the	prey	of jack-	als.
9.	both now	and	for- ev-	er —
10.	for ages unend-	ing.	A-	men.

78. WE HAVE RECEIVED, O GOD, YOUR MERCY

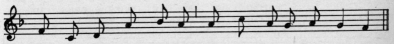

We have re-ceived, O God, your mer-cy in this tem-ple.

79. THE LORD HAS SAVED HIS PEOPLE

The Lord has saved his peo - ple, al - le - lu - ia.

1. Declare the word of joy,
2. The Lord has saved his peo- ple!
3. Sing praise to his great name,
4. Come and see the work of God;
5. Glory be to the Father and to the Son
6. As it was in the beginning,
   is now and ev- er shall be,

1. let it be heard even at the ends of the earth.
2. Shout with joy to God, all the earth.
3. sing glory, to his maj- es- ty.
4. how striking are his plans for men.
5. and to the Ho- ly Spir- it.
6. world without end. A- men.

80. I WILL BE GLAD AND EXULT

I will be glad and ex - ult in you;

I will sing praise to your name most high.

81. GOD HAS CALLED US OUT OF DARKNESS

God has called us out of dark - ness in - to

his mar - vel - ous light, al - le - lu - ia.

Choir

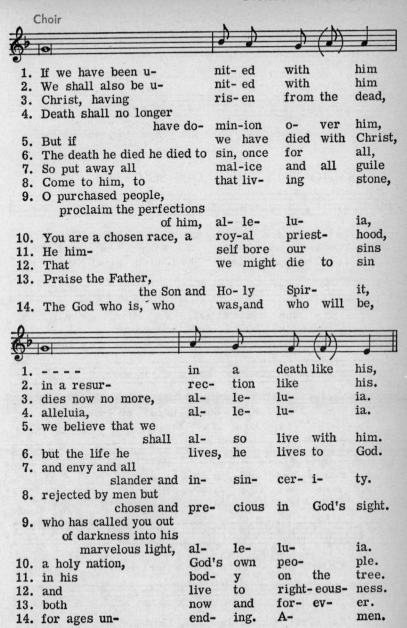

1. If we have been u- nit-ed with him
2. We shall also be u- nit-ed with him
3. Christ, having ris-en from the dead,
4. Death shall no longer have do- min-ion o- ver him,
5. But if we have died with Christ,
6. The death he died he died to sin, once for all,
7. So put away all mal-ice and all guile
8. Come to him, to that liv- ing stone,
9. O purchased people, proclaim the perfections of him, al- le- lu- ia,
10. You are a chosen race, a roy-al priest- hood,
11. He him- self bore our sins
12. That we might die to sin
13. Praise the Father, the Son and Ho- ly Spir- it,
14. The God who is, who was, and who will be,

1. - - - - in a death like his,
2. in a resur- rec- tion like his.
3. dies now no more, al- le- lu- ia.
4. alleluia, al- le- lu- ia.
5. we believe that we shall al- so live with him.
6. but the life he lives, he lives to God.
7. and envy and all slander and in- sin- cer- i- ty.
8. rejected by men but chosen and pre- cious in God's sight.
9. who has called you out of darkness into his marvelous light, al- le- lu- ia.
10. a holy nation, God's own peo- ple.
11. in his bod- y on the tree.
12. and live to right-eous- ness.
13. both now and for- ev- er.
14. for ages un- end- ing. A- men.

82. HE WHO EATS MY FLESH

He who eats my flesh and drinks my

blood a - bides in me and I in him.

83. TO JESUS CHRIST OUR SOVEREIGN KING

1. To Je - sus Christ, our sov - 'reign King, Who
2. Thy reign ex - tend, O King be - nign, To
3. To Thee and to Thy Church, great King, We

1. is the world's sal - va - tion, All
2. ev - 'ry land and na - tion; For
3. pledge our hearts' ob - la - tion; Un-

1. praise and hom - age do we bring And
2. in Thy King - dom Lord di - vine, A -
3. til be - fore Thy throne we sing In

1. thanks and ad - o - ra - tion.
2. lone we find sal - va - tion.
3. end - less ju - bi - la - tion.

Refrain

Christ Je - sus, Vic - tor! Christ Je - sus,

Rul - er! Christ Je - sus, Lord God and Sav - ior!

84. O GOD, ALMIGHTY FATHER

1. O God, al-might-y Fa-ther, Cre-a-tor of all
2. O Je-sus, Word in-car-nate, Re-deem-er most a-
3. O God, the Ho-ly Spir-it, Who lives with-in our

1. things, The heav-ens stand in won-der, While
2. dored, All glo-ry, praise and hon-or Be
3. soul, Send forth thy light and lead us To

Refrain

1. earth thy glo-ry sings. O most ho-ly Trin-i-ty,
2. thine, our sov'reign Lord.
3. our e-ter-nal goal.

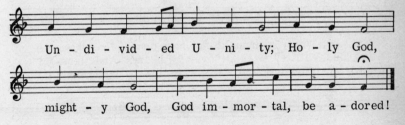

Un-di-vid-ed U-ni-ty; Ho-ly God,

might-y God, God im-mor-tal, be a-dored!

85. PRAISE THE LORD OF HEAVEN

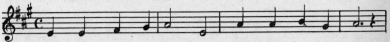

1. Praise the Lord of heav-en; Praise him in the height!
2. Praise the Lord, ye foun-tains Surg-ing from the seas,
3. Praise him, birds and cat-tle, Princ-es and all kings;

1. Praise him all ye an-gels; Praise him, stars and light;
2. Rocks and hills and moun-tains, Ce-dars and all trees;
3. Praise him, men and maid-ens, All cre-at-ed things;

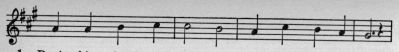

1. Praise him, clouds and wa - ters, All things in the skies;
2. Praise him, clouds and va - pors, Snow and hail and fire,
3. Glo - ri - ous and might - y Is . his name a - lone;

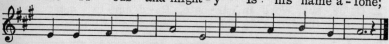

1. When his Word com-mand- ed, Struc-tured did a - rise.
2. Storm-y wind ful - fill-ing On - ly his de - sire.
3. Mak-ing earth his foot-stool, Mak - ing heav'n his throne.

86. NOW THANK WE ALL OUR GOD

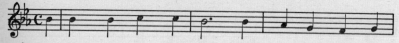

1. Now thank we all our God With heart and hands and
2. O may this gra - cious God Through all our life be
3. All praise and thanks to God The Fa - ther now be

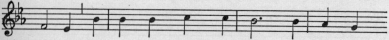

1. voic- es, Who won-drous things has done, In whom his
2. near us, With ev - er joy - ful hearts, And bless- ed
3. giv - en; The Son and Spir - it blest, Who reigns in

1. world re - joic-es; Who from our moth-er's arms Has
2. peace to cheer us; Pre-serve us in his grace, And
3. high-est heav-en, E - ter - nal, tri - une God, Whom

1. blessed us on our way With count - less
2. guide us in dis - tress, And free us
3. earth and heav'n a - dore; For thus it

1. gifts of love, And still is ours to _ day.
2. from all sin, Till heav - en we pos - sess.
3. was, is now, And shall be ev - er - more.

87. NOW THANK WE ALL OUR GOD

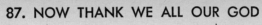
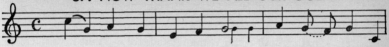

1. Now   thank we   all   our   God   with heart and hands and
2. Oh,—   may   this   gra-cious God   Through all our life   be
3. All —   praise   and   thanks   to   God The   Fa-ther —   now   be

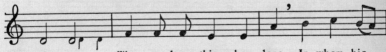

1. voic - es,   Who won-drous things has done, In whom his
2. near   us,   With ev - er   joy - ful hearts, And bless – ed
3. giv - en; The   Son   and ——   Spir - it   blest, Who reigns in

1. world re - joic - es;   Who from   our moth-er's arms Has
2. peace to   cheer   us;   Pre - serve   us   in his grace, And
3. high - est heav - en,   E - ter -   nal, Tri - une God, Whom

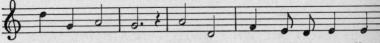

1. blessed   us   on   our   way   With   count - less
2. guide   us   in   dis - tress,   And   free   us
3. earth   and heav-en a - dore;   For   thus   it

1. gifts   of   love,   And——   still   is   ours   to - day.
2. from   all   sin,   Till——   heav- en   we   pos - sess.
3. was,   is   now,   And——   shall   be   ev - er - more.

88. ALL GLORY, PRAISE AND HONOR

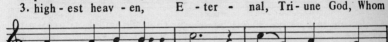

1.   All   glo - ry, praise, and   hon - or   To
2.   True King   art   thou, Lord   Je - sus   Of
3.   The saints and   an - gels praise thee,   While

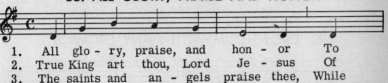

1.   thee, Re - deem - er   King!   To whom the lips   of
2.   Da - vid's roy - al   line!   Our King by right e-
3.   men   on   earth pro - claim   Thy rule of love and

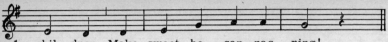

1. chil - dren Make sweet ho - san - nas ring!
2. ter - nal Both hu - man and di - vine!
3. mer - cy, In hearts that bless thy name!

Chorus

All glo-ry, praise, and hon-or to thee, Re-deem-er King!

To whom the lips of chil-dren make sweet ho-san-nas ring!

89. FROM ALL WHO DWELL BENEATH THE SKIES

1. From all who dwell be-neath the skies Let praise to
2. E - ter - nal are thy mer- cies, Lord, E - ter - nal,
3. Praise God, from whom all bless-ings flow. Praise him, all

1. our Cre - a - tor rise. Let praise to his great
2. too, thy ven-geance-sword; Thy praise shall sound from
3. crea-tures here be - low. Praise him a - bove, ye

1. name be sung Through ev - 'ry land, by ev -'ry tongue.
2. shore to shore Till suns shall rise and set no more.
3. heav'n-ly host. Praise Fa - ther, Son, and Ho - ly Ghost.

90. CROWN HIM WITH MANY CROWNS

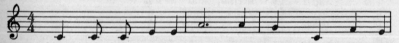

1. Crown him with man- y crowns, The Lamb up - on his
2. Crown him the Lord of love; Be - hold his hands and
3. Crown him the Lord of life, Who tri - umphed o'er the

1. throne; Hark! how   the heav'n-ly   an-them drowns All
2. side, Rich wounds, yet vis - i - ble a - bove, In
3. grave, And rose vic - to - rious in the strife For

1. mu - sic but its own; A - wake, my soul, and sing Of
2. beau- ty glo - ri-fied; His prais - es now we sing Who
3. those he came to save; All hail, Re-deem- er, hail! For

1. him who died for thee, And hail him as thy
2. died and rose on high, Who died, e - ter - nal
3. thou hast died for me; Thy praise shall nev - er,

1. lov - ing King Through all e - ter - ni - ty.
2. life to bring, And lives that death may die.
3. nev - er fail Through - out e - ter - ni - ty. A - men.

91. THE HEAV'NS DECLARE THY GLORY

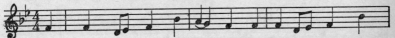

1. The heav'ns de-clare thy glo-ry, The fir-ma-ment thy
2. All heav'n on high re-joic-es To do its Mak-er's

1. pow'r; Day un - to day the sto - ry Re -
2. will; The stars with sol - emn voic - es Re -

1. peats from hour to hour; Night un - to night re -
2. sound thy prais - es still; So let my whole be -

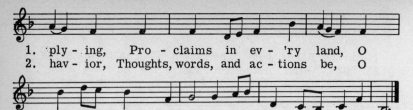

1. ply - ing, Pro - claims in ev - 'ry land, O
2. hav - ior, Thoughts, words, and ac - tions be, O

1. Lord, with voice un - dy - ing, The won - ders of thy hand.
2. Lord, my strength, my Sav - ior, One cease - less song to thee.

92. O PRAISE WE CHRIST OUR KING

1. O praise we Christ our King! the source of man's sal -
2. O hail, to Christ our King! we sing in ad - o -

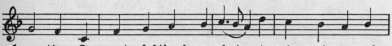

1. va - tion. Our grate - ful thanks we bring to sing in ex - ul -
2. ra - tion; The Cen - ter of all hearts, he pleads our con - se -

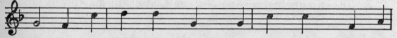

1. ta - tion. O Christ, our strength and ref - uge be as
2. cra - tion. To thee al - le - giance we pro - claim, O

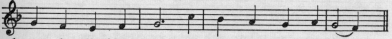

1. we in thy blest Name De - vote our lives to thee.
2. may thy king - dom come; Thy glo - ry is our aim.

93. PRAISE CHRIST JESUS, KING OF HEAVEN

1. Praise Christ Je - sus, King of heav - en; To his
2. Praise him for his grace and fa - vor To our
3. Fa - ther - like he tends and spares us; Well our
4. An - gels, help us to a - dore him; You be -

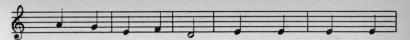

1. throne due trib - ute bring; Ran - somed, healed, re -
2. fa - thers in dis-tress; Praise him tru - ly
3. weak-ness-es he knows; In his hands he
4. hold him face to face; Sun and moon, bow

1. stored, for-giv - en, Grate - ful - ly your love now sing:
2. who is ev - er Slow to chide, and swift to bless:
3. gen - tly bears us, Res - cues us from all our foes.
4. down be- fore him, Dwell- ers all in time and space.

1. Al - le-lu - ia! Al-le-lu-ia! Praise the ev - er - last-ing King.
2. Al - le-lu - ia! Al-le-lu-ia! Glo - rious in his faith-ful-ness.
3. Al - le-lu - ia! Al-le-lu-ia! Wide - ly yet his mer - cy flows.
4. Al - le-lu - ia! Al-le-lu-ia! Praise with us the God of grace.

94. MAY THE GRACE OF CHRIST OUR SAVIOR

1. May the grace of Christ our Sav - ior And the Fa-ther's
2. Thus may we a- bide in un - ion With each oth - er

1. bound-less love, With the Ho - ly Spir- it's fa - vor,
2. and the Lord, And pos-sess, in sweet com - mun - ion,

1. Rest up - on us from a - bove.
2. Joys which earth can - not af - ford. A - men.

95. PRAISE THE LORD; YOU HEAV'NS ADORE HIM

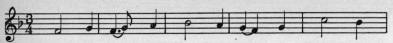

1. Praise the Lord; you heav'ns a-dore him; Praise him,
2. Praise the Lord, for he is glo-rious; Nev - er

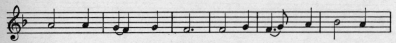

1. an - gels, in the height; Sun and moon, re - joice be-
2. shall his prom-ise fail: God has made his saints vic-

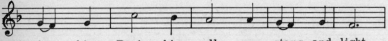

1. fore him; Praise him, all you stars and light.
2. to - rious; Sin and death shall not pre - vail.

1. Praise the Lord, for he has spo-ken; Worlds his
2. Praise the God of our sal-va-tion; Hosts on

1. might-y voice o - beyed: Laws which nev - er shall be
2. high, his pow'r pro-claim; Heav'n and earth and all cre-

1. bro - ken For their guid - ance he has made.
2. a - tion, Laud and mag - ni - fy his name.

96. PRAISE GOD FROM WHOM ALL BLESSINGS FLOW

Praise God from whom all bless-ings flow; Praise him,

all crea-tures here be-low; Praise him a-bove, ye

heav'n-ly host: Praise Fa-ther, Son, and Ho-ly Ghost. A-men.

97. HOLY GOD, WE PRAISE THY NAME

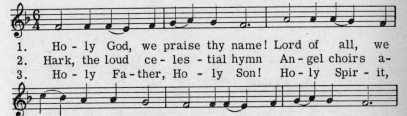

1. Ho-ly God, we praise thy name! Lord of all, we
2. Hark, the loud ce-les-tial hymn An-gel choirs a-
3. Ho-ly Fa-ther, Ho-ly Son! Ho-ly Spir-it,

1. bow be-fore thee! All on earth thy scep-tre 'claim,[1]
2. bove are rais-ing! Cher-u-bim and Ser-a-phim,
3. Three we name thee, While in es-sence on-ly One,

1. All in heaven a-bove a-dore thee. In-fi-nite thy
2. In un-ceas-ing cho-rus prais-ing, Fill the heavens with
3. Un-di-vid-ed God we 'claim thee; And a-dor-ing

1. vast do-main, Ev-er-last-ing is thy reign!
2. sweet ac-cord; Ho-ly, ho-ly, ho-ly Lord!
3. bend the knee, While we own the mys-ter-y.

[1] Abbreviated form for *acclaim* here and in verse three.

PSALMS

This selection of 33 psalms and a canticle offers choice excerpts from the psalter to be used for personal prayer or for parish recitation.

Following the precedent set in the psalter of *A Short Breviary*, the psalms are marked for singing according to given psalm tone melodies; an acute

accent indicates the syllable on which the rising inflection is made; a cir-
cumflex indicates the syllable on which the melody is lowered. The same
accents will hold for other psalm tones than those indicated; and by ignoring
the accents the psalms may be sung to other melodies or simply recited.

Some of the occasions on which these psalms could be used would be:

1. with the Offertory or Communion antiphon
2. at Bible vigils
3. for penance after confession
4. special parish devotions

> The first five "seasonal antiphons and psalms" are par-
> ticularly appropriate during Advent, Christmas, Lent,
> Easter, Pentecost (see also Nos. 110-115). In parish sing-
> ing it may at times be preferable to repeat the antiphon
> only after two or more verses of the psalm chanted by a
> cantor or choir group.

98. COME, LORD, DO NOT DELAY

Advent

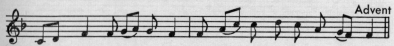

Come, Lord, do not de-lay! For-give the sins of your peo-ple.

6F

Ps. 24: Advent

1 To you I lĭft up my soul, *
    Ō Lord, my God.
2 In you I trust; let me not bē put to shame, *
    let not my enemies ēxult over me.
3 No one who waits for you shall bē put to shame; *
    those shall be put to shame who heedlēssly break faith.
4 Your ways, O Lord, mãke known to me; *
    teãch me your paths,
5 Guide me in your truth ānd teach me, *
    for you are Gõd my savior.
6 Remember that your compassīon, O Lord, *
    and your kindnēss are from of old.
7 The sins of my youth and my frailties rēmember not; *
    because of yoūr goodness, O Lord.
8 Good and uprĭght is the Lord; *
    that he shõws sinners the way.

9   He guides the humble tõ justice, *
      he teaches thē humble his way.

10   All the paths of the Lord are kindness ãnd constancy *
      toward those who keep his covenãnt and his decrees.

11   For your name's sāke, O Lord, *
      you will pardon my guilt, greãt as it is.

The Glory be to the Father . . . *may be added as the concluding verses
to any of the psalms or canticles.*

99. CHRIST IS BORN TO US

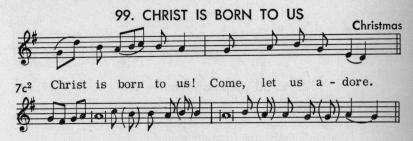

Christmas

7c² Christ is born to us! Come, let us a - dore.

Ps. 95: Christmas — Epiphany

1   Sing to the Lórd a new song; *
      sing to the Lórd, all you lands.

2   Sing to the Lórd; bless his name; *
      announce his salvátion, day after day.

3   Tell his glory amóng the nations; *
      among all peoples, hís wondrous deeds.

4   Splendor and majesty gó before him; *
      praise and grandeur are ín his sanctuary.

5   Give to the Lord, you fámilies of nations, *
      give to the Lord the glóry due his name!

6   Bring gifts, and énter his courts; *
      worship the Lord in hóly attire.

7   Tremble befóre him, all the earth; *
      say among the nátions: The Lord is king.

8   Let the heavens be glád and the earth rejoice; *
      let the sea and what fílls it resound;

9   Let the plaíns be joyful *
      and áll that is in them!

10   Then shall all the trees of the forest exúlt before the Lord, *
      for he cómes to rule the earth.

11   He shall rule the wórld with justice *
      and the peoples wíth his constancy.

100. WE ADORE YOU, O CHRIST

Lent

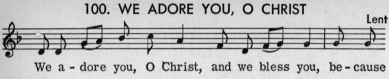

We a - dore you, O Christ, and we bless you, be - cause

by your ho - ly cross you have re - deemed the world.

Peregrinus

Ps. 50: Septuagesima — Lent

1 Have mercy on me, O God, in your goodness; *
   in the greatness of your compassion wipe out my offense.

2 Thoroughly wash me from my guilt *
   and of my sin cleanse me.

3 For I acknowledge my offense, *
   and my sin is before me always:

4 "Against you only have I sinned, *
   and done what is evil in your sight" —

5 Behold, you are pleased with sincerity of heart, *
   and in my inmost being you teach me wisdom.

6 Cleanse me of sin with hyssop, that I may be purified; *
   wash me, and I shall be whiter than snow.

7 Let me hear the sounds of joy and gladness; *
   the bones you have crushed shall rejoice.

8 Turn away your face from my sins, *
   and blot out all my guilt.

9 A clean heart create for me, O God, *
   and a steadfast spirit renew within me.

10 Cast me not out from your presence, *
    and your holy spirit take not from me.

11 Give me back the joy of your salvation, *
    and a willing spirit sustain in me.

12 O Lord, open my lips, *
    and my mouth shall proclaim your praise.

13 My sacrifice, O God, is a contrite spirit; *
    a heart contrite and humbled, O God, you will not spurn.

101. LIGHT FROM CHRIST RISEN

Easter

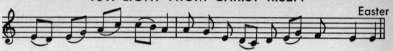

Light from Christ ris-en aid me to see the Fa-ther's glo-ry.

4g

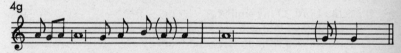

Ps. 117: Easter

1   Give thanks to the Lõrd, for he is good, *
    for his mercy endures forēver.

2   The joyful shout of victory in the tĕnts of the just: *
    "The right hand of the Lord has struck with pŏwer.

3   The right hand of the Lord ĭs exalted; *
    the right hand of the Lord has struck with pŏwer."

4   I shãll not die, but live *
    and declare the works of the Lõrd.

5   Though the Lord has indēed chastised me, *
    yet he has not delivered me to dĕath.

6   The stone which the buildĕrs rejected *
    has become the cornĕrstone.

7   By the Lõrd has this been done; *
    it is wonderful in our ēyes.

8   This is the dãy the Lord has made; *
    let us be glad and rejoice ĭn it.

9   Blessed is he who comes in the nãme of the Lord; *
    we bless you from the house of the Lõrd.

10 Give thanks to the Lõrd, for he is good; *
    for his kindness endures forēver.

102. THROUGH THE INDWELLING OF HIS SPIRIT

Pentecost

Through the in - dwell - ing of his Spir - it, God's love

floods in up - on us, Al - le - lu - ia.

1g²

Ps. 103: Pentecost

1 Bless the Lórd, O my soul! *
   O Lord, my God, yõu are great indeed!
2 You are clothed with májesty and glory, *
   robed in līght as with a cloak.
3 You have spread out the heavens líke a tent-cloth; *
   you have constructed your palace upõn the waters.
4 You make the cloúds your chariot; *
   you travel on the wīngs of the wind.
5 You make the wínds your messengers, *
   and flaming fīre your ministers.
6 How manifold áre your works, O Lord! *
   In wisdom you have wrought them all — the earth is full õf
      your creatures;
7 The sea álso, great and wide, *
   in which are schools without number
      of living thīngs both small and great.
8 Théy all look to you *
   to give them foõd in due time.
9 When you give it to thém, they gather it; *
   when you open your hand, they are fīlled with good things.
10 If you hide your fáce, they are dismayed; *
   if you take away their breath, they perish and return tõ their
      dust.
11 When you send forth your spirit, they áre created, *
   and you renew the face õf the earth.
12 May the glory of the Lord endúre forever; *
   may the Lord be glad īn his works!

103. ALLELUIA, ALLELUIA, ALLELUIA

Al - le - lu - ia, al - le - lu - ia, al - le - lu - ia.

6F

Ps. 1

1 Happy the man whō follows not *
   the counsels ōf the wicked

2 Nor walks in the way ōf sinners, *
   nor sits in the company ōf the insolent, *

3 But delights in the lāw of the Lord *
   and meditates on his lāw day and night.

4 He is like a tree planted near runnīng water, *
   that yields its fruit īn due season,

5 And whose leāves never fade. *
   Whatever hē does, prospers.

6 Not so the wickēd, not so; *
   they are like chaff which thē wind drives away.

7 Therefore in judgment the wickēd shall not stand, *
   nor shall sinners, in the assemblȳ of the just.

8 For the Lord watches over the wāy of the just, *
   but the way of the wīcked vanishes.

9 Glory be to the Father ānd to the Son *
   and to the Hōly Spirit;

10 As it was in the beginning, is now and evēr shall be, *
   world wīthout end. Amen.

104. WITHOUT CEASING WE SHALL ADORE

With - out ceasing we shall a - dore

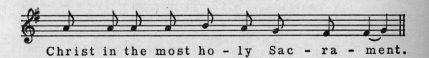

Christ in the most ho - ly Sac - ra - ment.

7c

Ps. 102

1   Bless the Lórd, O my soul; *
     and all my being, bléss his holy name.

2   Bless the Lórd, O my soul, *
     and forget not áll his benefits;

3   He pardons all yoúr iniquities, *
     he heáls all your ills.

4   He redeems your life fróm destruction, *
     he crowns you with kindness ánd compassion.

5   He fills your lífetime with good; *
     your youth is renewed líke the eagle's.

6   The Lord sécures justice *
     and the rights of áll the oppressed.

7   Merciful and grácious is the Lord, *
     slow to anger and aboúnding in kindness.

8   He will nót always chide, *
     nor does he keep his wráth forever.

9   Not according to our sins does hé deal with us, *
     nor does he requite us accórding to our crimes.

10   For as the heavens are hígh above the earth *
     so surpassing is his kindness toward thóse who fear him.

11   As far as the eást is from the west, *
     so far has he put our transgréssions from us.

12   As a father has compassion ón his children, *
     so the Lord has compassion on thóse who fear him,

13   For he knóws how we are formed; *
     he remembers thát we are dust.

14   Man's days áre like those of grass; *
     like a flower of thé field he blooms;

15   The wind sweeps over hím and he is gone, *
     and his place knóws him no more.

16   But the kindness of the Lord is from éternity *
     to eternity toward thóse who fear him,

17   And his justice toward chíldren's children *
     among those who keép his precepts.

18   Glory be to the Father ánd to the Son *
     and to the Hóly Spirit;

19   As it was in the beginning, is now and éver shall be, *
     world withóut end. Amen.

105. CHRIST HAS CONQUERED

Christ has con - quered! Christ is reign - ing! O - ver all Christ now is King!

106. CHRIST, THE KING OF KINGS

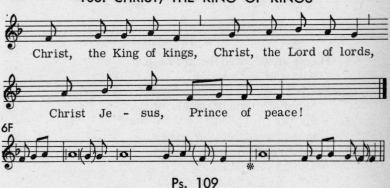

Christ, the King of kings, Christ, the Lord of lords,

Christ Je - sus, Prince of peace!

6F

Ps. 109

1 The Lord said to my Lord: "Sit at mȳ right hand *
   till I make your enemiẽs your footstool."

2 The sceptre of your power the Lord will stretch forth frõm Sion: *
   "Rule in the midst õf your enemies.

3 Yours is princely power in the day of your birth, in holȳ splendor; *
   before the daystar, like the dew, I hãve begotten you."

4 The Lord has sworn, and he wīll not repent: *
   "You are a priest forever, according to the order õf Melchisedech."

5 The Lord is at yoūr right hand; *
   he will crush kings on the dãy of his wrath.

6 He will do judgment on the nations, heaping ūp corpses; *
   he will crush heads ovẽr the wide earth.

7 From the brook by the waysīde he will drink; *
   therefore will hẽ lift up his head.

8 Glory be to the Father ãnd to the Son *
   and to the Hõly Spirit;

9 As it was in the b̃eginning, is now and evẽr shall be, *
   world wīthout end. Amen.

107. WHERE TRUE CHARITY AND LOVE DWELL

Where true char-i-ty and love dwell, sure-ly God is there.
U - bi ca-ri-tas et a-mor De-us i-bi est.

6F

Ps. 127

1 Happy are you whõ fear the Lord, *
   who wãlk in his ways!

2 For you shall eat the fruit of yoũr handiwork; *
   happy shall you bẽ, and favored.

3 Your wife shall be like ã fruitful vine *
   in the recesses õf your home;

4 Your children lĩke olive plants *
   aroũnd your table.

5 Behold, thus is thẽ man blessed *
   whõ fears the Lord.

6 The Lord bless you frõm Sion: *
   may you see the prosperity of Jerusalem
   all the dãys of your life;

7 May you see your childrẽn's children, *
   Peace be ũpon Israel.

8 Glory be to the Father ãnd to the Son *
   and to the Hõly Spirit;

9 As it was in the beginning, is now and evẽr shall be, *
   world wĩthout end. Amen.

Ps. 130

1 O Lord, my heãrt is not proud, *
   nor are mỹ eyes haughty;

2 I busy not myself wĩth great things, *
   nor with things toõ sublime for me.

3   Nay, rather, I have stilled ānd quieted *
     my soul līke a weaned child.

4   Like a weaned child on īts mother's lap, *
     so is my soūl within me.

5   O Israel, hōpe in the Lord, *
     both now ānd forever.

6   Glory be to the Father ānd to the Son *
     and to the Hōly Spirit;

7   As it was in the beginning, is now and evēr shall be, *
     world wīthout end. Amen.

Ps. 132

1   Behold, how good it is, and hōw pleasant, *
     where brethren dwēll in unity!

2   It is as when the precious ointment ūpon the head *
     runs down over the beard, the beārd of Aaron,

3   Till īt runs down *
     upon the cōllar of his robe.

4   It is a dew like that ōf Hermon, *
     which comes down upon the mountaīns of Sion;

5   For there the Lord has pronounced hīs blessing, *
     līfe forever.

6   Glory be to the Father ānd to the Son *
     and to the Hōly Spirit;

7   As it was in the beginning, is now and evēr shall be, *
     world wīthout end. Amen.

Ps. 133

1   Come, bless the Lord, all you servānts of the Lord *
     who stand in the house of the Lord
     during thē hours of night.

2   Lift up your hands toward thē sanctuary, *
     ānd bless the Lord.

3   May the Lord bless you frōm Sion, *
     the maker ōf heaven and earth.

4   Glory be to the Father ānd to the Son *
     and to the Hōly Spirit;

5   As it was in the beginning, is now and evēr shall be, *
     world wīthout end. Amen.

108. PRAISE BE TO YOU, O LORD, KING OF GLORY

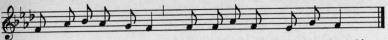

Praise be to you, O Lord, King of glo-ry, King a-dored!

2d

Ps. 144

1 I will extol you, O my Gód and King, *
    and I will bless your name forever ãnd ever.

2 Every day will I bléss you, *
    and I will praise your name forever ãnd ever.

3 Great is the Lord and highly tó be praised; *
    his greatness is ũnsearchable.

4 Generation after generation praises yoúr works *
    and proclaĩms your might.

5 The Lord is gracious and mérciful, *
    slow to anger and of greãt kindness.

6 The Lord is goód to all *
    and compassionate toward ãll his works.

7 The Lord is faithful in áll his words *
    and holy ĩn all his works.

8 The Lord lifts up all who are fálling *
    and raises up all who ãre bowed down.

9 The eyes of all look hopefully tó you, *
    and you give them their food ĩn due season;

10 You open yoúr hand *
    and satisfy the desire of every lĩving thing.

11 The Lord is just in áll his ways *
    and holy ĩn all his works.

12 The Lord is near to all who call upón him, *
    to all who call upon hĩm in truth.

13 He fulfills the desire of those who feár him, *
    he hears their cry ãnd saves them.

14 The Lord keeps all who lóve him, *
    but all the wicked hẽ will destroy.

15 May my mouth speak the praise óf the Lord, *
    and may all flesh bless his holy nãme forever.

16   Glory be to the Father and tó the Son *
       and to the Hōly Spirit;

17   As it was in the beginning, is now and ever sháll be, *
       world without ēnd. Amen.

109. THE LORD HAS DONE GREAT THINGS FOR ME

The Lord has done great things for me, and ho-ly is his name.

7c²

The Magnificat
Luke 1:46-55

1   My soul mágnifies the Lord, *
      and my spirit rejoices in Gód my savior,

2   Because he has regarded the lowliness óf his handmaid, *
      for behold, henceforth all generations shall cáll me blessed.

3   Because he who is mighty has dóne great things for me, *
      and hóly is his name:

4   And his mercy is from generation to géneration *
      toward thóse who fear him.

5   He has shown míght with his arm; *
      he has scattered the proud in the conceít of their heart.

6   He has put down the míghty from their thrones *
      and has exálted the lowly.

7   The hungry he has fílled with good things *
      and the rich he has sent émpty away.

8   He has given help to Israél his servant, *
      mindful óf his mercy —

9   As he prómised our fathers — *
      toward Abraham and his descéndants forever.

10   Glory be to the Fáther and to the Son *
       and to the Hóly Spirit;

11   As it was in the beginning, is now and éver shall be, *
       world wíthout end. Amen.

7a

110. RESTORE US, O GOD OUR SAVIOR
Ps. 84: Advent

1   Restore us, O Gód our savior, *
    and abandon your displeásure against us.
2   Show us, O Lórd, your kindness, *
    and grant us yoúr salvation.
3   I will heár what God proclaims; *
    the Lord — for hé proclaims peace
4   To his people, and tó his faithful ones, *
    and to those who pút in him their hope.
5   Near indeed is his salvation to thóse who fear him, *
    glory dwélling in our land.
6   Kíndness and truth shall meet; *
    jústice and peace shall kiss.
7   Truth shall spring oút of the earth, *
    and justice shall look dówn from heaven.
8   The Lord himself will gíve his benefits; *
    our land shall yiéld its increase.
9   Justice shall wálk before him, *
    and salvation, along the wáy of his steps.

1f

111. O GOD, WITH YOUR JUDGMENT ENDOW THE KING
Ps. 71: Christmas — Epiphany

1   O God, with your júdgment endow the king, *
    and with your justîce, the king's son;
2   He shall govern your peóple with justice *
    and your afflicted õnes with judgment.
3   He shall be like rain coming dówn on the meadow, *
    like showers watēring the earth.
4   Justice shall flówer in his days, *
    and profound peace, till the moõn be no more.
5   May he rúle from sea to sea, *
    and from the River to the ēnds of the earth.
6   The kings of Tharsis and the Ísles shall offer gifts; *
    the kings of Arabia and Saba shāll bring tribute.

7   All kings shall páy him homage, *
    all natiõns shall serve him.

8   For he shall rescue the poor man whén he cries out, *
    and the afflicted when he has no õne to help him.

9   He shall have pity for the lówly and the poor; *
    the lives of the poõr he shall save.

10 May his name be bléssed forever; *
    as long as the sun his nãme shall remain.

11 In him shall all the tribes of the eárth be blessed; *
    all the nations shall proclãim his happiness.

12 Blessed be the Lord, the Gód of Israel, *
    who alone dões wondrous deeds.

13 And blessed forever be his glórious name; *
    may the whole earth be filled wĩth his glory.

8G

112. YOU WHO DWELL IN THE SHELTER OF THE MOST HIGH
Ps. 90: Septuagesima — Lent

1   You who dwell in the shelter of the Móst High, *
    who abide in the shadow of thẽ Almighty,

2   Say to the Lord, "My refuge and my fórtress, *
    my Gõd, in whom I trust."

3   With his pinions he will cóver you, *
    and under his wings yõu shall take refuge;

4   Because you have the Lord for your réfuge; *
    you have made the Most Hĩgh your stronghold.

5   No evil shall befáll you, *
    nor shall afflictiõn come near your tent,

6   For to his angels he has given command abóut you, *
    that they guard yõu in all your ways.

7   Upon their hands they shall beár you up, *
    lest you dash your foõt against a stone.

8   You shall tread upon the asp and the víper; *
    you shall trample down the lion ãnd the dragon.

9   Because he clings to me, I will delíver him; *
    I will set him on high because he acknowlẽdges my name.

10 He shall call upon me, and I will ánswer him; *
    I will be wĩth him in distress;

11 I will deliver him and glorifý him; *
    with length of days I will gratify him and will show him mỹ
    salvation.

7c

113. OUT OF THE DEPTHS I CRY TO YOU, O LORD
Ps. 129: Septuagesima — Lent

1   Out of the depths I crý to you, O Lord; *
     Lórd, hear my voice!
2   Let your éars be attentive *
     to my voice in súpplication:
3   If you, O Lord, márk iniquities, *
     Lórd, who can stand?
4   But with yoú is forgiveness, *
     that yoú may be revered.
5   I trúst in the Lord; *
     my soul trústs in his word.
6   My soul waíts for the Lord *
     more than sentinels waít for the dawn.
7   More than sentinels waít for the dawn, *
     let Israel waít for the Lord,
8   For with the Lórd is kindness *
     and with him is plenteóus redemption;
9   And he will redeém Israel *
     from áll their iniquities.

2d

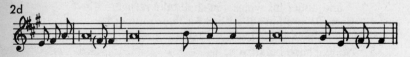

114. SHOUT JOYFULLY TO GOD, ALL YOU ON EARTH
Ps. 65: Easter

1   Shout joyfully to God, all yoú on earth, *
     sing praise to the glory õf his name;
2   Proclaim his glorious praise. Sáy to God, *
     "How tremendous ãre your deeds!"
3   Let all on earth worship and sing praíse to you, *
     sing praise tõ your name.
4   Come and see the wórks of God, *
     his tremendous deeds ãmong men,
5   He has given life to oúr souls, *
     and has not let oũr feet slip.

6 For you have tested ús, O God! *
   You have tried us as silver īs tried by fire.
7 We went through fire and wáter, *
   but you have led us out to rēfreshment.
8 Hear now, all you who feár God, *
   while I declare what he has dõne for me.
9 God has heard; he has listened to the sound óf my prayer. *
   He refused me not my prayer or hīs kindness.

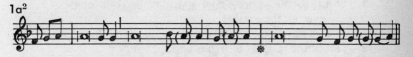

115. THE LORD IS MY LIGHT AND MY SALVATION
Ps. 26: Pentecost

1 The Lord is my light and mý salvation; *
   whõm should I fear?
2 The Lord is mý life's refuge; *
   of whom shoūld I be afraid?
3 Though an army encámp against me, *
   my heãrt will not fear;
4 Though war be wáged upon me, *
   even thēn will I trust.
5 One thing I ásk of the Lord; *
   thīs do I seek:
6 To dwell in the hoúse of the Lord *
   all the dãys of my life,
7 That I may gaze on the lóveliness of the Lord *
   and contemplãte his temple.
8 For he will hide me ín his abode *
   in the dãy of trouble;
9 He will conceal me in the shélter of his tent, *
   he will set me hīgh upon a rock.
10 Of you my heart speaks; yoú my glance seeks; *
   your presēnce, O Lord, I seek.
11 Hide nót your face from me; *
   do not in anger repēl your servant.
12 You are my helper: cást me not off; *
   forsake me not, O Gõd my savior.
13 Though my father and my móther forsake me, *
   yet will the Lõrd receive me.

1g³

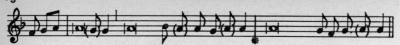

116. O LORD, HOW GLORIOUS IS YOUR NAME
OVER ALL THE EARTH
Ps. 8

1   O Lord, our Lord, how glorious is your name
    óver all the earth!*
    You have exalted your majesty abõve the heavens.

2   Out of the mouths of bábes and sucklings *
    you hãve fashioned praise.

3   When I behold your heavens, the wórk of your fingers, *
    the moon and the stars whĭch you set in place —

4   What is man that you should be míndful of him, *
    or the son of man that yõu should care for him?

5   You have made him little léss than the angels, *
    and crowned him with glorȳ and honor.

6   You have given him rule over the wórks of your hands, *
    putting all things ũnder his feet:

7   All sheép and oxen, *
    yes, and the beãsts of the field,

8   The birds of the air, the físhes of the sea, *
    and whatever swims the pãths of the seas.

9   Ó Lord, our Lord, *
    how glorious is your name õver all the earth!

2d

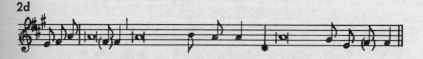

117. THE HEAVENS DECLARE THE GLORY OF GOD
Ps. 18

1   The heavens declare the glory óf God, *
    and the firmament proclaims hĭs handiwork.

2   Day pours out the wórd to day, *
    and night to night impãrts knowledge;

3   Not a word nor a díscourse *
    whose voice ĭs not heard;

4   Through all the earth their voíce resounds, *
       and to the ends of the world, theîr message.

5   The law of the Lord is pérfect, *
       refreshĭng the soul;

6   The decree of the Lord is trustwórthy, *
       giving wisdom to thē simple.

7   The precepts of the Lórd are right, *
       rejoicĭng the heart;

8   The command of the Lórd is clear, *
       enlightēning the eye;

9   The fear of the Lórd is pure, *
       enduring fŏrever;

10   The ordinances of the Lórd are true, *
       all ŏf them just;

11   They are more precious thán gold, *
       than a heap ŏf purest gold;

12   Sweeter also than sýrup *
       or honēy from the comb.

13   Though your servant is careful óf them, *
       very diligent ĭn keeping them,

14   Yet who can detect faílings? *
       Cleanse me from mȳ unknown faults!

15   From wanton sin especially, restrain your sérvant; *
       let it not rūle over me.

16   Then shall I be blameless and ínnocent *
       ŏf serious sin.

17   Let the words of my mouth and the thought of my heart
       find favor befóre you, *
       O Lord, my rock and my rēdeemer.

8G*

118. THE LORD IS MY SHEPHERD
Ps. 22

1   The Lord is my shepherd; I sháll not want.*
       In verdant pastures he gīves me repose;

2   Beside restful waters he leáds me; *
       he refrēshes my soul.

3 He guides me in ríght paths *
   fõr his name's sake.
4 Even though I walk in the dark válley *
   I fear no evil; for yõu are at my side
5 With your rod and yoúr staff *
   that gĭve me courage.
6 You spread the table befóre me *
   in the sĭght of my foes;
7 You anoint my heád with oil; *
   mỹ cup overflows.
8 Only goodness and kindness fóllow me *
   all the dãys of my life;
9 And I shall dwell in the house óf the Lord *
   fõr years to come.

8G

119. I WILL BLESS THE LORD AT ALL TIMES
Ps. 33

1 I will bless the Lord at áll times; *
   his praise shall be ẽver in my mouth.
2 Let my soul glory ín the Lord; *
   the lowly will heãr me and be glad.
3 Glorify the Lórd with me, *
   together let ũs extol his name.
4 I sought the Lord, and he ánswered me *
   and delivered mẽ from all my fears.
5 Look to him that you may be radiant wíth joy, *
   and your faces mãy not blush with shame.
6 Taste and see how good the Lórd is; *
   happy the man who takes rẽfuge in him.
7 Fear the Lord, you his hóly ones, *
   for naught is lacking to thõse who fear him.
8 The great grow poor and húngry; *
   but those who seek the Lord wãnt for no good thing.
9 Come, children, heár me; *
   I will teach you the feãr of the Lord.

10   Which of you desíres life, *
       and takes delight in prŏsperous days?

11   Keep your tongue from évil *
       and your lĭps from speaking guile;

12   Turn from evil, and dó good; *
       seek peace, and fŏllow after it.

13   The Lord has eyes fór the just, *
       and eărs for their cry.

14   The Lord confronts the evildóers, *
       to destroy remembrance õf them from the earth.

15   When the just cry out, the Lord heárs them, *
       and from all their distrĕss he rescues them.

16   The Lord is close to the brokenheárted; *
       and those who are crushed in spĭrit he saves.

17   Many are the troubles of the júst man, *
       but out of them all the Lõrd delivers him.

5

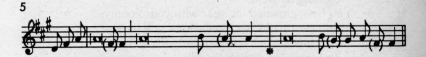

120. O GOD, YOU ARE MY GOD WHOM I SEEK
Ps. 62

1   O God, you are my Gód whom I seek; *
       for you my flesh pines and my soul thirsts like the earth,
       parched, lifeless and wíthout water.

2   Thus have I gazed toward you in the sánctuary *
       to see your power ánd your glory,

3   For your kindness is a greáter good than life; *
       my lips shall glórify you.

4   Thus will I bléss you while I live; *
       lifting up my hands, I will cáll upon your name.

5   As with the riches of a banquet shall my soúl be satisfied, *
       and with exultant lips my moúth shall praise you.

6   I will remember yoú upon my couch, *
       and through the night-watches I will méditate on you:

7   That yoú are my help, *
       and in the shadow of your wíngs I shout for joy.

8   My soúl clings fast to you; *
       your right hánd upholds me.

Peregrinus

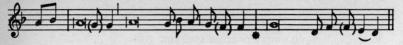

121. TO YOU WE OWE OUR HYMN OF PRAISE
Ps. 64

1 To you wē owe our hymn of praise, *
   O God, īn Sion;
2 You have visited thē land and watered it; *
   greatly have you ēnriched it.
3 God's watērcourses are filled; *
   you have prēpared the grain.
4 Thus have you prepared the land: drēnching its furrows, *
   breakīng up its clods,
5 Softenīng it with showers, *
   blessīng its yield.
6 You have crowned the yeār with your bounty, *
   and your paths overflow with a rīch harvest;
7 The untilled meadōws overflow with it, *
   and rejoicīng clothes the hills.
8 The fields are garmented with flocks
   and the vallēys blanketed with grain. *
   They shout ānd sing for joy.

7a

122. MAY GOD HAVE PITY ON US AND BLESS US
Ps. 66

1 May God have pity ón us and bless us; *
   may he let his face shíne upon us.
2 So may your way be knówn upon earth; *
   among all nations, yoúr salvation.
3 May the peoples praíse you, O God; *
   may all the peóples praise you!
4 May the nations be glád and exult *
   because you rule the peóples in equity;

5   May the peoples praíse you, O God; *
        may all the peóples praise you!
6   The earth has yiélded its fruits; *
        God, our Gód, has blessed us.
7   Máy God bless us, *
        and may all the énds of the earth fear him!

8c

123. HOW LOVELY IS YOUR DWELLING-PLACE
Ps. 83

1   How lovely is your dwélling-place, *
        Ō Lord of hosts!
2   My soul yeárns and pines *
        for the coūrts of the Lord.
3   My heart and mý flesh *
        cry out fōr the living God.
4   Even the sparrow fínds a home, *
        and the swallow a nest in whīch she puts her young —
5   Your altars, O Lórd of hosts, *
        my Kīng and my God!
6   Happy they who dwell in yoúr house! *
        continuallý they praise you.
7   O Lord of hosts, heár my prayer; *
        hearken, O Gōd of Jacob!
8   O God, behóld our shield, *
        and look upon the face of yoūr anointed.
9   I had rather one day ín your courts *
        than a thoūsand elsewhere;
10   I had rather lie at the threshold of the house óf my God *
        than dwell in the tents ōf the wicked.
11   For a sun and a shield is the Lórd God; *
        grace and glorȳ he bestows;
12   The Lord withholds no goód thing *
        from those who walk īn sincerity.
13   O Lórd of hosts, *
        happy the mēn who trust in you!

1g

124. THE LORD IS KING, IN SPLENDOR ROBED
Ps. 92

1 The Lord is kíng, in splendor robed; *
   robed is the Lord and gĩrt about with strength;
2 And he has máde the world firm, *
   nõt to be moved.
3 Your throne stands fírm from of old; *
   from everlastĩng you are, O Lord.
4 The floods lift up, O Lord, the floóds lift up their voice; *
   the floods lift ũp their tumult.
5 More powerful than the roar of many waters,
      more powerful than the breákers of the sea — *
   powerful on hĩgh is the Lord.
6 Your decrees are wórthy of trust indeed; *
   holiness befits your house, O Lõrd, for length of days.

1a

125. SING TO THE LORD A NEW SONG
Ps. 97: Marian Feasts

1 Sing to the Lórd a new song, *
   for he hãs done wondrous deeds;
2 His right hand has won víctory for him, *
   hĩs holy arm.
3 The Lord has máde his salvation known: *
   in the sight of the nations he has reveãled his justice.
4 All the énds of the earth have seen *
   the salvãtion by our God.
5 Sing joyfully to the Lórd, all you lands; *
   break ĩnto song; sing praise.
6 Sing praise to the Lórd with the harp, *
   with the harp and melõdious song.
7 With trumpets and the soúnd of the horn *
   sing joyfully befõre the King, the Lord.

8   Let the sea and what fílls it resound, *
       the world and thõse who dwell in it;

9   Let the rívers clap their hands, *
       the mountains shoût with them for joy

10   Before the Lórd, for he comes, *
       for he cõmes to rule the earth;

11   He will rule the wórld with justice *
       and the peoplẽs with equity.

8c

126. PRAISE THE LORD, ALL YOU NATIONS
Ps. 116

1   Praise the Lord, all you nátions, *
       sing his glory, āll you peoples.

2   For he has proven to us his loving-kíndness, *
       the Lord is true to his wõrd forever.

3   Glory be to the Father and tó the Son, *
       and to the Hõly Spirit.

4   As it was in the beginning, is now and ever sháll be, *
       world withoût end. Amen.

6F

127. HOW I LOVE YOUR LAW, O LORD!
Ps. 118

1   How I love yoûr law, O Lord! *
       It is my meditãtion all the day.

2   Your command has made me wiser than mỹ enemies, *
       for it is ẽver with me.

3   I have more understanding than all mỹ teachers *
       when your decrees are my mẽditation.

4   I have more discernment than thẽ elders, *
       because I obsẽrve your precepts.

5   From every evil way I wĩthhold my feet, *
       that Ĩ may keep your words.

6   From your ordinances I tŭrn not away, *
     for you hãve instructed me.

7   How sweet to my palate are yoŭr promises, *
     sweeter than hõney to my mouth!

8   Through your precepts I gain dĭscernment; *
     therefore I hate evẽry false way.

9   Oh, that I might be fĭrm in the ways *
     of keepĭng your statutes!

10   Happy are they who obsẽrve his decrees, *
     who seek him wĭth all their heart,

11   Happy are they whose wãy is blameless, *
     who walk in the lãw of the Lord.

7c²

128. GIVE THANKS TO THE LORD, FOR HE IS GOOD
Ps. 135

1   Give thanks to the Lórd, for he is good, *
     for his mercy endúres forever;

2   Give thánks to the God of gods, *
     for his mercy endúres forever;

3   Give thánks to the Lord of lords, *
     for his mercy endúres forever.

4   Who alóne does great wonders, *
     for his mercy endúres forever;

5   Who made the heávens in wisdom, *
     for his mercy endúres forever;

6   Who spread out the earth upón the waters, *
     for his mercy endúres forever;

7   Who máde the great lights, *
     for his mercy endúres forever;

8   The sun to rule óver the day, *
     for his mercy endúres forever;

9   The moon and the stars to rule óver the night, *
     for his mercy endúres forever.

10   Who remembered us ín our abjection, *
     for his mercy endúres forever;

11   And freed ús from our foes, *
     for his mercy endúres forever.

12 Who gives foód to all flesh, *
      for his mercy endúres forever.
13 Give thanks to the Gód of heaven, *
      for his mercy endūres forever.

4g

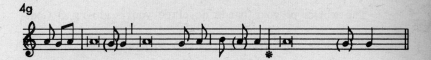

129. PRAISE THE LORD IN HIS SANCTUARY
Ps. 150

1 Praise the Lord in his sãnctuary, *
      praise him in the firmament of hĭs strength.
2 Praise him fŏr his mighty deeds, *
      praise him for his sovereign majĕsty.
3 Praise him with the blast õf the trumpet, *
      praise him with lyre ãnd harp.
4 Praise him with tĭmbrel and dance, *
      praise him with strings ãnd pipe.
5 Praise him with soŭnding cymbals, *
      praise him with clanging cymbãls.
6 Let everythĩng that has breath *
      praise thẽ Lord!

130. BLESSED IS HE WHO DELIGHTS IN THE LAW
Gelineau Ps. 1

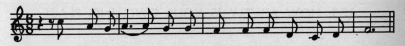

Bless-ed is he   who de-lights in the law of the Lord.

Text and melody for the psalms accompanying these antiphons are given in **Thirty Psalms and Two Canticles** for Gelineau Pss. 1, 18, 33, 83, 84, 95, 150; in **Twenty-four Psalms and a Canticle** for Gelineau Pss. 8, 22, 23, 41, 50, 94, 99, 122, 125, 129, 135, Luke 1:46-54; both books are available from: Gregorian Institute of America, 2132 Jefferson Avenue, Toledo, Ohio.

131. THE WORKS OF YOUR HANDS
Gelineau Ps. 18a

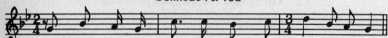

The works of your hands de-clare your glo-ry, O God.

132. TEACH ME TO DO YOUR WILL
Gelineau Ps. 18b

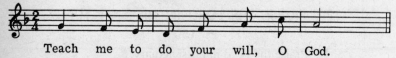

Teach me to do your will, O God.

133. LET US GLORIFY THE LORD
Gelineau Ps. 33

Let us glo-ri-fy the Lord and ex-alt his name for ev-er.

134. TASTE AND SEE
Gelineau Ps. 33

Taste and see that the Lord is good.

135. HOW LOVELY IS YOUR DWELLING PLACE
Gelineau Ps. 83

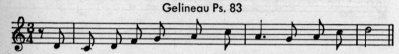

How love-ly is your dwell-ing place, O Lord of hosts.

136. SHOW US YOUR MERCY, O LORD
Gelineau Ps. 84

Show us your mer-cy, O Lord, and give us your sav-ing help.

137. BRING AN OFFERING
Gelineau Ps. 95

Bring an of - fer - ing and en - ter his courts:

in his tem - ple wor - ship the Lord.

138. LET EVERYTHING THAT LIVES PRAISE THE LORD
Gelineau Ps. 150

Let ev - 'ry - thing that lives praise the Lord.

139. HOW GREAT IS YOUR NAME, O LORD
Gelineau Ps. 8

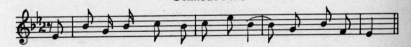

How great is your name, O Lord our God, through all the earth!

140. MY SHEPHERD IS THE LORD
Gelineau Ps. 22

My shep-herd is the Lord, noth-ing in-deed shall I want.

141. HIS GOODNESS SHALL FOLLOW ME ALWAYS
Gelineau Ps. 22

His good-ness shall fol-low me al-ways, to the end of my days.

142. SEEK THE FACE OF THE LORD
Gelineau Ps. 23

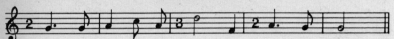

Seek the face of the Lord, and yearn for him.

143. MY SOUL IS THIRSTING FOR THE LORD
Gelineau Ps. 41

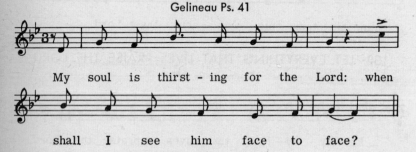

My soul is thirst-ing for the Lord: when

shall I see him face to face?

144. HAVE MERCY, LORD
Gelineau Ps. 50

Have mer-cy, Lord; cleanse me from all my sins.

145. O COME, LET US WORSHIP
Gelineau Ps. 94

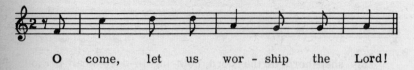

O come, let us wor-ship the Lord!

146. ARISE, COME TO YOUR GOD
Gelineau Ps. 99

A-rise, come to your God, sing him your songs of re-joic-ing.

147. WE LIFT OUR EYES TO THE LORD
Gelineau Ps. 122

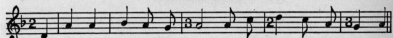

We lift our eyes to the Lord till he show us his mer-cy.

148. THOSE WHO SOW IN TEARS AND SORROW
Gelineau Ps. 125

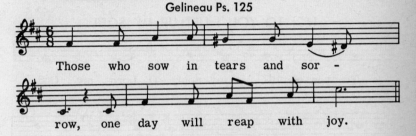

Those who sow in tears and sor -

row, one day will reap with joy.

149. I PLACE ALL MY TRUST IN YOU
Gelineau Ps. 129

I place all my trust in you, my

God: all my hope is in your mer - cy.

150. FOR HIS GREAT LOVE IS WITHOUT END
Gelineau Ps. 135

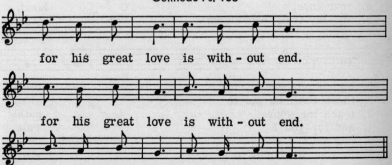

for his great love is with - out end.

for his great love is with - out end.

for his great love is with - out end.

151. THE LORD HAS DONE MARVELS FOR ME
Gelineau Magnificat (Luke 1:46-54)

The Lord has done mar-vels for me: ho-ly—— is his name.

152. TO YOU I LIFT UP MY SOUL

All

To you I lift up my soul, O Lord my God.

Choir

1. In you, O God, I trust!
2. No one who waits for you
3. Your way, O Lord,
4. For you are God,
5. Remember that your com-pas-sion,
6. The sins of my youth

1. Let me not be put to shame;
2. shall be put to shame;
3. make known to me,
4. God my sav-ior;
5. your love, O Lord,
6. and my frailties remem-ber not;

1. let not my en- e- mies
2. those shall be put to shame
3. teach me your paths;
4. and for you I wait
5. and your kind- ness
6. in your kindness remember me

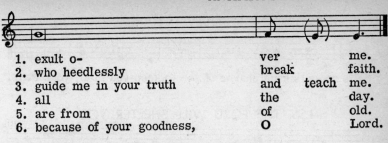

1. exult o-	ver	me.
2. who heedlessly	break	faith.
3. guide me in your truth	and teach	me.
4. all	the	day.
5. are from	of	old.
6. because of your goodness,	O	Lord.

153. THE LORD WILL GIVE US HIS BLESSING

All

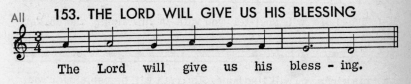

The Lord will give us his bless - ing.

154. THE LORD HIMSELF WILL GIVE US GOOD THINGS

All

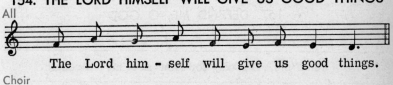

The Lord him - self will give us good things.

Choir

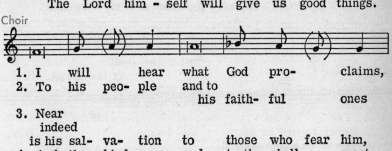

1. I will hear what God pro- claims,
2. To his peo- ple and to
    his faith- ful ones
3. Near
   indeed
   is his sal- va- tion to those who fear him,
4. And then kind- ness and truth shall meet
5. Truth
   shall spring from out the earth,

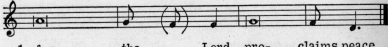

1. for	the	Lord pro-	claims peace
2. and	to	those who put	
		in him their	hope.
3. glo-	ry	dwel- ling in	our land —
4. justice	and	peace, they	shall kiss;
5. and justice	shall	look down	from heaven.

155. HIS ANGELS HAVE CHARGE OF YOU

All

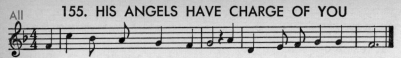

His an-gels have charge of you to keep you in all your ways.

156. THE LORD WILL SHELTER YOU

All

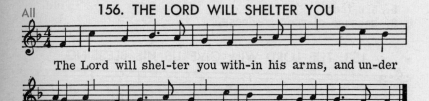

The Lord will shel-ter you with-in his arms, and un-der

his wings you will find hope. His truth will be a shield for you.

157. DEFEND ME, O GOD

All

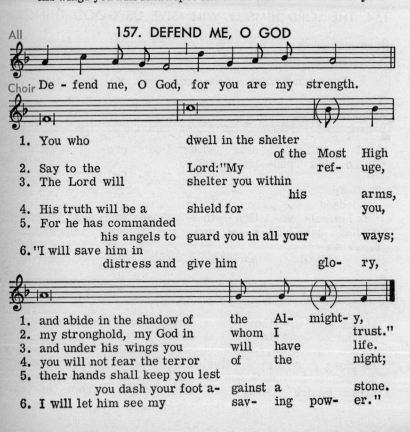

Choir De - fend me, O God, for you are my strength.

1. You who dwell in the shelter of the Most High
2. Say to the Lord: "My ref- uge,
3. The Lord will shelter you within his arms,
4. His truth will be a shield for you,
5. For he has commanded his angels to guard you in all your ways;
6. "I will save him in distress and give him glo- ry,

1. and abide in the shadow of the Al- might- y,
2. my stronghold, my God in whom I trust."
3. and under his wings you will have life.
4. you will not fear the terror of the night;
5. their hands shall keep you lest you dash your foot a- gainst a stone.
6. I will let him see my sav- ing pow- er."

158. TO YOU I LIFT UP MY SOUL

All

To you I lift up my soul.

159. ABIDE IN ME

All

Choir   A - bide in me and I in you.

1. I   am   the true vine and
                    my Father is the vine-   dress- er;
2. And   ev-   ery branch that
                    bears fruit he   will   cleanse
3. A-   bide   in me and   I   in   you;
4. I   am   the vine and you
                    are the branch-   es;
5. For   with- out me you can do noth-   ing;
6. As   the   Father has loved
                    me I also have loved   you;
7. In   this   is my Father   glo-   ri-   fied—
8. These things I have spoken to
                    you that my joy may be in   you

1. every branch in me that
                    bears no fruit he   will   take a-   way.
2. that   it   may   bear   more   fruit.
3. a-   bide   in   my   love.
4. he who abides in me and I in him   will   bear   much   fruit.
5. a-   bide   in   my   love.
6. a-   bide   in   my   love.
7. that you become   my   dis-   ci-   ples.
8. and that your   joy   may   be   full.

160. LORD, LISTEN TO MY CRY

All

Lord, lis - ten to my cry and hear my plea;

my King, my God, re-ceive my prayer.

Choir

1. If the Lord does not build the house,
2. If the Lord does not watch over the cit- y,
3. In vain is your ear- li- er ris- ing,
4. You who toil for the bread you eat:
5. O blessed are those who fear the Lord
6. By the labor of your hands you shall eat;
7. May the Lord bless you from Si- on
8. Praise the Father, Son and Ho- ly Spir- it,

1. in vain do its build- ers la- bor;
2. in vain does the watchman keep vig- il.
3. your going later to rest,
4. when he pours gifts on his beloved while they slum- ber.
5. and walk in his ways!
6. you will be happy and pros- per.
7. all the days of your life!
8. both now and forever. A- men.

All

161. O COME, LORD JESUS, COME

O come, Lord Je- sus, come.

Choir

1. Turn your ear, O Lord, and give an- swer,
2. Preserve my life for I am faith- ful;
3. You are my God! Have mercy on me, O Lord,
4. Give joy, O Lord, to your serv- ant,
5. O Lord, you are good and for- giv- ing —
6. Hear my prayer, O Lord,

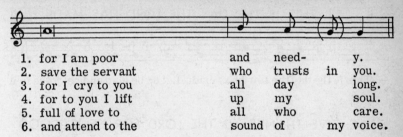

1.	for I am poor	and	need-		y.
2.	save the servant	who	trusts	in	you.
3.	for I cry to you	all	day		long.
4.	for to you I lift	up	my		soul.
5.	full of love to	all	who		care.
6.	and attend to the	sound	of	my	voice.

162. ALLELUIA! ALLELUIA! CHRIST OUR PASCH

All Antiphons Nos. 163, 164, 165 may be sung to the following psalm.

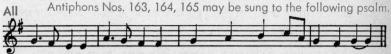

Al-le-lu-ia, al-le-lu-ia! Christ, our Pasch, is sac-ri-ficed.

Choir

1.	The Lord	is my Shepherd;	I	shall	not	want;
2.	Be-side	restful waters	he	leads		me,
3.	He guides	me	in	right		paths
4.	E-ven	though I walk				
		in the	dark	val-		ley
5.	With your	rod	and	your		staff
6.	You spread	a table	be-	fore		me
7.	You a-	noint	my	head	with	oil,
8.	On-ly	goodness and				
		kind-	ness	fol-	low	me
9.	And I	shall dwell in				
		the house	of	the		Lord

1.	in verdant pastures	he	gives	me	re-	pose;
2.	he re-	fresh-	es	my		soul.
3.	- - - -	for	his	name's		sake.
4.	I fear no evil; for					
	you	are	at	my		side—
5.	that	give	me	cour-		age.
6.	in the	sight	of	my		foes;
7.	my	cup	o-	ver-		flows.
8.	all the	days	of	my		life;
9.	- - - -	for	years	to		come.

163. THIS IS THE DAY THE LORD HAS MADE

All

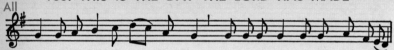

This is the day the Lord has made! Let us be glad and re-joice in it!

164. GIVE THANKS TO THE LORD FOR HE IS GOOD

All

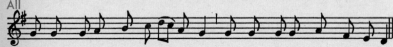

Give thanks to the Lord for he is good; his mer-cy en-dures for ev-er.

165. LET ALL ON EARTH ADORE THE LORD

All

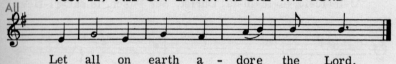

Let all on earth a - dore the Lord.

Choir

1. Let all the earth adore you,   God,
2. Shout with joy to the   Lord;
3. Hear now, all you who revere   God,
4. When I prayed to   him,
5. God has heard my   cry,
6. All people, bless our   God,
7. Glory be to the   Fa- ther,
8. As it was in the beginning, is   now,

1. and sing   praise   to   you,
2. all the earth to his   name   sing praise;
3. while I tell you what he has   done   for   me;
4. his praise was   on   my   tongue,
5. he has listened   to   my   plea;
6. loudly   sound   his   praise;
7. and   to   the   Son,
8. and   e'er   shall be,

1. O Most High! Let it glori- fy your name.
2. give glory to his maj- es- ty.
3. listen to his glo- ri- ous deeds.
4. his glory on my lips.
5. he has an- swered my prayer.
6. he has given life to our souls.
7. and to the Ho- ly Spir- it.
8. world without end. A- men.

166. O PEOPLE IN SION, BEHOLD

All

O peo-ple in Si-on, be-hold! the Lord shall come.

Choir

1. The Lord
   comes to
   save the na- tions, and the
                    glory of his   voice
2. O   shep- herd of Isra- el heark- en,
3. From your throne upon the
                    cher- u-   bim
4. Rouse your pow- er and come to save us;
5. O Lord of
   hosts, how   long will you
                    burn with an-   ger?
6. You have fed us with the
                    bread of   tears,

1. will   be   heard in the joy
                                of your   heart.
2. O guide of the flock of Jo- seph—
3. shine forth
   before Eph- ra- im, Benjamin
                    and Ma- nas- seh.
4. O Lord of hosts, re- store us.
5. If your face
   shine up- on us, then we
                    shall be   safe.
6. have given us tears to drink
                    in a- bun- dance.

167. COME, THOU LONG-EXPECTED SAVIOR

1. Come, thou long-ex-pect-ed Sav-ior, Born to set   thy
2. Born   thy peo-ple to de-liv-er, Born a child, and

1. peo-ple free; From our fears and sins re-lease us; Let us
2. yet a King, Born to reign in us for- ev - er, Now thy

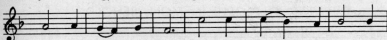

1. find our rest in thee. Is-rael's strength and con - so-
2. gra-cious king-dom bring. By thine   own   e - ter - nal

1. la -tion, Hope of all the earth thou art; Fond de -
2. Spir- it   Rule in all our hearts a - lone; By thine

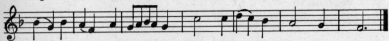

1. sire of ev - 'ry na-tion, Joy of ev-'ry long-ing heart.
2. all-suf-fi-cient mer-it Raise us to thy glo-rious throne.

168. BEDEW US, HEAVENS, FROM ABOVE

Refrain

Be - dew   us,   heav - ens, from a - bove!

O clouds, rain down the   Just One!

Cantor

1. With - hold your wrath from us, O Lord, and re - mem-

ber no more our e - vil - do - ing. Lo, the cit - y of the

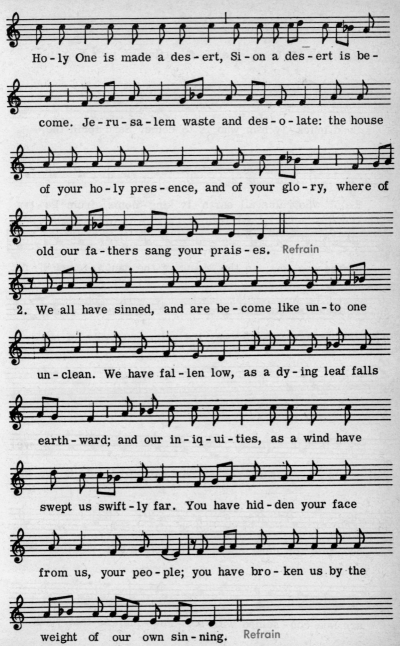

Ho-ly One is made a des-ert, Si-on a des-ert is be-

come. Je-ru-sa-lem waste and des-o-late: the house

of your ho-ly pres-ence, and of your glo-ry, where of

old our fa-thers sang your prais-es. *Refrain*

2. We all have sinned, and are be-come like un-to one

un-clean. We have fal-len low, as a dy-ing leaf falls

earth-ward; and our in-iq-ui-ties, as a wind have

swept us swift-ly far. You have hid-den your face

from us, your peo-ple; you have bro-ken us by the

weight of our own sin-ning. *Refrain*

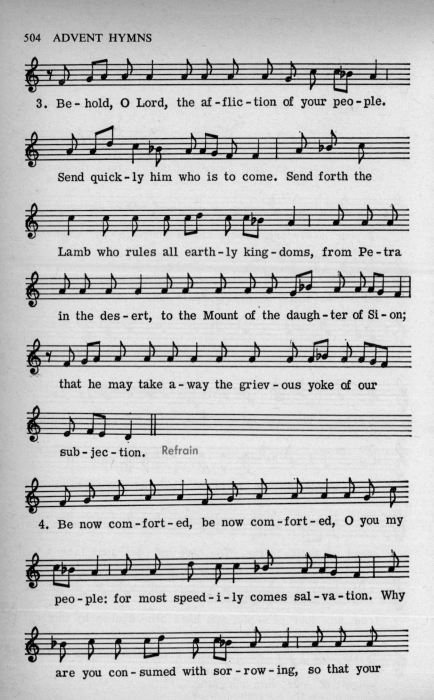

3. Be - hold, O Lord, the af - flic - tion of your peo - ple.

Send quick - ly him who is to come. Send forth the

Lamb who rules all earth - ly king - doms, from Pe - tra

in the des - ert, to the Mount of the daugh - ter of Si - on;

that he may take a - way the griev - ous yoke of our

sub - jec - tion.   Refrain

4. Be now com - fort - ed, be now com - fort - ed, O you my

peo - ple: for most speed - i - ly comes sal - va - tion. Why

are you con - sumed with sor - row - ing, so that your

grief has quite trans-formed you? I come to save,

be no more fear-ful. For know you not that I am your

God and Mas-ter, Is-rael's Ho-ly One, your sole

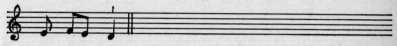

Re-deem-er. Refrain

169. ON JORDAN'S BANK

1. On   Jor-dan's bank the Bap-tist's cry An-nounc-
2. Then cleansed be   ev-'ry heart from sin; Make straight
3. For   you   are   our sal-va-tion, Lord, Our   ref-
4. To   God   the   Son all glo-ry   be! His   ad-

1. es that the Lord   is   nigh;   A-wake and heark-en
2. the way of God   with-in.   Let each one his   own
3. uge and our great   re-ward; Once more up-on   your
4. vent set all   na-tions free. Him   with the   Fa-ther

1. for   he brings Glad   ti-dings of   the King of kings.
2. heart pre-pare   For Christ   to come   and en-ter there.
3. peo-ple shine, And   fill   the world with love di-vine.
4. we   a-dore, And Ho-ly Spir-it   ev-er-more.

170. THE SEVEN "O" ANTIPHONS OF ADVENT

1. O SAPIENTIA (December 17)

1. O come, thou Wis - dom, Son di - vine, Our weak - ened

1. wills to thee in - cline! And shed thy light o'er life's

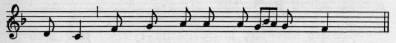

1. dark way, Lest, lured by sin, we go a - stray.

Refrain

Re-joice! Re-joice! O Is-ra-el! To thee shall come Im-man-u-el.

2. O ADONAI (December 18)

O come, O come, thou LORD OF MIGHT,
Who, midst the clouds on Sinai's height,
To Moses didst reveal thy Law,
In fiery majesty and awe!
  Rejoice! Rejoice! O Israel!
  To thee shall come Immanuel.

3. O RADIX IESSE (December 19)

O come, thou SPROUT OF JESSE'S TREE,
Free us from Satan's tyranny!
From fires of hell thy people save,
And give us vict'ry o'er the grave.
  Rejoice! Rejoice! O Israel!
  To thee shall come Immanuel.

4. O CLAVIS DAVID (December 20)

O KEY OF DAVID, make us free,
That we in heaven.thee may see!
Unlock the doors which sin did close,
That in thy grace we may repose.
  Rejoice! Rejoice! O Israel!
  To thee shall come Immanuel.

5. O ORIENS (December 21)

O come, thou RISING DAYSTAR clear,
And may thy light divine appear!
Enlighten all who sin and err,
With grace do thou our souls bestir!
  Rejoice! Rejoice! O Israel!
  To thee shall come Immanuel.

6. O REX GENTIUM (December 22)

O come, thou KING OF ALL THE EARTH,
That we may share thy wondrous birth!
Come, rule our heart and mind and will,
That we thy precepts may fulfill.
  Rejoice! Rejoice! O Israel!
  To thee shall come Immanuel.

7. O IMMANUEL (December 23)

O come, O come, IMMANUEL,
And ransom captive Israel,
That lives in earthly exile here,
Until the Son of God appear.
  Rejoice! Rejoice! O Israel!
  To thee shall come Immanuel.

171. HARK, A HERALD VOICE IS CALLING

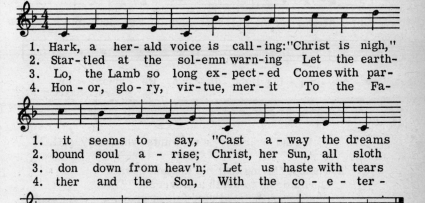

1. Hark, a her-ald voice is call-ing: "Christ is nigh,"
2. Star-tled at the sol-emn warn-ing Let the earth-
3. Lo, the Lamb so long ex-pect-ed Comes with par-
4. Hon-or, glo-ry, vir-tue, mer-it To the Fa-

1. it seems to say, "Cast a-way the dreams
2. bound soul a-rise; Christ, her Sun, all sloth
3. don down from heav'n; Let us haste with tears
4. ther and the Son, With the co-e-ter-

1. of dark-ness, O ye chil-dren of the day."
2. dis-pell-ing Shines up-on the morn-ing skies.
3. of sor-row, One and all to be for-giv'n.
4. nal Spir-it While e-ter-nal a-ges run.

172. CREATOR OF THE STARS OF NIGHT

1. Cre - a - tor   of   the stars of night, The peo-ple's ev-
2. As once through Mar-y's flesh you came, To save us from
3. And when   on   that last judg-ment day, We rise to glo-

1. er-last-ing light, Re - deem-er - Sav - ior of us   all,
2. our sin and shame, So   now, Re-deem-er, by your grace,
3. ry from de - cay, Then come a - gain, O Sav-ior blest,

1.   O   hear your serv - ants when they call.
2. Come, heal   a - gain our   fal - len race.
3. And bring us   to   e - ter - nal rest. A - men.

173. CREATOR OF THE STARS OF NIGHT

Cre - a - tor of the stars of night, Thy peo - ple's

ev - er - last - ing light, Je - sus Re - deem - er,

save us all And hear thy serv - ants when they call.

2. Thou, grieving that the ancient curse
   Should doom to death a universe,
   Hast found the med'cine full of grace
   To save and heal a ruined race.

3. Thou cam'st the Bridegroom of the Bride,
   As drew the world to eventide,
   Proceeding from a Virgin shrine
   The spotless Victim all divine.

4. At whose dread name majestic now
   All knees must bend, all hearts must bow;
   All things celestial thee do laud,
   All things terrestrial, mighty God.

5. To God the Father, God the Son
   And God the Spirit, three in one,
   Praise, honor, might and glory be
   From age to age eternally.

174. O JESUS, SAVIOR OF ALL MEN

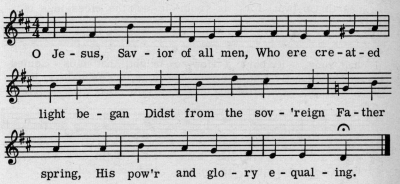

O Je-sus, Sav-ior of all men, Who ere cre-at-ed light be-gan Didst from the sov-'reign Fa-ther spring, His pow'r and glo-ry e-qual-ing.

2. The Father's light and splendor thou,
   Their endless hope to thee that bow;
   Accept the prayers and praise today
   That through the world thy servants pay.

3. The heav'ns above, the rolling main
   And all that earth's wide realms contain,
   With joyous voice now loudly sing
   The glory of their new-born King.

4. And we who by thy precious blood
   From sin redeemed are marked for God,
   On this the day that saw thy birth
   Sing the new song of ransomed earth.

5. All honor, praise and glory be,
   O Jesus, Virgin-born, to thee;
   All glory as is ever meet
   To Father and to Paraclete.

175. BEHOLD, A ROSE OF JUDAH

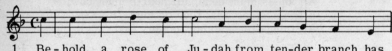

1 Be-hold, a rose of Ju-dah from ten-der branch has
2. This rose of roy-al beau-ty of which I - sa - iah
3. We pray thee, Vir - gin Moth- er, the Queen of heav'n and

1. sprung! A rose from root of Jes - se, as proph-ets long
2. sings, Is Mar - y, maid- en Moth-er, and Christ the flow'r
3. earth: Ob-tain for us from Je- sus the bless-ings of

1. had sung. It bore a flow - er bright, that blos - somed
2. she brings. By God's u-nique de-sign, re - main - ing
3. his birth. By his hu- mil - i - ty, may we live

1. in the win - ter when half - spent was the night.
2. still a vir - gin, she bore her Child di - vine.
3. as God's chil-dren, in peace and u - ni - ty.

176. ANGELS, FROM THE REALMS OF GLORY

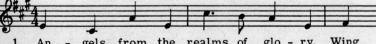

1. An - gels, from the realms of glo - ry, Wing
2. Shep - herds in the fields a - bid - ing, Watch-
3. All cre - a - tion, join in prais-ing God

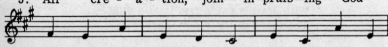

1. your flight o' er all the earth; You who sang cre-
2. ing o'er your flocks by night, God with man is
3. the Fa - ther, Spir - it, Son; Ev - er - more your

1. a - tion's sto - ry, Now pro - claim Mes - si -
2. now re - sid - ing, Bright - ly shines the in -
3. voic - es rais-ing To th'E - ter - nal Three

Refrain

1. ah's birth: Come and wor - ship, come and wor - ship,
2. fant Light:
3. in   One:

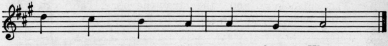

Wor - ship Christ,   the   new - born King.

177. HARK! THE HERALD ANGELS SING

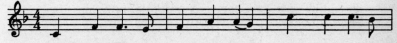

1. Hark! the her - ald   an - gels sing, "Glo - ry to the
2. Christ, by high-est heav'n a - dored, Christ, the ev - er-

1. new-born King; Peace on earth, and mer - cy mild, God
2. last - ing Lord! Late in time be -hold him come, Off -

1. and sin-ners rec - on - ciled!" Joy- ful, all ye na-
2. spring of the Vir-gin's womb. Veiled in flesh the God -

1. tions, rise, Join the tri-umph of the skies; With th'an-
2. head see; Hail th'in-car-nate De - i - ty, Pleased as

1. gel - ic host pro-claim,"Christ is born in Beth-le-hem!"
2. man with men to dwell, Je - sus, our Im-man-u - el.

Refrain

Hark! the her-ald an-gels sing,"Glo-ry to the new-born King. "

178. FROM LANDS THAT SEE THE SUN ARISE

1. From lands that see the sun a-rise To earth's re-
2. Blest Au-thor of this earth-ly frame To take a
3. The man-ger and the straw he bore, The cra-dle
4. All hon-or, praise and glo-ry be, O Je-sus

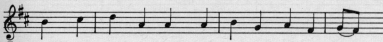

1. mot-est bound-a-ries, The Vir-gin-born to-day
2. serv-ant's form he came, That lib-er-at-ing flesh
3. he did not ab-hor; A lit-tle milk his in-
4. Vir-gin-born, to thee; All glo-ry, as is ev-

1. we sing The Son of Mar-y, Christ the King.
2. by flesh Whom he had made might live a-fresh.
3. fant fare Who feed-eth all the fowl of air.
4. er meet, To Fa-ther and to Par-a-clete.

179. WHILE SHEPHERDS WATCHED THEIR FLOCKS

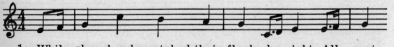

1. While shep-herds watched their flocks by night, All seat-
2. "Fear not," said he — for might-y dread Had seized

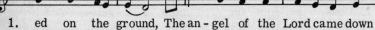

1. ed on the ground, The an-gel of the Lord came down
2. their trou-bled mind—"Glad ti-dings of great joy I bring

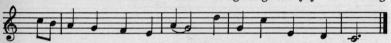

1. And glo-ry shone a-round, And glo-ry shone a-round.
2. To you and all man-kind, To you and all man-kind."

3. "To you, in David's town this day,
   Is born of David's line,
   The Savior, who is Christ, the Lord,
   And this shall be the sign:
   And this shall be the sign:

4. "The heav'nly Babe you there shall find
To human view displayed,
All meanly wrapped in swathing bands,
And in a manger laid,
And in a manger laid."

5. Thus spoke the seraph, and forthwith
Appeared a shining throng
Of angels praising God, who thus
Addressed their joyful song:
Addressed their joyful song:

6. "All glory be to God on high,
And to the earth be peace:
Good will henceforth, from heav'n to men,
Begin and never cease!
Begin and never cease!"

180. AWAY IN A MANGER

1. A - way in   a man-ger, No crib for a   bed,   The
2. The cat-tle are low-ing, The Ba - by a - wakes, But
3. Be near me, Lord Je - sus, I   ask you to stay Close

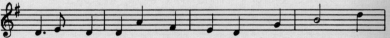

1. lit-tle Lord Je-sus Laid down his sweet head; The
2. lit-tle Lord Je-sus No   cry - ing   he   makes; I
3. by me for ev - er, And love me, I   pray; Bless

1. stars in   the   sky   Looked down where he
2. love you, Lord Je - sus! Look down from the
3. all   the   dear chil - dren In   your   ten - der

1. lay, The lit - tle Lord Je-sus, A - sleep on the hay.
2. sky, And stay by my cra-dle, Till morn-ing is nigh.
3. care, And fit us for heav-en, To live with you there.

181. IT CAME UPON THE MIDNIGHT CLEAR

It came up-on the mid-night clear, That glo-rious song of

old, From an-gels bend-ing near the earth To

touch their harps of gold: "Peace on the earth, good

will to men, From heav'n's all-gra-cious King:" The

world in sol-emn still-ness lay, To hear the an-gels sing.

182. GOOD CHRISTIAN MEN, REJOICE

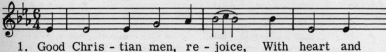

1. Good Chris - tian men, re - joice, With heart and
2. Good Chris - tian men, re - joice, With heart and
3. Good Chris - tian men, re - joice, With heart and

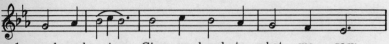

1. soul and voice; Give ye heed to what we say:
2. soul and voice; Now ye hear of end - less bliss:
3. soul and voice; Now ye need not fear the grave:

1. Je - sus Christ is born to - day; Earth and heav'n be-
2. Je - sus Christ was born for this! O-pened he the
3. Je - sus Christ was born to save! Calls you one and

1. fore him bow, And he is in the man-ger now.
2. heav'n-ly door, And man is bless-ed ev - er - more.
3. calls you all To gain his ev - er - last-ing hall.

1. Christ is born to-day! Christ is born to-day!
2. Christ was born for this! Christ was born for this!
3. Christ was born to save! Christ was born to save!

183. O LITTLE TOWN OF BETHLEHEM

1. O lit - tle town of Beth-le-hem, How still we see thee
2. For Christ is born of Mar - y; And gath-ered all a-
3. O ho - ly Child of Beth-le-hem, De-scend to us, we

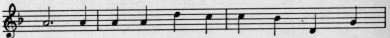

1. lie; A - bove thy deep and dream-less sleep The
2. bove, While mor-tals sleep, the an - gels keep Their
3. pray; Cast out our sin, and en - ter in, Be

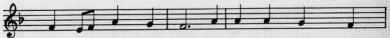

1. si - lent stars go by: Yet in thy dark streets
2. watch of won-d'ring love. O morn-ing stars, to -
3. born in us to - day. We hear the Christ - mas

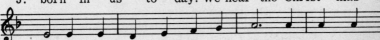

1. shin-eth The ev - er-last-ing light; The hopes and
2. geth-er Pro-claim the ho - ly birth; And prais - es
3. an - gels The great glad ti-dings tell; O come to

1. fears of all the years Are met in thee to-night.
2. sing to God the King, And peace to men on earth.
3. us, a-bide with us, Our Lord Im-man-u - el.

184. JOY TO THE WORLD

1. Joy to the world! the Lord is come: Let earth re-
2. Joy to the earth! the Sav-ior reigns: Let men their
3. He rules the world with truth and grace, And makes the

1. ceive her King; Let ev - 'ry heart pre - pare him
2. songs em - ploy; While fields and floods, rocks, hills, and
3. na - tions prove The glo - ries of his right-eous-

1. room, And heav'n and na - ture sing, And heav'n and
2. plains Re - peat the sound-ing joy, Re - peat the
3. ness, And won - ders of his love, And won - ders

1. na - ture sing, And heav'n, and heav'n and na - ture sing.
2. sound-ing joy, Re - peat, re - peat the sound-ing joy.
3. of his love, And won - ders, won - ders of his love.

185. O COME, ALL YE FAITHFUL

1.

O come, all ye faithful, joyful and triumphant,
O come, ye, O come, ye, to Bethlehem.
Come and behold him, born the King of angels,
O come, let us adore him,
O come, let us adore him,
O come, let us adore him,
Christ, the Lord.

2.

Sing, choirs of angels, sing in exultation,
Sing, all ye citizens of heaven above:
Glory to God, God in the highest.
O come, let us adore him,
O come, let us adore him,
O come, let us adore him,
Christ, the Lord.

186. ADESTE, FIDELES

1.

Adeste, fideles, laeti triumphantes,
Venite, venite in Bethlehem.
Natum videte, Regem angelorum.
  Venite, adoremus,
  Venite, adoremus,
  Venite, adoremus Dominum.

2.

Aeterni Parentis splendorem aeternum
Velatum sub carne videbimus;
Deum Infantem, pannis involutum
  Venite, adoremus,
  Venite, adoremus,
  Venite, adoremus Dominum.

187. SILENT NIGHT, HOLY NIGHT

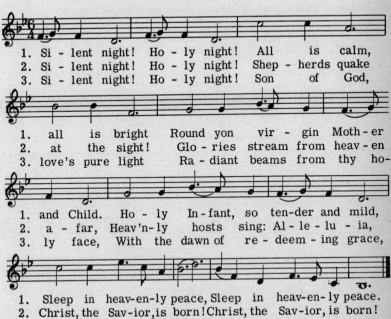

1. Si - lent night! Ho - ly night! All is calm,
2. Si - lent night! Ho - ly night! Shep - herds quake
3. Si - lent night! Ho - ly night! Son of God,

1. all is bright Round yon vir - gin Moth - er
2. at the sight! Glo - ries stream from heav - en
3. love's pure light Ra - diant beams from thy ho-

1. and Child. Ho - ly In - fant, so ten - der and mild,
2. a - far, Heav'n-ly hosts sing: Al - le - lu - ia,
3. ly face, With the dawn of re - deem - ing grace,

1. Sleep in heav-en-ly peace, Sleep in heav-en-ly peace.
2. Christ, the Sav-ior, is born! Christ, the Sav-ior, is born!
3. Je - sus, Lord, at thy birth, Je - sus, Lord, at thy birth.

188. ANGELS WE HAVE HEARD ON HIGH

1.

Angels we have heard on high, sweetly singing o'er the plains;
And the mountains in reply, echo still their joyous strains:
    Gloria in excelsis Deo!
    Gloria in excelsis Deo!

2.

Shepherds, why this jubilee? Why your joyous strain prolong?
Say, what may the tidings be which inspire your heav'nly song?
    Gloria in excelsis Deo!
    Gloria in excelsis Deo!

3.

Come to Bethlehem and see him, whose birth the angels sing;
Come, adore on bended knee, Christ the Lord, the new-born King.
    Gloria in excelsis Deo!
    Gloria in excelsis Deo!

189. SEE, AMID THE WINTER'S SNOW

See, a-mid the win-ter's snow, Born for us on earth be-low,

See the ten-der Lamb ap-pears, Prom-ised from e-ter-nal years.

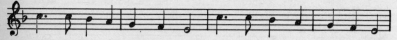

Hail, thou ev-er bless-ed morn! Hail, sal-va-tion's hap-py dawn!

Sing through all Je-ru-sa-lem, Christ is born in Beth-le-hem.

2. Lo, within a manger lies
   He who built the starry skies:
   He who, throned in height sublime,
   Sits amid the Cherubim.

3. Say, ye holy shepherds, say,
   What your joyful news today?
   Wherefore have ye left your sheep
   On the lonely mountain steep?

4. "As we watched at dead of night,
   Lo! we saw a wondrous light;
   Angels singing, 'Peace on earth,'
   Told us of the Savior's birth."

5. Sacred Infant, all divine,
   What a tender love was thine,
   Thus to come from highest bliss
   Down to such a world as this!

6. Teach, O teach us, holy Child,
   By thy face so meek and mild,
   Teach us to resemble thee,
   In thy sweet humility.

190. ALL MY HEART THIS NIGHT REJOICES

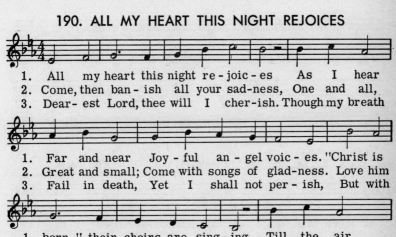

1. All   my heart this night re - joic - es   As   I   hear
2. Come, then ban - ish all your sad-ness, One   and   all,
3. Dear- est Lord, thee will   I   cher-ish. Though my breath

1. Far   and near   Joy - ful   an - gel voic - es. "Christ is
2. Great and small; Come with songs of glad-ness. Love him
3. Fail in death, Yet   I   shall not per - ish, But with

1. born," their choirs are sing-ing   Till   the   air
2. who   with love is glow-ing; Hail the   star,
3. thee   a - bide for ev - er There on high,

1. Ev -'ry-where Now with joy is ring - ing.
2. Near and far   Light and joy be - stow - ing.
3. In that joy Which can van - ish nev - er.

191. A CHILD IS BORN
192. THE MAGI KINGS

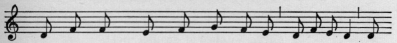

1. A Child is born in Beth-le-hem, al-le-lu-ia; Re-
2. Our Broth-er in the flesh is he, al-le-lu-ia; Our
3. By grace this Child is born a-gain, al-le-lu-ia; In

1. The Ma-gi kings come from a-far, al-le-lu-ia; Led
2. Gold, in-cense, myrrh they of-fer him, al-le-lu-ia; And

1. joice, re-joice Je-ru-sa-lem, al-le-lu-ia, al-le-lu-ia.
2. King for all e-ter-ni-ty, al-le-lu-ia, al-le-lu-ia.
3. ev-'ry heart he frees from sin, al-le-lu-ia, al-le-lu-ia.

1. on by faith in heav-en's star, al-le-lu-ia, al-le-lu-ia.
2. bend-ing low they wor-ship him, al-le-lu-ia, al-le-lu-ia.

Refrain

Let grate-ful hearts now sing a song of joy and

ho-ly praise to Christ the new-born King!

193. O MORE THAN MIGHTY CITIES KNOWN

O more than might-y cit-ies known, Dear Beth-le-

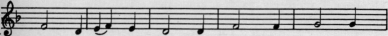

hem, in thee a-lone Sal-va-tion's Lord from

heav'n took birth In hu-man form up-on the earth.

2. And from a star that far outshone
   The radiant circle of the sun
   In beauty, swift the tidings ran
   Of God on earth in flesh of man.

3. The wise men, seeing him so fair,
   Bow low before him, and with prayer
   Their treasured Orient gifts unfold
   Of incense, myrrh and royal gold.

4. The fragrant incense which they bring,
   The gold, proclaim him God and King:
   The bitter spicy dust of myrrh
   Foreshadows his new sepulcher.

5. All glory, Lord, to thee we pay
   For thine Epiphany today;
   All glory, as is ever meet,
   To Father and to Paraclete.

194. SONGS OF THANKFULNESS AND PRAISE

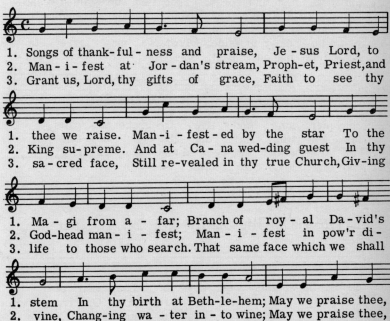

1. Songs of thank-ful-ness and praise, Je-sus Lord, to
2. Man-i-fest at Jor-dan's stream, Proph-et, Priest, and
3. Grant us, Lord, thy gifts of grace, Faith to see thy

1. thee we raise. Man-i-fest-ed by the star To the
2. King su-preme. And at Ca-na wed-ding guest In thy
3. sa-cred face, Still re-vealed in thy true Church, Giv-ing

1. Ma-gi from a-far; Branch of roy-al Da-vid's
2. God-head man-i-fest; Man-i-fest in pow'r di-
3. life to those who search. That same face which we shall

1. stem In thy birth at Beth-le-hem; May we praise thee,
2. vine, Chang-ing wa-ter in-to wine; May we praise thee,
3. see In that great e-piph-a-ny, When we praise thee,

1. ev - er - blest, God in man made man - i - fest!
2. ev - er - blest, God in man made man - i - fest!
3. ev - er - blest, God in man made man - i - fest!

195. THROUGHOUT THESE FORTY DAYS, O LORD

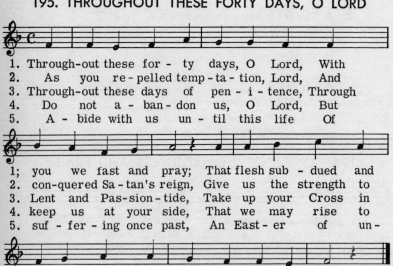

1. Through-out these for - ty days, O Lord, With
2. As you re - pelled temp - ta - tion, Lord, And
3. Through-out these days of pen - i - tence, Through
4. Do not a - ban - don us, O Lord, But
5. A - bide with us un - til this life Of

1; you we fast and pray; That flesh sub - dued and
2. con-quered Sa - tan's reign, Give us the strength to
3. Lent and Pas-sion-tide, Take up your Cross in
4. keep us at your side, That we may rise to
5. suf - fer - ing once past, An East - er of un-

1. spir- it freed, Your will we may o - bey.
2. con-quer sin And live by grace a - gain.
3. us a - gain, In us be cru - ci - fied.
4. life a - new, Re - deemed and glo - ri - fied.
5. end-ing joy, We may at - tain at last.

196. FROM THE DEPTHS WE CRY TO THEE

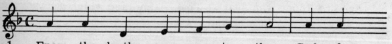

1. From the depths we cry to thee, God of
2. Though our con - scienc - es pro - claim Our trans-
3. Lord, ac - cept our Lent- en fast And for-

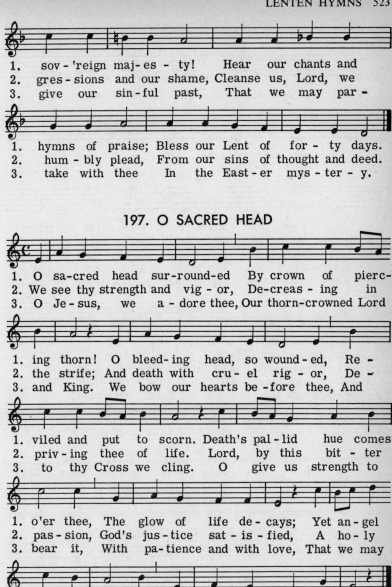

1. sov-'reign maj-es-ty! Hear our chants and
2. gres-sions and our shame, Cleanse us, Lord, we
3. give our sin-ful past, That we may par-

1. hymns of praise; Bless our Lent of for-ty days.
2. hum-bly plead, From our sins of thought and deed.
3. take with thee In the East-er mys-ter-y.

197. O SACRED HEAD

1. O sa-cred head sur-round-ed By crown of pierc-
2. We see thy strength and vig-or, De-creas-ing in
3. O Je-sus, we a-dore thee, Our thorn-crowned Lord

1. ing thorn! O bleed-ing head, so wound-ed, Re-
2. the strife; And death with cru-el rig-or, De-
3. and King. We bow our hearts be-fore thee, And

1. viled and put to scorn. Death's pal-lid hue comes
2. priv-ing thee of life. Lord, by this bit-ter
3. to thy Cross we cling. O give us strength to

1. o'er thee, The glow of life de-cays; Yet an-gel
2. pas-sion, God's jus-tice sat-is-fied, A ho-ly
3. bear it, With pa-tience and with love, That we may

1. hosts a-dore thee, And trem-ble as they gaze.
2. peo-ple fash-ion, Re-deemed and sanc-ti-fied.
3. tru-ly mer-it A glo-rious crown a-bove.

198. HEAR OUR ENTREATIES, LORD

Refrain

Hear our en - treat - ies, Lord, and show thy mer - cy;

for we are sin - ners be - fore thee.

Cantor

1. King high ex - alt - ed all the world's
2. Right hand of God - head, head - stone of
3. We, thy e - ter - nal maj - es - ty
4. Hum - bly con - fess - ing all our sins
5. Led a - way cap - tive, guilt - less, un -

1. Re - deem - er, to thee thy child - ren lift
2. the cor - ner, path of sal - va - tion, gate
3. en - treat - ing, make lam - en - ta - tion in
4. a - gainst thee, all our mis - do - ings, hid -
5. re - sist - ing, brought by false wit - ness un -

1. their eyes with weep - ing; Christ, we im -
2. of heav - en's king - dom: cleanse thou thy
3. thy ho - ly hear - ing; gra - cious - ly
4. den now no long - er; thou our Re -
5. to death for sin - ners; Christ do thou

1. plore thee, hear our sup - pli - ca - tion.
2. peo - ple, stained with much trans - gress - ing.
3. grant thou to our sins in - dul - gence.
4. deem - er, by thy love grant par - don.
5. keep us whom thy blood has ran - somed.

199. LOFTY TREE, BEND DOWN YOUR BRANCHES

1. Loft-y Tree, bend down your branch-es To em-brace
2. Tree u-nique! You were found worth-y Earth's great vic-
3. Hon-or, bless-ing ev - er - last-ing To th'im-mor-

1. your sa-cred load; Oh, re-lax the cru-el ten-sion
2. tim to sus-tain, Har-bor from the rag-ing tem-pest,
3. tal De - i - ty: To the Fa-ther, Son and Spir-it

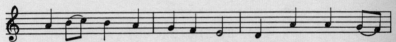

1. Of that all too rig-id wood; Gen-tly, gen-tly
2. Ark that saved the world a-gain, Tree with sa-cred
3. E-qual prais-es ev - er be: Glo-ry through the

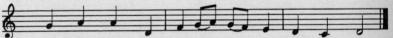

1. bear the mem-bers Of your dy-ing King and God.
2. blood a-noint-ed Of the Lamb for sin-ners slain.
3. earth and heav'n To Trin-i-ty in u-ni-ty.

200. SING, MY TONGUE, THE SAVIOR'S GLORY, TELL HIS TRIUMPH

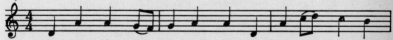

1. Sing, my tongue, the Sav-ior's glo-ry, Tell his tri-umph
2. Eat-ing of the tree for-bid-den, Man had sunk in
3. Hon-or, bless-ing ev - er-last-ing To th'im-mor-tal

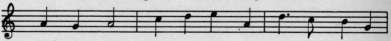

1. far and wide; Tell a-loud the fa-mous sto-ry
2. Sa-tan's snare, When his pit-y-ing Cre-a-tor
3. De - i - ty: To the Fa-ther, Son and Spir-it

1. Of his bod - y cru - ci - fied; How up - on the
2. Did this sec - ond tree pre-pare, Des-tined man - y
3. E - qual prais-es ev - er be: Glo - ry through the

1. Cross a vic - tim Van-quish-ing in death he died.
2. a - ges lat - er That first e - vil to re - pair.
3. earth and heav'n to Trin - i - ty in u - ni - ty.

201. BY THE CROSS

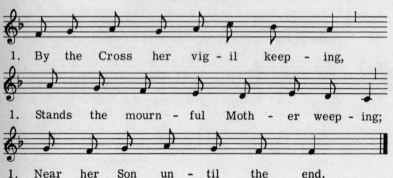

1. By the Cross her vig - il keep - ing,

1. Stands the mourn - ful Moth - er weep - ing;

1. Near her Son un - til the end.

2. Through her heart a sword is driv-en,
   And her soul to an-guish giv-en,
   More than we can com-pre-hend.

3. Who can con-tem-plate God's Moth-er,
   At the feet of Christ, our Broth-er;
   And no sym-pa-thy ex-press?

4. Who can see her so af-flict-ed
   By the wounds our sins in-flict-ed;
   And not share in her dis-tress?

5. She be-holds his des-o-la-tion,
   For the sins of his own na-tion,
   Dy-ing as a com-mon thief.

6. In her soul she feels those bruis-es,
   Ev-'ry drop of blood he los-es,
   Yet she can-not give re-lief.

7. Moth-er, let us share thy sor-row,
   From thy heart may we each bor-row,
   Love for Je-sus cru-ci-fied.

8. May our souls, with fer-vor burn-ing,
   All our thoughts to Je-sus turn-ing,
   Be trans-fixed here at thy side.

202. O MERCIFUL REDEEMER

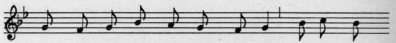

1. O mer - ci - ful Re - deem - er, hear; in pit - y
2. Our hearts are o - pen, Lord, to thee, and know-ing
3. Our sins are great, our wills are weak, but thy for-
4. O, grant most ho - ly Trin - i - ty, thou un - di -

1. now in - cline thine ear; ac - cept the con - trite
2. our in - iq - ui - ty, pour out on us thy
3. give-ness, Lord, we seek, and for the glo - ry
4. vid - ed U - ni - ty, that these our ho - ly

1. pray'rs we raise in this our fast of for - ty days.
2. heal - ing grace, re - store to life a fall - en race.
3. of thy name, do thou our wound-ed souls re - claim.
4. Lent - en days in-crease our mer - it and thy praise.

203. THE LAMB'S HIGH BANQUET WE AWAIT

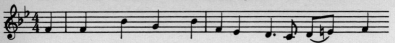

The Lamb's high ban - quet we a - wait In snow - white

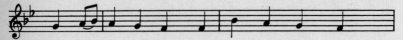

robes of roy - al state; And now, the Red Sea's

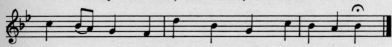

chan - nel past, To Christ our Prince we sing at last.

2. Upon the altar of the Cross
His body has redeemed our loss;
And tasting of his precious blood
Our life is hid with him in God.

3. Now Christ our paschal Lamb is slain,
The Lamb of God that knows no stain,
The true oblation offered here,
Our own unleavened Bread sincere.

4. We pray thee, King with glory decked,
In this our paschal joy protect
From ills that sin and death effect,
Thy ransomed flock, thine own elect.

5. To thee, who dead, again dost live,
All glory, Lord, thy people give;
All glory, as is ever meet,
To Father and to Paraclete.

204. JESUS CHRIST IS RISEN TODAY

1. Je - sus Christ is ris'n to - day, Al - le - lu - ia!
2. Hymns of praise then let us sing, Al - le - lu - ia!
3. But the pains which he en-dured, Al - le - lu - ia!
4. Sing we to our God a - bove, Al - le - lu - ia!

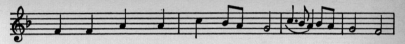

1. Our tri - um - phant ho - ly day, Al - le - lu - ia!
2. Un - to Christ our heav'n-ly King, Al - le - lu - ia!
3. Our sal - va - tion have pro-cured; Al - le - lu - ia!
4. Praise e - ter - nal as his love; Al - le - lu - ia!

1. Who did once, up - on the Cross, Al - le - lu - ia!
2. Who en-dured the Cross and grave, Al - le - lu - ia!
3. Now on high he is our King, Al - le - lu - ia!
4. Praise him, all ye heav'n-ly host, Al - le - lu - ia!

1. Suf - fer to re-deem our loss. Al - le - lu - ia!
2. Sin - ners to re-deem and save. Al - le - lu - ia!
3. Where the an-gels ev - er sing. Al - le - lu - ia!
4. Fa - ther, Son, and Ho - ly Ghost. Al - le - lu - ia!

205. YE SONS AND DAUGHTERS

Al - le - lu - ia, al - le - lu - ia, al - le - lu - ia.

1. Ye sons and daugh - ters of the Lord,
2. And those who die with Christ to sin,

1. The King of heav - en, the King a - dored, From
2. By grace can rise to life a - gain, With

1. death to life has been re - stored. Al-le-lu-ia.
2. him e - ter - nal vic - t'ry win. Al-le-lu-ia.

206. THE STRIFE IS O'ER, THE BATTLE DONE

Al - le - lu - ia! Al - le - lu - ia! Al - le - lu - ia!

1. The strife is o'er, the bat - tle done; The
2. The three sad days have quick - ly sped; He
3. Lord, by the stripes which wound - ed thee, From

1. vic - to - ry of life is won; The song of
2. ris - es glo - rious from the dead: All glo - ry
3. death's dread sting thy serv - ants free, That we may

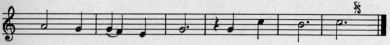

1. tri - umph has be - gun. Al - le - lu - ia!
2. to our ris - en Head! Al - le - lu - ia!
3. live and sing to thee, Al - le - lu - ia!

207. CHRIST, THE LORD, IS RISEN TODAY

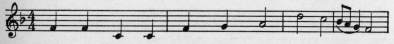

1. "Christ the Lord is risen to - day," Al - le - lu - ia!
2. Vain the stone, the watch, the seal; Al - le - lu - ia!
3. Lives a - gain our glo - rious King; Al - le - lu - ia!
4. Hail, the Lord of earth and heav'n! Al - le - lu - ia!

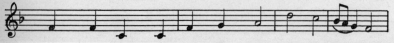

1. Sons of men and an - gels say; Al - le - lu - ia!
2. Christ has burst the gates of hell: Al - le - lu - ia!
3. Where, O death, is now thy sting? Al - le - lu - ia!
4. Praise to thee by both be giv'n; Al - le - lu - ia!

1. Raise your joys and tri - umphs high; Al - le - lu - ia!
2. Death in vain for - bids his rise; Al - le - lu - ia!
3. Once he died, our souls to save; Al - le - lu - ia!
4. Thee we greet tri - um - phant now; Al - le - lu - ia!

1. Sing, ye heav'ns, and earth, re - ply; Al - le - lu - ia!
2. Christ has o - pened par - a - dise. Al - le - lu - ia!
3. Where thy vic - to - ry, O grave? Al - le - lu - ia!
4. Hail, the Res - ur - rec - tion thou! Al - le - lu - ia!

208. CHRIST, THE LORD, IS RISEN TODAY

1. Christ, the Lord, is risen to - day; Al - le - lu - ia!
2. For the sheep the Lamb has bled, Al - le - lu - ia!
3. Christ, the Vic - tim un - de - filed, Al - le - lu - ia!

1. Chris - tians, haste your vows to pay; Al - le - lu - ia!
2. Sin - less in the sin - ner's stead; Al - le - lu - ia!
3. God and man has rec - on - ciled; Al - le - lu - ia!

1. Of - fer now your prais - es meet, Al - le - lu - ia!
2. Christ is ris'n to - day we cry; Al - le - lu - ia!
3. When in strange and dread-ful strife, Al - le - lu - ia!

1. At the pas-chal Vic - tim's feet. Al - le - lu - ia!
2. Now he lives no more to die. Al - le - lu - ia!
3. Met to - geth - er death and Life. Al - le - lu - ia!

209. JESUS CHRIST IS RISEN TODAY

1. Je - sus Christ is ris'n to - day! Al - le - lu - ia!
2. See the ho - ly wom - en come, Al - le - lu - ia!
3. Go tell all his breth-ren dear Al - le - lu - ia!
4. Glo - ry, Je - sus! be to thee! Al - le - lu - ia!

1. Sin - ners, wipe your tears a - way! Al - le - lu - ia!
2. Bear - ing spic - es to the tomb; Al - le - lu - ia!
3. "He is ris'n, he is not here! Al - le - lu - ia!
4. Your own might has set you free! Al - le - lu - ia!

1. He whose death up - on the Cross Al - le - lu - ia!
2. Hear the white-clad an - gel's voice Al - le - lu - ia!
3. Seek him not a - mong the dead; Al - le - lu - ia!
4. Come! for par - a - dise re - stored. Al - le - lu - ia!

1. Saves all men from end-less loss. Al - le - lu - ia!
2. Bid the u - ni - verse re - joice. Al - le - lu - ia!
3. He is ris - en as he said!" Al - le - lu - ia!
4. Let us bless our pas-chal Lord! Al - le - lu - ia!

210. BE JOYFUL, MARY

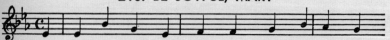

1. Be joy - ful, Mar - y, heav'n - ly Queen, be joy - ful,
2. The Son you bore by heav - en's grace, be joy - ful,
3. The Lord has ris - en from the dead, be joy - ful,
4. Then pray to God, O Vir - gin fair, be joy - ful,

1. Mar-y! Thy grief is changed to joy se-rene.
2. Mar-y! Did by his death our guilt e-rase.
3. Mar-y! He rose in glo-ry as he said.
4. Mar-y! That he our souls to heav-en bear.

Refrain

Al-le-lu-ia, re-joice, re-joice, O Mar-y!

211. LET HYMNS OF JOY

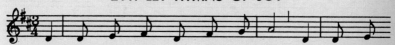

1. Let hymns of joy to grief suc-ceed. We know that
2. The morn had spread her crim-son rays, When rang the
3. To God the Fa-ther let us sing; To God the

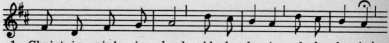

1. Christ is ris'n in-deed: Al-le-lu-ia, al-le-lu-ia!
2. skies with shouts of praise: Al-le-lu-ia, al-le-lu-ia!
3. Son, our ris-en King: Al-le-lu-ia, al-le-lu-ia!

1. We hear his white-robed an-gel's voice, And
2. Earth joined the joy-ful hymn to swell That
3. And e-qual-ly let us a-dore The

Refrain

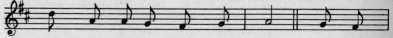

1. in our ris-en Lord re-joice. Al-le-
2. brought de-spair to van-quished hell.
3. Ho-ly Spir-it ev-er-more.

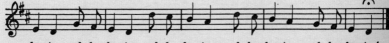

lu-ia, al-le-lu-ia, al-le-lu-ia, al-le-lu-ia, al-le-lu-ia!

212. ALLELUIA, LET THE HOLY ANTHEM RISE

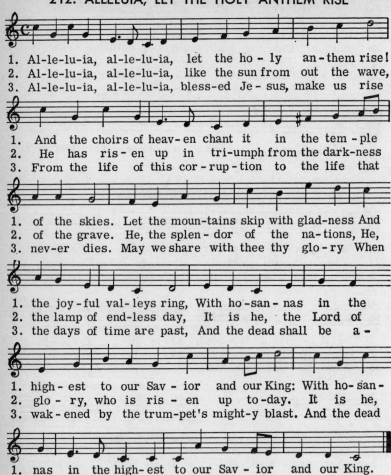

1. Al-le-lu-ia, al-le-lu-ia, let the ho - ly an-them rise!
2. Al-le-lu-ia, al-le-lu-ia, like the sun from out the wave,
3. Al-le-lu-ia, al-le-lu-ia, bless-ed Je - sus, make us rise

1. And the choirs of heav-en chant it in the tem -ple
2. He has ris - en up in tri-umph from the dark-ness
3. From the life of this cor - rup -tion to the life that

1. of the skies. Let the moun-tains skip with glad-ness And
2. of the grave. He, the splen - dor of the na-tions, He,
3. nev-er dies. May we share with thee thy glo-ry When

1. the joy-ful val-leys ring, With ho -san- nas in the
2. the lamp of end-less day, It is he, the Lord of
3. the days of time are past, And the dead shall be a -

1. high - est to our Sav - ior and our King: With ho-san-
2. glo - ry, who is ris - en up to-day. It is he,
3. wak - ened by the trum-pet's might-y blast. And the dead

1. nas in the high-est to our Sav - ior and our King.
2. the Lord of glo - ry, who is ris - en up to-day.
3. shall be a- wak-ened by the trum-pet's might-y blast.

213. O QUEEN OF HEAVEN, REJOICE

1. O Queen of heav-en, re-joice now, al - le - lu - ia; re-joice
2. Re - gi - na cae - li, lae - ta - re, al - le - lu - ia; Qui a

1. for he to whom you once gave birth, al - le - lu - ia,
2. quem me-ru - i - sti por - ta - re, al - le - lu - ia;

1. Is now ris-en, as he fore-told, al - le - lu - ia:
2. Re-sur-re-xit, sic-ut dix - it, al - le - lu - ia:

1. Pray for us to the Fa-ther, al - le - lu - ia.
2. O - ra pro no-bis De - um, al - le - lu - ia.

℣. Rejoice and be glad, Virgin Mary, alleluia.
℟. For the Lord has truly risen, alleluia.

Let us pray. O God, you were pleased to give joy to the world through the resurrection of your Son, our Lord Jesus Christ. Grant, we beseech you, that through the mediation of the Virgin Mary, his Mother, we may come to possess the joys of life everlasting. Through the same Christ, our Lord. ℟. Amen.

214. SING WE TRIUMPHANT HYMNS

1. Sing we tri - um-phant hymns of praise To greet our
2. In won-d'ring awe his faith -ful band Up - on the

1. Lord these fes-tive days. Al - le - lu - ia, al - le - lu - ia!
2. Mount of Ol-ive's stand. Al - le - lu - ia, al - le - lu - ia!

1. Who by a road be - fore un - trod As - cend-
2. And with the Vir - gin Moth - er see Their Lord

Refrain

1. ed to the throne of God. Al - le - lu - ia,
2. as - cend in maj - es - ty.

al - le - lu - ia, al - le - lu - ia, al - le - lu - ia, al - le - lu - ia!

215. COME, HOLY GHOST, IN NATURE ONE

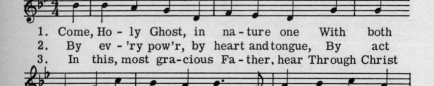

1. Come, Ho - ly Ghost, in na - ture one With both
2. By ev - 'ry pow'r, by heart and tongue, By act
3. In this, most gra - cious Fa - ther, hear Through Christ

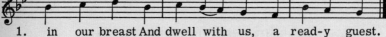

1. the Fa - ther and the Son, Shed forth thy grace with-
2. and deed thy praise be sung; In-flame with per - fect
3. thy e - qual Son our prayer, Who with the Ho - ly

1. in our breast And dwell with us, a read - y guest.
2. love each sense That oth - er souls may kin-dle thence.
3. Ghost and thee Doth live and reign e - ter-nal - ly.

216. COME, HOLY GHOST, CREATOR BLEST

1. Come, Ho - ly Ghost, Cre - a - tor blest, And in our
2. O Com-fort - er, to thee we cry, Thou gift of
3. Praise be to thee, Fa - ther and Son, And Ho - ly

1. hearts take up thy rest; Come with thy grace and heav'n-
2. God sent from on high, Thou font of life and fire
3. Spir - it, with them one; And may the Son on us

1. ly aid To fill the hearts which thou hast made.
2. of love, The soul's a - noint - ing from a - bove.
3. be-stow All gifts that from the Spir - it flow.

217. COME, HOLY SPIRIT, GOD-HEAD ONE

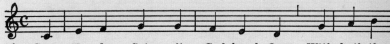

1. Come, Ho - ly Spir - it, God-head One With both the
2. With all our strength of mind and tongue, In word and
3. To God the Fa - ther, with the Son And Ho - ly

1. Fa - ther and the Son, Pour out thy grace with - in
2. deed thy praise be sung: May burn-ing love our hearts
3. Spir - it, God - head One, All glo - ry, praise and hon -

1. our breast, And be our souls' in - dwell - ing guest.
2. in - spire, In - flam - ing oth - ers with its fire.
3. or be, In time and in e - ter - ni - ty.

218. CREATOR SPIRIT ALL DIVINE

1. Cre - a - tor Spir - it all di - vine, Come vis - it
2. O gift of God, thine is the sweet Con - sol - ing
3. To us, through thee, the grace be shown To know the

1. ev - 'ry soul of thine And fill with thy ce -
2. name of Par - a - clete, Thou spring of life and
3. Fa - ther and the Son; And Spir - it of them

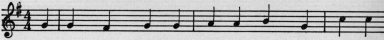

1. les - tial flame The hearts which thou thy- self did frame.
2. fire of love And sav - ing unc-tion from a - bove.
3. both, may we For - ev - er rest our faith in thee.

219. HOLY SPIRIT, TRUTH DIVINE

1. Ho - ly Spir - it, Truth di - vine, Dawn up - on
2. Ho - ly Spir - it, Love di - vine, Glow with - in
3. Ho - ly Spir - it, Pow'r di - vine, Strength - en this

1. this soul of mine; Breath of God and in - ward
2. this heart of mine; Kin - dle ev - 'ry high de -
3. weak will of mine; May thy sure sup - port pre -

1. Light, Wake my spir - it, clear my sight.
2. sire; Con - quer self in thy pure fire!
3. cede Ev - 'ry thought and word and deed.

220. JESUS CHRIST, THE KING OF AGES

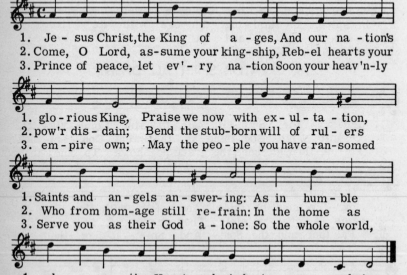

1. Je - sus Christ, the King of a - ges, And our na - tion's
2. Come, O Lord, as - sume your king-ship, Reb-el hearts your
3. Prince of peace, let ev'- ry na -tion Soon your heav'n-ly

1. glo - rious King, Praise we now with ex - ul - ta - tion,
2. pow'r dis - dain; Bend the stub-born will of rul - ers
3. em - pire own; May the peo - ple you have ran-somed

1. Saints and an - gels an - swer- ing: As in hum - ble
2. Who from hom-age still re-frain: In the home as
3. Serve you as their God a - lone: So the whole world,

1. ad - o - ra - tion Hearts and minds to you we bring.
2. in the cit - y Be su-preme, O Christ, and reign.
3. filled with bless-ing, Shall be gath- ered 'round your throne.

221. O JESUS VICTIM-PRIEST

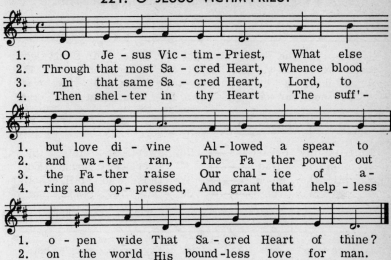

1. O Je - sus Vic - tim - Priest, What else
2. Through that most Sa - cred Heart, Whence blood
3. In that same Sa - cred Heart, Lord, to
4. Then shel - ter in thy Heart The suff'-

1. but love di - vine Al - lowed a spear to
2. and wa - ter ran, The Fa - ther poured out
3. the Fa - ther raise Our chal - ice of a -
4. ring and op - pressed, And grant that help - less

1. o - pen wide That Sa - cred Heart of thine?
2. on the world His bound - less love for man.
3. ton - ing love In sac - ri - fice and praise.
4. sin - ners there May find true peace and rest.

222. NAME ONCE GIVEN BY THE ANGEL

1. Name once giv - en by the an - gel To the maid of
2. Name of maj - es - ty and pow - er, Strength and cour - age

1. Naz - a - reth; Name a - bove all names ex - alt - ed
2. to the weak; Peace and com - fort to the dy - ing,

1. In the tri - umph o - ver death! Je - sus, name of
2. Truth, in - deed, to those who seek; May our lips in

1. bound - less mer - cy, Bless us till our fi - nal breath.
2. ho - ly rev - 'rence That great name of Je - sus speak.

223. JESUS, THE VERY THOUGHT OF THEE

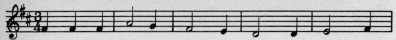

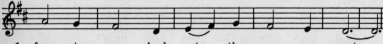

1. Je - sus, the ver - y thought of thee With sweet - ness
2. No voice can sing, no heart can frame, Nor can the
3. O hope of ev - 'ry con - trite heart, O joy of
4. Je - sus, our on - ly joy be thou, That with thee

1. fills my breast, —— But sweet - er far thy
2. mem - 'ry find —— A sweet - er sound than
3. all the meek, —— To those who fall, how
4. we may be; —— Je - sus, be thou our

1. face to see And in thy pres - ence rest.
2. thy blest name, O Sav - ior of man - kind!
3. kind thou art! How good to those who seek!
4. glo - ry now And through e - ter - ni - ty.

224. O CHRIST, OUR HOPE, OUR HEART'S DESIRE

1. O Christ, our hope, our heart's de - sire, Re - demp - tion's
2. How vast the mer - cy and the love Which free - ly
3. But now the bonds of death are burst, The ran - som
4. O Christ, you are our last - ing joy, Our ev - er

1. on - ly spring! Cre - a - tor of the world are
2. bears our sins, And suf - fer - ing a cru - el
3. has been paid; And you are on your Fa - ther's
4. great re - ward! Our on - ly glo - ry may it

1. you, Its Sav - ior and its King.
2. death, For us sal - va - tion wins.
3. throne, In glo - rious robes ar - rayed.
4. be To glo - ry in the Lord. A - men.

225. OF THE FATHER'S LOVE BEGOTTEN

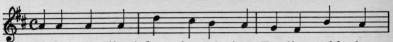

1. Of the Fa-ther's love be-got-ten Ere the worlds be-
2. O that birth for-ev-er bless-ed, When the Vir-gin
3. O ye heights of heav'n a-dore him, An-gel hosts, his

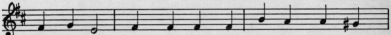

1. gan to be. He is first and last and al-ways,
2. full of grace, By the Ho-ly Ghost con-ceiv-ing,
3. prais-es sing; Pow'rs, Do-min-ions, bow be-fore him

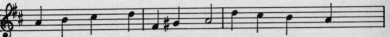

1. He the source, the end-ing he, Of the things that
2. Bore the Sav-ior of our race; And the Babe, the
3. And ex-tol our God and King. Let no tongue on

1. are, that have been, And that fu-ture years shall see.
2. world's Re-deem-er, First re-vealed his sa-cred face.
3. earth be si-lent, Ev'-ry voice in con-cert ring.

226. O SAVING VICTIM

1. O sav-ing Vic-tim o-p'ning wide The gate of
2. To thy great name be end-less praise, Im-mor-tal

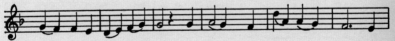

1. heav-en to man be-low! Our foes press on from ev-'ry
2. God-head, one in three; Oh, grant us end-less length of

1. side Thine aid sup-ply, thy strength be-stow.
2. days In our true na-tive land with thee. A-men.

227. SING MY TONGUE! ACCLAIM CHRIST PRESENT

1. Sing, my tongue! Ac - claim Christ pres - ent,
2. Heav - en's prom - ised gift to man - kind,
3. Din - ing with his twelve a - pos - tles
4. Word - made - flesh makes bread his bod - y,
5. Bow - ing low, then, of - fer hom - age
6. Praise and glo - ri - fy the Fa - ther,

1. Veiled with - in this sa - cred sign:
2. Born to vir - gin full of grace,
3. On the night be - fore he died,
4. Con - se - crates it by his word.
5. To a Sac - ra - ment so great!
6. Bless his Son's life - giv - ing Name,

1. Pre - cious blood and ris - en bod - y
2. Plants the seed of faith se - cure - ly
3. Tak - ing for the Pas - chal sup - per
4. Wine be - comes the blood of Je - sus:
5. Here is new and per - fect wor - ship;
6. Sing - ing their e - ter - nal God - head,

1. Un - der forms of bread and wine:
2. While he dwells with Ad - am's race.
3. Foods the law had spec - i - fied.
4. He it is whose voice is heard.
5. All the old must ter - mi - nate.
6. Pow - er, maj - es - ty and fame,

1. Blood once shed for man's re - demp - tion
2. Ends his mis - sion, leaves a sym - bol
3. Lo, he sets new bread be - fore them,
4. Minds in doubt need faith's as - sur - ance;
5. Sens - es can - not grasp this mar - vel;
6. Of - fer - ing their Ho - ly Spir - it

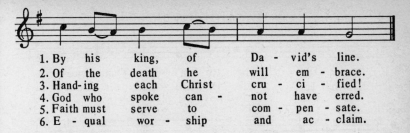

1. By his king, of Da - vid's line.
2. Of the death he will em - brace.
3. Hand-ing each Christ cru - ci - fied!
4. God who spoke can - not have erred.
5. Faith must serve to com - pen - sate.
6. E - qual wor - ship and ac - claim.

228. TANTUM ERGO
229. BOWING LOW, THEN, OFFER HOMAGE

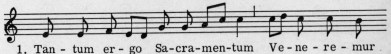

1. Tan - tum er - go Sa-cra-men-tum Ve - ne - re - mur
2. Ge - ni - to - ri Ge - ni - to - que Laus et iu - bi-

1. Bow - ing low, then, of-fer hom - age To a sac - ra-
2. Praise and glo - ri - fy the Fa - ther, Bless his Son's life-

1. cer - nu - i, Et an - ti-quum do - cu-men-tum No-
2. la - ti - o, Sa - lus, ho - nor, vir - tus quo - que Sit

1. ment so great! Here is new and per-fect wor - ship; All
2. giv-ing name, Sing-ing their e - ter - nal God-head, Pow-

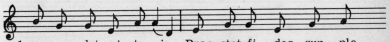

1. vo ce - dat ri - tu - i; Prae-stet fi - des sup - ple-
2. et be - ne - di - cti - o: Pro - ce-den - ti ab u-

1. the old must ter-mi - nate. Sens - es can - not grasp this
2. er, maj - es - ty and fame, Of - fer-ing their Ho - ly

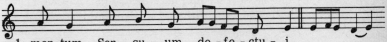

1. men-tum, Sen - su - um de - fe - ctu - i.
2. tro - que Com-par sit lau-da - ti - o. A - men.

1. mar - vel: Faith must serve to com-pen-sate.
2. Spir - it E - qual wor-ship and ac- claim. A - men.

230. O SALUTARIS HOSTIA

1. O sa - lu - ta - ris Ho - sti - a, Quae cae - li
2. U - ni tri - no - que Do - mi - no Sit sem - pi -

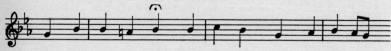

1. pan - dis o - sti - um: Bel - la pre - munt ho - sti - li -
2. ter - na glo - ri - a, Qui vi - tam si - ne ter - mi -

1. a, Da ro - bur, fer au - xi - li - um.
2. no No - bis do - net in pa - tri - a. A - men.

231. BOWING LOW, THEN, OFFER HOMAGE

1. Bow - ing low, then, of - fer hom - age To a Sac - ra -
2. Praise and glo - ri - fy the Fa - ther, Bless his Son's life -

1. ment so great! Here is new and per - fect wor - ship;
2. giv - ing name, Sing-ing their e - ter - nal God - head,

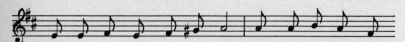

1. All the old must ter - mi - nate. Sens - es can - not grasp
2. Pow - er, maj - es - ty and fame, Of - fer-ing their Ho -

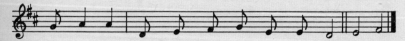

1. this mar - vel: Faith must serve to com - pen - sate.
2. ly Spir - it E - qual wor - ship and ac-claim. A - men.

232. THE CHURCH'S ONE FOUNDATION

1. The Church's one foun-da-tion   Is   Je - sus Christ her
2. E - lect from ev - 'ry na-tion,   Yet one o'er   all   the

1. Lord; She   is   his new cre - a - tion   By   wa -
2. earth, Her char - ter   of   sal - va - tion: One Lord,

1. ter and   the word: From heav'n he came and
2. one faith, one birth; One   ho - ly name she

1. sought her To   be   his ho-ly bride; With his own
2. bless - es, Par - takes one ho-ly food, And to one

1. blood he bought her, And for her   life he died.
2. hope she press - es, With ev -'ry grace en-dued. A-men.

233. WHO IS SHE THAT STANDS TRIUMPHANT

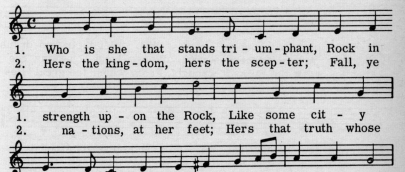

1.   Who   is she that   stands tri - um - phant, Rock in
2.   Hers the king-dom, hers the scep - ter; Fall, ye

1.   strength up - on the Rock, Like some cit - y
2.   na - tions, at her feet; Hers that truth whose

1. crowned with tur - rets, Brav-ing storm and earth-quake shock?
2. fruit   is free-dom, Light her yoke, her bur - den sweet.

1. Moth - er Church, her arms ex - tend - ed, Bless-ing thus a
2. As the moon its splen-dor bor-rows from a sun un-

1. world re-stored, All the an - thems of cre - a - tion,
2. seen at night, So from Christ, the Sun of jus-tice,

1. Lift-ing to cre - a - tion's Lord; All the an - thems
2. Ev - er-more she draws her light; So from Christ, the

1. of cre- a -tion, Lift-ing to cre - a - tion's Lord.
2. Sun of jus-tice, Ev - er - more she draws her light.

234. THE GOD WHOM EARTH AND SEA AND SKY

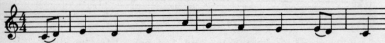

1. The God whom earth and sea and sky A - dore
2. How blest that Moth - er, in whose shrine The world's
3. Blest in the mes- sage Ga- briel brought, Blest by
4. All hon - or, praise and glo - ry be, O Je -

1. and laud and mag-ni - fy, Who o'er their won-drous
2. wise Ar - chi-tect di - vine, Whose hand con-tains the
3. the work the Spir - it wrought, From whom the great De-
4. sus, Vir- gin-born, to thee; All glo - ry, as is

1. struc-ture reigns The Vir - gin's spot-less womb con-tains.
2. earth and sky, Has deigned as in his ark to lie.
3. sire of earth Took hu - man flesh and hu-man birth.
4. ev - er meet, To Fa - ther and to Par - a-clete.

235. HAIL, HOLY QUEEN

1. Hail, ho- ly Queen   en - throned a - bove, Sal-ve Re-gi-na!
2. Our life, our sweet-ness   here be- low, Sal-ve Re-gi-na!
3. Our ad - vo - cate with   God on high, Sal-ve Re-gi-na!

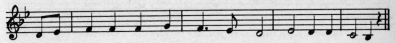

1. Hail, Queen of mer - cy, Queen of love, Sal-ve Re-gi-na!
2. From you all grace and com-fort flow, Sal-ve Re-gi-na!
3. To   you our plead -ing voic - es cry, Sal-ve Re-gi-na!

Chorus

Sing her praise, ye Cher - u - bim! Join our

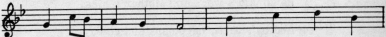

song, ye Ser - a - phim! Heav'n and earth re -

sound the hymn: Sal - ve, Sal - ve, Sal - ve Re - gi - na!

236. HAIL, O STAR OF OCEAN

1. Hail,   O star of   o - cean, God's own Moth-er blest,
2. Show thy-self a Moth - er, May the Word di - vine,
3. Keep our life all spot - less, Make our way se-cure,
4. Praise to God the Fa - ther, Hon - or to the Son,

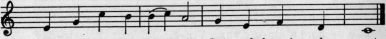

1. Ev - er sin-less Vir-gin, Gate of heav'n - ly   rest.
2. Born for us thine In - fant, Hear our prayer through thine.
3. Till we find in Je - sus Joy that shall   en - dure.
4. In the Ho - ly Spir- it Be the glo - ry one.

237. COME, O CHILDREN, GIVE SWEET VOICE

Come, O chil-dren, give sweet voice, Songs of our glad Moth-er,

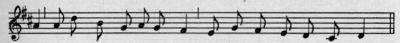

sing; In her joys let us re-joice For she bore our Sav-ior-King..

2. Angel entered maiden's room,
   Mary faithfully believed;
   God-man entered Mary's womb,
   By the Spirit's pow'r conceived.

3. Ever Virgin, she gave birth;
   Who has known such joy as this!
   Nurturing the Lord of earth,
   Handmaid's worship, Mother's kiss.

4. Led by star through dark and cold,
   Magi found the little Boy;
   With their worship, offered gold;
   He beheld their gifts with joy.

5. Jesus, O thou gracious One,
   Flooding Mary with thy light,
   And thou Godhead, three in one,
   May we sing thy glory bright.

238. VOICE OF CELEBRATION, SING!

Voice of cel-e-bra-tion, sing! Bells of ju-bi-la-tion, ring!

May we hold a sin-gle ray, Vir-gin, of your joys to-day.

2. You who from the Father won
   Spirit's grace to bear his Son,
   Bring us, sons of God by grace,
   To behold his holy face.

3. You who served your cousin old,
   Help us as our works unfold;
   You whose fruit was Deity,
   Give us glad eternity.

4. You who saw the Magi bow
   To your Babe, O help us now;
   You who, joyful, found your Boy,
   Lead us to eternal joy.

5. You who saved your Son from death,
   Strengthen us in dying breath;
   As we enter heaven, won,
   Mary, take us to your Son.

6. Christ, your Mother's sheer delight,
   Be the lamp in sinner's night;
   May our love be melody,
   Music of eternity.

239. MAY CROWNING HYMN

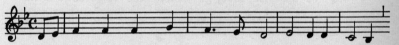

1. We gath-er 'round your shrine to-day, Sal-ve Re-gi-na!
2. This di-a-dem of flow-ers fair, Sal-ve Re-gi-na!

1. To crown you as our Queen of May, Sal-ve Re-gi-na!
2. Is in-ter-twined with love and pray'r. Sal-ve Re-gi-na!

Refrain

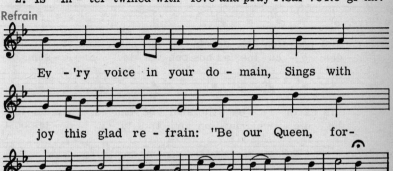

Ev-'ry voice in your do-main, Sings with

joy this glad re-frain: "Be our Queen, for-

ev-er reign!" Sal-ve, Sal-ve, Sal-ve Re-gi-na!

240. MARY, WE GREET THEE

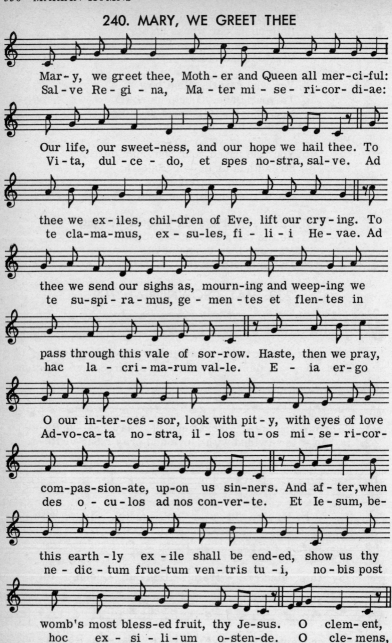

Mar - y, we greet thee, Moth - er and Queen all mer - ci - ful:
Sal - ve Re - gi - na, Ma - ter mi - se - ri - cor - di - ae:

Our life, our sweet-ness, and our hope we hail thee. To
Vi - ta, dul - ce - do, et spes no-stra, sal - ve. Ad

thee we ex - iles, chil-dren of Eve, lift our cry-ing. To
te cla-ma-mus, ex - su-les, fi - li - i He - vae. Ad

thee we send our sighs as, mourn-ing and weep-ing we
te su-spi - ra - mus, ge - men -tes et flen-tes in

pass through this vale of sor-row. Haste, then we pray,
hac la - cri-ma-rum val-le. E - ia er-go

O our in-ter-ces - sor, look with pit - y, with eyes of love
Ad-vo-ca-ta no - stra, il - los tu - os mi - se - ri-cor-

com-pas-sion-ate, up-on us sin-ners. And af - ter,when
des o - cu-los ad nos con-ver-te. Et Ie - sum, be-

this earth - ly ex - ile shall be end-ed, show us thy
ne - dic - tum fruc-tum ven-tris tu - i, no - bis post

womb's most bless-ed fruit, thy Je-sus. O clem-ent,
hoc ex - si - li - um o-sten-de. O cle-mens,

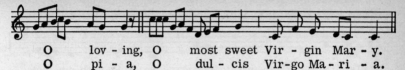

O   lov - ing, O   most sweet Vir - gin Mar - y.
O   pi - a, O   dul - cis Vir-go Ma - ri - a.

℣. Pray for us, holy Mother of God.
℟. Make us worthy of the promises of Christ.

Let us pray. All powerful, eternal God, by the cooperation of the Holy
Spirit you made ready the body and soul of the glorious Virgin Mother
Mary to be a fit dwelling-place for your Son. As we celebrate her memory
with joy, grant that through her motherly intercession we may be pre-
served from evil in this world and from eternal death. Through the same
Christ, our Lord. ℟. Amen.

241. HEART OF MARY

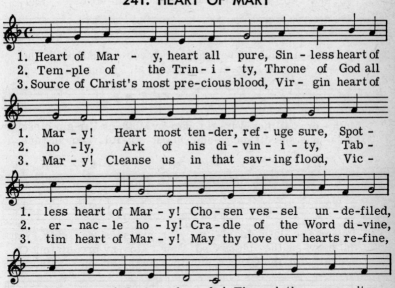

1. Heart of Mar - y, heart all pure, Sin - less heart of
2. Tem -ple of   the Trin - i - ty, Throne of God all
3. Source of Christ's most pre-cious blood, Vir - gin heart of

1. Mar - y! Heart most ten -der, ref - uge sure, Spot -
2. ho - ly,   Ark of his di - vin - i - ty, Tab -
3. Mar - y! Cleanse us in that sav - ing flood, Vic -

1. less heart of Mar - y! Cho - sen ves - sel un - de-filed,
2. er - nac - le ho - ly! Cra - dle of the Word di -vine,
3. tim heart of Mar - y! May thy love our hearts re-fine,

1. Lil - y chal - ice ho - ly! Through the   mer - its
2. Show us Christ our Broth - er, Heart of   Mar - y
3. Bless our con - se - cra - tion; May our hearts be

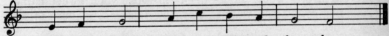

1. of thy Child, Make us pure and ho - ly.
2. mys - tic shrine, Show thy - self our Moth - er.
3. one with thine, Mak - ing rep - a - ra - tion.

242. DAILY SING IN PRAISE OF MARY

1. Dai - ly sing in praise of Mar - y, Sing with joy her
2. She is might - y in her plead-ing, Ten - der in her

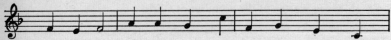

1. prais-es due! All her feasts, her ac-tions hon - or,
2. lov - ing care; Ev - er watch-ful, un - der - stand - ing,

1. With the heart's de - vo-tion true. Lost in won - d'ring
2. All our sor - rows she will share. Ad-vo-cate and

1. con-tem - pla-tion, Be her maj-es - ty con-fessed! Call her
2. lov-ing Moth-er, Me-di - a-trix of all grace! Heav-en's

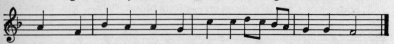

1. Moth - er, call her Vir-gin, Hap-py Moth-er Vir-gin blest!
2. bless-ings she dis-pens-es, On our sin-ful hu-man race.

243. IMMACULATE MARY

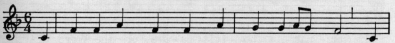

1. Im - mac - u - late Mar - y, your prais-es we sing. You
2. In heav-en the bless - ed your glo - ry pro-claim, On
3. We pray for the Church, our true Moth - er on earth, And

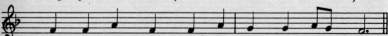

1. reign now in splen - dor with Je - sus our King.
2. earth we your chil - dren in-voke your sweet name.
3. beg you to watch o'er the land of our birth.

Refrain

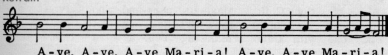

A - ve, A - ve, A - ve Ma - ri - a! A - ve, A - ve Ma - ri - a!

244. HYMN TO THE SORROWFUL MOTHER

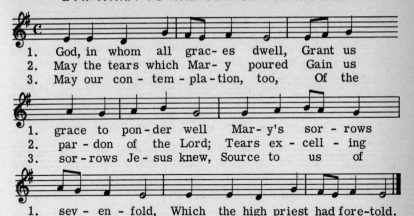

1. God, in whom all grac- es dwell, Grant us
2. May the tears which Mar- y poured Gain us
3. May our con - tem - pla-tion, too, Of the

1. grace to pon - der well Mar- y's sor - rows
2. par - don of the Lord; Tears ex - cell - ing
3. sor - rows Je - sus knew, Source to us of

1. sev - en - fold, Which the high priest had fore-told.
2. in their worth All the pen - anc - es of earth.
3. bless - ing be Through-out all e - ter - ni - ty.

245. MARY IMMACULATE, STAR OF THE MORNING

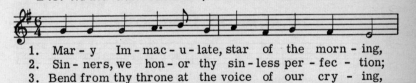

1. Mar - y Im - mac - u - late, star of the morn - ing,
2. Sin - ners, we hon - or thy sin - less per - fec - tion,
3. Bend from thy throne at the voice of our cry - ing,

1. Cho - sen be - fore the cre - a - tion be - gan!
2. Fall - en and weak, for thy mer - cy we plead.
3. Look to this earth which thy foot - steps have trod.

1. Des - tined to bring, through the light of thy dawn - ing,
2. Grant us the shield of thy might-y pro - tec - tion,
3. Stretch out thy arms to us liv - ing and dy - ing,

1. Con - quest of Sa - tan and res - cue to man!
2. Meas - ure thine aid by the depth of our need.
3. Mar - y Im - mac - u - late, Moth - er of God.

246. HAIL, THOU STAR OF OCEAN

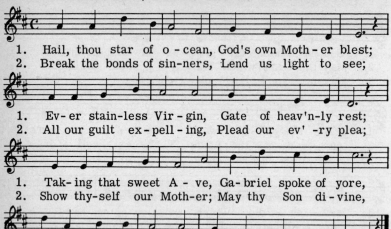

1. Hail, thou star of o - cean, God's own Moth - er blest;
2. Break the bonds of sin-ners, Lend us light to see;

1. Ev- er stain-less Vir - gin, Gate of heav'n-ly rest;
2. All our guilt ex- pell - ing, Plead our ev' -ry plea;

1. Tak- ing that sweet A - ve, Ga- briel spoke of yore,
2. Show thy-self our Moth-er; May thy Son di -vine,

1. E- va's name re-vers-ing, Peace for us im -plore.
2. Born for our sal- va - tion, Grant our prayers through thine.

247. HYMN TO SAINT JOSEPH

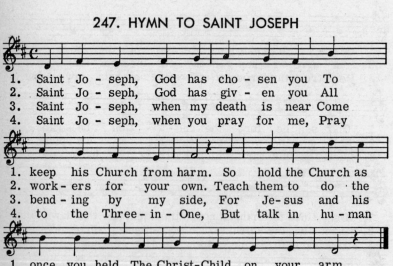

1. Saint Jo - seph, God has cho - sen you To
2. Saint Jo - seph, God has giv - en you All
3. Saint Jo - seph, when my death is near Come
4. Saint Jo - seph, when you pray for me, Pray

1. keep his Church from harm. So hold the Church as
2. work- ers for your own. Teach them to do the
3. bend - ing by my side, For Je- sus and his
4. to the Three- in - One, But talk in hu - man

1. once you held The Christ-Child on your arm.
2. best they can With steel and wood and stone.
3. Moth- er bent To help you when you died.
4. words with him Who let you call him son.

248. NOW LET THE EARTH WITH JOY RESOUND

Feast of an Apostle

1. Now let the earth with joy re-sound And heav'n the
2. Sick-ness and health your voice o - bey, At your com-
3. So when the world is at its end And Christ to
4. All hon - or, praise and glo - ry be, O Je - sus,

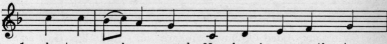

1. chant re - ech - o round; Nor heav'n nor earth too
2. mand they go or stay; From sin's dis- ease our
3. judg-ment shall de-scend, May we be called those
4. Vir - gin -born, to thee; All glo - ry, as is

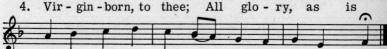

1. high can raise The great a - pos-tles' glo-rious praise!
2. souls re-store, In good con-firm us more and more.
3. joys to see Pre-pared from all e-ter-ni - ty.
4. ev - er meet, To Fa - ther and to Par - a - clete.

249. LET SAINTS ABOVE AND MEN BELOW

St. Benedict

1. Let saints a - bove and men be- low Their ho - ly
2. Thy sons, well taught, their voic-es raise To sing our
3. Praise, hon - or, glo - ry be to thee, Most bless-ed

1. joy and love now show, That Ben-e-dict with glo-ry
2. God's e - ter - nal praise. For us ob-tain, O Fa-ther
3. ho - ly Trin - i - ty! Whose love in ev - er - last-ing

1. crowned, E - ter - nal bliss in heav'n has found.
2. dear, Of high - er paths a vi - sion clear.
3. rest O'er-flows our saint's en - rap - tured breast.

250. JOYFUL, JOYFUL WE ADORE THEE

1. Joy-ful, joy-ful we a-dore thee, God of
2. All thy works with joy sur-round thee, Earth and
3. Thou art giv-ing and for-giv-ing, Ev - er
4. Mor-tals, join the might-y cho-rus Which the

1. glo - ry, Lord of love; Hearts un - fold like flow'rs
2. heav'n re-flect thy rays, Stars and an-gels sing
3. bless-ing, ev - er blest, Well-spring of the joy
4. morn-ing stars be-gan; Fa - ther-love is reign-

1. be-fore thee, Prais-ing thee, their Sun a - bove.
2. a-round thee, Cen - ter of un - bro-ken praise:
3. of liv - ing, O - cean-depth of hap-py rest!
4. ing o'er us, Broth-er - love binds man to man.

1. Melt the clouds of sin and sad - ness, Drive the
2. Field and for - est, vale and moun-tain, Flow - 'ry
3. Thou our Fa - ther, Christ our Broth-er, All who
4. Ev - er sing-ing, march we on-ward, Vic - tors

1. dark of doubt a - way; Giv - er of im-mor-tal
2. mead-ow, flash-ing sea, Chant-ing bird and flow-ing
3. live in love are thine; Teach us how to love each
4. in the midst of strife; Joy - ful mu - sic lifts us

1. glad-ness, Fill us with the light of day.
2. foun - tain, Call us to re - joice in thee.
3. oth - er, Lift us to the joy di - vine.
4. sun - ward In the tri - umph song of life.

251. PRAISE WE OUR GOD WITH JOY

1. Praise we our God with joy And glad - ness nev - er
2. All praise and thanks to God The Fa - ther now be

1. end - ing; An - gels and saints with us Their
2. giv - en, The Son, and Ho - ly Ghost En -

1. grate - ful voic - es blend - ing. He is our Shep-herd
2. throned in high - est heav - en; The one, e - ter - nal

1. true, With watch - ful care and love; His
2. God, Whom earth and heav'n a - dore; For

1. mer - cies with - out end He show-ers from a - bove.
2. thus it was, is now, And shall be ev - er - more.

252. PRAISE THE LORD OF HEAVEN
Psalm 148

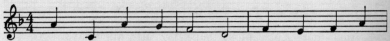

1. Praise the Lord of heav - en, Praise him in the
2. Praise the Lord, ye foun - tains Surg - ing from the
3. Praise him, birds and cat - tle, Princ - es and all

1. height, Praise him, all ye an - gels, Praise him,
2. seas, Rocks and hills and moun - tains, Ce - dars
3. kings; Praise him, men and maid - ens, All cre-

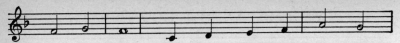

1. stars and light; Praise him, clouds and wa - ters,
2. and all trees; Praise him, clouds and va - pors,
3. a - ted things; Glo - ri - ous and might - y

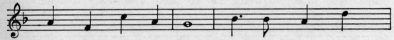

1. All things in the skies, When his Word com -
2. Snow and hail and fire, Storm - y wind ful -
3. Is his name a - lone; Mak - ing earth his

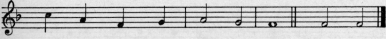

1. mand - ed, Struc - tured did a - rise.
2. fill - ing On - ly his de - sire.
3. foot- stool, Mak - ing heav'n his throne. A - men.

253. PRAISE TO THE HOLIEST IN THE HEIGHT

1. Praise to the Ho - liest in the height, And in
2. O lov - ing wis - dom of our God! When all

1. the depth be praise; In all his words most
2. was sin and shame, A sec - ond Ad - am

1. won - der - ful, Most sure in all his ways.
2. to the fight And to the res - cue came. A - men.

3. O wisest love! that flesh and blood,
   Which did in Adam fail,
   Should strive afresh against the foe,
   Should strive, and should prevail;

4. And that a higher gift than grace
   Should flesh and blood refine,
   God's presence and his very self
   And essence all divine.

5. O generous love! that he who smote
   In man for man the foe,
   The double agony in man
   For man should undergo;

6. And in the garden secretly,
   And on the Cross on high,
   Should teach his brethren, and inspire
   To suffer and to die.

7. Praise to the Holiest in the height,
   And in the depth be praise;
   In all his words most wonderful,
   Most sure in all his ways. Amen.

254. SONGS OF PRAISE THE ANGELS SANG

1. Songs of praise the an - gels sang, Heav'n with
2. Songs of praise a - woke the morn When the

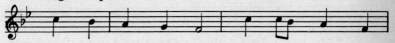

1. al - le - lu - ias rang, When cre - a - tion
2. Prince of peace was born; Songs of praise a -

1. was be - gun, When God spoke and it was done.
2. rose when he Cap - tive led cap-tiv- i - ty. A-men.

3. Heaven and earth must pass away,
   Songs of praise shall crown that day;
   God will make new heavens and earth,
   Songs of praise shall hail their birth.

4. Saints below with heart and voice
   Still in songs of praise rejoice;
   Learning here, by faith and love,
   Songs of praise to sing above.

5. Hymns of glory, songs of praise,
   Father, unto thee we raise,
   Jesus, glory unto thee,
   With the Spirit, ever be. Amen.

255. BLESSED BE THE HOLY TRINITY

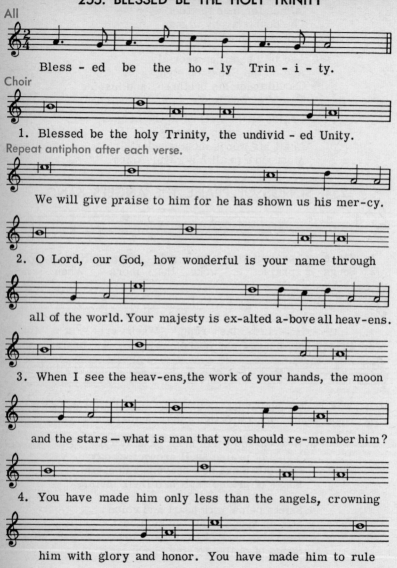

All

Bless - ed be the ho - ly Trin - i - ty.

Choir

1. Blessed be the holy Trinity, the undivid - ed Unity.

Repeat antiphon after each verse.

We will give praise to him for he has shown us his mer-cy.

2. O Lord, our God, how wonderful is your name through

all of the world. Your majesty is ex-alted a-bove all heav-ens.

3. When I see the heav-ens, the work of your hands, the moon

and the stars — what is man that you should re-member him?

4. You have made him only less than the angels, crowning

him with glory and honor. You have made him to rule

over the works of your hands.

5. You have given men charge of all things, the world you made.

O Lord, how your majesty fills all of the earth!

256. ROUND THE LORD IN GLORY SEATED

1. Round the Lord in   glo-ry seat-ed, Cher-u-bim
2. Heav'n is still with glo-ry ring-ing, Earth takes up
3. With the an-gels there a-round him, With his ho-

1. and ser - a - phim Filled his tem-ple, and re-peat-
2. the an-gels' cry, "Ho-ly, ho-ly, ho-ly," sing-
3. ly Church be-low, Now to-geth-er we a-dore

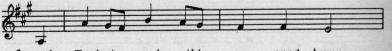

1. ed Each to each this sa - cred hymn:
2. ing, "Lord of hosts, our God Most High!"
3. him In the hal-lowed words all know:

Refrain

"Lord, thy glo-ry fills the heav-en, Earth is with its full-ness

stored; Un-to thee be glo-ry giv-en, Ho-ly, ho-ly, ho-ly Lord!"

257. GIVE TO OUR GOD IMMORTAL PRAISE

1. Give to our God im - mor - tal praise, Mer - cy and
2. Give to the Lord of lords re - nown, The King of

1. truth are all his ways. Won - ders of grace to
2. kings with glo - ry crown, His mer - cies ev - er

1. God be - long, Re - peat his mer - cies in your song.
2. shall en - dure, When time and tears are known no more.

258. THANK THE LORD FOR HE IS GOOD

Cantor

1. Thank the Lord for he is good:
2. He in wis - dom made the skies:
3. With a might - y sav - ing arm:
4. In our grief he com - forts us:

All

E - ter - nal is his mer - cy.

Cantor

1. Thank the Lord, the God of gods:
2. Light in heav - en he has made:
3. He has shat - tered E - gypt's might:
4. He from e - vil saves our souls:

All

E - ter - nal is his mer - cy.

Cantor

1. Thank our God, the Lord of lords, for
2. Sun he fash - ioned for the day, the
3. Res - cued Is - ra - el from death, and
4. He gives life and food to men: So

1. he a - lone does wond - rous works:
2. moon and stars to rule the night:
3. led them to the prom - ised land:
4. thank our God, the Lord of lords:

All

E - ter - nal is his mer - cy!

259. O GOD OF LOVE, O KING OF PEACE

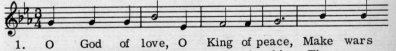

1. O God of love, O King of peace, Make wars
2. Re - mem - ber, Lord, your works of old, The won -
3. Whom shall we trust but you, O Lord? Where rest
4. Where saints and an - gels dwell a - bove All hearts

1. through-out the world to cease; The plans of sin - ful
2. ders that our fa - thers told; Re - mem - ber not our
3. but on your faith - ful word? None ev - er called on
4. are one in ho - ly love; May we to that high

1. man re-strain; Give peace, O God, give peace a-gain.
2. sin's dark stain; Give peace, O God, give peace a-gain.
3. you in vain; Give peace, O God, give peace a-gain.
4. state at - tain; Give peace, O God, give peace a-gain. A-men.

260. LORD, HAVE MERCY and OUR FATHER

Lord, have mer-cy. Christ, have mer-cy. Lord, have mer-cy.

Our Fa-ther, who art in heav-en, hal-lowed be thy

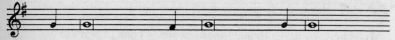

name; thy kingdom come; thy will be done on earth as it

is in heav-en. Give us this day our daily bread; and

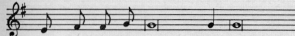

for-give us our trespass-es, as we forgive those who

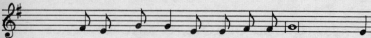

tres-pass a-gainst us; and lead us not into temptation,

but deliver us from e-vil.

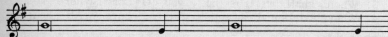

The Lord be with you.   All: And with your spir-it.

Let us pray . . .

261. O GOD, WHOSE HAND DID MAKE THE SKY

1.   O   God, whose hand did make the sky   And all   its
2.   En-light-en   thou the hearts of men, Our tar-nished
3. Hear thou our prayer, al-might-y King! Hear thou our

1. shin - ing hosts on high, Then paint-ing it with fi -
2. souls make pure a- gain, Un - loose the bands of guilt
3. prais - es while we sing, A - dor - ing with the heav'n-

1. 'ry light Made it so beau-teous and so bright.
2. with - in, Re - move the bur - den of our sin.
3. ly host The Fa - ther, Son and Ho - ly Ghost.

262. O GOD, OUR HELP IN AGES PAST

O God, our help in a-ges past, Our hope for years to come,

Safe shel-ter while our life shall last, And our e-ter-nal home.

2. Before the hills in order stood,
Or earth received her frame,
From everlasting thou art God,
To endless years the same.

3. A thousand ages in thy sight
Are like an evening gone;
Short as the watch that ends the night
Before the rising sun.

4. Time, like an ever-rolling stream,
Bears all its sons away;
They vanish swiftly as a dream
Dies at the op'ning day.

5. O God, our help in ages past,
Our hope for years to come,
Be thou our guide while troubles last,
And our eternal home.

263. ETERNAL FATHER, STRONG TO SAVE

1. E - ter - nal Fa - ther, strong to save, Who
2. O Sav - ior, whose al - might - y word The
3. O sa - cred Spir - it who did brood Up-
4. O Trin - i - ty of love and power, Our

1. cleans us in the wa - ter's wave, Who bids
2. winds and waves sub - mis - sive heard, Who walked
3. on the cha - os dark and rude, Who bade
4. breth - ren shield in dan - ger's hour; From fear

1. the might - y o - cean deep, Its own ap -
2. up - on the foam - ing deep, And calm a -
3. its an - gry tu - mult cease, And gave to
4. and tem - pest, fire and foe, Pro - tect them

1. point - ed lim - its keep; O hear us when we
2. mid the storm did sleep: O hear us when we
3. man light, life and peace: O hear us when we
4. where - so - e'er they go; Thus ev - er - more shall

1. cry to thee For those who long thy face to see.
2. cry to thee For those who long thy face to see.
3. cry to thee For those who long thy face to see.
4. rise to thee Glad hymns of praise from land and sea.

264. OUR FATHER'S GOD WHOSE EVER-MIGHTY HAND
Space Hymn

1. Our fa - thers' God, whose ev - er - might - y hand
2. And as we float a - long through out - er space,
3. Re - fresh your peo - ple on their toil - some way,

1. Leads forth in beau - ty all the star - ry band,
2. Past gal - ax - ies a - glow in dark's em - brace,
3. Lead us from night to nev - er - end - ing day;

1. Bright shin-ing worlds in splen-dor through the skies,
2. Toward oth - er worlds where broth-ers may a - wait,
3. Your love di - vine will guide us safe - ly past

1. Our grate-ful songs be - fore your throne a - rise.
2. Do care for us now in our weight-less state.
3. All e - vil snares and on to heav'n at last.

Refrain

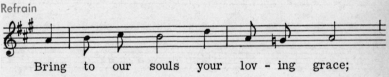

Bring to our souls your lov - ing grace;

Glo - ry to God in ev - 'ry time and place.

265. MY FAITH LOOKS UP TO THEE

1. My faith looks up to thee, Thou Lamb of
2. May thy rich grace im - part Strength to my

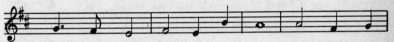

1. Cal - va - ry, Sav - ior di - vine! Now hear me
2. coward - ly heart, My zeal in - spire. As thou hast

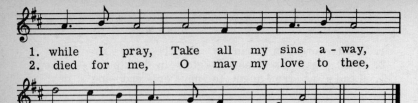

1. while I pray, Take all my sins a - way,
2. died for me, O may my love to thee,

1. O let me from this day Be whol - ly thine.
2. Sin - cere and con - stant be, A liv - ing fire. A - men.

266. ONWARD, CHRISTIAN SOLDIERS

On - ward, Chris - tian sol - diers, March - ing as to war,

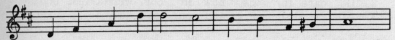

With the Cross of Je - sus Go - ing on be - fore:

Christ the roy - al Mas - ter Leads a - gainst the foe;

For - ward in - to bat - tle, See, his ban - ners go.

On - ward, Chris - tian sol - diers, March - ing as to war,

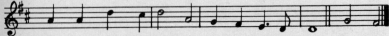

With the Cross of Je - sus Go - ing on be - fore. A - men.

2. Like a mighty army Moves the Church of God;
Brothers, we are treading Where the saints have trod;
We are not divided, All one body we,
One in hope and doctrine, One in charity.

3. Crowns and thrones may perish, Kingdoms rise and wane,
   But the Church of Jesus Constant will remain;
   Gates of hell can never 'Gainst that Church prevail;
   We have Christ's own promise, And that cannot fail.

4. Onward, then, ye people, Join our happy throng,
   Blend with ours your voices In the triumph song;
   Glory, laud, and honor Unto Christ the King;
   This through countless ages Men and angels sing.

267. BLESSED THE POOR IN SPIRIT

Cantor

1. Bless - ed   are   the   poor   in   spir - it:
2. Bless - ed   they   who   suf - fer   sor - row:
3. Bless - ed   they   who   prac - tice mer - cy:
4. Blest are   men   of   peace   for - ev - er:

All

1. Heav - en's   king - dom   shall   be   theirs;
2. Heav - en's   com - fort   shall   be   theirs;
3. Heav - en's   mer - cy   shall   be   theirs;
4. Heav - en's   son - ship   shall   be   theirs;

Cantor

1. Bless - ed   are   the   meek   and   gen - tle:
2. Bless - ed   those   who   seek   for   jus - tice:
3. Bless - ed   are   the   pure   of   con - science:
4. Blest are   they   who   die   for   jus - tice:

All

1. Theirs   the   love   of   God.
2. Theirs   the   grace   of   God.
3. Theirs   the   peace   of   God.
4. Theirs   the   sight   of   God.

268. FAITH OF OUR FATHERS!

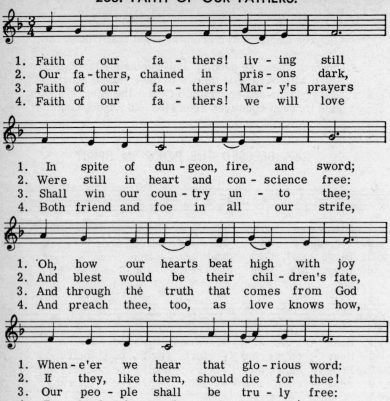

1. Faith of our fa - thers! liv - ing still
2. Our fa - thers, chained in pris - ons dark,
3. Faith of our fa - thers! Mar - y's prayers
4. Faith of our fa - thers! we will love

1. In spite of dun - geon, fire, and sword;
2. Were still in heart and con - science free:
3. Shall win our coun - try un - to thee;
4. Both friend and foe in all our strife,

1. Oh, how our hearts beat high with joy
2. And blest would be their chil - dren's fate,
3. And through the truth that comes from God
4. And preach thee, too, as love knows how,

1. When - e'er we hear that glo - rious word:
2. If they, like them, should die for thee!
3. Our peo - ple shall be tru - ly free:
4. By kind - ly words and vir - tuous life:

Refrain

Faith of our fa-thers, ho-ly faith! We will be true to thee till death.

269. O BLESSED DAY, THAT FIXED MY CHOICE

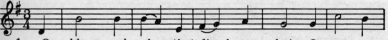

1. O bless - ed day, that fixed my choice On you, my
2. O bless - ed bond, that seals my vows To him who
3. 'Tis done! the great ob - la - tion's done! I am my
4. High heav'n, that heard the sol - emn vow, That vow re-

1. Sav - ior and my God! Well may my hap- py soul re-
2. mer - its all my love! Let cheer-ful an-thems fill his
3. Lord's, and he is mine; He drew me, and I fol-lowed
4. newed shall dai-ly hear, Till in life's lat- est hour I

1. joice, And tell its peace to all a-broad.
2. house, While in this sa - cred shrine I move.
3. on, Re - spon-sive to his voice di-vine.
4. bow, And bless in death a bond so dear. A-men.

270. O PERFECT LOVE, ALL HUMAN THOUGHT TRANSCENDING

1. O per-fect Love, all hu - man thought tran-scend-ing,
2. O per-fect Life, be thou their full as - sur-ance
3. Grant them the joy which bright-ens earth - ly sor- row;
4. Hear us, O Fa - ther, gra-cious and for - giv - ing,

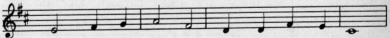

1. Low - ly we kneel in prayer be-fore thy throne,
2. Of ten-der char - i - ty and stead-fast faith,
3. Grant them the peace which calms all earth - ly strife,
4. Through Je -sus Christ, thy co - e - ter - nal Word,

1. That theirs may be the love which knows no end - ing,
2. Of pa - tient hope, and qui - et, brave en - dur-ance,
3. And to life's day the glo - rious un - known mor-row
4. Who with the Ho - ly Ghost, by all things liv - ing

1. Whom thou for ev - er -more dost join in one.
2. With child-like trust that fears nor pain nor death.
3. That dawns up - on e - ter - nal love and life.
4. Now and to end-less a - ges art a-dored.

271. WHEN MORNING GILDS THE SKIES

1. When morn - ing gilds the skies, My heart a -
2. The night be - comes as day When from the
3. Ye na - tions of man- kind, In this your
4. Be this, while life is mine, My can - ti -

1. wak - ing cries, May Je - sus Christ be praised: A -
2. heart we say, May Je - sus Christ be praised: The
3. con - cord find, May Je - sus Christ be praised: Let
4. cle di - vine, May Je - sus Christ be praised: Be

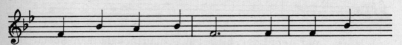

1. like at work and prayer To Je - sus
2. pow'rs of dark - ness fear When this sweet
3. all the earth a - round Ring joy - ous
4. this th'e - ter - nal song, Through all the

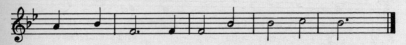

1. I re - pair; May Je - sus Christ be praised!
2. chant they hear, May Je - sus Christ be praised!
3. with the sound, May Je - sus Christ be praised!
4. a - ges long, May Je - sus Christ be praised!

272. NOW THAT THE DAYLIGHT FILLS THE SKY

1. Now that the day-light fills the sky We lift our
2. Would guard our hearts and tongues from strife; From an-ger's
3. So we, when this new day is gone And night in
4. To God the Fa - ther and the Son And Ho -ly

1. hearts to God on high, That he, in all we
2. din would hide our life; From e - vil sights would
3. turn is draw-ing on, With con-science by the
4. Spir - it, three in one, Be end - less glo - ry

1. do or say, Would keep us free from harm to - day.
2. turn our eyes; Would close our ears to van-i - ties.
3. world un-stained Shall praise his name for vic-t'ry gained.
4. as be - fore The world be - gan, so ev - er- more.

273. CREATOR OF THE WORLD

1. Cre - a - tor of the world, we pray, As twi-light brings
2. Keep far from us dis - turb-ing dreams, All fan - ta - sies
3. To God the Fa-ther and the Son And Ho - ly Spir -

1. the end of day, That you in your great mer - cy
2. and Sa -tan's schemes; Lest by him tempt - ed and be -
3. it, God-head One, All glo-ry, praise and hon - or

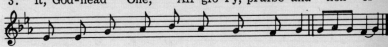

1. might Pro-tect and guard us through the night.
2. guiled, Our souls and bod-ies be de-filed.
3. be, In time and in e - ter - ni - ty. A - men.

274. ALL PRAISE TO THEE, MY GOD, THIS NIGHT

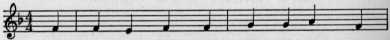

1. All praise to thee, my God, this night For
2. For - give me, Lord, through Christ thy Son, The
3. Praise God, from whom all bless-ings flow; Praise

1. all the bless-ings of the light! Keep me, O keep me,
2. ill that I this day have done, That with the world, my-
3. him, all crea-tures here be - low; Praise him a - bove, ye

1. King of kings, Be - neath thine own al - might - y wings!
2. self, and thee, Be - fore I sleep, at peace may be.
3. heav'n-ly host; Praise Fa - ther, Son, and Ho - ly Ghost.

275. TO THEE, BEFORE THE CLOSE OF DAY

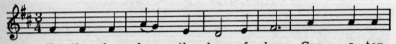

1. To thee, be - fore the close of day, Cre - a - tor
2. From e - vil dreams de - fend our eyes, From night-ly
3. O Fa-ther, grant that this be done Through Je - sus

1. of the world, we pray That with thy wont - ed fa -
2. fears and fan - ta - sies; Tread un - der foot the wick-
3. Christ thy on - ly Son, Who with the Ho - ly Ghost

1. vor thou Wouldst be our guard and keep - er now.
2. ed foe That no de - file - ment we may know.
3. and thee Shall live and reign e - ter - nal - ly.

276. PRAYER FOR OUR COUNTRY

Cantor: Let us pray for our coun - try.

Cantor:

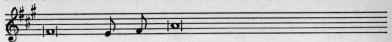

1.   That our   country may ever en-
4. That   we may   share your good gifts with our
7. That you may pro- tect and guide our rulers and
                                             their officials ac-
10. That   you may bless all men of science and
13.   That all   men may come to acknowledge you

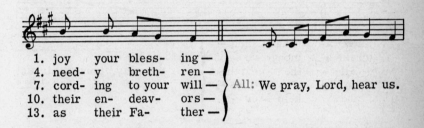

1. joy   your bless- ing —
4. need- y   breth- ren —
7. cord- ing to your will — } All: We pray, Lord, hear us.
10. their en- deav- ors —
13. as   their Fa- ther —

Cantor:

2. That your   sunshine and rain may visit our land
                                     in due meas-
5. That from   plague, famine and war you
8. That you may guide the decisions of magis-
11. That the dis- coveries of science may help us to live in
                                     prosperity,
14. And   Jesus Christ as your Son

2. ure   and   sea- son —
5. may   de-   liver us —
8. trates and judg- es — } All: We pray, Lord, hear us.
11. peace and uni- ty —
14. and   their Sav- ior —

Cantor:

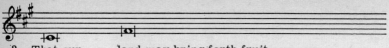

3. That our   land may bring forth fruit
6. That   anger, hatred and all ill will may
9. That your   justice and your peace may abound in
                                   our country and in
12. That   brotherly love may pervade all
                                   deliberations between
15. That they may look to your Holy Spirit as their Comforter

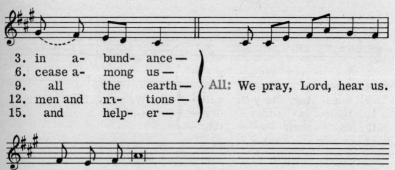

3. in   a-   bund-   ance —
6. cease a-   mong   us —
9. all   the   earth —   All: We pray, Lord, hear us.
12. men and   na-   tions —
15. and   help-   er —

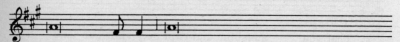

Priest: All this we ask of you through our Lord Jesus Christ

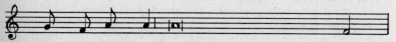

your on - ly Son, who lives and reigns with you and the

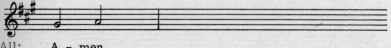

Ho - ly Spir - it for ages upon endless a - ges.

All: A - men.

277. I SING THE MIGHTY POWER OF GOD

1. I sing the might-y power of God, That made the moun-tains rise; That spread the flow-ing seas a-broad, And built the loft-y skies. I sing the wis-dom that or-dained The sun to rule the day; The moon shines full at his com-mand, And all the stars o-bey.

2. I sing the good-ness of the Lord, That filled the earth with food; He formed the crea-tures with his word, And then pro-nounced them good. Lord, how thy won-ders are dis-played, Wher-e'er I turn my eye: If I sur-vey the ground I tread, Or gaze up-on the sky!

3. There's not a plant or flower be-low, But makes thy glo-ries known; And clouds a-rise, and tem-pests blow, By or-der from thy throne; While all that bor-rows life from thee Is ev-er in thy care, And ev-'ry-where that man can be, Thou, God, art pres-ent there. A-men.

278. ALL CREATURES OF OUR GOD AND KING

1. All crea-tures of our God and King, Lift up your
2. Thou rush-ing wind that art so strong, Ye clouds that

1. voice and with us sing, Al - le - lu - ia! Al - le - lu - ia!
2. sail in heav'n a- long, Oh, praise him! Al - le - lu - ia!

1. Thou burn-ing sun with gold - en beam, Thou sil- ver
2. Thou ris - ing morn, in praise re-joice, Ye lights of

1. moon with soft-er gleam, Oh, praise him! Oh, praise
2. eve - ning, find a voice! Oh, praise him! Oh, praise

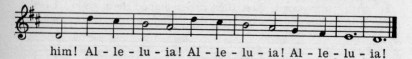

him! Al - le - lu - ia! Al - le - lu - ia! Al - le - lu - ia!

3. Thou flowing water, pure and clear,
   Make music for thy Lord to hear,
   Alleluia! Alleluia!
   Thou fire so masterful and bright,
   That givest man both warmth and light,
   Oh, praise him! Oh, praise him!
   Alleluia! Alleluia! Alleluia!

4. Dear mother earth, who day by day
   Unfoldest blessings on our way,
   Oh, praise him! Alleluia!
   The flowers and fruits that in thee grow,
   Let them his glory also show!
   Oh, praise him! Oh, praise him!
   Alleluia! Alleluia! Alleluia!

5. And all ye men of tender heart,
   Forgiving others, take your part.
   Oh, sing ye! Alleluia!
   Ye who long pain and sorrow bear,
   Praise God and on him cast your care!
   Oh, praise him! Oh, praise him!
   Alleluia! Alleluia! Alleluia!

6. And thou, most kind and gentle death,
   Waiting to hush our latest breath,
   Oh, praise him! Alleluia!
   Thou leadest home the child of God,
   And Christ our Lord the way hath trod:
   Oh, praise him! Oh, praise him!
   Alleluia! Alleluia! Alleluia!

7. Let all things their Creator bless,
   And worship him in humbleness.
   Oh, praise him! Alleluia!
   Praise, praise the Father, praise the Son,
   And praise the Spirit, three in one!
   Oh, praise him! Oh, praise him!
   Alleluia! Alleluia! Alleluia!

279. FROM ALL WHO DWELL BENEATH THE SKIES

1. From all who dwell be-neath the skies Let the Cre - a -
2. E - ter-nal are your mer-cies, Lord, E - ter-nal truth

1. tor's praise a - rise; Let the Re - deem- er's name
2. at - tends your word; Your praise shall sound from shore

1. be sung Through ev - 'ry land, by ev-'ry tongue.
2. to shore, Till suns shall rise and set no more. A-men.

280. FOR THE BEAUTY OF THE EARTH

1. For the beau-ty of the earth, For the beau-ty
2. For the beau-ty of each hour Of the day and
3. For the joy of hu - man love, Broth - er, sis - ter,
4. For thy-self, best gift di - vine! To our race so

1. of the skies, For the love which from our birth
2. of the night, Hill and vale, and tree and flow'r,
3. par-ent, child, Friends on earth and friends a-bove,
4. free-ly giv'n, For that great, great love of thine,

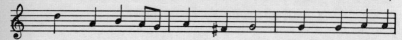

1. O - ver and a - round us lies, Christ, our God, to
2. Sun and moon and stars of light, Christ, our God, to
3. For all gen - tle thoughts and mild, Christ, our God, to
4. Peace on earth and joy in heav'n, Christ, our God, to

1. thee we raise This our sac - ri - fice of praise.
2. thee we raise This our sac - ri - fice of praise.
3. thee we raise This our sac - ri - fice of praise.
4. thee we raise This our sac - ri - fice of praise. A - men.

281. O LOVING MOTHER OF OUR SAVIOR

1. O lov-ing Moth-er of our Sav-ior, man-kind's read-y
2. Al - ma Re-dem-pto-ris Ma-ter, quae per - vi - a

1. en-trance in-to heav-en, and star of the sea: Oh has-
2. cae - li por-ta ma - nes, Et stel-la ma-ris, suc-cur-

1. ten to aid us, who oft fall-ing strive to rise a - gain. You
2. re ca-den-ti, sur-ge-re qui cu -rat po-pu - lo: Tu

1. gave birth, dear Moth-er, while na-ture stood in awe to
2. quae ge - nu - i - sti, na-tu - ra mi-ran-te, tu-

1. your own all - ho - ly Mak-er. Ev - er Vir-gin af - ter and
2. um san-ctum Ge-ni - to -rem: Vir-go pri - us ac pos-te -

1. be -fore you re - ceived from Ga - bri - el that first
2. ri - us Ga-bri - e - lis ab o - re su-mens

1. sol - emn A-ve: have com-pas-sion on us sin - ners.
2. il - lud A-ve, pec - ca - to-rum mi-se-re - re.

℣. during Advent The Angel of the Lord made the announcement to Mary.

℟. And she conceived by the Holy Spirit.

Prayer Let us pray. Pour out Your grace into our hearts, O Lord! By the voice of an angel we have learned of the incarnation of Christ, Your Son; lead us, by His passion and His Cross, to the glory of the resurrection. Through the same Christ, our Lord.

℟. Amen.

℣. from the first Vespers of Christmas Even after giving birth, you remained a Virgin.

℟. Mother of God, intercede for us.

Prayer Let us pray. O God, who through the fruitful virginity of Blessed Mary gave all men the riches of eternal salvation, we entreat You to let us feel the intercession of her who gave us the Author of life, our Lord Jesus Christ, Your Son.

℟. Amen.

282. QUEEN OF THE HEAVENS, WE HAIL THEE

1. Queen of the heav-ens, we hail thee, Queen of an-gel hosts,
2. A - ve Re - gi - na cae-lo - rum, A - ve Do-mi - na

1. we sa-lute thee. Thou the root and thou the por-tal, Thou
2. an-ge - lo -rum: Sal-ve ra - dix, sal-ve por-ta, Ex

1. the fount of light im-mor-tal. Hail, thou Vir-gin robed in glo-
2. qua mun-do lux est or - ta. Gau-de Vir - go glo - ri - o-

1. ry, Crown of all cre- a -tion's sto-ry! Beau-ty ex-cel-ling,
2. sa, Su- per om-nes spe-ci - o-sa: Va-le, o val-de

1. we greet thee, Oh be-seech thy Son for us, we pray thee.
2. de - co - ra, Et pro no - bis Chri-stum ex-o - ra.

℣. Let me praise you, most holy Virgin.
℞. Give me strength against your enemies.

Prayer Let us pray. O God of mercy, be the support of our weakness, and we shall celebrate in a fitting manner the memory of the holy Mother of God; thus by her intercession may we rise from our sins! Through the same Christ, our Lord. ℞. Amen.

283. O KING OF MIGHT AND SPLENDOR

1. O King of might and splen-dor, Cre-a - tor most a -dor ed,
2. Thy bod-y thou hast giv - en, thy blood thou hast out-poured

1. This sac - ri -fice we ren-der To thee as sov'-reign Lord. May
2. That sin might be for-giv-en, O Je- sus, lov - ing Lord. As

1. these our gifts be pleas-ing Un - to thy Maj-es-ty, Man-
2. now with love most ten - der Thy death we cel- e-brate, Our

1. kind from sin re - leas-ing Who have of -fend-ed thee.
2. lives in self - sur- ren - der To thee we con - se-crate.

284. O LORD, IN THIS GREAT MYSTERY

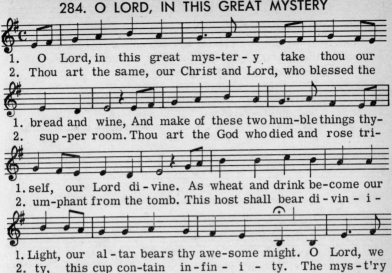

1. O Lord, in this great mys-ter-y take thou our bread and wine, And make of these two hum-ble things thy-self, our Lord di-vine. As wheat and drink be-come our Light, our al-tar bears thy awe-some might. O Lord, we of-fer thee the gift that lies be-fore thy sight.

2. Thou art the same, our Christ and Lord, who blessed the sup-per room. Thou art the God who died and rose tri-um-phant from the tomb. This host shall bear di-vin-i-ty, this cup con-tain in-fin-i-ty. The mys-t'ry fills our souls with love, O ho-ly Maj-es-ty.

285. HUMBLY WE ADORE THEE

1. Hum-bly we a-dore thee, Christ Re-deem-er King; Thou art Lord of
2. God, the Might-y, thou hast come, Bear-ing gifts of grace; Son of Ad-am
3. Je-sus, Lord, we thank thee For this won-drous Bread; In our land thou
4. We who share this mys—t'ry, In thee are made one; Ev-'ry act we
5. Thou who died to save us, Live on as our light; Though our eyes are
6. Christ, do thou be mer-ci-ful, Lamb for sin-ners slain; We in grief con-
7. Make us one in lov-ing thee, One in mind and heart; From this ho-ly

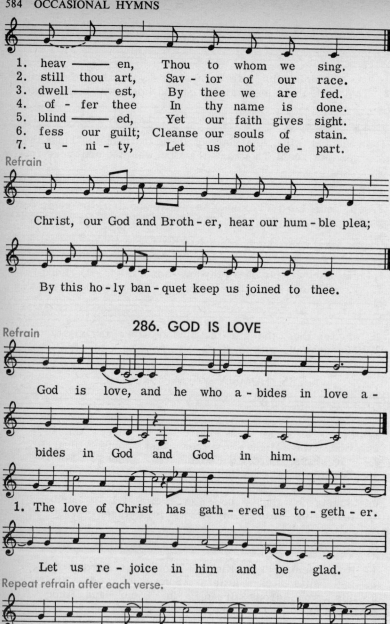

1. heav —— en,   Thou to whom we sing.
2. still thou art,   Sav - ior of our race.
3. dwell —— est,   By thee we are fed.
4. of - fer thee   In thy name is done.
5. blind —— ed,   Yet our faith gives sight.
6. fess our guilt; Cleanse our souls of stain.
7. u - ni - ty,   Let us not de - part.

Refrain

Christ, our God and Broth - er, hear our hum - ble plea;

By this ho - ly ban - quet keep us joined to thee.

286. GOD IS LOVE

Refrain

God is love, and he who a - bides in love a -

bides in God and God in him.

1. The love of Christ has gath - ered us to - geth - er.

Let us re - joice in him and be glad.

Repeat refrain after each verse.

2. By this shall all know that we are his dis - ci - ples,

If we have love one for an - oth - er.

3. Owe no man an-y-thing ex-cept to love one an-oth-er. For

he who loves his neigh-bor will ful-fill the whole law.

4. O car - ry one an - oth - er's bur - dens

And so you will ful - fill the law of Christ.

5. The cup of bless - ing which we bless, Is

it not fel - low - ship in the blood of Christ?

6. The bread which we break, Is

it not fel - low - ship in the bod - y of Christ?

7. We man - y are one bread, one bod - y, For

we all par - take of the one Bread.

8. This is the Bread that came down from heav - en;

He who eats this Bread shall live for - ev - er.

9. We who eat his flesh and drink his blood have life

ev - er - last - ing, And he will raise us up on the last day.

10. He is the vine, we the branch - es; We

who a - bide in him shall bear fruit.

287. WHERE TRUE CHARITY AND LOVE DWELL

Choir 1 Where true char-i-ty and love dwell, sure-ly God is there.

Choir 2 Where true char-i-ty and love dwell, sure-ly God is there.

Ch. 1 It is Christ's love that has gath-ered us to-geth-er.

Ch. 2 Let us all be joy-ful in him and ex-ul-tant. Ch. 1 Let

us live in fear and love of the liv-ing God. Ch. 2 And

from the heart sin-cere-ly love one an - oth - er.

Ch. 1 Where true char-i-ty and love dwell, sure-ly God is there.

Ch. 2 There-fore when we are as one gath - ered to - geth - er.

Ch. 1 Let us make dou - bly sure that there are no fac - tions.

Ch. 2 Let all con-ten-tion and strife be gone for - ev - er.

Ch. 1 And may there dwell in our midst Christ, who is our God.

Ch. 2 Where true char-i-ty and love dwell, sure-ly God is there.

Ch. 1 We now pray, O Christ our God, that you will make us

Ch. 2 See your face in glo - ry with your saints in heav - en.

Ch. 1 And your - self be our im - mense joy and ho - ly prize.

Ch. 2 **For ev-er and through the ev-er-last-ing a - ges.**

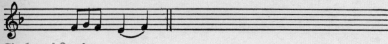

Ch. 1 and 2   **A - men.**

All   **288. ALL GLORY AND POWER BELONG TO YOU**[1]

All glo-ry and power be-long to you through

Je - sus Christ, now and for - ev - er!

Repeat antiphon after each verse.
Cantor

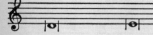

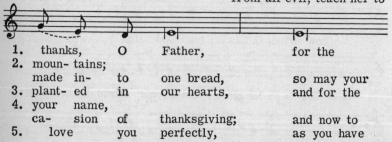

1. We   give you
2. The   elements of this bread we have broken were
                        once scattered over the
   as they were gathered together and
3. We give you thanks, O Father, for your holy name which
                        you have
4. All things, sovereign Lord, you created for the glory of
   you gave   food and drink to men for their enjoyment
                        as an oc-
5. Re-   member, O Lord, to deliver your Church
                        from all evil; teach her to

1. thanks,   O   Father,   for the
2. moun- tains;
    made in-   to   one bread,   so may your
3. plant- ed   in   our hearts,   and for the
4. your   name,
    ca-   sion of   thanksgiving;   and now to
5. love   you   perfectly,   as you have

[1] Text of this hymn adapted from the *Didache*; the full, original form may be found in *Early Christian Prayers*, page 178, published by Longmans, Green & Co., New York.

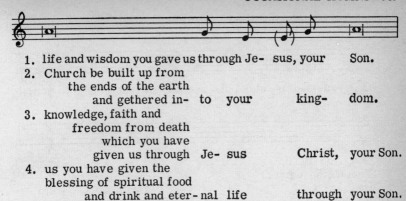

1. life and wisdom you gave us through Je- sus, your Son.
2. Church be built up from
   the ends of the earth
   and gethered in- to your king- dom.
3. knowledge, faith and
   freedom from death
   which you have
   given us through Je- sus Christ, your Son.
4. us you have given the
   blessing of spiritual food
   and drink and eter- nal life through your Son.
5. made her holy; build her
   up from the four winds
   and gather her into
   the kingdom you have set for her.

289. THE EARTH IS FILLED WITH THE LORD'S GOODNESS

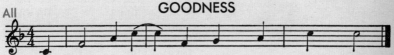

The earth is filled with the Lord's good - ness.

1. With the mercy of the Lord
2. The word of the Lord
3. May all upright persons triumph in the Lord;
4. Blessed are people whose God is the Lord,
5. Glory be to the Father and to the Son
6. As it was in the beginning, is now
   and ev- er shall be,

1. the earth is filled, al-le-lu-ia.
2. makes the heav- ens strong, al-le-lu-ia.
3. it is right to give him praise, al-le-lu-ia.
4. whom he has chosen to be his own, al-le-lu-ia.
5. and to the Ho- ly Spir- it, al-le-lu-ia.
6. world without end. A- men. al-le-lu-ia.

290. O JERUSALEM, STAND AND SEE

All

O Je-ru-sa-lem, stand and see the joy that comes to you!

Choir

1. God, the Lord,	has	spo-	ken
2. From Sion perfect	in	beau-	ty
3. Be-	fore		him
4. He summons	the	heav-	ens,
5. "Gather my faith-	ful		ones;
6. Loudly	the	heav-	ens

1. and has	sum-	moned the	earth
2. our	God	shines	forth;
3. is a de-	vour-	ing	fire,
4. the heavens	from	a-	bove,
5. be-	fore	me; gath-	er
6. pro-	claim	his jus-	tice,

1. from the	sun's	own ris-	ing
2. may he come	speed-	i-	ly
3. and	all	a- round	him
4. and	calls	the	earth
5. those who have	made	a cov-	'nant
6. for	God	him-	self

1. to	its	set-	ting.
2. and not be deaf	to		us.
3. is a rag-	ing		storm.
4. to the trial of	his	peo-	ple.
5. with me by sac-	ri-		fice."
6. is	the		judge.

291. GIVE THANKS TO THE NAME OF THE LORD

All

Give   thanks   to   the   name   of   the   Lord.

Choir

1. I rejoiced because they said to me, "We will go up to

the house of the Lord. / 2. And now we have set foot

within your gates, O Je - ru - sa - lem. / 3. Jerusalem,

built as a cit - y with com - pact u - ni - ty. / 4. To it

the tribes go up, the tribes of the Lord, according to

the de - cree for Is - ra - el, to give thanks to the name

of the Lord. / 5. In it are set up judg - ment seats,

seats for the house of Da - vid. / 6. Pray for the peace

of Je - ru - sa - lem. May those who love you pros -

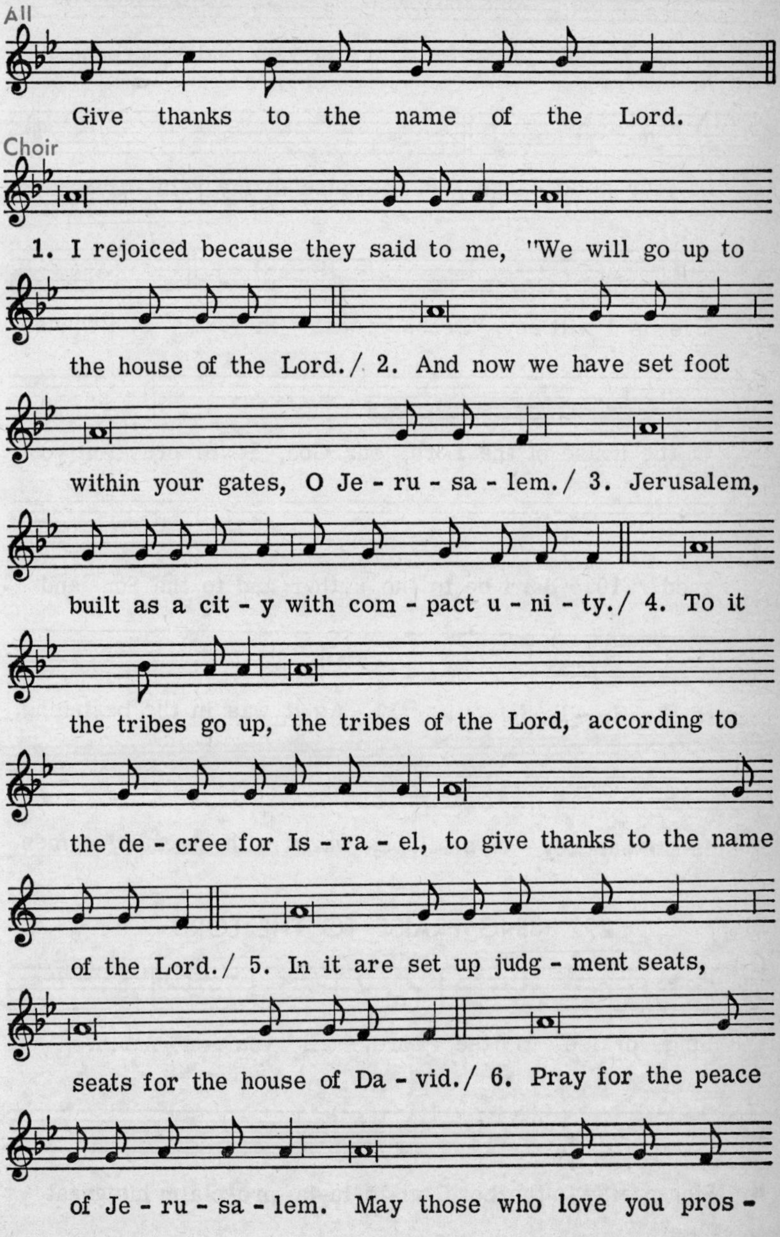

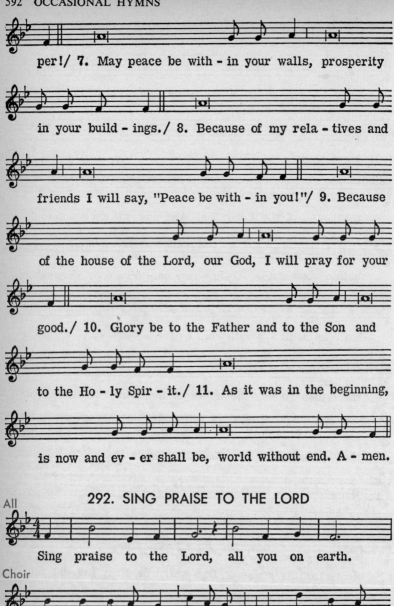

per!/ 7. May peace be with - in your walls, prosperity

in your build - ings./ 8. Because of my rela - tives and

friends I will say, "Peace be with - in you!"/ 9. Because

of the house of the Lord, our God, I will pray for your

good./ 10. Glory be to the Father and to the Son and

to the Ho - ly Spir - it./ 11. As it was in the beginning,

is now and ev - er shall be, world without end. A - men.

292. SING PRAISE TO THE LORD

All

Sing praise to the Lord, all you on earth.

Choir

Sing praise to the Lord, al-le-lu-ia; pro-claim his great

name, al-le-lu-ia; glo-ri-fy his maj-es-ty, al-le-lu-ia.

Repeat antiphon.

Al - le - lu - ia, al - le - lu - ia, al - le - lu - ia,

al - le - lu - ia, al - le - lu - ia, al - le - lu - ia.

Repeat antiphon.

Come and see the works of God, al - le - lu - ia; how

splen - did are his plans for men, al - le - lu - ia;

wonderful your deeds, O God, al - le - lu - ia.

Repeat antiphon.

Al - le - lu - ia, al - le - lu - ia, al - le - lu - ia,

al - le - lu - ia, al - le - lu - ia, al - le - lu - ia.

Repeat antiphon.

He has changed the sea to land, al - le - lu - ia. Through

the Red Sea Is - ra - el passed on foot, al - le - lu - ia.

Let us then be glad in him, al - le - lu - ia.

Repeat antiphon.

Al - le - lu - ia, al - le - lu - ia, al - le - lu - ia,

al - le - lu - ia, al - le - lu - ia, al - le - lu - ia.

Repeat antiphon.

Bless our God, you peo - ples, al - le - lu - ia;

loud - ly sound his prais - es, al - le - lu - ia; he

has given our souls life, al - le - lu - ia.

Repeat antiphon.

Al - le - lu - ia, al - le - lu - ia, al - le - lu - ia,

al - le - lu - ia, al - le - lu - ia, al - le - lu - ia.

Repeat antiphon.

Glory to the Fa - ther, al - le - lu - ia; glo - ry to the

Son, al - le - lu - ia; glory to the Spir - it, al - le - lu - ia.

Repeat antiphon.

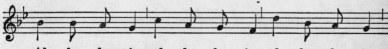

Al - le - lu - ia, al - le - lu - ia, al - le - lu - ia,

al - le - lu - ia, al - le - lu - ia, al - le - lu - ia.

Repeat antiphon.

All

293. YOU ARE PETER

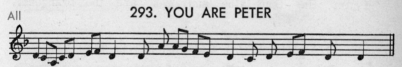

You are Pe-ter, and up-on this rock I will build my Church.

Choir

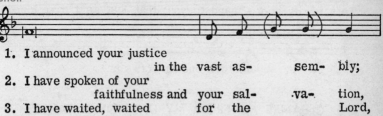

1.	I announced your justice	in the	vast as-	sem-	bly;
2.	I have spoken of your faithfulness and	your	sal-	va-	tion,
3.	I have waited, waited	for	the		Lord,
4.	He drew me out of the pit	of	de-	struc-	tion,
5.	He set my feet up-	on	a		crag;
6.	He put a new song in-	to	my		mouth,
7.	Though I am afflict-	ed	and		poor,
8.	You are my help and	my	de-	liv- er-	er;
9.	Praise the Father, the Son and	Ho-	ly	Spir-	it,
10.	The God who is, who was	and	who	will	be,

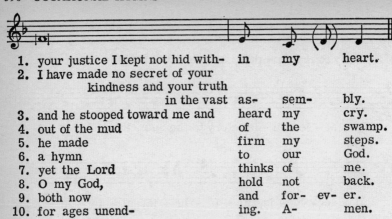

1. your justice I kept not hid with- in   my   heart.
2. I have made no secret of your
      kindness and your truth
                in the vast as- sem-   bly.
3. and he stooped toward me and   heard my   cry.
4. out of the mud   of   the   swamp.
5. he made   firm my   steps.
6. a hymn   to   our   God.
7. yet the Lord   thinks of   me.
8. O my God,   hold not   back.
9. both now   and for- ev- er.
10. for ages unend-   ing. A-   men.

294. I AM THE TRUE VINE

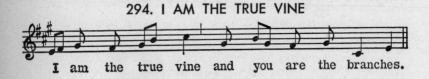

I am   the true vine and you are the branches.

295. THIS IS MY COMMAND TO YOU

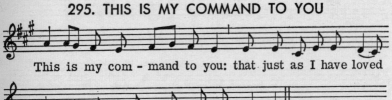

This is my com - mand to you: that just as I have loved

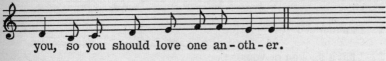

you, so you should love one an - oth - er.

296. CLEANSE ME FROM MY UNKNOWN FAULTS

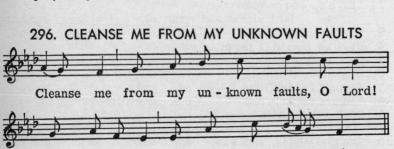

Cleanse me from my un - known faults, O Lord!

From wan-ton sin re - strain your serv - ant.

297. COME, BLESSED OF MY FATHER

Come, bless-ed of my fa-ther, re-ceive the king-dom, al-le-

lu-ia, which has been pre-pared for you from the be-gin-

ning of the world. Al-le-lu-ia, al-le-lu-ia, al-le-lu-ia!

298. GLORY BE TO THE FATHER

Glo-ry be to the Fa-ther, and to the Son, and to the

Ho-ly Spir-it; As it was in the be-gin-ning, is now

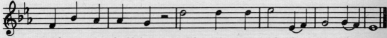

and ev-er shall be, world with-out end. A-men, A-men.

299. THREEFOLD AMEN

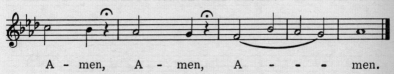

A - men, A - men, A - - - men.

300. WE PRAISE YOU, O GOD

1. We praise   you, O   God: we ac-claim you Lord and
2. Te De-um lau-da-mus: te Do-mi-num con-fi-

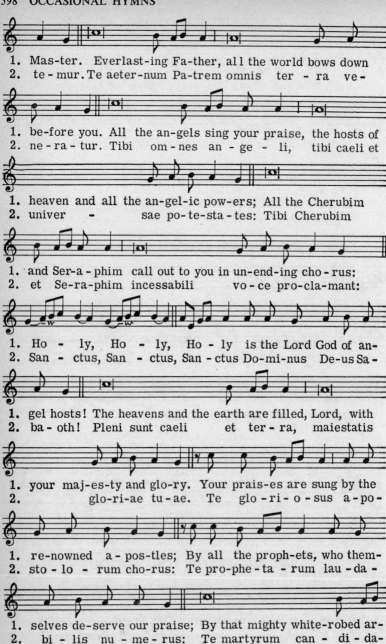

1. Mas-ter. Everlast-ing Fa-ther, all the world bows down
2. te - mur. Te aeter-num Pa-trem omnis ter - ra ve-

1. be-fore you. All the an-gels sing your praise, the hosts of
2. ne - ra - tur. Tibi om - nes an - ge - li, tibi caeli et

1. heaven and all the an-gel-ic pow-ers; All the Cherubim
2. univer - sae po-te-sta-tes: Tibi Cherubim

1. and Ser-a-phim call out to you in un-end-ing cho-rus:
2. et Se-ra-phim incessabili vo-ce pro-cla-mant:

1. Ho - ly, Ho - ly, Ho - ly is the Lord God of an-
2. San - ctus, San - ctus, San - ctus Do-mi-nus De-us Sa-

1. gel hosts! The heavens and the earth are filled, Lord, with
2. ba - oth! Pleni sunt caeli et ter - ra, maiestatis

1. your maj-es-ty and glo-ry. Your prais-es are sung by the
2. glo-ri-ae tu-ae. Te glo-ri-o-sus a-po-

1. re-nowned a-pos-tles; By all the proph-ets, who them-
2. sto-lo-rum cho-rus: Te pro-phe-ta-rum lau-da-

1. selves de-serve our praise; By that mighty white-robed ar-
2. bi-lis nu-me-rus: Te martyrum can-di-da-

1. my who shed their blood for Christ. And to the ends of the
2. tus lau - dat ex - er - ci - tus. Te per or-bem ter-ra-

1. earth, the holy Church pro-claims her faith in you: Fa -
2. rum sancta confi - te - tur Ec - cle - si - a: Pa -

1. ther, whose maj - es - ty is bound-less; Your only Son,who
2. trem im - men-sae ma-ies - ta - tis: Venerandum tu-

1. is true God, and who is to be a-dored; The Ho - ly
2. um ve - rum et u - ni-cum Fi-li - um: San-ctum quo-

1. Ghost, sent to be our Ad-vo-cate. O Christ, the King
2. que Pa - ra-cli-tum Spi-ri-tum. Tu Rex glo-ri-

1. of glo - ry! You a-lone are the Fa-ther's e-ter-nal Son.
2. ae Chri-ste. Tu Pa-tris sem-pi-ter- nus es Fi-li-us.

1. When you were to become man so as to save man-kind,
2. Tu ad liberandum suscep - tu-rus ho - mi-nem,

1. you did not shrink back from the chaste Vir-gin's womb.
2. non horruisti Vir - gi - nis u - ter - rum.

1. When you trium-phant-ly de-stroyed death's sting, you
2. Tu devicto mor-tis a - cu - le - o, a-

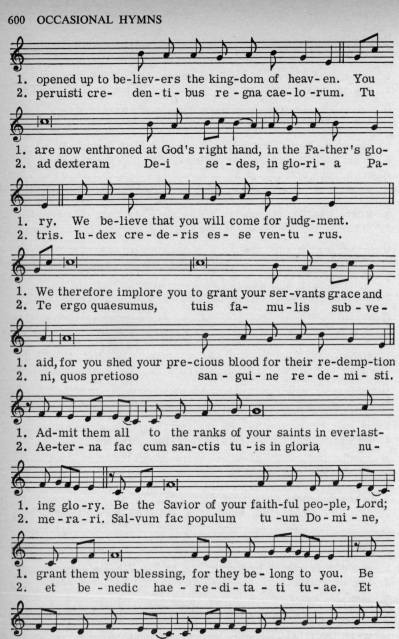

1. opened up to be-liev-ers the king-dom of heav-en. You
2. peruisti cre- den-ti-bus re-gna cae-lo-rum. Tu

1. are now enthroned at God's right hand, in the Fa-ther's glo-
2. ad dexteram De-i se-des, in glo-ri- a Pa-

1. ry. We be-lieve that you will come for judg-ment.
2. tris. Iu-dex cre-de-ris es- se ven-tu-rus.

1. We therefore implore you to grant your ser-vants grace and
2. Te ergo quaesumus, tuis fa-mu-lis sub-ve-

1. aid, for you shed your pre-cious blood for their re-demp-tion
2. ni, quos pretioso san-gui-ne re-de-mi-sti.

1. Ad-mit them all to the ranks of your saints in everlast-
2. Ae-ter-na fac cum san-ctis tu-is in gloria nu-

1. ing glo-ry. Be the Savior of your faith-ful peo-ple, Lord;
2. me-ra-ri. Sal-vum fac populum tu-um Do-mi-ne,

1. grant them your blessing, for they be-long to you. Be
2. et be-nedic hae-re-di-ta-ti tu-ae. Et

1. their Shep-herd, Lord; up-hold and ex-alt them for-ev-er
2. re-ge e-os, et ex-tol-le il-los us-que in

1. and ev - er. Day by day we praise you, dai-ly we ac -
2. ae-ter - num. Per singu- los   di - es be-ne-di-ci -

1. claim you. We will confess and glorify your ho-ly name now
2. mus . te. Et laudamus nomen tuum   in   sae-cu-lum, et

1. and for all   e - ter-ni-ty. In your great mercy, Lord,
2. in sae-cu-lum sae-cu-li. Dignare, Domine, di -

1. throughout this day,   keep us free from sin by your pro-tec-
2.   e is - to   si -ne peccato   nos cu - sto-di-

1. tion. Have mercy on us, we hum-bly pray; Lord, have
2. re. Miserere no - stri, Do - mi - ne,   mi - se -

1. mer - cy on   us. May your mercy, Lord,   your lov-
2. re - re no - stri. Fi - at   misericordia tua, Domi -

1. ing-kindness, always re - main with us; for we have
2.   ne, su - per nos, quemadmodum

1. placed our con - fi - dence in you. In you a - lone, Lord,
2. spe-   ra -vi - mus in te. In te, Do - mi - ne,

1. I   have hoped; may I   not be dis-ap-point-ed.
2. spe - ra - vi: non con-fun-dar in ae-ter num.

HOLY BAPTISM

Baptism is our birth as Christians, our birth as "other Christs." Through many centuries Christians loved to view the baptismal font as the womb of holy Mother Church; for at the font her children come forth alive with a new and higher life — that of God himself.

This second birth into God's own family at the sacred font is the source of new and wonderful privileges. The first of the baptismal graces which needs emphasis in twentieth-century America is that of our incorporation into Christ, the fact of the Mystical Body. Baptism makes us members of Christ: "We were all baptized into one Body . . . you are the Body of Christ and severally his members" (1 Cor. 12:13, 27). Our head is Christ, and consequently the thoughts which fill our minds must be his thoughts: "We have the mind of Christ" (1 Cor. 2:16). As in a body many cells share the same dignity, so the many individuals who form Christ's Body all share the same godlike dignity; there is then no place for mutual indignities or antagonisms; fraternal charity must reign supreme. Because baptism has made us all one in Christ, the efforts of each are to the advantage of all, the suffering of one brings tears to many, a single song of praise gladdens countless hearts.

Baptism, secondly, makes us the dwelling-place of the Blessed Trinity, makes each of us a holy temple, for "holy is the temple of God, and this temple you are" (1 Cor. 3:17). God's active, energizing presence in the baptized soul transforms it into a creature most pleasing to himself. Too frequently we may have limited our attention to the negative aspect of holy baptism, that is, its power to remit sin and to cleanse away all guilt. More marvellous is its fulfillment of Jesus' last prayer: "If any one love me, he will keep my word, and my Father will love him, and *we will come to him and will make our abode with him*" (St. John 14:23). And where Father and Son are, their Spirit must of necessity be: "Do you not know that the Spirit of God dwells in you?" (1 Cor. 3:16). As we become conscious of this unspeakable gift our hearts spontaneously welcome the command: "Glorify and bear God in your body" (1 Cor. 6:10).

Though baptism confers such great gifts, it is not a final stage in God's generosity toward us — it is only a beginning. Baptism plants the seed; the remaining sacraments bring it to harvest. All the sacraments are directed toward the holy Eucharist, particularly baptism. Baptism gives me the right to receive the holy Eucharist while the holy Eucharist preserves and makes fruitful my baptismal privileges. Baptism, by making me share in the priesthood of Christ through the "character" it imprints, enables me to share in the offering of the one only Sacrifice; by offering this Sacrifice with Christ I again renew my baptismal descent with Christ into death in order to rise again with him in newness of life. Baptism makes me a cell in Christ's Body; the Eucharist nourishes that cell, makes it healthy, makes it function in a loving, sacrificial spirit of unity with countless other cells, makes it ever a more fitting dwelling for the triune God.

Baptism is our birth as Christians. A little reflection, and this age-old truth becomes fresh and dynamic. Its power produced the age of martyrs and the glories of patristic Christianity. If we but give holy baptism the thought and attention it deserves, its power will vitalize and transform our weak devotions into a spirituality strong with the strength of Christ our Head and holy with the holiness of the indwelling Trinity. Its power will make us pleasing and acceptable to the eternal Father, for through it we have been enabled to offer the perfect Sacrifice in and through his Son Christ Jesus. Truly, holy baptism is a great sacrament, making us Christians, making us "a kingdom of priests, a holy people" (1 Pet. 2:9).

THE RITE FOR BAPTISM

I. Reception of the Candidate

The rite begins with the priest meeting the candidate for baptism at the door of the church. The candidate states his request and is informed of the fundamental Christian obligation of loving God and his neighbor. Through her minister the Church claims him for God and commands the spirit of evil to leave. The priest signs him with the sign of the Cross in token of his new allegiance and claims him as a child of Mother Church by laying his hand upon him. He commends the candidate to the charity of God and places on his tongue a pledge of wisdom and grace under the symbol of salt.

Vested in surplice and stole and having spent some moments in prayer before the altar, the priest comes to the entrance of the church and greets those waiting there with the child, saying:

Peace be with you.

He then asks the name of the infant:

What is your name?

The sponsors answer: N.

The priest asks the infant: N., **what do you ask of the Church of God?**

Sponsors: **Faith.**

Priest: **What does faith offer you?**

Sponsors: **Eternal life.**

Priest: **If, then, you wish to enter into life, keep the commandments: you shall love the Lord your God with your whole heart, and with your whole soul, and with your whole mind, and your neighbor as yourself.**

He then blows gently three times on the face of the infant (as if blowing away the evil spirit), while saying once:[1]

Depart from him, unclean spirit, and give place to the Holy Spirit, the Consoler.

Depart from her, unclean spirit, and give place to the Holy Spirit, the Consoler.

With his thumb the priest makes the sign of the Cross on the forehead and on the breast of the infant, saying:

Receive the mark of the Cross on your +forehead and within your +heart. Embrace the faith with its divine teachings. So live that you will indeed be a temple of God.

The priest continues:

Prayer

Let us pray. We beg you, Lord God, graciously hear our prayers. Guard your chosen one, N., with the never-failing power of the Cross of Christ, with which he has been marked. Protect him so that, remaining true to the first lessons he has learned about the great glory you will confer upon him, he may, by keeping your commandments, attain to the glory of a new birth. Through Christ our Lord.

℟. Amen.

Let us pray. We beg you, Lord God, graciously hear our prayers. Guard your chosen one, N., with the never-failing power of the Cross of Christ, with which she has been marked. Protect her so that, remaining true to the first lessons she has learned about the great glory you will confer upon her, she may, by keeping your commandments, attain to the glory of a new birth. Through Christ our Lord.

℟. Amen.

The priest places his hand upon the head of the child; then with hand extended he says:

Let us pray. Almighty and eternal God, Father of our Lord Jesus Christ, look with favor upon this your servant, N., whom you have[2] called to take his first steps in the faith. Take from him all blindness of heart. Free him from the snares of Satan which until now have held him. Open to him, Lord, the gate of your mercy. Then, sea-

Let us pray. Almighty and eternal God, Father of our Lord Jesus Christ, look with favor upon this your servant, N., whom you have[2] called to take her first steps in the faith. Take from her all blindness of heart. Free her from the snares of Satan which until now have held her. Open to her, Lord, the gate of your mercy. Then, sea-

[1] When a prayer is given in two columns, the left column refers to males, the right to females.

[2] If the child has already been baptized privately and this is only a supplementary ceremony, the priest adds the word **already**.

soned by the salt which is symbolic of your wisdom, may he be relieved of the corruption of evil desires; and, finding pleasure in the keeping of your commandments, may he serve you in your Church and make progress from day to day in the way of perfection.[3] Through the same Christ our Lord.

℞. Amen.

soned by the salt which is symbolic of your wisdom, may she be relieved of the corruption of evil desires; and, finding pleasure in the keeping of your commandments, may she serve you in your Church and make progress from day to day in the way of perfection.[3] Through the same Christ our Lord.

℞. Amen.

The priest blesses salt. After the salt has once been blessed, it may be used at any time thereafter for the same purpose, and in such instances the following prayer is omitted.

Blessing of Salt

O salt, creature of God, I exorcise you in the name of God † the Father almighty and in the love of our Lord Jesus † Christ and in the strength of the Holy † Spirit. I exorcise you by the living † God, the true † God, the holy † God, the God † who brought you into being to safeguard the human race, and commanded you to be consecrated by his servants for the benefit of those who are coming into the faith, so that by the power of the Holy Trinity you might become a health-giving sacrament to put the enemy to flight. Therefore, we beg you, O Lord our God, to sanctify † by your power of sanctification this salt which you have created and to bless † it with your blessing, so that it may become a perfect medicine for all who receive it and may remain always in every fiber of their being. In the name of our Lord Jesus Christ, who will come to judge the living and the dead and the world by fire.

℞. Amen.

As a pledge that the candidate for baptism may have a taste for heavenly wisdom and that he may be preserved from the corruption of sin, the priest places a few grains of blessed salt in his mouth while saying:

N., receive the salt, which is a symbol of wisdom. May it bring you God's favor for life everlasting.

℞. Amen.

[3] If this is a supplementary ceremony the priest adds:

and, by tasting the salt that heals, he may be ready to profit by the grace of your baptism that he has received. Through the same Christ our Lord. ℞. Amen.

and, by tasting the salt that heals, she may be ready to profit by the grace of your baptism that she has received. Through the same Christ our Lord. ℞. Amen.

Priest: **Peace be with you.**

℞. And with your spirit.

Prayer

Priest: **Let us pray. God of our fathers, God, the author of all truth, we humbly ask you to look with favor on this your servant N., who has had his first[4] taste of blessed food in the form of salt. Satisfy him with the bread of heaven, so that he may be forever fervent in spirit, joyful in hope, and zealous in your service.[5] We ask you, Lord, to lead him to the waters in which he will be born again, so that he, with all who believe in you, may obtain the unending rewards which you have promised. Through Christ our Lord.**

℞. Amen.

Priest: **Let us pray. God of our fathers, God, the author of all truth, we humbly ask you to look with favor on this your servant N., who has had her first[4] taste of blessed food in the form of salt. Satisfy her with the bread of heaven, so that she may be forever fervent in spirit, joyful in hope, and zealous in your service.[5] We ask you, Lord, to lead her to the waters in which she will be born again, so that she, with all who believe in you, may obtain the unending rewards which you have promised. Through Christ our Lord.**

℞. Amen.

II. Preparatory Purification

A solemn exorcism now follows. In God's name and by his authority the priest commands the spirit of evil to withdraw from the body and from the life of the person to be baptized. The sign of the Cross is traced upon his forehead as evidence of the power behind the command. His soul is commended again to the divine favor by prayer and the imposition of the priest's right hand.

The priest prays:

I exorcise you, unclean spirit, in the name of the Father † and of the Son † and of the Holy † Spirit. Come forth, depart from this servant of God, N., for he commands you, accursed and

The priest prays:

I exorcise you, unclean spirit, in the name of the Father † and of the Son † and of the Holy † Spirit. Come forth, depart from this servant of God, N., for he commands you, accursed and

---

[4] In a supplementary ceremony the word **first** is omitted.

[5] In a supplementary ceremony the priest finishes this prayer as follows:

And we ask you, Lord, that he whom you led to the waters in which he was born again, with all who believe in you, may obtain the unending rewards which you have promised. Through Christ our Lord.

℞. Amen.

And we ask you, Lord, that she whom you led to the waters in which she was born again, with all who believe in you, may obtain the unending rewards which you have promised. Through Christ our Lord.

℞. Amen.

damned spirit, he who walked upon the sea and extended his right hand to Peter as he was sinking.

Therefore, accursed devil, acknowledge your condemnation and pay homage to the true and living God; pay homage to Jesus Christ, his Son, and to the Holy Spirit, and depart from this servant of God, N., for Jesus Christ, our Lord and God, has called him to his holy grace and blessing, and to the font of baptism.

With his thumb the priest makes the sign of the Cross upon the forehead of the child while saying:

Accursed devil, never dare to desecrate this sign of the holy † Cross which we are tracing upon his forehead. Through the same Christ our Lord.

℟. Amen.

The priest lays his hand upon the head of the infant, and then with hand extended continues:

Prayer

Let us pray. Lord, holy Father, almighty and eternal God, source of all light and truth, I humbly beg your never-ending and most holy mercy upon this servant of yours, N. May it please you to grant him the light of your own wisdom. Cleanse him and make him holy. Give him true knowledge,[6] so that he may be made worthy of the grace of your baptism and main-

6 In a supplementary ceremony the priest finishes this prayer as follows:

so that he may be made worthy of the grace of your baptism which he has already received and may maintain firm hope, sound judgment, and a grasp of holy doctrine, so that he may be fit to keep that baptismal grace. Through Christ our Lord.

℟. Amen.

damned spirit, he who walked upon the sea and extended his right hand to Peter as he was sinking.

Therefore, accursed devil, acknowledge your condemnation and pay homage to the true and living God; pay homage to Jesus Christ, his Son, and to the Holy Spirit, and depart from this servant of God, N., for Jesus Christ, our Lord and God, has called her to his holy grace and blessing, and to the font of baptism.

Accursed devil, never dare to desecrate this sign of the holy † Cross which we are tracing upon her forehead. Through the same Christ our Lord.

℟. Amen.

Let us pray. Lord, holy Father, almighty and eternal God, source of all light and truth, I humbly beg your never-ending and most holy mercy upon this servant of yours, N. May it please you to grant her the light of your own wisdom. Cleanse her and make her holy. Give her true knowledge,[6] so that she may be made worthy of the grace of your baptism and main-

so that she may be made worthy of the grace of your baptism which she has already received and may maintain firm hope, sound judgment, and a grasp of holy doctrine, so that she may be fit to keep that baptismal grace. Through Christ our Lord.

℟. Amen.

tain firm hope, sound judgment, and a grasp of holy doctrine. Through Christ our Lord.
℟. Amen.

tain firm hope, sound judgment, and a grasp of holy doctrine. Through Christ our Lord.
℟. Amen.

III. Admittance into the Church and Progress to the Font

The person to be baptized is led by the priest from the entrance of the church into the house of God. This act symbolizes leaving the realm of Satan to enter the kingdom of God. A formal renunciation of all attachment to evil and a profession of faith are the final acts before the sacramental ablution.

The priest places the end of his stole (symbol of priestly power) which hangs from his left shoulder upon the child, and leads the child and sponsors into the church while saying:

N., enter the temple of God, so that you may have part with Christ in everlasting life.
℟. Amen.

The group enters the church with the priest leading the way to the font. As they proceed they say the Apostles' Creed and the Our Father in the name of the child (all others present may laudably join in).

Priest: Say the Apostles' Creed.

Priest and sponsors together: I believe in God, the Father almighty, Creator of heaven and earth; and in Jesus Christ, his only Son, our Lord, who was conceived by the Holy Spirit, born of the Virgin Mary, suffered under Pontius Pilate, was crucified, died, and was buried. He descended into hell; the third day he arose again from the dead; he ascended into heaven, sitteth at the right hand of God, the Father almighty; from thence he shall come to judge the living and the dead.

I believe in the Holy Spirit, the holy Catholic Church, the communion of saints, the forgiveness of sins, the resurrection of the body, and life everlasting. Amen.

Priest: Say the Our Father.

Priest and sponsors together: Our Father, who art in heaven, hallowed be thy name; thy kingdom come; thy will be done on earth as it is in heaven. Give us this day our daily bread; and forgive us our trespasses as we forgive those who trespass against us; and lead us not into temptation, but deliver us from evil. Amen.

At the entrance to the baptistry the spirit of evil is given a final injunction to desist from further interference with the candidate's consecration to God's service. With his back to the entrance of the baptistry, the priest says:

I exorcise you, every unclean spirit, in the name of God, the Father † almighty, and in the name of his Son, Jesus † Christ, our Lord and judge, and in the strength of the Holy † Spirit, that you may depart from this creature of God, N., whom our Lord has called to his holy temple in order that he may become[7] a temple of the living God and that the Holy Spirit may dwell in him. Through the same Christ our Lord, who will come to judge the living and the dead and the world by fire.

R⁷. Amen.

I exorcise you, every unclean spirit, in the name of God, the Father † almighty, and in the name of his Son, Jesus † Christ, our Lord and judge, and in the strength of the Holy † Spirit, that you may depart from this creature of God, N., whom our Lord has called to his holy temple in order that she may become[7] a temple of the living God and that the Holy Spirit may dwell in her. Through the same Christ our Lord, who will come to judge the living and the dead and the world by fire.

R⁷. Amen.

The Gospel on the eleventh Sunday after Pentecost tells how Jesus cured a deaf and dumb man by touching his ears and tongue. The Church imitates the example of Christ, showing that only through the grace of this sacrament is one enabled to hear fruitfully the word of God and worthily declare his praises.

The priest takes saliva from his mouth with his thumb (the use of saliva in touching the ears and nostrils of the infant may be omitted for a reasonable cause, to safeguard cleanliness or to avoid the danger of contracting or spreading disease) and he touches the ears and nostrils of the infant. While he touches the ears, first the right, then the left ear, he says:

Ephpheta, which means "Be opened,"

Touching the nostrils he continues:

so that you may perceive the fragrance of God's sweetness. But you, O devil, depart; for the judgment of God has come.

[7] In supplying ceremonies, the following is said:

in order that he might become a temple of the living God and that the Holy Spirit might dwell in him. Through the same Christ our Lord, who will come to judge the living and the dead and the world by fire.

R⁷. Amen.

in order that she might become a temple of the living God and that the Holy Spirit might dwell in her. Through the same Christ our Lord, who will come to judge the living and the dead and the world by fire.

R⁷. Amen.

Through a series of formal questions the person to be baptized is now given a chance publicly to renounce all attachment to the kingdom of Satan.
The priest interrogates the candidate:

N., **do you renounce Satan?**
The sponsors answer: **I do renounce him.**
Priest: **And all his works?**
Sponsors: **I do renounce them.**
Priest: **And all his allurements?**
Sponsors: **I do renounce them.**

Having dipped his thumb in the oil of the catechumens (OS or OC), the priest anoints the infant on the breast and between the shoulders (to signify the anointing of the whole body) in the form of a cross; as he anoints he says once:

I anoint you with the oil † **of salvation in Christ Jesus our Lord, so that you may have everlasting life.**
℞. **Amen.**

The priest wipes his thumb and the places anointed on the child with cotton. Then he changes his violet stole for a white one to signify the Church's joy over the prospective new member. Having entered the baptistry proper together with the sponsors and the child, the priest asks the candidate to profess his faith and loyalty publicly.

IN THE BAPTISTRY

N., **do you believe in God, the Father almighty, Creator of heaven and earth?**
Sponsors: **I do believe.**
Priest: **Do you believe in Jesus Christ, his only Son, our Lord, who was born into this world and who suffered?**
Sponsors: **I do believe.**
Priest: **Do you believe also in the Holy Spirit, the holy Catholic Church, the communion of saints, the forgiveness of sins, the resurrection of the body and life everlasting?**
Sponsors: **I do believe.**

(In a supplementary ceremony the priest omits what follows up to the anointing with holy chrism.)
Addressing the infant by name the priest asks:

N., **do you wish to be baptized?**
Sponsors: **I do.**

IV. The Sacramental Washing

Having explicitly renounced the devil and publicly professed faith in Christ Jesus, the candidate is ready for the saving waters of holy baptism. It is with a sense of deepest reverence that we assist at this transformation of a soul into a member of Christ's Mystical Body.

The godfather or godmother holds the child — if there are two sponsors the godfather places his hand under the child's shoulder. The priest takes baptismal water in a small vessel and pours it three times upon the head of the child in the form of a cross; while doing so he says once only, but distinctly and attentively:

N., I baptize you in the name of the Father †

(he pours the first time)

and of the Son †

(he pours a second time)

and of the Holy † Spirit

(he pours the third time).

Should there be doubt as to whether the infant has been previously baptized, the following form is used:

N., if you are not baptized, I baptize you in the name of the Father † and of the Son † and of the Holy † Spirit.

V. The Royal Anointing and the Bestowal of Gifts

Holy chrism is the sacred oil of priesthood. The newborn child of God is anointed with this fragrant oil as a sign that through baptism he has become a member of Christ who is the High Priest of God's new kingdom; because of this he is now qualified to take part, according to his station, in Christ's priestly work of worshipping and sanctifying. This interior transformation is further symbolized by two symbolic gifts: a white garment (sanctifying grace), and a burning candle (the living presence of Christ).

The priest dips his thumb into the holy chrism, and in the form of a cross anoints the child on the crown of the head; while doing so he says:

May almighty God, the Father of our Lord Jesus Christ, who has given you a new birth by means of water and the Holy Spirit and forgiven all your sins, (here he anoints) **anoint you with the chrism † of salvation in the same Christ Jesus our Lord, so that you may have everlasting life.**

℟. **Amen.**

Priest: **Peace be with you.**

℟. **And with your spirit.**

> The priest wipes his thumb and the place anointed on the child with cotton. He then clothes him with a white garment, or as a substitute, places a linen cloth upon his head as he says:

Receive this white garment. Never let it become stained, so that when you stand before the judgment seat of our Lord Jesus Christ, you may have life everlasting.

℟. **Amen.**

> The priest gives the baptized or his sponsor a lighted candle, saying:

Receive this burning light, and keep the grace of your baptism throughout a blameless life. Observe the commandments of God. Then, when the Lord comes to his heavenly wedding feast, you will be able to meet him with all the saints in the halls of heaven, and live for ever and ever.

℟. **Amen.**

> Lastly, the priest bids farewell to the newly baptized in the peace of Christ:

N., go in peace, and the Lord be with you.

℟. **Amen.**

> The following prayer may be said after the rite of baptism, if one so wishes.

Almighty and everlasting God, merciful Father, because you have on this day adopted as your child this your servant, N., we implore of you, that, strengthened by the Holy Spirit and nourished by the bread of heaven, he (she) may grow to full maturity in Christ.

And may he (she) always keep in mind his (her) patron saint, so that by imitating him (her), he (she) may attain to the eternal home of his (her) heavenly Father. Through Christ our Lord.

℟. **Amen.**

THE RITE FOR CONFIRMATION

Baptism brought us into the divine family of the three Persons of the Blessed Trinity. Confirmation puts us into closer relationship with the Holy Spirit. The apostles received the Holy Spirit on Pentecost Sunday. The bishop communicates the Holy Spirit in a very special way to each baptized person on the day of confirmation.

The bishop is the ordinary minister of confirmation, as he is of holy orders; for the bishop is at the head of the lay apostles of his diocese, just as he is the first priest. When an unconfirmed person is in danger of death, however, the Church authorizes certain priests (pastors and some chaplains) to administer confirmation, using the holy chrism blessed by the bishop on the previous Holy Thursday.

Confirmation may be conferred during Mass, which may be the Mass of the day or a second-class votive Mass of the Holy Spirit (page 220). The ceremony will follow the Gospel and homily, and it will include numbers II and III below, starting on page 614.

If confirmation is administered outside of Mass, it is preceded by a liturgy of the Word.

I. The Liturgy of the Word

The ceremony begins with an entrance hymn or chant. There follows the reading of the Epistle and Gospel of the votive Mass of the Holy Spirit. A lector reads the Epistle:

EPISTLE: Acts 8:14-17

It is through the sacrament of confirmation that the Holy Spirit is communicated to the faithful in a special way.

Lector: A reading from the Acts of the Apostles.

In those days, when the apostles in Jerusalem heard that Samaria had accepted God's message, they sent Peter and John, who went down to the Samaritans and prayed that they might receive the Holy Spirit. For it had not yet fallen on any of them; they had only been baptized in the name of the Lord Jesus. Then the two laid hands on them and they received the Holy Spirit.

Between the readings from Scripture, psalm verses or other chants may be sung. Then a deacon or priest reads the Gospel.

GOSPEL: John 14:23-31

The new law, Christ's word, is not written on tablets of stone, but engraved in our hearts. It is the Holy Spirit working within us who makes us understand the full import of the Gospel and reveals to us all the demands of charity.

Deacon (or Priest):   **The Lord be with you.**

All: **And with your spirit.**

Deacon (or Priest):   **† A reading from the holy Gospel according to John.**

All: **Glory to you, O Lord.**

At that time Jesus said to his disciples: "If anyone loves me, he will keep my word. Then my Father will love him, and we shall come to him and make our dwelling-place with him. Whoever does not love me does not keep my words; yet the word that you hear is not my own but comes from the Father who sent me. All this have I spoken to you during my stay with you. But the Paraclete, the Holy Spirit, whom the Father will send in my name, will teach you everything and remind you of all that I told you myself.

"'Peace' is my farewell to you. My 'peace' is my gift to you, and I do not give it to you as the world gives it. Do not let your hearts be troubled or fearful. You have heard me say to you, 'I am going away,' and 'I am coming back to you.' If you loved me, you would rejoice to have me go to the Father, for the Father is greater than I.

"But I have told you this now even before it happens so that, when it does happen, you may believe.

"I shall no longer speak at length with you, for the Prince of the world is coming. Actually, he has no hold on me; but the world must recognize that I love the Father and that I do exactly as the Father has commanded me."

Other readings from the missal, approved by the National Conference of Bishops, may be substituted. The homily will follow the Gospel, unless the officiating prelate wishes to change the order.

II. The Renewal of Baptismal Promises

Without baptism there would be no confirmation. Baptism gave us supernatural faith, together with the sanctifying grace which is the life of our soul. Confirmation gives us the strength to bear witness before the world to that faith which was given us in baptism. Hence it is fitting that we first renew our baptismal promises.

Bishop: Let us renew the promises of holy baptism, by which we once renounced Satan and his works, as well as that world which is the enemy of God, and promised to serve God faithfully in the holy Catholic Church.

Bishop: Do you renounce Satan?

All: We do renounce him.

Bishop: And all his works?

All: We do renounce them.

Bishop: And all his allurements?

All: We do renounce them.

Bishop: Do you believe in God, the Father almighty, Creator of heaven and earth?

All: We do believe.

Bishop: Do you believe in Jesus Christ, his only Son, our Lord, who was born into this world and who suffered?

All: We do believe.

Bishop: Do you believe also in the Holy Spirit, the holy Catholic Church, the communion of saints, the forgiveness of sins, the resurrection of the body and life everlasting?

All: We do believe.

Bishop: Now let us pray to God together, as our Lord Jesus Christ has taught us to pray:

All: Our Father, who art in heaven, / hallowed be thy name; / thy kingdom come; / thy will be done on earth as it is in heaven. / Give us this day our daily bread; / and forgive us our trespasses / as we forgive those who trespass against us; / and lead us not into temptation, / but deliver us from evil. Amen.

Bishop: And may almighty God, the Father of our Lord Jesus Christ, who has given us a new birth by means of water and the Holy Spirit and forgiven all our sins, keep us by his grace in the same Jesus Christ our Lord, so that we may have life everlasting.

All: Amen.

III. The Sacrament of Confirmation

The prophet Isaiah (11:2-3) mentioned seven gifts destined for the Messiah, the Anointed One. Before anointing us, the bishop prays that we may share in these seven gifts. The bishop faces those to be confirmed. They kneel before him, and he sings or says:

Bishop: **May the Holy Spirit descend upon you and the power of the Most High preserve you from sin.**

All: **Amen.**

Bishop: **Our help is in the name of the Lord.**

All: **Who made heaven and earth.**

Bishop: **O Lord, hear my prayer.**

All: **And let my cry come to you.**

Bishop: **The Lord be with you.**

All: **And with your spirit.**

He extends his hands toward those to be confirmed.

Bishop: **Let us pray. Almighty and eternal God, who in your kindness gave to these your servants a new birth through water and the Holy Spirit, and granted to them remission of all their sins, send forth from heaven upon them your sevenfold Spirit, the Holy Consoler.**

All: **Amen.**

Bishop: **The Spirit of wisdom and understanding.**

All: **Amen.**

Bishop: **The Spirit of counsel and fortitude.**

All: **Amen.**

Bishop: **The Spirit of knowledge and piety.**

All: **Amen.**

Bishop: **Mercifully fill them with the Spirit of your fear, and seal them with the sign of the Cross of Christ, that they may obtain everlasting life. Through the same Jesus Christ, your Son, our Lord, who lives and reigns with you in the unity of the Holy Spirit, God, forever and ever.**

All: **Amen.**

The oil with which we were anointed before baptism made us more like Christ, the Anointed One. After baptism and here again in confirmation we are anointed most appropriately with holy chrism. In the chrism, there is balm mixed with the oil; and this perfume symbolizes the attraction which the Christian life should have for unbelievers. The apostolate is not a propaganda or a conquest by force; it is an authentic and disinterested act of bearing witness. The confirmed person is consecrated to be a witness to Christ, and if necessary a martyr.

The bishop receives the mitre and crosier, and he is informed regarding the name chosen by each of the per-

sons to be confirmed. Each one is presented by a spon-
sor, and regularly should kneel while being confirmed.
The bishop dips the tip of the thumb of his right hand in
the chrism, lays his hand on the head of the candidate
and with his thumb makes the sign of the Cross on the
candidate's forehead, saying:

N., I sign you with the sign of the Cross.

He continues:

And I confirm you with the chrism of salvation.

He makes the sign of the Cross over the person:

In the name of the Father and of the Son and of the Holy Spirit.

The newly confirmed answers:

Amen.

The bishop strikes the newly confirmed gently on the
cheek (recalling the kiss of peace given at this point
in ancient times):

Peace be with you.

After all have been confirmed, while the bishop washes
his hands, the following antiphon is recited or sung:

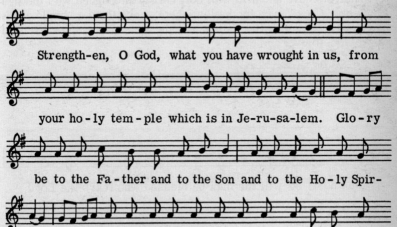

Strength-en, O God, what you have wrought in us, from
your ho-ly tem-ple which is in Je-ru-sa-lem. Glo-ry
be to the Fa-ther and to the Son and to the Ho-ly Spirit. As it was in the begin-ning is now and ev-er shall

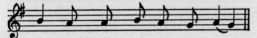

be world with-out end. A-men.

Repeat antiphon.

The bishop's mitre is removed, and he stands facing the altar, with his hands joined, and sings or says:

Bishop: Show us, O Lord, your mer-cy.
All: And grant us your sal - va-tion.

Bishop: O Lord, hear   my prayer.
All: And let my cry come to you.

Bishop: The Lord be with you.
All: And with your spir-it.

Bishop: Let us pray. O God, you gave the Holy Spirit to your apostles, and willed that through them and their successors he be given to the rest of the faithful. Look with favor upon our humble service, and grant that the Holy Spirit, descending into the hearts of those whose foreheads we have anointed with holy chrism and signed with the sign of the holy Cross, may, by dwelling there, make them a temple of his glory. You who with the Father and the same Holy Spirit live and reign, God, forever and ever.

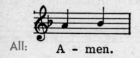

All: A - men.

Then he sings or says:

Be - hold! so will the man be blessed who fears the Lord.

Turning toward the newly confirmed and taking his crosier, he makes the sign of the Cross over them, singing or saying:

May the Lord bless you from Si - on, so that you may

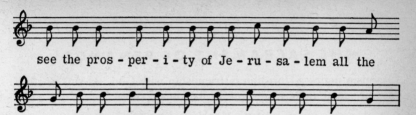

see the pros - per - i - ty of Je - ru - sa - lem all the

days of your life and may have life ev - er - last - ing.

All: A - men.

It is traditional that the Our Father, the Hail Mary and the Apostles' Creed are recited as a part of the confirmation rite. Benediction regularly follows confirmation when given outside Mass; see page **643**.

THE SACRAMENT OF PENANCE

Baptism unites a Christian in friendship with God. By sin, whether grave or venial, this friendship is broken or impaired.

a) LORD, I HAVE SINNED

Sin is not only the violation of a rule or commandment. It is above all a betrayal of God's love, for the love of God is shown us by his will, his law and his commandments. Sin is disobedience to God.

1. It is a BREAK with God, a revolt against him, infidelity to his love that singled us out before we were born. The Bible calls sin "adultery."

2. It is a DISRUPTION of the human community founded by God (Prayer over the Assembly, page 208): it is separation from the Church.

3. It is the DESTRUCTION of the sinner's own being, resembling that effected by sickness and death, the symbols of sin.

In these three ways the sinner separates himself from the source of life. If he dies in a state of grave sin, he will go to hell, that is, to eternal death, cut off forever from God, from his brothers and from himself.

A mortal sin is a *conscious and willed* (or at least clearly accepted) *refusal* to obey a *serious command* of God.

A venial sin (one easier to wipe out) is a *less conscious or less voluntary refusal* to obey a serious command, or the conscious and willed refusal of a *less important command*. It weakens the fervor of our Christian life and opens the door to mortal sin. If it is not wiped out before death, we must be purified of it in purgatory before entering heaven.

Above all, to rise again from sin we must recognize that we are sinners (Gospel, page 130).

b) I WILL COME BACK TO YOU, MY FATHER

By the sacrament of penance, the sinner re-enters into friendship with God and man, and regains peace with himself.

1. It is a RETURN from captivity to the Father who awaits our return as did the father of the prodigal son (Luke 15:11-32) and restores us to spiritual life. On the sinner's part this presumes a change of direction, a "conversion" (Gospel, page 23) and regret for sins committed. Forgiveness is made possible by Jesus Christ, the servant of God who took upon himself the burden of removing the sins of the

world: the sinner must immerse himself in the redeeming Blood of the Savior (Epistle, page 121).

2. It is a RECONCILIATION with the Church: "If you forgive any-one's sins, they shall be forgiven; if you hold anyone's sins back, they shall be held back," said the one Shepherd who wishes to gather his dispersed sheep together under his guidance (Gospel, page 95).

3. It is the REBUILDING of the temple, of the spiritual dwelling, thanks to the Holy Spirit given by the risen Jesus. It is life given back by Jesus, the healer of souls, who in his earthly life at the same time forgave sins and healed the sick (Gospel, page 148).

A Christian knows that there are no limits to love, and he desires ceaselessly to purify himself so as to intensify the love of God within him (Epistle, page 139). And so he should conduct himself with due moderation and without presumption (Epistles, pages 127 and 67).

I. EXAMINATION OF CONSCIENCE

The following examination of conscience draws attention to various sins, errors and omissions which are not ordinarily listed but which still prevent or hinder the freedom and spontaneity of the soul. It is an examination to help adults recognize their sins and failings.[1]

TOWARD OURSELVES

By mediocrity

Deliberately to accept our mediocrity and not to try to rise above it.

To excuse our sins by the fact that they are habits or that "everybody does it."

Habitually, not to put forth our best efforts.

To remain intellectually, politically, spiritually childish.

To remain ignorant of the great movements of thought and action of our times.

To act by whim or caprice.

Not to organize our time.

To become so over-organized as to be incapable of a spontaneously generous action.

To waste time on futilities.

By ambition

To love money.

To desire wealth.

To desire honors.

---

[1] This examination reproduces, with the permission of its authors (Fathers Lebret and Suavet) and its editor, a leaflet entitled "Examination of conscience" (Ed. Ouvriers).

To deprive ourselves or our families of what is essential for the sake of appearance.

To envy the condition of others.

To have more ambition than worth.

To have ambition that is not directed toward service.

By weakness

To lack the courage to defend truth or justice.

To deceive, to however small an extent, for the sake of attention, advancement, money.

To cringe before the wealthy and powerful.

By lack of moderation

To have gone beyond our strength or thrown our lives out of balance without a serious reason for doing so.

To lack self-mastery.

To get uselessly angry against things or people.

By disorder and lack of organization

Not to avail ourselves of some good put within our reach.

Habitually to do our work badly or carelessly.

Thoughtlessly to commit ourselves.

Not to consider the ultimate effects of our negligence, and also of our lack of knowledge or of professional formation.

To become or to risk becoming the cause of grave or fatal accidents.

To lack the strength to make decisions.

To lack continuity in carrying out what we have undertaken.

Not to finish, without serious reason, whatever we have begun.

Not to look ahead.

Not to consider the effects of delays, trials or great weariness on other people.

To be discouraged in the face of difficulties or after trials.

Not to make time for moments of solitude, reflection, recollection.

By pride and vanity

To be overbearing, vain, proud, conceited.

To attribute to our personal worth the respect we are given because of our office.

To remain very sensitive to slights.

To act from the desire to shine, or from ambition.

Always to think we are right.

Not to consider our limitations and to accept them.

To speak pompously.

To speak about things we do not know about.

To make hasty judgments in order to dominate discussions.

Against our bodies

To neglect to take normal care of ourselves or to do what is prescribed by the doctor.

To be excessively concerned about our health and waste time on it.

To abuse food, alcoholic drinks, tobacco, etc.

Not to get enough sleep.

To take pleasure in gross amusements.

In avoiding grossness, to lose ourselves in excessive refinement.

To exhaust ourselves in pleasures at the expense of our work.

To accept the current notions about sex; not to believe that there can be sexual sins.

To believe that we cannot help letting ourselves go and to deny our responsibility for doing so.

To take pleasure in a hectic atmosphere and find it natural.

To seek for sexual pleasure outside of marriage.

In marriage, to seek sexual pleasure for itself, while avoiding the normal consequences of our actions.

AGAINST OTHERS

Against charity

Not to be able to say in all sincerity that we love our neighbor as ourselves.

To love selfishly.

To wish to snatch another's affection. To be jealous.

To think only of ourselves.

To lack initiative in undertaking tasks for the common good.

Not to feel anguish at another's misery.

To pass by the unfortunate with indifference.

Consciously or unconsciously to despise another person, that is to say,

In dealing with another person, whoever he may be, not to think of him as a person, not to treat him as a person, and not to realize that we should, in some way, help him toward self-development. To have stifled his development in some way.

To talk only about ourselves and not to let others express themselves.

Not to seek to understand other people.

To refuse to render a service out of selfishness or human respect.

To let ourselves be waited on out of laziness or pride.

To have been able to relieve some distress and not to have done so.

Not to bring our neighbor help when he is in danger.

To seek the company only of persons whose friendship might be useful.

To abandon our friends in difficulties.

In our words and actions, habitually to despise poor people or those of a class or degree of culture inferior to our own.

To wish to be respected without ourselves respecting others.

Frequently to make other people wait for us.

To forget or miss engagements.

Not to be sufficiently accessible to others, sufficiently agreeable.

Not to give the other person our full attention during a conversation.

To wound others by our words.

To harm others by calumnies, scandals or merely idle talk.

To betray a confidence, to divulge confidences. To involve ourselves indiscreetly by words or attitudes in the personal life of others.

To beat down those who oppose us.

To give scandal by our appearance, our speech or our actions.

To give scandal by the gulf between the life we lead and the principles we adhere to.

Against truth

To lie.

Through fear or timidity to be silent when we should speak up for the truth.

To make use of Christianity and not to give the witness of a life according to the Gospel.

To uphold positions contrary to Christian teaching (abortion, divorce, sterilization of the unfit, etc.).

Against justice

To be directly or indirectly the cause of someone's death. To cooperate by suggestion, advice or action in procuring an abortion.

Not to be concerned with social problems.

To take refuge behind the laws.

Not to be concerned with human ills, in particular with inhuman institutions and customs.

To ridicule those who are so concerned.

To trust public opinion or the press in making a judgment on someone.

To profit from the needs or misery of another in order to exploit him.

To use our influence to keep ourselves from suffering the effects of our actions.

To attribute to "economic laws" the evils which flow from our negligence or greed.

To delay in paying our debts.

To keep for too long, or even forget to give back what we have borrowed — particularly books.

To think that things or advantages can be owned absolutely, with no regard for the common good or the needs of others. To consider the defense of such ownership more important than justice.

Not to join in organizations for the defense of justice and the common good.

Not to speak out in group discussions but to let selfish interests win out.

To accept an easy and comfortable life unjustified by the requirement of the service we render to society.

To keep for ourselves what we have over and above our needs. To "make" money without working.

Against our duties to our family

To shut ourselves up in our family life and its preoccupations.

To sacrifice our family to other concerns.

Not to help one another in family life.

To take over for our own use an important share of the resources of the whole family.

Not to respect the personality of another, even a child.

To demand of children more than we have the courage to practice ourselves.

To think it normal that parents should deprive themselves of essentials in order to give extras to their children.

To shut ourselves up against our parents, to refuse them tokens of affection.

To scorn their experience. To think of ourselves as superior to them, forgetting that in most cases it is due to them that we have acquired our learning and culture.

To mention indiscreetly the faults of members of the family.

TOWARD THE CHURCH

By thought

To think of the Church as a sect or a party and not as the Mystical Body of Christ.

To limit our view of the Church to the horizons of the visible Church, in particular to forget the suffering Church.

To reduce the role of the Church to the administration of the sacraments; to slight, in particular, the role of the teaching Church.

Never to read thoughtfully the books of the New Testament.

To be ignorant of papal teachings since Leo XIII.

To criticize these teachings without having studied them.

Not to retain anything but the conclusions of these teachings instead of entering into their Gospel inspiration.

To wish to understand only what is favorable to a position we have already taken.

To doubt the effectiveness of the Church in bringing the message of the Gospel to today's world.

Not to feel ourselves responsible for our share in the inadequacy of Christians.

To consider Catholics of the Eastern rite as less Catholic than ourselves.

To consider non-Catholic Christians as enemies rather than separated brethren.

By words

To identify the Church with the clergy alone. In speaking of the Church, to say "they" rather than "we."

To speak or act in the name of the Church without any mandate to do so.

Lightly to criticize the hierarchy or the clergy or any Christian effort of any kind.

To criticize the decisions of the magisterium, seeing only their consequences on our own concerns or our immediate environment and forgetting that the Holy Father speaks to the whole world.

By action

To consider ourselves exempt from the laws binding on all the faithful under the pretext that religion is a personal matter or that our circumstances are exceptional.

To lack fidelity to discipline and to lose authentic Christian values under the pretext of adaptation.

To compromise the Church by attitudes contrary to the Gospel.

To use our Christianity in order to obtain temporal benefits.

To attempt to put the organizations or the values of the Church at the service of our temporal interests.

To display in public the internal difficulties of the Church.

To call in non-Christians to settle difficulties arising between Christians.

By omission

Not to contribute in any way to Catholic action or to the Church's missionary work.

Not to seek to make the Church purer, more vital, more radiant.

By negligence, snobbism or on principle, not to take part in the daily life of the Church and its extraordinary manifestations.

To make inadequate contributions to the material needs of the Church.
Never to pray for the Pope or for priests.

TOWARD GOD

Not to ascend from the contemplation of nature and of human life to
the thought of God.

To wait for God to manifest himself rather than seeking him in the
midst of the contradictions of the present life.

Not to try to enter into the plan of God as deeply as possible.

Not to believe in God as he who, finally, guides the world.

Not to find and love God in our brothers.

Not to love our brothers in God.

Never to think about the Trinity.

Not to consider Jesus Christ as our brother who is always near us. To
cease to take him as our model.

Not to make an effort to bear the sin of the world with him, in particular the sins of our own kind of people and our country.

To place the Cross on our walls and not in our life.

To speak of Christ, but not to try to live according to the Gospel.

Not to be wholly taken over by the love of God.

Not to find time to pray.

To measure out like a miser the time to be given to God.

To pray only in obedience to a command or from habit.

To pray only with our lips.

In difficulties, in the face of the realization of our inadequacy, not to
have recourse to prayer.

To build our whole life without God and then ask him to intervene.

To pray only to ask favors, never to adore God, to thank him, to adhere to him, to love him.

To consider the spiritual life as an obligation to be carried out only
when we have fulfilled all our other duties.

When we have reached a certain stage in the spiritual life, to be content not to go any further.

II. SORROW FOR SINS

God does not pardon our sins unless we are truly sorry for them and
desire to do everything possible to keep from sinning again.

To gain true sorrow for our sins, we can pray, thinking

—of the sufferings and death of Christ nailed to the Cross to save us
and to give men the splendor of his own divine life;

—of the Father's love that expects from us something quite different
from the ungratefulness of sin;

—of the evil and the death that are attacking our souls and exposing it to the danger of hell;

—of the evil that we spread around us, instead of radiating goodness. The world is poisoned by innumerable public and secret sins.

So we become capable of saying to Christ in all sincerity:

"*Yes, Lord, I love you; wipe away my sins.*"

And we can be sure that we shall go out from the confessional with a soul revitalized, divinized by Christ's grace.

If we have to wait before our turn comes for confession, we can use this time to increase our sorrow for sin.

To help us in our resolve to aim at perfection, we might read the Gospel of the beatitudes, page 212.

III. HOW TO GO TO CONFESSION

The principal requirements are to confess our sins, at least all our grave sins, and to be sorry for them.

No formula is indispensable. What follows is the customary way of going to confession.

(The act of contrition should be said before confession; the penitent may then listen to the words of absolution, or repeat it during the absolution.)

ACT OF CONTRITION

O my God, I am heartily sorry for having offended thee, and I detest all my sins, because of thy just punishments, but most of all because they offend thee, my God, who art all-good and deserving of all my love. I firmly resolve, with the help of thy grace, to sin no more and to avoid the near occasions of sin. Amen.

1) The sign of the Cross:

"In the name of the Father and of the Son and of the Holy Spirit."

2) "Bless me, Father, for I have sinned."

3) "My last confession was —— days (weeks, months) ago. These are my sins."

4) Now tell your sins.

Then ask the confessor any questions that may be troubling you.

5) Answer the confessor's questions, if he asks any.

Listen to his advice.

Fix in your memory the penance he imposes.

6) While the priest is giving you absolution, repeat the act of contrition given above or the following simpler form:

"O my God, I am heartily sorry for having offended you because you are infinitely good and sin displeases you. I firmly resolve, with the help of your grace, to sin no more and to do penance."

The confession ends with the absolution. The priest says:

"May almighty God have mercy on you, forgive you your sins, and bring you to life everlasting. Amen."

Then, with his right hand elevated toward the penitent, he says:

"May the almighty and merciful Lord grant you pardon, absolution and remission of your sins. Amen.

"May our Lord Jesus Christ absolve you, and by his authority I absolve you from every bond of excommunication and interdict, to the extent of my power and your need. Finally I absolve you from your sins, in the name of the Father and of the Son † and of the Holy Spirit. Amen."

"May the Passion of our Lord Jesus Christ, the merits of the Blessed Virgin Mary and of all the saints, and also whatever good you do and evil you endure be cause for the remission of your sins, the increase of grace, and the reward of everlasting life. Amen."

IV. AFTER CONFESSION

Now we are purified, free and strong. With all our hearts, we should thank Jesus Christ. From now on we are much more closely united with him.

We should decide what efforts we are to make to improve our life; we should ask God to help us, and not be afraid of being generous.

We should carry out as soon as possible the prayers or acts which the priest assigned as penance for our sins. This penance does away with the punishments due our sins and obtains for us a more powerful grace not to fall into them again.

We should entrust our life and our resolutions to the Holy Virgin, our Mother.

And, if we have any time left, we should express our gratitude to Gor for his mercy, perhaps by praying Psalm 135, page 488, or Psalm 102, page 470.

V. IN OUR LIVES

Life is not always easy; we do not always know what we should do and we often the lack the strength to do it.

God ordinarily gives us his light and his help through the voice of a priest. We should realize the need to ask advice, above all when we are young and in serious crises of life, and to open our soul to a priest in whom we have confidence.

FORTY HOURS DEVOTION

This service in honor of Christ in the Holy Eucharist consists of:

1. holy Mass;
2. procession and Litany of the Saints;
3. exposition, adoration and Benediction of the Blessed Sacrament.

The Mass formulary may be the Votive Mass of the Most Holy Eucharist, page 215 (with *Glory to God* but not the Creed), the Votive Mass for Peace, page 225, or the Mass of the day depending upon its rank.

The procession is begun after the celebrant, holding the monstrance and facing the people, intones the hymn, "Sing, My Tongue! Acclaim Christ Present"; the last two stanzas of this hymn are not sung until the Blessed Sacrament is placed on the altar after the procession.

For private adoration of the Blessed Sacrament or for the parish evening service on days of the Forty Hours Devotion the formularies for a Bible Vigil would serve admirably well, for instance, that in honor of the Holy Eucharist, page 683.

The following hymns and chants for this devotion may be used although alternates and additional melodies may be selected:

301. SING, MY TONGUE! ACCLAIM CHRIST PRESENT

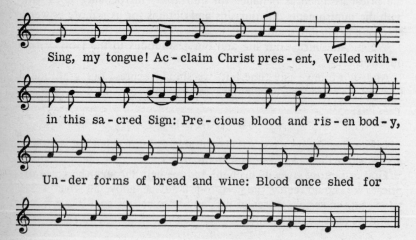

Sing, my tongue! Ac-claim Christ pres-ent, Veiled with-in this sa-cred Sign: Pre-cious blood and ris-en bod-y, Un-der forms of bread and wine: Blood once shed for man's re-demp-tion By his king, of Da-vid's line.

Heaven's promised gift to mankind,
Born to us of one most pure,
Spends his earthly days among us
Plants the seed of faith secure,
Ends his mission, leaves a symbol
Of the death he will endure:

Dining with his twelve apostles
On the night before he died,
Taking for the paschal supper
Foods the Law had specified,
Lo, he sets new bread before them,
Handing each — Christ crucified!

Word-made-flesh makes bread his body,
Consecrates it by his word.
Wine becomes the blood of Jesus:
He it is whose voice is heard.
Minds in doubt need faith's assurance:
God who spoke can not have erred.

Bowing low, then, offer homage
To a Sacrament so great!
Here is new and perfect worship;
All the old must terminate.
Senses cannot grasp this marvel:
Faith must serve to compensate.

Praise and glorify the Father,
Bless his Son's life-giving name,
Singing their eternal Godhead,
Power, majesty and fame,
Offering their Holy Spirit
Equal worship and acclaim. Amen.

302. THE LITANY OF THE SAINTS [1]

The first five invocations of the litany may be repeated.

Lord, have mer - cy on us.
Christ, have mer - cy on us.
Lord, have mer - cy on us.

[1] The English text of this Litany of the Saints is taken from *The Hours of the Divine Office in English and Latin*, an officially approved form of the Roman Breviary.

Christ, hear us.

All: Christ, lis-ten to us.

Cantors: God, the heaven-ly Fa-ther,

All: have mer-cy on us.

God the Son, Redeem- er of the world,
God the Ho- ly Spir- it,
Holy Trini- ty, one God,

Ho- ly Mar- y,
Holy Moth- er of God,
Holy Virgin, first a- mong vir- gins,
Saint Mi- chael,
Saint Ga- bri- el,
Saint Raph- a- el,

All: pray for us

All you holy Angels and Arch- an- gels,
All you holy ranks of bless- ed Spir- its,
Saint John the Bap- tist,
Saint Jo- seph,
All you holy Patriarchs and Proph- ets,

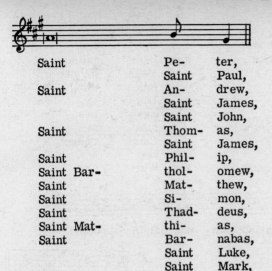

Saint	Pe-	ter,
	Saint	Paul,
Saint	An-	drew,
	Saint	James,
	Saint	John,
Saint	Thom-	as,
	Saint	James,
Saint	Phil-	ip,
Saint Bar-	thol-	omew,
Saint	Mat-	thew,
Saint	Si-	mon,
Saint	Thad-	deus,
Saint Mat-	thi-	as,
Saint	Bar-	nabas,
	Saint	Luke,
	Saint	Mark,

All you holy Apostles and	e-	van-	gelists,
All you holy disci-		ples	of	the Lord,
All you ho-		ly	In-	nocents,
Saint			Ste-	phen,
Saint			Law-	rence,
Saint			Vin-	cent,
Saints Fabian and		Se-	bas-	tian,
Saints			John	and Paul,
Saints Cosmas		and	Da-	mian,
Saints Gervase		and	Pro-	tase,
All you ho-		ly	Mar-	tyrs,
Saint		Syl-	ves-	ter,
Saint			Greg-	ory,
Saint			Am-	brose,
Saint		Au-	gus-	tine,
			Saint	Jerome,
Saint			Mar-	tin,
Saint			Nich-	olas,
All you holy Bishops and		Con-	fes-	sors,
All you ho-		ly	Doc-	tors,
Saint			An-	thony,
Saint			Ben-	edict,
Saint			Ber-	nard,

Saint		Dom-	inic,
Saint		Fran-	cis,
All you holy Priests	and	Cler-	ics,
All you holy Monks	and	Her-	mits,
Saint Mar-	y	Mag-	dalen,
Saint		Ag-	atha,
Saint		Lu-	cy,
Saint		Ag-	nes,
Saint	Ce-	cil-	ia,
Saint		Cath-	erine,
Saint An-	as-	ta-	sia,
All you holy Virgins	and	Wid-	ows,

All you holy men and wom- en, Saints of God,

All: plead for us.

Be mer - ci - ful,

All: spare us, O Lord.

Be mer - ci - ful,

All: lis - ten to us, O Lord.

From ev - 'ry e - vil,

All: de - liv - er us, O Lord.

From ev - 'ry sin,

From your an - ger,

From im - mi - nent dan - gers,

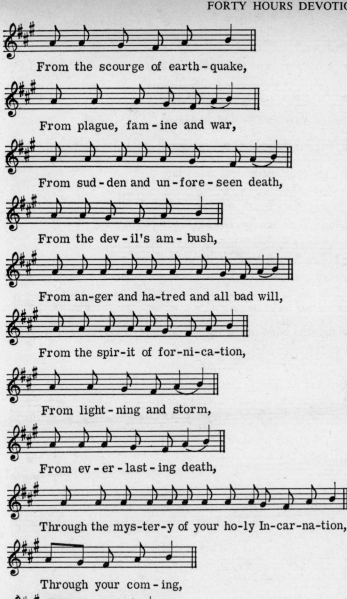

From the scourge of earth-quake,

From plague, fam-ine and war,

From sud-den and un-fore-seen death,

From the dev-il's am-bush,

From an-ger and ha-tred and all bad will,

From the spir-it of for-ni-ca-tion,

From light-ning and storm,

From ev-er-last-ing death,

Through the mys-ter-y of your ho-ly In-car-na-tion,

Through your com-ing,

Through your birth,

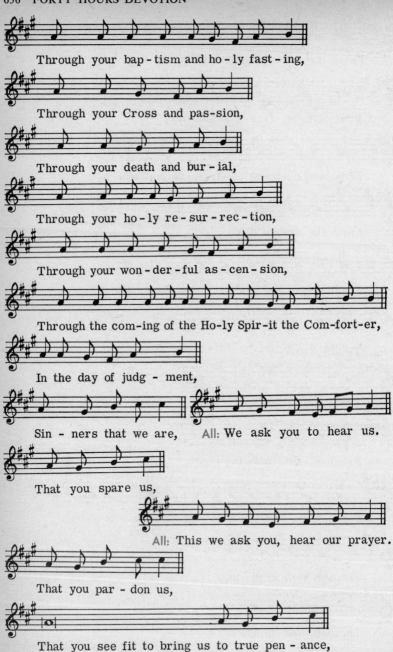

Through your bap - tism and ho - ly fast - ing,

Through your Cross and pas - sion,

Through your death and bur - ial,

Through your ho - ly re - sur - rec - tion,

Through your won - der - ful as - cen - sion,

Through the com - ing of the Ho - ly Spir - it the Com - fort - er,

In the day of judg - ment,

Sin - ners that we are,   All: We ask you to hear us.

That you spare us,

All: This we ask you, hear our prayer.

That you par - don us,

That you see fit to bring us to true pen - ance,

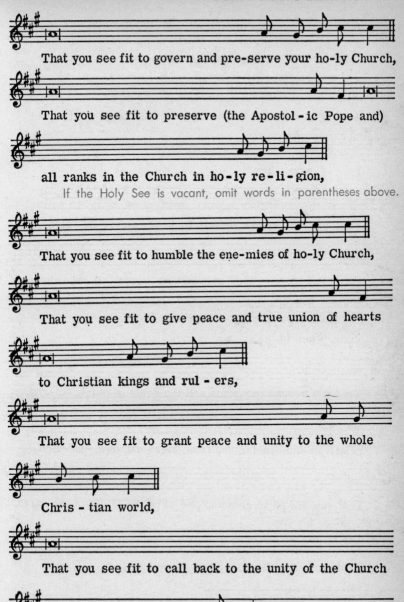

That you see fit to govern and pre-serve your ho-ly Church,

That you see fit to preserve (the Apostol - ic Pope and)

all ranks in the Church in ho-ly re-li-gion,

If the Holy See is vacant, omit words in parentheses above.

That you see fit to humble the ene-mies of ho-ly Church,

That you see fit to give peace and true union of hearts

to Christian kings and rul - ers,

That you see fit to grant peace and unity to the whole

Chris - tian world,

That you see fit to call back to the unity of the Church

all who have strayed from the truth, and lead all un-

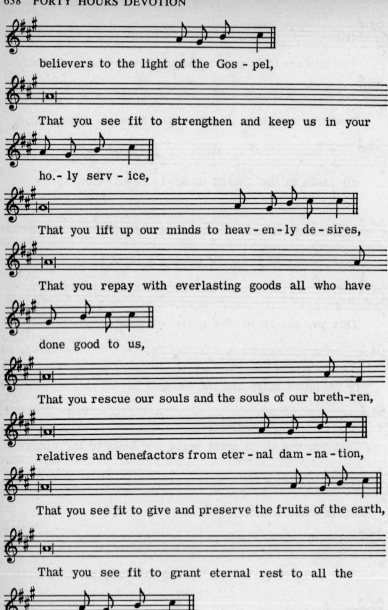

believers to the light of the Gos - pel,

That you see fit to strengthen and keep us in your

ho. - ly serv - ice,

That you lift up our minds to heav - en - ly de - sires,

That you repay with everlasting goods all who have

done good to us,

That you rescue our souls and the souls of our breth-ren,

relatives and benefactors from eter - nal dam - na - tion,

That you see fit to give and preserve the fruits of the earth,

That you see fit to grant eternal rest to all the

faith - ful de - part - ed,

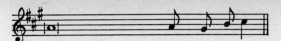

That you see fit to lis - ten to us,

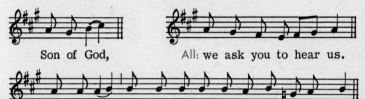

Son of God,   All: we ask you to hear us.

Lamb of God, you who take a-way the sins of the world,

All: spare us, Lord.

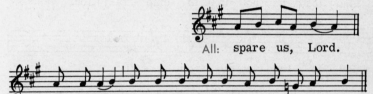

Lamb of God, you who take a-way the sins of the world,

All: lis - ten to us, Lord.

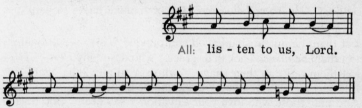

Lamb of God, you who take a-way the sins of the world,

All: have mer - cy on us.

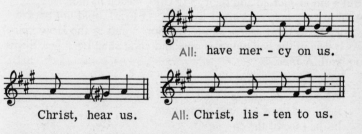

Christ, hear us.   All: Christ, lis - ten to us.

Lord, have mer - cy on us.

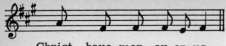

Christ, have mer - cy on us.

Lord, have mer - cy on us.   Our Fa - ther
(silently)

And lead us not in - to temp - ta - tion.

All: But de - liv - er us from e - vil.

Deign, O God, to res-cue me;*O Lord, make haste to help me.

2. Let them be put to shame *and* confounded * who seek *my* life.
3. Let them be *turned* back in disgrace * who desire my *ruin*.
4. Let them retire *in* their shame * who say to me, "aha, *aha*!"
5. But may *all* who seek you * exult and be glad *in* you,
6. And may those who love *your* salvation * say ever, "God be glor-*ified*!"
7. But I am af-*flict*-ed and poor; * O God, hasten *to* me!
8. You are my help and *my* deliverer; * O Lord, hold *not* back.
9. Glory be to the Fa-*ther* and to the Son * and to the Holy Spir-*it*.
10. As it was in the beginning, is now and *ev*-er shall be, * world with-out end. A-*men*.

Priest: Save your serv-*ants*.
All: Who hope in you, *my* God.
Priest: Be to us, Lord, a tower of *strength*.
All: In the face of the en-*emy*.
Priest: Let the enemy have no power o-*ver* us.
All: And the son of iniquity be unable to harm *us*.
Priest: Lord, do not deal with us according to our *sins*.
All: Nor repay us according to our mis-*deeds*.

The following invocation is omitted if the Holy See is vacant.

Priest: Let us pray for our Pope *N*.

All: May the Lord preserve him and give him life / and make him blessed on earth, / and not deliver him up to the will of his en-*emies*.

Priest: Let us pray for our benefac-*tors*.

All: May you see fit, Lord, to bestow eternal life / on all those who do good to us for your sake. A-*men*.

Priest: Let us pray for the faithful depart-*ed*.

All: Eternal rest grant unto them, O Lord, / and let perpetual light shine upon *them*.

Priest: May they rest *in* peace.

All: A-*men*.

Priest: For our absent breth-*ren*.

All: Save your servants who hope in you, *my* God.

Priest: Send them help, O Lord, from the sanc-*tuary*.

All: And out of Sion defend *them*.

Priest: O Lord, hear *my* prayer.

All: And let my cry come *to* you.

A procession may intervene at this point; if so, hymn No. 301, page 630, is sung; the final two verses or the *Tantum Ergo Sacramentum* follow after the monstrance is replaced on the altar. The celebrant then continues with

Priest: You gave them Bread from heaven (P.T. Alleluia).

All: Containing all that is delicious (P.T. Alleluia).

If a procession does not intervene at this point, the prayers continue as follow:

Priest: The Lord be with you.

All: And with your spirit.

Priest: Let us pray. Lord Jesus, in a wonderful sacrament you have left us the memorial of your passion. Grant us the grace to adore the hidden presence of your Body and Blood with such faith that we may always feel within ourselves the effects of your redemption.

During Advent:

It was your will, O Lord, that your divine Word should become flesh in the womb of the Blessed Virgin Mary when the angel made his announcement. Grant that your faithful who believe in this divine motherhood may have their prayers heard through Mary's intercession.

From Christmas through February 1:

O God, who through the fruitful virginity of Blessed Mary gave all men the riches of eternal salvation, we entreat you to let us feel the intercession of her who gave us the author of life, our Lord Jesus Christ, your Son.

From February 2 through Passiontide and after Paschaltide until Advent:

Lord God, grant that your children may always enjoy health of soul and body; may the intercession of the glorious Virgin Mary deliver us from the sorrows of this world and make us share your happiness throughout eternity.

In Paschaltide:

O God, you were pleased to give joy to the world through the resurrection of your Son, our Lord Jesus Christ. Grant, we beseech you, that through the mediation of the Virgin Mary, his Mother, we may come to possess the joys of life everlasting.

All-powerful, eternal God, have mercy on your servant, our Pope N.; in your kindness, guide him on the way to eternal salvation. With your help, he will desire only the things that please you and put all his strength into doing those things.

O God, our refuge and our strength, listen to your Church; with love she prays to you, and you are the one who can teach her to love. What we ask of you with loyal hearts, therefore, grant that we may obtain without fail.

All-powerful, eternal God, sovereign Master of the living and the dead, you know in advance those who, by their faith and their works, will one day be numbered among your elect; have mercy on them. We have come to pray for some whom the present life still holds in the bonds of flesh, and for others who have put off their bodies and have already entered into the next life. To all these, Lord, grant in your goodness, through the intercession of all the saints, the forgiveness of all their sins. This we ask of you through our Lord Jesus Christ, your Son, who lives and reigns with you in the unity of the Holy Spirit, God, forever. All: A-men.

Priest: O Lord, hear *my* prayer.

All: And let my cry come *to* you.

Priest: May the all-powerful and merciful Lord listen *to us*.

All: A-*men*.

Priest (on a lower tone): And may the souls of the faithful departed through the mercy of God rest in peace. All: Amen.

BENEDICTION OF THE BLESSED SACRAMENT PRAYERS

℣. Panem de cælo præstitísti eis (P.T. Alleluia).

℟. Omne delectaméntum in se habentem (P.T. Alleluia).

Orémus. Deus, qui nobis sub Sacraménto mirábili, passiónis tuæ memóriam reliquísti: tríbue, quǽsumus, ita nos Córporis et Sánguinis tui sacra mystéria venerári; ut redemptiónis tuæ fructum in nobis iúgiter sentiámus: Qui vivis et regnas in sǽcula sæculórum.

℟. Amen.

℣. You gave them Bread from heaven (P.T. Alleluia).

℟. Containing all that is delicious (P.T. Alleluia).

Let us pray. Lord Jesus, in a wonderful sacrament you have left us the memorial of your passion. Grant us the grace to adore the hidden presence of your Body and Blood with such faith that we may always feel within ourselves the effects of your redemption. This we ask of you, who live and reign forever. ℟. Amen.

THE DIVINE PRAISES

Blessed be God.
Blessed be his holy Name.
Blessed be Jesus Christ, true God and true Man.
Blessed be the Name of Jesus.
Blessed be his most sacred Heart.
Blessed be his most precious Blood.
Blessed be Jesus in the most holy Sacrament of the altar.
Blessed be the Holy Spirit, the Paraclete.
Blessed be the great Mother of God, Mary most holy.
Blessed be her holy and immaculate conception.
Blessed be her glorious assumption.
Blessed be the name of Mary, Virgin and Mother.
Blessed be St. Joseph, her most chaste spouse.
Blessed be God in his angels and in his saints.

303. THE DIVINE PRAISES

1. Blessed be God.   2. Blessed be his ho - ly name.

3. Blessed be Je - sus Christ, true God and true man.

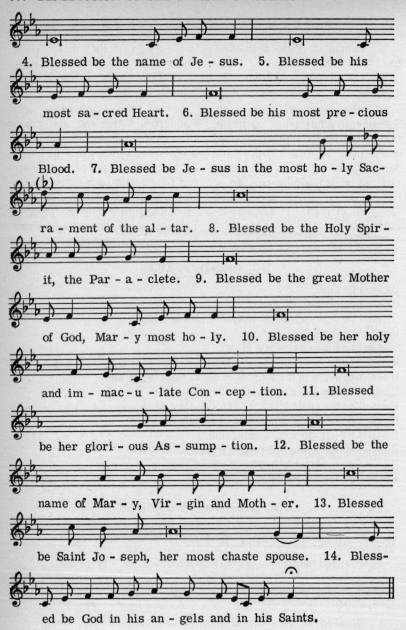

4. Blessed be the name of Je - sus.   5. Blessed be his

most sa - cred Heart.   6. Blessed be his most pre - cious

Blood.   7. Blessed be Je - sus in the most ho - ly Sac-

ra - ment of the al - tar.   8. Blessed be the Holy Spir-

it, the Par - a - clete.   9. Blessed be the great Mother

of God, Mar - y most ho - ly.   10. Blessed be her holy

and im - mac - u - late Con - cep - tion.   11. Blessed

be her glori - ous As - sump - tion.   12. Blessed be the

name of Mar - y, Vir - gin and Moth - er.   13. Blessed

be Saint Jo - seph, her most chaste spouse.   14. Bless-

ed be God in his an - gels and in his Saints.

LITANY OF THE SACRED HEART OF JESUS

Lord, have mercy on us.

Christ, have mercy on us.

Lord, have mercy on us.

Christ, hear us.

Christ, graciously hear us.

God the Father of heaven, have mercy on us.*

God the Son, Redeemer of the world,

God the Holy Spirit,

Holy Trinity, one God,

Heart of Jesus, Son of the eternal Father,

Heart of Jesus, formed by the Holy Spirit in the womb of the Virgin Mother,

Heart of Jesus, substantially united to the Word of God,

Heart of Jesus, infinite in majesty,

Heart of Jesus, sacred temple of God,

Heart of Jesus, tabernacle of the Most High,

Heart of Jesus, house of God and gate of heaven,

Heart of Jesus, burning furnace of charity,

Heart of Jesus, abode of justice and love,

Heart of Jesus, full of goodness and love,

Heart of Jesus, abyss of all virtues,

Heart of Jesus, most worthy of all praise,

Heart of Jesus, king and center of all hearts,

Heart of Jesus, in whom are all the treasures of wisdom and knowledge,

Heart of Jesus, in whom dwells the fullness of divinity,

Heart of Jesus, in whom the Father was well pleased,

Heart of Jesus, of whose fullness we have all received,

Heart of Jesus, desire of the everlasting hills,

Heart of Jesus, patient and most merciful,

Heart of Jesus, enriching all who call upon thee,

Heart of Jesus, fountain of life and holiness,

Heart of Jesus, atonement for our sins,

Heart of Jesus, loaded down with opprobrium,

Heart of Jesus, bruised for our offenses,

Heart of Jesus, obedient unto death,

Heart of Jesus, pierced with a lance,

Heart of Jesus, source of all consolation,

Heart of Jesus, our life and resurrection,

Heart of Jesus, our peace and reconciliation,

Heart of Jesus, victim for sin,

Heart of Jesus, salvation of those who trust in thee,

Heart of Jesus, hope of those who die in thee,

Heart of Jesus, delight of all the saints,

Lamb of God, who take away the sins of the world, spare us, O Lord.

*After each invocation: "Have mercy on us."

Lamb of God, who take away the sins of the world, graciously hear us, O Lord.

Lamb of God, who take away the sins of the world, have mercy on us.

℣. Jesus, meek and humble of heart.

℟. Make our hearts like unto thine.

Prayer

Let us pray. Almighty and everlasting God, look upon the heart of your dearly beloved Son, and upon the praise and satisfaction he offers you in the name of sinners and for those who seek your mercy. Be appeased, and grant us pardon in the name of the selfsame Jesus Christ, your Son, who lives and reigns with you forever and ever. ℟. Amen.

ACT OF CONSECRATION OF THE HUMAN RACE TO THE SACRED HEART OF JESUS

Most sweet Jesus, Redeemer of the human race, look down upon us humbly prostrate before thy altar. We are thine, and thine we wish to be; but to be more surely united with thee, behold, each one of us freely consecrates himself today to thy most Sacred Heart. Many indeed have never known thee; many too, despising thy precepts, have rejected thee. Have mercy on them all, most merciful Jesus, and draw them to thy Sacred Heart. Be thou King, O Lord, not only of the faithful who have never forsaken thee, but also of the prodigal children who have abandoned thee; grant that they may quickly return to their Father's house lest they die of wretchedness and hunger. Be thou King of those who are deceived by erroneous opinion, or whom discord keeps aloof, and call them back to the harbor of truth and unity of faith, so that soon there may be but one flock and one Shepherd. Grant, O Lord, to thy Church assurance of freedom and immunity from harm; give peace and order to all nations, and make the earth resound from pole to pole with one cry: Praise be to the divine Heart that wrought our salvation; to it be glory and honor forever. Amen.

LITANY OF ST. JOSEPH

Lord, have mercy on us.

Christ, have mercy on us.

Lord, have mercy on us.

Christ, hear us.

Christ, graciously hear us.

God the Father of heaven, have mercy on us.

God the Son, Redeemer of the world, have mercy on us.

God the Holy Spirit, have mercy on us.

Holy Trinity, one God, have mercy on us.

Holy Mary, pray for us.*

St. Joseph,

Illustrious son of David,

Splendor of patriarchs,

Spouse of God's Mother,

Chaste guardian of the Virgin,

Foster-father of the Son of God,

Watchful defender of Christ,

Head of the Holy Family,

*After each invocation: "Pray for us."

Joseph most just,
Joseph most pure,
Joseph most prudent,
Joseph most courageous,
Joseph most obedient,
Joseph most faithful,
Mirror of patience,
Lover of poverty,
Model of laborers,
Glory of family life,
Protector of virgins,
Mainstay of families,
Solace of the afflicted,
Hope of the sick,
Patron of the dying,
Terror of demons,
Protector of holy Church,
Lamb of God, who take away the sins of the world, spare us, O Lord.

Lamb of God, who take away the sins of the world, graciously hear us, O Lord.
Lamb of God, who take away the sins of the world, have mercy on us.

℣. He has made him master of his household.
℟. And ruler of all his possessions.

Prayer

Let us pray. Your divine Providence, Lord Jesus, chose St. Joseph to be the spouse of your most holy Mother. As you place us under his protection here below, grant that we may deserve to have him as our intercessor in heaven. This we ask of you, Lord Jesus. ℟. Amen.

LITANY OF THE BLESSED VIRGIN MARY

Lord, have mercy on us.
Christ, have mercy on us.
Lord, have mercy on us.
Christ, hear us.
Christ, graciously hear us.
God the Father of heaven, have mercy on us.
God the Son, Redeemer of the world, have mercy on us.
God the Holy Spirit, have mercy on us.
Holy Trinity, one God, have mercy on us.
Holy Mary, pray for us.*
Holy Mother of God,
Holy Virgin of virgins,
Mother of Christ,
Mother of divine grace,
Mother most pure,
Mother most chaste,
Mother inviolate,

Mother undefiled,
Mother most amiable,
Mother most admirable,
Mother of good counsel,
Mother of our Creator,
Mother of our Savior,
Virgin most prudent,
Virgin most venerable,
Virgin most renowned,
Virgin most powerful,
Virgin most merciful,
Virgin most faithful,
Mirror of justice,
Seat of wisdom,
Cause of our joy,
Spiritual vessel,
Vessel of honor,
Singular vessel of devotion,
Mystical rose,
Tower of David,
Tower of ivory,

*After each invocation: "Pray for us."

House of gold,
Ark of the covenant,
Gate of heaven,
Morning star,
Health of the sick,
Refuge of sinners,
Comforter of the afflicted,
Help of Christians,
Queen of angels,
Queen of patriarchs,
Queen of prophets,
Queen of apostles,
Queen of martyrs,
Queen of confessors,
Queen of virgins,

Queen of all saints,
Queen conceived without original sin,
Queen taken into heaven,
Queen of the most holy rosary,
Queen of peace,
Lamb of God, who take away the sins of the world, spare us, O Lord.
Lamb of God, who take away the sins of the world, graciously hear us, O Lord.
Lamb of God, who take away the sins of the world, have mercy on us.

The following prayers are added, in accordance with the season of the church year:
From the first Sunday in Advent until Christmas:

℣. The angel of the Lord made the announcement to Mary.
℟. And she conceived by the Holy Spirit.

Prayer

Let us pray. It was your will, O Lord, that your divine Word should become flesh in the womb of the Blessed Virgin Mary when the angel made his announcement. Grant that your faithful who believe in this divine motherhood may have their prayers heard through Mary's intercession. This we ask of you through our Lord Jesus Christ.
℟. Amen.

From Christmas until Candlemas:

℣. Even after giving birth, you remained a virgin.
℟. Mother of God, intercede for us.

Prayer

Let us pray. O God, who through the fruitful virginity of Blessed Mary gave all men the riches of eternal salvation, we entreat you to let us feel the intercession of her who gave us the author of life, our Lord Jesus Christ, who lives and reigns with you.
℟. Amen.

From Candlemas until Easter and from the end of Paschaltide until Advent:

℣. Pray for us, holy Mother of God.
℟. Make us worthy of the promises of Christ.

Prayer

Let us pray. Lord God, grant that your children may always enjoy health of soul and of body; may the intercession of the glorious Virgin

Mary deliver us from the sorrows of this world and make us share your happiness throughout eternity. This we ask of you through our Lord Jesus Christ.

℟. Amen.

During Paschaltide:

℣. Rejoice and be glad, Virgin Mary, alleluia!
℟. For the Lord has truly risen, alleluia!

Prayer

Let us pray. O God, you were pleased to give joy to the world through the resurrection of your Son, our Lord Jesus Christ. Grant, we beseech you, that through the mediation of the Virgin Mary, his Mother, we may come to possess the joys of life everlasting. Through our Lord Jesus Christ.

℟. Amen.

ROSARY OF THE BLESSED VIRGIN MARY

The Joyful Mysteries
(Usually said on all Mondays and Thursdays)

The Annunciation
The Visitation
The Nativity of our divine Lord
The Presentation
The Finding of the Child Jesus in the Temple

The Sorrowful Mysteries
(Usually said on all Tuesdays and Fridays)

The Agony in the Garden
The Scourging at the Pillar
The Crowning with Thorns
The Carrying of the Cross
The Crucifixion

The Glorious Mysteries
(Usually said on all Sundays, Wednesdays and Saturdays)

The Resurrection
The Ascension
The Descent of the Holy Spirit upon the Apostles
The Assumption of the Blessed Virgin into Heaven
The Coronation of the Blessed Virgin in Heaven

Prayer

Let us pray. Lord God, your only-begotten Son, by his life, his death and his resurrection, won salvation for us. We relive these mysteries in the Rosary of the Blessed Virgin Mary; give us the grace to follow the examples they set before us and to obtain the rewards they promise. Through the same Christ, our Lord.

℟. Amen.

CHAIR OF UNITY OCTAVE

January 18 to 25

Since the time of Pope Benedict XV, the Chair of Unity Octave has been observed throughout the Christian world during the week preceding the feast of the conversion of St. Paul. Following are the intentions given for each day and the official text of the prayers to be said. A Bible vigil for this intention may be found on page 692.

DAILY INTENTIONS

Jan. 18 For the unity of all Christians in the Church
Jan. 19 For our separated brethren
Jan. 20 For Anglicans
Jan. 21 For European Christians
Jan. 22 For American Christians (or for Christians of one's native land)
Jan. 23 For the spiritual renewal of Catholics
Jan. 24 For the Jewish people
Jan. 25 For the extension of the Church in all lands

THE OFFICIAL OCTAVE PRAYER

Antiphon That they all may be one, as thou, Father, in me and I in thee; that they also may be one in us; that the world may believe that thou hast sent me (John 17:21).

℣. I say unto thee thou art Peter;
℟. And upon this rock I will build my Church.

Prayer O Lord Jesus Christ, who saidst unto thine apostles: Peace I leave with you, my peace I give unto you: regard not our sins, but the faith of thy Church, and grant unto her that peace and unity which are agreeable to thy will. Who livest and reignest God forever and ever. Amen.

NOVENA TO THE HOLY SPIRIT

Bible Vigil

The following formulary is intended primarily for parish or community use during the nine days between Ascension and Pentecost. It would serve equally well as preparation for the sacrament of Confirmation, for times of parish renewal or special need. This form could likewise be used separately as a Bible Vigil by the addition of a homily, and, if desired, additional readings from holy Scripture. The choice and number of hymns will depend upon time and circumstances.

COME, HOLY SPIRIT, LORD OF LOVE

℣. O God, come to our assistance.

℟. O Lord, make haste to help us.

℣. Glory be to the Father, and to the Son, and to the Holy Spirit,

℟. As it was in the beginning, is now and ever shall be world without end. Amen. Alleluia.

Antiphon

All: When I shall be sanctified in you, * I will gather you together out of all the countries, / and I will give you a new spirit, alleluia.

Psalm 103:24, 27-35 or alternate from pages 464-489.

All: How manifold are your works, O Lord! In wisdom you have wrought them all; / the earth is full of your creatures:

They all look to you / to give them food in due time.

When you give it to them, they gather it; / when you open your hand they are filled with good things.

If you hide your face, they are dismayed; / if you take away their breath, they perish and return to their dust.

When you send forth your spirit, they are created, / and you renew the face of the earth.

May the glory of the Lord endure forever; / may the Lord be glad in his works!

He who looks upon the earth, and it trembles; / who touches the mountains, and they smoke!

I will sing to the Lord all my life; / I will sing praise to my God while I live.

Pleasing to him be my theme; / I will be glad in the Lord.

May sinners cease from the earth, and may the wicked be no more. / Bless the Lord, O my soul!

Glory be to the Father, and to the Son, / and to the Holy Spirit,

As it was in the beginning, is now and ever shall be / world without end. Amen.

Antiphon

All: When I shall be sanctified in you, I will gather you together out of all the countries, / and I will give you a new spirit, alleluia.

Reading (John 14:15-18) or alternate as selected.

Leader: If you love me, keep my commandments. And I will ask the Father and he will give you another Advocate to dwell with you forever, the Spirit of truth whom the world cannot receive, because it neither sees him or knows him. But you shall know him, because he will dwell with you, and be in you. I will not leave you orphans; I will come to you.

℟. Thanks be to God.

℣. Give thanks to the Lord, for he is good,

℟. For his goodness endures forever.

℣. Lord, have mercy on us.

℟. Christ, have mercy on us. Lord, have mercy on us.

All: Our Father . . .

℣. The Lord be with you.

℟. And with your spirit.

Prayer

Leader: Let us pray. Make the splendor of your divine glory shine on us, God all-powerful; and let a ray of your light enter the hearts of those who have been reborn through your grace, to give them the strength and the enlightenment of the Holy Spirit. Through Christ our Lord.

℟. Amen.

℣. The Lord be with you.

℟. And with your spirit.

℣. Let us bless the Lord.

℟. Thanks be to God.

℣. May the souls of the faithful departed through the mercy of God rest in peace.

℟. Amen.

SCRIPTURE SERVICES

Scripture services or Bible vigils have become a recognized part of parish worship. Each of the following 16 forms has three sections; it is by no means necessary to use all three sections at one service. The priest will choose the appropriate vigil or parts thereof; likewise hymns other than those suggested may be selected.

I. ADVENT

Come, Lord Jesus, come

ALL STAND

Entrance hymn, No. 167 or alternate.

1. CHRIST'S COMING IN THE FLESH

Priest: Christmas is not just a "birthday celebration" to commemorate Christ's birth in Bethlehem when the Word appeared in the flesh. In a mysterious but real manner, Christ is reborn in each of us to transform us into his likeness. St. Luke's Gospel specifies for us the exact date of Christ's historical coming. It asks us also to "prepare the road of the Lord" for his present, mysterious coming.

Reader: In the fifteenth year of the reign of Emperor Tiberius — when Pontius Pilate was governor of Judea; Herod, tetrarch of Galilee; his brother Philip, tetrarch of Iturea and Trachonitis; and Lysanias, tetrarch of Abilene — Annas and Caiaphas being high priests of the Jews, the word of God came to John, son of Zachary, in the desert.

He went about the whole Jordan region, preaching a baptism of repentance for the forgiveness of sins, according to what is written in the book of the oracles of the prophet Isaias:

"A voice cries in the desert:
Prepare the road of the Lord, straighten his paths!
Fill up all the hollows, level the mountains and the hills!
Straighten the crooked ways, smooth the rough roads!
And every man will see the salvation sent by God!" (Luke 3:1-6)

ALL KNEEL

Priest: Eternal, only-begotten Son of God, in this holy season of Advent, prepare our hearts to celebrate your birth.

All: Cleanse our hearts through sincere penance, / and grant us the spirit of silence / which we need to celebrate your mysteries.

Priest: O Lord, you give yourself to all men of good will.

All: See how our hearts long for you.

Priest: Come and free us from the slavery of sin.

All: Come and bring us new life.

Priest: Make our hearts your worthy dwelling-place.

All: Deliver us from tepidity and indifference in your service.

Priest: That we may meet you with confidence.

All: When you will come in glory to judge the living and the dead.

Priest: Lord, teach us your ways!

All: Lord, show us your paths!

Priest: Rouse your power, O Lord, and come to save us.

All: Come and let your face shine upon us.

Priest: Come, Lord, and do not delay.

All: Come, Lord Jesus, come!

Priest: **Let us pray.** Pause for personal prayer.

O God, you gladden us year after year with the promise of our redemption. Grant, we beseech you, through the intercession of the Blessed Virgin Mary, that we who now prepare for the coming of the Redeemer may also behold him without fear when he comes as our judge, our Lord Jesus Christ, who with you lives and reigns forever.

All: **Amen.**

ALL STAND

Hymn No. 281.

2. CHRIST'S COMING IN THE HEARTS OF MEN

ALL SIT

Priest: **Let us listen to the prophet Isaias as he foretells how the Messiah will establish universal peace by bringing all men together around God.**

Reader: In those days the prophet Isaias uttered this oracle:

It will come about, in the course of time, that the mountain of the Lord's house will dominate all other mountains, will rise above all the hills. All the nations will stream toward it; many peoples will make their way to it. "Come," they will say, "let us climb the Lord's mountain, let us go to the temple of the God of Jacob. He will teach us his ways, and we shall walk in his paths."

For it is from Sion that the law will go out; and from Jerusalem, the word of the Lord. He will be the judge of the nations; he will establish justice over the many peoples. Then those peoples will forge plough-shares out of their swords, and pruning-hooks out of their spears. The nations will no longer take up arms against one another, nor learn how to wage war.

House of Jacob, come: let us walk in the light of the Lord our God (Is. 2:2-5).

Priest: **The Messiah whose birth we shall celebrate at Christmas has already come, but many still do not know him, or refuse to serve him. We pray for his advent in their hearts and in our own.**

ALL KNEEL

Priest: **Drop down dew, you heavens, from above, and let the clouds rain down the Just One.**

All: **Let the earth be opened and bud forth the Savior.**

Priest: **Lord Jesus, eternal Wisdom —**

All: **In your merciful love, / you came down to earth to expel the darkness / with the brightness of your divine life.**

Priest: **You removed the wall which sin had raised between God and us.**

All: **You opened the gates / behind which the devil made prisoners of men.**

Priest: **Through you we regained access to God.**

All: **You have reconciled us with the heavenly Father.**

Priest: But many still have not yet seen your light.

All: And many are the hearts that have not yet known / your heavenly peace.

Priest: Our own hearts too, O Lord, are still dark and sinful.

All: We cry to you, in this holy season of Advent: / Come anew and save us!

Priest: Rouse your power, O Lord, and come to save us.

All: Come and let your face shine upon us.

Priest: Come, O Lord, and do not delay.

All: Come, Lord Jesus, come!

Priest: Let us pray. Pause for personal prayer.

Merciful God and Savior, you sent your Son, Jesus Christ, to save what was lost. You made him shine through the darkness of this world as the true daybreak. We pray you, with the sweet radiance of your grace illumine our dark hearts and the hearts of all those who still sit in the shadow of paganism, and guide our feet in the way of peace, unto your glorious kingdom. Through the same Christ our Lord.

All: Amen.

ALL STAND

Hymn No. 174.

3. CHRIST'S COMING IN GLORY

Priest: For each one of us, Christ will come on the day of our death. By his own words, in the Gospel of St. Luke, we are advised to be always ready.

Reader: At that time Jesus said to his disciples, "Be always dressed for service, a lighted lamp in your hand: be like servants awaiting their master on his return from the wedding: when he comes and knocks, they will open to him at once.

"Happy are those servants whom the master on his return finds awake. Actually, I tell you, he will be the one who tucks his robe under his girdle to go to work: he will have *them* recline at table and will make the rounds, waiting on them. Whether he comes back before midnight or after, if he finds them awake, it will go well with those servants.

"You are right in supposing that if the head of the household knew just when the thief was coming, he would remain awake and not let his house be broken into. That is how you should be: be ready, for the Son of Man will come at a time when you are not expecting him" (Luke 12:35-40).

ALL SIT

The priest may now give a homily developing the following points:

1. Advent prepares not merely for a commemoration of Christ's birth, but for a real, though mysterious, coming of Christ at the present time.

2. Advent is not only the immediate preparation for Christmas. Every

year Christians prepare for the last coming of the Lord, who will judge the world and present his kingdom to the Father.

ALL KNEEL

Priest: Beloved, let us live in this world with temperance, justice and piety.

All: Let us wait for the blessed hope and glorious coming / of our great God and Savior, Jesus Christ.

Priest: Heaven and earth will pass away.

All: But your words, O Lord, will not pass away.

Priest: What you foretold shall be accomplished: you will come to judge the living and the dead.

All: You will reward everyone according to his deeds.

Priest: Lord, imbue our hearts with holy fear of you and your justice.

All: But above all fill us with a joyful longing for your coming / and for the salvation that you will bring.

Priest: Keep us from being engulfed in worldly desires.

All: For at an unexpected hour / the Son of Man will come.

Priest: Grant us, O Lord, to be always on the watch.

All: That we may meet you with burning lamps on your return.

Priest: Lord, remember not our transgressions.

All: For with you, O Lord, is kindness / and plentiful redemption.

Priest: Rouse your power, and come to save us.

All: Come and let your face shine upon us.

Priest: Come, O Lord, and do not delay.

All: Come, Lord Jesus, come!

Priest: Let us pray. Pause for personal prayer.

Almighty, eternal God, stir our hearts and grant us to be steadfast in fervent prayer, in holy fear and childlike confidence, so that one day we may joyfully meet your Son and our Lord, Jesus Christ, when he comes on the clouds of heaven to judge the world. Through the same Christ our Lord.

All: Amen.

ALL STAND

Hymn No. 168.

ALL KNEEL

> If there is Benediction of the Blessed Sacrament, the following prayers may be said after the hymn of exposition.

Priest: Prince of peace and Lord Jesus Christ, Father of the world to come, you will return with power and glory on the clouds of heaven. Now you dwell among us in the Blessed Sacrament, not as our judge, but as our brother who wishes to share with us the riches of his inheritance. Hear, we beseech you, the petitions of your people!

All: Have mercy, O Lord, have mercy!

Priest: Prepare our hearts for a fervent celebration of your nativity.

All: We beseech you, hear us!

Priest: Inspire in us sincere conversion and penance.

All: We beseech you, hear us!

Priest: Lead all those who doubt and disbelieve to acknowledge your divine glory.

All: We beseech you, hear us!

Priest: Help the poor, console the afflicted, and deliver the oppressed.

All: We beseech you, hear us!

Priest: Banish from our midst all quarrels and wars, lies, treachery and injustice; and make us all one in you.

All: We beseech you, hear us!

Priest: Grant that, amidst the joys and sorrows of this life, we may always long for your coming.

All: We beseech you, hear us!

Priest: Have mercy on us on the day of the judgment, and lead us all to the glory of eternal life.

All: We beseech you, hear us!

Priest: For you are he who is to come in the splendor of the heavenly armies. You gather your people at the eucharistic table, as you will one day gather them from all times and all nations to the wedding feast in your kingdom, where you live and reign with the Father in the unity of the Holy Spirit, in all eternity.

All: Amen.

ALL STAND

Final hymn, No. 173.

II. CHRISTMAS SEASON

A Child is born to us today

ALL STAND

Entrance hymn, No. 174.

1. JESUS, OUR LORD

Priest: The beginning of St. John's Gospel has us meditate on the mysterious, intimate relations that unite the Word to the Father. Then it tells us how the Word of God has been expressed progressively in the world: first through the works of creation, then by the revelation made to the people of Israel, finally "by making himself flesh and dwelling among us."

Reader: Before all things, there was the Word; the Word was united to God, and the Word was God. From all eternity he was with God. It was through him that the Creator made all things; and nothing that exists was made without him. In him was life, and that life is the light of men. That light shines in the darkness, and the darkness has not been able to stop it.

There came a man sent from God: he was called John the Baptist. He came to serve as a witness, to bear witness on behalf of the light, that through him all men might have faith. He was not the light, but he was here to bear witness on behalf of the light.

The Word, the true light that enlightens every man, was making his entrance into this world. He was in the world — this world which God had created through him — and the world did not recognize him. He came home, and his own people did not welcome him.

But to all those who did welcome him he gave the power to become sons of God. For those who believe in him are not sons of blood or of carnal desire or of a human will; they are the sons of God.

Yes, the Word was made flesh and he established his dwelling-place among us. We have seen his glory, the glory which the Father has given his only-begotten Son by filling him with grace and truth (John 1:1-14).

ALL KNEEL

Priest: Jesus, child born of Mary, you are our Lord and our God.

All: We believe in you.

Priest: Helpless child, you lay in the manger.

All: King of glory, you reign in heaven.

Priest: You are fed with a little milk.

All: But you give food to all living creatures.

Priest: You are God's eternal Word.

All: But you became a speechless babe for us.

Priest: A child is born to us, and a son is given to us.

All: Government is upon his shoulder, / and he shall be called wonderful, counselor, God the mighty, / the father of the world to come, the prince of peace.

Priest: You are the image of the invisible God.

All: The splendor of his glory.

Priest: You are the Word of the Father through whom and for whom all things were created in heaven and on earth.

All: You are before all creatures, / and in you all things hold together.

Priest: You are the only-begotten Son of God.

All: Born of the Father before all ages.

Priest: God of God, Light of Light.

All: True God of true God.

Priest: For us men and for our salvation, you came down from heaven.

All: By the Holy Spirit, / you were made flesh of the Virgin Mary, / and became man.

Priest: Jesus Christ, born of the Virgin Mary.

All: We believe that you are the Son of the living God.

Priest: Let us pray. Pause for personal prayer.

Almighty, eternal God, whose only-begotten Son appeared in the substance of our flesh, grant, we beseech you, that by him in whom outwardly we recognize our likeness, we may deserve to be inwardly created anew. Through the same Christ, our Lord.

All: Amen.

ALL STAND

Hymn No. 177.

2. JESUS, OUR SAVIOR

Priest: In contrast to the majesty of the eternal birth of the Word, the Gospel according to St. Luke tells of the birth of Jesus at Bethlehem, humble and glorious at the same time.

Reader: It was during their stay at Bethlehem that the time came for her to give birth.

Mary brought her firstborn Son into the world, wrapped him in swaddling clothes and laid him in the manger of a stable, for there was no room for them in the inn.

In the countryside nearby, there were shepherds staying awake all night to watch their flocks. Suddenly the angel of the Lord stood by them, and the glory of the Lord surrounded them with light. They trembled with fear, but the angel said to them, "Do not be afraid, for I bring you good news, which will be a great joy for all the people: today, in the city of David, there is born to you a Savior: it is the Messias, the Lord! Here is how you will recognize him: you will find a newborn infant, wrapped in swaddling clothes and laid in a manger."

Suddenly a band of heavenly spirits joined the angel; they were praising God, saying:

"Glory to God in the heights of heaven, and peace on earth to men of good will!" (Luke 2:6-14).

ALL KNEEL

Priest: Listen to the good tidings of great joy for all the people.

All: This day is born to us a Savior, / who is Christ the Lord.

Priest: The Word was made flesh. Alleluia!

All: He dwelt among us. Alleluia!

Priest: We saw his glory.

All: The glory of the only-begotten Son of the Father.

Priest: He is full of grace and truth.

All: From his fullness we have all received, / grace for grace.

Priest: True peace has come down from heaven. Alleluia!

All: The day of salvation has shone for us. Alleluia!

Priest: The Lord has made known his salvation.

All: In the sight of the nations / he has revealed his justice!

Priest: With the Lord is kindness.

All: And plentiful redemption.

Priest: He does not judge as the eye sees.

All: He judges the poor with justice.

Priest: The Spirit of the Lord is upon you, because he has anointed you.

All: He has sent you to bring good news to the poor.

Priest: To proclaim to the captives their release, and to give the blind their sight again.

All: To liberate the oppressed / and to announce the acceptable time of the Lord.

Priest: Behold what manner of love the Father has bestowed upon us.

All: We are called children of God, / and such we are.

Priest: We are his children.

All: And it has not yet appeared what we shall be.

Priest: When he appears, we shall be like him.

All: For we shall see him just as he is.

Priest: Jesus Christ, Savior of the world!

All: We thank you for our redemption.

Priest: Let us pray. Pause for personal prayer.

Almighty, eternal God, in creating human nature you wonderfully dignified it, and you still more wonderfully restored it. Grant, we beseech you, that we may share in the divine nature of your only-begotten Son, who deigned to partake of our human nature. Through the same Christ, our Lord.

All: Amen.

ALL STAND

Hymn No. 188.

3. JESUS, OUR LIFE

ALL SIT

Priest: St. Paul's letter to Titus reminds us that Christmas was the manifestation of salvation. This historical fact, the import of which is perceived only by our faith, changes our relations with God even now; moreover, it announces the triumphant manifestation of salvation which will take place on the last day.

Reader: Here we see manifested the grace of God, ready to save all men!

It teaches us to reject irreverence and worldly ambitions and to lead our life here below in sobriety, justice and love of God.

It makes us look to the happiness that we hope for: of seeing Jesus Christ, our great God, our Savior, revealed in His glory (Titus 2:11-13).

The priest may now give a homily developing the following points:

1. Jesus our Lord, true God and true man, has come to effect our salvation. This sums up the message of Bethlehem.

2. Jesus our Savior is God's "last, deepest and loveliest word spoken to man."

3. The birth of Jesus is a forceful reminder that human life is good and worth living.

ALL KNEEL

Priest: Bless the Lord, O my soul!

All: Forget not any of his benefits.

Priest: He has visited us and wrought the redemption of his people.

All: He has established an everlasting covenant with us.

Priest: It was not enough for you to be our Creator and Lord.

All: You wished also to become our brother, / that we might become children of God, / heirs to the kingdom.

Priest: You made of us a chosen race, a royal priesthood, a holy nation.

All: That we might proclaim the perfections of him / who has called us out of darkness into his marvelous light.

Priest: For we were once in darkness.

All: Now we are the light of the world.

Priest: Let us walk, then, as children of light.

All: In all goodness, justice and truth.

Priest: Let us put on the new man.

All: Who has been created according to God, / in justice and holiness.

Priest: Let us bear with one another and forgive one another.

All: As the Lord has forgiven us, / so let us also forgive.

Priest: Above all, let us have charity.

All: And may the peace of Christ reign in our hearts.

Priest: May the Word of God dwell in us abundantly.

All: Let us sing psalms and hymns to God.

Priest: Whatever we do, let us do it in the name of the Lord Jesus.

All: Giving thanks to God the Father through him.

Priest: Let us mind the things that are above.

All: For we have died / and our life is hidden with Christ in God.

Priest: One day, Christ, our life, will appear.

All: Then we too shall appear with him in glory.

Priest: Let us pray. Pause for personal prayer.

Grant, we beseech you, O Lord, that, celebrating with joy the mysteries of the nativity of our Lord Jesus Christ, we may express them by worthy lives, and so deserve one day to join him who lives and reigns with you in the unity of the Holy Spirit, for ever and ever.

All: Amen.

ALL STAND

Hymn No. 191.

ALL KNEEL

If there is Benediction of the Blessed Sacrament, the following prayers may be said after the hymn of exposition.

Priest: Lord Jesus, divine Child, bless the children in our community, bless the children in the whole world, for love of whom you became a child.

All: We beseech you, O Lord.

Priest: Bless the sick, the blind and the dumb, the invalids and all the infirm for love of whom you made our flesh your own.

All: We beseech you, O Lord.

Priest: Bless the poor, the widows and the orphans, for love of whom you became poor.

All: We beseech you, O Lord.

Priest: Bless the abandoned, the refugees, the prisoners and all the forsaken, for love of whom you were exiled in Egypt.

All: We beseech you, O Lord.

Priest: Bless the oppressed and those who are in the abyss of desolation, for love of whom you, the living Word, have been silent and have shed tears.

All: We beseech you, O Lord.

Priest: Lord, the Son begotten of the Father.
All: Have mercy.
Priest: Christ, child born of Mary.
All: Have mercy.
Priest: Eternal God, as brethren of your Son, we make bold to say:
All: Our Father, who art in heaven, etc.
Priest: Lord Jesus, you are here present in our midst in the form of bread. You did not refuse to descend into the womb of a Virgin, to take on our human nature. You came to us, and we were reborn to a new life. Take us with you, when you are about to hand over the kingdom to your Father, that God, to whom be praise for all eternity, may be all in all.
All: Amen.
ALL STAND
Hymn No. 193.

III. THE LENTEN SEASON

This is the time of salvation

ALL STAND
Entrance hymn, No. 195.

1. GOD'S CALL TO REPENTANCE

ALL SIT
Priest: Even in Old Testament times, the prophet Joel, who invites us to a communitarian fast, is speaking to us about God's kindness and giving us a glimpse of forgiveness.
Reader: Word of the Lord God:
"With all your heart, turn back to me. Fast, weep and mourn. What must be torn as a sign of penance is not your garments; it is your hearts."

Return to the Lord your God, for he is kind and good, patient and full of mercy, always ready to hold back the evil he is sending upon you. Who knows whether he is not going to change his mind, forget his anger and leave his blessing for you, and something out of which you may present offerings and sacrifices to the Lord your God?

Sound the trumpet in Sion and proclaim a fast, call the assembly, gather the people, sanctify the community. Summon the old men, gather the children and the infants who are nursing; make the bride and the bridegroom leave their new home.

Between the porch and the altar let the priests, servants of the Lord, weep before God and say to him:

"Spare, O Lord, spare your people, and do not let your heritage be shamed. Do not permit the triumph of strangers, who would say, 'If their God existed, he would save them.' "

Yes, God's heart has been touched by love for his land; he has taken pity on his people. He has answered his people, "I am going to send you more than enough grain, wine and oil; and strangers will no longer insult you."

Word of the Lord all-powerful (Joel 2:12-19).

ALL KNEEL

Priest: Your beloved Son did penance for forty days and was tempted in the desert.

All: Make us steadfast in self-denial, / persevering in prayer / and generous in good works.

Priest: In sackcloth and ashes your Church keeps vigil during this holy Lenten season.

All: Cleanse us, O Lord, from our sins, / and give us the grace to prepare for the glory of Easter.

Priest: The season of penance opens the gates of paradise.

All: Therefore let us put on the new man, / who has been created according to God, / in justice and holiness that stream from truth.

Priest: Almighty, eternal God, through your prophet you have said, "In an acceptable time I shall hear you, and on the day of salvation I shall help you." Now we pray to you:

All: Open our hearts to your voice that calls to us in this holy season.

Priest: For forty years you dwelt among your people in the desert.

All: We pray you, be with us also / during these forty blessed days.

Priest: Our fathers hardened their hearts and tempted you in the desert, and none of them entered into your rest.

All: Grant that we may repent of our sins now, / lest, suddenly overtaken by death, / we seek time for penance and be unable to find it.

Priest: Let us pray. Pause for personal prayer.

All-powerful, eternal God, you always seek life, not death, for sinners. Grant us, in this sacred season, to fight as soldiers of Christ, that, sharing his trials and penance, we may also partake of the glory of his resurrection. Through the same Christ our Lord.

All: Amen.

ALL STAND

Hymn No. 197.

2. SINNERS BEFORE GOD

Priest: Telling us of the dinner that followed his own call to be an apostle, St. Matthew reminds us that Christ came to call sinners, not the just.

Reader: Now as Jesus was at table in Matthew's house, it happened that many publicans and sinners came to take their places with Jesus and his disciples.

Seeing this, the pharisees said to his disciples, "How can your master eat with the publicans and sinners!"

Jesus heard them. "It is not those in good health who need a physician," he said, "but the sick. Go and find out what this saying of the Scripture means: 'I desire mercy and not sacrifices.' I have not come to call the 'just,' you see, but the sinners" (Matthew 9:10-13).

ALL KNEEL

Priest: Almighty and merciful God, we come before you to acknowledge our sins and to accept punishment for them.

All: Compared to our evil deeds, / the pains we suffer are lighter than what we deserve.

Priest: Our weakness is crushed under your blows, but our malice is not amended.

All: Sadness fills our hearts, / but our stiff necks refuse to bow before you.

Priest: When you spare us in your mercy, we are not converted; when you punish us, we rebel against you.

All: In our sufferings we acknowledge the evil we have done, / but after the trial we forget what we have confessed.

Priest: When you extend your punishing arm, we promise amendment; once you withdraw it, we fail to keep our promise.

All: When you strike us, we implore your mercy; / once you spare us, we provoke you anew.

Priest: Before you, O Lord, we acknowledge our guilt. If you will not forgive us, we shall surely perish.

All: Almighty Father, you created us / that we might live with you forever. / Look down with mercy on the work of your hands.

Priest: Let us pray. Pause for personal prayer.

Holy and merciful God, look with favor upon those who bow in repentance before your majesty. Do not remember our former iniquities nor repay us according to our sins, but forgive us for your name's sake, through your beloved Son who shed his blood as the price of our redemption, Jesus Christ our Lord.

All: Amen.

ALL STAND

Hymn No. 198.

3. CREATE IN US A NEW HEART

ALL SIT

Priest: In his letter to the Ephesians, St. Paul tells us that we must make the best possible use of the time given us on earth and, by our docility to the Holy Spirit, we must already live as citizens of the heavenly city.

Reader: Be careful of your behavior: do not live as thoughtless people do, but rather like those who are thoughtful. Make the best possible use of the time allotted you, for we are passing through evil days.

It is not enough just to live along heedlessly; you must understand what is the will of God.

Do not drink too much wine; it leads to debauchery.

Fill yourselves rather with the Holy Spirit. In your assemblies, speak to God by means of psalms, hymns and canticles; with all your heart, sing to the Lord and praise him. Whatever happens, always give thanks to God our Father for it, in the name of our Lord Jesus Christ (Eph. 5:15-20).

The priest may now give a homily developing the following points:

1. Repentance is the door to God's kingdom. God's call to repentance (Matthew 4:17) sounds throughout salvation-history. This call also sounds for us during Lent.

2. Christ came to call sinners. If we say that we have no sin, we deceive ourselves (1 John 1:8) and we have no share with Christ.

3. Christian penance does not end in sorrow. It consists in stripping off the old self and putting on the new man who is created after the image of God (Eph. 4:24). Lent is a time of renewal or "re-creation."

ALL KNEEL

Priest: Almighty God, rich in grace and mercy, you have said, "If your sins be as scarlet, they shall be made as white as snow."

All: Like the sinful woman in the Gospel, we pray you; / like the lepers, we implore you —

Priest: Cleanse us of our sins, that we may be purified.

All: Wash us, and we shall be whiter than snow.

Priest: Turn away your face from our sins.

All: Blot out all our iniquities.

Priest: Create clean hearts within us.

All: Take not your Holy Spirit away from us.

Priest: Give us back the joy of your salvation.

All: And strengthen us with a perfect spirit.

Priest: Before we were afflicted, we went astray.

All: But now we hope in your promise.

Priest: It is good for us to be afflicted.

All: That we may learn your statutes.

Priest: Instruct us in your laws, that we may exactly observe them.

All: Lead us in the path of your commands, / for in them do we delight.

Priest: Incline our hearts to your decrees, and turn our eyes away from vanities.

All: A lamp to our feet is your word, O Lord, / a light on our path.

Priest: Open our lips, and our mouths shall declare your praise.

All: We shall teach your ways to the unjust, / and they shall be converted to you.

Priest: Let us pray. Pause for personal prayer.

O God, whose mercies are without number and whose goodness is infinite, we give thanks to you for graciously forgiving us. Grant, we beseech you, that, mindful of your Holy Spirit, we may share forever in the glory of the resurrection of our Lord Jesus Christ, who with you lives and reigns forever.

All: Amen, so be it, Lord, amen.

ALL STAND

Hymn No. 196.

ALL KNEEL

If there is Benediction of the Blessed Sacrament, the following prayers may be said after the hymn of exposition.

Priest: Lord Jesus Christ, Son of the living God, who want all to have life and no one to be lost.

All: Have mercy, O Lord, have mercy.

Priest: Divine Sower who spread the seed of the word of God.

All: Have mercy, O Lord, have mercy.

Priest: Mighty Lord, who have broken the power of the evil one.

All: Have mercy, O Lord, have mercy.

Priest: In this holy Lenten season, sanctify your Church and prepare her to celebrate the paschal solemnities.

All: We beseech you, hear us!

Priest: Move our hearts to sincere prayer, penance and good works.

All: We beseech you, hear us!

Priest: Prepare the catechumens for the sacrament of rebirth.

All: We beseech you, hear us!

Priest: To all who have left the right path, grant the grace of conversion.

All: We beseech you, hear us!

Priest: For our dear departed, shorten their sufferings in purgatory.

All: We beseech you, hear us!

Priest: Help us also, O Lord, during these days of grace, to cleanse ourselves of whatever displeases you in us. *Pause for personal prayer.* For you are the one who came to save what was lost. You are the good Shepherd of our souls. Honor to you with the Father and the Spirit in your holy Church.

All: Amen.

IV. PASSIONTIDE
The passion and death of Christ, our Lord

ALL STAND

Entrance hymn, No. 200.

1. THE BLOOD OF THE COVENANT

ALL SIT

Priest: Covenant, blood of the lamb, Passover, holy of holies — these were realities which constituted the very heart of Israelite religion and hence of Israelite life also. They spelled one central truth: God, the Savior of Israel!

Little wonder, then, that the first Christians found it so natural to express the mystery of Christ their Redeemer in terms of these same realities. For in him were fulfilled the law and the prophets. He was the culmination of Old Testament history, as indeed of all history.

In the celebration of her liturgy, the Church has always clung to the rich imagery of salvation-history in presenting the mystery of Christ's passion and death to her children. In this spirit we too will approach the Cross — to see how our redemption was wrought "with the precious blood of Christ, as of a lamb without blemish and without spot."

ALL STAND

All: **Before the feast of the Passover, / Jesus, knowing that the hour had come / for him to pass out of this world to the Father, / having loved his own who were in the world, / loved them to the end.**

Priest: To him who has loved us, and washed us from our sins in his own blood, and made us to be a kingdom, and priests to God his Father — to him belong glory and dominion forever and ever. Amen.

All: Before the feast of the Passover, / Jesus, knowing that the hour had come / for him to pass out of this world to the Father, / having loved his own who were in the world, / loved them to the end.

ALL SIT

Priest: Christ's sacrificial death on the Cross is foreshadowed in the Old Testament by the paschal lamb. By sprinkling the blood of the slaughtered lamb on their doorposts, the Israelites were delivered from the shadow of death which darkened the land of Egypt.

This was a type, a symbol, a foreshadowing of our deliverance from sin and the power of Satan by Christ's bloody sacrifice on Calvary. The reading is from the book of Exodus.

Reader: The Lord said to Moses and Aaron in the land of Egypt, "This month shall stand at the head of your calendar; you shall reckon it the first month of the year. Tell the whole community of Israel: On the tenth of this month every one of your families must procure for itself a lamb, one apiece for each household. If a family is too small for a whole lamb, it shall join the nearest household in procuring one and shall share in the lamb in proportion to the number of persons who partake of it. The lamb must be a year-old male and without blemish. You may take it from either the sheep or the goats. You shall keep it until the fourteenth day of this month, and then, with the whole assembly of Israel present, it shall be slaughtered during the evening twilight. They shall take some of its blood and apply it to the two doorposts and the lintel of every house in which they partake of the lamb. That same night they shall eat its roasted flesh with unleavened bread and bitter herbs. It shall not be eaten raw or boiled, but roasted whole, with its head and shanks and inner organs. None of it must be kept beyond the next morning; whatever is left over in the morning shall be burned up.

"This is how you are to eat it: with your loins girt, sandals on your feet and your staff in hand, you shall eat like those who are in flight. It is the Passover of the Lord. For on this same night I will go through Egypt, striking down every first-born of the land, both man and beast, and executing judgment on all the gods of Egypt — I, the Lord! But the blood will mark the houses where you are. Seeing the blood, I will pass over you; thus, when I strike the land of Egypt, no destructive blow will come upon you.

"This day shall be a memorial feast for you, which all your generations shall celebrate with pilgrimage to the Lord, as a perpetual institution" (Exod. 12:1-14).

ALL KNEEL

Priest: Let us pray, recalling that it is the Lord our God who has delivered men from death — the Israelites by the blood of the lamb, all mankind by the Blood of his only-begotten Son.
 Pause for personal prayer.

> Fear not, for I have redeemed you;
> I have called you by name: you are mine.

All: My strength and my courage is the Lord,
and he has been my savior.

Priest: When you pass through the water, I will be with you:
in the rivers you shall not drown.

All: My strength and my courage is the Lord,
and he has been my savior.

Priest: When you walk through fire, you shall not be burned;
the flames shall not consume you.

All: My strength and my courage is the Lord,
and he has been my savior.

Priest: For I am the Lord, your God,
the Holy One of Israel, your savior.

All: My strength and my courage is the Lord,
and he has been my savior.

Priest: Let all the nations gather together,
let the peoples assemble!

All: My strength and my courage is the Lord,
and he has been my savior.

Priest: Who among them could have revealed this,
or foretold to us the earlier things?

All: My strength and my courage is the Lord,
and he has been my savior.

Priest: It is I, I the Lord;
there is no savior but me.

All: My strength and my courage is the Lord,
and he has been my savior.

Priest: It is I who foretold, I who saved;
I made it known, not any strange god among you.

All: My strength and my courage is the Lord,
and he has been my savior.

Priest: I am the Lord, your Holy One,
the creator of Israel, your King.

All: My strength and my courage is the Lord.
and he has been my savior.

Priest: I am the first and I am the last;
there is no God but me.

All: My strength and my courage is the Lord,
and he has been my savior.

ALL STAND

Hymn No. 201.

2. THE NEW AND ETERNAL SACRIFICE

ALL SIT

Priest: Not only the paschal lamb but all Old Testament sacrifice found its fulfillment in the bloody offering of the eternal High Priest, Jesus Christ. Let us hear this truth proclaimed in the Epistle to the Hebrews.

Reader: The first covenant also had ritual ordinances and a sanctuary, though an earthly one. In the temple of Jerusalem, the sanctuary consisted first of all in a tent housing the lamp-stand, the table and the bread offered to the Lord. This first part was called the "holy." Behind a second veil, the tent called "holy of holies" contained the golden altar for the incense and the ark of the covenant, all covered with gold. In the latter was a golden urn holding the manna, Aaron's rod which had budded, and the tablets of the covenant. Above the ark, the cherubim of glory stretched out their wings over the propitiatory. About all that there is no room to speak here in detail.

Things being so arranged, the priests always used to enter the first tent to perform the acts of worship. But the second tent no one entered except once a year, then the high priest alone, and moreover he entered only with the blood offered for his sins and those of the people.

The Holy Spirit shows us by these means that access to the "holy of holies" was shut off as long as the first tent lasted. A parable for our times: it means that the gifts and the sacrifices are incapable of making perfect the conscience of the one who offers them. These questions of food, of drink, of various ablutions, purely material regulations, did not have any meaning except in anticipation of the better days to come.

But Christ has come, high priest of this long-awaited happiness. Having ingress to a temple greater and more perfect than that of Jerusalem, a temple which is not built by the hands of men and is not of this world, he entered once for all into the sanctuary of heaven, not with blood of goats or of calves, but covered with his own Blood, the Blood that paid the price of our deliverance for eternity.

If the blood of goats and of bull calves and the ashes of a heifer, with which those who have been defiled are sprinkled, sanctify them by obtaining purity of body for them, how much more must the Blood of Christ — who, prompted by the Holy Spirit, offered himself to God as a victim all-pure — purify our soul of all sin and make us true adorers of the living God!

It is he who has concluded the new covenant between God and men. It is his death that has destroyed sin, that sin which remained under the former covenant. It is his death that puts us in possession of the eternal inheritance, to which God is calling us in Jesus Christ our Lord (Heb. 9:1-15).

ALL KNEEL

Priest: Let us pray to Christ Jesus, our High Priest, who has inaugurated the new and eternal covenant by the shedding of his most precious Blood.

Pause for personal prayer. This is he who came in water and in blood, Jesus Christ; not in the water only, but in the water and in the blood.

All: For thou wast slain, and hast redeemed us for God with thy Blood.

Priest: And there are three that bear witness on earth; the Spirit, and the water, and the blood; and these three are one.

All: For thou wast slain, and hast redeemed us for God with thy Blood.

Priest: The cup of blessing that we bless, is it not the sharing of the Blood of Christ?

All: For thou wast slain, and hast redeemed us for God with thy Blood.

Priest: We have fellowship with one another, and the Blood of Jesus Christ, his Son, cleanses us from all sin.

All: For thou wast slain, and hast redeemed us for God with thy Blood.

Priest: For Christ, our Passover, has been sacrificed.

All: For thou wast slain, and hast redeemed us for God with thy Blood.

Priest: Therefore let us keep festival, not with the old leaven of malice and wickedness, but with the unleavened bread of sincerity and truth.

All: For thou wast slain, and hast redeemed us for God with thy Blood.

Priest: Unless you eat the flesh of the Son of Man, and drink his Blood, you shall not have life in you.

All: For thou wast slain, and hast redeemed us for God with thy Blood.

Priest: We adore you, O Christ, and we bless you.

All: For thou wast slain, and hast redeemed us for God with thy Blood.

ALL STAND

Hymn No. 199.

3. THE LAMB WHO TAKES AWAY THE SINS OF THE WORLD

Priest: "Behold, the Lamb of God, who takes away the sin of the world!" With these words, John pointed to him who was prefigured in the paschal lamb, to his sacrifice which was foreshadowed in its ritual slaying, to our redemption which had its type in the deliverance of Israel from death. Let us listen to St. John's account of the death of Christ.

Reader: Standing near the Cross of Jesus were his mother, his mother's sister Mary, wife of Cleophas, and Mary Magdalene. Seeing his mother and, standing near her, the disciple whom he loved, Jesus said to his mother, "Woman, here is your son." Then he said to the disciple, "Here is your mother."

And from that hour the disciple took her into his home.

After that, knowing that now everything was accomplished and wanting to fulfill all the sayings of the Scripture, Jesus said, "I am thirsty." There was a receptacle there filled with a vinegar drink. Someone dipped a sponge into it and put it on a stalk of hyssop to reach it up to his mouth. After taking the vinegar, Jesus said, "All is accomplished," and, bowing his head, he gave up his spirit.

Since it was the Preparation and since they did not want to leave the bodies on the cross on the Sabbath day — especially since this Sabbath was a great feast day — the Jews asked Pilate to have the legs of the cruci-fied men broken, so that they could be taken away.

The soldiers came, therefore. They broke the legs of the first, then of the second of the two who were crucified with Jesus. Finally they came to Jesus himself. Seeing that he was already dead, they did not break his legs; but one of the soldiers opened his side with the thrust of a lance, and blood and water flowed out immediately.

He who saw this bears witness to it, and his testimony is true — and he knows well that he is telling the truth — that you also may have the faith. For all these things happened in order to fulfill the Scripture: "Not one of his bones must be broken"; and another text again says, "They will raise their eyes toward him whom they have pierced" (John 19:25-37).

ALL SIT

The priest may now give a homily developing the following points:

1. Christ's sacrificial death was a true deliverance from the power of sin and Satan which had engulfed the human race since the fall of Adam.

2. The fruits of redemption come to us through the sacraments, especially the eucharistic sacrifice which is the memorial and renewal of Christ's redemptive act.

ALL KNEEL

Priest: Let us pray, pondering with the psalmist the sufferings of our Redeemer and begging the Lamb to wash us forever clean in the sanctifying stream of his Blood.

Pause for personal prayer.

> My God, my God, why have you forsaken me,
> far from my prayer, from the words of my cry?

All: Lamb of God, who take away the sins of the world, have mercy on us.

Priest: O my God, I cry out by day, and you answer not;
> by night, and there is no relief for me.

All: Lamb of God, who take away the sins of the world, have mercy on us.

Priest: But I am a worm, not a man;
> the scorn of men, despised by the people.

All: Lamb of God, who take away the sins of the world, have mercy on us.

Priest: All who see me scoff at me;
> they mock me with parted lips, they wag their heads.

All: Lamb of God, who take away the sins of the world, have mercy on us.

Priest: I am like water poured out;
> all my bones are racked.

All: Lamb of God, who take away the sins of the world, have mercy on us.

Priest: They have pierced my hands and my feet;
> I can count all my bones.

All: Lamb of God, who take away the sins of the world, have mercy on us.

Priest: They look on and gloat over me;
they divide my garments among them,
and for my vesture they cast lots.

All: Lamb of God, who take away the sins of the world, have mercy on us.

Priest: "Worthy is the Lamb who was slain
to receive power and divinity
and wisdom and strength
and honor and glory and blessing."

All: Lord God, Lamb of God, Son of the Father,
who take away the sins of the world, have mercy on us.

Priest: Let us pray that God will indeed have mercy on us and make us a holy people through the passion and death of his Son, Jesus Christ, our Savior. Pause for personal prayer. O Lord our God, you were pleased to accept your beloved Son, Jesus, as a fitting holocaust for the sins of man on the altar of the Cross. We beg you to cleanse us in the saving stream of his Blood and to sanctify us in the water that flowed from his side so that, forever freed from sin and the power of Satan, we may serve you as a living sacrifice and a holy priesthood; through the same Christ our Lord.

All: Amen! Before the feast of the Passover, / Jesus, knowing that the hour had come / for him to pass out of this world to the Father, / having loved his own who were in the world, / loved them to the end.

Priest: To him who has loved us, and washed us from our sins in his own Blood, and made us to be a kingdom, and priests to God his Father — to him belong glory and dominion forever and ever. Amen.

All: Before the feast of the Passover, / Jesus, knowing that the hour had come / for him to pass out of this world to the Father, / having loved his own who were in the world, / loved them to the end.

V. EASTER SEASON
This is the day the Lord has made!

ALL STAND
Hymn No. 203.

1. CHRIST, OUR PASSOVER, HAS BEEN SACRIFICED

ALL SIT

Priest: On the third day Christ rose again from the dead! Thus did the apostles preach, and thus did Christians believe. The good tidings of the resurrection echoed loud and clear in the hymns and prayers of the early liturgy, and found its most vivid expression in the words of St. Paul: Christ our Pasch, Christ our Passover!

To share Paul's vision of the risen Lord, we must first recapture the meaning of the Jewish Passover. It was the greatest feast of the Jewish people, for it looked to the greatest event in their history. Passover was the yearly memorial of the exodus, the passage out of Egypt into the promised land. God himself had intervened in the life of Israel, and the memory of his saving action became enshrined in the hearts of the people. This was the Pasch — their "passing over" from the misery of slavery in Egypt to a new life in a new land.

To the first Christians, the resurrection was a second and more wonderful exodus. It was, too, the inauguration of a new era. But now, for the first time, the shadows of Old Testament history receded, and eyes of faith saw in the brilliant light of Easter the real meaning of Passover and the true identity of the sacrificial Lamb. With Christ they also had risen. He was their Passover. They had been snatched from the fatal grip of sin. From Satan's tyranny they had come into the freedom of sons of God; they had passed from death's dominion into the realm of everlasting life. Christ himself was their Pasch.

ALL STAND

All: Christ, our Passover, has been sacrificed.

Priest: Therefore let us keep festival, not with the old leaven, nor with the leaven of malice and wickedness, but with the unleavened bread of sincerity and truth.

All: Christ, our Passover, has been sacrificed.

ALL SIT

Priest: Let us hear how Yahweh, the God of Israel, entered into the history of his chosen people. By the might and power of his saving action, he led them across the Red Sea and into the promised land. The reading is from the book of Exodus.

Reader: Pharaoh was already near when the Israelites looked up and saw that the Egyptians were on the march in pursuit of them. In great fright they cried out to the Lord. And they complained to Moses, "Were there no burial places in Egypt that you had to bring us out here to die in the desert? Why did you do this to us? Why did you bring us out of Egypt? Did we not tell you this in Egypt, when we said, 'Leave us alone. Let us serve the Egyptians'? Far better for us to be the slaves of the Egyptians than to die in the desert." But Moses answered the people, "Fear not! Stand your ground, and you will see the victory the Lord will win for you today. These Egyptians whom you see today you will never see again. The Lord himself will fight for you; you have only to keep still."

Then the Lord said to Moses, "Why are you crying out to me? Tell the Israelites to go forward. And you, lift up your staff and, with hand outstretched over the sea, split the sea in two, that the Israelites may pass through it on dry land. But I will make the Egyptians so obstinate that they will go in after them. Then I will receive glory through Pharaoh and all his army, his chariots and charioteers. The Egyptians shall know that I am the Lord, when I receive glory through Pharaoh and his chariots and charioteers."

The angel of God, who had been leading Israel's camp, now moved and went around behind them. The column of cloud also, leaving the front, took up its place behind them, so that it came between the camp of the Egyptians and that of Israel. But the cloud now became dark, and thus the night passed without the rival camps coming any closer together all night long. Then Moses stretched out his hand over the sea, and the Lord swept the sea with a strong east wind throughout the night and so turned it into dry land. When the water was thus divided, the Israelites marched into the midst of the sea on dry land, with the water like a wall to their right and to their left.

The Egyptians followed in pursuit; all Pharaoh's horses and chariots and charioteers went after them right into the midst of the sea. In the night watch just before dawn the Lord cast through the column of the fiery cloud upon the Egyptian force a glance that threw it into a panic; and he so clogged their chariot wheels that they could hardly drive. With that the Egyptians sounded the retreat before Israel, because the Lord was fighting for them against the Egyptians.

Then the Lord told Moses, "Stretch out your hand over the sea, that the water may flow back upon the Egyptians, upon their chariots and their charioteers." So Moses stretched out his hand over the sea, and at dawn the sea flowed back to its normal depth. The Egyptians were fleeing head on toward the sea, when the Lord hurled them into its midst. As the water flowed back, it covered the chariots and the charioteers of Pharaoh's whole army which had followed the Israelites into the sea. Not a single one of them escaped. But the Israelites had marched on dry land through the midst of the sea, with the water like a wall to their right and to their left. Thus the Lord saved Israel on that day from the power of the Egyptians. When Israel saw the Egyptians lying dead on the seashore and beheld the great power that the Lord had shown against the Egyptians, they feared the Lord and believed in him and in his servant Moses (Exod. 14:10-31).

ALL KNEEL

Priest: Let us pray in the words of Moses and the Israelites, giving praise to the Lord our God. He has won an eternal victory over the enemies of our salvation, and has led us safely into the promised land of grace and redemption and life.

Pause for personal prayer.

I will sing to the Lord, for he is gloriously triumphant;
horse and chariot he has cast into the sea.

All: This is the day the Lord has made;
let us be glad and rejoice in it.

Priest: Your right hand, O Lord, magnificent in power,
your right hand, O Lord, has shattered the enemy.

All: This is the day the Lord has made;
let us be glad and rejoice in it.

Priest: Who is like to you among the gods, O Lord?
Who is like to you, magnificent in holiness?

All: This is the day the Lord has made;
let us be glad and rejoice in it.

Priest: In your mercy you led the people you redeemed;
in your strength you guided them to your holy dwelling.

All: This is the day the Lord has made;
let us be glad and rejoice in it.

Priest: "The right hand of the Lord has struck with power:
  the right hand of the Lord is exalted;
  the right hand of the Lord has struck with power."
All: This is the day the Lord has made;
  let us be glad and rejoice in it.
Priest: I shall not die, but live,
  and declare the works of the Lord.
All: This is the day the Lord has made;
  let us be glad and rejoice in it.
Priest: Though the Lord has indeed chastised me,
  yet he has not delivered me to death.
All: This is the day the Lord has made;
  let us be glad and rejoice in it.
ALL STAND
Hymn No. 204.

2. SEEK THE THINGS THAT ARE ABOVE

ALL SIT

Priest: Christ's resurrection must be mirrored in our own daily lives through death to sin and a life that is alive with the power of grace. Let us listen to God's saving word in the letter of Paul to the Colossians.

Reader: Therefore, if you have risen with Christ, seek the things that are above, where Christ is seated at the right hand of God. Mind the things that are above, not the things that are on earth. For you have died and your life is hidden with Christ in God. When Christ, your life, shall appear, then you too will appear with him in glory.

Therefore mortify your members, which are on earth: immorality, uncleanness, lust, evil desire and covetousness (which is a form of idol-worship). Because of these things the wrath of God comes upon the unbelievers, and you yourselves once walked in them when they were your life. But now do you also put them all away: anger, wrath, malice, abusive language and foul-mouthed utterances. Do not lie to one another. Strip off the old man with his deeds and put on the new, one that is being renewed unto perfect knowledge "according to the image of his Creator." Here there is not "Gentile and Jew," "circumcised and uncircumcised," "Barbarian and Scythian," "slave and freeman"; but Christ is all things and in all.

Put on therefore, as God's chosen ones, holy and beloved, a heart of mercy, kindness, humility, meekness, patience. Bear with one another and forgive one another, if anyone has a grievance against any other; even as the Lord has forgiven you, so also do you forgive. But above all these things have charity, which is the bond of perfection. And may the peace of Christ reign in your hearts; unto that peace, indeed, you were called in one body. Show yourselves thankful. Let the word of Christ dwell in you abundantly: in all wisdom teach and admonish one another by psalms, hymns and spiritual songs, singing in your hearts to God by his grace. Whatever you do in word or in work, do all in the name of the Lord Jesus, giving thanks to God the Father through him (Col. 3:1-17).

ALL KNEEL

Priest: Let us pray, thanking God our Father for the victory that Jesus, his Son and our Brother, has won by his death and resurrection. It is for us that he has triumphed. Pause for personal prayer. Christ died for all, in order that they who are alive may live no longer for themselves, but for him who died for them and rose again.

All: Thanks be to God who has given us the victory through our Lord Jesus Christ.

Priest: If then any man is in Christ, he is a new creature: the former things have passed away: behold, they are made new.

All: Thanks be to God who has given us the victory through our Lord Jesus Christ.

Priest: For God, who commanded light to shine out of darkness, has shone in our hearts, to give enlightenment concerning the knowledge of the glory of God, shining on the face of Christ Jesus.

All: Thanks be to God who has given us the victory through our Lord Jesus Christ.

Priest: For you were once darkness, but now you are light in the Lord.

All: Thanks be to God who has given us the victory through our Lord Jesus Christ.

Priest: Walk, then, as children of light (for the fruit of the light is in all goodness and justice and truth), testing what is well pleasing to God.

All: Thanks be to God who has given us the victory through our Lord Jesus Christ.

Priest: For if we live, we live to the Lord, or if we die, we die to the Lord.

All: Whether we live or die, we are the Lord's.

Priest: You were buried together with him in baptism, and in him also rose again through faith in the working of God who raised him from the dead.

All: Whether we live or die, we are the Lord's.

Priest: "Death is swallowed up in victory! O death, where is your victory? O death, where is your sting?"

All: Thanks be to God who has given us the victory through our Lord Jesus Christ.

ALL STAND

Hymn No. 206.

3. BY RISING AGAIN YOU RESTORED OUR LIFE

Priest: Let us hear now the good tidings of the resurrection of our Lord Jesus Christ from the dead. The reading is from St. Matthew's gospel.

Reader: Now late in the night of the Sabbath, as the first day of the week began to dawn, Mary Magdalene and the other Mary came to see the sepulcher. And behold, there was a great earthquake; for an angel of the Lord came down from heaven, and drawing near rolled back the stone, and sat upon it. His countenance was like lightning, and his raiment like snow. And for fear of him the guards were terrified, and became like dead men. But the angel spoke and said to the women, "Do not be afraid; for I know that you seek Jesus, who was crucified. He is not here, for he has risen even as he said. Come, see the place where the Lord was laid. And go quickly, tell his disciples that he has risen; and behold, he goes before you into Galilee; there you shall see him. Behold, I have foretold it to you."

And they departed quickly from the tomb in fear and great joy, and ran to tell his disciples. And behold, Jesus met them, saying, "Hail!" And they came up and embraced his feet and worshipped him. Then Jesus said to them, "Do not be afraid; go, take word to my brethren that they are to set out for Galilee; there they shall see me."

Now while they were going, behold, some of the guards came into the city and reported to the chief priests all that had happened. And when they had assembled with the elders and had consulted together, they gave much money to the soldiers, telling them, "Say, 'His disciples came by night and stole him while we were sleeping.' And if the procurator hears of this, we will persuade him and keep you out of trouble." And they took the money, and did as they were instructed; and this story has been spread abroad among the Jews even to the present day.

But the eleven disciples went into Galilee, to the mountain where Jesus had directed them to go. And when they saw him they worshipped him; but some doubted. And Jesus drew near and spoke to them saying, "All power in heaven and on earth has been given to me. Go, therefore, and make disciples of all nations, baptizing them in the name of the Father, and of the Son, and of the Holy Spirit, teaching them to observe all that I have commanded you; and behold, I am with you all days, even unto the consummation of the world" (Matthew 28:1-20).

ALL SIT

The priest may now give a homily developing the following points:

1. Christ's death and resurrection are together the central mystery of our faith. Baptism makes us enter into this mystery; each eucharistic sacrifice is the renewal and increase of the Christ-life within us.

2. To die to sin and to live for Christ should be the central theme of our Christian living. This is the whole significance of the liturgy of the Easter Vigil.

ALL KNEEL

Priest: Let us pray, giving praise and thanksgiving to the true paschal Victim, Christ our Lord. By dying he destroyed our death and by rising again he restored our life.

Pause for personal prayer.

I will proclaim your name to my brethren;
in the midst of the assembly I will praise you.

All: You are the true Lamb! / For by dying you destroyed our death, / and by rising again you restored our life.

Priest: Lord Jesus, with you we have passed over into the promised land; we have entered the new Jerusalem, the holy city of light and life.

All: You are the true Lamb! / For by dying you destroyed our death, / and by rising again you restored our life.

Priest: You have wiped away every tear from our eyes; because of you, death shall be no more.

All: You are the true Lamb! / For by dying you destroyed our death, / and by rising again you restored our life.

Priest: Because of you, the former things have passed away; mourning, crying and pain shall be no more.

All: You are the true Lamb! / For by dying you destroyed our death, / and by rising again you restored our life.

Priest: "Worthy is the Lamb who was slain to receive power and divinity and wisdom and strength and honor and glory and blessing."

All: From him and through him and unto him are all things, / to him be the glory forever.

Priest: "To him who sits upon the throne, and to the Lamb, blessing and honor and glory and dominion, forever and ever."

All: From him and through him and unto him are all things, / to him be the glory forever.

Priest: Jesus Christ is the same, yesterday and today, yes and forever.

All: From him and through him and unto him are all things, / to him be the glory forever, amen.

Priest: Let us pray that almighty God, hearing the hymn of praise we offer to the eternal Lamb, may graciously grant us a full sharing in the sacrifice of his death and resurrection. Pause for personal prayer. O most merciful God, you have brought your loving design of salvation for all men to a glorious fulfillment by the resurrection of your only begotten Son, Jesus, from the dead. We beg you to extend this same marvelous power over our lives so that, continuing the pattern of redemption begun at baptism, we may daily die to sin and live a life of grace and holiness with our risen Savior, who lives and reigns forever.

All: Amen! Christ, our Passover, has been sacrificed.

Priest: Therefore let us keep festival, not with the old leaven, nor with the leaven of malice and wickedness, but with the unleavened bread of sincerity and truth.

All: Christ, our Passover, has been sacrificed.

VI. PENTECOST SEASON
Love poured out

ALL STAND
Hymn No. 216.

1. THE SPIRIT WHOM WE HAVE RECEIVED

ALL SIT

Priest: We all know that love consists in deeds rather than words, and that the lover shares all that he has and possesses with his beloved. Our daily, human experience of life and of love tells us that these things are true.

But all our human experience of love is only a shadow and a trace of what God's love is. God is love without end. He is love without boundary or limit. God is love without regret, without caution, without a breaking-point. If love means to make a gift of oneself to the beloved, then God is the greatest lover of all time and beyond time: God our Father sends us his Spirit to join us to the Body of Christ his Son. Standing in the presence of the Creator of heaven and earth, we are not called his servants, but his friends. And, by way of response, God makes upon us the simple demands of love: "My son, give me your heart" (Prov. 26:26).

ALL STAND

All: The love of God has been poured out in our hearts / by the Holy Spirit, whom we have received.

Priest: I am sure that neither death, nor life, nor angels, nor principalities, nor things present, nor things to come, nor any other creature will be able to separate us from the love of God which is in Christ Jesus our Lord.

All: The love of God has been poured out in our hearts / by the Holy Spirit, whom we have received.

ALL SIT

Priest: Let us listen to the inspired words of the psalmist, who gives us a hymn of praise for the wonders of creation, the gift of God's love to us.

Reader: O Lord, my God, you are great indeed!

> You are clothed with majesty and glory,
>> robed in light as with a cloak.
> You have spread out the heavens like a tent-cloth;
>> you have constructed your palace upon the waters.
> You make the clouds your chariot;
>> you travel on the wings of the wind.
> You fixed the earth upon its foundation,
>> not to be moved forever.
> You water the mountains from your palace;
>> the earth is replete with the fruit of your works.
> You raise grass for the cattle,
>> and vegetation for men's use,
> Producing bread from the earth,
>> and wine to gladden men's hearts,
> So that their faces gleam with oil,
>> and bread fortifies the hearts of men.
> You made the moon to mark the seasons;
>> the sun knows the hour of its setting.
> You bring darkness and it is night;
>> then all the beasts of the forest roam about.
> The sea also, great and wide,
>> in which are schools without number
>> of living things both small and great:
> They all look to you
>> to give them food in due time.

When you give it to them, they gather it;
when you open your hand, they are filled with good things.
How manifold are your works, O Lord!
In wisdom you have wrought them all —
the earth is full of your creatures (Ps. 103).

ALL KNEEL

Priest: Let us pray, giving thanks to God for the love he has shown us in the wonders of creation. Pause for personal prayer. All things have been created through Christ, and are to be restored through Christ to the Father.

All: Father, accept the offering we make / with Christ our Brother.

Priest: Christ has made all the earth holy.

All: Father, accept the offering we make / with Christ our Brother.

Priest: Christ has sanctified the seasons of nature's year.

All: Father, accept the offering we make / with Christ our Brother.

Priest: Christ has sanctified the hours of both day and night.

All: Father, accept the offering we make / with Christ our Brother.

Priest: Christ has sanctified all that the earth yields.

All: Father, accept the offering we make / with Christ our Brother.

Priest: Christ has sanctified everything that lives on the earth, in the sea and in the skies.

All: Father, accept the offering we make / with Christ our Brother.

Priest: Christ has sanctified man and all the works of man.

All: Father, accept the offering we make / with Christ our Brother.

Priest: Christ has sanctified our deepest thoughts, every plan that we make, every hope that we possess, our every act of love.

All: Glory be to the Father, and to the Son, and to the Holy Spirit, / as it was in the beginning, is now, and ever shall be, world without end. Amen.

ALL STAND

Hymn No. 218.

2. FILL OUR HEARTS WITH THE FIRE OF YOUR LOVE

ALL SIT

Priest: Let us listen now to the first letter of St. John, whose inspired words teach us that our Christian life is a life of love.

Reader: Beloved, let us love one another, for love is from God. And everyone who loves is born of God, and knows God. He who does not love does not know God; for God is love. In this has the love of God been shown in our case, that God has sent his only-begotten Son into the world that we may live through him. In this is the love, not that we have loved God, but that he has first loved us, and sent his Son a propitiation for our sins. Beloved, if God has so loved us, we also ought to love one another.

No one has ever seen God. If we love one another, God abides in us and his love is perfected in us. In this we know that we abide in him and he in us, because he has given us of his Spirit. And we have seen, and do testify, that the Father has sent his Son to be Savior of the world. Whoever confesses that Jesus is the Son of God, God abides in him and he in God. And we have come to know, and have believed, the love that God has on our behalf. God is love, and he who abides in love abides in God, and God in him (1 John 4:7-16).

ALL KNEEL

Priest: Let us pray, asking Christ to send his own Spirit into our hearts, so that we may love as he first loved us. Pause for personal prayer. In this we know that we abide in him and he in us, because he has given us of his Spirit.

All: Come, Holy Spirit, fill our hearts with the fire of your love.

Priest: Beloved, let us love one another, for love is from God.

All: Come, Holy Spirit, fill our hearts with the fire of your love.

Priest: He who does not love does not know God; for God is love.

All: Come, Holy Spirit, fill our hearts with the fire of your love.

Priest: There is no fear in love; but perfect love casts out fear.

All: Come, Holy Spirit, fill our hearts with the fire of your love.

Priest: Let us therefore love, because God first loved us.

All: Come, Holy Spirit, fill our hearts with the fire of your love.

Priest: If anyone says, "I love God," and hates his brother, he is a liar.

All: Come, Holy Spirit, fill our hearts with the fire of your love.

Priest: In this we have come to know his love, that he laid down his life for us; and we likewise ought to lay down our life for the brethren.

All: Glory be to the Father, and to the Son, and to the Holy Spirit, / as it was in the beginning, is now, and ever shall be, world without end. Amen!

ALL STAND

Hymn No. 219.

3. YOUR FRUIT SHOULD REMAIN

Priest: Let us hear now our Lord's last declarations and commandments concerning love, made on the night before he died. The reading is from the Gospel according to St. John.

Reader: As the Father has loved me, I also have loved you. Abide in my love. If you keep my commandments you will abide in my love, as I also have kept my Father's commandments, and abide in his love. These things I have spoken to you that my joy may be in you, and that your joy may be made full.

This is my commandment, that you love one another as I have loved you. Greater love than this no one has, that one lay down his life for his friends. You are my friends if you do the things I command you. No longer do I call you servants, because the servant does not know what his master does. But I have called you friends, because all things that I have heard from my Father I have made known to you. You have not chosen me, but

I have chosen you, and have appointed you that you should go and bear fruit, and that your fruit should remain; that whatever you ask the Father in my name he may give you. These things I command you, that you may love one another (John 15:9-17).

ALL SIT

The priest may now give a homily developing the following points:

1. God our Father has shared with us every good thing, but his love is made especially manifest by his gift to us of Christ and the Holy Spirit.

2. Even the power and ability to respond to our Father's love is itself a gift of God's grace; we accept this grace and willingly surrender our whole selves to the Lord.

ALL KNEEL

Priest: Let us pray, begging God for the grace to offer our whole selves in a sacrifice of love to him. Pause for personal prayer. He who has my commandments and keeps them, he it is who loves me.

All: Take, O Lord, and receive all my liberty, / my memory, my understanding and my entire will.

Priest: He who loves me will be loved by my Father, and I will love him and manifest myself to him.

All: Take, O Lord, and receive all that I have and possess.

Priest: If anyone love me, he will keep my word, and my Father will love him, and we will come to him and make our abode with him.

All: Lord, you have given me everything. / I return it all to you.

Priest: As the Father has loved me, I also have loved you. Abide in my love.

All: Lord, dispose of everything that I have / according to your holy will.

Priest: Greater love than this no one has, that one lay down his life for his friends.

All: Lord Jesus, only give us your love and your grace: / this is sufficient for us.

Priest: Let us pray, asking the Lord for the grace of a whole-hearted generosity in the love that we return to him. Pause for personal prayer. O God our Lord, teach us to be generous. Teach us to serve you as you deserve: to give and not to count the cost; to fight and not to heed the wounds; to toil and not to seek for rest; to labor and not to ask for any reward, save that of knowing that we do your will; through Christ our Lord.

All: Amen! The love of God has been poured out in our hearts / by the Holy Spirit, whom we have received.

Priest: I am sure that neither death, nor life, nor angels, nor principalities, nor things present, nor things to come, nor any other creature will be able to separate us from the love of God which is in Christ Jesus our Lord.

All: The love of God has been poured out in our hearts / by the Holy Spirit, whom we have received.

VII. THE HOLY EUCHARIST
We are one in his body and one in his love

ALL STAND
Entrance hymn No. 285.

1. TASTE AND SEE HOW GOOD THE LORD IS

ALL SIT
Priest: Our life in Christ is made possible by the sacrificial death and resurrection of the Lord. The Eucharist is the sacrament of Christ's death and resurrection and so is the whole source and center of the Church's life. The eucharistic meal is a sacrificial meal: Christ is priest and victim, just as he was the first time that the sacrifice was offered. All through the centuries of man's life, Christ continues to offer himself to the Father in the one and same sacrifice. In the sacrifice, Christ gathers all men to himself, to present us to his Father. Holy Mass, in these days of the Church, is the sacrifice of the whole Christ, head and members.

Let us listen to God's word in the Scripture as we are taught about our participation in the sacrificial meal. The sacred banquet, in which we feast upon the Lord, is the food of our eternal life in God.

ALL STAND
All: Taste and see how good the Lord is; / happy the man who takes refuge in him.
Priest: If anyone eat of this bread he shall live forever; and the bread that I will give is my flesh for the life of the world.
All: Taste and see how good the Lord is; / happy the man who takes refuge in him.

ALL SIT
Priest: Let us listen to the story of God's miraculous feeding of his people in the desert as he led them from Egypt to the promised land. The reading is from the book of Exodus.
Reader: Having set out from Elim, the whole Israelite community came into the desert of Sin, which is between Elim and Sinai, on the fifteenth day of the second month after their departure from the land of Egypt. Here in the desert the whole Israelite community grumbled against Moses and Aaron. The Israelites said to them, "Would that we had died at the Lord's hand in the land of Egypt, as we sat by our fleshpots and ate our fill of bread! But you had to lead us into this desert to make the whole community die of famine!"

Then the Lord said to Moses, "I will now rain down bread from heaven for you. Each day the people are to go out and gather their daily portion; thus will I test them, to see whether they follow my instructions or not. On the sixth day, however, when they prepare what they bring in, let it be twice as much as they gather on the other days."

So Moses and Aaron told all the Israelites, "At evening you will know that it was the Lord who brought you out of the land of Egypt; and in the morning you will see the glory of the Lord, as he heeds your grumbling against him. But what are we that you should grumble against us? When the Lord gives you flesh to eat in the evening," continued Moses, "and in the morning your fill of bread, as he heeds the grumbling you utter against him, what then are we? Your grumbling is not against us, but against the Lord."

Then Moses said to Aaron, "Tell the whole Israelite community: Present yourselves before the Lord, for he has heard your grumbling."

When Aaron announced this to the whole Israelite community, they turned toward the desert and lo, the glory of the Lord appeared in the cloud! The Lord spoke to Moses and said, "I have heard the grumbling of the Israelites. Tell them: In the evening twilight you shall eat flesh, and in the morning you shall have your fill of bread, so that you may know that I, the Lord, am your God."

In the evening quail came up and covered the camp. In the morning a dew lay all about the camp, and when the dew evaporated, there on the surface of the desert were fine flakes like hoarfrost on the ground.

On seeing it, the Israelites asked one another, "What is this?" for they did not know what it was.

But Moses told them, "This is the bread which the Lord has given you to eat" (Exod. 16:1-15).

ALL KNEEL

Priest: Let us pray, giving thanks to the Lord for the great deeds which he has performed on man's behalf. Pause for personal prayer. The Israelites asked one another, "What is this?" for they did not know what it was. But Moses told them, "This is the bread which the Lord has given you to eat.

All: The loving mercy of the Lord will last forever and ever.

Priest: Give thanks to the Lord, for he is good,

All: for his mercy endures forever.

Priest: Give thanks to the God of gods,

All: for his mercy endures forever.

Priest: Who alone does great wonders,

All: for his mercy endures forever.

Priest: Who smote the Egyptians in their first-born,

All: for his mercy endures forever.

Priest: And brought out Israel from their midst,

All: for his mercy endures forever.

Priest: Who led his people through the wilderness,

All: for his mercy endures forever.

Priest: Who remembered us in our abjection,

All: for his mercy endures forever.

Priest: And freed us from our foes,

All: for his mercy endures forever.

Priest: Who gives food to all flesh,

All: for his mercy endures forever.

Priest: Give thanks to the God of heaven,
   All: for his mercy endures forever.
ALL STAND
Hymn No. 68.

2. WE, THOUGH MANY, ARE ONE BODY

ALL SIT
Priest: Let us listen now to St. Paul's account of the last supper. The reading is from the first letter to the Corinthians.
Reader: As for me, I have taught you what I myself learned as coming from the Lord. On the night when he was betrayed, the Lord Jesus took bread and, after giving thanks, broke it and said, "Take some of this and eat it. This is my Body, which is going to be sacrificed for you. Do this in remembrance of me." Similarly, at the end of the meal, he took the cup of wine, saying, "This chalice is the new alliance in my Blood. Whenever you drink it, do so in remembrance of me."

Every time you eat this bread and drink this chalice, therefore, you are proclaiming the death of the Lord; and this you will do until he comes again. That is why anyone who eats the bread and drinks the chalice of the Lord in an unworthy manner will have to answer for the way he has mistreated the Lord's Body and Blood.

Let each one examine himself, then, before eating this bread and drinking this chalice. For he who eats and drinks as if there were no question of the Lord's Body, eats and drinks to his own damnation (1 Cor. 11:23-30)

ALL KNEEL
Priest: Let us pray, giving thanks to the Lord who has bestowed upon us the great mystery of his love in the eucharistic meal. Pause for personal prayer. Because the bread is one, we though many, are one body, all of us who partake of the one bread.
   All: We are one in his body and one in his love.
Priest: This is my Body which shall be given up for you; do this in remembrance of me.
   All: We are one in his body and one in his love.
Priest: A new commandment I give you, that you love one another; that as I have loved you, you also love one another.
   All: We are one in his body and one in his love.
Priest: As the Father has loved me, I also have loved you. Abide in my love.
   All: We are one in his body and one in his love.
Priest: Do not labor for the food that perishes, but for that which endures unto life everlasting, which the Son of Man will give you.
   All: We are one in his body and one in his love.
Priest: I am the bread of life. He who comes to me shall not hunger, and he who believes in me shall never thirst.
   All: We are one in his body and one in his love.

Priest: Now you are the body of Christ, member for member.
All: We are one in his body and one in his love.
ALL STAND
Hymn No. 71.

3. I AM THE LIVING BREAD

Priest: Let us listen now to the Gospel of St. John, in which we are given Christ's explanation of the mystery of the eucharistic meal.

Reader: "I am the bread of life. Your fathers ate the manna in the desert, and they are dead. Here is the bread that comes down from heaven; he who eats it will not die. I am the living bread that comes down from heaven. If anyone eats some of this bread, he will live for eternity. And the bread that I shall give is my flesh, delivered up for the life of the world."

The Jews then quarreled among themselves. "How can this man give us his flesh to eat?" they were saying.

Jesus said to them, therefore, "This is the solemn truth: If you do not eat the flesh of the Son of Man and if you do not drink his blood, you shall not have life in you. But he who eats my flesh and drinks my blood possesses life eternal; and I myself will raise him up on the last day. For my flesh is a true food, and my blood is a true drink. He who eats my flesh and drinks my blood dwells in me, and I dwell in him.

"The Father, the living God, has sent me, and it is he who makes me live. Similarly, when someone eats me, it is I who make him live. This is the bread that has come down from heaven. It is not like the manna which your fathers ate: they died none the less. He who eats this bread will live for-ever" (John 6:48-59).

ALL SIT
The priest may now give a homily developing the following points.

1. The manna which God gave to the Jews in the desert was a fore-shadowing of the eucharistic meal.

2. To partake of the Eucharist is to deepen our life in Christ's body, the Church, for in the Eucharist we are made one with Christ and one with the members of Christ's body.

ALL KNEEL
Priest: Let us give thanks to the Lord for his loving mercy. Pause for personal prayer. Come, holy people of God, receive Christ's Body and drink his holy Blood by which we have been redeemed.
All: We have feasted on the Lord; / let us give thanks, / for his Body and Blood have won our redemption.
Priest: The sacrament of his Body and Blood has saved us all from the jaws of hell.
All: We have feasted on the Lord; / let us give thanks, / for his Body and Blood have won our redemption.
Priest: Christ, the Son of God, has brought us salvation; by his Cross and Blood he has rescued the world.
All: We have feasted on the Lord; / let us give thanks, / for his Body and Blood have won our redemption.

Priest: The sacrifice was offered for all men; the Lord was both priest and victim.

All: We have feasted on the Lord; / let us give thanks, / for his Body and Blood have won our redemption.

Priest: He gives the bread of heaven to the hungry and refreshing drink to those who thirst.

All: We have feasted on the Lord; / let us give thanks, / for his Body and Blood have won our redemption.

Priest: The beginning and the end, Christ the Lord, who will come to judge mankind, has come to us.

All: Glory be to the Father, and to the Son, and to the Holy Spirit, / as it was in the beginning, is now, and ever shall be, world without end. Amen!

Priest: Through the mystery of his love, we are one with Christ in his flesh and blood. Let us pray that he will deepen that life in us.

Pause for personal prayer.

O Lord our God, you fed our fathers in the desert and gave up your Son to be sacrificed for our salvation. Grant, we pray you, that by our sharing in the eucharistic meal we may draw close to one another in your holy Church; through the same Christ our Lord.

All: Amen! taste and see how good the Lord is; / happy the man who takes refuge in him.

Priest: If anyone eat of this bread he shall live forever; and the bread that I will give is my flesh for the life of the world.

All: Taste and see how good the Lord is; / happy the man who takes refuge in him.

VIII. THE BLESSED VIRGIN MARY
Blessed art thou among women

ALL STAND

Entrance hymn No. 243.

1. MARY, DAWN OF THE WORLD'S SALVATION

ALL SIT

Priest: Let us listen to three passages from the book of Genesis. The first tells of God's command; the second, of the transgression, original sin. The third, called the protoevangelium, or first gospel, includes the first promise of a Redeemer.

Reader: The Lord God took the man and placed him in the garden of Eden to till it and to keep it. And the Lord God commanded the man thus, "From every tree of the garden you may eat; but from the tree of the knowledge of good and evil you must not eat; for the day you eat of it, you must die."

Now the serpent was more cunning than any beast of the field which the Lord God had made. He said to the woman, "Did God say, 'You shall not eat of any tree of the garden'?"

The woman answered the serpent, "Of the fruit of all trees in the garden we may eat; but 'Of the fruit of the tree in the middle of the garden,' God said, 'you shall not eat, neither shall you touch it, lest you die.'"

But the serpent said to the woman, "No, you shall not die; for God knows that when you eat of it, your eyes will be opened and you will be like God, knowing good and evil."

Now the woman saw that the tree was good for food, pleasing to the eyes, and desirable for the knowledge it would give. She took of its fruit and ate it, and also gave some to her husband and he ate.

Then the Lord God said to the woman, "Why have you done this?"

The woman said, "The serpent deceived me and I ate."

Then the Lord God said to the serpent:

"Because you have done this,
  cursed are you among all animals,
    and among all beasts of the field;
On your belly shall you crawl,
  dust shall you eat,
    all the days of your life.
I will put enmity between you and the woman,
  between your seed and her seed;
He shall crush your head,
  and you shall lie in wait for his heel"
(Gen. 2:15-17; 3:1-6, 13-15).

ALL KNEEL

Priest: Lord, your revelation teaches us that at the beginning of man's history stands an injustice, a rebellion against your holy commandment. Our first parents committed grievous sin against your eternal majesty.

All: We beseech you, Lord, have pity on us.

Priest: This sin of our first parents has caused us to lose the right to eternal happiness in heaven, a loss we cannot repair by ourselves.

All: We beseech you, Lord, have pity on us.

Priest: In your love for us, you chose Mary from eternity to be the Mother of our Savior.

All: We thank you, Lord, for your infinite love.

Priest: You made Mary the holiest of all virgins.

All: We praise you, Lord, for you are great.

Priest: You have made Mary the kindest of all mothers.

All: We praise you, Lord, for you are wonderful.

Priest: You have made Mary the purest of all your daughters.

All: We praise you, Lord, for you are powerful.

Priest: You have made Mary the fairest of all women.

All: We praise you, Lord, for you are good.

Priest: Of Mary was born your divine Son who came to redeem us from Satan's yoke.

All: We thank you, Lord, for your great mercy.

Priest: Through Mary the world has seen again the light from heaven that dispels the darkness.

All: We thank you, Lord, for your goodness.

Priest: Through Mary, sinful mankind obtains forgiveness for its sins.

All: We thank you, Lord, for your infinite love.

Priest: Through Mary the world has seen the new hope of salvation.

All: We thank you, Lord, for your wisdom.

Priest: Let us pray. Pause for personal prayer.

O God, your providence in the ordering of things does not falter. We humbly pray that with Mary the Mother of your divine Son pleading for us, you will remove from us every misfortune and grant all that is for our good.

All: Amen.

ALL STAND

Hymn No. 240.

2. MARY, MOTHER OF THE REDEEMER

Priest: The Gospel according to St. Matthew shows us that the Son of Mary is also the Son of God.

Reader: After the birth of Jesus at Bethlehem of Juda, under the reign of Herod, Magi from the East arrived in Jerusalem, asking, "Where can we find the king of the Jews who was just born? For we have seen his star in the East, and we have come to pay homage to him."

At this news King Herod was disturbed, and all Jerusalem with him. He called together the chief priests and the scribes and asked them where the Christ was to be born.

"In Bethlehem of Juda," they answered. "For the prophet has written, 'And you, Bethlehem, land of Juda, you are not the least of the towns of Juda; for from you shall come forth a leader, the shepherd of Israel, my people.'"

Then Herod had the Magi come to him secretly, and he found out from them the exact date on which they had seen this star. And he told them to go to Bethlehem. "Go and make careful inquiries about this child," he said; "and, when you have found him, report to me, that I too may go and pay him homage."

After listening to the king, the Magi set out on their way again. And there was the star they had seen in the East, moving along before them, until it came to where the Child was; then it stopped. The sight of the star filled them with joy.

Entering the house, they found the Child with his Mother Mary; and they fell to their knees and paid him homage. Then, opening their treasures, they offered him gold, frankincense and myrrh.

They were advised in a dream not to return to Herod; and so they went back to their country by another route.

After the departure of the Magi, the angel of the Lord appeared to Joseph in a dream and told him, "Get up, take the Child and his Mother, flee into Egypt and stay there until I give you further notice. For Herod is going to search for the Child, and do away with him if he can."

That very night Joseph got up, took the Child and his Mother and withdrew into Egypt. There he stayed until Herod's death. Thus was fulfilled what the Lord had said through his prophet, "Out of Egypt I have called my Son" (Matthew 2:1-15).

ALL KNEEL

Priest: You are blessed, O Virgin Mary, for God has chosen you as the dwelling-place of his Son.

All: Blessed are you among women, / for from you has risen the Sun of justice, / Christ our Lord, / through whom we have been redeemed.

Priest: You are blessed, O Virgin Mary, because you are the Mother of him who created all things.

All: Praise to you, O Virgin Mary, / for you gave birth to him who made you, / while remaining virgin forever.

Priest: Praise to you, O Virgin Mary, for from you comes the one who builds up the kingdom of God throughout the world.

All: Mary, dear Mother of our Savior, / we greet you and thank you / for having brought us salvation.

Priest: With the angel Gabriel we greet you. Hail, Mary, blessed are you among women, for the Most High has chosen you as the Mother of the Messiah.

All: In Bethlehem you gave birth / to the Redeemer of the world. / With pure maternal love / you nourished from your breast God, the Creator.

Priest: No woman here below is equal to you in power and in grandeur, for the King of heaven and earth is with you.

All: No woman is more beautiful and glorious, / for through you proceeds the light shining in the darkness.

Priest: O Virgin Mary, your motherhood heralds joy to all the world, for through you the gate of heaven is opened to us.

All: Show yourself to be a mother, O Virgin Mary, / and teach us to know and to love your Son, / Jesus Christ our Lord.

Priest: O Virgin Mary, teach us to be humble and pure, that, like you, we may receive the Savior into our hearts.

All: Show us the way of charity and love, / that by our words and deeds / we may bring Christ to the world.

Priest: Praised be the Father, the Son and the Holy Spirit, both now and forever.

All: The God who is, who was and who is to come / at the end of the ages. Amen.

Priest: Let us pray. Pause for personal prayer.

Lord, it was your will that at the annunciation, the Word should become incarnate in the womb of the Blessed Virgin Mary. Our humble prayer is that we be helped by her intercession with you. For we believe that she is truly the Mother of God. Through Jesus Christ our Lord.

All: Amen.

ALL STAND

Hymn No. 241.

3. MARY, MOTHER OF ALL CHRISTIANS

Priest: The apostle John calls himself the disciple whom Jesus loved. The whole of Christian tradition has been pleased to see in him the representative of all of us.

Reader: Standing near the Cross of Jesus were his Mother, his Mother's sister Mary, wife of Cleophas, and Mary Magdalene. Seeing his Mother and, standing near her, the disciple whom he loved, Jesus said to his Mother, "Woman, here is your son." Then he said to the disciple, "Here is your Mother."

And from that hour this disciple took her into his home (John 19:25-27).

ALL SIT

The priest may now give a homily developing the following points:

1. As the sin of the world started with the disobedience of the first woman, Eve, so the redemption of the world was to be prepared for by another woman, the second Eve. As Eve brought natural life to the world, Mary was to bring supernatural life to mankind through her Son, Jesus Christ.

2. By his eternal birth Christ is truly the Son of God, and by his temporal birth he is truly the Son of Mary.

3. Mary is the Mother not only of the person of Christ, but also of his Mystical Body, all members of his Church, because she is intimately associated with the whole redemptive work of her Son.

ALL KNEEL

Priest: We thank you, O Jesus, for giving us the Blessed Virgin to be our Mother.

All: We beseech you, O Jesus, that, like you, / we may be faithful and obedient children of Mary.

Priest: With full joy we receive you, O Blessed Virgin Mary, as a Mother most beloved among mothers.

All: Filled with hope, / we come to you, beloved Mother, / to seek your protection.

Priest: In the Cenacle you gathered around yourself your first children, all the disciples of Christ, waiting in prayer for the Holy Spirit.

All: Dear Mother, / you comforted and inspired the infant Church / in her trials and sufferings.

Priest: We all hasten to you, O Mary, like children to a beloved mother, like orphans to a mother whom they love.

All: Your tenderness, O Mary, and your goodness / surpass all that can be found of these here below.

Priest: You are the consoler of all the afflicted.

All: We beseech you, dear Mother, / that through your motherly love / we may be protected from all misfortune.

Priest: You are the refuge of sinners.

All: We beseech you, dear Mother, / that through your prayers / our sins may be forgiven by your Son Jesus Christ.

Priest: You are our powerful advocate before God.

All: We beseech you, dear Mother, / that through your intercession / we may obtain heavenly blessings in abundance.

Priest: Through you alone, dear Mother, we have access to the Son, and through the Son we shall reach the Father.

All: Through your merits, dear Mother, / protect us from all evils. / Through your prayers, / deliver us from all perils.

Priest: To you, dear Mother, we recommend all our wishes, desires, our joys and sorrows — our whole life, and especially its end.

All: Into your care, dear Mother, / take the whole Church, / our beloved Pontiff . . ., / all bishops, priests, religious, / and all followers of Christ in the world.

Priest: That the world may come to know the true Church of Christ and join the great family of God.

All: That all Christians may be finally united / in love and charity / in one fold and under one shepherd.

Priest: Praised be the Father, the Son and the Holy Spirit, both now and forever.

All: The God who is, who was and who is to come / at the end of the ages. Amen.

Priest: Let us pray. Pause for personal prayer.

Lord Jesus Christ, you have given us your Mother Mary as a mother always ready to help us. Enable us who earnestly seek her assistance to enjoy the fruits of your redemption, and by her holy intercession make us live together in peace and charity, we beseech you, O Lord who live and reign for ever and ever.

All: Amen.

ALL STAND
Final hymn, No. 246.

IX. FOR THE UNITY OF CHRISTIANS

One flock and one shepherd

ALL STAND
Entrance hymn, No. 232.

1. THAT ALL MAY BE ONE

Priest: In the Gospel according to St. John, Jesus reveals his plan to save all men by gathering them into the one sheepfold of God.

Reader: "I am the good shepherd; I know my sheep, and my sheep know me — just as my Father knows me and I know my Father — and I sacrifice my life for my sheep.

"I have still other sheep who are not of this fold; I must put myself at the head of them also; they will hear my voice. Then there will be but one flock and one shepherd" (John 10:14-16)

ALL KNEEL

Priest: Lord Jesus Christ! You are here upon the altar among those who believe in you. We adore you. We come to you devoutly. Look down in mercy on existing separations, even among those who acknowledge you. Many millions baptized in your name do not benefit from the fullness of life in your Church. You have constituted it alone as the never-failing fountain of grace and truth. To it you have entrusted the inexhaustible plenitude of riches originating from your passion, death and resurrection. You have given it the pledge of everlasting aid, when you spoke to Peter:

All: I say to you: / You are Peter (the Rock), / and on this rock I will build my Church; / and the gates of hell will not prevail against it.

Priest: Through no merits of our own, you have given us the grace to be called the children of this Church.

All: We are grateful to you, Lord!

Priest: Yes, Lord, we are grateful. But we cannot presume on this holy favor of having an integral faith by forgetting all those who still stand outside your visible Church.

All: Lead them too into your fold, / that they may hear your voice, / and that there be but one fold and one shepherd.

Priest: With great trust we bring this prayer for unity directly to you, Lord, in the sacrament of unity. You yourself, in the solemn hour when you left us this sacrament of unity, prayed to the Father:

All: Let them all be one, / just as you, Father, are in me, and I in you; / let them all be one, / that the world may believe that you have sent me.

Priest: In this sacrifice-sacrament you wish to unite us in a bond of love, of unity and of faith. And so the apostle Paul writes:

All: Is not the bread we break / communion with the body of Christ? / Since it is one bread, / so we build up only one body. / Indeed, we all take part / in this one bread.

Priest: Let us pray. Pause for personal prayer.

Lord Jesus Christ, you have left us the Blessed Eucharist as a bond of love and union, and we sincerely hope that all may be joined in that unity. Through you and in you we offer each day all holy Masses and Communions and all our prayers at the altar of sacrifice. We plead without ceasing: Through your holy Church lead everyone who believes in you along the way of peace and love. Direct those of partial faith into the one fold of your Church and lead the unbelieving to the light of your gospel — you who live and reign everlastingly.

All: Amen.

ALL STAND

Hymn No. 263.

2. LOOK NOT UPON OUR SINS

ALL SIT

Priest: In a magnificent passage of his letter to the Ephesians, St. Paul shows that Christians must be united among themselves as the members of one body are, because their vocation and their baptism make them the Body of Christ. He shows us also on what conditions of reciprocal love, truth and understanding we shall be able to realize this unity.

Reader: I entreat you, conduct yourselves in a manner worthy of the vocation to which God is calling you. Practice humility, gentleness, patience among one another, supporting one another by love, being careful to preserve that peace which unites you to one another, that you may be one in the Spirit.

All together you are but one body, but one spirit, as you have but one hope — that of the same heaven to which you are all called — one Lord, Christ, one faith, one baptism, one God, who is the Father of us all, who is above all, who acts in all and who is in all.

Yet each one of us has received grace in the measure in which Christ has seen fit to grant it to him; that is, until all of us together come to be one in the faith and in the knowledge of the Son of God, until all together constitute that complete man, that man in all his maturity, who embodies the fullness of Christ.

From that time on, we should no longer be children tossed about by the least wave and carried off by the winds of all those doctrines to which we are exposed by the wickedness of men and the deceitful cleverness of error. Living according to the truth in charity, we shall grow in every way in him who is the head of our body, Christ. For it is from Christ that the entire body, thanks to the connections which subordinate all the members to him, draws its cohesion and its unity; and it is through Christ that the body, thanks to the regular activity of each one of its members, achieves its growth and rises up, like a new building, in charity.

That is why — I ask you and beseech you in the Lord — you must no longer live as the pagans do, following their own frivolous thoughts. Their intellect is plunged in darkness; they are strangers to the life of God, under the spell of the profound ignorance into which their blinded heart has cast them. With their conscience hardened, are they not abandoned to debauchery and made slaves to all impurities and to the cult of money?

As for you, on the contrary, that is not what you have learned in the school of Christ. Not, that is, if the word you have heard is really his, and if it is really in him that you have been formed. For the truth is in Jesus Christ our Lord (Eph. 4:1-7, 13-21).

ALL KNEEL

Priest: Lord Jesus Christ! Our responsibility lies heavily upon us. The separation of Christians is a scandal to the world. It weakens us in our contacts with the unbelieving, with those who despise God. It hinders the missionary work of your Church. We are fearful in trying to fulfill your desire for our unity. Above all, as true believers, we experience with deepest sorrow the divisions regarding faith in your sacramental presence. Because of human guilt, a sad state prevails among us. With humility and sorrow we confess that the children of your Church are not without guilt in this matter. Loose not your righteousness against your people, Lord!

All: Think no more upon our former sins. / Grant a merciful hearing to the prayer of your people, / and bless our effort toward unity of faith in Christ.

Priest: Do not overlook, O Lord, the prayers and endeavors of our separated brothers. They bear your name as we do. In baptism they have become children of your Father; they believe in you; they love you. And many of them pray today with us sincerely for the unity you desire. But this is not attained by our good will alone. The roots of division penetrate too deeply through the course of centuries.

All: You alone can bring all / to the full truth of faith / and to the plenitude of grace in your Church.

Priest: Lord, you can sanctify souls. In an instant you changed Saul, a man wild with hate for you in your Church, into Paul. With greater ease you can effect Christian unity in souls who love you already!

All: You are the true light, / enlightening every man. / Drive out all darkness of error, / and lead all who love your name / to the fellowship of Christian unity.

Priest: Let us pray. Pause for personal prayer.

Lord Jesus Christ, you have said to your apostles: My peace I leave with you, my peace I give to you. Consider not our sins but the faith of your Church, and give it peace and unity according to your merciful will. For you live and reign eternally.

All: Amen.

ALL STAND

Hymn No. 265.

3. CHURCH UNITY PETITIONS

Priest: In the priestly prayer which concludes the discourse after the last supper as recorded in the Gospel according to St. John, Christ asks his Father to bring all men together into unity, that they may truly become his Body and may join him in heaven.

Reader: "It is for them that I pray: not for the world, but for those whom you gave me, because they are yours (indeed all that is mine is yours, and all that is yours is mine), and because I have been glorified in them.

"Even now, I am no longer in the world, but they are staying in the world while I am going to you.

"Holy Father, in your name guard those whom you have given me, that they may be one, as we are.

"When I was with them I kept them in your name. I kept those whom you gave me, and not one of them perished, except the one who was to destroy himself; for the Scripture must be fulfilled. But now I am coming to you, and I am pronouncing these words in the world that they may have in themselves the fullness of my joy. I have communicated your word to them; and the world has taken a loathing to them, for they are not of the world, just as I am not of the world. I do not ask that you take them out of the world, but that you keep them from evil. They are not of the world, just as I am not of the world.

"Sanctify them in truth: your word is truth. Just as you have sent me into the world, so I also am sending them into the world. And I am consecrating myself for them, that they in turn may be consecrated in truth.

"But I am praying not only for them; I am praying also for those who, thanks to their word, will believe in me; that all may be one, as you, Father, are in me and I am in you; that they also may be one in us, and that thus the world may believe that I am your envoy.

"As for me, the glory that you have given me I have given them, that they may be one, as we are one: I in them and you in me; that their unity may be perfect" (John 17:9-23).

ALL SIT

The priest may now give a homily developing the following points:

1. The unity of knowledge and love in the Blessed Trinity is the model of the unity which Christ desires among his followers.

2. The separated brothers of our day are not formally heretics and schismatics. We can achieve unity with them, not by denouncing them, but by good example, by understanding of our own beliefs and theirs, by love and by prayer.

ALL KNEEL

Priest: Lord Jesus Christ! Let us bring our petitions to you for the unity of men in your Church humbly, trustfully:

That you give to all baptized in your name the earnest desire for unity,

All: Please grant our petition.

Priest: That you give to us humility, sincere understanding, and genuine love for one another,

All: Please grant our petition.

Priest: That you unite everyone who believes in you in working for those without God and those who despise him,

All: Please grant our petition.

Priest: That you grant us, the children of your Church, the grace to live according to our faith,

All: Please grant our petition.

Priest: That you give us manly courage to acknowledge our faith to the world,

All: Please grant our petition.

Priest: That you humble the enemies of the Church for the sake of their own salvation,

All: Please grant our petition.

Priest: That you grant Christian peoples peace and real unity,

All: Please grant our petition.

Priest: That you enlighten those groping for full truth with the light of your revelation,

All: Please grant our petition.

Priest: That you lead all unbelievers to the light of the gospel,

All: Please grant our petition.

Priest: That you number that nation, once your chosen people, into your new and eternal covenant,

All: Please grant our petition.

Priest: Let us pray. Pause for personal prayer.

Redeem us, God, Father in heaven, and gather us from among heathens, so we may praise your name in the Church of your Son, our Lord Jesus Christ, who lives and reigns with you and the Holy Spirit, God eternally.

All: Amen.

ALL STAND

Final hymn, No. 224.

X. THANKSGIVING
Let us give thanks to the Lord our God

ALL STAND

Entrance hymn, No. 258.

1. GIVE THANKS TO THE LORD FOR HE IS GOOD

ALL SIT

Priest: Like the people of Israel, we are the chosen ones of God, and we can apply to ourselves what is promised in the book of Exodus.

Reader: In the third month after their departure from the land of Egypt, on its first day, the Israelites came to the desert of Sinai. After the journey from Raphidim to the desert of Sinai, they pitched camp.

While Israel was encamped here in front of the mountain, Moses went up to the mountain of God. Then the Lord called to him and said, "Thus shall you say to the house of Jacob: tell the Israelites: You have seen for yourselves how I treated the Egyptians and how I bore you up on eagle wings and brought you here to myself. Therefore, if you hearken to my voice and keep my covenant, you shall be my special possession, dearer to me than all other people, though all the earth is mine. You shall be to me a kingdom of priests, a holy nation. That is what you must tell the Israelites" (Exod. 19:1-6).

ALL KNEEL

Priest: Give thanks to the Lord for he is good; for his great love is without end.

All: Give thanks to the Lord for he is good; / for his great love is without end.

Priest: Out of all nations, God has chosen the people of Israel as his own, and promised them the land of Canaan.

All: Give thanks to the Lord for he is good; / for his great love is without end.

Priest: He made his people prosper; and he made them stronger than their foes.

All: Give thanks to the Lord for he is good; / for his great love is without end.

Priest: He led them out of Egypt, the land of slavery, and rescued them from their distress.

All: Give thanks to the Lord for he is good; / for his great love is without end.

Priest: He brought them across the waters of the Red Sea, and led them like a flock through the desert.

All: Give thanks to the Lord for he is good; / for his great love is without end.

Priest: Like the people of Israel, we were living in darkness and in chains. But God sent his only-begotten Son to save us.

All: Give thanks to the Lord for he is good; / for his great love is without end.

Priest: When we were dead because of our sins, he brought us to life through water and the Holy Spirit, and made us members of his household.

All: Give thanks to the Lord for he is good; / for his great love is without end.

Priest: He has rescued us from the power of darkness and taken us into the kingdom of his beloved Son, in whom we obtain redemption and the remission of sins.

All: Give thanks to the Lord for he is good; / for his great love is without end.

Priest: In the sacrament of baptism he has marked us with his seal and made us a chosen race and a holy nation.

All: Give thanks to the Lord for he is good; / for his great love is without end.

Priest: He has called us into the kingdom of his Son, the holy Church, that he may show us the overflowing riches of his grace.

All: Give thanks to the Lord for he is good; / for his great love is without end.

Priest: He nourishes us with the eucharistic food of immortality and clothes us with his countless blessings and graces.

All: Give thanks to the Lord for he is good; / for his great love is without end.

Priest: As he led the people of Israel to the promised land, he leads us also, his chosen people, to our heavenly home.

All: Give thanks to the Lord for he is good; / for his great love is without end.

Priest: He will seat us in heaven together with his Son Jesus Christ, and he will give us the perfect and unfading inheritance of the glory of heaven.

All: Give thanks to the Lord for he is good; / for his great love is without end.

Priest: Let us pray. Pause for personal prayer.

O God, whose mercies are without number, and whose goodness is an inexhaustible treasure, we render thanks to your most kind majesty for calling us into your holy Church to be your chosen people. We beseech you, O God, that, with the help of your grace, we may always be faithful to your calling, on the road to the heavenly promised land. Through Jesus Christ our Lord.

All: **Amen.**

ALL STAND

Hymn No. 279.

2. GIVE THANKS TO GOD WHO HAS MADE US HIS CHILDREN

ALL SIT

Priest: In the language of St. Paul's letter to the Romans, the flesh designates our human nature with its egoistic tendencies which close us upon ourselves; the Spirit designates the grace that acts in us, the Holy Spirit who communicates the divine life to us and opens us up to the love of God and of our neighbor.

Reader: Since we have received the Spirit of God, we no longer owe anything to the flesh. It is not for the flesh to direct our life. But if you do live according to the flesh, you are heading for death. If, on the contrary, the Spirit is directing you, you are condemning to death the tendencies of your flesh, but you are headed for life!

All those who allow themselves to be led by the Spirit of God are the sons of God.

For the Spirit whom you have received makes you no longer slaves obeying out of fear. He makes you sons whom God adopts, and he makes us cry out to God, "Abba!", that is to say, "Father!"

It is the Spirit himself who makes our spirit certain of this: to God, we are sons. Being sons, we are heirs, the heirs of God, sharing the heritage of Christ (Rom. 8:12-17).

ALL KNEEL

Priest: **We thank you, O Lord, our God and our Father, our Creator and our Savior. We thank you for the innumerable blessings you have shown us, especially for the grace of calling us to be your children.**

All: Praise and thanks be to you, / O God our Father.

Priest: **You have wrought for us marvelous works; and you have made the skies and the earth in your wisdom.**

All: Praise and thanks be to you, / O God our Father.

Priest: **You have called us out of nothing, and keep us in existence. You remember us in our distress and give food to all living things.**

All: Praise and thanks be to you, / O God our Father.

Priest: **By reason of our sins, we were dead, but out of your great love you have brought us to life, for you predestined us to be adopted through Jesus Christ as your children.**

All: Praise and thanks be to you, / O God our Father.

Priest: **You have granted us poor creatures to be rich in faith and heirs of the kingdom promised to those who love you.**

All: Praise and thanks be to you, / O God our Father.

Priest: **You have begotten us again through the resurrection of Jesus**

Christ from the dead, unto a living hope, unto an incorruptible inheritance reserved for us in heaven.

All: Praise and thanks be to you, / O God our Father.

Priest: From you we have received, through the bath of regeneration, not a spirit of bondage, but a spirit of adoption as sons, so that we may cry, "Abba, Father!"

All: Praise and thanks be to you, / O God our Father.

Priest: As a father has compassion on his sons, so also you have pity on those who love you; and you bless them with daily wonders of the salvation that is happening in the holy Church.

All: Praise and thanks be to you, / O God our Father.

Priest: Through the sacraments you give us a share in your divine life and riches.

All: Praise and thanks be to you, / O God our Father.

Priest: You are a Father of compassion and love, slow to anger and generous in mercy. You do not treat us according to our sins, nor repay us according to our faults.

All: Praise and thanks be to you, / O God our Father.

Priest: Let us pray. Pause for personal prayer.

Almighty, everlasting God, who have seen fit to regenerate us your servants by water and the Holy Spirit and have made us your children, grant that we may always be grateful for your fatherly love and that we may become more and more like your beloved Son Jesus Christ. Through the same Christ our Lord.

All: Amen.

ALL STAND

Hymn No. 73.

3. GIVE THANKS TO GOD WHO HAS PROMISED US THE HEAVENLY PARADISE

Priest: In the Gospel according to St. Matthew, the parable of the talents is a reminder of the heavenly reward promised to those who make good use of the graces God has given them.

Reader: Addressing his disciples, Jesus proposed this parable: "A man who was going on a trip called his servants and entrusted his goods to them: to one he handed over five talents; to another, two; to a third, only one, according to the abilities of each one. He went off, and immediately the one who had received five talents set about making profitable use of them: he gained another five; the one who had received two talents gained two more in the same way; but the third dug a hole in the ground and hid the talent he had received.

"After a long absence the master came back and settled accounts with them. The one who had received the five talents came forward and presented five more: 'Master, you entrusted five talents to me; here are five more that I have gained.'

" 'Fine work! Good, faithful servant! Since you have proved faithful in little things, I am going to put you in charge of bigger things; receive a share now in your master's joy.'

"In his turn the one who had received the two talents came forward: 'Master, you entrusted two talents to me; here are two more that I have gained.'

" 'Fine work! Good, faithful servant! Since you have proved faithful in little things, I am going to put you in charge of bigger things; receive a share now in your master's joy' " (Matthew 25:14-23)

ALL SIT

The priest may now give a homily developing the following points:

1. Through baptism we were called into the Church, the new people of God. We have, then, the privilege and the duty to serve him and to love him as our God. He will treat us as his own, protecting us from all evil and taking care of us in all our needs.

2. God has not only chosen us to serve him; he has also made us his own children by giving us his life through the sacrament of baptism. God's fatherly love for us should stir up in our hearts a sincere and filial gratitude.

3. The earth where we live is not our lasting dwelling-place. God has prepared for his chosen ones eternal life and glory, honor and peace in his own dwelling-place.

ALL KNEEL

Priest: O God, our Father, to those who are afflicted and who labor for your glory you have promised eternal rest in heaven.

All: We thank you, O God; / and grant us, we pray you, / that we may rejoice in you here on earth / in the midst of adversity.

Priest: O God, our Father, to all those who believe in you, you have promised treasures in heaven where neither rust nor moth consumes, nor thieves break in and steal.

All: We thank you, O God; / and grant us, we pray you, / that we may not seek earthly goods, / which rust and moth consume, / but everlasting possessions in heaven.

Priest: O Jesus, our Lord and God, to all those who follow your commandment of charity, you have promised a kingdom prepared from the foundation of the world.

All: We thank you, our Lord. / Grant us, we pray you, / that we may always do our best / to bring assistance and joy to the hungry and thirsty, / to the afflicted and to all those who are in need.

Priest: O Jesus, our Lord and God, to all those who believe and follow you, you have promised a part in the eternal banquet with all the saints in the kingdom of heaven.

All: We thank you, our Lord; / and grant us, we pray you, / that we may ever remember / that we are pilgrims and strangers here on earth.

Priest: O Jesus, our Lord and God, for all your faithful servants you have prepared the eternal joy and the unfading crown of glory in heaven.

All: We thank you, our Lord; / and grant us, we pray you, / that we may always despise worldly pleasures and honor, / and thus deserve to receive from you an eternal reward.

Priest: O Jesus, our Lord and God, you have said, "Every one who has left house or brothers or sisters or father or mother or wife or children or lands for my name's sake, shall receive a hundredfold and shall possess life everlasting."

All: We thank you, our Lord; / and grant us, we pray you, / that we may always put the first things first / and seek above all the kingdom of heaven and its justice.

Priest: O Jesus, our Lord and God, to all your faithful ones you will give the crown of life, which cannot be touched by a second death.

All: We thank you, our Lord; / and grant us, we pray you, / that we may have a strong hope to live with you / in the heavenly paradise.

Priest: O Jesus, our Lord and God, to all those who overcome the world you will give permission to sit with you upon your throne judging the world and seeing God face to face.

All: We thank you, our Lord; / and grant us, we pray you, / that we may have a living faith / to overcome all difficulties on the road to heaven / and be able to reach our eternal home.

Priest: O God, our Father, you have revealed to us that there shall no longer be hunger or thirst, nor shall the sun strike us with its heat. For the Lamb will guide us to the fountains of the waters of life, and you will wipe away every tear from our eyes.

All: We thank you, O God; / and grant us, we pray you, / that with joy we may always be expecting / the day of your visitation, / when you will bring us to your eternal kingdom in heaven.

Priest: Let us pray. Pause for personal prayer.

We beseech you, almighty God and merciful Father, that in thanking you for the gifts we receive here on earth, we may obtain yet greater gifts which you have promised for our life in heaven. Through Jesus Christ our Lord.

All: Amen.

ALL STAND

Final hymn, No. 96.

XI. THE SPIRIT OF RENEWAL
Thy Spirit shall renew the face of the earth

ALL STAND

Entrance hymn, No. 215.

1. BEHOLD! I MAKE ALL THINGS NEW

Priest: Men wear down with time. It is not only our bodies and our great stores of energy which suffer this depletion; the bright light of good intention, too, grows dim with the passage of weeks and years. The sense of commitment, perhaps vivid and preoccupying for so long, fades to a shadow and receives little of our attention or devotion. At the center, sin brings darkness and death, and leaves its mark upon us. We are in profound need of conversion and renewal.

But it is now as it was in the beginning. There was, in the beginning, darkness and the abyss — but God's spirit was there too, moving over the waters. We need to open our darkness and chaos to the Spirit, who will enliven and renew us!

ALL STAND

All: I am about to create new heavens and a new earth; / the things of the past shall not be remembered or come to mind.

Priest: If the Spirit of him who raised Jesus from the dead dwells in you, then he who raised Jesus Christ from the dead will also bring to life your mortal bodies because of his Spirit who dwells in you.

All: I am about to create new heavens and a new earth; / the things of the past shall not be remembered or come to mind.

ALL SIT

Priest: Israel was given a promise of restoration and renewal. Let us listen to the prophet Ezechiel.

Reader: The hand of the Lord came upon me, and he led me out in the spirit of the Lord and set me in the center of the plain, which was now filled with bones. He made me walk among them in every direction so that I saw how many they were on the surface of the plain. How dry they were!

He asked me: Son of man, can these bones come to life?

"Lord God," I answered, "you alone know that."

Then he said to me: Prophesy over these bones, and say to them: Dry bones, hear the word of the Lord! Thus says the Lord God to these bones: See! I will bring spirit into you, that you may come to life. I will put sinews upon you, make flesh grow over you, cover you with skin, and put spirit in you so that you may come to life and know that I am the Lord.

I prophesied as I had been told, and even as I was prophesying I heard a noise; it was a rattling as the bones came together, bone joining bone. I saw the sinews and the flesh come upon them, and the skin cover them, but there was no spirit in them.

Then he said to me: Prophesy to the spirit, prophesy, son of man, and say to the spirit: Thus says the Lord God: From the four winds come, O spirit, and breathe into these slain that they may come to life.

I prophesied as he told me, and the spirit came into them; they came alive and stood upright, a vast army.

Then he said to me: Son of man, these bones are the whole house of Israel. They have been saying, "Our bones are dried up, our hope is lost, and we are cut off." Therefore, prophesy and say to them: Thus says the Lord God: O my people, I will open your graves and have you rise from them, and bring you back to the land of Israel. Then you shall know that I am the Lord, when I open your graves and have you rise from them, O my people! I will put my spirit in you that you may live, and I will settle you upon your land; thus you shall know that I am the Lord. I have promised, and I will do it, says the Lord (Ez. 37:1-14).

ALL KNEEL

Priest: Let us pray, asking the Lord that we may remain always open to the invasion of our life by the Spirit. Pause for personal prayer. You have been washed, you have been sanctified, you have been justified in the name of our Lord Jesus Christ, and in the Spirit of our God.

All: The spirit of the Lord God is upon me, / because the Lord has anointed me.

Priest: O my people! I will put my spirit in you that you may live.

All: The spirit of the Lord God is upon me, / because the Lord has anointed me.

Priest: You were sealed with the Holy Spirit of the promise.

All: The spirit of the Lord God is upon me, / because the Lord has anointed me.

Priest: Whoever are led by the Spirit of God, they are the sons of God.

All: The spirit of the Lord God is upon me, / because the Lord has anointed me.

Priest: I will give you a new heart and place a new spirit within you.

All: The spirit of the Lord God is upon me, / because the Lord has anointed me.

Priest: You shall live in the land I gave your fathers; you shall be my people and I will be your God.

All: The spirit of the Lord God is upon me, / because the Lord has anointed me.

Priest: Your light has come, the glory of the Lord shines upon you.

All: The spirit of the Lord God is upon me, / because the Lord has anointed me.

Priest: The Lord shall be your light forever, your God shall be your glory.

All: The spirit of the Lord God is upon me, / because the Lord has anointed me.

Priest: Behold, I make all things new!

All: The spirit of the Lord God is upon me, / because the Lord has anointed me.

ALL STAND

Hymn No. 268.

2. SPIRIT OF GOD, FILL US WITH YOUR LIFE

ALL SIT

Priest: The Spirit of the Lord gave life and power to the young Church at Pentecost. Let us listen to the reading from the Acts of the Apostles.

Reader: When the feast of Pentecost came, the disciples were all gathered in the same house. Suddenly there came from the sky a great noise, like that of a violent wind, and the whole house was filled with it.

What appeared to them then was like tongues of fire separating to take their places over each of them. At the same time they were all filled with the

Holy Spirit, and they began to speak various tongues, according to the inspiration they received from the Spirit.

Now on these festival days there were at Jerusalem devout Jews, who had come on pilgrimage from every nation under heaven. Attracted by the noise, a crowd of them gathered and stood there amazed, for each one of them heard the apostles speaking his own language.

In their astonishment and wonder they were saying, "These people who are speaking are all Galileans! Then how does it happen that each one of us hears them speaking his own native language? Whether we are Parthians, Medes or Elamites, whether we live in Mesopotamia, Judea or Cappadocia, on the shores of the Black Sea or in Asia, whether we come from Phrygia, Pamphylia, Egypt or Cyrenaic Libya, whether we are visitors from Rome, Jews, converts to Judaism, Cretans, Arabians — we hear them telling in our own languages of the great things God has done!"

And all were amazed and perplexed, asking one another, "What's the meaning of this?"

Some, however, laughed it off. "They're full of new wine," they said.

But Peter came forth with the eleven and, in a loud voice, addressed the crowd as follows:

"Men of Judea, and all you who live in Jerusalem, let this be known to you, and pay attention to what I say. No, these men are not drunk as you suppose. Why, it is only nine o'clock in the morning. But this is the prophecy of Joel being fulfilled:

" 'In the last days, says God, I will pour out my Spirit on all mankind. Then your sons and your daughters shall prophesy, your young men shall see visions, and your old men shall have dreams. Yes, on my servants and my handmaids I will pour out my Spirit in those days, and they shall prophesy. I will make prodigies appear in the heavens above, and signs on the earth below: blood, fire, clouds of smoke. The sun will grow dark, the moon will take on the color of blood, before the great day comes, the glorious day of the Lord. But whoever calls upon the name of the Lord shall be saved" (Acts 2:1-21).

ALL KNEEL

Priest: Let us pray that the Holy Spirit may come down upon us just as he came to renew the lives of the apostles. Pause for personal prayer. Lord, send us your Spirit and renew the face of the earth.

All: Spirit of God, Gift of God, / fill us with your life.

Priest: Come, Spirit of the new creation, make us into new men.

All: Spirit of God, Gift of God, / fill us with your life.

Priest: We call upon you by name: Helper of men, Source of new life, burning Fire within us!

All: Spirit of God, Gift of God, / fill us with your life.

Priest: Sevenfold Gift of God, be a new Light to our darkness.

All: Spirit of God, Gift of God, / fill us with your life.

Priest: Spirit of the love between us, pour your love into our hearts.

All: Spirit of God, Gift of God, / fill us with your life.

Priest: Give us, we pray you, new strength in our weakness.
All: Spirit of God, Gift of God, / fill us with your life.
Priest: Keep the enemy far from us; lead us to salvation.
All: Spirit of God, Gift of God, / fill us with your life.
Priest: Spirit of the promise, remain with us in peace all our days.
All: Spirit of God, Gift of God, / fill us with your life.

ALL STAND

Hymn No. 266.

3. PREFER DEEDS TO WORDS

Priest: Our risen Savior sends us his own Spirit to accomplish the renewal of our lives. The reading is from the Gospel according to St. John.
Reader: "If you love me, keep my commandments. And I will ask the Father and he will give you another Advocate to dwell with you forever, the Spirit of truth whom the world cannot receive, because it neither sees him nor knows him. But you shall know him, because he will dwell with you, and be in you" (John 14:15-17).

ALL SIT

The priest may now give a homily developing these points:

1. Our dry bones need to be brought to life, and so we must open ourselves to the Spirit who will renew us.

2. The presence of the Spirit in the Church, always at work there, provides us with a continually new Pentecost.

ALL KNEEL

Priest: Let us pray that we may always express in our actions the life of the Spirit within us. Pause for personal prayer.
     That we may be true sons of the Church in the Spirit of Christ—
All: Let us pray to the Lord.
Priest: That the Spirit of Christ make us a light to the world around us —
All: Let us pray to the Lord.
Priest: That the Spirit of Christ make us like a city on a mountain top —
All: Let us pray to the Lord.
Priest: That we might long for the unity of all men in the Spirit of Christ —
All: Let us pray to the Lord.
Priest: That our real love for one another be a sign to all men of the Spirit of Christ in our midst —
All: Let us pray to the Lord.
Priest: That we might not speak of possessing the truth until the truth has possessed us in the Spirit of Christ —
All: Let us pray to the Lord.
Priest: That we might have the maturity to begin tasks that are larger and longer than our lives, in the Spirit of Christ —
All: Let us pray to the Lord.

Priest: That we might prefer deeds to words, and our brothers to ourselves, in the Spirit of Christ —

All: Let us pray to the Lord.

Priest: Let us pray that the Spirit of the Lord take full possession of us.

Pause for personal prayer.

O Lord our God, we stand empty and poor in your sight. Look with mercy upon us, we pray you, and send us your Holy Spirit to renew our life and enrich us with his bright presence; through Christ our Lord.

All: I am about to create new heavens and a new earth; / the things of the past shall not be remembered or come to mind.

Priest: If the Spirit of him who raised Jesus from the dead dwells in you, then he who raised Jesus Christ from the dead will also bring to life your mortal bodies because of his Spirit who dwells in you.

All: I am about to create new heavens and a new earth; / the things of the past shall not be remembered or come to mind.

XII. VOCATION

Speak, Lord, for your servant is listening

ALL STAND

Entrance hymn, No. 132.

1. FOR VOCATIONS TO THE PRIESTHOOD

Priest: The call of Samuel as told in the first book of Kings may be understood as a type of the individual vocations to the priesthood of the New Law.

Reader: At that time, while the youth Samuel was minister to the Lord under Heli, a revelation of the Lord was uncommon and vision infrequent.

One day Heli was asleep in his usual place. His eyes had lately grown so weak that he could not see. The lamp of God was not yet extinguished, and Samuel was sleeping in the temple of the Lord, where the ark of God was. The Lord called to Samuel, who answered, "Here I am." He ran to Heli and said, "Here I am. You called me."

"I did not call you," Heli said. "Go back to sleep." So he went back to sleep.

Again the Lord called Samuel, who rose and went to Heli. "Here I am," he said. "You called me."

But he answered, "I did not call you, my son. Go back to sleep." At that time Samuel was not familiar with the Lord, because the Lord had not revealed anything to him yet.

The Lord called Samuel again, for the third time. Getting up and going to Heli, he said, "Here I am. You called me."

Then Heli realized that the Lord was calling the youth. So he said to Samuel, "Go to sleep, and if you are called, reply, 'Speak, Lord, for your servant is listening.'"

When Samuel went to sleep in his place, the Lord came and revealed his presence, calling out as before, "Samuel, Samuel!"

Samuel answered, "Speak, for your servant is listening" (1 Kings 3:1-10)

ALL KNEEL

Prayer of Pope Pius XII for Priestly Vocations:

Priest: Christ Jesus, in your merciful love you are mindful of the miseries of men. You hear their plea for leaders to guide them along the rough ways of this earth to light and life.

All: Send to those men who are yours / priests garbed in justice / for the joy of your devoted souls.

Priest: Set up as models all those to whom you have entrusted this lofty and exalted office of truth.

All: Enlighten their spirits / to recognize the priceless grace of your calling. / Make their wills strong / that they might overcome worldly allurements.

Priest: Do not let them shrink from sacrifice. Through acceptance of the Cross, let them rise to Calvary's heights.

All: Let their parents realize / how great and beautiful it is / to give their sons to you.

Priest: Inspire noble souls with the willingness to assist financially those whom poverty would prevent from following your call.

All: Grant that their teachers and professors / carefully foster your calling, / until the day when they ascend your altar / with zealous, love-filled hearts.

Priest: Above all, good Jesus, grant that they may be holy guides for your holy people:

All: Men who prefer God's love to man's;

Priest: Men of love, who renounce the joys of an earthly family,

All: To father the parish family, / who give their love to the poor and weak, / to those suffering and sinned against;

Priest: Men of light,

All: Who, beacon-like, / bring the light of faith / to human hearts;

Priest: Men of sacrifice,

All: Who willingly walk an added mile / to aid a brother, / white or colored, / foreigner or friend;

Priest: Men of counsel and strength,

All: Eager to listen, / wise in words, / schooled in patience;

Priest: Men of grace,

All: To purify and ennoble;

Priest: Men of peace, who at the last moments of life inspire delightful longing and love for you, who send souls home to the blessed embrace of your peace;

All: Who open the gates of heaven, / where you will be the unending light and everlasting joy / of all hearts eternally. Amen.

ALL STAND

Hymn No. 260.

2. FOR VOCATIONS TO THE RELIGIOUS LIFE

Priest: A few words of Christ recorded in the Gospel according to St. Luke show the complete renunciation of the world that is required for the religious life.

Reader: As Jesus and his disciples were going along the road, a man said to him, "I will follow you wherever you go."

Jesus answered him, "The foxes have holes, and the birds of the sky have nests, but the Son of Man has nowhere to lay his head."

To another man he said, "Follow me."

He replied, "Let me first go and bury my father."

Jesus answered, "Let the dead bury their own dead; but you, come, proclaim the kingdom of God."

Another man said to him, "Lord, I will follow you; but first let me take leave of those at home."

Jesus said to him in reply, "No one who puts his hand to the plow and then looks back is fit for the kingdom of God" (Luke 9:57-62).

ALL KNEEL

Priest: Look down from heaven, Lord, and see.

All: Take care of this vine, / and protect what your right hand has planted.

Priest: Behold, how good it is, and how pleasant, where brethren dwell at one!

All: For there the Lord has pronounced his blessing.

Priest: O Lord, my heart is not proud nor are my eyes haughty;

All: I busy not myself with great things, / nor with things too sublime for me.

Priest: Nay rather, I have stilled and quieted my soul, like a weaned child on its mother's lap: so is my soul within me.

All: O Israel, hope in the Lord, / both now and forever.

Priest: Who can ascend the mountain of the Lord? Or who may stand in his holy place?

All: He whose hands are sinless, / whose heart is clean,

Priest: Who desires not what is vain, nor swears deceitfully to his neighbor.

All: He shall receive a blessing from the Lord, / and a reward from God his Savior.

Priest: Happy they who dwell in your house, O Lord! Continually they praise you.

All: Break forth in blossoms and yield a smell. / And bring forth leaves in grace. / And praise with canticles, / and bless the Lord in his works.

Priest: Let us pray. Pause for personal prayer.

Look down with kindness on your family, Lord, and keep adding new offspring to it. May the various religious communities of your Church guide their children to the goals of holiness they have set for themselves, and make them at the same time a powerful instrument for the salvation of others. Through Christ our Lord.

All: Amen.

ALL STAND

Hymn No. 75.

3. FOR THE LAY LIFE

ALL SIT

Priest: In his first letter to the Corinthians and in his letter to the Ephesians, St. Paul stresses the diversity of members in the Mystical Body of Christ.

Reader: The body is not one member, but many. If the foot says, "Because I am not a hand, I am not of the body," is it therefore not of the body? And if the ear says, "Because I am not an eye, I am not of the body," is it therefore not of the body?

If the whole body were an eye, where would be the hearing? If the whole body were hearing, where would be the smelling? But as it is, God has set the members, each of them, in the body as he willed. Now if they were all one member, where would the body be? But as it is, they are indeed many members, yet but one body. And the eye cannot say to the hand, "I don't need your help"; nor again the head to the feet, "I have no need of you."

Each one of us has received grace, in the measure in which Christ has seen fit to grant it to him. As the psalm says, "Ascending to the heights, with captives in his train, he loaded men with gifts."

The expression "He ascended" indicates that he had previously descended to this world below; but he who had descended is the same one who has ascended beyond all the heavens, in order to fill us all with his gifts.

He it is who has made some apostles, some prophets, others again evangelists, or pastors and teachers of the faith, organizing the faithful in this way, with consummate wisdom, that they may work at this great task: the building of the body of Christ. This continues until all of us together come to be one in the faith and in the knowledge of the Son of God, until all together constitute that complete man, that man in all his maturity, who embodies the fullness of Christ (1 Cor. 12:14-21; Eph. 4:7-13).

The priest may now give a homily developing these points:

1. St. Paul's teaching on the diversity of members may be applied not only to the callings he mentions, which pertain mostly to the priesthood and the religious life, but also to marriage, the single life in the world, and the various professions and occupations of lay people.

2. All are called to work at building the Body of Christ through their priesthood, through their religious life, through their marriage, through their single state, through their occupation.

ALL KNEEL

Priest: Provident Father, by your call and by the breathing of the Spirit, give us the members we need to build up the Body of your Son, Jesus Christ.

That we may have priests who are instruments of your love,

All: Please grant our petition.

Priest: That we may have religious, contemplative and active, to pray and work for our sanctification,

All: Please grant our petition.

Priest: That we may have missionaries, clerical, religious and lay, zealous to spread your kingdom throughout the world,

All: Please grant our petition.

Priest: That we may have teachers and writers devoted to improving the mind by which man resembles you,

All: Please grant our petition.

Priest: That we may have government officials and civil servants working always for the common good of our country and of the world,

All: Please grant our petition.

Priest: That we may have lawyers who aim to be successful only by making justice prevail,

All: Please grant our petition.

Priest: That we may have doctors and nurses who strive to heal the body for the sake of the whole man created in your image,

All: Please grant our petition.

Priest: That we may have farmers and fishermen to provide us and all the world with good food to sustain a worthy human life,

All: Please grant our petition.

Priest: That we may have men in trade and business who place honesty and human dignity above selfish gain and greed,

All: Please grant our petition.

Priest: That we may have workers who shape the things of your creation for the proper use of men,

All: Please grant our petition.

Priest: That we may have workers who serve other persons in a spirit of love, seeing Christ in all,

All: Please grant our petition.

Priest: That we may have husbands and wives, fathers and mothers who make their marriage and their family life a way leading to heaven,

All: Please grant our petition.

Priest: You sons of men, bless the Lord.

All: Praise and exalt him above all forever.

Priest: Priests of the Lord, bless the Lord.

All: Praise and exalt him above all forever.

Priest: Servants of the Lord, bless the Lord.

All: Praise and exalt him above all forever.

Priest: Spirits and souls of the just, bless the Lord.

All: Praise and exalt him above all forever.

Priest: Holy men of humble heart, bless the Lord.
  All: Praise and exalt him above all forever.
Priest: Let us bless the Father and the Son and the Holy Spirit.
  All: Let us praise and exalt God above all forever.
ALL STAND
Final hymn, No. 135.

XIII. SIN

The wages of sin is death

ALL STAND
Entrance hymn, No. 136.

1. SIN, A REFUSAL TO LOVE

ALL SIT
Priest: The great mystery of God's plan for us is not an impersonal and mechanically conceived blueprint, without life and affection. Nothing could be further from the truth. God's plan is a loving invitation to share his life, offered in terms of love and seeking a response of love from us.

Only by understanding that God is love can we fully understand the meaning of sin. Sin means the refusal of God's love. When we sin, we reject the life of love that we share in the Church, united with Christ and our brothers. Sin makes us an island: it cuts us off from life; it puts us to death. God has given us everything. He has given us his Son — and still we resist him!

ALL STAND
  All: Have mercy on me, O God, in your goodness;
       in the greatness of your compassion wipe out my offense.
Priest: O my people, what have I done to you,
       or how have I wearied you? Answer me!
  All: Have mercy on me, O God, in your goodness;
       in the greatness of your compassion wipe out my offense.
ALL SIT
Priest: Let us listen to the account of man's first sin, which has been passed on to all of us. The reading is from the book of Genesis.
Reader: Now the serpent was more cunning than any beast of the field which the Lord God had made. He said to the woman, "Did God say, 'You shall not eat of any tree of the garden'?"

The woman answered the serpent, "Of the fruit of all the trees in the garden we may eat; but 'Of the fruit of the tree in the middle of the garden,' God said 'you shall not eat, neither shall you touch it, lest you die.'"

But the serpent said to the woman, "No, you shall not die; for God knows that when you eat of it, your eyes will be opened and you will be like God, knowing good and evil."

Now the woman saw that the tree was good for food, pleasing to the eyes, and desirable for the knowledge it would give. She took of its fruit and ate it, and also gave some to her husband and he ate. Then the eyes of both were opened, and they realized that they were naked; so they sewed fig-leaves together and made themselves coverings.

When they heard the sound of the Lord God walking in the garden in the cool of the day, the man and his wife hid themselves from the Lord God among the trees of the garden. But the Lord God called the man and said to him, "Where are you?"

And he said, "I heard you in the garden, and I was afraid because I was naked; and I hid."

Then he said, "Who told you that you were naked? You have eaten then of the tree of which I commanded you not to eat."

The man said, "The woman you placed at my side gave me fruit from the tree and I ate."

Then the Lord God said to the woman, "Why have you done this?"

The woman said, "The serpent deceived me and I ate" (Gen. 3:1-13).

ALL KNEEL

Priest: Let us pray, asking God for the light to see how sin has brought us to ruin. Pause for personal prayer.

> Does any other nation change its gods? —
> yet they are not gods at all!
> But my people have changed their glory
> for useless things.

All: I acknowledge my offense, / and my sin is before me always.

Priest: O Lord, in your anger punish me not, in your wrath chastise me not.

All: I acknowledge my offense, / and my sin is before me always.

Priest: There is no health in my flesh because of your indignation; there is no wholeness in my bones because of my sins.

All: I acknowledge my offense, / and my sin is before me always.

Priest: For my iniquities have overwhelmed me; they are like a heavy burden, beyond my strength.

All: I acknowledge my offense, / and my sin is before me always.

Priest: I am stooped and bowed down profoundly; all the day I go in mourning.

All: I acknowledge my offense, / and my sin is before me always.

Priest: I am numbed and severely crushed; I roar with anguish of heart.

All: I acknowledge my offense, / and my sin is before me always.

Priest: My heart throbs; my strength forsakes me; the very light of my eyes has failed me.

All: I acknowledge my offense, / and my sin is before me always.

ALL STAND

Hymn No. 260.

2. HAVE MERCY ON ME, LORD

All SIT

Priest: The mystery of God's love for us completely escapes our human understanding. Let us listen to the propecy of Isaias, who tells us how Christ takes our sins on himself and suffers on our behalf.

Reader: There was in him no stately bearing to make us look at him,
   nor appearance that would attract us to him.
He was spurned and avoided by men.
   a man of suffering, accustomed to infirmity,
One of those from whom men hide their faces,
   spurned, and we held him in no esteem.
Yet it was our infirmities that he bore,
   our sufferings that he endured,
While we thought of him as stricken,
   as one smitten by God and afflicted.
But he was pierced for our offenses,
   crushed for our sins;
Upon him was the chastisement that makes us whole,
   by his stripes we were healed.
We had all gone astray like sheep,
   each following his own way;
But the Lord laid upon him
   the guilt of us all.
Though he was harshly treated, he submitted
   and opened not his mouth;
Like a lamb led to the slaughter
   or a sheep before the shearers,
   he was silent and opened not his mouth.
Oppressed and condemned, he was taken away,
   and who would have thought any more of his destiny?
When he was cut off from the land of the living,
   and smitten for the sin of his people,
A grave was assigned him among the wicked
   and a burial place with evildoers,
Though he had done no wrong
   nor spoken any falsehood (Is. 53:2-9).

ALL KNEEL

Priest: Let us pray, begging God our Lord to give us a deep sense of shame and sorrow because we have offended him so grievously. Pause for personal prayer.

   "Come, all you who pass by the way,
    look and see
   Whether there is any suffering like my suffering,
    which has been dealt me
   When the Lord afflicted me
    on the day of his blazing wrath."

All: What is man that you should be mindful of him,
   or the son of man that you should care for him?

Priest: The favors of the Lord are not exhausted,
         his mercies are not spent.
All: What is man that you should be mindful of him,
         or the son of man that you should care for him?
Priest: I have waited, waited for the Lord,
         and he stooped toward me and heard my cry.
All: What is man that you should be mindful of him,
         or the son of man that you should care for him?
Priest: Many shall look on in awe
         and trust in the Lord.
All: What is man that you should be mindful of him,
         or the son of man that you should care for him?
Priest: For all about me are evils beyond reckoning;
         my sins so overcome me that I cannot see.
All: What is man that you should be mindful of him,
         or the son of man that you should care for him?
Priest: Though I am afflicted and poor,
         yet the Lord thinks of me.
All: What is man that you should be mindful of him,
         or the son of man that you should care for him?

ALL STAND
Hymn No. 142.

3. FORGIVE US OUR TRESPASSES

ALL STAND

Priest: We learn the full extent and malice of our sin in the presence of our crucified Lord. Let us listen to St. Luke's account of the crucifixion of Christ.

Reader: When they arrived at the place called the Skull, they crucified him there, and the criminals, one on his right, the other on his left. And Jesus was saying, "Father, forgive them; they do not know what they are doing." They made a division of his clothes and drew lots for them.

And the people were there, looking on. Their leaders kept scoffing, "He saved others. Let him save himself if he is the Messiah, God's chosen one!" The soldiers kept making fun of him too. They would offer him vinegar to drink, saying, "If you're the King of the Jews, then save yourself!"

Over his head there was an inscription written in Greek, Latin and Hebrew characters: "The King of the Jews."

One of the crucified criminals insulted him: "If you're the Messiah, save yourself, and us with you."

But the other one rebuked him: "Have you no fear of God? We're condemned to the same punishment, and for us it's a just one: we're paying for what we've done. But this man— he's done nothing wrong." And he said to Jesus, "Lord, remember me when you come into the glory of your kingdom!"

And Jesus answered, "Truly, I tell you, this very day you shall be with me in paradise" (Luke 23:33-43).

ALL SIT

The priest may now give a homily developing the following points:

1. The enormity of man's sin is revealed by a consideration of the sufferings which Christ our Lord endured.

2. The same consideration of the suffering Christ shows forth the mercy and love which God has for us.

ALL KNEEL

Priest: Let us pray, begging God for the grace to despise all our sins and for the strength to avoid offending him again. Pause for personal prayer. As obedient children, do not conform to the lusts of former days when you were ignorant; but as the one who called you is holy, be you also holy in all your behavior; for it is written, "You shall be holy, because I am holy."

All: Lord, make us holy as you are holy.

Priest: Take heed, brethren, lest perhaps there be in any of you an evil, unbelieving heart that would turn away from the living God.

All: Lord, make us holy as you are holy.

Priest: If anyone does not abide in me, he shall be cast outside as the branch and wither; and they shall gather them up and cast them into the fire, and they shall burn.

All: Lord, make us holy as you are holy.

Priest: It is a fearful thing to fall into the hands of the living God.

All: Lord, make us holy as you are holy.

Priest: For it is better, if the will of God should so will, that you suffer for doing good than for doing evil. Because Christ also died once for sins, the just for the unjust, that he might bring us to God.

All: Lord, make us holy as you are holy.

Priest: Since Christ therefore has suffered in the flesh, do you also arm yourselves with the same intent.

All: Lord, make us holy as you are holy.

Priest: Let us pray, asking God for the grace of lasting fidelity to his invitation of love. Pause for personal prayer.

O God our Lord, you created us out of nothingness and formed us anew by the sacrificial death and resurrection of your Son. Grant, we pray you, that, transformed by the life of your grace, we may leave aside forever the sinful wanderings of past days and remain always faithful to our holy vocation in Christ Jesus our Lord.

All: Amen! Have mercy on me, O God, in your goodness;
in the greatness of your compassion wipe out my offense.

Priest: O my people, what have I done to you, or how have I wearied you? Answer me!

All: Have mercy on me, O God, in your goodness;
in the greatness of your compassion wipe out my offense.

XIV. PENANCE
Out of the depths I cry to you, O Lord

ALL STAND

Entrance hymn, No. 147.

1. I WILL GET UP AND GO TO MY FATHER

ALL SIT

Priest: By our sin, we have rejected God's love for us and turned our backs to his invitation to share in his own divine life. But we are not without hope, for our God is a God of mercy.

Though our sin has made us dead men, alien to God and to the family and household of our brothers in the Church, God does not give us up. In the sacrament of penance, the Lord returns our lost life to us; we are reconciled to him and to our brother members of Christ's Body, the Church. Let us open our hearts to the word which the Lord speaks to us today: it is a message of mercy and pardon.

ALL STAND

All: I will get up and go to my father, / and will say to him: / Father, I have sinned against heaven and before you. / I am no longer worthy to be called your son.

Priest: But to the penitent he provides a way back, he encourages those who are losing hope! Return to the Lord and give up sin, pray to him and make your offenses few.

All: I will get up and go to my father, / and will say to him: / Father, I have sinned against heaven and before you. / I am no longer worthy to be called your son.

ALL SIT

Priest: Let us listen to the book of Wisdom, where we are told of the Lord's loving mercy for sinners.

Reader: And in return for their senseless, wicked thoughts, which misled them into worshiping dumb serpents and worthless insects,

You sent upon them swarms of dumb creatures for vengeance, that they might recognize that a man is punished by the very things through which he sins.

For not without means was your almighty hand, that had fashioned the universe from formless matter, to send upon them a drove of bears or fierce lions,

Or new-created, wrathful, unknown beasts to breathe forth fiery breath,

Or pour out roaring smoke, or flash terrible sparks from their eyes.

Not only could these attack and completely destroy them; even their frightful appearance itself could slay.

Even without these, they could have been killed at a single blast, pursued by retribution and winnowed out by your mighty spirit;

But you have disposed all things by measure and number and weight.

For with you great strength abides always; who can resist the might of your arm?

Indeed, before you the whole universe is as a grain from a balance, or a drop of morning dew come down upon the earth.

But you have mercy on all, because you can do all things; and you overlook the sins of men that they may repent.

For you love all things that are and loathe nothing that you have made; for what you hated, you would not have fashioned.

And how could a thing remain, unless you willed it; or be preserved, had it not been called forth by you?

But you spare all things, because they are yours, O Lord and lover of souls, for your imperishable spirit is in all things!

Therefore you rebuke offenders little by little, warn them, and remind them of the sins they are committing, that they may abandon their wickedness and believe in you, O Lord! (Wis. 11:15–12:2).

ALL KNEEL

Priest: Let us pray that the God of such great mercy will have mercy on us! Pause for personal prayer.

Help us, O God our Savior, because of the glory of your name;
Deliver us and pardon our sins for your name's sake.

All: Out of the depths I cry to you, O Lord;
Lord, hear my voice!

Priest: Yet even now, says the Lord,
return to me with your whole heart,
with fasting, and weeping, and mourning.

All: Out of the depths I cry to you, O Lord;
Lord, hear my voice!

Priest: Rend your hearts, not your garments,
and return to the Lord, your God.

All: Out of the depths I cry to you, O Lord;
Lord, hear my voice!

Priest: For gracious and merciful is he,
slow to anger, rich in kindness,
and relenting in punishment.

All: Out of the depths I cry to you, O Lord;
Lord, hear my voice!

Priest: Perhaps he will again relent
and leave behind him a blessing.

All: Out of the depths I cry to you, O Lord;
Lord, hear my voice!

Priest: I trust in the Lord;
my soul trusts in his word.

All: Glory be to the Father, and to the Son, and to the Holy Spirit, as it was in the beginning, is now, and ever shall be, world without end. Amen!

ALL STAND

Hymn No. 262.

2. I CONFESS THAT I HAVE SINNED

ALL SIT

Priest: Let us listen to St. John, who tells us that sin not only disrupts our union of love with God but also destroys the fellowship of love that we share with all the members of Christ's Body, the Church. Christ will free us from our sin, if we turn to him.

Reader: The message which we have heard from him and announce to you, is this: that God is light, and in him is no darkness. If we say that we have fellowship with him, and walk in darkness, we lie, and are not practicing the truth. But if we walk in the light as he also is in the light, we have fellowship with one another, and the Blood of Jesus Christ, his Son, cleanses us from all sin.

If we say that we have no sin, we deceive ourselves, and the truth is not in us. If we acknowledge our sins, he is faithful and just to forgive us our sins and to cleanse us from all iniquity. If we say that we have not sinned, we make him a liar, and his word is not in us.

My dear children, these things I write to you in order that you may not sin. But if anyone sins, we have an advocate with the Father, Jesus Christ the just; and he is propitiation for our sins, not for ours only but also for those of the whole world (1 John 1:5–2:2).

ALL KNEEL

Priest: Let us pray, acknowledging our guilt before God and our brothers in the Church. Pause for personal prayer.

  Can a mother forget her infant,
   be without tenderness for the child of her womb?
  Even should she forget, I will never forget you.
  See, upon the palms of my hands I have written your name.

All: I confess to almighty God that I have sinned.
  I confess to the Virgin Mary that I have sinned.
  I confess to the angels of God that I have sinned.
  I confess to John the Baptist that I have sinned.
  I confess to Peter and Paul that I have sinned.
  I confess to the holy Church that I have sinned.
  I confess to you, my brothers in Christ, that I have sinned.
  I confess to myself that I have sinned.

ALL STAND
Hymn No. 81.

3. MY SON HAS COME TO LIFE AGAIN

Priest: Let us hear now the beautiful story of the prodigal son, as recorded by St. Luke.

Reader: Jesus proposed this parable: "A man had two sons. The younger one said to his father, 'Father, give me the share of the estate that I have coming to me.' And the father divided his property between them. A few days later, having got all that was coming to him, this younger son went off to a distant country and wasted his fortune by living extravagantly.

"He had spent everything when a desperate famine swept over that land, and the hard days began for him. He hired himself out to one of the citizens of that country, who sent him to his farm to feed the pigs. He would have been glad to stuff himself with the husks that the swine were feeding on, but there were none for him.

"Looking into himself, then, he thought: How many hired hands at my father's house have all the bread they want, while I am dying here of hunger! My resolution is made; I will return to my father and say to him, 'Father, I have sinned against heaven and against you; I no longer deserve to be called your son; treat me like one of your hired hands.'

"He set out, therefore, and returned to his father.

"While he was still at a distance, his father caught sight of him. Overcome with emotion, he ran to meet him, fell upon his neck and kissed him. Then the son began, 'Father, I have sinned against heaven and against you; I no longer deserve to be called your son —'

"But the father said to the servants, 'Quick! Bring the finest clothes and put them on him, slip a ring on his finger and put shoes on his feet. Kill the fattened calf, let us eat and celebrate. This son of mine was dead, and here he is alive; he was lost, and now he is found!'

"And they began to have a feast" (Luke 15:11-24).

ALL SIT

The priest may now give a homily, developing the following points:

1. Repentance is first of all the work of God; we are able to return to him only because God gives us the grace to do so.

2. Pardon for our sins means reconciliation with God and reconciliation with our brothers; once more we may live the life of the Church and share fully in the sacrifice which she offers.

ALL KNEEL

Priest: Let us pray, asking God our Lord that he will accept our plea for forgiveness. Pause for personal prayer.

This my son was dead, and has come to life again; he was lost, and is found.

All: If you allow me, I will return,
    for you are the Lord, my God.

Priest: Give thanks to the Lord, for he is good,
    for his kindness endures forever.

All: If you allow me, I will return,
    for you are the Lord, my God.

Priest: Happy are they who observe what is right,
    who do always what is just.

All: If you allow me, I will return,
    for you are the Lord, my God.

Priest: We have sinned, we and our fathers;
    we have committed crimes; we have done wrong.

All: If you allow me, I will return,
    for you are the Lord, my God.

Priest: And the Lord grew angry with his people,
        and abhorred his inheritance.
  All: If you allow me, I will return,
        for you are the Lord, my God.
Priest: Yet he had regard for their affliction
        when he heard their cry.
  All: If you allow me, I will return,
        for you are the Lord, my God.
Priest: And for their sake he was mindful of his covenant
        and relented, in his abundant kindness.
  All: Save us, O Lord our God,
        and gather us from among the nations,
     That we may give thanks to your holy name
        and glory in praising you.
Priest: We have wandered far from our Father's house. Let us pray that we may be attentive to his invitation to return. Pause for personal prayer.

O Lord our God, in your loving mercy you overlook our sins and call us to return to share your life. Grant, we beg you, that, strengthened by your grace, we may rise up from our death of sin and remain always devoted to your holy will; through Christ our Lord.

  All: Amen! I will get up and go to my father, / and will say to him: / Father, I have sinned against heaven and before you. / I am no longer worthy to be called your son.

Priest: But to the penitent he provides a way back, he encourages those who are losing hope! Return to the Lord and give up sin, pray to him and make your offenses few.

  All: I will get up and go to my father, / and will say to him: / Father, I have sinned against heaven and before you. / I am no longer worthy to be called your son.

XV. FOR THE NEEDS OF MEN
Our help is in the name of the Lord

ALL STAND
Entrance hymn, No. 263.

1. FOR THE SICK AND SUFFERING

ALL SIT
Priest: That God has a special love toward the sick and suffering is evident in many, many passages of the Bible. Psalm after psalm voices the gratitude of persons upon receiving the healing power of God. From the book of Isaias we have this account of the sickness and recovery of King Ezechias.

Reader: In those days, when Ezechias was mortally ill, the prophet Isaias, son of Amos, came and said to him: "Thus says the Lord: Put your house in order, for you are about to die; you shall not recover."

Then Ezechias turned his face to the wall and prayed to the Lord: "O

Lord, remember how faithfully and wholeheartedly I conducted myself in your presence, doing what was pleasing to you!" And Ezechias wept bitterly.

Then the word of the Lord came to Isaias: "Go, tell Ezechias: Thus says the Lord, the God of your father David: I have heard your prayer and seen your tears. I will heal you: in three days you shall go up to the Lord's temple; I will add fifteen years to your life. I will rescue you and this city from the hand of the king of Assyria; I will be a shield to this city."

Isaias then ordered a poultice of figs to be taken and applied to the boil, that he might recover. Then Ezechias asked, "What is the sign that I shall go up to the temple of the Lord?"

Isaias answered: "This will be the sign for you from the Lord that he will do what he has promised: See, I will make the shadow cast by the sun on the stairway to the terrace of Achaz go back the ten steps it has advanced."

So the sun came back the ten steps it had advanced (Is. 38:1-8).

ALL KNEEL

Priest: Our help is in the name of the Lord,
   All: Who made heaven and earth.
Priest: We must glory in the Cross of our Lord Jesus Christ,
   All: In whom is our salvation, / our life, and our resurrection.
Priest: It is through the cross of sickness and suffering
   All: That we most surely become identified with the power of Christ on Calvary.
Priest: It was through the Cross that Christ entered into his glory.
   All: It is through the cross of suffering that we share that glory.
Priest: Steadfastly our Savior set his face to go up to Jerusalem and his sacred passion.
   All: Give to us and to your sick, O Lord, / the grace of patient endurance.
Priest: Through pain and suffering we fulfill most perfectly these words of Christ:
   All: Take up your cross and follow me.
Priest: Our consolation is that the sufferings of this time cannot be compared with the glory that awaits us.
   All: No eye has seen, nor ear heard, / nor has it entered into the heart of man, / what God has prepared for those who love him.
Priest: Let us pray. O Lord God, you said through your apostle James: "Is anyone sick among you? Let him bring in the priests of the Church, and let them pray over him, anointing him with oil in the name of the Lord. And the prayer of faith will save the sick man, and the Lord will raise him up, and if he be in sins, they shall be forgiven him."

We implore you, our Redeemer, that by the grace of the Holy Spirit you cure the illness of our sick and heal their wounds; forgive their sins, and drive away from them all pains of mind and body. In your mercy give them health, inward and outward, so that they may once more be able to take up their work, restored by the gift of your mercy. You who live and reign with the Father and the Holy Spirit, God, for ever and ever.

All: Amen.

ALL STAND
Hymn No. 265.

2. PETITIONS FOR OUR PERSONAL NEEDS

ALL SIT

Priest: The letter of St. James reminds us that when we ask for rain or sun as the prophets did, these material goods are to be related to spiritual progress.

Reader: Confess your sins to one another, and pray for one another, that you may be healed.

For it is very powerful, the fervent prayer of the just man. Look at the prophet Elias. He was a man like us, subject to the same miseries. He prayed that it might not rain; and for three and a half years there was no rain in that land. He prayed again, and the sky gave rain and the earth gave its fruits.

My brethren, if one of you strays from the truth and another brings him back, be assured that he who brings back a sinner to the right way will save that man's soul from death and will cover a multitude of sins (James 5:16-20).

ALL KNEEL

Priest: Lord, have mercy on us.

All: Christ, have mercy on us.

Priest: Lord, have mercy on us. Christ, hear us.

All: Christ, graciously hear us.

Priest: God, Father of heaven,   All: Have mercy on us.
God the Son, Redeemer of the world,
God the Holy Spirit,
Holy Trinity, one God,
God, in whom we live, move, and have our being,
You have created the heavens, land, and seas,
You have ordered all things according to their
    size, number and weight,
You hold the heavens in your hand, you have set
    shores about the seas,
You fashion all things in the wisdom of your will,
Almighty and all-wise God,
You open your hand to fill all living things with
    blessings,
You let your sun shine on good and evil men,
You send rain on the just and sinners,
You feed the birds of the air and clothe the lilies
    of the field,
All-good and merciful God,

You turn all things to good for those who love you,
You send trials to test and improve us,
You heal the sick and comfort the broken-hearted,
You reward Christian patience with profound joy,
Father of mercy and God of all consolation,

Priest: Be merciful,
All: Spare us, O Lord.
Priest: Be merciful,
All: Hear us, O Lord.

Priest: From all evil,   All: Deliver us, O Lord.
From all sin,
From your anger,
From pestilence, hunger, and war,
From lightning and tempests,
From hail and cloudbursts,
From crop-failure and famine,
From murmuring and complaints against your holy
    decrees,
From meanness and impatience,
From the spirit of discrimination,
From undue concern for temporal things,
From misuse of your gifts and benefits,
From lack of love toward our neighbor races,
On the day of judgment,

Priest: We are poor sinners,   All: Please grant our petition.
That we may always trust in your divine
    providence,
That we may not become insolent in good fortune
    and despairing in misfortune,
That we may obey promptly all your designs,
That we may praise your name, whether you give
    or take away,
That you give us what we need for sustaining life,
That you bless our toil and labor,
That you grant us strength and patience in all
    adversities,
That you lead us to improve our lives through trials,
That you grant us eternal joys for present pain and
    grief,

Priest: Lamb of God, you take away the sins of the world,
All: Spare us, O Lord.
Priest: Lamb of God, you take away the sins of the world,
All: Hear us, O Lord.
Priest: Lamb of God, you take away the sins of the world,
All: Have mercy on us.
Priest: Christ, hear us.
All: Christ, graciously hear us.

Priest: Come to our aid, strong God and Lord:
All: Show us your face, and we shall be saved.
Priest: Let us pray. Pause for personal prayer.

God, from you come all good things. Graciously grant that through your inspiration we may recognize what is right, and accomplish it with your help. Almighty God, we beg you to aid us, that in all our work we may trust in your goodness, and through your protection, be secure in all adversities. O God, your providence is unfailing in its accomplishments; we humbly beg you to turn away all harm from us, and impart to us all good, through Christ our Lord.

All: Amen.

ALL STAND
Hymn No. 148.

3. PETITIONS FOR OUR PEOPLE AND COUNTRY

Priest: In the Gospel according to St. Luke, Christ himself tells us how to make our prayers of petition.
Reader: Jesus said to his disciples, "Suppose that one of you goes to find a friend in the middle of the night and says to him, 'My friend, lend me three loaves of bread. Someone has come to see me, and I have nothing to offer him.' And this answer comes to you from within: 'Don't bother me. The door is barred; my children and I are in bed; I can't get up to give you anything.' Let me tell you, keep knocking on the door. If friendship does not prompt him to get up, your insistence will, and, to have some peace for himself, he will give you everything you need.

"Thus, I tell you: Ask and you shall receive, seek and you shall find, knock and it shall be opened to you. For he who asks, receives; he who seeks, finds; he who knocks, sees the door open up for him.

"What father among you, when his son asks him for bread, gives him a stone? or, when his son asks him for fish, gives him a serpent? or, when his son asks him for an egg, gives him a scorpion? If you, therefore, evil as you are, know how to give your children what is good, with how much more reason you can expect that your Father in heaven will give the Holy Spirit to those who ask him!" (Luke 11:5-13).

ALL SIT
The priest may now give a homily developing the following points:

1. God is our Father. Let us address our petitions to him trustingly and insistently.

2. But let us not forget that he knows better than we what is good, and that the only true good is the Holy Spirit.

ALL KNEEL
Priest: Provident God, humbly but with great trust we come to you to pray for our people and country.

That you maintain our people in your grace,
All: Please grant our petition.

Priest: That you bring back the many who have wandered from the way of salvation to the truth of the faith and the observance of your commandments,

All: Please grant our petition.

Priest: That you continue to give our country an honored place among the nations of the world,

All: Please grant our petition.

Priest: That you give us men who will lead our people with true wisdom and strength,

All: Please grant our petition.

Priest: That you free us from worry and distress,

All: Please grant our petition.

Priest: That you further social justice to its fullness among our people,

All: Please grant our petition.

Priest: That you overcome all class distinctions through the Spirit of your love,

All: Please grant our petition.

Priest: That you bless our farms and factories, wherever we work, and our culture,

All: Please grant our petition.

Priest: That you detach men from greed for money and positions,

All: Please grant our petition.

Priest: That you give light and comfort to the many who suffer from age, sickness and disease,

All: Please grant our petition.

Priest: That you prepare our young people for suitable and worthwhile careers,

All: Please grant our petition.

Priest: That you guard our people from doing injustice,

All: Please grant our petition.

Priest: That you grant your peace to all peoples on earth,

All: Please grant our petition.

Priest: That you give your eternal peace to all our many departed,

All: Please grant our petition.

Priest: Bless, O Lord, our people, that they may always fulfill your will for their true welfare, for the good of other peoples, and for the glory of your name — you who live and reign eternally.

All: Amen.

ALL STAND

Hymn No. 276.

ALL KNEEL

If there is Benediction of the Blessed Sacrament, the following prayers may be said after the hymn of exposition.

Priest: Strong God of eternity, Lord and Father in heaven! See our need, our misery; look upon our distress with the eyes of your boundless mercy.

All: Have mercy on your people.

Priest: Merciful Father, spare us from further well-deserved punishments, present and future dangers, social turmoil, sadness and sickness and worry, troubled and needy times.

All: Strengthen our parishes and pastors in your Spirit / and bless their work for peace and harmony among men.

Priest: We beg you, Lord, take our country under your continued protection. Endow our leaders with insight and sympathy.

All: Make them realize what promotes the moral welfare of the people, / and let them accomplish what is right / with your help.

Priest: Enkindle in us zeal for your love.

All: Make us sensitive to justice, / zealous for social improvements, / that, as your people, / we may witness genuinely to the gospel ideals.

Priest: Therefore, too, we pray for our enemies and friends, for sinners and the sick, for the mentally ill, for those suffering in our hospitals, for those detained in purgatory.

All: O Lord, may all our deeds and omissions, our works and projects, our life and death / be always dedicated to you.

Priest: Earnestly we seek your grace,

All: That both now and ever, with all the elect, / we may praise, honor and glorify you, in blessedness and deepest joy.

Priest: Grant us this, Lord, Father in heaven.

All: Through Jesus Christ, your Son, / our Lord and Savior, / who lives and reigns with you and the Holy Spirit / equally as God, forever. Amen.

ALL STAND
Final hymn, No. 66.

XVI. FOR THE FAITHFUL DEPARTED
Eternal rest grant unto them, O Lord

ALL STAND
Entrance hymn, page 330.

1. HE WHO HAS FAITH IN ME SHALL LIVE

ALL SIT
Priest: At the period of the Machabees, in the course of the persecutions they had to undergo, the Jews, inspired by God, proclaimed their faith in the immortality of the soul and the resurrection of bodies. It is this belief, confirmed by Christ's teaching, that gives meaning to our prayer for the departed.

Reader: After the battle, the valiant Judas Machabeus, having made a collection, sent two thousand drachmas of silver to Jerusalem, that a sacrifice might be offered in expiation for the sins of the dead; a fine, noble thought, inspired by his belief in the resurrection.

For, if he had not believed that those who had fallen would rise again, it would have been useless and superfluous to pray for the dead. But it was his considered opinion that great mercy is in store for those who have fallen asleep with the love of God.

It is a holy and pious thought, therefore, to pray for the dead, that they may be freed from their sins (2 Mach. 12:43-46).

ALL KNEEL

Priest: Come, let us adore the King unto whom all things live:

All: Let us adore the Lord of the living and dead.

Priest: Lord Jesus Christ, King unto whom all things live, you are present and active here in the sacramental rites, especially the eucharistic liturgy, not to judge the world, but to continue your saving, redemptive work.

All: We adore you, O Lord, / in the mysteries of your love.

Priest: With great confidence we come before you, Lord, to pray for all our beloved dead, for those who have not yet entered eternal life — for souls not yet completely cleansed from guilt.

All: Eternal rest grant unto them, O Lord; / and let perpetual light shine upon them!

Priest: Being weak creatures, they sinned, but they retained faith in you — that faith, as you promised, worthy of eternal life. After your friend Lazarus died, you said to his sister Martha: "I am the Resurrection and the Life. Whoever has faith in me shall live, although he be dead. And everyone who keeps faith in me will not die forever. Do you believe this?"

All: Yes, Lord, we believe that you are the Christ, / the Son of the living God, / who came into this world.

Priest: Remember, Lord, your servants and handmaids who have gone before us with the sign of faith and sleep in peace.

All: Reward them in your mercy / with a place of refreshment, light, and peace.

Priest: Eternal rest grant unto them, O Lord.

All: And let perpetual light shine upon them.

Priest: May they rest in peace!

All: Amen.

ALL STAND

Hymn No. 19.

2. LIFE FROM THE CROSS

ALL SIT

Priest: St. Paul in his first letter to the Thessalonians teaches that the life after death comes to mankind through the death and resurrection of Christ.

Reader: I want you to know the truth about your dead, in order that you may not grieve as others do, who have no hope.

The fact is, if we know that Jesus died and rose again, then we should believe that those who have fallen asleep in the love of Jesus will be brought by God with his Son.

What I am going to say to you is in accordance with the words of the Lord: when the Lord comes back on earth, the living, the survivors, will not get ahead of those who died before them. For the Lord himself, at the given signal, at the voice of the archangel, at the sound of the divine trumpet, will come down from heaven; and those who have died in the love of Christ will be the first to rise. Then the living, the survivors, united with those who have risen, will be taken up with them into the air, to meet Christ. And from then on, forever, we shall be with the Lord.

May these words help you console one another! (1 Thess. 4:13-18).

ALL KNEEL

Priest: Lord Jesus Christ, Redeemer of the world! To give us life, you sacrificed your own, in accordance with the Father's will. Trusting in this love, we ask you:

All: Christ Jesus crucified, / show mercy to the souls in purgatory.

Priest: Because you endured your agony in Gethsemane, were scourged and crowned with thorns, because you suffered on the way to Golgotha and on the Cross:

All: Show mercy to the souls in purgatory.

Priest: Humiliated to the utmost on the Cross, you chose to experience the bitterness of being far from God. You cried out: My God, my God, why have you abandoned me?

All: Show mercy to those souls / being purified by fire, / far from the holy face of God.

Priest: Here in the eucharistic rites you have left us the memorial of your atoning death and saving resurrection. Each day you most wondrously renew the sacrifice of redemption. Because of your limitless love for us we beg you:

All: Show mercy to the souls in purgatory.

Priest: Let your heart's Blood flow down from the sacrificial altar of the Cross into purgatory:

All: Let those souls be cleansed / by the fire of your love.

Priest: Once you said: When I am lifted up above the earth, I will draw all things to myself.

All: Draw the souls in purgatory / to your most holy heart!

Priest: Lord, hear our prayer,

All: And let our cry rise up to you.

Priest: Let us pray. Pause for personal prayer.

O God, Father in heaven, you are rich in mercy and desire the happiness of all. Therefore we beg of that mercy: by the prayers of the holy and pure Virgin Mary and of all the saints, call our brothers and relatives, friends and benefactors who have passed from this life on earth to everlasting blessedness, through Christ our Lord.

All: Amen.

Priest: Eternal rest grant unto them, O Lord.

All: And let perpetual light shine upon them.

Priest: May they rest in peace!

All: Amen.

ALL STAND. Hymn No. 115.

3. WHOEVER EATS OF THIS BREAD SHALL LIVE FOREVER

Priest: In the Gospel according to St. John we hear Christ's promise of the Eucharist as a pledge of the resurrection of our body.

Reader: Jesus said to the Jewish crowd, "I am the living bread that comes down from heaven. If anyone eats some of this bread, he will live for eternity. And the bread that I shall give is my flesh, delivered up for the life of the world."

The Jews then quarreled among themselves. "How can this man give us his flesh to eat?" they were saying.

Jesus said to them, therefore, "This is the solemn truth: If you do not eat the flesh of the Son of Man and if you do not drink his blood, you shall not have life in you. But he who eats my flesh and drinks my blood possesses life eternal; and I myself will raise him up on the last day" (John 6:51-55).

ALL SIT

The priest may now give a homily developing the following points:

1. Prayer for the dead is meaningful only because of our faith in the final resurrection, and this in turn depends on our faith in the resurrection of Christ. Through baptism we have become one with Christ: we shall rise with him and rise as he did.

2. The Eucharist renews in us every day the eternal life received at baptism. And the communion in Christ's Body is a pledge of the resurrection of our body.

ALL KNEEL

Priest: Divine Redeemer! In you we behold the unspeakably great love of the Father for us. For this is the will of the Father who sent you: that everyone who beholds you and believes in you should obtain eternal life. You are the true bread of heaven which the Father gives us.

All: Whover eats of this bread / will live forever.

Priest: We pray to you with confidence for our beloved dead, who must suffer still in purgatory. With believing hearts they ate this bread which the Father in heaven gives his children — your very self, O Lord, in this sacrifice-sacrament.

All: Give them that life now / which you have promised.

Priest: As the living Father has sent you, and you live by the Father,

All: So now let those who have eaten your flesh / have life through you.

Priest: Yes, they have life already; at this moment they stand in your grace as children of your Father. Yet we pray:

All: Let them have the fullness of life / in your glory.

Priest: Lord, hear our prayer,

All: And let our cry rise up to you.

Priest: Let us pray. Pause for personal prayer.

Lord Jesus Christ, Creator and Redeemer of the faithful, give to the souls of your servants and handmaids forgiveness of all their sins. On earth you let them approach your table; let them enter now into the wedding feast of eternal life, that they may praise the Father and you, the Son, and the Holy Spirit eternally.

All: **Amen.**

ALL STAND

Hymn No. 113.

ALL KNEEL

If there is Benediction of the Blessed Sacrament, the following prayers may be said after the hymn of exposition.

Priest: **Christ Jesus, Lord of life, Redeemer of the world: in the spirit of that love which you prescribed for us, we pray to you for our departed:** That you grant eternal rest to all the faithful departed,

All: **Please grant our petition.**

Priest: **That you lead our parents, relatives and friends whom you have called from this life to their eternal home,**

All: **Please grant our petition.**

Priest: **That you reward our departed benefactors with eternal blessedness,**

All: **Please grant our petition.**

Priest: **That you receive into your peace the souls of our brothers who in war gave their lives for us,**

All: **Please grant our petition.**

Priest: **That you accept the sacrifices of those who died for civil rights and reward them with fellowship among the saints,**

All: **Please grant our petition.**

Priest: **That you allow us to be happily reunited with our loved ones,**

All: **Please grant our petition.**

Priest: **Divine Redeemer, by your ascension you preceded us in order to prepare a dwelling with your Father for your followers. We beg you to allow the souls of our departed ones to take possession of this eternal home in peace and blessedness, where sorrow and war and death are forgotten. May your holy angels keep watch at their tombs until resurrection day when you will call their bodies also to glory, you who live and reign eternally.**

All: **Amen.**

Priest: **Lord, give to the living your grace; and to the dead, eternal rest.**

All: **Let perpetual light shine upon them.**

Priest: **May they rest in peace!**

All: **Amen.**

ALL STAND

Final hymn, No. 160.

THE WAY OF THE CROSS
304. AT THE CROSS HER STATION KEEPING

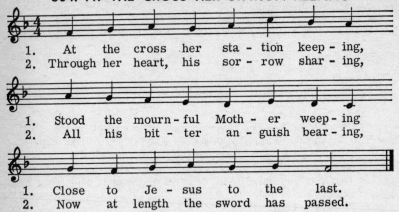

1. At the cross her sta-tion keep-ing,
2. Through her heart, his sor-row shar-ing,

1. Stood the mourn-ful Moth-er weep-ing
2. All his bit-ter an-guish bear-ing,

1. Close to Je-sus to the last.
2. Now at length the sword has passed.

In the name of the Father and of the Son and of the Holy Spirit. Amen.

In humble attitude and with a repentant spirit we offer you, eternal Father, this tribute of our worship, that it may redound to your honor and glory and may benefit all who have the faith, Christians alive or dead, in the forgiveness of their sins and the attainment of life everlasting.[1]

℣. We should glory in the Cross of our Lord Jesus Christ.
℟. In him we find salvation, life and resurrection.[2]

Let Us Pray

In the passion of your Son, O God, / you showed us the path to eternal glory, / the way of the Cross. / By our prayers we now follow him to Calvary. / In your kindness grant that for all eternity / we may share his triumph / with him who lives and reigns with you forever. Amen.[3]

Oh, how sad and sore distressed
Was that Mother highly blessed
Of the sole-begotten One!

Christ above in torment hangs;
She beneath beholds the pangs
Of her dying glorious Son.

INDULGENCES ATTACHED TO THE WAY OF THE CROSS—A plenary indulgence can be gained every time the Way of the Cross is made. If for some reasonable cause the holy exercise is not completed, an indulgence of ten years is granted for each station. An additional plenary indulgence can be gained if Holy Communion is received on the same day as the Stations are made. (No. 164, *Preces et Pia Opera*)

[1] Compiled from Offertory prayers of the Mass.   [2] Entrance Chant of Holy Thursday.
[3] Rite of the erection of the Stations of the Cross.

FIRST STATION

Jesus Is Condemned to Death

℣. We adore you, O Christ, and we praise you.
℟. Because by your holy Cross you have redeemed the world.[1]

As soon as it was morning, the chief priests deliberated with the elders, the scribes and the whole Council. Jesus was bound and led out to be handed over to Pilate. And they all condemned him and said, "He deserves death." Then Pilate sat in his judgment-seat and handed him over to them to be crucified.[2]

℣. God did not spare even his own Son.
℟. He delivered him up for us all.[3]

Let Us Pray

Lord Jesus Christ, / from the glory of the Father in heaven / you came down upon earth, / and you poured out your precious Blood / for the remission of our sins. / We humbly entreat you that on the day of judgment, / placed at your right hand, / we may be able to hear you say, "Come, you blessed." / This we ask of you, who live and reign forever. Amen.[4]

> Who, on Christ's dear Mother gazing
> Pierced by anguish so amazing,
> Born of woman, would not weep?

---

[1] Tract of Votive Mass of the Holy Cross.   [2] Mark 15:1; Matthew 26:66; John 19:16.
[3] First antiphon of Lauds for Good Friday (Rom. 8:32).   [4] Collect, Votive Mass of the Passion of Our Lord.

SECOND STATION

Jesus Takes Up His Cross

℣. We adore you, O Christ, and we praise you.

℟. Because by your holy Cross you have redeemed the world.

Carrying his own Cross, he went out to the place called the "Skull" (or Calvary). Hail, O Christ, our King! You alone have had pity on the folly of our sins. Obedient to the Father, you are led forth to be crucified, like an innocent lamb to the slaughter. To you be glory; to you be triumph and victory; to you the crown of highest honor and acclaim.[1]

℣. The Lord has laid on him the iniquity of us all.

℟. For the wickedness of his people he has stricken him.[2]

Let Us Pray

Lord, you have said, / "My yoke is sweet and my burden is light." / Grant that we may be able to carry that burden / so as to obtain grace from you who live and reign forever. Amen.[3]

> Who, on Christ's dear Mother thinking,
> Such a cup of sorrow drinking,
> Would not share her sorrows deep?

---

[1] John 19:17 and Alleluia verse of Votive Mass of the Passion of Our Lord. [2] Is. 53:6, 8.
[3] Vesting prayer before Mass.

III

THIRD STATION

Jesus Falls the First Time under the Cross

℣. We adore you, O Christ, and we praise you.
℟. Because by your holy Cross you have redeemed the world.

Our Lord Jesus Christ debased himself and became obedient to the point of death — even death on a cross. That is why God has exalted him to the highest degree and given him the Name that is above all other names. Come, let us bow down in worship before God; let us weep in the presence of the Lord who made us; for he is indeed the Lord our God.[1]

℣. It was really our sufferings that he bore.
℟. Our sorrows with which he burdened himself.[2]

Let Us Pray

We are weak, O God all-powerful, / and we lose heart in the midst of so many trials. / Through the merits of your Son's passion, / give us a new birth of hope. / This we ask of you through him who lives and reigns forever. Amen.[3]

> Bruised, derided, cursed, defiled,
> She beheld her tender Child
> All with bloody scourges rent.

---

[1] Epistle of Palm Sunday (Phil. 2:8-9) and Ps. 94:6-7.   [2] Is. 53:4.   [3] Collect, Monday in Holy Week.

IV FOURTH STATION

Jesus Meets His Afflicted Mother

℣. We adore you, O Christ, and we praise you.
℟. Because by your holy Cross you have redeemed the world.

To what can I liken or compare you, O daughter Jerusalem? For great as the sea is your distress. O Mother of mercy, grant that we may ever realize in ourselves the death of Jesus and may share with him in his saving passion.[1]

℣. A sword of sorrow has pierced your soul.
℟. And has filled your heart with bitter pain.[2]

Let Us Pray

At the hour of your passion, Lord Jesus Christ, / the most holy soul of the Virgin Mary, your Mother, / was pierced with a sword of sorrow. / May she plead, now and at the hour of our death, / for your clemency on our behalf. / This we ask of you who live and reign forever. Amen.[3]

> O thou Mother, font of love,
> Touch my spirit from above,
> Make my heart with thine accord.

---

[1] Lam. 2:13 and *Stabat Mater*.   [2] Luke 2:35; Job 9:18.   [3] Collect, Votive Mass of the Seven Sorrows of the Blessed Virgin Mary.

FIFTH STATION

Simon of Cyrene Is Forced to Take Up the Cross

℣. We adore you, O Christ, and we praise you.
℞. Because by your holy Cross you have redeemed the world.

While they were leading him away, they commandeered a certain Simon, from Cyrene, a passerby, and made him take up the Cross of Jesus. And they laid the Cross on him, to carry after Jesus. If anyone wishes to come after me, let him deny himself, and take up his cross daily, and follow me.[1]

℣. He who will not carry his cross and walk in my footsteps.
℞. Cannot be my disciple.[2]

Let Us Pray

Let your heart be touched, O Lord, by our offerings. / Our wills resist your grace; / Lord, bring them back to yourself! / Through Christ our Lord. Amen.[3]

> For the sins of his own nation
> Saw him hang in desolation,
> Till his spirit forth he sent.

---

[1] Matthew 27:32; Mark 15:21; Luke 23:26; 9:23.   Luke 14:27.   [3] Prayer
over the Offerings, Saturday of Fourth Week in Lent.

SIXTH STATION

Veronica Wipes the
Face of Jesus

℣. We adore you, O Christ, and we praise you.
℟. Because by your holy Cross you have redeemed the world.

He had no beauty nor grace to attract our gaze. An object of scorn, a castoff from mankind, a man of sorrows, worn out by suffering; like one of those in whose presence men hide their faces, we scorned him and disdained him! His look was marred beyond that of man, and his appearance beyond that of mortals. Yet he is fairer than the sons of men, and by his wounds we are healed.[1]

℣. Hide not your face from us.
℟. Do not in anger repel your servants.[2]

Let Us Pray

By the precious Blood of Jesus Christ, your Son, / you remake us to your own image, O God. / Guide our footsteps in your paths, / that we may truly obtain the gift of your divine charity. / Through the same Christ our Lord. Amen.[3]

> Make me feel as thou hast felt;
> Make my soul to glow and melt
> With the love of Christ my Lord.

---

[1] Is. 53:3, 52:14; Ps. 44:3.　　[2] Ps. 26:9.　　[3] Prayer over the Offerings, for Charity.

VII

SEVENTH STATION

Jesus Falls a Second Time

℣. We adore you, O Christ, and we praise you.
℟. Because by your holy Cross you have redeemed the world.

They have given me over to the impious, and among the wicked they have cast me, and have not spared my life. The powerful have gathered together against me, and like giants they stand against me. They have inflicted cruel wounds on me, and they have mocked me.[1]

℣. I am a worm, not a man.
℟. The scorn of men, despised by the people.[2]

Let Us Pray

Lord, by the humiliation of your Son / you have lifted up our fallen world; / grant that your children may live in joy. / You have rescued them from falling to eternal death: / lead them always toward eternal happiness. / Through the same Jesus Christ our Lord. Amen.[3]

> Holy Mother, pierce me through.
> In my heart each wound renew
> Of my Savior crucified.
>
> Let me share with thee his pain,
> Who for all my sins was slain,
> Who for me in torments died.

---

[1] Seventh Responsory, Tenebrae of Good Friday; First Responsory, *ibid.* [2] Ps. 21:7.
[3] Collect, Second Sunday after Easter.

EIGHTH STATION

Jesus Meets the Women of Jerusalem

℣. We adore you, O Christ, and we praise you.

℟. Because by your holy Cross you have redeemed the world.

There was a great throng of people following Jesus, especially women who were beating their breasts and wailing over him. Jesus turned toward them. "Women of Jerusalem," he said, "do not weep over me, but rather weep over yourselves and over your children! Yes, the days are coming when people will say, "What a blessing it is for a woman to be sterile, never to have borne children and never to have nursed them!" [1]

℣. Those that sow in tears.

℟. Shall reap rejoicing.[2]

Let Us Pray

Lord, you do not like to punish: / you would rather take pity on those who hope in you. / Make us weep as we should for the evil we have committed / and thus obtain the favor of being consoled by you. / Through Christ our Lord. Amen.[3]

> Let me mingle tears with thee,
> Mourning him who mourned for me,
> All the days that I may live.

---

[1] Luke 23:27-29.   [2] Ps. 125:5.   [3] Prayer for the People, Saturday of Fourth Week in Lent.

IX

Jesus Falls a Third Time

℣. We adore you, O Christ, and we praise you.
℟. Because by your holy Cross you have redeemed the world.

My people, what have I done to you? Or in what have I grieved you? Answer me! I brought you out of the land of Egypt, and you brought me to the Cross. Forty years I rained manna on you in the desert, and you rained blows and scourges on me. What more should I have done for you that I have not done? [1]

℣. Like the sheep that is led to the slaughter-house.
℟. Like the lamb that lets itself be shorn in silence / he did not even open his mouth. [2]

Let Us Pray

O Lord, in your goodness, guard your Church always. / Without you, our human nature cannot help failing: / help us avoid what is harmful, / and direct our steps toward that which furthers our salvation. / Through Christ our Lord. Amen. [3]

> By the Cross with thee to stay,
> There with thee to weep and pray:
> This I ask of thee to give.

---

[1] Reproaches of Good Friday. [2] Is. 53:7. [3] Collect, Fourteenth Sunday after Pentecost.

TENTH STATION

Jesus Is Stripped of His Garments

℣. We adore you, O Christ, and we praise you.
℟. Because by your holy Cross you have redeemed the world.

Having arrived at the place called "Golgotha," that is, "Place of the Skull" (or Calvary), they gave him wine mixed with gall. He tasted it, but would not drink it. And they divided his clothes among them by drawing lots. (This action fulfilled the prophet's prediction: "They distributed my clothes among them, and for my garment they cast lots.")[1]

℣. They put gall in my food.
℟. And in my thirst they gave me vinegar to drink.[2]

Let Us Pray

Strip us, O Lord, of our former self with its evil deeds and ways; / and clothe us with that new nature / which has been created according to justice and true holiness. / Through Christ our Lord. Amen.[3]

> Virgin, of all virgins blest!
> Listen to my fond request:
> Let me share thy grief with thee.

---

[1] Matthew 27:33-35.   [2] Ps. 68:22.   [3] Rite of religious profession.

ELEVENTH STATION

Jesus Is Nailed to the Cross

℣. We adore you, O Christ, and we praise you.
℟. Because by your holy Cross you have redeemed the world.

When they arrived at the place called Calvary, they crucified him there, and two criminals, one on his right, the other on his left. My people, what have I done to you? I have raised you up with great power, and you have hanged me on the Cross.[1]

℣. They have pierced my hands and my feet.
℟. I can count all my bones.[2]

Let Us Pray

By the passion of your only-begotten Son, O Lord, / and by the blood flowing from his five wounds, / you repaired the evil wrought by sin in our human nature. / Here on earth we revere the wounds he received; / grant, we pray you, that in heaven / we may win the fruit of his most precious Blood. / Through the same Christ our Lord. Amen.[3]

> Let me to my latest breath,
> In my body bear the death
> Of that dying Son of thine.

---

[1] Luke 23:33; John 19:18; Reproaches of Good Friday.   [2] Ps. 21:17-18.
[3] Collect, Feast of the Five Wounds.

TWELFTH STATION

Jesus Dies on the Cross

℣. We adore you, O Christ, and we praise you.
℟. Because by your holy Cross you have redeemed the world.

Seeing his Mother and, standing near her, the disciple whom he loved, Jesus said to his Mother, "Woman, here is your son." Then he said to the disciple, "Here is your Mother." After taking the vinegar, Jesus said, "All is accomplished." Then he cried out in a loud voice, "Father, into your hands I commit my spirit." And, bowing his head, he gave up his spirit.[1]

℣. Christ for our sake became obedient to death.
℟. Even to death on a cross.[2]

Let Us Pray

Lord Jesus Christ, Son of the living God, / at midday you mounted the gibbet of the Cross for the redemption of the world, / and you poured out your precious Blood for the remission of our sins. / We humbly entreat you: / grant that after our death / we may enter with joy the gates of paradise. / This we ask of you who live and reign forever. Amen.[3]

> Let his stripes and scourging smite me,
> At his holy Cross requite me,
> Let his Blood refresh me there.

---

[1] John 19:26, 27, 30; Luke 23:46 (Fifth Responsory of Tenebrae on Good Friday).
[2] Versicle of Good Friday (Phil. 2:8).
[3] Postcommunion, Votive Mass of the Passion of Our Lord.

THIRTEENTH STATION

The Body of Jesus Is Placed in the Arms of His Mother

℣. We adore you, O Christ, and we praise you.
℟. Because by your holy Cross you have redeemed the world.

O all you who pass by the way, look and see whether there is any sorrow like my sorrow. Worn out from weeping are my eyes, within me all is in ferment; my gall is poured out on the ground, as I behold the cruel death of my Son, for the enemy has prevailed against him. Do not call me Noemi (that is, beautiful). Call me Mara (that is, bitter), for the Almighty has made it very bitter for me.[1]

℣. The tears are on her cheeks.
℟. And there is none to comfort her.[2]

Let Us Pray

Your passion, Lord, / plunged into the soul of the Virgin Mary, your Mother, / the sword of sorrow foretold by Simeon. / We reverently call her sufferings to mind; / grant that we may profit by the happy effects of your redemption. / This we ask of you who live and reign forever. Amen.[3]

> When the flames of hell would end me
> At the judgment day, defend me,
> Gentle Virgin, with thy prayer.

---

[1] Lam. 1:12, 2:11, 1:16; Ruth 1:20.   [2] Lam. 1:2.   [3] Collect, Feast of the Seven Sorrows of the Blessed Virgin Mary.

XIV

FOURTEENTH STATION

Jesus Is Laid in the Tomb

℣. We adore you, O Christ, and we praise you.

℟. Because by your holy Cross you have redeemed the world.

Taking the body of Jesus, Joseph wrapped it in a white shroud and placed it in his own tomb, a new tomb which he had hollowed out in a rock. Then he rolled a great stone to the entrance of the tomb.[1]

℣. You will not abandon my soul to the nether world.
℟. Nor will you suffer your faithful One to undergo corruption.[2]

Let Us Pray

O Lord, you left us a record of your passion / in the holy shroud in which Joseph wrapped your sacred body / when it was taken down from the Cross. / In your mercy grant that through your death and burial / we may be brought to the glory of your resurrection. / This we ask of you who live and reign forever. Amen.[3]

> Christ, when thou shalt call me hence,
> Be thy Mother my defense,
> Be thy Cross my victory.
>
> While my body here decays,
> May my soul thy goodness praise,
> Safe in paradise with thee.

Let Us Pray

Submissive to your will, O God, / your Son suffered the torment of the Cross for us / to rescue us from the power of the devil. / We are your servants; / grant that we may obtain the grace of rising with him. / Through the same Christ our Lord. Amen.[4]

---

[1] Matthew 27:59-60. [2] Ps. 15:10. [6] Collect, Feast of the Holy Shroud.
[4] Second Collect, Wednesday of Holy Week; Collect, Votive Mass of the Holy Cross.

SELECTED BLESSINGS

BLESSING OF A WOMAN BEFORE THE BIRTH OF A CHILD

℣. Our help is in the name of the Lord.

℟. Who made heaven and earth.

℣. Save your servant.

℟. Who trusts in you, my God.

℣. Be a tower of strength for her, O Lord.

℟. Against the attack of the enemy.

℣. Let the enemy have no power against her.

℟. And let not the son of evil draw near to harm her.

℣. Send her aid, O Lord, from your holy place.

℟. And watch over her from Sion.

℣. O Lord, hear my prayer.

℟. And let my cry come to you.

℣. The Lord be with you.

℟. And with your spirit.

Let us pray. Almighty, everlasting God, you have permitted to your servants, in their profession of the true faith, to acknowledge the glory of the eternal Trinity and to adore its unity in the power of its majesty. We ask that by her constancy in that faith, your servant, N., may ever be strengthened against all adversity. Through Christ our Lord.

℟. Amen.

Let us pray. O Lord God, Creator of all things, mighty and awe-inspiring, just and merciful, you alone are kind and loving. You set Israel free from every evil, making our fathers your beloved people, and sanctified them by the power of your Spirit. By the co-working of the Holy Spirit, you prepared the body and soul of the glorious Virgin Mary to become a worthy home for your Son. You filled John the Baptist with the Holy Spirit, making him leap with joy in his mother's womb. Receive the sacrifice of the contrite heart and the ardent desire of your servant, N., who humbly asks you for the welfare of the child which you permitted her to conceive. Guard the work which is yours and defend it from all the deceit and harm of our bitter enemy, so that the hand of your mercy may assist her delivery, and her child may come to the light of day without harm, be kept safe for the holy birth of baptism, serve you always in all things, and attain to everlasting life. Through our Lord Jesus Christ, your Son, who lives and reigns with you in the unity of the Holy Spirit, God, for ever and ever.

℟. Amen.

Then the priest sprinkles the woman with holy water. Then the following psalm is said:

Psalm 66

May God have pity on us and bless us; *
    may he let his face shine upon us.
So may your way be known upon earth; *
    among all nations, your salvation.
May the peoples praise you, O God; *
    may all the peoples praise you!
May the nations be glad and exult
    because you rule the peoples in equity; *
    the nations on the earth you guide.
May the peoples praise you, O God; *
    may all the peoples praise you!
The earth has yielded its fruits; *
    God, our God, has blessed us.
May God bless us, *
    and may all the ends of the earth fear him!
Glory be to the Father and to the Son *
    and to the Holy Spirit.
As it was in the beginning, is now and ever shall be, *
    world without end. Amen.

℣. Let us bless the Father, and the Son, and the Holy Spirit.
℟. Let us praise and glorify him forever.
℣. God has given his angels charge over you.
℟. To keep you in all your ways.
℣. O Lord, hear my prayer.
℟. And let my cry come to you.
℣. The Lord be with you.
℟. And with your spirit.

Let us pray. Visit, we pray you, O Lord, this house, and drive far from it and from this your servant, N., the enemy with all his plots. May your holy angels dwell here to keep her and her child in peace, and may your blessing † be always upon her. Save them, O almighty God, and grant them your unfailing light. Through Christ our Lord.
℟. Amen.

May the blessing of almighty God, the Father and the Son † and the Holy Spirit, descend upon you and your child and remain forever.
℟. Amen.

BLESSING OF A MOTHER AFTER CHILDBIRTH AND OF HER CHILD

Vested in surplice and white stole, the priest with his server proceeds to the entrance of the church where the

mother with her baptized child awaits him holding a
lighted candle. He sprinkles them and all the others present with holy water, saying:

Peace be with you.

Then he says to the mother:

**Come into the temple of God; adore the Son of the Blessed Virgin
Mary, adore him who granted that you should bear a child.**

The priest leads the mother with her child and the others
to the altar, where she places the lighted candle in a
candlestick and goes to a kneeler. The priest proceeds
to the altar; with the priest leading, all pray the

Magnificat (Luke 1:46-54)

My soul magnifies the Lord, *
  and my spirit rejoices in God my savior,
Because he has regarded the lowliness of his handmaid, *
  for behold, henceforth all generations shall call me blessed,
Because he who is mighty has done great things for me, *
  and holy is his name;
And his mercy is from generation to generation *
  toward those who fear him.
He has shown might with his arm; *
  he has scattered the proud in the conceit of their heart.
He has put down the mighty from their thrones *
  and has exalted the lowly.
The hungry he has filled with good things *
  and the rich he has sent empty away.
He has given help to Israel his servant, *
  mindful of his mercy,
As he promised our fathers, *
  toward Abraham and his descendants forever.
Glory be to the Father and to the Son *
  and to the Holy Spirit.
As it was in the beginning, is now and ever shall be, *
  world without end. Amen.

After the Magnificat all kneel while the priest, standing,
says:

Lord, have mercy.
Christ, have mercy.
Lord, have mercy.
Our Father (silently as far as:)

℣. And lead us not into temptation.
℞. But deliver us from evil.
℣. O Lord, hear my prayer.
℞. And let my cry come to you.
℣. The Lord be with you.
℞. And with your spirit.

Let us pray. Almighty, everlasting God, by the childbearing of the Blessed Virgin Mary, you turned the pains of childbearing into joy for your faithful. Look with kindness on this your servant who comes rejoicing to your holy temple to give thanks to you, and grant that after this life she and her child may, by the merits and intercession of the Blessed Virgin Mary, attain to the joys of everlasting life. Through Christ our Lord.
℞. Amen.

If the mother has come to the church without the child, the following prayer for the child is omitted.
Then the priest blesses the child:

Let us pray. O Lord Jesus Christ, Son of the living God, begotten in eternity, you willed to be born in time. You love the innocence of childhood, and lovingly embraced and blessed the little children who were brought to you. Anticipate the needs of this child (these children) with your tender blessings, and grant that no evil may corrupt his (her, their) mind, but that, advancing in age, in wisdom, and in grace, he (she, they) may live so as to please you always. You who live and reign with God the Father in the unity of the Holy Spirit, God, for ever and ever.
℞. Amen.

Finally, the priest sprinkles the mother and the child with holy water, blessing them:

May the peace and blessing of almighty God, the Father and the Son † and the Holy Spirit, descend upon you and remain forever.
℞. Amen.

BLESSING FOR WEDDING ANNIVERSARIES

The spouses who are giving thanks on the occasion of the celebration of their wedding anniversary, go to the altar or to the sanctuary entrance and kneel. The pastor or another priest, vested in surplice and white stole or in the Mass vestments (except the maniple), begins:

℣. Our help is in the name of the Lord.
℞. Who made heaven and earth.

℣. O Lord, hear my prayer.
℟. And let my cry come to you.
℣. The Lord be with you.
℟. And with your spirit.

Let us pray. Direct, O Lord, we ask you, all our actions by your inspiration and carry them on by your assistance, that every prayer and work of ours may always begin from you and through you be brought to completion. Through Christ our Lord. ℟. Amen.

Then, if it is customary, the priest addresses the spouses, urging them to renew their intention to remain constant in married life and in God's love until death. The spouses may then renew their matrimonial consent in this way:

Priest: N., do you renew and conform your taking of N. here present for your wedded wife?

Husband: I do.

Priest: N., do you renew and confirm your taking of N. here present for your wedded husband?

Wife: I do.

The spouses join their right hands, and the priest blesses them, saying:

May the blessing of almighty God, the Father and the Son † and the Holy Spirit, descend upon you and remain forever.

℟. Amen.

BLESSING

Ant. Behold, thus is the man blessed who fears the Lord.

Psalm 127

Happy are you who fear the Lord, *
    who walk in his ways!
For you shall eat the fruit of your handiwork; *
    happy shall you be, and favored.
Your wife shall be like a fruitful vine *
    in the recesses of your home;
Your children like olive plants *
    around your table.
Behold, thus is the man blessed *
    who fears the Lord.
The Lord bless you from Sion: *
    may you see the prosperity of Jerusalem
    all the days of your life;
May you see your children's children. *
    Peace be upon Israel!

Glory be to the Father and to the Son *
   and to the Holy Spirit.
As it was in the beginning, is now and ever shall be, *
   world without end. Amen.

or Psalm 116

Praise the Lord, all you nations; *
   glorify him, all you peoples!
For steadfast is his kindness toward us, *
   and the fidelity of the Lord endures forever.
Glory be to the Father and to the Son *
   and to the Holy Spirit.
As it was in the beginning, is now and ever shall be, *
   world without end. Amen.

The antiphon is repeated:

Ant. Behold, thus is the man blessed who fears the Lord.
Lord, have mercy.
Christ, have mercy.
Lord, have mercy.
Our Father (silently as far as:)
℣. And lead us not into temptation.
℞. But deliver us from evil.
℣. O Lord, hear my prayer.
℞. And let my cry come to you.
℣. The Lord be with you.
℞. And with your spirit.

Let us pray. Almighty, everlasting God, look with kindness on these
your servants, who with gladness approach your holy temple to give
thanks, and grant that, after this life they may (with their children) attain to the joys of eternal happiness. Through Christ our Lord.
℞. Amen.

Then the priest sprinkles the spouses with holy water in
the usual way.
The Mass of the day may be celebrated or a votive Mass
of the Holy Trinity or of the Blessed Virgin Mary, as a
votive Mass of class II, with the prayer of thanksgiving
added under one conclusion. After the Mass the Te Deum
may be added with the versicles and prayer of thanksgiving.

Te Deum

O God, we praise you: *
   we acknowledge you to be the Lord.

All the earth, eternal Father, *
   worships you.
To you all the angels, to you the heavens *
   and all the powers:
To you the cherubim and seraphim *
   cry aloud without ceasing:
Holy, holy, holy *
   Lord God of hosts.
The heavens and the earth *
   are full of the majesty of your glory.
To you *
   the glorious choir of apostles,
To you *
   the wonderful company of prophets,
To you *
   the white-robed army of martyrs, all give praise.
To you *
   holy Church throughout the whole world pays homage,
Father *
   of infinite majesty,
Your true and only Son *
   who is to be adored,
The Holy Spirit *
   the Consoler.
You, O Christ, *
   are the king of eternal glory.
You are *
   the eternal Son of the Father.
About to take on our human nature in order to redeem us, *
   you did not disdain the Virgin's womb.
You conquered the sting of death, *
   and opened the kingdom of heaven
   to those who believe in you.
You sit at the right hand of God, *
   in the glory of the Father.
We believe *
   that you will come again as judge.
And so, we implore you, help your servants, *
   whom you have redeemed with your precious Blood.
Let them be numbered among your saints, *
   in everlasting glory.
Save your people, O Lord, *
   and bless your inheritance.

And rule them, *
and raise them on high forever.
Day by day *
do we bless you.
And we praise your name forever, *
for ever and ever.
In your goodness, O Lord, *
keep us this day without sin.
Have mercy on us, O Lord, *
have mercy on us.
Let your mercy, O Lord, come upon us, *
for we have hoped in you.
In you, O Lord, have I hoped: *
let me not be put to shame forever.

℣. Blessed are you, O Lord, the God of our fathers.
℟. Praised, worthy and exalted above all forever.
℣. Let us bless the Father and the Son and the Holy Spirit.
℟. Let us praise him and exalt him above all forever.
℣. Bless the Lord, O my soul.
℟. And forget not all he has done for you.
℣. O Lord, hear my prayer.
℟. And let my cry come to you.
℣. The Lord be with you.
℟. And with your spirit.

Let us pray. O God, whose mercy is unlimited and whose goodness is inexhaustible, we thank you for all that you in your loving majesty have given us. We ask that you, who always answer those who pray, may in your mercy not abandon them, but prepare them to receive eternal rewards. Through Christ our Lord.
℟. Amen.

BLESSING OF CANDLES AND THROATS

FEAST OF SAINT BLAISE, BISHOP AND MARTYR
FEBRUARY 3

℣. Our help is in the name of the Lord.
℟. Who made heaven and earth.
℣. The Lord be with you.
℟. And with your spirit.

Let us pray. O God most powerful and most kind, you created all the different things in the world by the Word alone and willed that this Word by which all things were made should become incarnate for the remaking of mankind. You are great and limitless, worthy of reverence and praise, the worker of wonders. For your sake the glorious martyr and bishop, Saint Blaise, joyfully gained the palm of martyrdom, never shrinking from any kind of torture in confessing his faith in you, and you gave to him, among other gifts, the prerogative of curing by your power every ailment of men's throats. Humbly we beg you in your majesty not to look upon our guilt but, pleased by his merits and prayers, in your awe-inspiring kindness, to bless † this wax created by you and to sanctify † it, pouring into it your grace. May all who in good faith have their throats touched by this wax be freed from every ailment of the throat through the merit of his suffering and, in good health and spirits, give thanks to you in your holy Church and praise your glorious name, which is blessed for ever and ever. Through our Lord Jesus Christ, your Son, who with you lives and reigns in the unity of the Holy Spirit, God, for ever and ever.

℞. Amen.

The priest sprinkles the candles with holy water.

Then he places two candles, arranged in the form of a cross, on the throat, under the chin, of each person to be blessed, as the latter kneels before the altar. The priest says:

Through the intercession of Saint Blaise, bishop and martyr, may God deliver you from ailments of the throat and from every other evil. In the name of the Father and of the Son † and of the Holy Spirit.

℞. Amen.

BLESSING OF A SICK CHILD

Sick children who have reached the use of reason so that the sacrament of anointing may be given to them should be assisted by the exhortations and prayers described in the Roman Ritual where the visitation and care of the sick are found, according to the circumstances and the capacity of the child.

For younger children, however, the following prayers may be used.

The priest enters the room of the sick child and begins:

℣. Peace to this house.

℞. And to all who dwell herein.

Then he sprinkles the sick child, the bed, and the room, saying nothing. Then he says the following psalm.

Ant. Praise the Lord, O children; praise the name of the Lord.

Psalm 112

Praise, you servants of the Lord, *
  praise the name of the Lord.
Blessed be the name of the Lord *
  both now and forever.
From the rising to the setting of the sun *
  is the name of the Lord to be praised.
High above all nations is the Lord; *
  above the heavens is his glory.
Who is like the Lord, our God, who is enthroned on high *
  and looks upon the heavens and the earth below?
He raises up the lowly from the dust; *
  from the dunghill he lifts up the poor
To seat them with princes, *
  with the princes of his own people.
He establishes in her home the barren wife *
  as the joyful mother of children.
Glory be to the Father and to the Son *
  and to the Holy Spirit.
As it was in the beginning, is now and ever shall be, *
  world without end. Amen.

Ant. Praise the Lord, O children; praise the name of the Lord.

After this the priest says:

Lord, have mercy.
Christ, have mercy.
Lord, have mercy.
Our Father (silently as far as:)
℣. And lead us not into temptation.
℟. But deliver us from evil. Amen.
℣. Our God is merciful.
℟. Who watches over little ones.
℣. Let the little ones come to me.
℟. For of such is the kingdom of heaven.
℣. O Lord, hear my prayer.
℟. And let my cry come to you.
℣. The Lord be with you.
℟. And with your spirit.

Let us pray. O God, by whose help all things grow to maturity and, once grown, are kept strong, stretch out your hand over this, your young servant, N., in his

Let us pray. O God, by whose help all things grow to maturity and, once grown, are kept strong, stretch out your hand over this, your young servant, N., in her sickness, that he, having regained his health and strength, may grow up to full manhood, and unfailingly offer you a loyal and pleasing service all the days of his life. Through Christ our Lord.

℟. Amen.

sickness, that she, having regained her health and strength, may grow up to full womanhood, and unfailingly offer you a loyal and pleasing service all the days of her life. Through Christ our Lord.

℟. Amen.

After the prayer, the priest places his right hand upon the head of the sick child and says:

"They shall lay their hands upon the sick and they shall recover." May Jesus, Son of Mary, the Lord and Savior of the world, through the merits and intercession of his holy apostles Peter and Paul, and of all the saints, be loving and merciful to you.

℟. Amen.

The following Gospel may be said at the choice of the priest, according to circumstances and the desire of the child's parents.

℣. The Lord be with you.

℟. And with your spirit.

A reading from the holy Gospel according to John.

℟. Glory to you, O Lord.

When the priest says **A reading,** etc., he makes the sign of the Cross as usual upon his forehead, mouth, and breast, and similarly upon the sick child, if the latter cannot sign himself.

John 1:1-14

In the beginning was the Word: the Word was in God's presence, and the Word was God. He was present with God in the beginning. Through him all things came into being, and apart from him not a thing came to be. That which came to be found life in him, and this life was the light of men. The light shines on in the darkness, for the darkness did not overcome it. (Now there was a man sent by God, named John, who came as a witness to testify to the light so that through him all men might believe. But only to testify to the light, for he himself was not the light.) He was the real light that gives light to every man; he was coming into the world. He was in the world, and the world was made by him; yet the world did not recognize him. To his own he came; yet his own people did not accept him. But all those who did accept him — those who believe in his name — he empowered to become God's children: those who were begotten, not by blood, nor the flesh, nor man's desire, but by God. And the Word became flesh and made his dwelling among us. And we have seen his glory, the glory of an only Son coming from the Father, rich in kindness and fidelity.

After this, the priest blesses the sick child, saying:

May the blessing of almighty God, the Father and the Son † and the Holy Spirit, descend upon you and remain forever.
℞. Amen.

Then the priest sprinkles the child with holy water.
If there are several sick children in the same room or place, the above prayers are said in the plural.

BLESSING OF A SICK ADULT

The priest enters the room of the sick person and says:

℣. Peace to this house.
℞. And to all who dwell herein.

He goes directly to the sick person and says:

℣. Our help is in the name of the Lord.
℞. Who made heaven and earth.
℣. O Lord, hear my prayer.
℞. And let my cry come to you.
℣. The Lord be with you.
℞. And with your spirit.

The priest may use one or more of the following prayers.

Let us pray. As I enter here with a sense of my own unworthiness, O Lord Jesus Christ, may your peace and your mercy enter with me. Let the demons with all their wickedness flee from this place; let the angels of peace be present, and let all hateful dissension take leave of this house. O Lord, show forth in us the greatness of your holy name, and bless whatever we do. You who are holy and loving, who live with the Father and the Holy Spirit for ever and ever.
℞. Amen.

Let us pray. O Lord, look upon your servant, N., laboring under bodily weakness, and cherish and revive the soul which you created, so that, purified by his sufferings, he may soon find himself healed by your mercy. Through Christ our Lord.
℞. Amen.

Let us pray. O Lord, look upon your servant, N., laboring under bodily weakness, and cherish and revive the soul which you created, so that, purified by her sufferings, she may soon find herself healed by your mercy. Through Christ our Lord.
℞. Amen.

Let us pray. O Lord, who in mercy console your faithful, we ask of you in your boundless love that as I, your lowly servant, enter here, you may visit this your servant, N., lying on his bed of pain, as you visited the mother of Peter's wife. In your kindness be with him, O Lord, so that he may regain his former strength, and be able to give thanks to you in your Church. Who live and reign, God, for ever and ever.

℟. Amen.

Let us pray. O Lord, who in mercy console your faithful, we ask of you in your boundless love that as I, your lowly servant, enter here, you may visit this your servant, N., lying on her bed of pain, as you visited the mother of Peter's wife. In your kindness be with her, O Lord, so that she may regain her former strength, and be able to give thanks to you in your Church. Who live and reign, God, for ever and ever.

℟. Amen.

Then, extending his right hand toward the sick person, the priest says:

May the Lord Jesus Christ be with you that he may defend you; within you that he may sustain you; before you that he may lead you; behind you that he may protect you; above you that he may bless you: he who lives and reigns with the Father and the Holy Spirit for ever and ever.

℟. Amen.

May the blessing of almighty God, the Father and the Son † and the Holy Spirit, descend upon you and remain forever.

℟. Amen.

Finally he sprinkles the sick person with holy water.

BLESSING OF ANY PLACE OR HOUSE

℣. Our help is in the name of the Lord.

℟. Who made heaven and earth.

℣. The Lord be with you.

℟. And with your spirit.

Let us pray. O Lord God almighty, bless † this place (house). In it may there be health, chastity, victory over sin, strength, humility, goodness of heart and gentleness, full observance of your law and gratefulness to God, the Father, and the Son, and the Holy Spirit. And may this blessing remain upon this place (house) and upon those who live here, now and for ever and ever.

℟. Amen.

The priest sprinkles the place with holy water.

BLESSING OF ANY KIND OF FOOD

℣. Our help is in the name of the Lord.

℟. Who made heaven and earth.

℣. The Lord be with you.

℟. And with your spirit.

Let us pray. O Lord, bless † this N., created by you, that it may be a means of good health for mankind. Grant by this invocation of your holy name that all who partake of it may receive health of body and protection of soul. Through Christ our Lord. ℟. Amen.

The priest sprinkles the food with holy water.

BLESSING OF AN AUTOMOBILE OR ANY KIND OF VEHICLE

℣. Our help is in the name of the Lord.

℟. Who made heaven and earth.

℣. The Lord be with you.

℟. And with your spirit.

Let us pray. O Lord God, listen favorably to our prayers, and with your right hand bless † this car (truck, wagon, etc.). Send your holy angels so that all who ride in it may be delivered and guarded from every danger. And as you granted faith and grace by your deacon, Philip, to the man from Ethiopia who was sitting in his chariot and reading holy Scripture, show the way of salvation to your servants, so that, helped by your grace and always intent on doing good works, they may, after all the trials of their pilgrimage and life on earth, attain to everlasting joys. Through Christ our Lord. ℟. Amen.

The priest sprinkles the vehicle with holy water.

BLESSING FOR ALL THINGS

For use when no special blessing is given.

℣. Our help is in the name of the Lord.

℟. Who made heaven and earth.

℣. The Lord be with you.

℟. And with your spirit.

Let us pray. O God, by whose word all things are made holy, pour down your blessing † on this — (these —) which you created. Grant that whoever, giving thanks to you, uses it (them) in accordance with your law and your will, may by calling upon your holy name receive through your aid health of body and protection of soul. Through Christ our Lord. ℟. Amen.

The priest sprinkles the object (or objects) with holy water.

THE LITURGY FOR AIDING THE SICK

PREPARATION

Those attending the sick person have the serious obligation of calling the priest *in time*. Do not delay until the patient is in a coma, or actually dying. Whenever there is real danger, whenever the illness becomes at all grave, call the priest immediately. Failure to do so, for fear of disturbing or frightening the sick person, is false charity; it means doing a grievous disservice to the sick person. For the better disposed the recipient of the sacraments is, the more fully will he receive of their fruits.

In the case of holy anointing, this is particularly important. For if the sacrament is meant to remove all the "remnants of sin" and to prepare the person for immediate entry into glory, a perfect disposition is prerequisite. And to have this, the mind must be clear and the will capable of making firm decisions. Calling the priest early enough may therefore spare your loved one much, if not all, of his time of purgation in the next world.

Moreover, holy anointing is meant to restore *bodily health* to the sick person, if such be God's holy will. This again is a weighty reason for summoning the priest in time; for we have no right to expect God to work miracles.

In case of *serious accident*, call a priest at once. Then, even if the person is seemingly unconscious, recite aloud for him the act of contrition and repeat the name of Jesus; he may be able to hear and follow mentally. In case of *sudden death*, too, do not fail to call a priest. The soul does not leave the body immediately, and the priest can still administer the sacraments.

THE PRIEST'S VISIT

1. Telephone your parish rectory. Give the priest your address accurately and fully. Station someone outside to direct him if he is not familiar with your residence. Help the sick person make a good preparation for receiving the sacraments by praying with him.

2. Prepare a small table, covered with a white cloth. On it place a crucifix, two blessed candles, holy water, a glass of drinking water, a spoon, a napkin, and some balls of cotton on a dish.

3. If the priest comes with the Blessed Sacrament, meet him at the door with a lighted blessed candle. Place a chair near the head of the sick person's bed. Light the candles on the table. During the confession leave the room, but return for the other rites; kneel and answer the prayers.

Afterwards, when the priest has left, throw the used cotton and water into fire. Continue to pray with the sick person or encourage him to pray by himself.

In some cases it may not be possible for the priest to hear the sick person's confession, confer the sacrament of holy anointing, and give Viaticum *in the order* in which they are here presented. If anything is to be omitted, the priest will say the Introductory Prayers (page 764) and proceed at once to the required rite.

THE LITURGY FOR ADMINISTERING
HOLY COMMUNION TO THE SICK

The liturgy for the administration of holy Communion begins with the following greeting as the priest enters the sick person's room:

℣. Peace to this house.

℟. And to all who dwell herein.

Wearing a white stole, the priest places the Blessed Sacrament on an appropriately prepared table,[1] genuflects and adores; all kneel. Then with holy water he sprinkles the sick person, room, and bystanders, as he says:

Sprinkle me, O Lord, with hyssop, and I shall be purified; wash me, and I shall be whiter than snow.

Ps. 50 Have mercy on me, O God, in your goodness.

Glory be to the Father and to the Son and to the Holy Spirit.

As it was in the beginning, is now and ever shall be, world without end. Amen.

Sprinkle me, O Lord, with hyssop, and I shall be purified; wash me, and I shall be whiter than snow.

℣. Our help is in the name of the Lord.

℟. Who made heaven and earth.

℣. O Lord, hear my prayer.

℟. And let my cry come to you.

℣. The Lord be with you.

℟. And with your spirit.

Let us pray. Hear us, Lord, holy Father, almighty and eternal God, and graciously send your holy angel from heaven to watch over, to cherish, to protect, to abide with, and to defend all who dwell in this house. Through Christ our Lord.

℟. Amen.

Should the sick person wish to go to confession, all others will leave the room. After changing his stole, the priest hears the confession, gives absolution, and says:

May the passion of our Lord Jesus Christ, the merits of the Blessed Virgin Mary and of all the saints, and whatever good you do and evil you endure be cause for the remission of your sins, the increase of grace, and the reward of everlasting life. Amen.

At a sign from the priest, relatives and friends return to the bedside. All present pray the Confiteor:

[1] A table covered with a white cloth, with a crucifix, two blessed candles, holy water, a glass of drinking water, a spoon and a napkin.

I confess to almighty God, to blessed Mary ever Virgin, to blessed Michael the Archangel, to blessed John the Baptist, to the holy apostles Peter and Paul, to all the saints, and to you, Father, that I have sinned exceedingly in thought, word, and deed; through my fault, through my fault, through my most grievous fault. Therefore I beseech blessed Mary ever Virgin, blessed Michael the Archangel, blessed John the Baptist, the holy apostles Peter and Paul, all the saints, and you, Father, to pray to the Lord our God for me.

The priest responds with the following invocations:

May almighty God have mercy on you, forgive you your sins, and bring you to life everlasting.

℟. Amen.

May the almighty and merciful Lord grant you pardon, absolution, † and remission of your sins.

℟. Amen.

After genuflecting, the priest takes the Blessed Eucharist, elevates it so that the sick person may look upon it, and says:

Behold the Lamb of God, * behold him who takes away the sins of the world.

He then says three times (in unison with the sick person and all present):

Lord, I am not worthy that you should come under my roof. * Speak but the word, and my soul will be healed.

He gives the Eucharist, saying:

The Body of Christ.

Communicant: Amen.

If the Blessed Eucharist is being received as holy Viaticum, the following form is used:

Receive, my brother, this food for your journey, the Body of our Lord Jesus Christ, that he may guard you from the wicked enemy and lead you into everlasting life. Amen.

Receive, my sister, this food for your journey, the Body of our Lord Jesus Christ, that he may guard you from the wicked enemy and lead you into everlasting life. Amen.

If death is imminent and there would be danger in delay, the priest says May almighty God have mercy, etc., and, omitting in whole or in part all the above prayers, he administers Viaticum immediately.

After the usual purification, the priest continues:

℣. The Lord be with you.

℟. And with your spirit.

Let us pray. O Lord, holy Father, almighty and eternal God, trustfully we beg of you that the most sacred Body of your Son, our Lord, may be a lasting remedy of both body and soul for our brother who has just received it. Through him who lives and reigns with you in the unity of the Holy Spirit, God, for ever and ever.

℟. Amen.

℣. The Lord be with you.

℟. And with your spirit.

Let us pray. O Lord, holy Father, almighty and eternal God, trustfully we beg of you that the most sacred Body of your Son, our Lord, may be a lasting remedy of both body and soul for our sister who has just received it. Through him who lives and reigns with you in the unity of the Holy Spirit, God, for ever and ever.

℟. Amen.

If there remains another host in the pyx, the priest genuflects and with it makes the sign of the Cross over the sick person; otherwise, he gives a blessing, using the customary form:

May the blessing of almighty God, the Father and the Son ✝ and the Holy Spirit, descend upon you and remain forever.

℟. Amen.

THE LAST RITES

AS GIVEN WITHOUT INTERRUPTION

Upon entering the place where the sick person lies, the priest says:

℣. Peace to this house.

℟. And to all who dwell herein.

If holy Communion is to be given, the priest places the Blessed Eucharist on the fittingly prepared table; all present kneel in adoration. He then places the holy oils alongside the burse, and changes his white stole for a violet one. With holy water, he sprinkles the sick person, those present, and the room, saying:

Sprinkle me, O Lord, with hyssop, and I shall be purified; wash me, and I shall be whiter than snow.

℣. Our help is in the name of the Lord.

℟. Who made heaven and earth.

℣. The Lord be with you.

℟. And with your spirit.

Let us pray. As I enter here with a sense of my own unworthiness, O Lord Jesus Christ, let abiding happiness enter with me; may the blessings of God and unmixed joy accompany my visit; may fruitful charity and lasting good health come with me. Let no evil spirit gain entrance here. May the angels of peace be present, and may all harmful discord leave this house. Strengthen me with your divine power and bless † what I am about to do. Unworthy though I be, may my entry be blessed by you who are holy, you who are merciful, you who abide with the Father and the Holy Spirit for ever and ever.

℟. Amen.

Let us pray and beg our Lord Jesus Christ to fill with his † blessings this house and all who dwell herein. May he give them his holy angel as their guardian; may he prompt them to serve him, mindful of the wonders of his law. May he ward off every hostile power; may he save them from fear and all anxiety, and keep them safe and sound in this house. Who lives and reigns with the Father and the Holy Spirit, God, for ever and ever.

℟. Amen.

Let us pray. Hear us, Lord, holy Father, almighty and eternal God, and graciously send your holy angel from heaven to watch over, to cherish, to protect, to abide with, and to defend all who dwell in this house. Through Christ our Lord.

℟. Amen.

These prayers may be wholly or partially omitted when circumstances warrant.

If the sick person wishes to receive the sacrament of penance, all present leave. After absolving the penitent the priest says:

May the passion of our Lord Jesus Christ, the merits of the Blessed Virgin Mary and of all the saints, and also whatever good you do and evil you endure be cause for the remission of your sins, the increase of grace, and the reward of everlasting life. Amen.

Relatives and friends return to the bedside. The sick person, or others present, say the Confiteor:

I confess to almighty God, to blessed Mary ever Virgin, to blessed Michael the Archangel, to blessed John the Baptist, to the holy apostles Peter and Paul, to all the saints, and to you, Father, that I have sinned exceedingly in thought, word, and deed; through my fault, through my fault, through my most grievous fault. Therefore I beseech blessed Mary ever Virgin, blessed Michael the Archangel, blessed John the Baptist, the holy apostles Peter and Paul, all the saints, and you, Father, to pray to the Lord our God for me.

May almighty God have mercy on you, forgive you your sins, and bring you to life everlasting.

℞. Amen.

May the almighty and merciful Lord grant you pardon, absolution, † and remission of your sins.

℞. Amen.

Before the holy anointing, the priest encourages those present to pray for the sick person. When circumstances permit, he may read the following excerpt from the Gospel or some other appropriate passage.

A reading from the holy Gospel according to Matthew.

Matthew 8:5-10, 13

At that time: After Jesus had entered Capharnaum, a centurion approached him with this request: "Lord, my boy is at home in bed paralyzed, suffering terribly." He said to him, "I will come and cure him." "Lord," replied the centurion, "I am not worthy to have you enter my house. Just give an order, and my boy will get better. I myself know how authority works. I have soldiers under me, and if I give one man the order, 'On your way,' off he goes; or another the order, 'Come here,' he comes. If I tell my slave, 'Do this,' he does it." Jesus was surprised to hear this and he remarked to his followers, "I assure you, I have never found an Israelite with faith as great as this." To the centurion Jesus said, "Go home. It shall be done in answer to your faith." The boy got better that very moment.

A series of versicles and responses follows:

Priest: Let us kneel down and pray.

Lord, have mercy.

Christ, have mercy.

Lord, have mercy.

℣. Lord, that you would visit and strengthen this sick man.

℞. We beseech you, hear us.

℣. That you would give him life and health.

℞. We beseech you, hear us.

℣. That you would grant him the grace of the Holy Spirit.

℞. We beseech you, hear us.

℣. Lamb of God, who take away the sins of the world.

℣. Lord, that you would visit and strengthen this sick woman.

℞. We beseech you, hear us.

℣. That you would give her life and health.

℞. We beseech you, hear us.

℣. That you would grant her the grace of the Holy Spirit.

℞. We beseech you, hear us.

℣. Lamb of God, who take away the sins of the world.

R̷. Spare us, O Lord.

V̷. Lamb of God, who take away the sins of the world.

R̷. Graciously hear us, O Lord.

V̷. Lamb of God, who take away the sins of the world.

R̷. Have mercy on us.

R̷. Spare us, O Lord.

V̷. Lamb of God, who take away the sins of the world.

R̷. Graciously hear us, O Lord.

V̷. Lamb of God, who take away the sins of the world.

R̷. Have mercy on us.

THE HOLY ANOINTING

The priest extends his right hand over the head of the sick person and says:

In the name of the Father † and of the Son † and of the Holy † Spirit. May any power that the devil has over you be utterly destroyed, as I place my hands on you and call upon the help of the glorious and holy Mother of God, the Virgin Mary, and of her illustrious spouse, Joseph, and of all the holy angels, archangels, patriarchs, prophets, apostles, martyrs, confessors, virgins, and all the saints. Amen.

Having moistened his thumb with holy oil, the priest anoints the eyes, ears, nostrils, mouth, hands, and feet of the sick person in the form of a cross as he prays:

ON THE EYES

May the Lord forgive you by this holy † anointing and his most loving mercy whatever sins you have committed by the use of your sight. Amen.

Immediately after each anointing the holy oil is removed with cotton.

ON THE EARS

May the Lord forgive you by this holy † anointing and his most loving mercy whatever sins you have committed by the use of your hearing. Amen.

ON THE NOSTRILS

May the Lord forgive you by this holy † anointing and his most loving mercy whatever sins you have committed by the use of your sense of smell. Amen.

ON THE MOUTH

with lips closed

May the Lord forgive you by this holy † anointing and his most loving mercy whatever sins you have committed by the use of your sense of taste and the power of speech. Amen.

ON THE HANDS

May the Lord forgive you by this holy † anointing and his most loving mercy whatever sins you have committed by the use of your sense of touch. Amen.

ON THE FEET

For any good reason the anointing of the feet may be omitted.

May the Lord forgive you by this holy † anointing and his most loving mercy whatever sins you have committed by the use of your power to walk. Amen.

In the case of extreme urgency, one anointing upon the forehead together with the following form suffices:

May the Lord forgive you by this holy † anointing whatever sins you have committed. Amen.

(If the sick person continues to live, the anointing of the other senses should be completed as described above.)

If the priest is doubtful whether the sick person is still alive, he uses the conditional formula, saying:

If you are alive, may the Lord forgive you by this holy † anointing whatever sins you have committed. Amen.

The priest purifies his hands. If there is sufficient time he continues with the following prayers (if not, he continues as on page 770).

Lord, have mercy.

Christ, have mercy.

Lord, have mercy.

Our Father (silently as far as:)

℣. And lead us not into temptation.

℟. But deliver us from evil.

℣. Save your servant.

℟. Who trusts in you, my God.

℣. Send him help, O Lord, from your sanctuary.

℟. And sustain him from Sion.

℣. Be a tower of strength for him, O Lord.

℟. Against the attack of the enemy.

℣. Let the enemy have no power over him.

℣. Send her help, O Lord, from your sanctuary.

℟. And sustain her from Sion.

℣. Be a tower of strength for her, O Lord.

℟. Against the attack of the enemy.

℣. Let the enemy have no power over her.

℟. And let not the son of evil dare to harm him.

℣. O Lord, hear my prayer.

℟. And let my cry come to you.

℣. The Lord be with you.

℟. And with your spirit.

Let us pray. O Lord God, you said through your apostle James: "Is anyone sick among you? Let him bring in the priests of the Church, and let them pray over him, anointing him with oil in the name of the Lord. And the prayer of faith will save the sick man, and the Lord will raise him up, and if he be in sins, they shall be forgiven him." We implore you, our Redeemer, that by the grace of the Holy Spirit you cure the illness of this sick man and heal his wounds; forgive his sins, and drive away from him all pains of mind and body. In your mercy give him health, inward and outward, so that he may once more be able to take up his work, restored by the gift of your mercy. You who live and reign with the Father and the Holy Spirit, God, for ever and ever.

℟. Amen.

Let us pray. We implore you, O Lord, look with kindness on your servant, N., who is growing weak as his body fails. Cherish the soul which you created, so that, purified and made whole by his sufferings, he may find himself restored by your healing. Through Christ our Lord.

℟. Amen.

℟. And let not the son of evil dare to harm her.

℣. O Lord, hear my prayer.

℟. And let my cry come to you.

℣. The Lord be with you.

℟. And with your spirit.

Let us pray. O Lord God, you said through your apostle James: "Is anyone sick among you? Let him bring in the priests of the Church, and let them pray over him, anointing him with oil in the name of the Lord. And the prayer of faith will save the sick man, and the Lord will raise him up, and if he be in sins, they shall be forgiven him." We implore you, our Redeemer, that by the grace of the Holy Spirit you cure the illness of this sick woman and heal her wounds; forgive her sins, and drive away from her all pains of mind and body. In your mercy give her health, inward and outward, so that she may once more be able to take up her work, restored by the gift of your mercy. You who live and reign with the Father and the Holy Spirit, God, for ever and ever.

℟. Amen.

Let us pray. We implore you, O Lord, look with kindness on your servant, N., who is growing weak as her body fails. Cherish the soul which you created, so that, purified and made whole by her sufferings, she may find herself restored by your healing. Through Christ our Lord.

℟. Amen.

Let us pray. Lord, holy Father, almighty and eternal God, by pouring the grace of your blessing into the bodies of the sick, you watch with all-embracing care over your creatures. Be present in your kindness as we call upon your holy name. Free your servant from sickness, restore him his health, raise him up by your right hand, strengthen him by your power, protect him by your might and give him back to your holy Church, with all that is needed for his welfare. Through Christ our Lord. ℟. Amen.

Let us pray. Lord, holy Father, almighty and eternal God, by pouring the grace of your blessing into the bodies of the sick, you watch with all-embracing care over your creatures. Be present in your kindness as we call upon your holy name. Free your servant from sickness, restore her her health, raise her up by your right hand, strengthen her by your power, protect her by your might and give her back to your holy Church, with all that is needed for her welfare. Through Christ our Lord. ℟. Amen.

When the case is urgent and the preceding prayers have been omitted, the priest continues with:

THE ADMINISTRATION OF VIATICUM

The priest removes his violet stole and puts on the white stole again. He genuflects, opens the pyx, and then may say:

Let us pray, beloved brothers, as our Lord himself taught us.

All present recite the Lord's Prayer aloud:

Our Father . . .

The priest then says:

We beg you, O Lord, at this moment above all, to deliver this your servant from all evil and to strengthen him with the bread of life, the Body of our Lord Jesus Christ, who lives and reigns with you for ever and ever. ℟. Amen.

We beg you, O Lord, at this moment above all, to deliver this your servant from all evil and to strengthen her with the bread of life, the Body of our Lord Jesus Christ, who lives and reigns with you for ever and ever. ℟. Amen.

The priest then genuflects and, raising up the host in the sight of the sick person, says:

Behold the Lamb of God, * behold him who takes away the sins of the world.

In the usual way, he then says three times:

Lord, I am not worthy that you should come under my roof. * Speak but the word, and my soul will be healed.

As is customary, the sick person and those assisting join in repeating this invocation. The priest then gives the Eucharist to the sick person, saying:

Receive, my brother, this food for your journey, the Body of our Lord Jesus Christ, that he may guard you from the wicked enemy and lead you into everlasting life. Amen.

Receive, my sister, this food for your journey, the Body of our Lord Jesus Christ, that he may guard you from the wicked enemy and lead you into everlasting life. Amen.

If death is very near and there is danger in delay, after the anointing the priest immediately holds up the host and says, Behold the Lamb of God, etc.

After purifying his fingers, the priest says:

℣. The Lord be with you.
℟. And with your spirit.

Let us pray. O Lord, holy Father, almighty and eternal God, trustfully we beg of you that the most sacred Body of your Son, our Lord, may be a lasting remedy of both body and soul for our brother who has just received it. Through him who lives and reigns with you in the unity of the Holy Spirit, God, for ever and ever.
℟. Amen.

Let us pray. O Lord, holy Father, almighty and eternal God, trustfully we beg of you that the most sacred Body of your Son, our Lord, may be a lasting remedy of both body and soul for our sister who has just received it. Through him who lives and reigns with you in the unity of the Holy Spirit, God, for ever and ever.
℟. Amen.

The priest and all those present say:

O holy banquet, in which Christ is received, the memory of his passion is renewed, the soul is filled with grace, and there is given to us a pledge of future glory.

℣. You have given them bread from heaven.
℟. Containing in itself all delight.
℣. The Lord be with you.
℟. And with your spirit.

Let us pray. O God, who in this wonderful sacrament left us a memorial of your passion, grant, we implore you, that we may so venerate the sacred mysteries of your Body and Blood as always to be conscious of the fruit of your redemption. You who live and reign for ever and ever.
℟. Amen.

THE APOSTOLIC BLESSING FOR THE HOUR OF DEATH

Let us pray. O God most kind, the Father of mercies and the God of all consolation, it is your will that no one who believes and hopes in you should perish. In your boundless mercy, look with kindness on your servant, N., for true faith and Christian hope commend him (her) to you. Come to him (her) in your saving power, and because of the passion and death of your only Son be pleased to grant him (her) remission and pardon of all his (her) sins, so that his (her) soul, when it leaves this life, may find you a most favorable judge and, cleansed from every stain by the Blood of your Son, may enter into life everlasting. Through Christ our Lord. ℞. Amen.

May our Lord Jesus Christ, the Son of the living God, who gave to Peter his apostle the power to bind and to set free, in his most loving mercy receive your confession and give back to you that robe of grace which was first given to you in baptism. And I, by the power given to me by the Apostolic See, grant you a full pardon and the remission of all your sins. In the name of the Father and of the Son † and of the Holy Spirit. ℞. Amen.

Through the most sacred mysteries of man's redemption, may almighty God remit all the punishments due to you in this life and in the life to come; may he open to you the gates of heaven, and lead you into everlasting joy. ℞. Amen.

May almighty God bless you, the Father and the Son † and the Holy Spirit. ℞. Amen.

When necessity demands, the following shorter form may be used:

By the power given me by the Apostolic See, I grant you a plenary indulgence and the remission of all your sins, and I bless you. In the name of the Father and of the Son † and of the Holy Spirit. ℞. Amen.

OFFICE OF THE DEAD

This Office is said in choir on the day of burial and on other days when the occasion is suitable or when the custom of the particular church calls for it: Matins together with Lauds after Lauds of the day, Vespers after Vespers of the day, immediately after the verse **Let us bless the Lord** and **Thanks be to God.** At the end of every psalm, however, there is said

Eternal rest * grant unto them, O Lord.

And let perpetual light * shine upon them.

always in the plural, even if the Office is being recited for one person only.

MATINS

The Hour begins directly with the invitatory.

Except on the day of the Commemoration of all the Faithful departed, there is a choice between saying all the Nocturns given below and saying one only. If the latter option is taken, then, aside from the day of burial, on which the first Nocturn is always said, the following order is observed:

Sunday, Monday and Thursday — first Nocturn;

Tuesday and Friday — second Nocturn;

Wednesday and Saturday — third Nocturn.

Invit. **The King for whom all things live, * Come, let us adore.**

Repeat **The King for whom all things live, come, let us adore.**

Psalm 94

Come, let us sing joyfully to the Lord; let us acclaim the Rock of our salvation. Let us greet him with thanksgiving; let us joyfully sing psalms to him.

The King for whom all things live, come, let us adore.

For the Lord is a great God, and a great king above all gods; in his hands are the depths of the earth, and the tops of the mountains are his.

Come, let us adore.

His is the sea, for he has made it, and the dry land, which his hands have formed. Come, let us bow down in worship; let us kneel before the Lord who made us. For he is our God, and we are the people he shepherds, the flock he guides.

The King for whom all things live, come, let us adore.

Oh, that today you would hear his voice: "Harden not your hearts as at Meriba, as in the day of Massa in the desert, where your fathers tempted me; they tested me though they had seen my works.

Come, let us adore.

"Forty years I loathed that generation, and I said: They are a people of erring heart, and they know not my ways. Therefore I swore in my anger: They shall not enter into my rest."

The King for whom all things live, come, let us adore.

Eternal rest grant unto them, O Lord, and let perpetual light shine upon them.

Come, let us adore.

The King for whom all things live, come, let us adore.

1st Nocturn

For Sunday, Monday and Thursday

Ant. 1 **Direct * my way in your sight, O Lord, my God.**

[1] Psalm 5

Hearken to my words, O Lord, * attend to my sighing.

Heed my call for help, * my king and my God!

To you I pray, O Lord; at dawn you hear my voice; * at dawn I bring my plea expectantly before you. —

For you, O God, delight not in wickedness; no evil man remains with you; * the arrogant may not stand in your sight.

You hate all evildoers; * you destroy all who speak falsehood;

The bloodthirsty and the deceitful * the Lord abhors. —

But I, because of your abundant kindness, * will enter your house;

I will worship at your holy temple * in fear of you, O Lord;

Because of my enemies, guide me in your justice; * make straight your way before me. —

For in their mouth there is no sincerity; * their heart teems with treacheries.

Their throat is an open grave; * they flatter with their tongue.

Punish them, O God; * let them fall by their own devices;

For their many sins, cast them out * because they have rebelled against you. —

But let all who take refuge in you be glad * and exult forever.

Protect them, that you may be the joy * of those who love your name.

For you, O Lord, bless the just man; * you surround him with the shield of your good will.

Eternal rest * grant unto them, O Lord.

And let perpetual light * shine upon them.

Ant. Direct my way in your sight, O Lord, my God.

Ant. 2 Turn to me, * Lord, and save my soul; for among the dead no one remembers you.

[2] Psalm 6

O Lord, reprove me not in your anger, * nor chastise me in your wrath.

Have pity on me, O Lord, for I am languishing; * heal me, O Lord, for my body is in terror;

My soul, too, is utterly terrified; * but you, O Lord, how long . . . ? —

Return, O Lord, save my life; * rescue me because of your kindness,

For among the dead no one remembers you; * in the nether world who gives you thanks? —

I am wearied with sighing; every night I flood my bed with weeping; * I drench my couch with my tears.

My eyes are dimmed with sorrow; * they have aged because of all my foes. —

Depart from me, all evildoers, * for the Lord has heard the sound of my weeping;

The Lord has heard my plea; * the Lord has accepted my prayer.

All my enemies shall be put to shame in utter terror; * they shall fall back in sudden shame.

Eternal rest.

Ant. Turn to me, Lord, and save my soul; for among the dead no one remembers you.

Ant. 3 Lest my soul * become like the lion's prey, while there is no one to redeem me or save me.

[3] Psalm 7

O Lord, my God, in you I take refuge; * save me from all my pursuers and rescue me,

Lest I become like the lion's prey, * to be torn to pieces, with no one to rescue me. —

O Lord, my God, if I am at fault in this, * if there is guilt on my hands,

If I have repaid my friend with evil, * I who spared those who without cause were my foes,

Let the enemy pursue and overtake me; let him trample my life to the ground, * and lay my glory in the dust. —

Rise up, O Lord, in your anger; rise against the fury of my foes; * wake to the judgment you have decreed.

Let the assembly of the peoples surround you; * above them on high be enthroned.

The Lord judges the nations. Do me justice, O Lord, because I am just, * and because of the innocence that is mine.

Let the malice of the wicked come to an end, but sustain the just, * O searcher of heart and soul, O just God. —

A shield before me is God, * who saves the upright of heart;

A just judge is God, * a God who punishes day by day.

Unless they be converted, God will sharpen his sword; * he will bend and aim his bow,

Prepare his deadly weapons against them, * and use fiery darts for arrows. —

He who conceived iniquity and was pregnant with mischief, * brings forth failure.

He has opened a hole, he has dug it deep, * but he falls into the pit which he has made.

His mischief shall recoil upon his own head; * upon the crown of his head his violence shall rebound.

I will give thanks to the Lord for his justice, * and sing praise to the name of the Lord Most High.

Eternal rest.

Ant. Lest my soul become like the lion's prey, while there is no one to redeem me or save me.

℣. From the gate of hell. ℟. Deliver their souls, O Lord.

Our Father silently throughout.

The lessons are read without absolution, blessings or title.

Lesson i   Job 7:16-21

Spare me, Lord, for my days are but a breath. What is man, that you make much of him, or pay him any heed? You observe him with each new day and try him at every moment! How long will it be before you look away from me, and let me alone long enough to swallow my spittle? Though I have sinned, what can I do to you, O watcher of men? Why have you set me up against you; or why should I be a burden to myself? Why do you not pardon my offense, or take away my guilt? For soon I shall lie down in the dust; and should you seek me in the morning, I shall be gone.

The lessons end without any other conclusion.

℟. I believe that my Redeemer lives, and that on the last day I shall rise from the earth, * And in my flesh I shall see God, my Savior. ℣. It will not be some other being, but I myself who see him: my own eyes shall look upon him. And.

Lesson ii   Job 10:1-7

I loathe my life. I will give myself up to complaint; I will speak from the bitterness of my soul. I will say to God: Do not put me in the wrong! Let me know why you oppose me. Is it a pleasure for you to oppress, to spurn the work of your hands, and smile on the plan of the wicked? Have you eyes of flesh? Do you see as man sees? Are your days as the days of a mortal, and are your years as a man's lifetime, that you seek for guilt in me and search after my sins, even though you know that I am not wicked and that none can deliver me out of your hand?

℟. You who raised Lazarus fetid from the tomb, * You, Lord, give them rest, and a place of pardon. ℣. You who are to come to judge the living and the dead, to judge the world by fire, You, Lord.

Lesson iii   Job 10:8-12

Your hands have formed me and fashioned me; will you then turn and destroy me? Oh, remember that you fashioned me from clay! Will you then bring me down to dust again? Did you not pour me out as milk, and thicken me like cheese? With skin and flesh you clothed me, with bones and sinews knit me together. Grace and favor you granted me, and providence has preserved my spirit.

℟. Lord, when you come to judge the earth, where shall I hide from your wrathful countenance? * For I have sinned exceedingly in my life. ℣. I am appalled at the sins I have committed, and I blush before you. Do not condemn me when you come to judge. For. Eternal rest grant unto them, O Lord, and let perpetual light shine upon them. For.

Then Lauds, as below **782** when only one Nocturn is said.

But if Lauds are omitted altogether, then after the 3rd responsory the **Our Father** and the *preces* are said, as below at Lauds **785**.

2nd Nocturn
For Tuesday and Friday

Ant. 4 **In verdant pastures * he gives me repose.**

[4]   Psalm 22

The Lord is my shepherd; I shall not want. * In verdant pastures he gives me repose.

Beside restful waters he leads me; * he refreshes my soul.

He guides me in right paths * for his name's sake.

Even though I walk in the dark valley * I fear no evil; for you are at my side

With your rod and your staff * that give me courage. —

You spread the table before me * in the sight of my foes;

You anoint my head with oil; * my cup overflows.

Only goodness and kindness follow me * all the days of my life;

And I shall dwell in the house of the Lord * for years to come.

Eternal rest.

Ant. In verdant pastures he gives me repose.

Ant. 5 **The sins * of my youth and my frailties remember not, O Lord.**

[5]   Psalm 24

To you I lift up my soul, * O Lord, my God.

In you I trust; let me not be put to shame, * let not my enemies exult over me.

No one who waits for you shall be put to shame; * those shall be put to shame who heedlessly break faith.

Your ways, O Lord, make known to me; * teach me your paths,

Guide me in your truth and teach me, for you are God my savior, * and for you I wait all the day.

Remember that your compassion, O Lord, * and your kindness are from of old.

The sins of my youth and my frailties remember not; in your kindness remember me, * because of your goodness, O Lord. —

Good and upright is the Lord; * thus he shows sinners the way.

He guides the humble to justice, * he teaches the humble his way.

All the paths of the Lord are kindness and constancy * toward those who keep his covenant and his decrees.

For your name's sake, O Lord, * you will pardon my guilt, great as it is.

When a man fears the Lord, * he shows him the way he should choose.

He abides in prosperity, * and his descendants inherit the land.

The friendship of the Lord is with those who fear him, * and his covenant, for their instruction. —

My eyes are ever toward the Lord, * for he will free my feet from the snare.

Look toward me, and have pity on me, * for I am alone and afflicted.

Relieve the troubles of my heart, * and bring me out of my distress.

Consider my affliction and my suffering, * and take away all my sins.

Behold, my enemies are many, * and they hate me violently.

Preserve my life and rescue me; * let me not be put to shame, for I take refuge in you.

Let integrity and uprightness preserve me, * because I wait for you, O Lord.

Redeem Israel, O God, * from all its distress!

Eternal rest.

Ant. The sins of my youth and my frailties remember not, O Lord.

Ant. 6 I believe that I shall see * the bounty of the Lord in the land of the living.

[6]   Psalm 26

The Lord is my light and my salvation; whom should I fear? * The Lord is my life's refuge; of whom should I be afraid?

When evildoers come at me to devour my flesh, * my foes and my enemies themselves stumble and fall.

Though an army encamp against me, my heart will not fear; * though war be waged upon me, even then will I trust. —

One thing I ask of the Lord; this I seek: * to dwell in the house of the Lord all the days of my life,

That I may gaze on the loveliness of the Lord * and contemplate his temple.

For he will hide me in his abode in the day of trouble; * he will conceal me in the shelter of his tent, he will set me high upon a rock.

Even now my head is held high * above my enemies on every side.

And I will offer in his tent sacrifices with shouts of gladness; * I will sing and chant praise to the Lord. —

Hear, O Lord, the sound of my call; * have pity on me, and answer me.

Of you my heart speaks; you my glance seeks; * your presence, O Lord, I seek.

Hide not your face from me; * do not in anger repel your servant.

You are my helper: cast me not

off; * forsake me not, O God my savior.

Though my father and mother forsake me, * yet will the Lord receive me. —

Show me, O Lord, your way, * and lead me on a level path, because of my adversaries.

Give me not up to the wishes of my foes; * for false witnesses have risen up against me, and such as breathe out violence.

I believe that I shall see the bounty of the Lord * in the land of the living.

Wait for the Lord with courage; * be stouthearted, and wait for the Lord.

Eternal rest.

Ant. I believe that I shall see the bounty of the Lord in the land of the living.

℣. May the Lord seat them with princes. ℟. With the princes of his people.

Our Father silently throughout.

Lesson iv   Job 13:22-28

Answer me. What are my faults and my sins? My misdeeds and my sins make known to me! Why do you hide your face and consider me your enemy? Will you harass a wind-driven leaf, or pursue a withered straw? For you draw up bitter indictments against me, and punish in me the faults of my youth. You put my feet in the stocks; you watch all my paths and trace out all my footsteps. I waste away like a rotten thing, like a garment that the moth has consumed.

℟. Remember me, O God, because my life is but wind, * And men will see me no more. ℣. Out of the depths I have cried to you, O Lord; Lord, hear my voice. And.

Lesson v   Job 14:1-6

Man, born of woman, is short-lived and full of trouble. Like a flower he springs up and fades; he flees like a shadow, and never continues in the same state. Upon such a one will you cast your eyes so as to bring him into judgment with you? Who can make clean one that is conceived of unclean seed? Who but you alone? Short are the days of man. You know the number of his months; you have fixed the limit which he cannot pass. Look away from him and let him be, while, like a hireling, he completes his day.

℟. Alas for me, Lord! I have sinned exceedingly in my life. Wretch that I am, what shall I do? Where shall I fly but to you, my God? * Have mercy on me when you come on the last day. ℣. My soul is greatly troubled; come to its aid, O Lord. Have mercy.

Lesson vi   Job 14:13-16

Who would grant me this, that you would hide me in the nether world and keep me sheltered till your wrath is past; that you would fix a time for me, and then remember me? When a man has died, do you think he will live again? All the days of my drudgery I shall wait, until my relief comes. You will call, and I shall answer you; you will offer support to the work of your hands. You have indeed counted my steps; but now, overlook my sins.

℟. Remember not my sins, O Lord, * When you come to judge the world by fire. ℣. Direct my way in your sight, O Lord, my God. When. Eternal rest grant unto them, O Lord, and let perpetual light shine upon them. When.

Then Lauds, as below 782, when only one Nocturn is said.

But if Lauds are omitted altogether, then after the last responsory the **Our Father** and the *preces* are said, as below at Lauds 785.

3rd Nocturn
For Wednesday and Saturday

Ant. 7 May it please you, * Lord, to deliver me: Lord, have regard to help me.

[7] Psalm 39

I have waited, waited for the Lord, and he stooped toward me * and heard my cry.

He drew me out of the pit of destruction, out of the mud of the swamp; he set my feet upon a crag; * he made firm my steps.

And he put a new song into my mouth, * a hymn to our God.

Many shall look on in awe * and trust in the Lord. —

Happy the man who makes the Lord his trust; * who turns not to idolatry or to those who stray after falsehood.

How numerous have you made, O Lord, my God, your wondrous deeds! * And in your plans for us there is none to equal you;

Should I wish to declare or to tell them, * they would be too many to recount. —

Sacrifice or oblation you wished not, * but ears open to obedience you gave me.

Holocausts or sin-offerings you sought not; * then said I, "Behold I come; in the written scroll it is prescribed for me,

To do your will, O my God, is my delight, * and your law is within my heart!" —

I announced your justice in the vast assembly; * I did not restrain my lips, as you, O Lord, know.

Your justice I kept not hid within my heart; * your faithfulness and your salvation I have spoken of;

I have made no secret of your kindness * and your truth in the vast assembly. —

Withhold not, O Lord, your compassion from me; * may your kindness and your truth ever preserve me.

For all about me are evils beyond reckoning; * my sins so overcome me that I cannot see;

They are more numerous than the hairs of my head, * and my heart fails me. —

Deign, O Lord, to rescue me; * O Lord, make haste to help me.

Let all be put to shame and confusion * who seek to snatch away my life.

Let them be turned back in disgrace * who desire my ruin.

Let them be dismayed in their shame * who say to me "Aha, aha!"

But may all who seek you exult and be glad in you, * and may those who love your salvation say ever, "The Lord be glorified."

Though I am afflicted and poor, * yet the Lord thinks of me.

You are my help and my deliverer; * O my God, hold not back!

Eternal rest.

Ant. May it please you, Lord, to deliver me: Lord, have regard to help me.

Ant. 8 Heal my soul, * Lord, for I have sinned against you.

[8] Psalm 40

Happy is he who has regard for the lowly and the poor; * in the day of misfortune the Lord will deliver him.

The Lord will keep and preserve him; he will make him happy on the earth, * and not give him over to the will of his enemies.

The Lord will help him on his sickbed, * he will take away all his ailment when he is ill. —

Once I said, "O Lord, have pity on me; * heal me, though I have sinned against you.

My enemies say the worst of me: * 'When will he die and his name perish?'

When one comes to see me, he speaks without sincerity; * his heart stores up malice; when he leaves he gives voice to it outside.

All my foes whisper together against me; * against me they imagine the worst:

'A malignant disease fills his frame'; * and 'Now that he lies ill, he will not rise again.'

Even my friend who had my trust * and partook of my bread, has raised his heel against me. —

But you, O Lord, have pity on me, and raise me up, * that I may repay them."

That you love me I know by this, * that my enemy does not triumph over me,

But because of my integrity you sustain me * and let me stand before you forever. —

Blessed be the Lord, the God of Israel, * from all eternity and forever. Amen. Amen.

Eternal rest.

Ant. Heal my soul, Lord, for I have sinned against you.

Ant. 9 Athirst * is my soul for the living God. When shall I come

and appear before the face of the Lord?

[9] Psalm 41

As the hind longs for the running waters, * so my soul longs for you, O God.

Athirst is my soul for God, the living God. * When shall I go and behold the face of God?

My tears are my food day and night, * as they say to me day after day, "Where is your God?"

Those times I recall, now that I pour out my soul within me, when I went with the throng * and led them in procession to the house of God,

Amid loud cries of joy and thanksgiving, * with the multitude keeping festival.

Why are you so downcast, O my soul? * Why do you sigh within me?

Hope in God! For I shall again be thanking him, * my savior and my God. —

Within me my soul is downcast; * so will I remember you from the land of the Jordan and of Hermon, from Mount Misar.

Deep calls unto deep in the roar of your cataracts; * all your breakers and your billows pass over me.

By day the Lord bestows his grace, * and at night I have his song, a prayer to my living God.

I sing to God, 'My Rock, why do you forget me? * Why must I go about in mourning, with the enemy oppressing me?"

It crushes my bones that my foes mock me, * as they say to me day after day, "Where is your God?"

Why are you so downcast, O my soul? * Why do you sigh within me?

Hope in God! For I shall again be thanking him, * my savior and my God.

Eternal rest.

Ant. Athirst is my soul for the living God. When shall I come and appear before the face of the Lord?

℣. Give not to the beasts the souls that praise you. ℟. Be not forever unmindful of the souls of your afflicted ones.

Our Father silently throughout.

Lesson vii   Job 17:1-3, 11-15

My spirit is broken, my lamp of life extinguished; my burial is at hand. I have not sinned, and my eye rests on bitter sights. Deliver me, Lord, and set me beside you, and it matters not whose hand fights against me. My days are passed away, my plans are at an end, leaving my heart tormented. Such men change the night into day; and after darkness I hope for light again. If I wait, the nether world is my dwelling, and I have spread my couch in the darkness. I have called corruption "my father," and the maggot "my mother" and "my sister." Where then is my hope, and who is concerned about my patience?

℟. The fear of death troubles me, as I sin daily and do not repent. * Since in hell there is no redemption, have mercy on me, O God, and save me. ℣. O God, by your name save me, and by your might deliver me. Since.

Lesson viii   Job 19:20-27

The flesh has been consumed, and my bones cleave to my skin, and nothing but lips are left about my teeth. Pity me, pity me, at least you my friends, for the hand of God has struck me! Why do you hound me as though you were divine, and insatiably prey upon me? Who will see to it that my words are written down? Who will do me the favor of inscribing them in a record, engraving them with an iron chisel in a plate of lead or cutting them in stone? But as for me, I know that my Redeemer lives, and that on the last day I shall rise out of the earth and be clothed again with my skin, and in my flesh I shall see my God. It will not be some other being, but I myself who see him: my own eyes shall look upon him. This my hope lies deep in my heart.

℟. O Lord, judge me not according to my deeds, for I have done nothing worthy in your sight; therefore I beseech your majesty * That you, O God, may wipe out my offense. ℣ Thoroughly wash me, O Lord, from my injustice, and of my sin cleanse me. That.

Lesson ix   Job 10:18-22

Why did you bring me forth from the womb? I should have died and no eye have seen me. I should have been as though I had never lived; I should have been taken from the womb to the grave. Are not the days of my life few? Let me alone, therefore, that I may lament my sorrow a little before I go whence I shall not return, to the land that is dark and covered with the mist of death, the land of misery and of darkness, where the shadow of death lies, and there is no order, only everlasting horror.

The following responsory is used when only the third Nocturn for the dead has been said.

℟. Deliver me, Lord, from the paths of hell. You have shattered the bronze doors, and visited hell, and given them light, that they might see you, * For they were suffering in darkness. ℣. "You have come, our Redeemer," they cried out. For. Eternal rest grant unto them, O Lord, and let perpetual light shine upon them. For.

The following responsory takes the place of the preceding one when three Nocturns for the dead have been said.

℞. Deliver me, O Lord, from eternal death on that dreadful day * When the heavens and the earth shall be shaken, * When you shall come to judge the world by fire. ℣. I am seized by fear and trembling as the judgment draws near and that future wrath. When the heavens. ℣. That day shall be a day of wrath and of ruin and of misery; that day so great, so very galling. When you. Eternal rest grant unto them, O Lord, and let perpetual light shine upon them. Deliver me, up to but not including the first ℣. I am seized.

Then, if Lauds are omitted altogether, after the last responsory the **Our Father** and the *preces* are said, as below at Lauds **785.**

If Matins, with a single Nocturn or with three Nocturns, is separated from Lauds, the following is added after the last responsory:

℣. The Lord be with you.
℞. And with your spirit.
Or: ℣. O Lord, hear my prayer.
℞. And let my cry come to you.

Then the Collect is said, as below at Lauds **785,** with the following added:

℣. Eternal rest grant unto them, O Lord.
℞. And let perpetual light shine upon them.

℣. May they rest in peace.
℞. Amen.

LAUDS

The Hour begins directly with the following:

Ant. 1 **Crushed bones * shall rejoice before the Lord.**

[1]   Psalm 50

Have mercy on me, O God, in your goodness; * in the greatness of your compassion wipe out my offense.

Thoroughly wash me from my guilt * and of my sin cleanse me. —

For I acknowledge my offense, * and my sin is before me always:

"Against you only have I sinned, * and done what is evil in your sight" —

That you may be justified in your sentence, * vindicated when you condemn.

Indeed, in guilt was I born, * and in sin my mother conceived me;

Behold, you are pleased with sincerity of heart, * and in my inmost being you teach me wisdom. —

Cleanse me of sin with hyssop, that I may be purified; * wash me, and I shall be whiter than snow.

Let me hear the sounds of joy and gladness; * the bones you have crushed shall rejoice.

Turn away your face from my sins, * and blot out all my guilt. —

A clean heart create for me, O God, * and a steadfast spirit renew within me.

Cast me not out from your presence, * and your holy spirit take not from me.

Give me back the joy of your salvation, * and a willing spirit sustain in me. —

I will teach transgressors your ways, * and sinners shall return to you.

Free me from blood guilt, O God, my saving God; * then my tongue shall revel in your justice.

O Lord, open my lips, * and my mouth shall proclaim your praise.

For you are not pleased with sacrifices; * should I offer a holocaust, you would not accept it.

My sacrifice, O God, is a contrite spirit; * a heart contrite and humbled, O God, you will not spurn. —

Be bountiful, O Lord, to Sion in your kindness * by rebuilding the walls of Jerusalem;

Then shall you be pleased with due sacrifices, burnt offerings and holocausts; * then shall they offer up bullocks on your altar.

Eternal rest.

Ant. Crushed bones shall rejoice before the Lord.

Ant. 2 O Lord, * hear my prayer; to you all flesh must come.

[2]   Psalm 64

To you we owe our hymn of praise, O God, in Sion; * to you must vows be fulfilled, you who hear prayers.

To you all flesh must come * because of wicked deeds.

We are overcome by our sins; * it is you who pardon them.

Happy the man you choose, and bring * to dwell in your courts.

May we be filled with the good things of your house, * the holy things of your temple! —

With awe-inspiring deeds of justice you answer us, * O God our savior,

The hope of all the ends of the earth * and of the distant seas.

You set the mountains in place by your power, * you who are girt with might;

You still the roaring of the seas, * the roaring of the waves and the tumult of the peoples.

And the dwellers at the earth's ends are in fear at your marvels; * the farthest east and west you make resound with joy. —

You have visited the land and watered it; * greatly have you enriched it.

God's watercourses are filled; you have prepared the grain. * Thus have you prepared the land:

Drenching its furrows, * breaking up its clods,

Softening it with showers, * blessing its yield.

You have crowned the year with your bounty, * and your paths overflow with a rich harvest;

The untilled meadows overflow with it, * and rejoicing clothes the hills.

The fields are garmented with flocks and the valleys blanketed with grain. * They shout and sing for joy.

Eternal rest.

Ant. O Lord, hear my prayer; to you all flesh must come.

Ant. 3 Your right hand * upholds me, O Lord.

[3]   Psalm 62

O God, you are my God * whom I seek;

For you my flesh pines and my soul thirsts * like the earth, parched, lifeless and without water.

Thus have I gazed toward you in the sanctuary * to see your power and your glory,

For your kindness is a greater good than life; * my lips shall glorify you. —

Thus will I bless you while I live; * lifting up my hands, I will call upon your name.

As with the riches of a banquet shall my soul be satisfied, * and with exultant lips my mouth shall praise you.

I will remember you upon my couch, * and through the night-watches I will meditate on you:

That you are my help, * and in the shadow of your wings I shout for joy.

My soul clings fast to you; * your right hand upholds me. —

But they shall be destroyed who seek my life, * they shall go into the depths of the earth;

They shall be delivered over to the sword, * and shall be the prey of jackals.

The king, however, shall rejoice in God; everyone who swears by him shall glory, * but the mouths of those who speak falsely shall be stopped.

Eternal rest.

Ant. Your right hand upholds me, O Lord.

Ant. 4 From the gate of hell * deliver my soul, O Lord.

[4]   Canticle of Ezechias
Is. 38:10-20

Once I said, "In the noontime of life I must depart to the gates of the nether world. * I am bereft of the rest of my years."

I said, "I shall see the Lord no more in the land of the living. * No longer shall I behold my fellow men among those who dwell in the world."

My dwelling, like a shepherd's tent, * is struck down and borne away from me.

I roll up my life like a weaver; he cuts me off from the thread. * Day and night you give me over to torment.

I cry out until the dawn. Like a lion he breaks all my bones; * day and night you give me over to torment.

Like a swallow I utter shrill cries; * I moan like a dove.

My eyes grow weak, gazing heavenward: * O Lord, I am in straits; be my surety! —

What shall I say? For he has told me and he has done it! I shall go on through all my years * despite the bitterness of my soul.

Those live whom the Lord protects, and among them the life of my spirit will go on; * you have healed me and kept me alive!

Thus is my bitterness transformed into salvation. You have preserved my life from the pit of destruction * when you cast behind you all my sins.

For it is not the nether world that gives you thanks, nor death that praises you; * neither do those who go down into the pit await your kindness.

The living, the living give you thanks, as I do today; * fathers declare to their sons your faithfulness.

The Lord keeps me; and so we will sing my psalms * all the days of our life in the house of the Lord.

Eternal rest.

Ant. From the gate of hell deliver my soul, O Lord.

Ant. 5 Let everything that has breath * praise the Lord!

[5]   Psalm 150

Praise the Lord in his sanctuary, * praise him in the firmament of his strength.

Praise him for his mighty deeds, * praise him for his sovereign majesty.

Praise him with the blast of the trumpet, * praise him with lyre and harp,

Praise him with timbrel and dance, * praise him with strings and pipe.

Praise him with sounding cymbals, praise him with clanging cymbals. * Let everything that has breath praise the Lord!

Eternal rest.

Ant. Let everything that has breath praise the Lord!

℣. I heard a voice from heaven saying. ℟. Blessed are the dead who die in the Lord.

Ant. (Ben.) I am * the resurrection and the life; he who believes in me, even if he die, shall live; and whoever lives and believes in me, shall never die.

Canticle of Zachary
Luke 1:68-79

Blessed be the Lord, the God of Israel, * because he has visited and wrought redemption for his people.

And has raised up a horn of salvation for us * in the house of David his servant.

. As he promised through the mouths of his holy ones, * the prophets from of old:

Salvation from our enemies * and from the hands of all our foes.

He has fulfilled his kindness to our fathers, * and been mindful of his holy covenant

In the oath to Abraham our father, * by which he swore to grant us

That, delivered from the hands of our enemies, * we should serve him without fear

In holiness and justice before him * all our days. —

And you, O child, shall be called the prophet of the Most High; * for you shall go before the Lord to prepare his ways.

To give his people knowledge of salvation * through forgiveness of their sins,

Because of the compassionate kindness of our God * with which the Orient from on high will visit us,

To shine on those who sit in darkness and the shadow of death, * to guide our feet into the way of peace.

Eternal rest.

Ant. I am the resurrection and the life; he who believes in me, even if he die, shall live; and whoever lives and believes in me, shall never die.

Then, kneeling:

Our Father then silently to

℣. And lead us not into temptation. ℟. But deliver us from evil.

℣. From the gate of hell.

℟. Deliver his (her, their) soul(s), O Lord.

℣. May he (she, they) rest in peace.

℟. Amen.

℣. O Lord, hear my prayer.

℟. And let my cry come to you.

(℣. The Lord be with you.

℟. And with your spirit.)

Let us pray.

The appropriate Collect is said from those that follow; then the ℣. **Eternal rest,** with the rest as below **787.**

On the day of burial of the deceased

Collect

We ask you, Lord, to pardon the soul of your servant (handmaid)

786 OFFICE OF THE DEAD: LAUDS

N. Now that he (she) is dead to this world, may he (she) live united to you! The sins that human weakness has led him (her) to commit in this life, wipe out by your forgiveness, you who are all mercy and goodness. This we ask of you through our Lord.

Or another Collect

To you alone, Lord, is it proper always to have mercy and to forgive. We implore you on behalf of the soul of your servant (handmaid) N. which you have taken out of this world today. Do not forget that soul forever and let the enemy take it; order your holy angels to receive it and carry it to heaven, its country. May the soul which has put its hope and its faith in you not have to suffer the pains of hell, but rather possess eternal joy. This we ask of you through our Lord.

On the third, the seventh and the thirtieth day after the burial of the deceased
Collect

Lord, it is now three (or seven or thirty) days since your servant (handmaid) N. was buried. Please grant to his (her) soul fellowship with your elect and your saints and the refreshment of your everlasting mercy. This we ask of you through our Lord.

On the anniversary
Collect

You are kindness itself, Lord. Grant to the soul of your servant (handmaid) N. (or servants and handmaids) the anniversary of whose burial we are celebrating today, a place of rest and of happiness in the splendor of your light. This we ask of you through our Lord.

For a deceased Pope
Collect

By a wonderful arrangement of your providence, Lord, you have been pleased to number your servant N. among your sovereign pontiffs. Grant that after having been the vicar on earth of your Son, he may be associated forever with the glory of your holy pontiffs in heaven. This we ask of you through the same Jesus Christ, our Lord and your Son, who lives and reigns with you in the unity of the Holy Spirit, God, forever.

For a deceased Bishop
Collect

In the priesthood which continues the work of the apostles, Lord, you have raised to the pontifical dignity your servant(s) N. (and N.); grant also that he (they) be associated in their eternal happiness. This we ask of you through our Lord.

For a Cardinal Bishop deceased, say: you have raised to the pontifical dignity your servant the Cardinal Bishop N.

For a Cardinal Priest who was also a Bishop: you have raised to the pontifical dignity your servant the Cardinal Priest N.

For a Cardinal Priest who was not a Bishop: you have raised to the priestly dignity your servant the Cardinal Priest N.

For a Cardinal Deacon who was a priest: you have raised to the priestly dignity your servant the Cardinal Deacon N.

For a Cardinal Deacon who was not a priest, however, the Collect Bend down O Lord, which is given a little further on, is to be said in this way: for the soul of your servant the Cardinal Deacon N. which has departed etc.

For a deceased priest
Collect

In the priesthood which continues the work of the apostles, Lord, you have raised to the priestly dignity your servant(s) N. (and N.); grant also that he (they) be associated in their eternal happiness. This we ask of you through our Lord.

Another Collect

While the soul of your priestly servant N. sojourned in this world, O Lord, you adorned it with sacred offices. Grant, we beseech you, that it may ever rejoice in the glory of its heavenly home. This we ask of you through our Lord.

For a deceased man
Collect

Bend down, O Lord, to hear our prayers: we humbly entreat your mercy for the soul of your servant N. which has departed from this world; establish his soul in a place of light and peace, and cause him to share the happiness of your saints. This we ask of you through our Lord.

For a deceased woman
Collect

Lord, in your mercy have pity on the soul of your handmaid N.; rid her of the infections of our mortal life and give her a share in eternal salvation. This we ask of you through our Lord.

For deceased brethren, relatives and benefactors
Collect

Lord, you desire to pardon us and to save us. We ask your clemency for our brethren, our relatives and our benefactors who have departed from this world. Grant, through the intercession of the Virgin Mary and of all the saints, that they may have a share in your eternal happiness. This we ask of you through our Lord.

For father and mother
Collect

You have commanded us, Lord, to honor our father and our mother. In your kindness have mercy on the souls of my father and my mother, forgive them their sins and grant that I may see them again in the joy of the eternal light. This we ask of you through our Lord.

If the Office is for several, say: on the souls of our parents, and we instead of I.

If it is for the father only, say the soul of my (or our) father.

If it is for the mother only, say the soul of my (or our) mother.

In the Office for the dead in general
Collect

O God, Creator and Redeemer of all the faithful, grant to your departed servants the forgiveness of all their sins. May our fervent prayers obtain for them this favor of yours which they have desired so much! This we ask of you, Lord Jesus, living and reigning with the Father in the unity of the Holy Spirit, God, forever.

After the Collect, there is said (always in the plural):

℣. Eternal rest grant unto them, O Lord.

℟. And let perpetual light shine upon them.

℣. May they rest in peace.

℟. Amen.

VESPERS

Vespers begin directly with the
Ant. I shall please the Lord *
in the lands of the living.

[1]   Psalm 114

I love the Lord because he has
heard * my voice in supplication,

Because he has inclined his ear
to me * the day I called.

The cords of death encompassed
me; the snares of the nether world
seized upon me; * I fell into distress
and sorrow,

And I called upon the name of
the Lord, * "O Lord, save my
life!" —

Gracious is the Lord and just; *
yes, our God is merciful.

The Lord keeps the little ones; *
I was brought low, and he saved me.

Return, O my soul, to your tranquility, * for the Lord has been good
to you.

For he has freed my soul from
death, * my eyes from tears, my
feet from stumbling.

I shall walk before the Lord *
in the lands of the living.

Eternal rest.

Ant. I shall please the Lord in
the lands of the living.

Ant. 2 Woe is me, O Lord, * that
my sojourn is prolonged.

[2]   Psalm 119

In my distress I called to the
Lord, * and he answered me.

O Lord, deliver me from lying
lip, * from treacherous tongue. —

What will he inflict on you, with
more besides, * O treacherous
tongue?

Sharp arrows of a warrior * with
fiery coals of brushwood. —

Woe is me that I sojourn in Mo-
soch, * that I dwell amid the tents of
Cedar!

All too long have I dwelt * with
those who hate peace.

When I speak of peace, * they are
ready for war.

Eternal rest.

Ant. Woe is me, O Lord, that my
sojourn is prolonged.

Ant. 3 The Lord guards you *
from all evil; may the Lord guard
your life.

[3]   Psalm 120

I lift up my eyes toward the
mountains; * whence shall help
come to me?

My help is from the Lord, * who
made heaven and earth. —

May he not suffer your foot to
slip; * may he slumber not who
guards you:

Indeed he neither slumbers nor
sleeps, * the guardian of Israel. —

The Lord is your guardian; * the
Lord is your shade; he is beside you
at your right hand.

The sun shall not harm you by
day, * nor the moon by night. —

The Lord will guard you from all
evil; * he will guard your life.

The Lord will guard your coming
and your going, * both now and
forever.

Eternal rest.

Ant. The Lord guards you from
all evil; may the Lord guard your
life.

Ant. 4 If you, O Lord, * mark
iniquities, Lord, who can stand?

[4]   Psalm 129

Out of the depths I cry to you,
O Lord; * Lord, hear my voice!

Let your ears be attentive * to
my voice in supplication: —

If you, O Lord, mark iniquities, * Lord, who can stand?

But with you is forgiveness, * that you may be revered. —

I trust in the Lord; * my soul trusts in his word.

My soul waits for the Lord * more than sentinels wait for the dawn. —

More than sentinels wait for the dawn, * let Israel wait for the Lord,

For with the Lord is kindness * and with him is plenteous redemption;

And he will redeem Israel * from all their iniquities.

Eternal rest.

Ant. If you, O Lord, mark iniquities, Lord, who can stand?

Ant. 5 Forsake not * the work of your hands, O Lord.

[5]   Psalm 137

I will give thanks to you, O Lord, with all my heart, * for you have heard the words of my mouth;

In the presence of the angels I will sing your praise; * I will worship at your holy temple

And give thanks to your name, * because of your kindness and your truth;

For you have made great above all things * your name and your promise.

When I called, you answered me; * you built up strength within me. —

All the kings of the earth shall give thanks to you, O Lord, * when they hear the words of your mouth;

And they shall sing of the ways of the Lord: * "Great is the glory of the Lord."

The Lord is exalted, yet the lowly he sees, * and the proud he knows from afar. —

Though I walk amid distress, you preserve me; against the anger of my enemies you raise your hand; * your right hand saves me.

The Lord will complete what he has done for me; your kindness, O Lord, endures forever; * forsake not the work of your hands.

Eternal rest.

Ant. Forsake not the work of your hands, O Lord.

℣. I heard a voice from heaven saying. ℟. Blessed are the dead who die in the Lord.

Ant. (Magn.) All * that the Father gives to me shall come to me, and him who comes to me I will not cast out.

Canticle of the Blessed Virgin Mary
Luke 1:46-55

My soul * magnifies the Lord,

And my spirit rejoices * in God my savior,

Because he has regarded the lowliness of his handmaid, * for behold, henceforth all generations shall call me blessed,

Because he who is mighty has done great things for me, * and holy is his name;

And his mercy is from generation to generation * toward those who fear him. —

He has shown might with his arm; * he has scattered the proud in the conceit of their heart.

He has put down the mighty from their thrones * and has exalted the lowly.

The hungry he has filled with good things * and the rich he has sent empty away. —

He has given help to Israel his servant, * mindful of his mercy

(As he promised our fathers) * toward Abraham and his descendants forever.

Eternal rest.

Ant. All that the Father gives to me shall come to me, and him who comes to me I will not cast out.

The following *preces* are said kneeling:

Our Father then silently to

℣. And lead us not into temptation. ℟. But deliver us from evil.

℣. From the gate of hell.

℟. Deliver his (her, their) soul(s), O Lord.

℣. May he (she, they) rest in peace.

℟. Amen.

℣. O Lord, hear my prayer.

℟. And let my cry come to you.

(℣. The Lord be with you.

℟. And with your spirit.)

Let us pray.

The appropriate Collect is said as above at Lauds **785.** After the Collect there is said (always in the plural):

℣. Eternal rest grant unto them, O Lord.

℟. And let perpetual light shine upon them.

℣. May they rest in peace.

℟. Amen.

INDEX OF HYMNS, ANTIPHONS, PSALMS, PEOPLE'S SUNG MASSES

INDEX OF PSALMS

CONTENTS